The Promise-Plan of GOD

Other Zondervan Works by Walter C. Kaiser Jr.

Toward an Old Testament Theology, 1978 (Portuguese 1980, Korean 1982, Chinese 1987, Spanish 1980, Indonesian 2000)

Toward Old Testament Ethics, 1983 (Chinese 1987, Korean 1990)

Toward Rediscovering the Old Testament, 1987 (Chinese 1990)

"Exodus" in *The Expositor's Bible Commentary*, vol. 2, 1990; revised ed. 2008

An Introduction to Biblical Hermeneutics: The Search for Meaning (co-author), 1994 (Korean 1996), 2nd ed. 2007

"Proverbs: Wisdom for Everyday Life," in *Great Books of the Bible* Series, 1995

"Psalms: Heart to Heart with God," in *Great Books of the Bible* Series, 1995

The Messiah in the Old Testament, 1995 (Korean 2001)

"The Law as God's Gracious Guidance for the Promotion of Holiness," in *Counterpoints: Five Views of Law and Gospel*, 1996

The NIV Archaeological Study Bible (executive editor), 2006

The Promise-Plan *of* GOD

A Biblical Theology *of the* Old *and* New Testaments

Based on *Toward an Old Testament Theology*

WALTER C. KAISER JR.

ZONDERVAN ACADEMIC

ZONDERVAN ACADEMIC

The Promise-Plan of God

Based in part on *Toward an Old Testament Theology*

Published by Zondervan, 3950 Sparks Drive SE, Suite 101, Grand Rapids, MI 49546, USA. Zondervan is a registered trademark of The Zondervan Corporation, L.L.C., a wholly owned subsidiary of HarperCollins Christian Publishing, Inc.

Requests for information should be addressed to customercare@harpercollins.com.

Zondervan titles may be purchased in bulk for educational, business, fundraising, or sales promotional use. For information, please email SpecialMarkets@Zondervan.com.

Library of Congress Cataloging-in-Publication Data

Kaiser, Walter C.
The promise-plan of God : a biblical theology of the Old and New Testaments : based on toward an Old Testament theology / Walter C. Kaiser.
p. cm.
ISBN 978-0-310-27586-2
1. Bible—Theology. 2. God—Promises. I. Title.
BS543.K35 2008
230'.041—dc22

2007044575

HarperCollins Publishers, Macken House, 39/40 Mayor Street Upper, Dublin 1, D01 C9W8, Ireland (https://www.harpercollins.com)

Interior design by Mark Sheeres

Printed in the United States of America

25 26 27 28 29 30 31 32 33 34 36 37 38 /TRM/ 25 24 23 22 21 20 19 18 17 16 15 14 13 12

Dedicated to
seven wonderful grandchildren
who love a good story,
especially the grand overarching story of the Bible:

Christine Margaret Coley
Sarah Elise Coley
Austin Jonathan Kaiser
Brittany Mae Kaiser
Kathleen Michelle Coley
Joshua Michael Christian Coley
Benjamin Matthew Isaac Coley

Psalm 128:5–6

Contents in Brief

Contents

Part 2. A Biblical Theology of the New Testament

Preface

In the new world of postmodern times, we have frequently suffered the loss of a universal framework of meaning for many of the great literary works, including the Bible. All too often, we have assumed that an emphasis on diversity is more in keeping with the pluralism and individualism of our day. But in coming to this conclusion and impasse, we have lost the power to see the grand narrative that united story after story and section after section of the Bible. The waning of the case for the unity of the Bible has led to a truncated Bible that loses the presentation of the overall plan and mind of God in the text of Scripture.

Jean-Francois Lyotard has argued in *The Postmodern Condition* that a postmodern view of the world calls for a "war on Totality."[1] This is nothing less than an attack on any claim to universal meaning, and it thereby attacks any worldview that argues for wholeness and unity in a work as well as in life itself! The problem with this view, of course, is that it wants to exempt its own view from this denial that there are no overarching unities or plans to life or to works such as the Bible.

But what if we began by taking the text on its own terms, using the American sense of jurisprudence that says that a person is innocent until proven guilty? What would such a treatment of the biblical text look like? I believe that the book in your hands will supply the answer. Elsewhere I have examined whether the claims of the text are true and whether the story of the Bible is reliable and comes in general from the era it purports to represent.[2] In this book, however, I want to state the case for the unity of the metanarrative and to return to the original mission of biblical theology as a diachronic ("through the times") discipline (rather than an iterative systematic theology) of each book or section. That is, I have tried to capture the distinctive theological note in each section or book as the plan of God unfolded through the historic times of Israel and the church.

The rejection of any metanarrative at all must not be the cause adopted by readers and students of the Bible. That is why I present *The Promise-Plan of God: A Biblical Theology of the Old and New Testaments* as an alternative to much of the work being done on the biblical theology of the Bible. I think you will enjoy the case as it unfolds from the text of Scripture itself.

---

1. Jean-Francois Lyotard, *The Postmodern Condition: A Report on Knowledge*, trans. Geoff Benington and Brian Massumi (Minneapolis: University of Minnesota Press, 1984), 82.
2. Walter C. Kaiser Jr., *Are the Old Testament Documents Reliable and Relevant?* (Downers Grove, IL: InterVarsity Press, 2001); idem, *A History of Israel: From the Bronze Age Through the Jewish Wars* (Nashville: Broadman and Holman, 1998).

It only remains for me to thank those who have been especially helpful to me in my writing this book, namely, Katya Covrett, Ben Irwin, Jim Ruark, Elizabeth Yoder, and Stan Gundry. I am deeply indebted to each one of you. You have each done your best to make this work as good as it could be; for this I am most appreciative.

June 2007

Abbreviations

Old Testament

Genesis	Ge
Exodus	Ex
Leviticus	Lev
Numbers	Nu
Deuteronomy	Dt
Joshua	Jos
Judges	Jdg
Ruth	Ru
1 Samuel	1Sa
2 Samuel	2Sa
1 Kings	1Ki
2 Kings	2Ki
1 Chronicles	1Ch
2 Chronicles	2Ch
Ezra	Ezr
Nehemiah	Ne
Esther	Est
Job	Job
Psalm(s)	Ps(s)
Proverbs	Pr
Ecclesiastes	Ecc
Song of Songs	SS
Isaiah	Isa
Jeremiah	Jer
Lamentations	La
Ezekiel	Eze
Daniel	Da
Hosea	Hos
Joel	Joel
Amos	Am
Obadiah	Ob
Jonah	Jnh
Micah	Mic
Nahum	Na
Habakkuk	Hab
Zephaniah	Zep
Haggai	Hag
Zechariah	Zec
Malachi	Mal

New Testament

Matthew	Mt
Mark	Mk
Luke	Lk
John	Jn
Acts	Ac
Romans	Ro
1 Corinthians	1Co
2 Corinthians	2Co
Galatians	Gal
Ephesians	Eph
Philippians	Php
Colossians	Col
1 Thessalonians	1Th
2 Thessalonians	2Th
1 Timothy	1Ti
2 Timothy	2Ti
Titus	Tit
Philemon	Phm
Hebrews	Heb
James	Jas
1 Peter	1Pe
2 Peter	2Pe
1 John	1Jn
2 John	2Jn
3 John	3Jn
Jude	Jude
Revelation	Rev

Bible Versions

Authorized Version	AV
Evangelical Standard Version	ESV
Jerusalem Bible	JB
King James Version	KJV
New American Standard Bible	NASB
New English Bible	NEB
New International Version	NIV
New Revised Standard Version	NRSV
Revised Standard Version	RSV
Revised Version	RV
Today's English Version	TEV

Introduction

God's Promise-Plan in Both Testaments

Diversity or Unity?

The emphasis on diversity within Scripture is so pervasive in our day that most biblical scholars would judge any other approach to biblical theology as being out of keeping with the current lines of thinking for this discipline. As Gerhard Maier noted:

> It is difficult to speak of a "center" of Scripture today, because the rubric "center of Scripture" is often separated from the "unity of Scripture." While the two were closely identified at the time of the Reformation, the Enlightenment disengaged them. Indeed, the "center of Scripture" practically replaced the lost "unity of Scripture."[1]

Accordingly, in an attempt to return to those pre-critical[2] times, especially as enjoyed in the Reformation, I will argue for a textually derived "center" that simultaneously parallels the case for the "unity of the Bible." I believe that a biblical center and its accompanying unity were strongly attested, especially by the writers of the New Testament, who taught that the doctrine of the Messiah, the Anointed One of God, was preserved as a record of the "promise" (or promise-plan) made by God; yet it first appeared in all parts of the Old Testament, even though it appeared there under a constellation of different but synonymous names (such as "word," "rest," "blessing," and the like).[3] This case can be presented by describing ten scriptural generalizations of the promise-plan of God. But first, let us seek to define the unifying plan that Scripture displays.

---

1. Gerhard Maier, *Biblical Hermeneutics*, trans. R. W. Yarbrough (Wheaton, IL: Crossway, 1994), 202.

2. "Pre-critical times" is not an altogether felicitous term, but it is often used these days to represent the interpretation of Scripture prior to the rise of the historical-critical approach to the text of the Bible that began in the eighteenth century.

3. For years now, I have been impressed with the thesis of Willis J. Beecher, *The Prophets and the Promise* (1905; reprint, Grand Rapids.: Baker, 1975). What follows is a close reworking of the case he set forth over a century ago in the famous Princeton Stone Lectures.

Definition of the Promise-Plan of God

In emphasizing the one unifying promise-plan of God as the theological center of the whole Bible rather than listing many random and scattered predictions (or even the absence of such an organizing mind behind revelation), this biblical theology differs from the task and results of the discipline known as *systematic theology*.

Systematic theology has traditionally organized its approach around topics and themes such as God, humanity, sin, Christ, salvation, the church, and last things. By contrast, biblical theology has, more often than not, been a discipline in search of a mission and a structure — often falling into the same topical and structural tracks gone over by systematic theology, even though it severely criticized and stood aloof from systematic theology, claiming it had imposed an external grid (derived from philosophy or the like) on its material.

Since its inception, biblical theology has had a strong diachronic strain that insists on tracing the historic development of doctrine as it appeared chronologically in the history of Israel and the church. Thus, while it had to be scriptural in *form* and *method* as well as in substance, it had to present itself in the order that God disclosed his revelation over the centuries or decades. It was to be a biblical theology, not a compilation of biblical *theologies* (on the alternative assumption that there was no unity or center to the canon). The use of the singular noun in biblical theology implied that there was an organizing center that could be discovered — that the whole canon expressed the unity of the one mind and unified purpose of God. This unity had to be uncovered before exploring the plan and purpose of God as revealed in the individual books and sections of Scripture.

The best proposal for such a unity is to be found exactly where Scripture itself pointed in its repeated references. I believe that the most suitable candidate for the unity or center of God's disclosure is to be found in the "promise-plan" of God as revealed in repeated references throughout Scripture. The promise form of biblical theology focuses on one all-embracing divine word of promise rather than on its many scattered predictions (which is what most think of when they hear the word "promise"), and it traces the growth of that declaration of God in the large teaching passages in each era of divine revelation. Usually in dogmatic or systematic theology, the texts used to support the doctrine discussed are scattered verses (rather than large "chair," or teaching chapters or pericopes) distributed over the length and breadth of the whole Bible.

Whereas systematic theology generally separates prediction from promise, omitting references to the threatening aspect of the promise and the judgments of God as well as the historic *means* that God used to keep his word alive and ultimately to bring his word to pass, biblical theology insists on keeping both the threatening aspects and the predictions of hope together as alternative parts of the same promise-plan. It also traces the intermediate historic means, or links by which that word was maintained in partial fulfillments until the final and complete fulfillment came in Christ. Thus the promise was not simply a predictive word that remained inert and in word form only until it was finally fulfilled in its end point; it was a word that was maintained over the centuries in a continuing series of historic fulfillments that acted as earnests, or down payments on that word that still pointed to the last or final fulfillment.

Willis J. Beecher, in his 1904 Princeton Stone Lectures, defined the promise in this way: "God gave a promise to Abraham, and through him to mankind; a promise eternally fulfilled and fulfilling in the history of Israel; and chiefly fulfilled in Jesus Christ, he being that which is principal in the history of Israel."[4]

Accordingly, the divine promise was given to the patriarchs — Abraham, Isaac, and Jacob — in Genesis. It was continued and renewed in the exodus narrative, emphasizing that the new nation Israel was Yahweh's son and his people, who were to be a kingdom of priests and a holy nation for the benefit of all humanity, yet out of whose "seed" would come God's Messiah for the whole world.

The same promise is restated and renewed with David as he is told that he and his "seed" are to be given a "throne," "a dynasty," and "a kingdom" (2Sa 7:16) that will serve as a "law/charter for all humanity" (2Sa 7:19, my trans.). From David's time onward, a stream of writing prophets composed the Psalms and the so-called historical books (better named the "Earlier Prophets"), along with the books of the "Latter Prophets." They too kept appealing to the promise-plan that God gave to the patriarchs and to David as the heart and soul of the message they had for their day and our own times as well.

It is little wonder, then, that the New Testament writers found the theme of the promise to be not only the unifying center around which they understood the Old Testament but also the way to trace the continued advancement and development of the metanarrative of the future work of God. The only addition I would make to Beecher's definition would be to take it back to the Edenic promise made to Eve about her "seed" crushing the head of the serpent, the evil one himself. My definition of the promise-plan of God would be as follows:

> The promise-plan is God's word of declaration, beginning with Eve and continuing on through history, especially in the patriarchs and the Davidic line, that God would continually *be* in his person and *do* in his deeds and works (in and through Israel, and later the church) his redemptive plan as his *means* of keeping that promised word alive for Israel, and thereby for all who subsequently believed. All in that promised seed were called to act as a light for all the nations so that all the families of the earth might come to faith and to new life in the Messiah.

Ten Characteristics of the Promise-Plan of God

This promise-plan can be described as having ten distinctive characteristics. These may be defined as follows:

1. *The doctrine of the Promised Messiah is found throughout all the Scriptures and not just in isolated or selected passages as understood by the Promise-Fulfillment Scheme.*

4. Beecher, *Prophets and the Promise*, 178.

Our Lord held the readers of the Old Testament accountable for knowing who he was and what would happen to him in Jerusalem. For example, the two disciples whom Jesus encountered on the road to Emmaus on the first Easter Sunday were soundly rebuked by our Lord for their failure to understand the message of the Old Testament and to grasp the significance of what was said about the coming Messiah:

> He said to them, "This is what I told you while I was still with you: Everything must be fulfilled that is written about me in the Law of Moses, the Prophets and the Psalms." (Lk 24:44)

> "How foolish you are, and how slow of heart to believe all that the prophets have spoken! Did not the Christ have to suffer these things and then enter his glory?" And beginning with Moses and all the Prophets, he explained to them what was said in all the Scriptures concerning himself. (Lk 24:25 – 27)

What the Old Testament contained only in the word of promise was precisely what our Lord held ordinary laypersons like Cleopas and his companion accountable for knowing, despite their obvious gloom over what they had thought was a tragic turn of events in the crucifixion of Jesus.

2. *The Old Testament Messianic teaching was regarded as the development of a single promise* (Gr. epangelia), *repeated and unfolded through the centuries with numerous specifications and in multiple forms but always with the same essential core.* So central is this article of faith that the apostle Paul, when he was on trial for his life, wrapped up his total life and ministry by saying:

> And now it is because of my hope in what God has *promised* our fathers that I am on trial here today. This is *the promise* our twelve tribes are hoping to see fulfilled as they earnestly serve God day and night ... that God raises the dead. (Ac 26:6 – 7a, emphasis mine)

Paul's appeal to King Agrippa was based, not on a number of scattered predictions throughout the Scriptures, but on "the promise" (that is, the one definite promise — note the article) that God had made long ago to the nation's ancestors (Abraham, Isaac, Jacob, David) and on "the promise" he had made to the "twelve tribes." As Beecher put it, "The thing he is speaking of he calls, not prediction, but promise; not promises, but promise; not a promise, but the promise. The word is singular and definite." The whole essential messianic truth, as he knows it, he sums up in this one formula, "the promise made of God unto our fathers."[5]

More than forty New Testament passages refer to this word "promise,"[6] which has as its most central and prominent feature the revelation concerning the Messiah. Around

5. Beecher, *Prophets and the Promise*, 180.

6. See the charts for the frequency and distribution of the use of *epangelia* in appendix 2.

this central motif all the teaching of the New Testament (as well as the Old Testament) can be grouped, according to the writers of the canon of Scripture.

3. *The New Testament writers equate this single, definite promise as the one made to Abraham when God called him from Ur of the Chaldeans.* Instead of treating this definite promise as one that was recently received in the New Testament era, the writer of the book of Hebrews linked it with the transaction God made with Abraham long ago:

> When God made his *promise* to Abraham ... he swore by himself, saying, "Surely I will bless you and give you many descendants." (Heb 6:13 – 14, emphasis mine)

> Because God wanted to make the unchanging nature of his purpose very clear to the heirs of what was *promised*, he confirmed it with an oath. (Heb 6:17; cf. Ge 22:17, emphasis mine)

> ... Isaac and Jacob ... were heirs with him of *the same promise.* (Heb 11:9, emphasis mine)

> These were all commended for their faith, yet none of them received what had been *promised* ... that only together with us would they be made perfect. (Heb 11:39 – 40, emphasis mine)

The apostle Paul makes the same argument in Romans:

> It was not through law that Abraham and his offspring received *the promise* that he would be heir of the world, but through the righteousness that comes by faith. For if those who live by law are heirs, faith has no value and *the promise* is worthless.... Yet he [Abraham] did not waver through unbelief regarding *the promise* of God, but was strengthened in his faith and gave glory to God. (Ro 4:13 – 14, 20, emphasis mine)

4. *While the New Testament writers occasionally speak of promises, using the plural form of the word, the manner in which they do so does not weaken the case for a single definite promise in the Scriptures.* In those rare instances where the New Testament writers use the plural word "promises," they do so to indicate that the one promise is made up of many specifications. The contemporary call for diversity in the Scripture tends only to show the influences of modernity and postmodernity rather than a search for the text's own system of organization. When we opt for this view, we demonstrate that we belong more to this current age (which values diversity and pluralism) than to the age of the Bible, for the Bible keeps claiming that it is reflecting the single mind and the unified will of God himself and not of the assortment of human writers who were used by the Spirit of God.

Note also that even with all these various specifications referred to as "promises," they exist within the broad scope of the single promise of God, and not to extraneous streams of parallel or opposing thought, as these examples from Romans demonstrate:

> Theirs [the people of Israel] is the adoption as sons; theirs the divine glory, the covenants, the receiving of the law, the temple worship and *the promises.* (Ro 9:4, emphasis mine)

> For I tell you that Christ has become a servant of the Jews on behalf of God's truth, to confirm *the promises* made to the patriarchs so that the Gentiles may glorify God for his mercy. (Ro 15:8 – 9, emphasis mine)

A brief sampling of some of the numerous specifications include the promise of the Holy Spirit, the resurrection of Messiah, the inheritance of the land of Canaan, the outreach to the Gentiles, the coming of the Messiah (both in his first and second coming), and the like. There are many other additional places where a plurality of specifications will be noted later. But these examples are enough to make the point that the one promise is made up of a host of related themes within the same whole plan.

5. *The New Testament writers regard this single, definite promise, composed of many specifications, to be the theme of both the Old and New Testaments.* If there ever was a case for the unity and a center to the whole Bible, it could especially be found in the claims made by the writers of the New Testament that it is best located under the label of the "promise." They traced the development of this messianic theme back to Eve, Abraham, and their descendants, including David and his lineage leading all the way to the first century AD. No one less than deacon Stephen traced this path for the Sanhedrin:

> Brothers and fathers, listen to me! The God of glory appeared to our father Abraham while he was still in Mesopotamia, before he lived in Haran. "Leave your country and your people," God said, "and go to the land I will show you." ... As the time drew near for God to fulfill his *promise* to Abraham, the number of our people in Egypt greatly increased." (Ac 7:2 – 3, 17, emphasis mine)

While the Old Testament does not have an exact verbal equivalent for the term "promise," the same concept is found under a constellation of terms. The earliest expression of the promise idea is found in the oft-repeated word "blessing" (*barakah*) that occurs rather frequently in Genesis 1 – 11 (e.g., Ge 1:22, 28; 2:3; 5:2; 9:1, 26).

But the Old Testament uses other terms besides "blessing." For example, Foster McCurley counted more than thirty examples where the verb *dibber* (usually translated "to speak") could better be rendered "to promise."[7] Add to these two terms God's "pledge," his "oath," and his "rest," along with the plethora of terms and metaphors pointing to his messianic privilege such as "Seed," "Branch," "Servant," "Stone," "Root," "Lion," and the list goes on.

6. *The promise made to Abraham is represented as both being partially fulfilled in the events of the exodus and yet still to be fully fulfilled in the distant future.* That was Stephen's point in Acts 7:17, for God was fulfilling the plan made to Abraham and in

7. Foster R. McCurley Jr., "The Christian and the Old Testament Promise," *Lutheran Quarterly* 22 (1970): 401 – 10; esp. 402, n. 2. Some of the items promised using this verb "to speak" or "to promise" included: (1) the land (Ex 12:25; Dt 9:28; 12:20; 19:8; 27:3; Jos 23:5, 10); (2) blessing (Dt 1:11; 15:6); (3) multiplication of the people of Israel (Dt 6:3; 26:19); (4) rest (Jos 22:4; 1Ki 8:56); (5) all good things (Jos 23:15); and (6) a Davidic dynasty, kingdom, and throne (2Sa 7:28; 1Ki 2:24; 8:20, 24 – 25; 1Ch 17:26; 2Ch 6:15 – 16; Jer 33:14) and the Hebrew noun *dabar*, "word," "promise" (1Ki 8:56; Ps 105:42).

the days of the exodus, which was later to be called "the promise." Paul showed the same method of interpretation, only he began with the exodus and zeroed in on the days of King Saul and King David:

> After removing Saul, he made David their king; ... From this man's descendants God has brought to Israel the Savior Jesus, as he *promised.* (Ac 13:22 – 23, emphasis mine)

Since this plan of God was seen as an ongoing process that reached through all of history, it was necessary to point out each of the events in the historical line leading toward the Messiah, all the while fulfilling parts of the promise while moving to its final and complete resolution and fulfillment.

That is why the events connected with the birth of John the Baptist and Jesus are treated both as fulfillments of the promise-plan and as further predictors of what was to come. John's father, Zechariah, saw the raising up of "a horn of salvation for us in the house of his servant David" (i.e., the Messiah, Lk 1:69) as a further fulfillment of "the oath he swore to our father Abraham" (Lk 1:73). Thus, the promise passed through Abraham and through David and could be seen at the beginning of the Christian era to have rested on both John the Baptist, as the forerunner of our Lord, and of Jesus himself.

7. *The New Testament writers not only declare that the promise-plan of God is seen through the whole Old Testament, but they adopt the Old Testament phraseology as part of their own way of expressing God's revelation to them.* Distinctive terms such as "the day of the LORD," "the last days," "The Servant of the LORD," "My Son," "My Firstborn," "My Messenger," "My Holy One," the "kingdom of God," and the "Messiah," were progressively added in the Old Testament and thus become almost routine for New Testament vocabulary.

8. *The New Testament writers teach that the promise of God is operating eternally and is irrevocable.* Despite the fact that "a hardening in part" has come over Israel (Ro 11:25), nevertheless, "God's gifts and his call are irrevocable" (Ro 11:29). Paul was adamant on this point:

> Brothers, let me take an example from everyday life. Just as no one can set aside or add to a human covenant that has been duly established, so it is in this case. *The promises* were spoken to Abraham and to his seed. The Scripture does not say "and to seeds," meaning many people, but "and to your seed," meaning one person, who is Christ. What I mean is this: the law, introduced 430 years later, does not set aside the covenant previously established by God and thus do away with *the promise.* For if the inheritance depends on the law, then it no longer depends on a *promise*; but God in his grace gave it to Abraham through a *promise.* (Gal 3:15 – 18, emphasis mine)

No less definitive was the announcement by the writer of Hebrews:

> When God made his *promise* to Abraham, since there was no one greater for him to swear by, he swore by himself....

> Because God wanted to make the unchanging nature of his purpose very clear to the heirs of what was *promised*, he confirmed it with an oath. God did this so that, by two unchangeable things [his word in Ge 12 and his oath in Ge 22] in which it is impossible for God to lie, *we* [the generations long after Abraham and his heirs] who have fled to take hold of the hope offered *to us* may be greatly encouraged. (Heb 6:13, 17 – 18, emphasis mine)

9. *The New Testament writers make a strong connection between the promise and a number of other doctrines.* God's promise, as originally given in Genesis 12:3, was not to be limited only to Abraham's people, but it was to be for all the Gentiles, families, and nations of the earth. In Galatians 3:6 – 8, Paul teaches three amazing truths: (1) Abraham received the gospel in advance of its later fuller explication; (2) the substance of the gospel was found in the words "All nations will be blessed through you"; and (3) the gospel given to Abraham is the same one by which all the nations/Gentiles on earth are to be saved at the hearing of the name of Jesus Christ (or its earlier synonyms). Paul taught that

> Abraham "believed God, and it was credited to him as righteousness." Understand, then, that those who believe are children of Abraham. Scripture foresaw that God would justify the Gentiles by faith, and *announced the gospel in advance* to Abraham [saying]: "All nations will be blessed through you." (Gal 3:6 – 8, emphasis mine)

Add to this Paul's continued argument in Galatians 3:29 that "if you belong to Christ, then you are Abraham's seed, and heirs according to *the promise*" (emphasis mine). Paul adds, "He [God] redeemed us [Jews] in order that the blessing given to Abraham might come to the Gentiles through Christ Jesus, so that by faith we might receive *the promise* of the Spirit" (Gal 3:14, emphasis mine).

The promise just mentioned is similar to another that is also connected with our sealing with the Holy Spirit, as Paul declared in Ephesians 1:13 ("you were marked in him with a seal, *the promised* Holy Spirit"), which is amazing, for we Gentiles "were separated from Christ, excluded from citizenship in Israel and foreigners to the covenant of *promise*" (Eph 2:11 – 12, emphasis mine). Surprisingly, we Gentiles are "heirs with Israel, members together of one body, and sharers together in *the promise* in Christ Jesus" (Eph 3:6, emphasis mine).

This promise-doctrine is also connected to the doctrine of the kingdom of God. So prominent and pervasive is this concept that Jesus came announcing in the gospel era that we need not rally the textual support at this time. However, it does introduce a further consideration: if the kingdom of God is that central, why isn't it the center and unifying factor instead of the promise?

Willis J. Beecher, whom we have been following throughout these ten arguments for the centrality and unifying nature of the promise doctrine, or promise-plan of God, made the following observation: "The most prominent thing in the New Testament is the proclamation of the kingdom and its anointed king. But it is on the basis of the divine promise that its preachers proclaim the kingdom, and when they appeal to the Old Testament in proof of Christian doctrine, they make the promise more prominent than the kingdom itself."[8]

In this connection, the promise carries with it eschatological teachings as well. They affirm the coming of the Lord along with the doctrine of the resurrection. For instance, 2 Peter 3:10 warned: "The Lord is not slow in keeping his *promise*.... But the day of the Lord will come like a thief. The heavens will disappear with a roar" (emphasis mine). Likewise, Hebrews 9:15 assures us that "those who are called may receive *the promised* eternal inheritance" (emphasis mine).

There are more doctrines connected with the promise, but this sampling should be enough to convince us that the promise doctrine is at once central enough, and yet broad enough, to embrace the entirety of what God had in store as he unfolded his plan in Scripture.

10. *The culmination of all the specifications (i.e., the individual predicted doctrines that support the one unifying promise-plan) are wrapped up in the one promise doctrine, or promise-plan, which focuses on Jesus Christ.* To preach Christ as the Messiah was to proclaim the promise. These were not numerous predictions arbitrarily and randomly scattered throughout the Old Testament and then fulfilled now and again in the New Testament. Instead, all three parts of the promise were repeatedly evidenced by the writers of both Testaments: (1) the promissory *word*, (2) the events of history that served as the *means*, or *links* for maintaining the promise until it reached its planned goal, and (3) the *final fulfillment* in history in accordance with the revelatory words spoken ahead of time by God's prophets and apostles.

These ten characteristics begin to show that the word *promise*, as used in Scripture, is not the same as what is meant by the term in the "promise-fulfillment" school of thought. The promise-fulfillment plan, despite some similarities with other schools of thought, misses one of the main distinctives between its view and that of the promise-plan of God: the *means*, or *links* God used in giving mini-fulfillments through the course of history that were an essential part of the final fulfillment but certainly not to the extent and awesomeness of the completion in space and time of the final word and fulfillment announced ages prior to its resolution.

An "Epangelical" Proposal for Doing Biblical Theology[9]

Traditionally, evangelicalism has seen two major proposals for locating a "unity of perspective" between the two Testaments: the Covenantal, also called the Reformed view,

8. Beecher, *Prophets and the Promise*, 178–79.

9. The word "Epangelical" is derived from the Greek word *epangelia*, meaning the "promise."

and the Dispensational perspective. Even though there are countless variations on how each of these views (and others closely or distantly related to them) relate the Old Testament to the New, these two perspectives have been the focus of most of the discussion in recent years. But more to the point, what is most important is how each decides if there exists one or two "people(s) of God" (i.e., Israel and the church) and one or two "program(s) of God" (i.e., a single redemptive-historical program or an earthly and a heavenly program for Israel and the church). But at the end of the day, answers to these questions form a large part of the heart of the problem of biblical unity and/or diversity and the amount apportioned to each in a biblical theology.

The older view, going back to the work of Johannes Cocceius[10] (1603 – 69), took the concept of *covenant* as the most significant theme in theology. The basic idea was that in paradise there was a "covenant of works," in which salvation was gained on the condition of perfect obedience. When Adam and Eve sinned, that offer was rescinded, and a "covenant of grace/redemption" was offered as a free gift of God. To be sure, Scripture explicitly mentions a covenant with Abraham (Ge 12:1 – 3) and with David (2Sa 7), as well as a new covenant (Jer 31:31 – 34), but Reformed, or covenant theology, tended to go beyond these exegetically derived covenants by mentioning additional, even hypothetical or implicit covenants, such as the "covenant of creation," the "covenant of redemption," the "covenants of works" or the "covenant of grace."

According to this view, the nation of Israel, because of her disobedience and failure to keep (what is alleged to be) the conditional covenant God made with her, has lost her distinctive part in the covenant and is no longer part of the covenant, especially as a nation, other than for those believing Jews who are now grafted into the church. In this way of approaching the text, Israel failed to keep her side of what was believed to be a bilateral ("two-sided") covenant, so the blessings originally offered to her were now transferred and given over to the believing church. The covenant, it is to be noticed, was understood as bilateral or conditional rather than a unilateral or unconditional covenant[11] made with Abraham, Isaac, Jacob, David, and the nation of Israel.

Dispensational theology, on the other hand, came much later in the nineteenth century and on into the twentieth century. The traditional or classic dispensationalist view held that there were two separate peoples in the Bible (Israel and the church) with two separate identities, destinies, and programs (an earthly and heavenly program). It viewed the present day as belonging to the "age of the church," but as existing during a parenthesis, or break — an intercalation in God's program for Israel in which Israel as a nation was set aside temporarily until the Davidic kingdom could be restored again to its greatest height ever toward the end of the historic process in the "age

10. Johannes Cocceius, *Summa doctrinae de foedere et testamento Dei* (1648) and *Opera Omnia*, 12 vols. Folio (1673 – 75).

11. See the case for an unconditional covenant in my treatment of the patriarchal revelation in Genesis 15 in chapter 2 below.

to come." Here the promise (*epangelia*) with Israel was seen as being unilateral and unconditional, based on the grace of God (who was the only one who went between the split-animals in the Genesis 15 covenant)[12] and not on the obedience of the nation. But classical dispensationalism bifurcated the one people of God and the one program of God into two separate plans and promises in the history of redemption.

Each of these two solutions of the relationship of Israel to the Christian church fails to reckon with one or more of the following primary assertions of Scripture:

1. The church is *grafted into the olive tree*, which stands for the nation of Israel, and not the other way around, which erroneously has Israel being grafted into the roots and the trunk of the church (Ro 9 – 11). The believing church is grafted into the roots and trunk of the olive tree of Israel. Without the roots and trunk of the tree, which represent the nation of Israel, the church has no anchoring or rootage in space and time or history.
2. The new covenant of Jeremiah 31:31 – 34 was explicitly made with "the house of Israel and the house of Judah"; it was not a covenant made with the church, even though the church may share in it, just as it shares in parts of the Abrahamic-Davidic covenant(s). There is no specific covenant in Scripture directly made for, or with, the church in either Testament!
3. Ever since the beginnings of human history, God has been raising up a *remnant* from all over the human race. The present-day believing church is part of that faithful remnant, which ever since Pentecost has been grafted into the trunk of the tree identified as Israel. Thus, there are *distinguishable* aspects between Israel and the church, just as there is a *distinguishable* aspect in the program of God, but there is not a *separation*, or a sharp division, between "the people of God" or the "kingdom of God." The continuity term for believing Israel and the church is the one "people of God," just as the continuity term for the one program of God is the "kingdom of God."

The word "epangelical" is derived from *epangelia*, the Greek word for "promise." This view maintains that there is only *one* "people of God" (even though there may be numerous aspects of that same singular group) and there is only *one* "program of God" (again, with several aspects all within that one umbrella term).

How did such a strong line of separation come between Israel and the believing community? Probably it came sometime around the ministry of Eusebius Pamphilus in the fourth century of the Christian era, when the church began to show evidences of an anti-Jewish stance that affected its theological constructions from then on. It also came as the Emperor Constantine was making Christianity a legal religion.

---

12. See the full discussion on "making/cutting a covenant" below in my discussion of Genesis 15.

It appears that during the reign of Constantine, Eusebius was aware of the fact that his views on Israel and the coming kingdom of God did not reflect those of earlier church fathers like Papias (ca. AD 60 – 130), the bishop of Hierapolis. Polycarp, another church father (ca. AD 60 – 155), praised Papias as "a man well-skilled in all manner of learning, and well acquainted with the Scriptures."[13] However, even while Eusebius recognized that most of the ecclesiastical writers of that day agreed with Papias that God would regather the nation of Israel in the final day and that Christ would rule on earth as his final kingdom reign began before it reached on into the eternal state, Eusebius propounded another view that left Israel out of the picture and also denied any rule and reign of Christ on earth as history concluded.

Origen may have contributed to the shift in thinking represented by Eusebius, for he championed the fact that the best way to understand the words of the Old Testament was to take them allegorically:

> If anyone wishes to hear and understand these words [of the Old Testament] literally, he ought to gather with the Jews rather than with Christians. But if he wishes to be a Christian and a disciple of Paul, let him hear Paul saying that "the Law is spiritual" [thereby] declaring that these words are "allegorical" when the law speaks of Abraham and his wife and sons.[14]

However, even more influential on Eusebius' thinking was the Emperor Constantine, who helped set this aspect of theology into concrete for generations to come. In Eusebius' letter to the churches over the Passover controversy, he redrew the line of separation precisely at the altar, which line Christ had abolished in his death when he tore down that middle wall of partition between Jew and Gentile. Eusebius, in an outburst of anti-Semitism, referred to the Jews as those "polluted wretches" who were "parricides and murders of our Lord."[15] Thus, the foundations for anti-Semitism were set by Eusebius.

But more to the point, when Emperor Constantine made Christianity a legal religion, it seems that the trade-off made by Eusebius and the church was to let the government have control and rights to the geopolitical aspects of the earthly kingdom, while in turn, the government of Constantine would leave the spiritual aspects of the kingdom of God to the church. As a result, the tide of the first three or four Christian centuries, which had taught almost with one voice that there were both physical and spiritual aspects of the kingdom of God, was now turned; the concept of an earthly rule and reign of Christ with his believing body was relinquished to a new geopolitical reality of the emperor and the church began to emphasize the spiritual and internal aspects of the rule and reign of Christ in the hearts and lives of believers.

13. As quoted in Eusebius Pamphilus, *The Ecclesiastical History of Eusebius Pamphilus*, trans. Christian Fredrick Cruse (Grand Rapids: Baker), Book III, ch. 36, p. 120.

14. Origen, *Homilies on Genesis and Exodus*, trans. Ronald E. Heine, in *The Fathers of the Church*, vol. 71 (Washington, DC: Catholic University Press, 1982), Homily VI, 121 – 22.

15. Eusebius, *Ecclesiastical History*, V.22, 51 – 54.

The importance of the preceding analysis can be seen in the discussion that follows. If a unifying plan of God is to be identified, then the way Israel is interfaced with the church will be extremely important.

Five Different Ways of Relating Israel and the Church

In the course of time, five different methods of relating Israel and the church developed: (1) the Replacement Covenant, (2) the Super Covenant, (3) the Dual Covenant, (4) the Separate Covenant, and (5) the Renewed Covenant.

The Replacement Covenant. In this view, the covenant is treated as a conditional or bilateral agreement which can be rendered null and void if either side defaults. Since Israel did not keep her side of the terms of the covenant, the promises made to her were nullified and she was replaced by the believing body, which today is the church. The blessings originally made out for Israel were now to be fulfilled in the new covenant and were made out instead to be with the church.

The problems with this view of the covenant are: (1) God never made a covenant with the church in Scripture; (2) the Abrahamic-Davidic covenant was not a conditional one, depending on a bilateral acceptance and maintenance, for in the case of the Abrahamic covenant, it was God alone who walked between the animal pieces in Genesis 15 and not Abraham, thus making it a unilateral and unconditional treaty; and (3) the New Testament clearly teaches that God has not cast off disobedient Israel (Ro 11:1, 25 – 26). In fact, even after the return from the Babylonian exile in 539 BC, the prophet Zechariah argues in 518 BC (well after the 536 BC return from the Babylonian captivity) that a return to the land was still scheduled to be fulfilled in the future (Zec 10:8 – 12).

The Super Covenant. This was the sixteenth-century version of what today is called "covenant theology." In its mature form, it saw Israel and the church as one and the same in the history of the human race. Using the extrabiblical terms "covenant of grace" or "covenant of redemption," it taught that this new plan replaced the expired extrabiblical "covenant of works" presumably made with Adam and Eve in the garden of Eden. The sign of this covenant formerly was circumcision, but it now is (usually infant) baptism, and the "people of God," formerly Israel, are now all believers in the church.

There are some problems with this view also. Besides the fact that the covenants that are used by the Scriptures to organize the unity of the Bible are not all mentioned by all the names assigned to them, there definitely is no covenant that exists with the church. Moreover, Jesus himself did not disavow the restoration of the nation of Israel, but specifically affirmed it (Ac 1:6 – 7; 3:21; 15:13 – 18). The apostle Paul can still simultaneously identify himself with his physical brethren, the Jews (Php 3:4 – 6; Ro 11:1) as well as with all believers. God's promise to the nation of Israel is "irrevocable" (Ro 11:29) and contemporary Jewish people too will be saved and have their sins taken away (Ro 11:26 – 27) one day in the future. On the positive side, this view has caught the unity of the plan of salvation in the whole Bible, but it has narrowed its soteriology so as to miss the centrality of the Jew in the plan of God (e.g., Jn 4:22). Moreover, Paul's great treatise on the plan of salvation throughout the book of Romans cannot be discussed without treating the issue of the Jew and the Gentile, as Paul noted in Romans 1:16 (and thereafter in the rest of the book of Romans): "I am not ashamed of the gospel, because it is the power of God that brings salvation to everyone who believes: first to the Jew, then to the Gentile."

The Dual Covenant. A Jewish philosopher named Franz Rosenzweig, who died in 1929, argued that Jewish people did not need the saving gospel of Jesus Christ, for they had a separate covenant, one made with Abraham. Therefore, evangelizing Jewish people was not only wrong, but it failed to recognize that God had already saved them in another covenant.

Despite the fact that this position earnestly attempted to offer a new way of smoothing out Jewish/believing church relationships (that avoided what many Jewish persons viewed as "proselytizing of Jews"), it too failed at some critical points: (1) the gospel offered Abraham is the same one offered today to all peoples and to the church (Ge 12:3; 15:6; Lk 1:73; Gal 3:8; Ro 4:13); (2) the object of faith in both the Abrahamic covenant and New Testament is the same: the "seed," "the Anointed One," "the Man of Promise" (i.e., Jesus); and (3) the "olive tree" into which the church is grafted is Jewish. There does not exist a distinct and separate existence for the message of salvation apart from the promise-plan of God (Ro 11:20–23).

The Separate Covenant. Traditional or classic dispensationalism affirmed that Israel and the church had separate identities, promises, programs, and destinies. Thus, dispensationalism in its classic forms distinguishes between the two peoples of God (Israel and the church) and the two programs of God (the kingdom of God and the kingdom of heaven). It argues that Jesus came with an offer of the kingdom to Israel, but they did not accept it, so the offer of the kingdom was "postponed," and thus Jesus was forced to go to the cross instead.

It must be recognized, however, that in recent years "progressive dispensationalism" has emerged. Proponents of this view, often former adherents to "classic dispensationalism," reject the idea of a postponed offer of the kingdom of God to the Jews of Jesus' day, while affirming that there is generally one people and one program of God in the whole Bible.

But the classic view still faced some real problems: (1) the early church preached her gospel directly from the Old Testament (e.g., the Bereans in Acts 17:11, who "examined the Scriptures [i.e., the Old Testament] every day to see if what Paul said was true"), for the New Testament did not exist yet; (2) the church was not based on a different promise-plan of God from that made with Israel, for the new covenant was, as dispensationalism itself argued, made with the "house of Israel and the house of Judah"; (3) the church is not an intercalation, a parenthetical interruption in the plan of God, but part of the continuation of God's promise-plan (Ro 11:5); (4) Israel and the church are not to be regarded as separate and distinct from each other, but as one body of believers (Eph 2:14 – 16; 4:4 – 6; Ac 15:11); and (5) the kingdom was not "postponed" when Israel refused to believe in Jesus while he was on earth, for the cross of Christ was not an alternative, or backup plan, but was in the divine order of things (Ac 4:27 – 28; Rev 13:8; Ps 110:1); thus, the church is part of the kingdom plan of Jesus related to the Jews (Mt 8:11 – 12; Lk 13:28 – 29; Ac 8:5, 12; 28:23, 28). Moreover, the Jews wanted to make Jesus their "king" (Jn 6:15) when they saw how he fed the five thousand, but he would not allow them to do so, for their desires were motivated by political aspirations alone and not by matters of the heart or soul. Dispensationalism believed there would be a future for the nation of Israel, but it often did so by maintaining too sharp a line of division between the earthly and heavenly peoples of God, with a hypothetical offer of salvation by works for those who (theoretically) perfectly kept the law, something no one, of course, was ever able to do (cf. Gal 3:21).

The Renewed Covenant. Following Willis J. Beecher's 1905 Stone Lectures at Princeton Seminary, this writer has focused on *epangelia*, the Greek word for "promise," thus calling this proposal "Epangelicalism." It agrees with the covenantal position that the plan of salvation in Scripture is *one* and that there is *one* "people of God." But in that one program and one people there are distinctions or various aspects that can be observed without making them into separate sets of peoples or programs.

The promise-plan of God, moreover, focused on the *contents* of the covenants in the Old Testament, rather than focusing on the *shape* and *form* of the covenant, or even the name of the covenant. It noted that the content of each of the covenants and promises in the Scripture was both retained and progressively enriched, enlarged, and incorporated into a body of foundational truths that carried the main burden of the whole message and plan of the Bible. It did all of this without jettisoning God's promises to the ancient nation of Israel or barring the door for the Gentile inclusion while grafting all believers, Jew and Gentile, into the same olive tree.

The new covenant, in this respect, is viewed as a "renewed covenant" (see the discussion of Jer 31:31 – 34 below) that repeated almost three-fourths of what God had included in the earlier covenants with the patriarchs and the Davidic line. However, there were new items as well in that renewed covenant of Jeremiah 31:31 – 34. This plan of God that began in Genesis 3:15 with the promise of an *heir*, the "seed," would go on to include the *inheritance* of a "land," and the *heritage* of the gospel, in which all the nations of the earth would be blessed. But all of this was merely a beginning of a constellation of specifications that were embraced in this one unifying plan of God called the promise.

It is this plan and the unity we have briefly depicted here that we will describe and trace in its grand overarching metanarrative that runs through the whole Bible. We trust that it will restore for all who study it both the coherence and cohesiveness that once was a hallmark of our presentations of the gospel. Enjoy!

Part 1

A Biblical Theology of the Old Testament

Chapter 1

Prolegomena to the Promise: The Pre-Patriarchal Period

Genesis (From the beginning to about 2150 BC)

Genesis 1–11

The Structure and Purpose of Genesis

The purpose and teaching of the book of Genesis are found in its literary structure. Eleven times, the phrase "This is the account of..." introduces each new section (Ge 2:4; 5:1; 6:9; 10:1; 11:10, 27; 25:12, 19; 36:1, 9; 37:2).[1] Accordingly, this repeated phrase serves as a framework for the whole book and shows that there was a continuum from creation to Adam's line, from Adam's line to Noah's line, from Noah's line to Noah's three sons, from them to his son Shem, and then on to Terah, the father of Abraham. About half of this literary framework appears in Genesis 1–11, thereby placing the story of these early chapters in the same historical context as the other half, with the same literary structure appearing in the patriarchal narrative of Genesis 12–50.

The theology of the whole book of Genesis is centered around the goodness of God in extending his "blessings" of the promise-plan so generously all the way from creation to the choice of Abraham's line to be the means by which God would bless the nations of the world with his gift of the good news. The word for the promise-plan of God that dominates the theology of Genesis is *blessing*, a word that occurs in both its verbal and nominal form some 88 times in the whole book of Genesis. However, it must always be remembered that the theology of Genesis is only a part of the whole, which in this case is the complete Torah, also called the Pentateuch, the teaching of the first five books of the Bible: Genesis, Exodus, Leviticus, Numbers, and Deuteronomy.[2]

---

1. T. D. Alexander, "Genealogies, Seed and Compositional Unity of Genesis," *Tyndale Bulletin* 44 (1993): 255–70.

2. D. J. A. Clines, *The Theme of the Pentateuch* (Sheffield, UK: University of Sheffield, 1978).

Genesis 1 – 11 provides the broadest, most universal and cosmic setting for the total promise-plan of God. The sweep of these initial chapters of the Bible strongly indicates that God's concern was for the whole world, even before he announced the role the patriarchs and their offspring would play in carrying out this mission for "all the families of the earth" (12:3).[3]

The hallmark of Genesis 1 – 11 is to be found in the "blessing" of God as expressed in the Edenic, Noachic, and Abrahamic covenants. He was the one who had promised to "bless" all created beings at the beginning of the pre-patriarchal narrative (1:22, 28), later at several strategic points in the course of its narrative (5:2; 9:1), and at the conclusion to this first section in the Bible (12:1 – 3). Thus, the promise-plan of God began using the theme of blessing or "to bless"[4] as one of the terms that signaled the introduction of the promise-plan of God, thereby insuring the unity, parameters, and center for the theology of Genesis 1 – 11, even though it did not use the term "promise," which would become the label of choice later in New Testament times.[5]

Unfortunately, this block of biblical materials has rarely been treated in its unified contribution to theology. All too often, as Claus Westermann observed,[6] theologians have restricted their attention to a discussion of creation, the fall, and humanity's personal sin before God. However, the canonical shape of the message as we have it in Genesis 1 – 11 asks of the interpreter much more than those meager results. Humanity is placed before God in the fall but is likewise located in a society and in the gifts of government and the state, according to Genesis 4 and 6. Accordingly, humanity was the recipient of much more than life and successive curses for disobedience — principally, that they would also receive the coming Man of promise.

The pattern of events in all eleven chapters is too closely interwoven to be left aside by the exegete or theologian. Structurally, they exhibit the juxtaposition of God's gift of blessing with humanity's revolt. The divine word of blessing initiates every type of increase and all legitimate dominion; it follows the central tragedy of the section — the flood — and concludes in the transitional section of Genesis 12:1 – 3 in the blessing of the gospel itself as described in Genesis 12:3b (cf. Gal 3:8).

Humanity's revolt, on the other hand, is evident primarily in the three catastrophes of the fall, the flood, and the "flop" of the tower of Babel. Here too, in each of these disasters and crises for human civilization, the divine word was present — only it was a word of judgment before it was a word of blessing.

But even this triple rhythm of blessing and curse, hope and doom, did not exhaust the basic structure and theology of the text in its wholeness. God's goal for history, while

3. T. W. Mann, "'All the Families of the Earth': The Theological Unity of Genesis," *Interpretation* 45 (1991): 35 – 53.

4. C. W. Mitchell, *The Meaning of BRK "To Bless" in the Old Testament* (Atlanta: Society of Biblical Literature, 1987).

5. See the diagrams of the New Testament use of "promise" in appendix 2.

6. Claus Westermann, *Creation*, trans. J. J. Scullion (Philadelphia: Fortress Press, 1974), 17 – 31. His analysis of Genesis 1 – 11 agrees at several points with conclusions we had already reached independently.

marked by the insertions of his word at critically important junctures, was opposed by humanity's continual rejection of these divine blessings in a doctrine of work (2:15), in the area of the family (4:1–16), in cultural achievements (vv. 17–24), in the development of the human race (Ge 5; 10; 11:10–32), and in the gift of government and the state (6:1–6).

The double line of humanity's failure and God's special word of grace or blessing can be represented this way:

Humanity's Failure:	God's Blessing:
1. The fall (Ge 3)	a. Promise of a seed (Ge 3:15)
2. The flood (Ge 6–8)	b. Promise of God's dwelling in Shem's tents (Ge 9:25–27)
3. The flop and the scattering (Ge 11)	c. Promise of worldwide blessing (Ge 12:1–3)

The Word of Creation

But as the theology of this section began, so did the world—by the divine word of a personal, communicating God. Ten times over, the text reiterated this lead-off statement: "And God said" (1:3, 6, 9, 11, 14, 20, 24, 26, 29; 2:18). Creation, then, was depicted as the result of the dynamic word of God. To call forth the world in direct response to God's spoken word was to act as Jesus of Nazareth did when, in response to his word, men and women were healed. For example, the centurion pleaded, "But just say the word, and my servant will be healed" (Mt 8:8). And his servant was healed at that very hour (Mt 8:13). So the word was likewise spoken in Genesis 1, and the world came into being. This theological affirmation appears later in the Psalms:

> By the *word of the Lord* the heavens were made,
> their starry host by the *breath of his mouth*....
> For he *spoke*, and it came to be;
> he commanded, and it stood firm.
>
> *(Psalm 33:6, 9, emphasis mine)*

Whether secondary causes were also thereby set into motion in effecting the result cannot be determined from the text. Every time the text would seem to imply a mediate creation (i.e., where the existing materials or forces of nature might be authorized or endowed by God to do the work of carrying out the creation order—the three instances being: "Let the earth bring forth" [Ge 1:11]; "Let the waters bring forth" [v. 20]; "Let the earth bring forth" [v. 24]), the next verse in two of the three instances (vv. 21, 25) attributes the same things as having been done directly by God. Only Genesis 1:11 (the land producing vegetation) might be an exception to representing God's work as immediate creation, since verse 12 continues that same way of speaking without the qualifying phrases seen in Genesis 1:21 and 25. However, that may simply be a way of highlighting the recipient (the earth or the waters) of the forthcoming benefits of God rather than textually providing for a mediate or secondary agency in these instances.

On the whole, the method of creation was as clear as its source: it was God who created, and the method he used was his word. But word-creation stresses more than method. It emphasizes that creation was in accordance with God's knowledge as embodied in his word. Likewise, his purposeful design and the predetermined function of all things was underscored, since he often *named* what he created. Thus the essence and purpose of his creation was outlined from its inception. And if he named these things, he then owned them, for one only names what one owns or is given jurisdiction over.[7]

Often the discussion of the time of creation consumes more time and energy than it should in our modern attempts to interpret the text. Biblical theology generally is disinterested in this discussion. However, the decision over whether Genesis 1 – 2 reported an *absolute beginning* or merely a *relative beginning* is central to the concern of theology.

Recently, many modern translations have preferred a "when ... then" construction for Genesis 1:1 – 3: "*When* God created,... the earth being without form,... *then* God said" (emphasis mine). While such a construction is possible on certain grammatical grounds, there are strong arguments against such an explanation or translation in this instance. Both the punctuation of the Hebrew Masoretic text and Greek transliterations of the Hebrew text into Greek letters show convincingly that there was quite a respectable history of interpretation that took the first word, *bᵉrēšît*, as an absolute noun, "in the beginning," rather than as a Hebrew construct noun, "in beginning of creating," or "When God began to create."[8] Therefore, Genesis 1:1 commits itself to the absolute beginning of everything ("heaven and the earth") outside of God.

The use of the verb *bārā'*, "create" (1:1, 21, 27; 2:3 – 4; 5:1 – 2; 6:7), does not appear to be as determinative for a creation out of nothing view as some might expect it to be. This is apparent in that apart from God himself, no language calls for such a concept for conversations among mortals. Therefore, in the Bible the verb is indeed restricted to God as its sole subject. It is never used with any agency of material and is rendered by the strongest Greek verb for "create" (*ktizō*) in the Greek Septuagint translation of the Old Testament, but it also appears in parallel usage to two other words in the creation narrative: *'āśâh*, "to make, do" (1:26 – 27; cf. also its later parallels in Isa 41:20; 45:18), and *yāṣar*, "to form, mold" (2:7; cf. its later usage in Isa 43:1; 45:18; Am 4:13). In Isaiah

7. In the ancient Near East, to "name" something was "to call one's name over" that person, place, or thing, thereby showing one's ownership and sovereignty over it.

8. For further support and additional arguments, see E. J. Young, *Studies in Genesis* (Nutley, NJ: Presbyterian and Reformed Publishing House, 1964), 1 – 14. See also the fine article by Gerhard F. Hasel, "Recent Translations of Genesis 1:1: A Critical Look," *Bible Translator* 22 (1971): 154 – 67.

45:18 all three verbs appear in parallelism, thus disallowing any major distinction or special nuances between them:

> For this is what the LORD says —
> he who created [*bārā*] the heavens,
>   he is God;
> he who fashioned [*yātsar*] and made [*'āśâh*] the earth,
>   he founded [*kûn*] it;
> he did not create [*bārā'*] it to be empty,
>   but formed [*yātsar*] it to be inhabited —
> he says:
> "I am the LORD,
>   and there is no other."

To be sure, "create" does appear at the outset of the creative order (Ge 1:1), at the first appearance of life (v. 21), and with the designation that man is made in the image of God (v. 27). But this cannot be used to support the untenable view of theistic evolution, as A. H. Strong and James Orr[9] argued at the beginning of the twentieth century by noting that there were three interruptions, as they would call them, in the divine work of creation: (1) at the creation of matter (1:1), (2) at the creation of life (1:21), and (3) at the infusion of the *imago Dei* into the man and the woman (1:26 – 27). The preceding evidence of parallel usage of creation verbs would discourage placing a higher value on the word *bārā* than on the other two verbs for "to make," and "to form" in order to claim that theistic evolution is taught in the biblical text.

We conclude, then, that God initiated the creation process out of nothing other than his word. More detailed statements will need to wait until Hebrews 11:3 states a doctrine of creation *ex nihilo*, "out of nothing," in definitive terms.

The Days of Creation. The "days" of creation climax in the creation of man and woman. They were the chief interest of our writer. For in typical style, observed throughout the whole work on Genesis, the writer quickly traced the smaller details of the creation picture before he entered into the subject or persons on which he wanted to focus. Adam and Eve both were made on the sixth day, but the duration of that "day" (*yôm*), and the details of how they were created are further explained in Genesis 2:4ff. By now the reader is aware of the author's elasticity in his use of the word "day": it shares the same range of meaning as is known in modern English. It is equal to daylight (as 1:5 attests); to our calendar days which make up the year (as 1:14 attests); and to the whole span of creation, or, as we would say, the "day of the horse and buggy" or the "day of Abraham Lincoln" (as 2:4 likewise uses the word).

9. A. H. Strong, *Systematic Theology, Vol. II: The Doctrine of Man* (Philadelphia: Judson Press, 1907); James Orr, *The Christian View of God and the World*, 9th ed. (New York: Scribner's, 1908), Lecture Notes III and IV.

The sixth creative period of time must also have lasted more than a twenty-four hour day, for it was long enough for Adam to grow lonely for a companion (2:20). Surely this loneliness took more than an afternoon's idle thought! Moreover, he busied himself with the task of naming the animals as his loneliness continued to build. Finally, God created a woman, and it was still that sixth "day."

Through the influence mainly of Augustine, the early church — up until the middle of the nineteenth century — held the majority view that there had been three creative "days" before the calendar type of days were created on the fourth day (1:14). Thus, the usage urged here is not a modern backward projection to an antiquated text that needed to be rescued from scientific embarrassment; it was the clear teaching of the text itself. God did not make a twenty-four hour day until three of these types of "days" in Genesis had passed!

Some of the details of what followed the divine word of Genesis 1:26 are now supplied in 2:4 – 7, which is not a second creation story but rather a fleshing out of the main emphasis of the story quickly traced in chapter 1. Adam was not "alive" (*nepeš ḥayyâh*), as it is more accurately rendered, even though some translate it in a more word-for-word manner as "living soul," until God had taken some of the dust of the ground, shaped it, and breathed into it the breath of life. Now to be sure, these are anthropomorphic expressions, but they surely are figures that say God was directly involved in the production of a man and a woman. Humanity's vitality was a direct gift from God, for prior to that he was not "alive" — that much the text carefully claimed!

Eve too was "built" (*bānâh*) by God, yet in such a way that her propinquity or closeness to Adam was assured. She was to be "bone of [his] bone and flesh of [his] flesh" (2:23). Together they originated from the hand of God. Man was so linked to the soil that as his fortunes went, so did the fortunes of nature; and woman was likewise linked to man, for she was "taken from man."

Both, however, shared equally in the highest gift given to any of the orders of creation: the image of God. Male and female shared alike, and both were fully equal as God gave this exclusive and highest mark yet set on anything in creation. Only later in New Testament terms will the definitional content of this image become clearer (e.g., the "image of God" will include "knowledge," Col 3:10; and "righteousness and holiness," Eph 4:24). In the Genesis record, the precise content of the image is less specific. We see it expressed in concepts such as the possibility of fellowship and communication with God, the exercise of responsible dominion and leadership over the creation owned by God, and the fact that in some way unspecified as yet, God is the prototype of which man and woman are merely copies, replicas (*ṣelem*, "carved or hewn statue or copy") and facsimiles (*d^{e}mût*, "likeness").[10]

10. The literature on the image of God is huge. Some of the more representative but recent contributions are D. J. A. Clines, "The Image of God in Man," *Tyndale Bulletin* 19 (1968): 55 – 103; James Barr, "The Image of God in the Book of Genesis — A Study in Terminology," *Bulletin of John Rylands University Library* 51 (1968): 11 – 26.

Word of Blessing. The word of creation was followed by a word of blessing. Accordingly, all creatures of sea and air were endowed with reproductive capabilities and given a divine mission:

> God blessed them by saying:
> "Be fruitful and multiply
> and fill the waters of the seas;
> and let the birds multiply on the earth." (Ge 1:22, my translation)

This part of the blessing humanity shares with the created order mentioned in verse 22, but an additional part of our blessing appears to stem decidedly from the gift of the image of God. Almost identical terms are used in verses 26 and 28 to amplify one part of the image that was foremost in the mind of God when he so graciously benefited that first couple: they were to subdue and "have dominion" over all creation (v. 28). Of course, the divine mission to "subdue" (*kābaš*) and to "dominate" (*rādâh*) was no license for humanity to abuse the creative orders. Human beings were not to be bullies or a law to themselves. They were to be God's viceroy and therefore accountable to him. Creation was to benefit humanity, but humanity also was to benefit God!

Once more, the divine word of blessing came: "Then God blessed the seventh day and made it holy, because on it he rested [*šābat*] from all the work of creating that he had done" (2:3). The day is called the Sabbath (*šabbāt*) because it was the day commemorating God's cessation (*šābat*) of his work. In this way he put a division between his work of creation and all subsequent work (usually termed the providential work of God). Thus history has the first of three great divine markers found in revelation: (1) the Sabbath; (2) the "it is finished" of Psalm 22:31; John 19:30 (the division between redemption promised and redemption accomplished); and (3) "it is done" of Revelation 21:6 (the division between history and eternity).

So God made the seventh "day" holy as a perpetual memorial to the fact that he had completed the entire universe and all that was in it. His "rest" was to be symbolic for man, both in his own rhythm of work and cessation from labor and for his eternal hopes. So decisive was this ending that the writer also abruptly stops his narration of events; he does not conclude with the expected "And there was evening and there was morning, a seventh day."

All had been completed. Everything had been done. It was all "good"; in fact, it was "very good" (1:31). Every function, every being, and every blessing necessary to carrying out life and its joys were now in hand. But this was all an untested goodness.

The First Word of Promise: The Seed

To test humanity's obedience and free decision to follow the Creator, God placed the tree of the knowledge of good and evil in the garden of Eden with the prohibition that Adam and Eve were not to eat its fruit. As such, the tree contained no magical enzymes or vitamins; it simply stood for the possibility of humanity's rebellion against the clear word of God. In eating the fruit, humankind would personally "know" (that is, experientially taste) the opposite side of all the good they currently experienced. The totality of experience — both good and bad — would be in their repertoire of sensations.

Another factor must be added before the theology of the fall can be understood. The serpent (*hannāḥāš*), the creature that was "more subtle than the beasts of field" (3:1), was also present in the garden. The craftiness and subtlety of the serpent was comparably greater than that of any of the beasts of the field.[11]

Most people know that the New Testament identified this serpent with Satan: "The God of peace will soon crush Satan under your feet" (Ro 16:20); "The great dragon was hurled down — that ancient serpent called the devil, or Satan, who leads the whole world astray" (Rev 12:9; 20:2); "just as Eve was deceived by the serpent's cunning ... for Satan himself masquerades as an angel of light" (2Co 11:3, 4). But few recognize that he acted in the garden of Eden in the same way.

Satan's form and shape are no more implied by his appellation "the serpent" than by the name "dragon." Nor is the curse on him determinative for setting his morphology. Genesis 3:14 only asserts that his conquest was so secure that it used the symbolic clause, "You will crawl on your belly" (cf. Ge 49:17; Job 20:14, 16; Ps 140:3; Isa 59:5; Mic 7:17), which pointed to Satan's eventual and total defeat. Also, his contemptible station and abject humility were so real that he would lick the dust or, as we say today to opponents on the athletic field, "Bite the dust." Both phrases were pictures from the ancient Near East of vanquished mortals: they were forced to lie face down, prostrate before the conquering monarchs, often forming for the conquering king the footstool for his throne.[12] Reptiles do not, of course, eat dirt as their food, but Satan would taste defeat as a result of his part in the temptation. Also observe carefully that God had already created "creatures that move along the ground" in Genesis 1:24 and had pronounced them "good" (v. 25). Therefore, the curse on Satan could not have been the reason God made "creepers" and pronounced a curse over them because of the action of Satan; this mode of locomotion already existed in the created order with no negative overtones.

The serpent consistently speaks on his own behalf in the dialog with the woman; he is not a surrogate for someone else. He was even party to what God had said; in fact, from his own knowledge he knew the possible alternatives and eventualities that would come from eating the fruit. To the woman, he was a person and not one of the animals, for she did not express surprise at being addressed by him. She was, however, offended by the distorted narrowness that he attributed to God and the limited freedom of the first couple. The serpent implied that it was grossly unfair for God to deny this couple the privilege of eating from any and all of the trees of the garden.

11. The Hebrew *mikkôl* could be taken in Genesis 3:1, 14 as a partitive, "*any* of the beasts of the field" — or as a comparative, "than the beasts of the field." But in 3:14 all agree that the construction must be comparative. Context also dictates in favor of our rendering. See Paul Haupt, "The Curse on the Serpent," *Journal of Biblical Literature* 35 (1916): 155–62.

12. Cf. the Amarna Tablets, E.A. 100:36; Psalm 72:9; Isaiah 49:23; Micah 7:17.

Deception worked its trick, however, and the woman succumbed to the heavy pressure and cunning argumentation of the tempter himself. Adam also disobeyed, but on less strenuous grounds than those laid upon the woman, for he just ate, even though he had had a greater advantage in that he had walked and talked with God in the garden for a longer time than had Eve. Thus the first failure of the three selected by the writer of Genesis for theological reflection set the scene for a new word of divine blessing. If any blessing was to come from any place, it would be from God.

A prophetic word of judgment and deliverance was addressed to the serpent (Ge 3:14 – 15), the woman (v. 16), and the man (vv. 17 – 19). The reason for the curse was stated in each case: (1) Satan beguiled the woman; (2) the woman listened to the serpent; and (3) the man listened to the woman — no one listened to God! Consequently, the ground would feel the effects of humanity's fall. It would bring forth thorns and thistles and result in the man's sweat. Meanwhile, children would be born with pain, and a woman's "turning" (*t^e^šûqâh*) (but not, as almost all translate it, as her "desire")[13] to her husband would result in the fact that he would "rule over" (*māšal*) her, that is, take unfair advantage of her. However, the serpent, for his part, would face the disgrace of certain, ultimate defeat and vanquishing.[14]

But in the midst of the dirge of gloom and rebuke came God's surprising word of prophetic hope (Ge 3:15). A divinely instigated hostility — "I will put enmity between you [the serpent] and the woman, and between your offspring [or seed] and hers — is climaxed with the triumphant appearance of a "he" — no doubt a representative person of the woman's seed. He would deliver a lethal blow to the head of Satan, while the best the serpent would be able or even permitted to do would be to nip the heel of this male descendant.

Who this male descendant was, was not immediately revealed. Perhaps Eve thought Cain was that one. She named her son Cain (Heb., *qayin*), saying she had "gotten (Heb., *qaniti*) a man, even the Lord" (4:1); at least, that is a fair way of rendering the enigmatic phrase.[15] Regardless of whether one agrees with this rendering, she was mistaken, and the biblical text only records her longings and perhaps gives us an insight into how clear an understanding she had of Genesis 3:15 — she expected that God would supply a person who would care for their sin that had occasioned the fall.

Yet God had not been silent. He had spoken, and his word prophesied of another day when a complete reversal of the serpent's temporary coup would happen as a result of the one who had spoken so authoritatively. Furthermore, the "blessing" of God's promise-plan to humankind did continue. The genealogy of the ten most significant men in the antediluvian period recorded in Genesis 5 was one type of evidence of that

13. The translation of *t^e^šûqâh* as "desire" dates to the Middle Ages when a sexual nuance was introduced for the first time. See Walter C. Kaiser Jr., "Correcting Caricatures: The Biblical Teaching on Women," *Priscilla Papers* 19, no. 2 (2005): 5 – 11, for more information on this matter and related issues.

14. Ibid.

15. This is a literal rendering of the Hebrew and is the way Luther interpreted the Hebrew in his German Bible.

blessing.[16] They were "fruitful" and they did "multiply," just as Genesis 5:2 reaffirmed that word, saying, "He created them male and female and blessed them." So they had "sons and daughters" as further evidence of the blessing of God.

Humankind was blessed in the fields (4:1 – 2) and also in cultural advances (vv. 17 – 22). Moreover, the selection of the twenty men in the two genealogies leading up to Abraham (apparently listing only the most important of that line and sequence), plotted the progress of that "seed" promised to Eve as well as the agents of that blessing for their contemporaries.

Meanwhile, the theme of judgment continued to mar the record. There was another notice of banishment from the immediate presence of the Lord. Just as Adam and Eve had been sent forth from the garden of Eden in Genesis 3:23 – 24, so Cain, the murderer of his brother Abel, was condemned to be "a fugitive and wanderer on the earth" (4:12 – 16).

The sense of God's presence had been so intimate that when offerings were brought to the Lord, it was the Lord himself who first inspected the man (4:4 – 5) and then looked at the offering itself. God valued the heart condition of the one making the offering more than the gift that was brought. Thus it was that jealousy broke out in the institution of the family, resulting in murder and the necessary imposition of the theme of judgment on Cain for the first murder in the Bible.

The Second Word of Promise: The God Who Will "Dwell" among Shem

The earth's second crisis came with the subversion of the institution of the state as it led an unruly populace to practice and perpetrate evil. Already a proud Lamech had begun to distort the purpose of government with his boastful tyranny and polygamy (4:23 – 24). According to his thinking, he was not to be challenged or rebuked by anyone. If Cain would be avenged by God sevenfold, then Lamech would be avenged seventy-seven times, he boasted.

In the midst of the blessing of God ("men began to multiply on the face of the earth," 6:1), came the heaping up of evil. The rulers of the day, having adopted for themselves the Near Eastern titulary of "sons of God,"[17] autocratically began to multiply as many wives for themselves as they pleased. Their lust for a "name" (Heb., *shem*, i.e., a "reputation," 6:4), led these autocratic rulers to compound their excesses and abuse the purposes of their office.

In exasperation, God gave up on humankind. His Spirit would not always continue to strive with men (6:3). Such "mighty men" (v. 4), or aristocrats (*n^{e}pilîm gibborîm*), must be halted in their wickedness. Once again the theme of expulsion will come, only in a much more tragic and final way: God would blot out humanity from the earth (v. 7).[18]

16. See Excursus A at the end of this chapter on the use of the numbers in the two genealogies in Genesis 5 and 11.

17. Meredith Kline, "Divine Kingship and Genesis 6:1 – 4," *Westminster Theological Journal* 24 (1961 – 62): 187 – 204.

18. See Excursus B at the end of this chapter on the identity of the "sons of god."

"But Noah found favor in the eyes of the LORD" (6:8), for he was "a righteous man, blameless among the people of his time" (v. 9). Thus the earth's second greatest time of need, according to this text, was to be relieved, as it had been in Genesis 3:15, with an enactment of the salvation from God. There was a righteous remnant — not by accident or by any means of partiality. Noah's father, Lamech, found in Noah — at the time of his birth — the "comfort" (for that is the meaning of "Noah") that his work in the earth, previously cursed by the Lord, would now be lightened with Noah's help (5:29).

The wickedness forcing the hand of God was not an inevitable fate allotted to all people now that the fall was a fait accompli. There had been righteous men during this same time. Consider Enoch, who "walked with God" for 365 years, not as a hermit in isolation, but as a man who raised a family of sons and daughters (5:22). So pleased was God with his life of obedience and faith that "he was not" on earth any longer, for God "took him" (v. 24). The text handles so easily the issue of mortal man being ushered into the very immortal presence of God that we are amazed that no further explanation follows. Did Enoch's translation serve as a paradigmatic model for Old Testament people until further revelation filled in the hiatus of information? The revelation of that fact would always be available if any wanted to ponder its implications.

Noah was of that stock. He found grace in the eyes of the Lord. Noah was righteous before God in his generation (7:1). Instructed by God, he built an ark. Thus he and his family experienced the salvation of God while judgment came on the rest of humanity.

The divine blessing, "Be fruitful and multiply and fill the earth," was again repeated, this time to Noah, his wife, his sons, their wives, and every living thing on the earth, in the air, and in the sea (8:17; 9:1, 7). Here God added his special covenant with nature. He would maintain "seedtime and harvest, cold and heat, summer and winter, day and night" without interruption as long as the earth remained (8:22). The contents of these promises formed an "everlasting covenant" between God and every living creature (9:8, 11, 16) as signified by the rainbow in the sky. Along with this note of God's blessing was his explicit promise "Never again will I curse (*qallēl*) the ground because of human beings" (8:21), a reminder of a similar curse on the ground in Genesis 3:17. Likewise the reference to the "inclination of the human heart" (*yēṣer lēb*) in 8:21 recalled a similar phrase using the same word, *yēṣer*, in Genesis 6:5. Given the repeated appearance of such features, it may be confidently asserted that the structural unity stretched from Genesis 1 to 11.[19]

19. See the informative discussion of R. Rendtorff, "Genesis 8:21 und die Urgeschichte des Yahwisten," *Kirche und Dogma* 7 (1961): 69 – 81, as cited by W. M. Clark, "The Flood and the Structure of the Prepatriarchal History," *Zeitschrift für die alttestamentliche Wissenschaft* 83 (1971): 205 – 10. Rendtorff argued that the age of curse and primeval history both concluded in Genesis 8:21. As Clark points out, Genesis 9:25ff. does raise the curse again, but it is of limited application to Canaan, and it is followed by an immediate blessing.

The word of judgment and salvation reached its highest point in the aftermath of the earth's second crisis. It came through Noah after he learned what his son Ham had done to him while he was sleeping off the effects of his wine.

The structure of Genesis 9:25 – 27 is a heptastich (a poem consisting of seven lines), which is divided into three parts by the repeated refrain of Canaan's servitude, a son of guilty Ham:

> He [Noah] said,
> "Cursed be Canaan!
> The lowest of slave
> will he be to his brothers."
>
> He also said,
> "Blessed be the LORD, the God of Shem!
> May Canaan be the slave of Shem.
>
> May God extend Japheth's territory;
> may Japheth live in the tents of Shem,
> and may Canaan be his slave."

Now the key issue is this: Who is the subject of the verb *w^{e}yiškōn*, "may he [here rendered 'Japheth'] live" in verse 27? We concur with the judgment of the Targum of Onkelos, Philo, Maimonides, Rashi, Aben Ezra, Theodoret, Baumgarten, and Delitzsch that the subject is God, not Japheth. Our reasons are these: (1) the subject of the previous clause is presumed to continue into the next clause where the subject is unexpressed, which was true in this instance since it only said "May he live/dwell"; (2) the use of the indirect object in the previous line as subject ("Japheth") of this line would require strong contextual reasons for doing so; (3) the context of the next several chapters designates Shem as the first in honor of blessings; and (4) the Hebrew phrase *w^{e}yiškōn b^e'oh^{o}lê šēm*, "and he will dwell [or live] in the tents of Shem," hardly makes sense if it is attributed to Japheth, for Japheth had already been granted the blessing of expansion.

The plan of the whole prophecy appears to devote the first strophe only to Canaan, the second to Shem and Canaan, and the third to all three brothers. On balance, then, the best option is to regard God as promising to Shem a special blessing. God himself would dwell with the Semitic peoples. The word for "dwell" is related to the later concept of Mosaic theology of the "Shekinah" glory of God, wherein the presence of God over the tabernacle was evidenced by the pillar of cloud by day and the pillar of fire by night. Hence, the man Shem would be the one through whom the "seed" promised earlier in 3:15 would now come. Had not God said, "Praise be to the LORD God of Shem" (9:26)? And why did he use this distinctive form of address? Could it be that the blessing and indwelling were linked? And could it be that they were God's next provision to earth's latest crisis?

The Third Word of Promise: A Blessing to All the Nations

The third and final crisis during this period of mixed blessing and curse was the concerted effort put forth by the human race to organize and preserve their unity around some architectural symbol. As they put it, "Let us make a name for ourselves and not be scattered over the face of the whole earth" (11:4).[20] Even though the blessing of God continued to be realized in their multiplication (11:10 – 32) and their filling the earth with some seventy nations (10:1 – 32), the thoughts of their hearts were again directed away from the glory of God or his provisions. The judgment of God came in the double form of the confounding of their speech and the scattering of the peoples over the earth. But again the sin-curse theme was closely matched with a divine grace-blessing theme.

Instead of uniting people around an ethno-political project aimed at the glorification of human beings and their ability to meet the needs of a disparate community of nations, God provided his word of blessing once again. It was a word that climaxed every blessing pronounced in the pre-patriarchal narrative. Five times in Genesis 12:1 – 3, a transitional section between the two time periods of Genesis, the word "blessing" is repeated. Nor was it any surprise that it was a word directed to one of Shem's descendants, Abraham. He was himself to be blessed; yet he was thereby to be a blessing to all the nations of the world. What the nations could not attain by their own organization and goals would now be given to them in grace.

The number of people included in "all the families of the earth" (*mišpᵉḥōt hāʾᵃdāmāh*) is the same as the list of nations in Genesis 10. Had not Genesis 10:32 concluded, "These are the families of the sons of Noah" (*mišpᵉḥōt bᵉnê nōaḥ*)? The promise, then, was universal and was limited in its participation only by the response of faith — even as it was so limited for Abraham's participation.

Thus earth's third crisis was again resolved with the gracious word of the same God who dealt justly with sin. We conclude that the theology of this section is a unified development, bracketed and advanced by the free, gracious word of God. It commenced in a word of creative power; it concluded in a word of promise.

The debacles of humanity's first disobedience in Genesis 3, the tyrannical distortion of political power in Genesis 6, and the haughty aspiration of unity on a humanistic basis in Genesis 11, led to the judgments of the fall, the flood, and the failed unification of humanity. They resulted instead in the dispersion of humankind. The theological factors found in each crisis, which perpetrated the judgment of God, were the thoughts, imaginations, and plans of an evil heart (3:5 – 6; 6:5; 8:21; 9:22; 11:4). But God's salvific word was equal to every default of earth's mortals. Alongside the sin-judgment themes came a new word about a "seed" (3:15), a race among whom God would personally take up his

20. Samuel Noah Kramer, "The 'Babel of Tongues': A Sumerian Version," *Journal of the American Oriental Society* 88 (1968): 108 – 11.

residence and "dwell" (9:27), and the blessing of what Paul would later call the "good news" of the gospel (Gal 3:8) offered to every nation on the face of the earth (12:3).

Excursus A: Can the Numbers in the Genealogies of Genesis Be Used to Calculate the Date of Adam's Birth?

The most important observation one can make about the theological use of the numbers of years at which the ten antediluvians of Genesis 5:3 – 32 and the nine or ten postdiluvians of Genesis 11:1 – 32 had children, and the total years they lived, is that nowhere does the biblical text add up these numbers or use them to make a chronological note as to when Adam was born or the total number of years that expired before and after the flood. However, the same author who recorded these numbers, Moses, will in another instance supply a numerical summary, as in Exodus 12:40, saying Israel was in Egypt 430 years. A later writer, in 1 Kings 6:1, will say that 480 years had elapsed from the exodus from Egypt to the fourth year of Solomon's reign, when he began to construct the temple. Again, in Judges 11:26, that writer will observe that three hundred years had expired from the entry into the land until the time of the judge Jepthah, who lived around 1100 BC. So there was no fear of giving such numerical summaries; it just was not done in Genesis 5 and 11.

But if the numbers in Genesis 5 and 11 are not to be added up, then what was the reason for recording them? There are two theological reasons for their inclusion. First, that the numbers for the total number of years that each lived move from somewhere close to a thousand years old down to around two hundred years old demonstrates that men and women had been built to be immortal but that the corrosive effects of sin could already be observed even in the physical side of life. Second, the same corrosive effects of sin could be seen in the declining years at which these mortals were able to bear children, as it also slides from a high of five hundred down to twenty-nine years.

Anglican Bishops J. B. Lightfoot (nineteenth century) and James Ussher (seventeenth century) were grossly mistaken to surmise, based on an inappropriate and nonbiblical use of these numbers, that Adam was created on October 24, 4004 BC at 9:30 a.m., 45th meridian time. Closer than that, being careful scholars, they would not venture! But what they failed to notice was that not only did the text refrain from doing what they had just done, but the genealogies in the Bible routinely exhibit considerable amounts of abridgement at times. Thus, Matthew 1:1 has Jesus as the son of David (about

1000 BC), who was in turn the son of Abraham (about 2100 BC). Moreover, the genealogy that followed in Matthew 1 reduced the line of Jesus to three sets of fourteen individuals, since the name of "David" (Hebrew *dvd*) adds up to fourteen: "D" = 4, the middle Hebrew letter, *waw* (*v*) = 6, and the last "D" = 4, for a total of 14.

Even in the two Genesis genealogies, there was a built-in warning not to use these numbers for purposes of gaining a perspective on a chronological extension of time. For example, in Genesis 11:26, it would appear at first blush that Abraham's father had triplets in his seventieth year. However, it will not all add up if that is the use we are going to assign to these numbers. Abram (also called Abraham), who is one of the so-called triplets, left Haran when his father died (Ge 12:4; Ac 7:4), but he was only 75 years old at the time. But Genesis 11:32 asserted that Terah had lived a total of 205 years. If Abram had been born in Terah's seventieth year, and he was 75 years old when his father died, that gives a total number of years for Terah of 145, not 205. Thus, we think that the seventieth year was the year he began having children, but the figures were of no value in calculating the total time that had elapsed, if one went from father to son, as Lightfoot and Ussher were proposing.

Accordingly, the list of names in Genesis 5 and 11 only record the very important persons who carry the line forward and name the next one in line, though the person may be several generations removed. Examples from late in Israel's history exhibit gaps of seven to ten generations that are more often than not skipped, yet the father is still said to "beget" the one who was removed by that many or more generations.

Few have equaled the fine study done on this issue by the late William Henry Green of Princeton Seminary in the nineteenth century. Green's patient tracing of a number of these genealogies reinforced the conclusion described here.[21]

Excursus B: The Sons of God and the Daughters of Men (Genesis 6:1–4)

There are three positions used to explain Genesis 6:1 – 4 that may be labeled: (1) the cosmologically mixed races view (the mingling of angels and humans),

21. This article, "Primeval Chronology," from *Bibliotheca Sacra* (April 1890), is reprinted in Walter C. Kaiser Jr., ed., *Classical Evangelical Essays in Old Testament Interpretation* (Grand Rapids: Baker, 1972), 13 – 28.

(2) the religiously mixed races view (the godly Sethites and the worldly Cainites), and (3) the sociologically mixed races view (despotic male aristocrats and beautiful female commoners).

The oldest and best-known view is that the sons of god were "angels" who left heaven and came to earth and had sexual relations "with the daughters of men," leaving a race of "giants" (Heb., *nephilim*). The pseudepigraphal book of Enoch from around 200 BC (Enoch 6:1 – 7:6) put forth this theory, as did the historian Josephus (*Antiquities* 1.3.1) and the Greek Septuagint translation of the Old Testament in the third century BC (though only the Alexandrian manuscript does so; the critical edition of the Septuagint by Alfred Rahlfs does not). They all explain "sons of God" as angels, but that use of the term only occurs in Job 1:6; 2:1; and 38:7 (with a possible parallel in Psalm 29:1 and 89:7 for "sons of the mighty").

Nowhere in Scripture are we told, either in this passage in Genesis 6 or elsewhere, that angels married human women. In fact, Mark 12:25 states that angels do not marry. Even more serious is the fact that if the problem began with the initiative of the "sons of God," who are equated in this view with angels, then why did God not flood heaven instead of bringing his judgment on earth? Some will still appeal to 1 Peter 3:18 – 20; 2 Peter 2:4; and Jude 6 – 7 for additional support for the angel theory, but these passages do not mention angelic marriages.

The religiously mixed races view fares no better than the cosmologically mixed races view. This view argued that the apostate line of Seth committed the sin of being unequally yoked with unbelieving "daughters of men," who are interpreted to mean those from the line of Cain. But this view also fails, for it used the term "men" in verse 1 in a different sense than in verse 2: in verse 1 it meant "humanity" generally, but in verse 2 it meant the "line of Cain" specifically. Also, why would a religiously mixed race have such dramatic physical results as a race of "giants," as the Hebrew phrase *nephilim gibborim* is understood? Religion is not known to affect the DNA in this sort of way!

The best view is the sociologically mixed races view. The "sons of God" title was an early but favored titulary for kings, nobles, and aristocrats in the ancient Near East. Such power-hungry despots were driven to be "men of renown" in their quest for a "name" (Ge 6:4). In this power drive, they despotically usurped control. They perverted the whole concept of God-given government by doing whatever they pleased, with no amelioration of any of earth's injustices or iniquities, for which relief God had given government in the first place (6:5 – 6). They also became polygamous (6:2).

The evidences for this preferred view are these: (1) the ancient Aramaic Targums rendered the "sons of God" as "sons of nobles"; (2) Symmachus's Greek translation rendered the same phrase as "the sons of kings or lords"; (3) the Hebrew word for "God/gods" is *'elohim*, which is used in Scripture and rendered already in many English Bibles as "magistrates," or "judges" (Ex 21:6; 22:8; Ps 82:1, 6); and (4) discoveries from the ancient Near East have validated the pagan use of a host of gods' and goddesses' names to give more prestige and clout to the authority and despotism of kings and rulers in that day.

On the matter of the so-called giants, the word *nephilim* occurs only here in 6:4 and Numbers 13:33, which in the Numbers passage does refer to the Anakim, who were people of great stature. The root of the word *nephilim* comes from *naphal*, "to fall." Moreover, the word *nephilim* is associated in some contexts with the word *gibborim*, which comes from *gibbor*, meaning "a man of valor," "strength," "wealth," or "power." For example, Nimrod, in Genesis 10:8, was such a *gibbor*. He also appears to be a king in the land of Shinar (i.e., probably, Babylon). Therefore, the meaning of *nephilim*, in this context, does not appear to be "giants," but something more like "aristocrats," "princes," or "great men" who ruled.

Genesis 6:1 – 4, therefore, is best understood as depicting ambitious, despotic, and autocratic rulers who seized power and women in any way they pleased and did so in an attempt to build their own reputations and notoriety. Not surprisingly, this spirit was also carried on by their progeny as well. The result was that every inclination of the hearts of men and women, from rulers on down to the populace, was increasingly wicked. That is why the flood had to come: humanity had to be judged for its perversion of the right, the good, and the just, along with judgment on the institution of the state and on government, which also had provoked God to the limit.

Chapter 2

The Provisions in the Promise: The Patriarchal Era

Genesis, Job (About 2100 – 1800 BC)

Genesis 12 – 50

The same structure observed in the first eleven chapters of Genesis continues into the patriarchal period: "The account of ..." (25:12, 19; 36:1, 9; 37:2). Many consider this formula, with a good deal of justification, to indicate the sources that Moses used under inspiration of God for the material that obviously predated his times.

The story picks up with God's call of Abraham, where God uses the term *bārak*, "to bless" five times in the transitional section between the pre-patriarchal and patriarchal times (12:1 – 3). Abraham (and later, his offspring) is to be a "blessing" to all the families of the earth (12:3). Thus the promise of God is embedded in the "blessing" of God, used in its verbal and nominal form some 88 times in Genesis.

A new progress in the divine revelation begins with Genesis 12. In this new era, there is to be a succession of individuals who now serve as God's appointed means of extending his word of blessing to all humanity. Under God's election for service and his call to personal and worldwide blessing, Abraham, Isaac, and Jacob became hallmarks of a new phase in the accumulating divine blessings in the promise-plan of God.

Word of Revelation

The emerging prominence assigned to the divine word in the pre-patriarchal era did not diminish in the patriarchal times; instead, it increased. In fact, it may be noted as one of the distinctive features of Genesis 12 – 50, for repeatedly the patriarchs were presented as the frequent and immediate recipients of various forms of divine revelation.[1] It is not surprising, then, that the record should treat them as "prophets" (Ge 20:7; and later in Ps 105:15), men who had immediate access to the word and ear of the living God.

At crucial junctures in their history, God addressed these men directly in spoken words (12:1, 4; 13:14; 15:1; 21:12; 22:1) with the introductory formula of "The word of the LORD came to him" or "The LORD said to him." Therefore it was not only Moses to whom God spoke clearly "mouth to mouth" (Nu 12:6 – 8), but God also spoke in some direct way also to Abraham, Isaac, and Jacob.

Even more startling was the fact that the Lord himself appeared (lit., "let himself be seen" [*wayyērā'*]) by these men in what has subsequently been called a theophany (18:1). The reality of the living God's presence underscored the importance and authenticity of his words of promise, comfort, and direction. These appearances (also known as epiphanies), brought humanity, God, and his purposes for men and women into a very close nexus. All three patriarchs experienced the impact of God's presence on their lives (12:7; 17:1; 18:1; 26:2 – 5, 24; 35:1, 7, 9). Each appearance of God marked a major development in the progress of revelation as well as in the lives of these men. There he would again bless them, rename them, or send them on a mission that carried with it major consequences for the patriarchs, if not for the whole scheme of theology to follow.

Coupled with these theophanies was the manifestation of "the angel of the LORD" (Ge 16:7).[2] This particular angel appears to have been more than just an angelic messenger from God. Frequently, he received the respect, worship, and honor that was usually only reserved for God, yet he was consistently distinguished from God. His role and appearance are even more obvious in the period of the judges; however, there was no scarcity of references in the patriarchal era either (16:7 – 11; 21:17; 22:11 – 18; 24:7, 40; 31:11, 13; 32:24 – 30; 48:15 – 16). Thus he carried an identity with God, yet he was also sent from him! To say that the patriarchs regarded him as equivalent to what the New Testament would call a christophany would not be far from the truth. One thing for sure, he was not the invisible God. And he acted and talked as the Lord. There the matter apparently rested until revelation clarified the enigma later on, when he was recognized as a pre-incarnate appearance of Christ.

God also spoke during this era through dreams (*ḥ^{a}lôm* — 20:3; 31:10 – 11, 24; 37:5 – 10; 40:5 – 16; 41:1 – 32) and visions (*maḥ^{a}zeh, mar'ōt* — 15:1; 46:2). The vision was a distinct mode of communicating new knowledge to Abraham in a dramatic setting in which Abraham was aware of a complete panorama of detail (chap. 15). Jacob experienced a similar vision urging him to go down to Egypt (chap. 46). However, dreams

1. P. V. Premsagar, "Theology of Promise in the Patriarchal Narratives," *Indian Journal of Theology* 23 (1974): 114.

2. See Aubrey R. Johnson, *The One and the Many in the Israelite Conception of God* (Cardiff: University of Wales Press, 1961), 28 – 33.

were more widely distributed to persons such as the Philistine king Abimelech; Jacob's uncle, Laban; the jailed Egyptian butler and baker; Pharaoh; and the young, inexperienced Joseph. In all such instances, the emphasis was on the dream as dream; its interpretation or revelation was not always an integral part of this form of God's address to men and nations.

Word of Promise

What a premium this era placed on the innovative and beneficial character of that word! Indeed, from the very outset of Genesis 12 – 50, the accent fell on God's word of blessing and promise. To Abraham, this one promise appeared in four stages of development, which are to be found in Genesis 12:1 – 3; 13:14 – 16; 15:4 – 21; and 17:4 – 16 (and perhaps also 22:15 – 18).

The content of this promise was basically threefold: a "seed," a "land," and a "blessing to all the nations of the earth" of the gospel. If one could select an emphasis in this series, pride of place would go to the last item. On five separate occasions the patriarchs were designated to be a blessing for all nations: Abraham in Genesis 12:3; 18:18; and 22:17 – 18; Isaac in 26:3 – 4; and Jacob in 28:13 – 14. Indeed, worldwide blessing was the whole purpose of God's promised blessing ever since the very first statement of that promise in 12:2 – 3.

Even before any technical vocabulary about entering into a covenant appeared, God promised to enter into a relationship with Abraham and thereby to be and to do something for Abraham that would benefit both him and all the nations of the earth. The writer presented Genesis 12:2 – 3 as the substance of that word of blessing and promise.

First, there were three short clauses addressed to Abraham alone, using the Hebrew cohortative[3] form of the verb.

1. "I will make you a great nation."
2. "I will bless you."
3. "I will make your name great."

The third clause states something that is almost certainly filled with irony. The quest for a "name," that is, renown, reputation, and even superiority, had been the driving ambition of those tyrannical kings called "sons of God" in Genesis 6:1 – 4 and the architects of the Tower of Babel in Genesis 11:4. Now God himself would give to one man, on God's own divine grounds, what others had so selfishly sought but failed to attain.

Moreover, the significance of this third clause and the previous two becomes clear for the first time when the next clause was added to the previous three. No doubt it is to be taken as a result or even a purpose clause. It stated the divine purpose and inten-

3. A cohortative form of the Hebrew verb expresses in the first person a resolve to do something. It is usually indicated by adding *– ah* to the end of the Hebrew verb in the first person in the prefix tense of the Hebrew verb.

tion for benefiting Abraham so generously: "So that [or in order that] it [or you] may be a blessing" (Ge 12:2). The Hebrew simply reads *wehᵉyēh bᵉrākâh*. Consequently, a preliminary goal has been achieved in this newly announced relationship. Abraham is to be: (1) a great nation, (2) personally blessed, and (3) the recipient of a great name. But all of this was *so that* he might be a blessing.

But to whom was Abraham to be a blessing? And how was Abraham to be a blessing? Those questions appear to be answered in the next three clauses. First, the Lord added two more promises in Genesis 12:3, again using the Hebrew cohortative form of the verbs.[4]

4. "I will bless those who bless you."
5. "I will curse those who curse you."

Not only did God thereby continue the promise, but he introduced a whole class of people who would respond variously to Abraham. Only then was the grand finale reached. This time the Hebrew verb shifted suddenly to the perfect tense,[5] in what again can only be a result (or purpose) clause: "So that [in order that] in you all the nations of the earth shall be blessed."

What a vast sweep was now included in what might have been so trite and so personal an exchange between a single individual and his God! Of course, most competent commentators remain skeptical about the passive rendering of the niphal (the passive stem for active verbs) form of the Hebrew verb,[6] but they fail to see that already the previous result clause had stated as much without specifying exactly to whom Abraham was to be a blessing. The text was so clearly a response to the needs of the swarming multitudes listed in the table of nations (chap. 10) and the multiplication of Shem's line (chap. 11), that it easily could be classified as one of the first great worldwide missionary texts of Scripture.

Thus far, the emphasis was on God's word of blessing. There was a deliberate attempt to connect this new phase of theology with the pre-patriarchal emphasis. Five times God had promised his blessing in the short space of two verses, but Abraham was to be the focus of attention: he was to be a great nation, he was to have a great name, and he was to be blessed by God and by all people. There was no direct reference yet in Genesis 12:1 – 3 to a "seed" or an "indwelling" in the tents of Abraham as was promised in Genesis 1 – 11. Nor was there a reference yet to a covenant (*bᵉrît*), which God would "cut" (*kārat*, 15:18), "give" (*nātan*, 17:2), "establish" (*hēqîm*, 17:7, 19, 21), or to which he

4. E. Kautzsch, *Gesenius' Hebrew Grammar* (Oxford: Clarendon Press, 1909), 325, says that cohortative following the imperative expresses either result or intention. Intention fits here very well.

5. I am indebted to H. C. Leupold, *Exposition of Genesis* (Grand Rapids: Baker, 1968), 1:411 – 14, for many of the observations in this analysis of Genesis 12:2 – 3.

6. See O. T. Allis's article, "The Blessing of Abraham," *Princeton Theological Review* 25 (1927): 263 – 98, which contained an irrefutable linguistic case on the passive rendering of this niphal. No one to this day has attempted a response to his evidence.

would "swear" to (*nišba*ʿ, 22:16). As the references show, that was to come later in God's disclosures. Just now it was a relationship with a man that served as a basis for blessing the peoples of the earth. Interestingly enough, the actual realization of the promise of nationhood would have to wait for several centuries until Israel was delivered from Egypt.

An Heir

When Yahweh appeared to Abraham, after the patriarch had arrived at Shechem, that ancient word about a "seed" (3:15) was again revived. Now, however, it was directed to Abraham (Ge 12:7). From there on, the importance of this gift of a child who would inherit the promises and blessings became one of the dominant themes in the patriarchal narrative, appearing, all told, some twenty-eight times.[7]

Eve had been promised both a "seed" and a male individual—apparently from that "seed." Now in the progress of revelation, with much greater specification added, the concept was elaborated both on the corporate (all who believed) and representative (Man of promise/"Seed") aspects of this promised heir. It was to encompass so great a number that, in hyperbolic fashion, they would rival the stars of heaven and the sands on the seashore. But this "seed" would also be another "son"—born at first to Abraham, when all hope of his ever having children was lost, and then continued in the one born to his son Isaac, and later to the one born to Isaac's son Jacob.

A line of successive representative sons of the patriarchs who were regarded as one with the whole group they represented matched the seminal idea already advocated in Genesis 3:15. Furthermore, in the concept of "seed" were the two aspects: (1) the seed as a future *benefit* and (2) the seed as the present *beneficiaries* of God's temporal and spiritual gifts. Consequently, "seed" was always a collective singular noun; few times did it have the meaning of a plural noun (as in "descendants"). Thereby the "seed" was marked as a unit, yet with a flexibility of reference: now referring to the *one* person, now to the *many* descendants of that family. This interchange of reference with its implied "corporate solidarity" was more than a cultural phenomena or an accident of careless editing; it was an integral part of its doctrinal intention. The best contemporary illustration of this phenomenon, which is called "corporate solidarity in biblical studies," can be seen in the Western world, where an individual who wished to sue a major corporation would see on the court docket their individual name listed versus the name of the corporation, which for purposes of law was always treated merely as another individual, even though that corporate name also functioned as a corporate label for all that that company stood for and owned. However, everyone would know that the corporate

7. Genesis 12:7; 13:15, 16 (2x); 15:13, 18; 16:10; 17:7, 8, 9, 10, 13, 16, 19; 21:12; 22:17 (2x), 18; 24:7; 26:3, 4 (3x), 24; 28:13, 14 (2x); 32:12; 35:12; 48:3, 4.

"individual" was a legal fiction, for behind that label stood a CEO or president of the corporation, all the employees, the board(s) of governors of that company, and all the stockholders of that company. Thus, we refer to the "one" and the "many" when we refer to the "seed," or "offspring," but the use of the translation "descendants" limited the reference only to the whole group who believed but did not include the representative of the whole group, the coming Messiah himself.

The drama of the possible obstacles and frustrations that could have permanently blocked the divine intention here made up a large part of the historical record in this era. Barrenness seemed to plague all three wives of the patriarchs: Sarah (16:1; 17:15 – 21); Rebekah (25:21); and Rachel (30:1). Old age was another threat in Abraham's case (17:17; 18:11 – 13).

Egyptian and Philistine monarchs nearly stole the wives away from the patriarchs, because of each husband's fearful lying (12:10 – 20; 20:1 – 18; 26:1 – 11). Added to this were the ravaging effects of famine (12:10), filial hostility (32:7 – 8), and later even the slaughter of infants conducted by Pharaoh (Ex 1:22). But through it all the meaning was precisely as God put the question to Sarah: "Is anything too miraculous ['wonderful' or 'difficult,' Heb., *h^{a}yippālē*] for the Lord?" (18:14).

Not even Abraham's attempt to preserve this seed was to count, for the entire life of this child (and each one that followed him) was completely a gift of God. Therefore, when God "tested" (*nissâh*) Abraham's faith by asking him to sacrifice his only son — yes, the very one on whom the whole plan and promise of God rested — he did not demur (Ge 22:1 – 10). He feared God (v. 12) and believed that God would "provide" (vv. 8, 14, *yir'eh*) so that he *and the lad* would be able to rejoin the party after the sacrifice with those who were waiting at the base of Mount Moriah (v. 5).

Isaac was also more than a mere foil. He too had a deep stake in what was happening. Yet he learned obedience and trust in this same Lord. Later in his life, when Isaac had selected Esau to receive his blessing and when everything humanly possible of going wrong was taking place as sons, mother, and father plotted over who would be the marked heir to carry the line of the "seed," again Isaac learned that the calling and election of God were not of human intellect or work. God made his selection of his heir apart from the tragic and ridiculous human attempts to upstage the divine plan and free gift.

An Inheritance

The promise of the land of Canaan to Abraham, Isaac, Jacob, and their seed ran through these narratives as the second of the three key themes (Ge 12:1, 7; 13:15, 17; 15:7 – 8, 18; 17:8; 24:7; 26:3 – 5 [pl. "lands"]; 28:13 – 14; 35:12; 48:4; 50:24; and later reaffirmed in Ex 3:8, 17; 6:6; 23:23 – 24, a total of some 20 times).

Genesis 15:18 describes the borders of this land as extending "from the river of Egypt to the Euphrates." Genesis 17:1 – 8 emphasizes that the land was to be an "everlasting possession." And Genesis 15:1 – 21 explains that the patriarch would possess the promised word about the land but that he would merely taste some of the reality of being personally in the land, for the full reality would be delayed until the "fourth generation" when "the iniquity of the Amorites [was] complete" (v. 16).

From the very first moment of God's call to Abraham, he had spoken of this "land" or "country" to which he was sending him (12:1). Albrecht Alt was wrong in rejecting the promise of land as being an authentic part of the patriarchal promise.[8] Likewise, Gerhard von Rad had no factual basis for denying that the entrance into the land by the twelve tribes was not exactly the same vision held by the patriarchs.[9] Only Martin Noth of these three scholars allowed both the land promise and the promise of a seed to be parts of patriarchal religion.[10] Faithfulness to the message of the text in the canonical shape as it has now come down to us demands that both promises be treated as equally authentic and necessary parts of God's message to the patriarchs.

The solemnizing of this offer of land took place in the so-called covenant of pieces (15:7 – 21). Acting on the instructions given by Yahweh, Abraham took various sacrificial animals and divided them into two. After sunset, "a smoking furnace and a flaming torch passed between the pieces" (v. 17), and Yahweh made a covenant to give to Abraham and his seed the whole land.

Such a material or temporal blessing was not to be torn apart from the spiritual aspects of God's great promise. Nor was it to be spiritualized or transmuted into some type of heavenly Canaan of which the earthly Canaan was only a model. The text is emphatic, especially in chapter 17, that this covenant was to be eternal. However, already in Genesis 13:15 the offer of the land in its entirety was given to Abraham "forever." And when Abraham was ninety-nine years old, this promise was made into "an everlasting covenant" (*b^e rît ʿôlām* — 17:7, 13, 19) and the land was to be for an "everlasting possession" (*ʾ^a ḥuzzat ʿôlām* — 17:8; also 48:4). The word *ʿôlām*, "everlasting," must add something more to the noun it went with, for in the case of covenant, there was already a strong idea of perpetuity.[11]

The ancestral promises were fulfilled in the later settlement of the land under Joshua. This, in turn, became a token or pledge of the complete land grant yet to come in the future, even as the earlier occupations were simultaneously recognized as "expositions, confirmations, and expansions of the promise."[12] Thus even Joshua's settlement of the land did not exhaust the promise of this land as a place chosen by Yahweh for his

8. Albrecht Alt, "The God of the Fathers," *Essays on Old Testament History and Religion*, trans. R. A. Wilson (Garden City, NY: Doubleday, 1968), 83 – 84.

9. Gerhard von Rad, *Old Testament Theology* (London: Oliver and Boyd, 1962), 1:168 – 70.

10. Martin Noth, *A History of Pentateuchal Traditions*, trans. B. W. Anderson (Englewood Cliffs, NJ: Prentice-Hall, 1972), 54 – 58, 79 – 115, 147 – 56.

11. See the somewhat unsatisfactory studies of E. Jenni, "Das Wort *ʿôlām* in AT," *Zeitschrift für die alttestamentliche Wissenschaft* 84 (1952): 197 – 248; idem, "Time," *Interpreter's Dictionary of the Bible* (Nashville: Abingdon, 1964), 4:644; James Barr, *Biblical Words for Time* (Naperville, IL: Allensons, 1962), 69, n.1.

12. Jürgen Moltmann, *Theology of Hope* (New York: Harper & Row, 1965), 105.

people. For just as the promise of a son had been enlarged to include in that sonship all the patriarch's descendants, so there was an "overspill" as well in the land promise from the time of Joshua's occupation of the land until the day when God brought Israel back from her times of exile.

A Heritage

The third and climactic element in the promise was that Abraham and each of the successive sons of promise were to be the source of genuine blessing; indeed, they were to be the touchstone of blessing to all other peoples on the earth. All nations of the world would be blessed by them, for each was the mediator of life to the nations (of Abraham — 12:3; 18:18; 22:17 – 18; of Isaac — 26:3 – 4; and of Jacob — 28:13 – 14).

The apostle Paul would later point to this phrase ("all the peoples on earth will be blessed through you," Ge 12:3), and declare that it was the same "gospel" he preached (Gal 3:8). Simply put, the good news was that "in [the promised seed] all the nations of the earth shall be blessed" (Gal 3:8). Thus the embryo of God's good news could be reduced to the linchpin word "blessing." The one who was blessed was now to be the conduit of blessing of universal proportions to the whole world. In contrast to the nations who sought a "name" merely for themselves, God made Abraham a great name so that he might be the means of blessing all the nations on earth.

But, it might be asked, how were the nations to receive this blessing mediated by Abraham or any of his successive sons? The method must be the same as it was for Abraham. It would be by faith: "Abram believed the LORD, and he credited it to him as righteousness" (Ge 15:6).

The literal rendering of Genesis 15:6 is simply he believed in Yahweh (*he*ᵉ*mîn ba YHWH*). This, of course, was more than a vague intellectual assent to a supreme deity in which he decided merely to become a theist. The object of his faith was to be found in the content of the total promise. As such, priority may be given to the oldest, most ancient, and most central part of that promise: the person or the man of promise signified by that male descendant who was to come from the seed (3:15). Indeed, when God first met Abraham, the issue of progeny was not specifically included but only inferred (12:1 – 3), for the first clause promised to make Abraham into a great nation. His trust, then, was in the Lord — but particularly in the Lord who had promised.

Conrad von Orelli's summation of this connection between Abraham and the faith of the nations is worth noticing:

> How Abraham himself, in virtue of his special relation to God, was a mediator of blessing to those about him, is shown in Gen. xx.7; that his people in the same way were to convey the divine blessing, the dispensation of God's grace to the whole world, see in Isa. xix.24; Zech. viii.13. In the present passage the import of the brief saying is expounded in [Gen. 12:]3, according to which God's relation to men depends on their attitude to Abraham (cf. xx.7), and the Lord will deal well with those who wish well to

> him and do homage to the divine grace revealing itself in him; and on the other hand, will make him feel His displeasure who despises and scorns one whom God has blessed. The singular number here is significant. It can only be single hardened sinners who so misunderstand one who is a source of blessing to all about him, as to condemn and hate him, and in him his God. The world, as a whole, will not withhold homage, and will therefore enjoy the benefit of this source of blessing. The latter is implied in the final words [of 12:3] which puts the crown on the promise.... But whether the subjective act of homage or the objective act of divine blessing lies in the niphal ["be blessed"], exegetes are not agreed. That one involves the other follows, however, from the preceding words.[13]

Since the verb "to believe" in Genesis 15:6 is the Hebrew hiphil form (the causative stem) of the verb *'āman* (cf. English "amen"), Geerhardus Vos pointed to the "causative-productive sense"[14] of the verb and to the preposition. Both, in his judgment, showed that faith had its source and its object in the personal Yahweh. For Abraham, it meant he had to renounce all his human efforts to secure the promise (as witnessed by his attempting at first to legally adopt Eliezer as his son and the inheritor of his estate, Ge 15:2), and he had to depend on the same divine person who had spoken of the future to work in the present as well as the future, to accomplish what he said he would do. Thus, Abraham possessed the *promises* of God, as yet unrealized, when he possessed the God of the promises and his trustworthy *word*, even though he never got to enjoy the reality of the content of the promise — the land itself — during his lifetime.

Some will object to describing the Abrahamic promises as being unconditional and unilateral, with all of the obligation for their fulfillment both in the present and the future on God and not on Abraham or his descendants. Five passages are often cited as examples of stipulations of obedience placed on Abraham in order that he might receive these blessings: Genesis 12:1; 17:1, 9 – 14; 22:16; 26:5.

The first is the imperative, "Go from your country, your people and your father's household to the land I will show you" (12:1). This imperative is followed by two imperfects and then a series of cohortative imperfects in verses 2 – 3. But does such a command amount to a formal condition on the divine intention to bless? While admitting that there is a certain conditional element present, Cleon Rogers correctly demonstrated that the accent of the passage was on the cohortatives, which emphasized intentionality rather than obligation, and that this type of construction occurred in Genesis 45:18 (where the stress was on what Joseph intended to do for his brothers) or Genesis 30:28 (what Laban intended to do for Jacob) and Genesis 27:3; 1 Samuel 14:12; 28:22; 2 Sam-

13. Conrad von Orelli, *The Old Testament Prophecy of the Consummation of God's Kingdom Traced in Its Historical Development*, trans. J. J. Banks (Edinburgh: T & T Clark, 1889), 107.

14. Geerhardus Vos, *Biblical Theology* (Grand Rapids: Eerdmans, 1954), 98. Von Rad, *Old Testament Theology*, 1:171, stressed that the object of faith was "something in the future," God's "plan for history (Gen. xv. 5)," and this is what Abraham believed and "'made himself secure' in."

uel 14:7.[15] Thus the summons to "Go," was an invitation to receive the gift of promise by faith.[16]

Genesis 17:1 – 2 would appear at first to impose another condition: "Walk before me faithfully and be blameless. Then I will make my covenant between me and you and will greatly increase your numbers." Once more the sequence was two imperatives followed by two cohortative imperfects. Therefore, what was true of 12:1 – 3 is also applicable here. Furthermore, the promise had already been repeated several times, in 12:1 – 3, 7; 13:14 – 17; 15:7 – 21; and 16:10. Consequently, some expositors have argued that the force of the verb translated "I will make" (*w*^{e}*'ett*^{e}*nâh*) does not mean "to set up" but rather "to put into force" or "make operative the one that is in force."[17] The identical argument would apply for 17:9 – 14, where circumcision might, at first blush, seem like another condition on the promise. But verse 11 completely settled the argument: circumcision was only a "sign" of the covenant, not its condition.

The last two passages are more difficult. In Genesis 22:16 – 18 Abraham was told, "Because (*kî ya'an ʾ*^{a}*šer*) you have done this and have not withheld your son, your only son, I will surely bless you ... because (*ʿēqeb ʾ*^{a}*šer*) you have obeyed me." In Genesis 26:5 the blessing is repeated to Isaac "because (*ʿēqeb ʾ*^{a}*šer*) Abraham obeyed me and did everything I required of him, keeping my commands, my decrees and my instructions." In my judgment, the conditionality was not attached to the promise, but only to the participants who would benefit from these abiding promises. If the condition of faith was not evident, then the patriarch would become a mere transmitter of the blessing without personally inheriting any of its gifts directly. Such faith must be evident also in an obedience that sprang from faith. Certainly, the promise was not initiated in either chapter 22 or 26; that had long since been settled. But each chapter did have a sensitive moment of testing or transition. Furthermore, the election of God had been with a purpose not only of blessing Abraham and the nation (18:18) but also of charging him and his household to "keep the way of the LORD by doing what is right and just, so that (*l*^{e}*maʿan*) the LORD will bring about for Abraham what he has promised him" (v. 19).

The connection is undeniable. The duty of obedience (law, if you wish) was intimately tied up with promise as a desired sequel. Therefore, the transition to the coming time of Mosaic law should not be all that difficult for any who had really adequately listened to the full revelation of the promise in the patriarchal era. But in no way was the promise-plan itself dependent on anyone's obedience; it only insured their participation in the benefits of the promise but not on its maintenance.

15. Cleon L. Rogers Jr., "The Covenant with Abraham and Its Historical Setting," *Bibliotheca Sacra* 127 (1970): 252 and n. 61.

16. Hans Walter Wolff also agrees; see Walter Brueggemann and Hans Walter Wolff, "The Kerygma of the Yahwist," *The Vitality of Old Testament Traditions* (Atlanta: Knox Press, 1975), 47.

17. Leupold, *Genesis*, 1:514; C. E. Keil and F. Delitzsch, *Biblical Commentary on the Old Testament* (Grand Rapids: Eerdmans, 1866), 1:223.

Word of Assurance

Throughout the patriarchal narratives one more theme rang out as another part of the "blessing" of the promise. It was simply God's pledge: "I will be with you."

Actually, the first time God's presence with men was explicitly mentioned was where the writer commented that God was "with" (*'et*) Hagar's son Ishmael (21:20). Then it appeared as a word in the Philistine mouths of Abimelech and Phicol to Abraham: "God is with (*'im*) you in everything you do" (21:22) and later to Isaac: "We can clearly see that the Lord was with (*'im*) you" (26:28).

Out of 104 examples of this formula of the divine presence employing the two Hebrew prepositions translated "with" (*'et* and *'im*) in the Old Testament, fourteen examples of God's assurance appear in the Isaac and Jacob narratives.[18] God appeared to Isaac with these comforting words: "Do not be afraid, for I am with (*'et*) you" (26:24). Or as he said in an earlier appearance, "Stay in this land, and I will be with (*'im*) you and will bless you" (26:3). For Jacob, it was a dream of a ladder with God's assurance as he set out for Haran: "Behold, I am with (*'im*) you and will watch over you wherever you go" (28:15).

To this Jacob vowed, "If God will be with (*'im*) me and will watch over me on this journey I am taking, ... then the LORD will be my God" (28:20–21). Again, when Jacob was about to return to Canaan, the Lord repeated his earlier promise: "I will be with (*'im*) you" (31:3). Accordingly, Jacob repeated to Laban that the Lord had indeed been with (*'im*) him (31:5; 35:3). Jacob's son Joseph likewise experienced that same divine presence of God (39:2, 3, 21, 23).[19] As Jacob had been favored and blessed by the God who knew of his problems with a scheming Laban, so Joseph was likewise rescued and blessed by the same Lord who followed his changing situation in Egypt.

Yahweh's active presence manifested his character, power, and ability to fulfill the repeated word of promise. It was preeminently a word of personal relationship. The divine presence, of course, had been felt by Abraham before the words were put into a promise-theology formula. For example, the victory Abraham won over Kedorlaomer in Genesis 14:13–24 was an illustration of this fact, even if the word was not present. Similarly, so was the intimacy of Abraham's cross-examination of God over his justice in dealing with Sodom and Gomorrah (18:23–33); the Judge of the whole earth would do what was right. Had he not been Abraham's "shield" and "exceeding great reward" (15:1)?

Abraham received the first part of what was to become the oft-repeated tripartite formula of the promise. For now, it was the divine promise: "I will ... be your God and the God of your descendants after you" (Ge 17:7). The sovereign God of all the universe would now condescend and call himself the God of Abraham and his seed.

18. Horst D. Preuss, "*'eth, 'im*," *Theological Dictionary of the Old Testament*, ed. G. J. Botterweck and H. Ringgren, trans. John T. Willis (Grand Rapids: Eerdmans, 1974–) 1:449–63, esp. 456.

19. Charles T. Fritsch, "God Was with Him: A Theological Study of the Joseph Narrative," *Interpretation* 9 (1955): 21–34.

Therein lay the essence of their personal relationship. No wonder James remarked that Abraham was "called God's friend" (Jas 2:23). Their relationship was one of love (18:19), action (19:29), and blessing in all that Abraham did (21:22).

Ruler of Promise

As the blessing Abraham received in Genesis 12:1 – 3; 15; and 17 was transferred to Isaac in 26:3 – 6 and then to Jacob in a dream at Bethel in 28:13 – 14, and especially at Paddan Aram (35:9 – 12; cf. 46:1 – 4), so Judah, the fourth son of the patriarch, received it from Jacob's blessing in 49:8 – 12.

True, Joseph did receive a double portion in the inheritance, since his two sons were in a sense adopted by Jacob (cf. *b^e^kōrāt* of 1Ch 5:1), but Judah became the "leader" (*nāgîd*) among his brethren. The oldest son, Reuben, lost his birthright because he dishonored his father's marriage bed (Ge 35:22). Simeon and Levi, Jacob's second and third sons, were bypassed because of their outrageous revenge on the Shechemites (34:13 – 29). So the mantle of leadership fell to Jacob's fourth son, Judah.

As Isaac had blessed his son Jacob in Genesis 27:29, so Jacob now transmitted the same supremacy over his brothers to his son Judah in 49:8. His prowess would make him a princely tribe, and he would maintain his superiority over his foes. His emblem would be the regal lion. To him were given the scepter (*šēbet*) and the ruler's staff (*m^e^ḥōqēq* — 49:10).

But what is the meaning of the phrase "until Shiloh comes" (*'ad kî yābō' šîlōh*)? Again, the opinion of von Orelli merits careful attention:

> The context on one hand, the oldest authorities in respect of reading on the other, conduct us to our translation. *Š^e^lloh* was the reading handed down from antiquity, and the LXX [Septuagint] rendered this neutrally: *heōs ean elthē ta apokeimena autō* [until there come the things stored up for him]. Instead of this abstract neuter subject we take the personal subject dominating everywhere here and render: *until he comes into that which belongs to him*, therefore *into his own*, his possession described on the sequel. Cf. especially the blessing of Moses on Judah, Deut. xxxiii.7: *w^e^'el 'ammô t^e^bî'ennû* ["to his people bring him"]. As champion of the other tribes, he will display untiring energy until he has won his territory without curtailment; and then not merely will the tribes of Israel do homage to him but other nations also will bow to his rule.[20]

Of the last phrase of Genesis 49:10, "he shall take to him the peoples" (*w^e^lô yiqq^e^hat 'ammîm*), he continued,

20. Von Orelli, *Prophecy*, 121 – 22. The Lucianic and Origenic recensions of the LXX read *heôs an elthē apokeitai*, "until he, to whom it is reserved, comes."

> [peoples] cannot apply to the Israelites merely,... but must refer to the more general national rule, which according to xxvii.29 is part of Jacob's heritage, and will be Judah's special portion.[21]

For Ezekiel, or later Jewish and Christian interpreters, to regard this as another addition to the doctrine of the seed to come is therefore not unwarranted. Neither was Ezekiel's allusion in 21:27, "until he to whom it rightfully belongs shall come, to him I will give it," out of bounds either.[22] The Man of promise would be overwhelmingly successful; he would reign over all the peoples of the earth because it was his right and destiny so to do. Furthermore, he would originate from the tribe of Judah in Israel!

Job and the Patriarchs

In his commentary on the book of Job, Edouard Dhorme noted "that the period which the sacred author had in mind ... was that of the patriarchs."[23] Dhorme went on to itemize some of the striking resemblances between the book of Job and the descriptions of the patriarchs in Genesis 12 – 50:

- The wealth of Job (1:3) and the prosperity of Isaac (Ge 26:13 – 14)
- Increase in Job's cattle (1:10) and Laban's increase of cattle (Ge 30:29 – 30)
- The preference for the divine name of Shaddai in Job and the patriarchs
- Non-priests offer sacrifice (1:5) as did the patriarchs
- Content of the sacrifice (7 bulls and 7 rams) (42:8) is the same offered by Balaam for King Balak (Nu 23:1 – 3)
- Job lived 140 years (42:16), which allowed him to see four generations (35 years for a generation) and Joseph lived 110 years, which allowed him to see three generations (about 36 years for a generation) (Ge 50:23)
- The currency of *qesitah* (42:11) is the same as in Jacob's day (Ge 33:19; Jos 24:32)

---

21. Ibid. See W. Gesenius, *Hebraisches und Aramaisches Handworterbuch*, 17th ed., F. Buhl, ed. (Leipzig, 1921), 596[b]. He concluded that *'ammim* is never used of Israel exclusively; it refers to all peoples or people outside Israel.

22. For further study, see W. L. Moran, "Genesis 49:10 and its use in Ezekiel 21:32," *Biblica* 39 (1958): 405 – 25. He would vocalize "Shiloh" as *šay* and *lôh* and change *yâbô'* to the hiphil *yûbâ'*, "until tribute is brought to him and his is the obedience of the people." Moran rightly rejects the reading *šîlu(m)* as an alleged Akkadian cognate meaning "Prince, ruler, king" (which does not occur in Akkadian, 405 – 9) and the reading "of the City Shiloh" (which is never spelled *šylh* in Hebrew, 410 – 11), but he also rejects *šello* (409 – 10, 14 – 16) because the unexpressed subject cannot be "the staff" or "the scepter" since this ruins the parallelism. (Orelli, of course, took the personal subject dominating the whole section.) Further, it should have been written *šellô hô'* and *še* as a relative pronoun is very improbable since that is a feature of the northern dialect. (In response to these last two problems, we call attention to the parallel between *welô* and *šîloh* in the two parallel lines and to the use of *še* in contexts not necessarily northern or late.)

23. Edouard Dhorme, *A Commentary on the Book of Job*, trans. Harold Knight (Nashville: Thomas Nelson, 1984), xx.

- The death of Job (42:7) is described in the exact terms of Abraham and Isaac (Ge 25:8; 35:29)

Thus we may safely regard Job as belonging to the era of the patriarchs.

The book of Job is not so much about why people suffer, or even why Job must suffer; it is more a book about God himself being on trial. Satan accused God of having a loyal clientele because he favored certain ones with so much blessing and wealth. If all of these material and physical goods were taken away from these mortals, he argued, they would soon drop their worship and service of God. God gave his permission for Satan to strip these material blessings from Job, who never knew, as we the readers know, that he had been divinely selected for this experiment. But Satan's power and authority were strictly limited by God himself. Though God was not the author of Job's suffering, he nevertheless had to give permission for things to go even as far as they did under the brutal sway of Satan.

Job's three friends carry the view of a God of retribution. This is a true attribution to God, but it is only one of eight reasons for suffering in the Old Testament.[24] Job, however, is more concerned over the problem that God does not seem to be listening to his cry for help. Job never directly accuses God of doing evil, but he cannot understand what appears to be divine passivity in his case.

God is the focus of every speech in the dialogue set in three acts, the wisdom poem of Job 28, the monologue of Elihu, the divine speeches, and even the concluding epilogue. Suffering is not, therefore, treated as a philosophical problem. The book of Job wanted to define the proper relationship between God and mortals. He is the Lord who will always be there in all his omnipotence and mercy, despite how the circumstances appear at the moment.

God of Promise

In the patriarchal narratives, there was a series of names for God. He was El Olam, "the Everlasting God" (Ge 21:33); El Elyon, "the Most High God" (14:18 – 20, 22); and Yahweh Yireh, "Yahweh will provide" (22:14). But the most frequent and important name was El Shaddai, usually translated "God Almighty" (17:1; 28:3; 35:11; 43:14; 48:3; cf. also 49:25 — *'et Shaddai*).

In the book of Job, El Shaddai is used some thirty times, beginning with Job 5:17. This is not unexpected since, as we have seen, there are good reasons for placing the events of Job in the patriarchal era. Regardless of what scholars ultimately decide the meaning of Shaddai is (whether "nourisher" or "God of the Mountain"),[25] the pattern of usage is clear in the six patriarchal references and in most of Job's more than thirty

24. For these eight reasons for suffering in the Old Testament, see Walter C. Kaiser Jr., *Grief and Pain in the Plan of God: Christian Assurance and the Message of Lamentations* (Ross-shire, UK: Christian Focus, 2004), 127 – 36.

25. From Ugaritic *ṯdy*, "mountains," or from *šd*, "breast"; contrast *šd*, "field."

references. This name stressed the might and power of God; thus the Septuagint rendered it in Job as *ho pantokratōr*, the "All-Ruler" or "Almighty." As Geerhardus Vos stated it,[26] El Shaddai emphasized the supernatural work of God's grace. As he overpowered nature and forced her to forward his plan of salvation, El Shaddai indicated God's ability to master nature. Thereby it linked together his work in creation and now his overpowering work in history to effect his plan.

Outside of these six references in Genesis and the thirty-one references in Job, this divine name appears three other places in the Pentateuch (Ex 6:3; Nu 24:4, 16), four times in the Prophets (Isa 13:6; Joel 1:15; Eze 1:24; 10:5), and in Psalms (68:15 [Heb.]; 91:1) and Ruth (1:20 – 21). Together they fit the general tenor of the name and its use in the patriarchal era; God is omnipotent and a great Sovereign who can and will act on behalf of those whom he loves and who are called according to his purpose and plan.

Thus, the theology of this section was intertwined around that *word* from on high: its *blessing* to a chosen seed, and its *assurance* of the divine presence that guaranteed the certainty of the promised heir, inheritance, and heritage or even the present success of the patriarchs. It was all God's word of encouragement.

So blessed were these men that their benefits overflowed to their neighbors. Hence Laban claimed that he was blessed of Yahweh on account of his proximity to Jacob (Ge 30:27, 30). In the same way, Pharaoh was blessed because of his proximity to Joseph (Ge 39:5).

Perhaps this same concept of physical proximity was involved in the act of communicating blessing from father to son, as H. Mowvley suggested.[27] Rather than locating the root for the verb to bless (*brk*) as Gesenius did in the root *brq*, "to break," that is, the bending of or breaking of one's knees when homage or thanks is given, he followed J. Pedersen, von Rad, and Procksch, who translate the verb *bārak* as "to place on the knees of." (Joseph may have placed his children on Jacob's knees, Ge 48.) Thus Isaac touched and kissed Jacob as he imparted his blessing to him (Ge 27:27). So Laban kissed his grandchildren and blessed them (31:55). Likewise, the one who wrestled with Jacob touched the hollow of his thigh (32:25 – 32).

Just as important as the act, however, was the word of blessing itself. The blessing was many things: a prediction, the gift itself resulting from blessing (33:11), a capacity given by God to ensure the fulfillment of the promise (17:16; 24:60), the reward of prosperity (15:1), the peace of the Lord (26:29), and nothing less than the presence of God himself (26:3, 28).[28]

The patriarchs' confidence that they survived death, even if the actual method or means was left undiscussed, appeared with the other blessings of the age. Abraham

26. Vos, *Theology*, 95 – 96. He noted the connection in Isaiah 13:6 and Joel 1:15 between *shaddai* and the Hebrew verb *šâdad*, "to overpower, destroy." Cf. Frank M. Cross, "Yahweh and the God of the Patriarchs," *Harvard Theological Review* 55 (1962): 244 – 50.

27. Harry Mowvley, "The Concept and Content of 'Blessing' in the Old Testament," *Bible Translator* 16 (1965): 74 – 80.

28. Ibid., 78 – 79.

believed that the almighty God could effect the deliverance of his son from death itself in Genesis 22. He had as much a right to this view as Gilgamesh had for his friend Enkidu, or the myth of Tammuz had for dead vegetation. Therefore, the patriarchal text always carefully distinguished the fact that each patriarch was "gathered to his people" from the act of burial in the "grave" (Ge 25:8 – 9; 35:29; 37:35; 49:29, 31, 33). Neither was their relationship to God or his continuing association with them canceled after death, for he repeatedly identified himself, the living personal God, as the "God of Abraham, Isaac, and Jacob" (Ex 3:6; cf. Mk 12:26; Lk 20:37).[29] No wonder the psalmist confidently expressed the fact that humankind continues to enjoy fellowship with God beyond the grave (Pss 16:10; 49:15; 73:24). Likewise, Job argues in 14:14 that man enjoys the same prospect of "sprouting forth/renewal/release" as does the felled tree that "it will sprout again" (Job 14:7).[30]

29. For fuller discussion, see James Orr, *Christian View of God and the World*, appendix to lecture 5 (Grand Rapids: Eerdmans, 1947), 200 – 210; Patrick Fairbairn, *The Typology of Scripture* (Grand Rapids: Zondervan, 1963), 1:343 – 59.

30. See a fuller discussion in chapter 6 on wisdom theology.

Chapter 3

The People of the Promise: The Mosaic Era

Exodus, Leviticus, Numbers (About 1475 – 1400 BC)

The Book of Exodus

There are three prominent theological subjects in the book of Exodus that also nicely cover the full scope and message of this second of the five books of the Torah. The three subjects are divine redemption, divine morality, and divine worship. As a whole, Exodus contains some of the richest, most foundational theology in all the Old Testament. In this book, the promise-plan of God is further elaborated on as the themes of God's "son," his "firstborn," and his "tabernacling/dwelling" with those he will call a "holy nation," "kings and priests," and his "treasured possession."

Some of the most detailed divine disclosures on the nature of God appear in Exodus 3, 6, 33, and 34. In disclosing the "name" of God, they highlight God's attributes of justice, truthfulness, mercy, faithfulness, and holiness. To know God's "name" is to know him and to know his character (3:13 – 15; 6:3). But the book of Exodus also reveals God as the Lord of history as well. There is no one like him, "majestic in holiness, awesome in glory, working wonders" (15:11). Pharaoh, the Egyptians, and all Israel would see the power and might of God as he moved to redeem his people from the land of bondage and slavery.

The theology of deliverance and redemption are demonstrated in the exodus of Israel from Egypt. One of the words for "redeem" (Heb., *ga'al*), showed that God was indeed a "kinsman redeemer" (6:6; 15:13). To further illustrate this truth, the Passover meal pointed to the Paschal lamb that was to be slain in connection with the nation's redemption. The apostle Paul would later point out that Jesus was that Paschal Lamb who was slain for our redemption (1Co 5:7), just as John the Baptist also pointed to Jesus as the "Lamb of God" who would take away the sins of the world (Jn 1:29).

Exodus also tells us how to live and how to worship. The foundation for biblical ethics and all morality was laid out in the Decalogue (chap. 20) and was illustrated in the Covenant Code (chaps. 21 – 23). This was followed by an elaborate and detailed presentation of the tabernacle and the proper way to worship God. The most amazing item in all the tabernacle teaching was that one of the words for the tabernacle was the place of God's "dwelling" (Heb., *mishkan*). Thus, the omnipotent, immortal, majestic God of the whole universe came and dwelt among the nation of Israel. This is the very God who was, and is, and is to come again in the second advent.

The Connection between Exodus and Genesis

In spite of the four hundred years of silence that separated the patriarchal times in Genesis 12 – 50 from the Mosaic era, the theology hardly misses a beat. For example, the brief review of Jacob's family concludes in Exodus 1:7 with seven words deliberately piled one on another. These evidence the fulfillment of God's promise that Jacob's seed had indeed been "fruitful," "increased greatly," "multiplied," and "grown exceeding strong." It was a clear allusion to the "blessing" promised in Genesis 1:28 and 35:11.

But the seed was now more than a mere family; it would soon be a people — indeed, even a nation. There lies the new distinction for this era. And their experience of the gracious acts of God was more than a collection of personal interventions for selected individuals. Here, as part of their confession, God's acts would be reaffirmed by the whole nation: "Yahweh delivered his people from Egypt." Nevertheless, it would all be traced back to the same comforting assurance: "I will be with you," for that was God's name and character. His name was "I am," that is, Yahweh, the God who would be dynamically, effectively present when he was needed and when people called on him.

The loyal love and dependable grace of this covenant-making God to his promises dominated the transition between these ages. He had heard Israel's groanings in Egypt, and his interest in them and action on their behalf were summed up as a "remembering" of his covenant with Abraham, Isaac, and Jacob (2:24). The God of the deliverance was one and the same as "the God of your fathers" (3:13); "the God of Abraham, the God of Isaac and the God of Jacob" (vv. 15 – 16).

Previously, God had appeared to Abraham, Isaac, and Jacob in the character and nature of El Shaddai; but now he would manifest himself as "Yahweh" (6:3) by delivering Israel and leading her into the land he had sworn to give to the three great patriarchs (6:8; 33:1). Again, all this divine activity could be subsumed under one concept: it was a "remembering" of his covenant (6:5). To "remember" in biblical terms was not a mere cognitive function of calling something to one's mind, but it also involved actively carrying out and responding to what one had just recalled to mind.

Hence, the author of Exodus connected the patriarchs and the exodus periods directly; for him the Sinaitic covenant was theologically and historically a continuation of the Abrahamic promise. Rather than treating Egypt and Sinai as an interruption to the previous promises, their needs became a new opportunity for another manifestation of God's divine loyalty to his oft-repeated promise-plan. Indeed, the book of Exodus, as do a good number of other books of the Old Testament, begins with the Hebrew letter *waw*, which means "and" and is left untranslated in most translations. But this surely was a sign that the book of Exodus is closely linked with the plan of God set forth in Genesis. In fact, Exodus 1:1 begins, "And these are the names of the sons of Israel," which is a virtual repetition of Genesis 46:8, where Israel's journey to Egypt was announced. Thus, the message of the Torah is one; we cannot separate promise from redemption, or promise from law, or promise from worship!

My Son, My Firstborn

Jacob's twelve sons and Joseph's two children multiplied until they became a great nation during the Egyptian bondage. After 430 years of slavery (Ex 12:40), the sons of Jacob had had enough; they cried out to God for help.

Help came in the person of Moses and in the miraculous interventions and words of the Lord. Moses' first act as the newly appointed spokesman for the living God was to command Pharaoh categorically, "Israel is my firstborn son: ... Let my son go" (4:22 – 23). Yahweh was now to be seen as a "Father" by what he did: he brought Israel into being as a nation; he fostered the nation and led it. That is what fatherhood is all about. So Moses would reason in his final speech to Israel: "Is he not your Father, your Creator, who made you and formed you?" (Dt 32:6).

The text pointedly uses the singular for the whole community of Israel collectively. When the Old Testament refers to individual Israelites, it uses the plural (e.g., "You are the children of the LORD your God" [Dt 14:1]). But the individual Israelite was also a "son of God" precisely because he was a member of the chosen people.

While it is true that it was commonplace in the ancient Near East for monarchs to claim that they were "sons" of one god or another — especially in Egypt, where the Pharaoh was thought to be derived from sexual union between the god and the queen — Israel carefully avoided any idea of divine sonship. Yet when God used the designation "my firstborn son," it was not a mindless epithet or a poetic indulgence. It was an integral part of God's call and his deliverance of Israel from Egypt.

Israel's sonship expressed a relationship:[1] Israel was the son of Yahweh but not merely in the sense of a citizen of a nation, a member of a craftsman's guild, or a disciple of a teacher. Hebrew *ben*, "son," can be understood in varying contexts in all of these senses. Here, however, it was a familial relationship: a people who made up the family of God. Israel was not a family in an adopted sense or a mere ethnic, political,

1. I am indebted to Dennis McCarthy for many of the insights here: "Israel, My Firstborn Son," *The Way* 5 (1965): 183 – 91.

or social unity. Rather, it was a family formed, saved, and guarded by God, the "Father" of this family.

As true sons, Israel must imitate its Father in activity. Everything the Father is, the son should aspire to be (e.g., "Be holy because I the LORD your God am holy," Lev 19:2 passim). The son, on his part, must respect the wishes of the Father and show his respect and gratitude by doing what his Father commands him to do. The Father, on the other hand, would demonstrate his love in his tender and loyal dealings with his son.

The title "firstborn" (*b*[e]*kôr*), on the other hand, usually meant the first child to be born (e.g., Ge 25:25; or "to open the womb," Ex 13:2 NRSV). In the transferred sense, as used here, it denotes "first in rank," "first in preeminence." As such, it bestows special rights and honors of inheritance and favor on its recipients.

The rights of primogeniture were superseded when another son was designated as "firstborn." What had previously rested on position and chronology was now removed and grounded in grace. So it was with Jacob, who was renamed Israel. Esau was the "first" in position of actual birth (Ge 25:25–26), but it was Jacob who received God's favor and the surprise of being called his "firstborn." Likewise Ephraim was Joseph's second child, but Jeremiah recognized him as God's "firstborn" (Jer 31:9).

The importance of both the meaning and the concept of "collective/corporate solidarity," in the terms "my son" and "my firstborn," are not always appreciated by readers and theologians of the Old Testament when they see the word "seed." As we have seen, in that one word, "seed," was the ultimate or final representative person who was to come as well as all those that key person represented. "My son" and "my firstborn" likewise functioned in the same dual capacity. They were collective terms that represented and included that *one* who was to come and the *many* who were believing on him.

Readers of the New Testament should not be surprised, then, when the same terms were used of Jesus the Messiah. He too was addressed by what had become, by then, technical terms. He too was delivered out of Egypt and was given the same familial term "my son" (Mt 2:15; cf. Hos 11:1). Moreover, He was God's "firstborn," *prōtotokos* (Ro 8:29; Col 1:15, 18; Heb 1:6; Rev 1:5). And the title *prōtotokoi* that he shared with all believers was just as true of all Israel in the Old Testament (Heb 12:23). The continuity of terms, identities, and meanings throughout both Testaments is more than a mere accident. It is a remarkable evidence of a single planned program and a unified single people of God.

My People, My Possession

Israel was more than a family or God's son; Israel had also become a *gōy*, a "nation" (Ex 19:6). This fact first became evident when the Lord told Moses at the burning bush, "I have indeed seen the misery of my people in Egypt" (3:7). This title Moses repeated to Pharaoh in God's categorical demand: "Let my people go" (5:1; 7:14; 8:1, 20; 9:1; 10:3).

To be called a "people" (*'am*)[2] meant that they were an ethnic social group with enough numerical strength and enough unity to be regarded as a corporate whole. Yet they were so intimately linked to Yahweh that he called them "my people."

Yahweh's loyalty to his people became evident in the events of the plagues, the exodus, and the wilderness journey. Israel was to be released from servitude to Pharaoh so that she might serve the Lord. However, when the Egyptian monarch consistently refused to yield to Yahweh's demands, his power — called the "finger of God" in Exodus 8:19 (cf. Ex 31:18; Ps 8:3; Lk 11:20) — was unleashed in increasing degrees of severity against Pharaoh, his people, and their lands and goods.

But the objective was never mere punishment for Pharaoh's obstinacy. The plagues had a salvific purpose for both Israel and Egypt. They were to convince Pharaoh that Yahweh indeed had spoken and had to be feared and obeyed. Israel had no choice and neither did the Egyptians.

Was this God chauvinistic and unfairly partial to Israel to the detriment of the Egyptians' economy? Not so again! The text insists that his plagues also had an evangelistic appeal to the Egyptians. Each catastrophe was invoked "so that you [Egyptians] will know that I, the LORD, am in this land" (8:22); "so that you may know that there is no one like me in all the earth" (9:14; cf. 8:10); to "show you my power and that my name might be proclaimed in all the earth" (9:16); and "that you may know that the earth is the LORD's" (19:29).

Egypt's gods were no gods at all. Only Yahweh was God, and he was such in all the earth, not just in the patriarchs' territory of Haran or Canaan. His name and power had to be published throughout the whole earth so that all nations of the earth might "fear him," that is, "believe him." Accordingly, some Egyptians did come to fear and trust him. Some of Pharaoh's servants "feared the word of the LORD [Yahweh]" (9:20) and did as Moses commanded. No doubt that is the explanation for the "mixed multitude" that left Egypt with Israel (12:38). It included those Gentiles who had come "to know" — that is, to experience personally — the Lord God of all the earth.

Even after the miraculous deliverance was accomplished on the evening of the Passover, many Egyptians still clung adamantly to their reckless course of direct confrontation with this incomparably great God. Patiently, the divine offer of grace remained open as they pursued Israel as she crossed the sea. They must "know that I am the LORD" (14:4), even as that God also received praise and glory from Israel for his mighty victory over Pharaoh, his chariots, and his horsemen (v. 18).

The effect on Israel was overwhelming. After she saw what God had finally done against the impervious Egyptians, they "feared the LORD and put their trust in him and in Moses his servant" (14:31). Together they sang:

2. Contrast our conclusions with those of Richard Deutsch, "The Biblical Concept of the 'People of God,'" *Southeast Asia Journal of Theology* 13 (1972): 4 – 12.

> Your right hand, O LORD,
> was majestic in power.
> Your right hand, O LORD,
> shattered the enemy. (Ex 15:6)
>
> Who among the gods
> is like you, O LORD?
> Who is like you —
> majestic in holiness,
> awesome in glory,
> working wonders? (Ex 15:11)

Israel's freedom was owed to the "loyal love" (*ḥesed* — Ex 15:13) that Yahweh had for his people. Other peoples heard and trembled, but God's people whom he had purchased (*qānâh* — 15:16) saw the "salvation of the LORD" (*y^ešû'at YHWH* — 14:13). Human manipulation was clearly excluded; it was God's deliverance (3:8; 6:6). He was Israel's "kinsman-redeemer" (*gô'el* — 6:6), who with miracles and an "outstretched arm" took them and called them "my own people" (v. 7).

The meaning of this event had been set forth in the ceremony of the Passover held on Israel's last night in Egypt. That rite was to be celebrated annually along with the accredited explanation supplied in Exodus 13:14 – 16. You must say, went the explanation to later generations, that "the LORD killed the firstborn of both people and animals in Egypt. This is why I sacrifice to the LORD the first male offspring of every womb and redeem [*pādâh*] each of my firstborn sons" (v. 15).

Thus Israel was constituted a "people." In fact, Exodus 12:3 called her a "congregation" (*'ēdâh*) for the first time as she began to prepare for the Passover meal in each family. Abraham had become numerous; indeed, he had now become a great nation, and God's two great redemptive acts of the Passover and the exodus had underscored the reality of this new fulfillment.

Most surprising of all was Israel's status as God's "choice" or "treasured possession" (*s^egûllâh* — 19:5). But what made Israel so valuable and what exactly did the phrase mean? The meaning of this special term was elucidated by Moshe Greenberg, who pointed to its Akkadian equivalent *sikiltum*,[3] and by C. Virolleaud, who noted Ugaritic *sglt*, which he translated "*proprieté*."[4] The basic root of this term was *sakālu*, "to set aside a thing or a property." It was the opposite of real property such as real estate, houses, and farms, which could not be moved. God's *s^egûllâh*, on the other hand, was his moveable treasure, such as jewelry and small valuables. Israel's value, then, came from God's love and affection, which he had set on her. She became his property, the object of his affection.

3. Moshe Greenberg, "Hebrew *s^egûllâ*: Akkadian *sikiltu*," *Journal of American Oriental Society* 71 (1951): 172ff.

4. As cited by Moshe Weinfeld, "The Covenant of Grant in Old Testament and Ancient Near East," *Journal of American Oriental Society* 90 (1970): 195, n. 103.

Later, in Deuteronomy, Israel was also called "holy" (*qādôš*) as well as a "treasured possession." But these passages were always linked with the concept of the "people" (*ʿam* — Dt 7:6; 14:2; 26:18–19; also, without *s^egûllâh* — 14:21; 28:9); thus, the same point was preserved. Israel was to be God's distinct treasure set aside for a marked purpose.

With this we have a fourth new term (along with God's "son," his "firstborn," and his "possession") to refer to Israel's standing before a God who had chosen and called her, not individually, but collectively, which gives the complete meaning of peoplehood and nationhood. The whole concept could be reduced to a single phrase: "I will take you as my own people" (6:7). That affirmation became the second part of the famous tripartite formula of God's promise-plan: "I will be your God and you shall be my people." Only the third part was lacking now: "And I will dwell in the midst of you." That will come momentarily.

But who was this God and who could be compared to him (15:11)? Moses and Miriam had celebrated the answer on the occasion of the Red Sea deliverance in a song that magnified God's incomparable greatness. His deliverance of his people from Egypt (15:1 – 12), which also signaled his future help in their pending entrance into Canaan (vv. 13 – 18), made his undisputed sovereignty over humanity, nations, and nature most clear: "The LORD will reign forever and ever" (v. 18).

Few passages are more pivotal for the discussion of God's name[5] and character than Exodus 6:2 – 8. The distinction between his appearance to the patriarchs as El Shaddai and his present manifestation to Moses as Yahweh (*YHWH*) has continued to be a source of scholarly debate and conjecture. Certainly the patriarchs were not without a knowledge of the name Yahweh, for that name did appear in the Genesis record well over one hundred times. What Exodus 6:3 stressed was the two reflexive verbs, *wāʾerāʾ* ("I appeared") and *nôdaʿtî* ("I did not make myself known"), and the Hebrew preposition *b^e* ("by") before El Shaddai, and by implication before Yahweh.

This preposition, known as a *beth essentiae*, is to be translated in this instance "as," and means that "God appeared to Abraham, to Isaac, and to Jacob *in the character of* (i.e., with the accompanying attributes of the name of) El Shaddai; but *in the character of* my name Yahweh I did not make myself known to them." The name, then, revealed the character, qualities, attributes, and essence of the person so designated.

Such an analysis of Exodus 6:3 may be confirmed by an examination of 3:13. When God promised to go with Moses when he stood before Pharaoh and the people, Moses queried, "Suppose I go to the Israelites and say to them, 'The God of your fathers [Abraham, Isaac, and Jacob] has sent me to you,' and they ask me, 'What is his name?' Then what shall I tell them?"

---

5. See W. C. Kaiser Jr., "Name," *Zondervan Pictorial Encyclopedia of the Bible* (Grand Rapids: Zondervan, 1975), 4:364.

As Martin Buber,[6] and others have noted, the Hebrew interrogative "what?" (*mâh*) is to be distinguished from "who?" (*mî*). The latter only asked for the title or designation of a person, while *mâh*, especially when connected with the word "name," sought out the qualities, character, powers, and abilities resident in that name.

Thus, the answer came back bluntly. His name was "I am has sent me to you" (3:14). It was not so much an ontological designation or a static notion of being (e.g., "I am that I am"); it was rather a promise of a dynamic, active presence — "I will be [there]." As God had revealed himself in his supernatural control over nature for the patriarchs, now Moses and Yahweh's son, Israel, would know his presence in a day-by-day experience as it never was known before. Later on, in Deuteronomy, this will develop into a name theology, in which the "name" came to represent the presence of God himself instead of merely experiencing the effects of his presence.

Kingly Priests

This uniquely owned, "treasured possession" was destined to be a royal priesthood composed of the entire congregation. Israel, the firstborn of the nations, was given the status of sonship, delivered from Egypt, and made ministers on behalf of themselves and the nations. This mediatorial role was announced in Exodus 19:3 – 6:

> This is what you are to say to the house of Jacob and what you are to tell the people of Israel: "You yourselves have seen what I did to Egypt, and how I carried you on eagles' wings and brought you to myself. Now if you obey me fully and keep my covenant, then out of all nations you will be my treasured possession. Although the whole earth is mine, you will be for me a kingdom of priests and a holy nation."

The entire world belonged to the Lord; yet in the midst of the nations he had placed Israel. To her he had given a special task. Few have captured the meaning of this text better than Charles A. Briggs:

> We have a further unfolding of the second Messianic prophecy [Gn 9:27] in that the dwelling of God in the tents of Shem becomes the reign of God as the King of the kingdom of Israel.
>
> The kingdom of God is a kingdom of priests, a holy nation. It has a sacred ministry of priesthood, as well as sovereignty with reference to the nations of the world. As holy, the Israelites are the subjects of their holy King, and as priests they represent Him and mediate for Him with the nations. Thus the third feature of the Abrahamic covenant is unfolded. As the essential thing to Abraham had been the promised seed, as the essential thing to Jacob had been the promised land, so now, when Israel had become a nation,

6. Martin Buber, *Kingship of God* (New York: Harper & Row, 1967), 104 – 6, 189 – 90; see also, J. A. Motyer, *The Revelation of the Divine Name* (London: Tyndale, 1956), 3 – 31.

> separating itself from the Egyptians, and entering into independent national relations to the various nations of the world, the essential thing became the relation which they were to assume on the one side to God their king, and on the other to the nations, and indeed first of all the positive side of that relation. This is represented in our promise: as a ministry of royalty and priesthood. They are a kingdom of priests, a kingdom and a priesthood combined in the unity of the conception, royal priests or priest kings.[7]

Briggs noted that the term "kingdom of priests" (*mamleket kōh^{a}nîm*) was more a compound noun than a construct relation of the genitive case. In fact, the terms were so closely combined in their unity that Israel was to be at once priest-kings and also royal priests. It was to be true of everyone in the nation as a whole, just as all had been included in sonship.[8]

William Moran[9] has argued convincingly that "kingdom of priests" is not a synonym for a "holy nation." It was a separate entity. Moreover, *mamleket* occasionally meant "king" (1Ki 18:10; Isa 60:11–12; Jer 27:7–8; Hag 2:22), especially in prose passages such as Exodus 19. For Moran, the style of the passage was remarkably personal. It began in verse 3 "to the sons of Israel" (*lib^{e}nê yiśrā'ēl*) and concluded in verse 6 "to the sons of Israel" (*'el b^{e}nê yiśrā'ēl*). In the message addressed to the people, verses 4–6, the first and last clauses, were introduced by the emphatic "you" (*'attem*). Other repetitions of references to persons stressed the deep personal address in the covenant of Exodus 19:3–6: "you" (*'etkem* [2x]), "to me" (*lî* [3x]), and alliteration "though all belongs to me" (*kî lî kol*, K-L-K-L).

The distinctive nature and special status given to this nation, God's personal possession, *s^{e}gûllâh*, was wrapped up in their universal priesthood. They were to be mediators of God's grace to the nations of the earth, even as in Abraham "all the nations of the earth were to be blessed."

Unfortunately for the people, they declined the privilege of being a national priesthood in preference to representation under Moses and Aaron (Ex 19:16–25; 20:18–21). Therefore, the original purpose of God was delayed (not scrapped or defeated forever) until New Testament times when the priesthood of all believers was again proclaimed (1Pe 2:9; Rev 1:6; 5:10). Nevertheless, Israel's role of being the agents chosen by God to minister to the needs of the nations was not rescinded.

The people keenly felt the magnificence and holiness of Yahweh's presence in the thunder of his voice and in the lightning effect of his presence that left the natural world in seismographic convulsions. Thus they begged Moses to approach God on their behalf and receive his communications for them. So Moses became the first Levite to represent the people.[10] Later, by divine authority, Moses consecrated Aaron and his

7. Charles Augustus Briggs, *Messianic Prophecy* (New York: Charles Scribner's Sons, 1889), 102.

8. Ibid., 102–3, n. 2.

9. William L. Moran, "A Kingdom of Priests," *The Bible in Current Catholic Thought*, ed. John L. McKenzie (New York: Herder & Herder, 1962), 7–20, esp. 14–16. See some mild revisions of Moran in Brevard S. Childs, *The Book of Exodus* (Philadelphia: Westminster Press, 1974), 367; yet cf. p. 342, n. 6 and p. 374, n. 6.

10. Note, however, that there apparently had been priests prior to this new provision (Ex 19:22, 24).

sons to function at the altar (28:1). Other jobs connected with the sanctuary and the cult were given to the whole tribe of Levi after they had proved their faithfulness during the golden calf incident (32:25 – 29).

Still, the whole scene had been an unprecedented event in the annals of human history. Of the original encounter with God at Sinai, Moses queried the people in Deuteronomy 4:33 – 36:

> Has any other people heard the voice of God speaking out of fire, as you have, and lived? . . .
>
> From heaven he made you hear his voice to discipline you. On earth he showed you his great fire and you heard his words from out of the fire. Because he loved your ancestors and chose their descendants after them, he brought you out of Egypt. . . .

But now God's voice was heard by Moses; and the mediatorial work for Israel must now be performed by the priests, Aaron and his sons, and the Levites. The representative nature of the Levitical priesthood was made even more graphic in Numbers 3:12 – 13. For every firstborn son in each Israelite family, a Levite was consecrated to God in lieu of the death of that firstborn son. Rather than completing the implied logical consequences of the death and sacrifice to the Lord of every firstborn thing to show Yahweh's ownership over the whole earth, this legislation halted that inference in the case of firstborn from men and women. In their case, God was pleased to provide the Levites as substitutes. Likewise, the high priest represented all the people, for he bore the names of all the tribes of Israel on his breastplate as he went into the sanctuary (28:29).

This priesthood was given to Aaron in a "perpetual statute" (29:9) and renewed again to Phinehas (Nu 25:13). It is important to notice that the *office*, the priesthood, was eternally secured, not the particular individuals or family. Thus it did not suffer abrogation when it later passed temporarily from Phinehas's descendants to Ithamar's line. The conclusion, once again, is the same: the *promise* remained permanent, but the *participation* in the blessings of that promise depended on the individual's spiritual condition.

A Holy Nation

Yet another title was given to Israel in Exodus 19:6. There was to be a nation, but not like the ordinary run of nations that did not know God. Israel was to be a "holy nation." But this promise was to be linked with the people's response and preparation for the theophany, the appearance of God. Such requirements were a "test" according to Exodus 20:20: "Do not be afraid. God has come to test you, so that the fear of God will be with you to keep you from sinning."

Was this covenant a deliberate change from the promissory covenant of the patriarchs to a conditional covenant in which "obedience was the absolute condition of blessing"?[11] Was God displeased with the response of the people who pledged, "We will do everything the LORD has said" (19:8; 24:3, 7)? Could this be interpreted as a "step downward" and a "mistake" tantamount to "rejecting God's gracious dealings with them"?[12] What was the relationship of the "if" statements (19:5; Lev 26:3ff.; Dt 11:13ff.; 28:1) and the command "Walk in all the way that the LORD your God has commanded you, so that (*l*ᵉ*maʿan*) you may live and prosper and prolong your days in the land that you will possess" (Dt 5:33)?

The contrast implied in these questions was too sharp for the text. If the alleged obligatory nature of this covenant should prove to be the new grounds for establishing a relationship with the covenantal God, then it should prove possible to demonstrate that the same logic can be applied to the conditional statements noticed in the chapter on patriarchal theology.[13]

The "if" is admittedly conditional. But what was it conditional to? It was a condition, in this context, to Israel's distinctive position among all the peoples of the earth, to her mediatorial role and her status as a holy nation. In short, it could qualify, hamper, or negate Israel's experience of sanctification and ministry to others; but it hardly could effect her election, salvation, or present and future transmission of the ancient promise to others. She must obey God's voice and heed his covenant, not "in order to" (*l*ᵉ*maʿan* — purpose clause) live and have things go well for her, but "with the result that" (*l*ᵉ*maʿan* — result clause)[14] she will experience authentic living and things going well for her (Dt 5:33).

Israel was to be separate and holy; she was to be separate and as no other people on the face of the earth. As an elect or called people now being formed into a nation under God, holiness was not an optional feature. Israel had to be holy, for her God, Yahweh, was holy (Lev 20:26; 22:31 – 33). As such, they could not be consecrated or set apart any further to any thing or person (27:26) or enter into any rival relationships (18:2 – 5).

THE BOOK OF LEVITICUS

Even though Leviticus is one of the most challenging books for modern readers, any initial discouragement left in the minds of most readers can be quickly dissipated when one learns the central concern and purpose of the book: "Be holy for I am holy" (Lev

11. James Freemen Rand, "Old Testament Fellowship with God," *Bibliotheca Sacra* 109 (1952): 153. Note C. I. Scofield, *Scofield Reference Bible* (New York: Oxford University Press, 1909), 20: "The Dispensation of Promise ended when Israel rashly accepted the law (Exod. 19:8)."

12. Rand, "Old Testament Fellowship," 155.

13. See Genesis 18:17ff.; 22:18; 26:5.

14. This Hebrew particle is used to indicate inevitable consequence as well as purpose; see S. R. Driver, *A Treatise on the Use of Tenses in Hebrew*, 4th ed. (Oxford: Clarendon Press, 1906), 200.

11:44–45; 19:2 passim). The Hebrew root *qodesh*, "holy," appears as a noun, verb, or adjective some 150 times in Leviticus.

The book is named for the Levites; however, oddly enough, they are only mentioned once, in Leviticus 25:32–34. But this book does belong to the five-sectioned Torah, which means "instruction," or "teaching." As such, it cannot be separated from the story of the promise or from the promise-plan of God.

The first seven chapters of Leviticus present the teaching on sacrifices, followed by a second section on the priesthood (Lev 8–10). Purity laws dominate chapters 11–15. Leviticus 16 is, in many ways, central to the life of the worshiping community with its instruction on the Day of Atonement. Finally, chapters 17 to 27 present what many have called the Holiness Law, with Leviticus 18–20 dealing with holiness in the family, especially in sexual activity, and 21–25 presenting holiness in ritual regulations such as in marriages, mourning rites, holy days, and days of fasts.

If there ever was a red-letter edition of the Old Testament, in which all that God said would be put in red letters, just like the red-letter New Testaments place the words of Jesus in red, then this book would be almost solid red; for the formula "The LORD said to Moses" appears fifty-six times, with seventeen of the twenty-seven chapters beginning with this formula.

Promise of Obedience as the Basis for Eternal Life?

It must be observed, first of all, that eternal life, or living in the benefits of the promise, was not now conditioned by a new law of obedience.[15] Nor did Leviticus 18:5 make it so when it said that "the [person] who obeys them will live by them." Andrew A. Bonar was wrong when he commented on this verse:

> But if, as most think, we are to take, in this place, the word [*sic*] "*live in* [by] *them*," as meaning "eternal life to be got by them," the scope of the passage is, that so excellent are God's laws, and every special minute detail of these laws, that *if a man were to keep these always and perfectly*, the very keeping would be eternal life to him. And the quotations in Rom. 10:5, and Gal. 3:12 would seem to determine this to be the true and only sense here [*italics his*].[16]

But this view misses the following points:

- Leviticus 18 begins and ends (vv. 2, 30) with the theological setting of "I am the LORD your God." Thus law-keeping here was Israel's sanctification and the grand evidence that the Lord was indeed her God already.

15. For parts of the following argument and further details see W. C. Kaiser Jr., "Leviticus and Paul: 'Do This and You Shall Live' (Eternally?)," *Journal of the Evangelical Theological Society* 14 (1971): 19–28.

16. Andrew A. Bonar, *A Commentary on Leviticus* (1846; reprint, London: Banner of Truth Trust, 1966), 329–30. So also agrees Charles L. Feinberg, *The Prophecy of Ezekiel* (Chicago: Moody Press, 1969), 110: "Obedience would have brought life physically and spiritually, temporally and eternally (see Deut. 4:40; 5:16)."

- Instead of imitating the customs of the surrounding pagans, Israel's happy privilege would be to manifest the life already begun in faith by her observance of God's instructions, teachings, or laws.
- "Those things" which Israel was to do were the Lord's statutes and judgments, which were sharply contrasted with the customs and ordinances of the Egyptians and Canaanites.

The same point made in Leviticus 18:5 will be made by Moses later on in Deuteronomy 16:20 and by Ezekiel in Ezekiel 20:11. G. A. Cooke summarized it succinctly: "The ancient mind fastened on the outward acts revealing the inward state, while the modern mind goes directly to the internal condition."[17] Patrick Fairbairn was of a similar mind:

> Neither Moses nor Ezekiel, it is obvious, meant that the life spoken of, which comprehends whatever is really excellent and good, was to be *acquired* by means of such conformity to the enactments of heaven; for life in that sense already was theirs.... Doing these things, they lived in them; because life thus had its due exercise and nourishment and was in a condition to enjoy the manifold privileges and blessings secured in the covenant. And the very same thing may be said of the precepts and ordinances of the [NT] gospel: a man lives after the higher life of faith only insofar as he walks in conformity with these; for though he gets life by a simple act of faith in Christ, he cannot exercise, maintain and enjoy it but in connection with the institutions and requirements of the gospel [*italics his*].[18]

Some more points:

- One of the ways of "doing" [obeying] the law was to recognize the imperfection of one's life and thus to make a sacrifice for the atonement of one's sins. Thus Leviticus 18:5 was not a hypothetical offer of eternal life as a reward for perfect law-keeping. The law itself assumed and provided for lawbreakers in the great sacrificial system that was a part of that covenant of law!
- Furthermore, the people had not spoken "rashly" in saying, in Exodus 19:8, "We will do everything the LORD has said." On the contrary, the Lord had spoken in glowing terms of approval in Deuteronomy 5:28–29: "Oh, that their hearts would be inclined to fear me and keep all my commandments always" (cf. 18:18).[19]

---

17. G. A. Cooke, *The Book of Ezekiel*, International Critical Commentary (Edinburgh: T & T Clark, 1967), 199.

18. Patrick Fairbairn, *An Exposition of Ezekiel* (Evansville: Sovereign Grace Publishers, 1960), 215–16.

19. Note also J. Oliver Buswell, *A Systematic Theology of the Christian Religion* (Grand Rapids: Zondervan, 1962), 313: "The words *en autç* [Rom. 10:5] and the corresponding words in Galatians 3:12, *en autois*, where the same Old Testament passage [Lev. 18:5] is quoted, should not be construed as instrumental, but as locative, indicating the sphere or horizon of life of a godly man.... Moses is obviously describing, not the means of attaining eternal life, but the horizon within which an earthly godly life ought to be lived." The *New Scofield Reference Bible*, ed. E. Schuyler English et al. (New York: Oxford University Press, 1969), 95, now says, "The 'if' of v. 5 is the essence of law" and hence "the fundamental reason why 'the law made nothing perfect' (Heb. 7:18–19; cp. Rom. 8:3)." We believe this still misses the point. Even the added observation about the order is not correct either: "To Abraham the promise preceded the requirement; at Sinai the requirement preceded the promise. In the New Covenant the Abrahamic order is followed (see Heb. 8:8–12)."

Let it be noted that even the Sinaitic covenant was initiated by Yahweh's love, mercy, and grace (Dt 4:37; 7:7 – 9; 10:15 passim). When Israel broke the law of God, she no more forfeited her inheritance to the promise and her sure transmission of the promise to her children than did the patriarchs or the Davidic royal line later. Even Israel's involvement in the golden calf incident did not end God's faithfulness (Ex 32). It only highlighted the necessity of obedience for those who claimed to have experienced the grace of God's deliverance in the exodus and the truth that the Lord God is "compassionate and gracious, slow to anger, and abounding in love and faithfulness" (34:6).

The Law of God

No formula appeared with greater insistence in this period of time than "I am Yahweh" or "I am Yahweh your God" (Lev 18:5, 30; 19:2, 4, 10, 12, 14, 16, 18, 25, 28, 30, 31, 32, 34, 37; 20:7, 8, 24, 26 passim). And that was the basis for any and all demands laid on Israel. Her Lord was Yahweh, the God who was dynamically present. What is more, he was holy; therefore, Israel had no choice in the matter of good and evil if she were to enjoy the constant fellowship of one whose very character did not and would not tolerate evil.

To aid the young nation recently released by centuries of bondage into the privileges and responsibilities of freedom, God gave his law. This single law had three aspects or parts: the moral law, the civil law, and the ceremonial law.[20]

The Moral Law. The context of God's moral demands was twofold: "I am Yahweh your God," and "I brought you out of the land of Egypt, out of the house of slavery" (Ex 20:2). Consequently, the standard of moral measurement in deciding what was right or wrong, good or evil, was fixed in the unwavering and impeccably holy character of Yahweh, Israel's God. His nature, attributes, character, and qualities provided the measuring stick for all ethical decision making. But there was, by the same token, an environment of grace — the free loving act of deliverance from Egypt. Israel did not need to keep the law in order to be released from Egypt. On the contrary, since she was so dramatically redeemed, the lever of obligation could not be easily rejected by Israel if Yahweh was her Lord and master.

Should anyone doubt that grace was in the foreground of the law, let that one carefully ponder the sequence of the exodus, the journey to Sinai, God's graciousness to Israel during the wanderings, and his forgiveness of the idolatrous and sexually distracted golden calf cultists.

The form of the moral law as found mainly in the Ten Commandments (Ex 20:2 – 17; Dt 5:6 – 21) was overwhelmingly negative. However, this had nothing to do with either

20. For a defense of God's single law having "heavier or weightier" parts to it, see W. C. Kaiser Jr., "The Weightier and Lighter Matters of the Law: Moses, Jesus, and Paul," *Current Issues in Biblical and Patristic Interpretation: Studies in Honor of Merrill C. Tenney*, ed. G. F. Hawthorne (Grand Rapids: Eerdmans, 1975), 176 – 92.

the tone or aim of that law. It was simply easier to express a believer's restrictions in much fewer words, for his or her freedom was so vast that it would take volumes to describe what one could do. Besides, all morality is double sided anyway — every moral act is at one and the same time a refraining from a contrary mode of action and the adoption of its opposite. It would make no difference if that law were stated negatively or positively. Furthermore, when an evil was prohibited, as for example murder, that law was not fulfilled when people merely abstained from violently snatching away the lives of their fellow humans. It was only "kept" when men and women did all that was in their power to aid their neighbors' lives. Human life was viewed as valuable since humanity was made in the image of God, and thus life was based on the character of God. Therefore, human life must be both preserved and enhanced. One could not refuse to do either — that is, to refuse to preserve, or to seek to improve, the lives of neighbors. Inactivity in the moral realm could never be a fulfilling of the law; that would be equivalent to a state of death. More was required of Israel than merely refraining from doing what was forbidden.

The Decalogue did, however, contain three positive statements: "I am the LORD your God" (20:2); "Remember the Sabbath day" (v. 8); and "Honor your father and your mother" (v. 12). To these three statements, which did not have a finite verbal form attached, the other seven negative statements were in turn subordinated.[21] These three positive injunctions introduced three spheres of human responsibility:

1. Humanity's relationship to God (20:2 – 7)
2. Humanity's relationship to worship (vv. 8 – 11)
3. Humanity's relationship to society (vv. 12 – 17)

In the first sphere of responsibility, people were told to love God with a proper internal and external veneration for his person and work. The second sphere declared God's sovereignty over how people spend their time, while the third spelled out the sanctity of life, marriage, property, truth, and internal desire.[22]

The Ceremonial Law. The same law that made such high demands on humanity also provided for the eventuality that there might also be a failure to reach those standards. For this eventuality there was an elaborate sacrificial system. But that was only one of the three strands belonging to the ceremonial law. One had also to take note, in the second place, of the tabernacle, with its theology of the "tabernacling" God (see below for a development of this point), and finally, in the third place, of the theology of uncleanness and purification.

To begin with the last first, it must be insisted that the "unclean" was not equated in the writer's mind with that which was dirty or forbidden. The teaching of this section of

21. J. J. Owens, "Law and Love in Deuteronomy," *Review and Expositor* 61 (1964): 274 – 83.

22. For further detail, see W. C. Kaiser Jr., "Decalogue," *Baker's Dictionary of Christian Ethics*, ed. C. F. H. Henry (Grand Rapids: Baker, 1973), 165 – 67.

Scripture was not that cleanliness was next to godliness. That may be all well and good, but the word of the text was *cleanness*, not cleanliness.

Simply put, cleanness meant the worshiper was qualified to meet Yahweh; "unclean" signified that the person lacked the necessary qualifications to come before the Lord. This doctrine was closely aligned with the teaching of holiness: "Be ye holy," urged the text repeatedly, for "I, the Lord your God, am holy." Similarly, holiness in its positive aspect was a *wholeness*: a life entirely dedicated to God and set apart for his use.

Many of the basic actions of life left one unclean. Some of these acts, such as caring for the dead or giving birth, were often unavoidable, but they nonetheless rendered one unclean. Instead of using this word as a rubric to teach hygiene or sanitary standards, Moses used it to fix in the worshipers' minds the "otherness" of God's being and morality as compared to humanity's.

Did not God tell Moses, back in the desert while he was shepherding his father-in-law's sheep, to remove his sandals from his feet because the ground on which he stood was holy? Why was he asked to do something as mundane as that? Wasn't Moses' inner heart attitude sufficient preparation for a proper meeting with God? Obviously, that was part of it, but not the whole picture, especially for real worship through which we meet God! Proper preparation for worship also led to external acts that involved the whole person and not just the heart. While primacy must be given to a repentant and open heart, human beings must still take a holistic view when preparation is being made to meet God, who is radically different from humanity.

But lawbreakers were not left without remedy. Fellowship with God was conditioned only on faith in the Lord himself and in what he had promised. If broken by sin, it was rectified by God's forgiveness on the basis of a ransom, as ordained by God. The principle was "The life of a creature is in the blood, and I have given it to you to make atonement for yourselves on the altar" (Lev 17:11). Hence the means of dealing with sin was provided by God himself in the system of sacrifices announced in the Torah.

Not all the sacrifices addressed the problem of the disruption of fellowship between God and man. Some, like the peace or fellowship offerings, were rich times of sharing with one another the gifts of God in his presence. But others, like the whole-burnt offering, sin offerings, or guilt offering, were specifically provided for the hiatus and rupture caused by sin's damaging effects.

The Theology of the Atonement. Divine forgiveness was not and could not be cheap, just as human forgiveness necessitated that someone pay if the reality of forgiveness were ever to be more than a cliché. Such payment was wrapped up in the theology of atonement (Heb. root *kpr*).

There are four basic Hebrew words using *kpr*: (1) a "lion," (2) a "village," (3) to "caulk" or smear a ship with pitch as in Noah's ark, and (4) "to ransom or to deliver by a substitute." It is this fourth word, *kipper*, that interests us here.

Some have argued that the fourth word was related to the third, "to caulk," and to a Near Eastern cognate word that meant "to cover." But Hebrew usage dictated differently. The noun form clearly indicated that a *substitute* of one kind or another was always meant (e.g., Ex 21:30; 30:12; Nu 35:31 – 32; Ps 49:8; Isa 43:3 – 4).[23] Thus, the denominative verb (i.e., a verb that was derived from the noun form) likewise meant "to deliver or ransom someone by a substitute." Mortals, by their sin against God, owed their very lives as a forfeiture to God; but God had provided that animals' lives should serve for the time being, as a picture of what God, who now granted his forgiveness, would one day do when the God-man would later give his life as the only proper and final substitute for the debt of our sins.

How many sins could be atoned by such a system in Israel? All sins of weakness or rashness were capable of being atoned, whether they were done knowingly or unwittingly. Leviticus specifically affirmed that the trespass offering was for sins such as lying, theft, fraud, perjury, or debauchery (Lev 6:1 – 7). And on the great Day of Atonement (Yom Kippur), "all" the sins of "all" Israel, of "all" who had truly repented ("afflicted their souls," Lev 16:29, 31; 23:27, 32 KJV) were forgiven. Indeed, the most persistent phrase in the Levitical sacrificial instructions was the assurance: "And he shall be forgiven" (Lev 1:4; 4:20, 26, 31, 35; 5:10, 16; 16:20 – 22). Therefore, the old but false distinction between "witting," that is, "sins done with a high hand," and "unwitting," as it was usually explained, sins done in ignorance of what the law said on the matter, was unwarranted. The unwitting sins (*bišᵉgāgâh*), or better still, sins "in error," involved all sin that sprang from the weakness of flesh and blood. But the sin of Numbers 15:27 – 36, the sin of a "high hand" (*bᵉyād rāmâh*), was plainly that of rebellion against God and his word. So Numbers 15:30 – 31 explained, "Anyone who sins defiantly . . . blasphemes the LORD . . . because they have despised the LORD's word and broken his commands." This is very similar to what the New Testament called blasphemy against the Holy Spirit or the unpardonable sin. It was high treason and revolt against God with the upraised, clenched fist: a picket against heaven! But this was not to be put in the same class as sins of murder, adultery, or the like. Treason or blasphemy against God was much more serious, for it attacked God himself.

If all sins, except the unpardonable and sustained revolt against God, were forgivable, what part did the sacrifices play and how efficacious were they? *Subjectively*, they were most effective.[24] The sinner did receive complete relief. His or her sins were forgiven on the basis of the word of a faithful God and the God-approved substitute. Of

23. Leon Morris, *The Apostolic Preaching of the Cross* (Grand Rapids: Eerdmans, 1955), 160 – 78, and J. Hermann, "Kipper and Kopper," *Theological Dictionary of the New Testament*, ed. Gerhard Kittel, and trans. G. W. Bromiley (Grand Rapids: Eerdmans, 1965), 3:303 – 10. Hermann concluded by saying, "It would be useless to deny that the idea of substitution is present to some degree," 310.

24. I was greatly aided in my understanding of parts of this argument by Hobart Freeman, "The Problem of Efficacy of Old Testament Sacrifices," *Bulletin of Evangelical Theological Society* 5 (1962): 73 – 79.

course, the efficacy did also depend on the internal state of the sinner's heart (Lev 16:29, 31; and later, Ps 50:10 – 13; Pr 21:27; Isa 1:11 – 14; Jer 6:20; 7:21; Hos 5:6; 6:6; Am 5:25; Mic 6:6 – 7). And the person did get relief from the penalty and memory of his or her sins. On the Day of Atonement there were two goats to indicate two parts of one act. One was a sin offering — a goat slain as the substitute, so that sins might be forgiven. The other goat was led away (*ʿaz* — "goat" — *ʾāzal* — "to lead away" — Lev 16:26), to picture the fact that those same sins were forgotten in the sense that God chose not to remember them or call them to mind against the forgiven person any more.

Nevertheless, sin was not *objectively* cared for as yet. The blood of bulls and goats could never take away or remove sin, and neither did the Old Testament claim it did (Heb 10:4)! These were substituted animals, not people; hence, they could only be symbols of that real sacrifice yet to come. Thus in the meantime there was a "passing by" (*parēsis* — Ro 3:25) of the sins of the Old Testament on the basis of God's declared word until he would later provide his own final substitute who was a true man, yet one who had not sinned.

The Civil Law. As far as theology is concerned, this aspect of God's law was a mere application of the moral law to selected parts of the community's life, especially where tensions were likely to develop in that day. True justice and holiness on the part of the judges and rulers were to be measured by the demands of the Decalogue and God's Holiness Code. Accordingly, the civil law illustrated its practice in the various cases or situations that confronted the leadership during the Mosaic era.

The Tabernacling God

The single most important fact in the experience of this new nation of Israel was that God had come to "tabernacle" (*šākan*), or "dwell," in her midst. Nowhere was this stated more clearly than in Exodus 29:42b – 46, where in connection with the tabernacle it was announced:

> There [at the entrance] I will meet you and speak to you; there also I will meet with the Israelites, and the place will be consecrated by my glory. So I will consecrate the Tent of Meeting and the altar. . . . I will dwell ["tabernacle"] among the Israelites and be their God. They will know that I am the LORD their God, who brought them out of Egypt so that I might dwell among them. I am the LORD their God.

Now the triad was complete. One of the most frequently repeated formulas of the promise-plan would be:

> I will be your [their] God;
> You [they] shall be my people.
> and I will dwell in the midst of you [them].

In its very first announcement, the dwelling of God was connected with the tabernacle. In fact, one of the names of the tent-sanctuary of God was *miškān*, which clearly was related to the verb *šākan*, "to tent, dwell, tabernacle." Ordinarily, Hebrew preferred to speak of a permanent dwelling as *yāšab*, "to sit, dwell," and so it did whenever it spoke of Yahweh dwelling in heaven. But as Frank Cross pointed out, invariably, when the text pointed to Yahweh's presence dwelling with human beings on earth or in the tabernacle and later in the temple, the verb was *šākan*.[25] Thus, it would appear, even as Cross suggested, that these two verbs contrasted the divine transcendence (*yāšab*) with divine immanence (*shakan*). And in the case of the tabernacle, it was the place where God would take up his temporary abode. A new sense of the "closeness" and active presence of God was to be Israel's.

The only exception to this distinction was to be found in the use of *yāšab* and its derivatives to express the fact that God was "enthroned," or sat on the throne,[26] especially in the use of this verb in connection with the central piece of furniture in the tabernacle: "who is enthroned between the cherubim" (1Sa 4:4; 2Sa 6:2; 1Ch 13:6; Ps 99:1; Isa 37:16). The ark of the covenant of God, with its mercy seat, or place of atonement, overspread by the two cherubim, was the most intimate of all the expressions of God's nearness to his people. Exodus 25:22 commented: "There, above the cover between the two cherubim that are over the ark of the covenant law, I will meet with you and give you all my commands for the Israelites."

The theology of the tabernacle was to be formed in the purpose statement of Exodus 25:8: "Make a sanctuary for me, and I will dwell [*šākan*] among them."[27] But the central feature, both in the theology of atonement and in the theology of the divine presence, was the ark of the covenant of God.

Yahweh's divine presence was so central and so significant in the Mosaic era that four other forms are used to speak of it: *pānîm*, the "face," "appearance," or "presence" of the Lord; *kābôd*, "glory"; *mal'ak YHWH*, "angel of the Lord"; and *šēm*, "name." The passage that connects most of these divine presence themes is Exodus 33.[28] There Moses had asked God to show him his "glory" (v. 18) so that he might be assured that God's "face," or "presence" (vv. 14–15) was indeed going before him. To this request God acceded by causing all his "goodness" to pass before Moses, and there God proclaimed in front of Moses the "name" Yahweh (v. 19). Protected by the "hand" of God while he waited "in the cleft of the rock," Moses saw the reality of God's presence, though only from the back, for "my face must not be seen" (vv. 21–23).

Of the angel that would accompany Israel, the promise had been equally clear. Exodus 23:20–21 declared:

25. Frank M. Cross Jr., "The Priestly Tabernacle," *The Biblical Archaeologist Reader*, eds. David N. Freedman and G. Ernest Wright (Garden City, NY: Anchor Books, 1961), 225–27.

26. Ibid., 226.

27. See, for further details, R. E. Clements, *God and Temple: The Presence of God in Israel's Worship* (Philadelphia: Fortress Press, 1965), 35ff. Gerhard von Rad argues that God's permanent dwelling was attached to the ark, while the *mô'ēd*, "meeting of God," was connected with the tent (*Old Testament Theology* [London: Oliver and Boyd, 1962], 1:234–36).

28. Page H. Kelley, "Israel's Tabernacling God," *Review and Expositor* 67 (1970): 488–89.

> See, I am sending an angel ahead of you to guard you along the way and to bring you to the place I have prepared. Pay attention to him and listen to what he says. Do not rebel against him; he will not forgive your rebellion, since my Name is in him.

He was that same one mentioned in Exodus 32:34 as "my angel [who] will go before you." If the name — the character, nature, or attributes — of God was "in him," could he be less than the pre-incarnate Word tabernacling among them? Indeed, God's presence was with Israel, and he would give her "rest" (Ex 33:14). To such a promise as this, God signed his name, as it were, in Exodus 29:46: "I am the LORD."

The theology of those days revolved around three dominating concepts: redemption (from Egypt), morality, and worship. As Bernard Ramm put it:

> Redeemed man is called to morality; moral man is called to worship. The redeemed man shows his repentance in the quality of his moral life; he shows his gratitude in his worship.[29]

The Book of Numbers

God had promised numerous descendants to the patriarch Abraham (Ge 13:16; 15:5; 17:2, 6; 22:17), but how numerous could this group reasonably get? For example, the census of the first generation of those who could carry out warfare appeared in Numbers 1 – 4, with a census of the second generation found in chapter 26. So shocking were the numbers and the graciousness of God that many stumble to this day over the huge increase given to the nation.[30]

From Harmony to Rebellion to Judgment

Numbers 1 – 10 tells of happy days for the people of Israel, but what followed in Numbers 11 – 21 were repeated instances of rebellion on the part of the nation that stirred the anger of God. Seven cases in which they refused to trust Yahweh are listed in these chapters. This pattern will begin to mark Israel and her relationship to God from here on out: at first a period of walking with God, followed by a time of unbelief and outright disobedience, ending in the judgment of God until once again the people come to their senses and turn back to God in repentance and revival in the mercy and grace of God.

A Star Witness to the Messiah

Most interpreters are stymied when it comes to evaluating the Mesopotamian Gentile prophet Balaam in Numbers 22 – 24. When the Israelites camped in the plains of

29. Bernard Ramm, *His Way Out* (Glendale, CA: Regal Books, 1974), 148.

30. See the Excursus that follows this chapter.

Moab, King Balak of Moab grew restless and sent to Pethor, near the Euphrates River, for Balaam the son of Beor[31] to come and put a curse on Israel, thereby guaranteeing Balak's success as he went out to fight against Israel — or so he thought!

At first Balaam refused to come, based on a warning from God that it was impossible to curse a people who were already blessed, but when Balak sent a more prestigious delegation with a bigger offer, Balaam decided he could not refuse, though he warned that he could not say or do anything more than what God would say.

When Balaam failed to produce the hoped-for curse on Israel after three attempts — and that under very auspicious circumstances — Balaam offered a fourth oracle, warning of what God was going to do against Moab and what he would do for Israel:

> A star will come out of Jacob;
> A scepter will rise out of Israel.
> He will crush the foreheads of Moab,
> The skulls of the sons of Sheth. (Nu 24:17)

This was another addition to the promise-plan of God concerning the Messiah who was to come in the future to rule and reign.

There would be other non-Israelite disclosures of true revelations from God (such as Nebuchadnezzar's experience in Daniel 4), but Scripture devoted almost a hundred verses to describing how God protected Israel and kept his promise both to his coming Messiah and to his people.

Even if Balaam began well as a genuine servant of the Lord, he did not end well. It appears that Balaam did not receive the expected honorarium for his work, but instead of returning back home to northern Mesopotamia, he stayed with the Moabite and Midianite contingent in their country. What most likely happened was that Balaam encouraged the Moabite and Midianite women to go to the Israelite men and urge them to join them in their idolatrous worship of the Baal of Peor, which involved forms of religious prostitution and some association of fire for the dead. He died in the battle God commanded Moses to lead against the five kings of Midian and their nation (Nu 31:8).

Israel had suffered loses for her involvement in this audacious idolatry — some 24,000 died in the plague. Yet the promises of God could not thereby be jettisoned or obliterated.

31. For more details, see Walter C. Kaiser Jr. "Balaam, Son of Beor, in Light of Deir 'Alla and Scripture: Saint or Soothsayer?" in *Go to the Land I Will Show You: Dwight Young Festschrift*, ed. Joseph Coleson and Victor Matthews (Winona Lake, IN: Eisenbrauns, 1996), 95 – 106.

Excursus: The Problem with the Numbers in Numbers

The theological blessing in the book of Numbers has become at the same time its largest apologetical and exegetical problem — its numbers! The statement that Israel had reached 603,550 fighting men who were twenty years old and older (Nu 1:46) seemed to most moderns to be far too large a number for a newly released slave nation. This number would imply a total population of some two million persons or more. Many biblical scholars are shocked by such a large number, for they estimate that the total population under King Solomon some five to six centuries later was less than one million. Various solutions have been proposed, including:

1. A misunderstanding of *'elph*, the Hebrew word usually translated as "thousand." In a few contexts *'elph* was rendered as "clan," "family unit," or "tribe" (cf. Jdg 6:15).[32]
2. All these numbers are the result of scribal errors.
3. The numbers are deliberately inflated by a factor of something like ten in order to give God more glory and praise.

However, there is an internal consistency about all these numbers. For example, Exodus 38:25 – 26 required a half-shekel for every one of the 603,550 fighting men, which amounted to "100 talents and 1,775 shekels." Since there are 3,000 shekels to a talent, then 3,000 times 100 equals 300,000 shekels, plus the 1,775 shekels would be 301,775. When this number is multiplied by two (to account for the half-shekel price), it equaled 603,550 fighting men!

Remember that Israel was in Egypt 430 years (Ex 12:40). Population tends to double every twenty-five years, according to Malthus.[33] If this estimate is correct, then the number of two million is not at all impossible. Surely, this was another vindication of God's promise that he would bless the seed of Abraham, for that is exactly what resulted in their experience.

32. See George E. Mendenhall, "The Census Lists of Numbers 1 and 26," *Journal of Biblical Literature* 77 (1958): 52 – 66, and Ronald Allen's Introduction to "Numbers," in *The Expositor's Bible Commentary*, ed. Frank E. Gaebelein (Grand Rapids: Zondervan, 1990), 2:686 – 91.

33. Thomas Robert Malthus (1766 – 1834) popularized this demographic figure. See A. Flew, "The Structure of Malthus' Population Theory," *Australasian Journal of Philosophy* 35 (1957).

Chapter 4

The Place of the Promise: The Pre-Monarchial Era

Deuteronomy, Joshua, Judges (About 1400 – 1050 BC)

The Book of Deuteronomy

The spirit and the theology of Deuteronomy extends far beyond the confines of the closing days of the Mosaic era or even the contents of a single work. Deuteronomy serves both as the completion of the Torah and as an introduction to most if not all of the former or earlier prophets: Joshua, Judges, Samuel, and Kings — also called the historical books by some. Martin Noth regarded Deuteronomy to 2 Kings as an original work that attempted to write a history of Israel from Moses to the exile and to interpret it from the vantage point of theology.[1] This interpretation was one of the most insightful contributions to Old Testament studies in this century. Whether Deuteronomy was all the work of one author who wrote most of Joshua to 2 Kings after the shadows of the fall of Samaria in 722 BC and fall of Jerusalem in 587 BC had passed is another matter. But of the basic theological motivation and general prophetic tone of these books there can be very little debate.

Deuteronomy, for the most part, consists of the final sermons of Moses. Therefore, these chapters bring to a close not only the life and ministry of Moses but the whole of the Torah. The emphasis of the book of Deuteronomy is not so much "the second law," as the Septuagint labeled this book (incorrectly based on the words of Deuteronomy 17:18), but rather the emphasis falls on the grace of God despite the nation's intrinsic bent toward sinfulness.

The book in many ways anticipated the benefits of the new covenant, especially in 30:1 – 14, summarized in verse 6: "The Lord your God will circumcise your hearts

1. Martin Noth, *Uberlieferungsgeschichtliche Studien 1, Die samm Inden under bearbeitenden Geschichtswerke im Alten Testament* (Tübingen: Max Niemeyer Verlag, 1943).

and the hearts of your descendants, so that you may love him with all your heart and with all your soul, and live." Israel's persistent refusal to obey God's laws will not be the last word; God's grace and the circumcision of their hearts will be the final word to history.

Deuteronomy also reflects the pattern of the second-millennium Near Eastern treaties between the great king and his subjects. This typical pattern, which was distinctive to the treaties of the middle of the second millennium BC, involved the following parts that match the flow of material in Deuteronomy:

A Preamble or Introduction (Dt 1:1 – 5)
A Historical Review of Past Relationships between the Parties (1:6 – 4:49)
The Basic Stipulations (5:1 – 26:19)
The Sanctions in the Form of Blessings and Curses (27:1 – 30:20)
The Witnesses to the Treaty (32:1 – 47)
The Provision for Reading and Storage of the Treaty (31:1 – 30; 32:48 – 34:12)

While there are some strong similarities between the ancient Near Eastern forms and the book of Deuteronomy, this structure also showed some independence from the pattern. Moses, however, seemed to write this book with the treaty/covenant pattern in mind so that both the structure of the book and the repeated exhortations would constantly bring the people back to the content of the covenant itself.

The close relationship between Deuteronomy and the books of Joshua through 2 Kings, which scholars delight in calling the work of the Deuteronomic Historian, can be seen everywhere. Foremost among these similarities is the Deuteronomic phraseology, which Moshe Weinfeld[2] has listed in great detail.

In addition to the influence of language and style, Deuteronomy has also contributed the basic theological framework of the Old Testament. According to Gordon J. Wenham,[3] the books of Deuteronomy and Joshua are bound together theologically by five *leitmotifs*: (1) the holy war of conquest; (2) the distribution of the land; (3) the unity of all Israel; (4) Joshua as the successor of Moses; and (5) the covenant. Each of these five themes appeared in the first chapter of Joshua: holy war (vv. 2, 5, 9, 11, 14); the land (vv. 3 – 4, 15); the unity of Israel (vv. 12 – 16); the role of Joshua (vv. 1 – 2, 5, 17); and the covenant (vv. 3, 7 – 8, 13, 17 – 18).[4]

Yet there is more. In these books the Abrahamic-Davidic covenant tradition will be linked with the Sinaitic-Mosaic covenant. For example, David and his successor recognized their obligation to obey the "law of Moses," to keep the statutes, commandments,

2. Moshe Weinfeld, *Deuteronomy and the Deuteronomic School* (Oxford: Clarendon Press, 1972), appendix A, 320 – 59. See also the list of S. R. Driver, A *Critical and Exegetical Commentary on Deuteronomy* (New York: Charles Scribner's Sons, 1916), lxxviii – lxxxiv.

3. Gordon J. Wenham, "The Deuteronomic Theology of the Book of Joshua," *Journal of Biblical Literature* 90 (1971): 140 – 48.

4. Ibid., 141.

and ordinances of God written there so that they might prosper in all that they did and be established (1Ki 2:1 – 4; 9:4 – 5). In fact, Solomon freely appealed to God's ancient work in the exodus and the promised gift of the land to that generation (1Ki 8:16, 20, 34, 36, 53).

But one of the most immediate concerns that linked the patriarchal and Mosaic traditions with the earlier prophets of Joshua – 2 Kings was the frequent reference made to the "place" that Yahweh would choose, or already had chosen, for his name to dwell. Closely tied with this concept was the theme of the "rest" — the "inheritance" that was to be Israel's possession when she entered the land. These two emphases emerge as the dominant theological themes of the pre-monarchical era.

However, the theology of the earlier prophets is more than just a collection of Deuteronomic themes. For these earlier prophets there were, as Dennis J. McCarthy has pointed out,[5] three programmatic statements that dominated both the history and the theology from the exodus to the exile: Deuteronomy 31, Joshua 23, and 2 Samuel 7. These three passages came from three of the most emotionally charged moments in the history of Israel: The swan song of Moses (Dt 31), the last speech of Joshua (Jos 23), and the unexpected divine announcement made to David when he was contemplating the construction of the house of God (2Sa 7). These key statements underscored the prophetic emphasis in the mouths of God's spokesmen for the most crucial moments in the history and the theology of Israel.

However, six other passages followed up these three programmatic statements with well-placed speeches by the leading actors in that history (Jos 1:11 – 15; 1Sa 12; 1Ki 8:14 – 61), or the writer's own assessment and summary of the times (Jos 12; Jdg 2:11 – 23; 2Ki 17:7 – 23). Actually, two passages were matched with each of the three programmatic texts. The resulting pattern was as follows:

- I. Deuteronomy 31
  - A. Joshua 1
  - B. Joshua 12
- II. Joshua 23
  - A. Judges 2:11 – 23
  - B. 1 Samuel 12
- III. 2 Samuel 7
  - A. 1 Kings 8
  - B. 2 Kings 17

While this structure will aid us in understanding the overall theological plan in the earlier prophets (Joshua – 2 Kings), it cannot form the total progress of theology for all of Israel's subsequent history from the exodus to the exile — too much would be

5. Dennis J. McCarthy, "II Samuel 7 and the Structure of the Deuteronomic History," *Journal of Biblical Literature* 84 (1965): 131 – 38.

neglected, for example, wisdom theology and the latter prophets. Neither does its adoption here detract from the theme already discovered in pre-patriarchal, patriarchal, or Mosaic eras — the promise-plan of God. The theme of the parting speeches of two of Israel's greatest leaders, Moses and Joshua, centered on the momentary fulfillment of that anciently announced promise: a land, a rest, and a place chosen by Yahweh (Dt 31:2 – 3, 5, 7, 11, 20, 23; Jos 23:1, 4, 5, 13, 15). These three features dominate the transition from the Mosaic era to the pre-monarchical era.

The Inheritance of the Land

Sixty-nine times, the writer of Deuteronomy repeated the pledge that Israel would one day "possess" and "inherit" the land promised to her. Sporadically, he made explicit links between this pledge and the word that Abraham, Isaac, and Jacob had received (Dt 1:8; 6:10, 18; 7:8; 34:4). Thus Israel was forced to relate the impending conquest of Canaan under Joshua to the promise of God and not to any feelings of national superiority.

The land of Canaan and the people of Israel alike were called the "inheritance (*naḥ^{a}lâh*) of Yahweh" (1Sa 26:19; 2Sa 21:3; 1Ki 8:36), or his "possession" (*$^{'a}$ḥuzzâh*, Jos 22:19; *y^{e}ruššah*, 2Ch 20:11). Ever since Exodus 19:5 had called Israel Yahweh's "treasured possession" (*s^{e}gûllâh*),[6] they had become a "treasured people" out of all the peoples of the earth (Dt 7:6; 14:2; 26:18) and a "people of inheritance" (*'am naḥ^{a}lâh*, Dt 9:26, 29; 32:8 – 9; 1Ki 8:51, 53; 2Ki 21:14).[7] Thus Israel became the promised people, and Canaan became the promised land.

In Deuteronomy the land became the special area of focus. Repeatedly, in some twenty-five references, the land was called a gift from Yahweh (Dt 1:20, 25; 2:29; 3:20; 4:40; 5:16 passim). And this gift was the same land that was promised to the "fathers" (Dt 1:8, 35; 6:10, 18, 23; 7:13; 8:1; 9:5; 10:11; 11:9, 21; 19:8; 26:3, 15; 28:11; 30:20; 31:7, 20 – 21, 23; 34:4). Why von Rad would confuse the issue and say that since the land belongs to Yahweh "it is now quite clear that this notion is of a totally different order from that of the promise of the land to the early patriarchs" is hard to understand.[8] His line of argument does not stand up to the blunt claims of the text. Surely, the fact that Yahweh is the true owner of the land is no mark of syncretism with features from Canaanite religion. While Baal may have been regarded as the Lord of the land and the giver of all blessings in pagan Canaanite religion, Yahweh was Lord of all the earth — his

6. The AV rendering "peculiar" derives from Latin *peculiaris* and that from *peculium*, a technical term meaning private property that a child or a slave was permitted to possess. At Alalakh, the cognate *sikiltu* is the "treasured possession" of the god. I am indebted to J. A. Thompson, *Deuteronomy* (Downers Grove, IL: InterVarsity Press, 1975), 74 – 75, n. 1, for this material.

7. Cf. J. Hermann, "*Nah^{a}lâh* and *Nâhal* in the Old Testament," *Theological Dictionary of the New Testament*, ed. Gerhard Kittel, trans. G. W. Bromiley (Grand Rapids: Eerdmans, 1965), 3:769 – 76. Also Patrick D. Miller Jr., "The Gift of God: The Deuteronomic Theology of the Land," *Interpretation* 22 (1969): 451 – 61.

8. Gerhard von Rad, "The Promised Land and Yahweh's Land in the Hexateuch," *The Problem of the Hexateuch and Other Essays*, trans. E. W. Truemen Dicken (New York: McGraw-Hill, 1966), 88; idem, *Old Testament Theology* (London: Oliver and Boyd, 1962), 1:296 – 301.

"creative word," to use a fine von Rad phrase, had settled that issue. Consequently, there were not two viewpoints on the inheritance of the land. It can only be Israel's, because it was first Yahweh's land and his to give to whomever he pleased for however long he pleased. Had not Deuteronomy begun with the same observation about some of the previous inhabitants of Transjordania? The Emim, the Horites, and the Zamzummim had been dispossessed and destroyed by the Lord (Dt 2:9, 12, 21), and their lands had been divinely given to Moab, Edom, and Ammon, just as Israel had similarly received Canaan from his hands. The comparison with Israel is made in that very context: "Just as Israel did in the land the Lord gave them as their possession" (Dt 2:12).

It is agreed that Yahweh did say, "The land is mine and you reside in my land as foreigners and strangers" (Lev 25:23). But was that at cross-purposes with the promise made to the patriarchs that they would possess the land? Never in Israel's history did she ever own the land, the earth, or the soil outright in our sense of the word; it was always granted to her by Yahweh as a fief-holder in which she could cultivate and live on it as long as she served him. But this land, like the whole earth, belonged to the Lord—and so did the abundance that was in it and the people who lived on it. That was the lesson taught to Pharaoh in the repeated plagues ("so that you might know that the earth is the Lord's," Ex 9:29) and to Job ("Everything under heaven belongs to me," 41:1) and later in Psalm 24:1 and in that great commentary on the Davidic covenant, Psalm 89:11.

Von Rad was likewise overly concerned over the fact that the word *naḥ^{a}lâh*, "inheritance," was persistently used to denote tribal lands but that nowhere in the Hexateuch (the first six books of the Bible) was the total land called Yahweh's "inheritance."[9] But there were examples of its use with the whole land. J. Hermann[10] noted that it was Joshua's job to lead Israel in taking the whole land as an "inheritance," or in the verbal form, "to inherit" it (Dt 1:38; 3:28; 31:7; Jos 1:6—hiphil form of the verb *nāḥal*). Of course, the emphasis of the hour was on each tribe. They had to be separately satisfied and do their part to receive their "share" (*ḥebel*—Jos 17:5, 14; 19:9), "portion" (*ḥēleq*—Dt 10:9; 12:21; 14:27; 18:1; Jos 18:5, 7, 9; 19:9), or "lot" (*gôrāl*—Jos 14:2; 15:11; 16:1; 17:1; 18:11; 19:1, 10, 17, 24, 32, 40, 51).

Previous to this, the patriarchs had only possessed a small part of that land, a burial place for Sarah, as an earnest of the fulfillment that was to come. Thus in a real sense Canaan was the "land of their sojourning" (Ge 17:8; 28:4; 36:7; 37:1; 47:1; Ex 6:4). The patriarchs possessed mainly the word of promise, but not the total reality itself.

The land was a gift, but Israel had to "possess" (*yāraš*) it; thus the reception of the gift had a corresponding action, a military action. Both of these notions, as Miller[11] pointed out, were located side by side in the expression "the land which Yahweh gives you to possess" (Dt 3:19; 5:31; 12:1; 15:4; 19:2, 14; 25:19). Divine sovereignty and human responsibility were complementary ideas rather than antithetic pairs.

9. Ibid., 82, 86.
10. Hermann, "*Nah^{a}lâh*," 771.
11. Miller, "Gift," 454.

What God gave could only be called a "good land" (Dt 1:25, 35; 3:5; 4:1 – 22; 6:8; 8:7, 10; 9:6; 11:17), just as his work in creation had received his word of approbation. It was "a land flowing with milk and honey" (Dt 11:9; 26:9, 15; 27:3; 31:20).[12] In every way, the promised inheritance was a delightful gift — owned by Yahweh and leased to Israel in partial fulfillment of his word of promise. In this land, Israel was to be blessed (Dt 15:4; 23:20; 28:8; 30:16), but special emphasis was placed on the blessing of the ground (28:8). Thus God's "blessing" in the promise-plan again became one of the connecting concepts that united the theology of the earlier periods with that of the pre-monarchical era.

Rest in the Land

One of the new provisions added to the expanding revelation of the promise-plan was the provision of "rest" for Israel.[13] So special was this rest that Yahweh would call it "my rest" (Ps 95:11; Isa 66:1). It was precisely this aspect of the promise theme that provided a key link between the end of the book of Numbers and the time of David, the two texts at opposite ends of the time period being Deuteronomy 12:9 – 10 and 2 Samuel 7:1, 11.

Nowhere in the patriarchal promises did "rest" (*m^enûḥâh*) appear as one of God's future blessings to the fathers or Israel. But when it first appeared in Deuteronomy 12:9, one gathers that it might already have been known in the tradition of the people:

> ... since you have not yet reached the resting place (*m^enûḥâh*) and the inheritance (*naḥ^alâh*) the LORD your God is giving you.

Yet it must be noted that Moses had been promised "rest" (*nûaḥ*) as early as Exodus 33:14, when he led Israel out of Egypt. Later, in Deuteronomy 3:20, Moses promised that "rest" (*nûaḥ*) would shortly come to all his fellow countrymen when they possessed the land of Canaan. Both of these words were cognates of the Deuteronomy 12:9 term. Indeed, the Hebrew root *nûaḥ*, "to rest," supplied the majority of words for the concept of rest. When the hiphil (the causative stem of the Hebrew word) of this root was followed by the preposition *l^e*, "to, for," plus a person or group, it usually assumed a technical status. Thus in some twenty instances of *hēnîaḥ l^e*, it was a place granted

12. J. A. Thompson, *Deuteronomy*, 120 – 21, noted that this same phrase appears in the Egyptian Tale of Sinuhe (*ANET*, 18 – 25, lines 80 – 90), four times in Exodus (3:8, 17; 13:5; 33:3), in Leviticus (20:24), four times in Numbers (13:27; 14:8; 10:13, 14), and five times in Deuteronomy (see above).

13. For a development of the ideas in this section see W. C. Kaiser Jr., "The Promise Theme and the Theology of Rest," *Bibliotheca Sacra* 130 (1973): 135 – 50. Also see Gerhard von Rad, "There Remains a Rest for the People of God: An Investigation of a Biblical Conception," *Hexateuch and Essays*, 94 – 102. A New Testament approach to the problem is E. Käsemann, *Das Wandernde Gottesvolk* (Göttingen: Vandenhoeck and Ruprecht, 1957); J. Frankowski, "Requies, Bonum Promissum populi Die in VT et in Judaismo (Heb. 3:1 – 4:11)," *Verbum Domini* 43 (1965): 124 – 49; O. Hoflus, *Katapausis: Die Vorstellung vom Endzeitlichen Ruheort im Hebräerbrief* (Tübingen: J. C. B. Mohr, 1970); David Darnell, "Rebellion, Rest and the Word of God: An Exegetical Study of Hebrews 3:1 – 4:13" (Ph.D. diss., Duke University, 1974); and Elmer H. Dyck, "A Theology of Rest" (M.A. diss., Trinity Evangelical Divinity School, 1975).

by the Lord (Ex 33:14; Dt 3:20; Jos 1:13, 15; 22:4; 2Ch 14:5); a peace and respite from enemies round about (Dt 12:10; 25:19; Jos 21:44; 23:1; 2Sa 7:1, 11; 1Ki 5:18 [5:4]; 1Ch 22:9, 18; 23:25; 2Ch 14:6; 15:15; 20:30; 32:22 [probable reading?]); or a cessation of sorrow and toil in the future (Isa 14:3; 28:12).

The noun *m*[e]*nûḥâh*, "resting place" or "rest," came to assume technical status as well. In Jacob's blessing of Issachar, the portion of land given to him was called a "resting place" (Ge 49:15). So far as we can see, this usage was not yet technical. But the strong associations of a geographical, spatial, and material "rest" in subsequent texts like Deuteronomy 12:9; 1 Kings 8:56; 1 Chronicles 22:9; Isaiah 28:12; and Micah 2:10 cannot be denied. This "rest" was a "place" where Yahweh would "plant" his people — a place where they could live without being disturbed anymore.

Yet there was more to this "rest" than geography. Rest was where the presence of God stopped in the wilderness wanderings (Nu 10:33) or where he dwelt (1Ch 28:2; Ps 132:8, 14; Isa 66:1). No doubt it was for this reason that David stressed the aspect of belief and trust as the basis of entering into that rest in Psalm 95:11. The condition was not an automatic one.

For the time being, "rest" would signify the quality of living in the land of inheritance when it was occupied. Yahweh himself would give Israel rest in the land (Dt 3:20; 12:10; 25:19). So Joshua 21:44 – 45 summarized the promise and its reality:

> The LORD gave them *rest* on every side, just as he had sworn to their forefathers. Not one of their enemies withstood them; the LORD handed all their enemies over to them. Not one of all the LORD's good promises to the house of Israel failed; every one was fulfilled.

But this only yielded a conundrum. If Joshua had fulfilled the promised rest, what was 2 Samuel 7:1, 11 claiming, coming as it did from a later time? And why would Solomon, later still, be called a "man of [peace and] rest" (1Ch 22:9; 1Ki 8:56)? Also, how are we to understand the spiritual and material aspects of rest? The resolution of these matters can be found in the Old Testament view of fulfillment. Specially named generations received their share of the completion of the single plan of God. This at once served as a partial confirmation of God's long-standing word and as a contemporaneous installment on the fulfillment. This, in turn, simultaneously functioned as a means of connecting that word to its ultimate or climactic fulfillment, since these periodic installment types of fulfillments were generically identical with that ultimate event and were viewed as one having one meaning. Thus there was a single meaning in the mind of the author, even though he might know of or experience multiple fulfillments of that single meaning! The promise was not to be thought of as having been given its final disclosure or fulfillment even in the aspect of the land.[14] Hence, rest was more

14. In a different connection, see von Rad, *Theology*, 2:383.

than the entry into and division of the land to all the tribes; it was also to be a final condition that pervaded the land. Thus after Israel entered the land, she was warned that she would only enjoy the quality of life God had intended for her if she continually obeyed his commandments (Dt 4:10; 12:1; 31:13). The extent of Israel's possession of the land was likewise important before the promise could be said to have been completely fulfilled. That was the way Stephen also put it in his speech in Acts 7:4 – 5:

> God sent him to this land where you are now living. He gave him no inheritance here, not even a foot of ground. But God promised him that he and his descendants after him would possess the land, even though at that time Abraham had no child.

The emphasis of Joshua 21:43 – 45 was still on the promised word, which had not failed Israel, nor would it. But whether Israel would retain her privilege of remaining in the land was another matter. She had to choose between life and death, good and evil. To choose life and the good was to "obey" one command that summarized all the others: Love the Lord your God. The presence of the conditional "if" did not pave the way for a "declension from grace into law,"[15] any more than it did for the patriarchs or the generation of Moses, much less the Davidic covenant to come! Therefore, the promise of the inheritance of God's rest was protected even in the event of subsequent sins by the recipient's descendants. Israel had to *transmit* the promise even if that generation would not *participate* in the promise. Rest was no blank check in which future generations could rest on their ancestors' laurels and slide by God's standards. This promise was to be theirs only if they would appropriate it by faith — that was the spiritual and immediate benefit of "rest."

In its final fulfillment, the God of rest — whose house of "rest" (*m^{e}nûḥâh*) contained the ark of the covenant of the Lord and functioned also as his footstool (1Ch 28:2) built by the "man of rest" to whom God had given respite from all his enemies (1Ch 22:9) — would again take up his rest in his temple in the future messianic era (Ps 132:14; cf. 2Ch 14:6). "In that day," says Isaiah, "the Lord will reach out his hand a second time to reclaim the surviving remnant of his people" (Isa 11:11). It is in this context that a series of Psalms (93 – 100) — variously designated as "Apocalyptic Psalms," "Theocratic Psalms" (Delitzsch), "Millennial Psalms" (Thorluck), "Songs of the Millennium" (Binnie), "Group of Millennial Psalms" (Herder), "Second Advent Psalms" (Rawlinson), "Enthronement Psalms" (Mowinckel), or "Royal Psalms" (Perowne) — depict the Lord as king reigning over all peoples and lands (Pss 93:1; 96:10; 99:1) and that Psalm 95 raises the offer of entering into God's rest again. For the psalmist, that ancient offer of rest was ultimately tied up with the events of the second advent of the return of Messiah to this earth. Every other rest, apparently, was only an "earnest," a down payment, on the final Sabbath rest yet to come in the second advent.[16]

---

15. As suggested by von Rad, "Promised Land," *Hexateuch and Essays*, 91.

16. See W. C. Kaiser, "Promise Theme," 142 – 43. See also my discussion of Hebrews 3:7 – 4:13 on 145 – 49 in that same article.

A Chosen Place in the Land

One of the most hotly debated phrases in the theology of Deuteronomy is the so-called centralization of sacrificial worship at a single sanctuary in Jerusalem. Indeed, this plank was the starting point and keystone from which all the other deductions are made in the Wellhausian system of literary criticism.[17] The claim was that the cultic requirements of Deuteronomy were a clear advance over the altar law of the Sinaitic "Book of the Covenant":

> Make an altar of earth for me and sacrifice on it your burnt offerings and fellowship offerings, your sheep and goats and your cattle. Wherever I cause my name to be honored, I will come to you and bless you. (Ex 20:24)

That is to say, the Sinaitic law limited the use of sacrifices only to those places sanctified by the divine presence — those places where God had appointed that his name should be remembered because he had met with his representative or people at that spot.

But was Deuteronomy reversing these Sinaitic directions when it ordered Israel: "But you are to seek the place [site] the Lord your God will choose from among all your tribes to put his Name there for his dwelling" (Dt 12:5, 11, 21; 14:23 – 24; 15:20; 16:2, 6, 11; 26:2)? Or "Offer them [sacrifices] only at the place the LORD will choose in one of your tribes" (Dt 12:14, 18, 26; 14:25; 16:7, 15 – 16; 17:8, 10; 18:6; 31:11; Jos 9:27)?

Both the laws of Deuteronomy and Exodus insisted that the place of sacrifice must be appointed and chosen by the Lord, not by people. Sacrifices may not be offered "anywhere you please" (Dt 12:13).[18] And when the context of Deuteronomy 12 is investigated, the contrast is found to be, not between many Yahweh altars and one such altar, but between those altars erected to other gods, whose names are to be destroyed, and that "place" where Yahweh's name shall abide (vv. 2 – 5). Thus, instead of revoking the Sinaitic legislation, Deuteronomy built on it. We again hear of a "place" (*māqôm*) where Yahweh will "cause his name to be remembered" (or "dwell"), where sacrifices and offerings may be made and where blessing will result.[19]

Scholarly attention, however, has focused on the article and number of the noun in the expression "the place" in Deuteronomy 12:5, 14. Oestreicher argued that the article was distributive and not restrictive and that the lack of an article in the expression "in one of your tribes" (v. 14) was to be given a general meaning due to an analogous expression in the fugitive slave law in Deuteronomy 23:16 [17].[20] Thus the translation of Deuteronomy 12:14 would be "in every place which Yahweh shall choose in any of

17. J. Wellhausen, *Prolegomena to the History of Israel*, trans. J. S. Black and A. Menzies (Edinburgh: T & T Clark, 1885), 368.

18. *Kol mâqôm* (cf. Ge 20:13; Dt 11:24; Jos 1:3), M. H. Segal, *The Pentateuch: Its Composition and Its Authorship* (Jerusalem: Magnes Press, 1967), 87, n. 17.

19. As argued by G. T. Manley, *The Book of the Law* (London: Tyndale Press, 1957), 132.

20. Th. Oestreicher, "Dtn xii.13f. im Licht von Dtn xxiii. 16f.," *Zeitschrift für alttestamentliche Wissenschaft* 43(1925): 246 – 49. Deuteronomy 23:16 would read, "He [the slave] shall dwell with you *in any place* which he shall choose within any of your gates" (italics mine).

your tribes." The singular number of the expression "the place" would denote a class and not a single locality even as it did in Deuteronomy 23:16.

E. W. Nicholson disagreed with this analogy, however. The subject of the Deuteronomy 23:16 law was a *class* of people, runaway slaves seeking asylum, while the subject of the Deuteronomy 12:5 – 7 law was Yahweh. Furthermore, he argued, the singular number of "place" is strange if the writer meant to say "in the places which Yahweh shall choose in your tribes."[21] Nicholson's counterarguments to Oestreicher are probably correct. But this still does not support a centralization hypothesis. The subject was not one Yahweh altar versus many Yahweh altars — nothing is said on that topic. It is only about Yahweh's intention to put his name in an as-yet-unnamed place after the people arrive in Canaan. In fact, Deuteronomy 27:1 – 8, with its injunction to build an altar on Mount Ebal, raises a fatal flaw to the centralized altar theory, according to Manley: "It manifestly commands that which the law is supposed to forbid and, to make matters worse, uses the very words of Exodus xx.24 which Deuteronomy is supposed to revoke."[22]

At most, Deuteronomy taught that Yahweh would select a site in Canaan after he had helped Israel to "inherit" the land and to find "rest" (Dt 12:10 – 11) in much the same way as he had done in the past. He would "make his name dwell" in the place of his election. This promise joined the Immanuel and Shekinah-glory theology of the patriarchal and Mosaic eras. And just as God had elected one man out of all humanity, Abraham, and one tribe out of the twelve sons of Jacob, Judah, so now he would choose one place in one of the tribes in which his name would dwell. There he would take up his dwelling (12:5), and there Israel would come to worship him. It would function in many ways as the tabernacle had done for so long.

Name Dwelling in the Land

There are three other theologically important expressions that are connected with the "place" promise. They are phrases in which Yahweh promises:

1. "To make his name dwell [*šākan*] there" (Dt 12:11; 14:23; 16:2, 6, 11; 26:2)
2. "To put [*śîm*] his name there" (Dt 12:5, 21; 14:24; 1Ki 9:3; 11:36; 14:21; 2Ki 21:4, 7; 2Ch 6:20; 33:7)
3. "That my name might be there" (1Ki 8:16, 29; 2Ki 23:27)

Too much is made of this material when some, following von Rad, make this "name-theology" a replacement for the older "glory-theology," in that no longer is Yahweh himself present at the ark of the covenant, but only his name is now present.[23] Von Rad himself noted, however, that the "name" was present already in Exodus 20:24 and

21. E. W. Nicholson, *Deuteronomy and Tradition* (Philadelphia: Fortress Press, 1967), 53 – 54. Cf. p. 53, n. 1 for list of those challenging his exegesis. To this add Manley, *Book of the Law*.

22. Manley, *Book of the Law*, 134; cf. also James Orr, *The Problem of the Old Testament* (London: J. Nisbet & Co., 1909), 174 – 80; Gordon J. Wenham, "Deuteronomy and the Central Sanctuary," *Tyndale Bulletin* 22 (1971): 103 – 18, esp. 110 – 14.

23. Gerhard von Rad, *Studies in Deuteronomy* (Chicago: Henry Regnery Co., 1953), 38 – 44.

Exodus 31. The "name" here, as in the antecedent theology, stood for the total being, character, and nature, just as name was used in the prohibition given at Sinai against taking the *name* of the Lord God in vain. Roland de Vaux could not agree with von Rad either. These three phrases meant "to claim ownership."[24] While it is true that God's "holy habitation" (*mᵉʿôn qōdeš* — Dt 26:15) and his "dwelling place" (*mᵉqôm šebet* — 1Ki 8:30, 39, 43, 49) is in heaven, the latter expression is also found in the Song of the Sea (Ex 15:17) in parallelism with the "sanctuary" of the Lord.

The point seems to be that God is transcendent in that his permanent abode (*yšb, šbt*) is in heaven; yet he is immanent in that he dwells (*škn*) on the earth (Ex 25:8; 29:45; Lev 26:11; Nu 16:3) in his glory, angel, name, and now in a "place" that he will yet select (Dt 12:5). There is no evidence that Deuteronomy or Moses in any way rejected this so-called dialectical conception of the divine abode. Heaven is not the exclusive dwelling place of God — he may "sit" or "be enthroned" there, but he also "tabernacled" on earth as well. And Deuteronomy added to the list of his manifestations of himself to Israel — the *place* where he will cause his name (his person) to dwell. What God owned he now openly possessed by having his name "put" on it or "called over" it.

The Book of Joshua

The book of Joshua (about 1450 to 1375 BC) forms a bridge from the five books of the Torah to the books of Judges and the other earlier prophets of Samuel and Kings. As the successor to Moses, Joshua was to exhort Israel to faithfulness and courageous action in conquering the land. The conquest of the land of Canaan was in direct fulfillment of the repeated promise-plan that the land was to be given to Abraham's offspring.

In addition to conquering and possessing the land, two ceremonies were dedicated to the renewal of the covenant. The first was on Mount Ebal, where Joshua built an altar to the Lord and offered sacrifices, copied the law of Moses, and read it for the people (Jos 8:30 – 35). The second was at Shechem (Jos 24), where Joshua wrote the words of Israel's covenant renewal in "the Book of the Law of God" and erected a large stone as a witness and a reminder of that agreement (Jos 24:25 – 27). As the work of the conquest was winding down, the issue for Israel was one of being faithful in everyday life to the Lord.

Conquest of the Land

Yahweh was known as a "man of war" after his celebrated victory at the Red Sea (Ex 15:3 KJV; "warrior" NIV). Even before there was a king to lead her, the Lord went out

24. As cited by Weinfeld, *Deuteronomy*, 194, n. 2.

at the head of Israel's army (Jdg 5:5, 13, 20, 23). And the rules for such wars had been given in explicit legal enactments in Deuteronomy:

1. The laws of battle (20:1 – 15)
2. The laws on beautiful captive women (21:10 – 14)
3. The destruction of Canaanite sanctuaries (12:1 – 4)
4. The extermination of previous inhabitants (20:16 – 20)
5. The purification for battle (23:9 – 14)
6. The war with Amalek (25:17 – 19)

These laws were illustrated in Joshua 1 – 11, where four full-length descriptions of this type of war were detailed:

1. Conquest of Jericho (Jos 6)
2. Second attack on Ai (Jos 8)
3. Southern campaign (Jos 10)
4. Northern campaign (Jos 11)

Two other descriptions recorded Israel's failure to conduct this type of war:

1. First attack on Ai (Jos 7)
2. Unapproved treaty with the Gibeonites (Jos 9)

Yahweh's Wars

Such wars have been named "holy wars" by Gerhard von Rad.[25] They were in actuality "Yahweh's wars" (1Sa 18:18; 25:28); therefore, such battles were not to be initiated by any leader or group without consulting the Lord first (1Sa 28:5 – 6; 30:7 – 8; 2Sa 5:19, 22, 23). After Israel had been assured by Yahweh that the anticipated battle was his own, then the trumpets were sounded and the cry went up: "Yahweh has given [the enemy] into your hands" (Jdg 3:28; 6:3; 7:15; 1Sa 13:3). The war began with Yahweh's promise of success and an exhortation to fight valiantly. Israel must only trust and not be afraid (Jos 1:6, 9; 6:2; 8:1; 10:8; 11:6). The men were then "consecrated" to the Lord, for their mission set them apart from all mundane activity (1Sa 21:6; 2Sa 11:11). Yahweh went before the army and dwelt in the camp (Dt 23:14; Jdg 4:14) and "fought" on behalf of Israel (Dt 1:30). The military leader of the army, though often specially endowed with powers, was ultimately dependent on the Lord, for the Lord could save by few or by many (Jdg 7:2ff.; 1Sa 13:15ff.). This is vividly brought out by Joshua's vision of the "commander of the LORD" who stood with sword in hand ready for action (Jos 5:13 – 15). At the climax of the battle, Yahweh sent terror or panic (*m*ᵉ*hûmâh, hāmam*) into the hearts of the enemy, bringing about their overthrow (Jos 10:10; Jdg 4:15; 1Sa 5:11; 7:10 passim).

25. Von Rad, *Studies in Deuteronomy*, 45 – 59; idem, *Der heilige Krieg im alten Israel* (Zurich: Zwingli Verlag, 1951); Gordon J. Wenham, "The Deuteronomic Theology of the Book of Joshua," *Journal of Biblical Literature* 90 (1971): 141 – 42.

The Ban

In this type of warfare, spoils were not to be taken by anyone, for everything in this war was under "ban" (*ḥērem* = *ḥāram*, "to utterly destroy" — Dt 20:17; 2:34; 3:6; 7:2). It was the exclusive property of the Lord; therefore, it was to be totally devoted to destruction (Jos 6:17 – 27; 1Sa 15:3). What could not be burned, such as silver, gold, or iron, was to be placed in the sanctuary of God. The "ban" was just the opposite of a voluntary whole-burnt offering in which the offerer willingly gave up the entire animal in an act of total submission (Lev 1; cf. Ro 12:1 – 2). Here, after much divine longsuffering and waiting, God called for everything that belonged to him in the first place — life, possessions, valuables — as an involuntary whole-burnt offering. Thus more was involved than mere destruction; it was a "religious punishment," which signified "the separation from the profane sphere and deliverance into the power of God."[26] As God had predicted to Abraham, he would wait "until the iniquity of the Amorite" was "complete" (Ge 15:16). And so he did — six hundred years! Now Joshua was fulfilling that word.

The theology of this type of conquest emphasized the pattern of the priority of the divine command and the fidelity to which that divine word was carried out. When men were responsibly obedient, then God was sovereignly present, as he was in Israel's southern campaign: "The LORD threw down great stones from heaven" (Jos 10:11), for "the LORD fought for Israel" (v. 14). But when Israel "did not inquire of the LORD" (Jos 9:14), when she attempted to attack Ai, or when Achan's personal sin of stealing from God those things in Jericho "dedicated to destruction" (under the "ban" or part of the *ḥerem*) left a cloud of moral pollution over *all* the people (7:11, 13, 19), the results were catastrophic and disgraceful.

The Book of Judges

The purpose of the book of Judges (about 1380 to 1050 BC) is to demonstrate that "in those days Israel had no king; everyone did as he saw fit" (Jdg 17:6; 21:25; cf. 18:1; 19:1).[27] The period of the judges stressed charismatic leadership under the working of the Holy Spirit. One ruler (here also called a "judge") after another was raised up and anointed in response to the people's exhaustion with their sin and disobedience.

---

26. Johannes Bauer, "Ban," *Sacranentum Verbi* (New York: Herder & Herder, 1970), 1:55. Cf. also G. R. Driver, "Hebrew Homonyms," *Vetus Testamentum Supplements* 16 (1967): 56 – 59, who sees two roots behind *ḥērem*: *hrm*, Akkadian *haramu*, "to cut off, separate," and *ḥrm*, Arabic *Ḥarama*, "prohibited, declared illicit." J. P. Lilley, "Understanding the *ḥerem*," *Tyndale Bulletin* 44 (1993): 169 – 77. K. L. Younger Jr., *Ancient Conquest Accounts* (Sheffield: University of Sheffield, 1990).

27. W. J. Dumbrell, "'In Those Days There Was No King in Israel; Every Man Did What Was Right in His Own Eyes,' The Purpose of the Book of Judges Reconsidered," *Journal for the Study of the Old Testament* 25 (1983): 23 – 33. F. E. Greenspahn, "The Theology of the Framework of Judges," *Vetus Testamentum* 36 (1986): 385 – 96.

The book begins with two editorial introductions (Jdg 1:1 – 2:5 and 2:6 – 3:6) and closes with two conclusions (17:1 – 18:31 and 19:1 – 21: 25). Sandwiched in between the introductions and conclusions were the cycles of judges such as Othniel, Ehud, Deborah and Barak, Gideon, Jephthah, and Samson.

Prophetic History in the Land

Beyond the fulfillment of the Abrahamic promise of the land with its anticipated conquest, distribution, rest, and place for the name of God to dwell, there was another major theological element in Deuteronomy and the earlier prophets. It was the structure found in Joshua to 2 Kings and mentioned earlier in this chapter. In the case of the book of Judges, the meaning and significance of the narratives was to be found in a familiar cycle of apostasy, punishment, repentance, divine compassion, deliverance, and rest in the land.

This cycle was first stated in Judges 2:11 – 3:6, but subsequently it served as an outline for the experiences of several generations. The most significant theological point was, as Carl Graesser Jr. has observed,[28] that the phrases, concepts, and theological emphases were those of the book of Deuteronomy. Compare, for example:

Judges 2:11 with Deuteronomy 4:25 and 6:3
Judges 2:12 with Deuteronomy 4:25 and 6:14
Judges 2:14 with Deuteronomy 6:15

The impact of Deuteronomy on Judges 2:11 – 14 was just as heavy as it had been on Joshua 1:2 – 9 where, according to Graesser, "more than fifty percent" of that speech could "be reproduced verbatim from verses in Deuteronomy."[29] Compare:

Joshua 1:2 with Deuteronomy 5:31
Joshua 1:3 – 4 with Deuteronomy 11:24
Joshua 1:5 with Deuteronomy 11:25 and 31:6
Joshua 1:6 with Deuteronomy 31:23
Joshua 1:7 – 8 with Deuteronomy 5:32
Joshua 1:9 with Deuteronomy 31:6

But what was the key or organizing concept that made this history more than just a dreary report of constant failure? What use was there in detailing these narratives for those days, much less for future generations? I believe Hans W. Wolff has correctly identified that lost piece of theology in the doctrine of repentance.[30]

---

28. Carl Graesser Jr., "The Message of the Deuteronomic Historian," *Concordia Theological Monthly* 39 (1968): 544, n. 10. For a complete list of "Deuteronomic language," see S. R. Driver, *Introduction to the Literature of the Old Testament* (New York: Meridian Books, 1956), 99 – 102. Also see Weinfeld, *Deuteronomy*, app. A, pp. 320 – 59, and S. R. Driver, *Commentary on Deuteronomy* (New York: Charles Scribner's Sons, 1916), lxxviii – lxxxiv.

29. Ibid., 545, n. 19.

30. Hans Walter Wolff, "The Kerygma of the Deuteronomic Historical Work," in *The Vitality of Old Testament Traditions*, coauthored by Walter Brueggemann and Hans W. Wolff (Atlanta: John Knox Press, 1975), 83 – 100.

Repentance and Blessing

"As long as Joshua lived," began Judges 2:7 on an ominous note, "the people served the LORD." However, from there on the story was the same: "They did evil in the sight of the LORD ... and departed from Yahweh ... and followed other gods ... [whereupon] the anger of the LORD was hot against Israel ... and he sold them into the clutches of their enemies round about" (Jdg 2:11 – 12, 14). Then "they cried to Yahweh" (Jdg 3:9; 4:3; cf. also 1Sa 12:19) — and there it was. Misery would finally find a voice, and in her despair, Israel would "return" (*šûb*) to the Lord.

The basis for this injunction was to be found in Deuteronomy 30:1 – 10. Three times the catchword "to return" (*shub*) was repeated (vv. 2, 8, 10). "If you will turn back to Yahweh your God with all your heart and with all your soul," then God will again bless his people.

The earliest prophetic use of the term to "repent" — to "return" to the Lord — appears in 1 Samuel 7:3:

> If you are returning (*šābîm*) to the LORD with all your hearts, then rid yourselves of the foreign gods and the Ashtoreths and commit yourselves to the LORD and serve him only, and he will deliver you out of the hand of the Philistines.

Wolff found 1Kings 8:46ff. to be "the most impressive connection" with Deuteronomy 30:1 – 10 — especially the rare phrase "to take something to heart" (*hēšîb 'el lēb* in Dt 30:1b and 1Ki 8:47a; see also 1Sa 7:3). Twice during his dedicatory prayer for the temple, Solomon prayed that God would be merciful to Israel if she "repented" and "turned" to him (1Ki 8:46 – 53).

Likewise 2 Kings 17:13 summarized the message "by all prophets and seers of Israel and Judah." It was simply "repent" (*šubû*):

> Turn (*šubû*) from your evil ways. Observe my commands and decrees, in accordance with the entire Law that I commanded your fathers to obey and that I delivered to you through my servants the prophets.

The same word could also be used as the highest accolade given to any Israelite king. Of King Josiah it was said in 2 Kings 23:25:

> Neither before nor after Josiah was there a king like him who turned (*šāb*) to the LORD as he did — with all his heart and with all his soul and with all his strength, in accordance with all the Law of Moses.

He was faithful to the Davidic type; yet he was also faithful to the Sinaitic commandment as well. There was no duality here. It was one and the same thing. In fact, so markedly different in morality and religion were the lives of the kings of Israel and Judah that David and Jeroboam became standards of piety and impiety respectively. Every northern king was condemned because he "walked in all the ways of Jeroboam, the son of Nebat, and in the sin which he made Israel to sin" (1Ki 14:16; 15:26, 30, 34; 16:26; 22:52; 2Ki 3:3; 10:29, 31; 13:2, 6; 14:24; 15:9, 18, 24, 28; 23:15; cf. 1Ki 12:30; 13:34; 2Ki 17:21 – 22). Of any good king of Judah it was said, "He walked before me as David his father walked" (1Ki 3:3, 14; 11:4, 6, 33, 38; 14:8; 15:3, 5, 11; 2Ki 14:3; 16:2; 18:3; 22:2).

Out of all the kings of Israel and Judah, only Hezekiah and Josiah are commended unconditionally, while six others — Asa, Jehoshaphat, Jehoash, Amaziah, Uzziah, and Jotham — received a qualified commendation. Consistently, the others scorned the commandments and proudly refused to repent.

Repentance was the basis for any new work of God after a time of failure. And the result of that repentance was the "good" (*tôb*) God would do to all Israel. Walter Brueggemann[31] pointed to this theme of "goodness" as a parallel to Wolff's "repentance" theme. For him the theme was a covenantal term. To speak "well" or "rightly" (*tôb*) in all that they said (Dt 5:28; 18:17) was for Israel to honor a formal treaty or covenant obligation (cf. the only two other instances, 1Sa 12:23; 1Ki 8:36; and perhaps 2Ki 20:3).[32]

But in a larger sense, Israel was also the recipient of "good." As such, "good" functioned as a synonym for *šālôm*, "peace" in its most comprehensive and most holistic sense, observed Brueggemann, while in Deuteronomy 30:15 "good" was a synonym for "life."[33] Thus every "blessing" (an old theological term by this time) was included in the good life, which included life itself (Dt 5:16, 33; 6:18, 24); longevity (4:40; 5:16; 22:7); the land (5:16, 33; 6:18); and the increase and multiplication of one's family (6:3). Israel was to "obey" in order that Yahweh might do her "good" (12:25, 28; 19:13; 22:7).

In the very text that Wolff found his programmatic threefold call to "repent" (Dt 30:2, 8, 10), Brueggemann found two divine offers to make Israel "more prosperous (*tôb*) and numerous than [her] ancestors" (vv. 5, 9). This "goodness" surpassed mere description and moved into the category of promises and confession. The land given to Israel was a "good land" (Dt 8:7 – 10), for Israel would "*bless* the LORD [her] God for the *good* land he had given [her]" (note also the word of promise about the land in Dt 1:8, 25; 6:10, 18).

The same word of goodness and blessing could be seen in the Davidic house, which did the "good" that Saul refused to do (1Sa 16:16; 20:7, 12, 31). Yet David was able to do the "good" because Yahweh granted it to him: "And when the Lord has dealt *well* with my lord" (1Sa 25:31; cf. 1Ki 8:66). Thus the key promise to David in 2 Samuel 7:28, which was to "endure" (eight times in that chapter there is the adverb "forever"), was called his "*good* [word] to [his] servant." Everything related to the well-being of David's realm could be summarized in this word "good" (2Sa 2:6).

Thus "repentance" has a counter theme: Israel was offered the blessing, promise, and assurance of God. This balance prevented the theologian, as Brueggemann correctly

31. Walter Brueggemann, "The Kerygma of the Deuteronomic Historian," *Interpretation* 22 (1968): 387 – 402.

32. Ibid., 389, nn. 6, 7 refer to Aramaic treaties where *tôb* occurs.

33. Ibid., 391.

commented, from finding in Deuteronomy only law, obedience, judgment, curse, and repentance; there were likewise the faithfulness and blessing of God to a covenant, and a word from which he does not renege.[34]

Predictive Word and Fulfilled Event

The prophetic historians especially found God's word "good." His words were fulfilled in history—"Not one good word of all that he had promised to the house of Israel had failed; all had come to pass" (Jos 21:45; 23:14; 1Ki 8:56; 2Ki 10:10). For that word was not an "empty" (*rēq*) word or a word "void" of power (Dt 32:47); once it was uttered, it reached its goal.

Such a series of "good" words uttered by the prophets could be made into another whole framework for another aspect of the single plan of God that embraced these days of entering into the promised inheritance, rest, and place where he would put his name. Gerhard von Rad[35] pointed out this thread of prophecy and fulfillment throughout the prophetic historians. Each divine word of prediction spoken by the prophets had its corresponding historical event, for example:

Promise	Topic	Fulfillment
2 Samuel 7:13	Solomon, the temple builder	1 Kings 8:20
1 Kings 11:29–36	Division of the kingdom	1 Kings 12:15
1 Kings 13:1–3	Josiah's pollution of Bethel altar	2 Kings 23:16–18
1 Kings 14:6–16	Uprooting of Jeroboam's kingdom	1 Kings 15:29
1 Kings 16:1–4	Uprooting of Baasha's kingdom	1 Kings 16:12
Joshua 6:26	Curse on rebuilding of Jericho	1 Kings 16:34
1 Kings 22:17	Death of Ahab in battle	1 Kings 22:35–38
1 Kings 21:21	Judgment on Ahab and his family	1 Kings 21:27–29; 2 Kings 9:7
2 Kings 1:6	Sick Ahaziah will die	2 Kings 1:17
2 Kings 21:10–16	Manasseh's sins will bring disaster	2 Kings 23:26; 24:2
2 Kings 22:15–20	Josiah will escape impending evil days	2 Kings 23:29–30

The Creative Word of God

This theology of history accented the priority of God's creative word. The northern ten tribes had their doom sealed with the apostasy of Jeroboam (1Ki 14:16). Yet because

34. Ibid., 38.

35. Von Rad, *Studies*, 74–91.

of Yahweh's word of promise to David, Judah continued to live on (1Ki 11:13, 32, 36). Yahweh wanted to leave "a light in Jerusalem" (1Ki 15:4) — an obvious allusion to the Davidic house and promise (2Sa 21:17; Ps 132:17; cf. 2Sa 14:7).

While David spoke this word to his son Solomon, "that the LORD may keep his promise to me,... you will never fail to have a man on the throne of Israel" (1Ki 2:4), Solomon realized the fulfillment of that blessing in his own life (1Ki 8:20, 25), which Yahweh also confirmed to Solomon directly (1Ki 9:5). Later on, Isaiah (55:3) reflected back on it, and called this "good" word the "sure mercies of David" (*has^{e}dê Dāwid*). Thus, the ancient words of blessing and promise were still being renewed, enlarged, and fulfilled. As von Rad put it, the prophets changed "the gears of history with a word of God."[36]

A Prophet Like Moses

Every reference made to the promised seed throughout the pre-patriarchal, patriarchal, and Mosaic eras had been generic in character; they portrayed the future redemption as the "seed" of the woman, the race of Shem, the "seed" of Abraham, the tribe of Judah, and the kingdom of Israel. But when Moses predicted in Deuteronomy 18:15 – 19 that Yahweh had said to him, "A prophet will I raise up for them, from the midst of their brethren, like you," the question now was: Did he mean a simple singular "prophet," a collective, or a generic idea? And was this "prophet" another messianic figure?

From the context one might, at first reading, only expect an individual prophet coming from Israel and compared with Moses. However, the prophetic office was not transmitted to Moses' successors like the Davidic line was. Rather, Moses' ministry and person were outside the usual class of prophets, for he had been placed over all God's house (Nu 12:7). He also had fulfilled the priestly functions before the Aaronic priesthood had been inaugurated (Ex 24:4 – 8). Furthermore, each of the parallel offices of "judge" (Dt 17:8 – 13), "king" (vv. 14 – 20), and "priest" (18:1 – 8) were collective and generic, not individual, in the immediate context.

Thus we can conclude that this promise is also generic. Moses recognized that his work was incomplete; yet he could see another prophet in view who unlike himself would complete the ministry of instruction and revelation of God. This coming prophet would be (1) an Israelite, "of thy brethren" (Dt 18:15, 18); (2) "like" Moses (vv. 15, 18); and (3) authorized to declare the word of God with authority (vv. 18 – 19). Such an expectation was common knowledge even before the days of Jesus. Philip found Nathanael and announced, "We have found the one Moses wrote about in the Law and about whom the prophets also wrote" (Jn 1:45). Likewise the Samaritan woman concluded that Jesus was that "prophet" (4:19, 29); and the multitude near the Sea of Galilee exclaimed, "Surely this is the Prophet who is to come into the world" (6:14). Peter likewise quoted our passage in his temple address and applied it to Jesus (Ac 3:22 – 26), as did Stephen (7:37).

36. Von Rad, *Theology*, 1:342.

The key to the theology of this period remained the inheritance of the land and the "rest" into which Israel entered by faith. Furthermore, in that very "place" Yahweh would cause his name to dwell. And Israel's history would be marked by the "good" if she would "repent" and receive the "good" prophetic word sent from God at those crucial junctures in her history.

The prophetic history, with its programmatic statements and its evaluative comments that were put in the mouths of key speakers, flows from the internal structure of the narration of how Israel succeeded or failed to fully enter into the "rest" that God had promised. In this sequence, it was the word of God through his messengers that led the way. The people followed in obedience or repentance — or in total collapse. Yet the promise of God continued to survive in David's house regardless of ineptitude present on every hand.

Excursus: A Theology of God and the Canaanite Genocide

One of the most frequently raised objections to the Old Testament teaching that God is just and loving is his command, as Joshua went into Canaan with the Israelites, to exterminate from the face of the earth all men, women, and children belonging to the seven or eight nations of Canaan that were in the land. The biblical teaching on God's fairness and mercy are hard-pressed, according to many, when such wholesale and blanket condemnation is demanded by God of all the inhabitants of Canaan at the time of Israel's arrival.

It is not as if Israel was so morally superior that they were in a position to cast the first stones. As Ronald Goetz said with some justification, "Israel is helped *in spite* of her sins, while the Canaanites are destroyed *because* of theirs."[37] But the answer, as Goetz himself observed, does not lie in the fact that Israel was vastly more righteous than the Canaanites, but instead it lies in the increasing degrees of guilt that had accrued to Canaan over the years and millennia prior to the time of Joshua's conquest. Therefore, without trying to mitigate or tone down the divine command to totally wipe out the population of Canaan, the text that places this whole question in perspective is Deuteronomy 9:5:

> It is not because of your righteousness or your integrity that you are going in to take possession of their land; but on account of the wickedness of these nations,

37. Ronald Goetz, "Joshua, Calvin and Genocide," *Theology Today* 32 (1975): 266.

the LORD your God will drive them out before you, to accomplish what he swore to your fathers, to Abraham, Isaac and Jacob.

God waited all during the days of the patriarchs, the days of the Egyptian bondage, and more, for the Canaanites to repent and turn away from the sins they had increasingly been heaping up against themselves. Genesis 15:16 makes it clear that even in the time of 2100 to 1800 BC it still would have been premature for Abraham, Isaac, or Jacob to have acted on the promise of God and to have invaded Canaan and taken it for themselves, "for the sin of the Amorites [had] not reached its full measure." Our Lord was waiting for the national "cup of iniquity" to reach the brim and run over!

The mercy, grace, and love of God caused him to act extremely slowly in carrying out the threat of judgment against Canaan. It must also be remembered that all prophecies (except those in the Abrahamic-Davidic-new covenant stream, which are unconditional) have an expressed or unexpressed "unless" or "if" connected to them and are therefore conditional in the threats they raise against nations. "If" Canaan had repented at any time along that timeline that stretched from Noah's observation that his grandson Canaan had the same sexual perversions as his father Ham (Ge 9:25), then God would have changed his indictment against that nation (Jer 18:7 – 10). We are unable to date the time of Noah's flood, but even if it were somewhere around 3500 BC, and God watched Canaan from that date all the way down to around 1400 or 1300 BC, then God waited more than two millennia before he gave the command for Joshua to destroy the inhabitants of that land.

God does not pervert justice (Job 8:3), but as Judge of all the earth, he does what is right (Ge 18:25). The issue here is the whole question of the legitimacy and meaning of divine anger (*ira Dei*). Too frequently mortals have tended to define anger as Aristotle did, as "the desire for retaliation,"[38] or the burning need to get even for some slight or actual harm that had been carried out against us. Some have even defined anger as a "brief madness,"[39] but it was the Church Father Lactantius (last half of the third century AD), who defined anger as "a motion of the soul rousing itself to curb sin."[40]

In the second century of the Christian era, arguments by Marcion against the God of the Old Testament as a "Demiurge" (a subordinate deity who was responsible for the creation of evil) forced the church to expel Marcion in AD

38. Aristotle, *De Anima* 1, 1. See the excellent discussion of this whole topic in Abraham Heschel, *The Prophets* (New York: Harper & Row, 1962), 2:1 – 86, esp. 60.

39. Horace, *Epistolae* 1:2:62. Also see J. C. Hardwick, "The Wrath of God and the Wrath of Man," *The Hibbert Journal* 39 (1940 – 41): 251 – 61.

40. Cited by Heschel, *Prophets*, 2:82.

144. Tertullian wrote his *Against Marcion* to answer many of Marcion's objections to the God of the Old Testament. But it was Lactantius's *De Ira Dei* ("On the Anger of God") that began to answer and correctly understand the passages dealing with the anger of God. He wrote:

> He who loves the good by this very fact hates the evil: and he who does not hate evil, does not love the good; because the love of goodness issues directly out of the hatred of evil, and the hatred of evil issues directly out of the love of goodness. No one can love life without abhorring death; and no one can have an appetency for light without an antipathy to darkness.[41]

God's anger and wrath are his legitimate expressions of his abhorrence of all that is sinful, wrong, unjust, and against his very nature and being. God did not flare up with an impetuosity against the Canaanites, but gave them centuries and millennia to get the point and right the wrong. In the end, he had to act or he would not be holy, just, righteous, and fair.[42]

41. Lactantius, *De Ira Dei*, 51.

42. See the four viewpoints on this subject in *Show Them No Mercy: Four Views on God and Canaanite Genocide*, ed. Stanley N. Gundry (Grand Rapids: Zondervan, 2003). The views are by C. S. Cowles, Eugene H. Merrill, Daniel L. Gard, and Tremper Longman III.

Chapter 5

The King of the Promise: The Davidic Era

Ruth, 1 and 2 Samuel, Psalms, 1 Kings (About 1050 – 970 BC)

The Book of Ruth

The book of Ruth, which has only four chapters, eighty-five verses, and 1,294 words, is theologically a very significant book if for no other reason than that it contains the genealogy of David, the great king of Israel (Ru 4:18 – 22).

Most of this slim volume is dialogue — in fact, fifty-five out of the eighty-five verses are dialogue. More than half of the words of this book (678 of them, or 52.4 percent) are from the lips of the book's main characters.[1] Only on two occasions does the narrator intervene (in Ru 1:6 and 4:13). God is mentioned twenty-three times in the book. Most of these references appear in prayers (9 times) or in descriptions of God's actions (7 times).[2]

The heart and purpose of the book is identified in Ruth 2:12, where Boaz prays that Ruth, a Moabitess, may find her reward for her kindness (*ḥesed*) under the wings (*kenapim*) of Yahweh. The same word for "wing" is used for the "skirt" that Ruth asked Boaz to spread over her (Ru 3:9).

The working of God can be seen in his providential answers to prayer, his ending of the famine that brings Ruth back to Judah, and in the grandchild born to Naomi, who later becomes the "father" of Jesse, and he, in turn, becomes the father of David (4:22). The book teaches, therefore, the blessing of God, the reward for all such deeds

1. These statistics are from Daniel Block, *The New American Commentary: Judges and Ruth* (Nashville: Broadman and Holman, 1999), 588, n. 5.

2. These numbers are from Ronald M. Hals, *The Theology of the Book of Ruth* (Philadelphia: Fortress, 1969). See also W. S. Prinsloo, "The Theology of the Book of Ruth," *Vetus Testamentum* 30 (1980): 330 – 41.

of kindness (*ḥesed*), the inclusion of the Gentiles in the blessings of the gospel, even in the promised Davidic line, and the works of God in providence.

But it is God's promise to Ruth's great-grandson, David, in 2 Samuel 7 that has to be among the most brilliant moments in the history of salvation, not only for this epoch of biblical history, but for the whole plan of redemption. It is matched in importance and prestige only by the promise made to Abraham in Genesis 12 and later to all Israel and Judah in Jeremiah's new covenant (Jer 31:31 – 34). Therefore, this forty-year segment out of the narratives of the prophetic historians (Joshua to 2 Kings) merits an extended and separate treatment even though it finds its basic location in the works of the earlier prophets.

However, there is more textual material to consider than a mere chapter, such as 2 Samuel 7, or its later commentaries such as Psalm 89. In our diachronic treatment of theology and in our desire to have biblical theology act as a basic aid primarily to exegetical theology rather than first of all to systematic theology, we will need to include the following in the Davidic era: (1) what scholars have referred to since Leonhard Rost[3] as the "succession narrative" (2Sa 9 – 20 and 1Ki 1 – 2; i.e., the remaining history of David from the end of 1Sa 16 – 31 and from 2Sa 1 – 8; 21 – 24), and (2) the royal psalms (Pss 2, 18, 20, 21, 45, 72, 89, 101, 110, 132, 144:1 – 11). Likewise, since David and the ark of the covenant were so intimately united in much of their theology, this chapter will also consider (3) the "history of the ark" (1Sa 4:1 – 7:2) and the momentous experience in David's life when he moved the ark to Jerusalem (2Sa 6).

A Promised King

Deuteronomy 17:14 – 15 had carefully specified the following:

> When you enter the land the Lord your God is giving you and you have taken possession of it and settled in it, and you say, "Let us set a king over us like all the nations around us," be sure to appoint over you the king the Lord your God chooses.

Therefore, kingship as such was not outside the plan of God. It had only to wait for the proper time and for God's selection. Up to this point, Israel's government had been what Josephus had labeled a "theocracy,"[4] in which the sovereignty and power belonged to God. Had not Israel also sung at the exodus, "The Lord will reign for ever and ever" (Ex 15:18)? But when would the promised kingship be set up under the theocracy?

A Usurping Ruler

In the interim, there were several false starts. Gideon had received the offer to "rule over" (*māšal*) the people of Israel after his stunning victory over Midian (Jdg 8:22). Not only was he to be their king, but the offer was an offer of a hereditary kingship: "You,

3. Leonhard Rost, *Die Überlieferung von der Thronnach-folge Davids* (Stuttgart: W. Kohlhammer Verlag, 1926).

4. Flavius Josephus, *Against Apion*, 2.16.164 – 166.

your son, and your grandson also." To all this Gideon declined unconditionally and instead asserted the principle, "The LORD will rule over you" (v. 23).

Gideon's son, however, was not that reluctant. After his father's death, he became king of Shechem (Jdg 9:15 – 18). This usurper (for so he would be if Yahweh were the real king and had not chosen him), son of Gideon's maidservant, took a new name, Abimelek (meaning "My father is king"). Martin Buber[5] has argued that "to appoint a name" is never used in connection with giving a name to a child at birth; rather, it is consistently the verb "to call." This expression means "to give a new name" (cf. 2Ki 17:34; Ne 9:7). If Gideon renamed his son, then he probably did so on the occasion of his rejection of the kingly office, declaring instead that God his father was his king; hence, *Abi*, "my father," is *melek*, "king." But the expression in Judges 8:31 can also be translated, "They appointed him," or even, "He appointed for himself," the name "my father [before me] was — [really] — a king!"

The irony is clearly brought out in Judges 9:6 where the root *mālak*, "to be king, to reign," appears literally two times: "And they kinged 'father-king' as king." The whole experiment ended in tragedy for Abimelek and his "kingdom."

The Books of Samuel

The key biblical-theological point of view in 1 and 2 Samuel is the way God's earlier promises given to the patriarchs and to Israel are being fulfilled in the appointment and reign of David. The books of Samuel (about 1100 to 970 BC) record the rise and ministry of the prophet Samuel (1Sa 1 – 7); the people's choice of Saul as king (1Sa 8 – 12); God's rejection of Saul as king (1Sa 13 – 15); God's choice of David as king to replace Saul (1Sa 16 – 31); David's success in ruling from Hebron (2Sa 1 – 5); David's victories over the Philistines, his return of the ark to Jerusalem, and God's great promise to David (2Sa 6 – 7); David's victories over the surrounding nations (2Sa 8 – 10); David's sin with Bathsheba and the consequences that followed (2Sa 11 – 20).[6]

The prospect of a coming king was a constant theme in the promise-plan of God, for it appeared in the promises to the patriarchs (Ge 17:6, 16; 35:11), in the prophecies of Balaam (Nu 24:7, 17 – 19) and in Deuteronomy (17:14 – 20). But the people had a false start with King Saul when they asked for a king for improper reasons. God's choice will fall to David in 2 Samuel 7, one of the most significant prophecies of the Bible.

5. Martin Buber, *Kingship of God*, 3rd ed., rev. and enl., trans. Richard Sheimann (New York: Harper & Row, 1967), 74.

6. See V. P. Long, *The Reign and Rejection of King Saul: The Case for Literary and Theological Coherence* (Atlanta: Scholars Press, 1989), and P. E. Satterthwaite, "David in the Books of Samuel: A Messianic Hope?" in *The Lord's Anointed: Interpretation of Old Testament Messianic Texts*, ed. P. E. Satterthwaite, R. S. Hess, and G. J. Wenham (Grand Rapids: Eerdmans, 1995).

A Rejected Ruler

Samuel's generation was no wiser than their predecessors when they prematurely demanded a king (1Sa 8:4 – 6) on the false assumption that God was powerless to help them now that Samuel had grown old and his sons were morally corrupt (vv. 1 – 3). This too was a rejection of Yahweh's kingship (8:7; 10:19). The whole situation grieved Samuel to no end (8:6).

Samuel's opposition appears strange at first in light of the promise of Deuteronomy 17:14 – 20, where directions had been given on how to act in the event that the people should desire a king. But Samuel's opposition, as was Yahweh's as well, was a condemnation of the people's spirit and motives for requesting a king: they wished to be "like all the nations" in having a king (8:5, 20). It was also a tacit statement of disbelief in the power and presence of God: they wanted a king to go before them and fight their battles (v. 20).

Graciously, God yielded to the people's requests after Samuel had done everything he could to make them aware of the responsibilities of being under a king (1Sa 8:10 – 19). They got what they had asked for: Saul. And Saul accomplished the task appointed him by God:

> He will deliver my people from the hand of the Philistines. I have looked upon my people, for their cry has reached me. (1Sa 9:16, cf. 10:1)

And so it was. Wherever Saul turned his hand, so mightily was the power of God on him as a Spirit-filled leader that he emerged victorious against every nation he fought (1Sa 14:47; cf. 2Sa 1:17 – 27 in David's lament). Saul also rooted out all kinds of superstition and the occult forbidden by Mosaic law (1Sa 28:9) and even seemed to be careful about such Levitical matters of detail as the eating of blood (14:34). He was "God's chosen" (10:24) and "anointed" (10:1).

But what of the perpetuity of that reign of Saul? Nowhere had Saul, or Samuel for that matter, been promised that the offer was a hereditary rule; yet 1 Samuel 13:13 – 14 showed that the possibility had been there nonetheless:

> [God] would have established your kingdom over Israel for all time. But now your kingdom will not endure; the LORD has sought out a man after his own heart and appointed him leader of his people, because you have not kept the LORD's command.

There would have been nothing unusual about this had not the promise of a ruler coming from the tribe of Judah already been given, but indeed that is exactly what had been promised in Genesis 49:10. The symbols of that office, a scepter and a ruler's staff, would not depart from Judah until the one to whom they legitimately belonged came. How then was the Lord able to offer Saul an everlasting kingdom — especially since he was from the tribe of Benjamin? There is no doubt that Israel was to have a king one day, for that had been made plain in Numbers 24:17 and Deuteronomy 17:14.

And Israel could have made several false — even premature — starts. But here the Lord himself said to Saul, in retrospect, that the kingdom could have been an everlasting kingdom — there is the difficulty.

The solution to this conundrum was not to be found in an allegedly treasonous act of Samuel, who, according to some, contrary to what Scripture claimed, was supposed to have single-handedly deposed Saul and chosen David instead. This particular issue could not be resolved by blaming the people alone for electing a king after their own heart (1Sa 12:13), for Saul was also the one whom "Yahweh had chosen" (9:16; 10:1, 24; 12:13). Patrick Fairbairn came closest to solving this issue:

> After the people had been solemnly admonished of their guilt in requesting the appointment of a king on *their* worldly principles, they were allowed to raise one of their number to the throne.... And to render the divine purpose in this respect manifest to all who had eyes to see and ears to hear, the Lord allowed the choice first to fall on one who — as representative of the people's earthly wisdom and prowess — was little disposed to rule in humble subordination to the will and authority of Heaven and was therefore supplanted by another who should act as God's representative, and bear distinctively the name of His servant.[7]

Thus the lesson was designedly allowed by God to show Israel that God alone was the supreme king and that any government had to function under his authority. Hence the lot temporarily fell to Benjamin (10:20) rather than Judah. Saul was incomparable[8] to all others because only he, to the exclusion of all others, was God's man, according to Samuel (v. 24). His stature (v. 23) was a sign, but his divine election was what really made him incomparable.

Whether God might have given Saul the "kingdom," later known as the northern ten tribes, which subsequently broke away and were given to Jeroboam, and kept only "one tribe" (note that Judah and Benjamin were here regarded as *one* tribe!) for David his servant that he might always have a "lamp" in Jerusalem, the city where God had chosen to place his name (1Ki 11:33 – 37), is ultimately unknown.[9] One thing is known, Ephraim had always had a chip on its shoulder and was ready to challenge or secede from the rest of the tribes at the slightest provocation all during the era of the judges (Jdg 8:1; 12:1). Consequently, a rift had been in the making for a long time. But it does suggest what might have been involved for Saul had he continued in obedience to God.

The permitted monarchy was — even as foreseen in Deuteronomy 17:14 – 20 — to be bound by certain restrictions. The people were not to appoint anyone who was not

---

7. Patrick Fairbairn, *The Typology of Scripture* (Grand Rapids: Zondervan, 1963), 1:121 – 22.

8. For a discussion of this formula of incomparability, see C. J. Labuschagne, *The Incomparability of Yahweh in the Old Testament* (Leiden: E. J. Brill, 1966), 9 – 10.

9. J. Barton Payne, "Saul and the Changing Will of God," *Bibliotheca Sacra* 129 (1972): 321 – 25. He distinguishes between God's permissive will and his directive will in allowing Saul to be the first king, but he failed to directly link Genesis 49:10 and 1 Samuel 13:13b to this discussion.

chosen by God, and the king was not to do his own will and pleasure: he was to rule according to the law of God. Thus Israel still had a theocracy of sorts, where the king merely reigned as a viceroy of Yahweh, the heavenly Sovereign.

It is commonplace in recent scholarship to divide the narratives on the institution of the monarchy into two basic sources: one favorable to the monarchy (1Sa 9:1 – 10; 11:1 – 11, 15; 13:2 – 14:46), and the other later, Deuteronomistic, and antimonarchical in its outlook (1Sa 7:3 – 8:22; 10:17 – 27; 12:1 – 25). More recently, Hans-Jochen Boecker[10] has shown that it is too simplistic to label 1 Samuel 8 and 12 as antimonarchical. These passages do give a more conditional acceptance of kingship as an institution from God, but that was mainly because the monarchy carried with it the greater danger of apostasy.

These chapters were no more antimonarchical than Jotham's fable of Judges 9:7 – 21 was. According to Eugene H. Maly's careful analysis,[11] this fable contained a caricature of Abimelek, the would-be king, and a figurative description of the impending destruction that awaited the Shechemites. The worthlessness of the bramble's (Abimelek's) rule and the prediction of the fire coming forth from the bramble to destroy the Shechemites was no general condemnation of kingship itself; rather, its criticism was directed at those who were foolish enough to look to such protection as this and at the worthless king himself. Again, the focus was on the response of people, not on the institution itself.

An Anointed Ruler

When Saul was rejected, the Lord looked for "a man after his own heart" (1Sa 13:14), and David, the son of Jesse, was his selection. He was first anointed by the prophet Samuel (1Sa 16:13), then anointed as king of Judah (2Sa 2:4), and finally anointed to rule over all Israel (2Sa 5:3). Even as Saul had ten times been called the "anointed of the Lord" (*māšîaḥ YHWH*, 1Sa 24:6 [7], 10 [11]; 26:9, 11, 16, 23; 2Sa 1:14, 16), so now David is "anointed" and "the Spirit of the LORD came mightily on [him] from that day forward" (1Sa 16:13). He too was called "the LORD's anointed" ten times. The oil of anointing, when used in worship, was a symbol of the divine Spirit; but in regal consecration it marked God's gift of his Spirit to aid the king of Israel in administering his rule. It marked David as the recipient and representative of the divine majesty. Saul too had received the "Spirit of God" (1Sa 11:6) as did the previous "judges" from Othniel to Samuel. But when Saul departed from the Lord after a brilliant beginning of delivering Israel from the Philistines (1Sa 9:16; 14:47), he became totally inept at governing the people.

Although this title of "the anointed one" was used twice by transference in Psalm 105:15 of the patriarchs, and once of Cyrus, a divinely called ruler, in Isaiah 45:1 (cf. 1Ki 19:15), the title was otherwise only used absolutely of the king. Subsequently, the word

10. As cited by Bruce C. Birch, "The Choosing of Saul at Mizpah," *Catholic Biblical Quarterly* 37 (1975): 447 – 48, n. 4.

11. Eugene H. Maly, "The Jotham Fable — Anti-Monarchical?" *Catholic Biblical Quarterly* 22 (1960): 299 – 305.

became the title for the great Davidite who was to come and to complete the expected kingdom of God. All together, the noun *māšîaḥ*, "anointed," occurs thirty-nine times in the Old Testament. Twenty-three times it is the title for the reigning king of Israel.[12]

This means that there were nine passages left where the "anointed one" denoted some coming person, usually in the line of David (1Sa 2:10; 2:35; Pss 2:2; 20:6; 28:8; 84:9; Hab 3:13; Da 9:25 – 26). He was Yahweh's king who would reign over his everlasting kingdom on earth; yet simultaneously he was that chosen man in the line of election who was entitled to sit as God's representative on the throne of David. Though this term was by no means the clearest or the most frequent in the Old Testament, usage fixed it as the most fitting term, in preference to all other titles, to describe the expected King — the Messiah.

A Promised Dynasty

More than a kingship was at stake, however. Next to the promise given to Abraham must rank the word of blessing poured out on David. The classical Old Testament passage dealing with this new addition to the ever-expanding promise-plan of God was 2 Samuel 7, with its duplicate in 1 Chronicles 17 and commentary in Psalm 89.[13] It was the account of David's proposal to build a "house," or temple for the Lord and the revelation Nathan received with God's counterproposal that he would not allow David to construct it. Instead, Yahweh would make a "house" out of David (2Sa 7:5 – 11)!

Historical and literary criticism have not always seen fit to treat 2 Samuel 7 in a uniform, much less a kind way. Probably the most violent estimate of the text came from R. H. Pfeiffer,[14] who charged that the author's mind was "muddled," his text "obscure, involved," "badly written," full of "bad grammar and dreary style," filled with "*repetition ad nauseam*" and "monkish drivel." The whole chapter, he opined, was a late-fourth-century BC Jewish *midrash* based on Psalm 89, having no literary or historical value!

While others, like Hermann Gunkel, reversed the direction of literary dependence and declared Psalm 89 a free poetic expansion of 2 Samuel 7, John L. McKenzie and C. J. Labuschagne[15] took the middle ground that both the historical book and the psalm writers drew from an original common source. And contrary to those who would regard 2 Samuel 7:13 as a "Deuteronomic addition," the verse is not only to be regarded as genuine, but it is precisely the point on which the theology of the whole passage pivots, as the following discussion will show.

12. In addition to the three exceptions named above, "anointed" was also used of the Levitical priests (Lev 4:3, 5, 16; 6:22 [15]).

13. For much of what follows and for greater detail, see W. C. Kaiser Jr., "The Blessing of David: A Charter for Humanity," in *The Law and the Prophets*, ed. John Skilton (Philadelphia: Presbyterian and Reformed Publishing House, 1974), 298 – 318.

14. R. H. Pfeiffer, *Introduction to the Old Testament* (New York: Harper & Row, 1953), 368 – 73.

15. John L. McKenzie, "The Dynastic Oracle: II Samuel 7," *Theological Studies* 8 (1947): 195; C. J. Labuschagne, "Some Remarks on the Prayer of David in II Samuel 7," *Studies on the Book of Samuel* (Stellenbosch, South Africa: 1960), 29. For details on the synoptic problem in these texts, see Kaiser, "Blessing of David," 300 – 303.

A House

It can be demonstrated that building a temple was closely connected with the establishment of a kingdom in the ancient Near East. Such a connection was demonstrated in F. Willesen's fine study.[16] Thus, according to 2 Samuel 7:13, the "house" of David had to be first established by Yahweh before a temple could be built. Temple building could only be the completion and crowning effect of Yahweh's creation of a kingdom. This same emphasis on the necessity of God's work of establishing the kingdom taking priority over the construction of a house of worship can also be seen in 7:11c, where the "you" is emphatically positioned in the Hebrew text: "The Lord declares to you that the Lord himself will establish a house for you" (cf. 7:13a, where "He [Solomon] is the one who will build a house for my Name"). The contrast, then, was between a kingdom established by human beings and one totally brought about by Yahweh.

God promised to make David a "house" (*bayit*). But what could this mean? *Bayit* referred to more than a residence; it was also a family: parents, children, and kin. For example, Noah went into the ark with his "whole house" (Ge 7:1), obviously not with the building of their residence; and Jacob ordered "his whole house" to get rid of their foreign gods (35:2). Later, all the tribes could be subdivided into "houses" (larger family groupings, Jos 7:14); and the posterity of a family, king, or dynasty would be called his "house" (Ex 2:1; 1Ki 11:38; 12:16; 13:2).

For 2 Samuel 7, the meaning of a "dynasty" was most fitting, especially since the expression "your house and your kingdom will be made sure forever" (v. 16) could only mean that David's "dynasty" would rule forever. This was the new addition to the promise plan: all that had been offered to the patriarchs and Moses was now being offered to David's dynasty. Nor was that all; it was to last on into the future (v. 19).

Eight times in 2 Samuel 7, Yahweh promised to make David "a house" (vv. 11, 13, 16, 19, 25, 26, 27, 29), not counting the instances of parallel ideas that use other terms. It was explained that David's "house" was a line of descendants (vv. 12, 16, 19, 26, 29) that the Lord would give to him in perpetuity. Usually monarchs worried, once they had succeeded in enforcing the peace after a long period of military gains, about the durability of their kingdom (cf. Nebuchadnezzar in Da 2). But David was relieved of this anxiety. His "dynasty," throne, and kingdom would be secure forever; it was established by the Lord.

A Seed

Even though the word "seed" is used only once (2Sa 7:12), this promise of a dynasty that would have a long line of descendants was a reminder of a similar word to Abra-

16. F. Willesen, "The Cultic Situation of Psalm 74," *Vetus Testamentum* 2 (1952): 289ff.

ham. "Seed" had a collective meaning of "posterity" even as it did in Genesis 3:15; 12:7; 13:15. But it simultaneously pointed to the one person who represented the whole group and was the earnest of a line of descendants yet to come. Thus David's "seed" would build the proposed temple (2Sa 7:13), meaning the single individual Solomon. But at the same time, the eternally enduring house would never lack a descendant to sit on the throne of David. In fact, in one expression in 2 Chronicles 22:10, Athaliah wanted to extirpate the "whole seed of the kingship" (*kol zera hammamlākâh*), the whole dynasty.

A Kingdom

As already noticed, one item in the promise during the era of the patriarchs and the exodus was that Israel would have "kings" (Ge 17:6, 16; 35:11; cf. 36:31), including a "kingdom" (Ex 19:6; Nu 24:7) and a "dominion" (Nu 24:19). Now that kingdom was being assigned to David and his family according to 2 Samuel 7:23–24, 26, 27.

It was not that God had abdicated his rule or that his reign had come to an end, for so closely linked with God's reign was this newly announced reign of David that the Davidic throne and kingdom were later called the Lord's own. Thus 1 Chronicles 28:5 speaks of Solomon sitting on "the throne of the kingdom of the LORD over Israel"; 2 Chronicles 13:8 refers to "the kingdom of the LORD"; and in 2 Chronicles 9:8, the king is placed by God "on his [God's] throne as king to rule for the LORD your God." Already in 1 Samuel 24:6 and 2 Samuel 19:21, he was called the "LORD's anointed." Accordingly, the theocracy and the Davidic kingdom, by virtue of their special place in the covenant, were regarded as one. They were so inseparably linked that in the future their destiny was identical.

A Son of God

Particularly surprising was the divine announcement: "I will be his father, and he will be my son" (2Sa 7:14). Now "father" must have been a title David used naturally of God, for he had named one of his children Absalom, "my Father (God) is peace." Indeed, Moses had already taught Israel the same when he asked, "Is he not your Father, your Creator?" (Dt 32:6).

Nor was the concept of sonship without its theological antecedents in times past. All the members of Israel were his sons, his firstborn (Ex 4:22; 19:4). Interestingly enough, "the whole diplomatic vocabulary of the second millennium was rooted in the familial sphere."[17] Hence, it was most appropriate for this covenant with David.

What was new was that Yahweh should now treat David's son in a manner that was clearly reminiscent of the patriarchal and Mosaic promises. This was more than the Near

17. Moshe Weinfeld, "The Covenant of Grant in the Old Testament and in the Ancient Near East," *Journal of the American Oriental Society* 90 (1970): 194.

Eastern titulary of divine sonship: "son of god-x"; it was a divine gift, not a proud human boast. It was also a particularization of the old word given to Israel (his "firstborn"), which now would be addressed to David's seed (Ps 89:27). In a totally unique way, David could now call him "my Father" (v. 26), for each Davidite stood in this relation of a son to his God. Yet it is not said that any single Davidite would ever realize purely or perfectly this lofty concept of divine sonship, but only that should any person qualify for this relationship, he would also need to be a son of David.

A Charter for Humanity

What God had promised David was no brand-new theme unrelated to the previous blessings of his promise-plan. Already there had been in vogue a long development of theology that could inform and contribute to David's covenant. Among the familiar themes already known to David in 2 Samuel 7, as they were again rehearsed in this word directed to him, were

1. "I will make thee a great name" (2Sa 7:9; cf. Ge 12:2; etc.).
2. "I will appoint a place for Israel and will plant them" (2Sa 7:10; cf. Ge 15:18; Dt 11:24–25; Jos 1:4–5).
3. "I will set up thy seed after thee" (2Sa 7:12; cf. Ge 17:7–10, 19).
4. "He shall be my son" (2Sa 7:14; cf. Ex 4:22).
5. "I will be to thee a God and you shall be to me for a people" (2Sa 7:23–24; cf. Ge 17:7–8; 28:21; Ex 6:7; 29:45; Lev 11:45; 22:33; 23:43; 25:38; 26:12, 44–45; Nu 15:41; Dt 4:20; 29:12–13 passim).
6. Yahweh's uniqueness (2Sa 7:22; cf. Ex 8:10; 9:14; 15:11; Dt 33:26; Pss 18:31[32]; 89:6[7], 8[9] passim).
7. Israel's uniqueness (2Sa 7:22; cf. Ex 1:9; Nu 14:12; Dt 1:28–31; 5:26; 7:17–19; 9:14; 11:23; 20:1; 33:29 passim; and esp. the plural verb in 2Sa 7:23: "Who are like your people, like Israel, one nation in the earth whom God has gone to redeem," a literal rendering of Dt 4:7–8 with the same peculiar grammar).[18]
8. The exceptional use of "Adonai Yahweh" (2Sa 7:18–19 [2x], 22, 28–29), which does not appear again in Samuel or Chronicles. Probably the special significance of this name, which appears only a total of five times prior to this, was caught by R. A. Carlson,[19] who noted that this was the name used when God promised Abraham a "seed" in Genesis 15:2, 8. Its repeated use in 2 Samuel 7 is too striking to be accidental.

---

18. For a list of twenty-four so-called Deuteronomistic similarities to 2 Samuel 7, see Frank M. Cross Jr., *Canaanite Myth and Hebrew Epic* (Cambridge: Harvard University Press, 1973), 252–54.

19. R. A. Carlson, *David the Chosen King: A Tradio-Historical Approach to the Second Book of Samuel*, trans. Eric Sharpe and Stanley Rudman (Stockholm: Almqvist and Wiksell, 1964), 127. The other five instances of "Adonai Yahweh" are Deuteronomy 3:24; 9:26; Joshua 7:7; Judges 6:22; 16:28. Note the promise content in each prayer. In Kings the double name occurs only in 1 Kings 2:26; 8:53, while "Adonai" appears in 1 Kings 3:10, 15; 22:6; 2 Kings 7:6; 19:23.

Thus the blessing of Abraham was continued in a blessing of David:

> "Now be pleased to bless the house of your servant, that it may continue forever in your sight; for you, O Sovereign LORD, have spoken, and with your blessing the house of your servant will be blessed forever." (2Sa 7:29)

But when David suddenly realized what had been given to him in this alternative proposal, he was completely overwhelmed. Sensing the solemnity and importance of the moment, he went into the presence of God and prayed a prayer which can be outlined as follows:

1. Thanksgiving for God's favor on him now (vv. 18 – 21)
2. Praise for God's work for Israel in the *past* (vv. 22 – 24)
3. Prayer for God's fulfillment of this promise in the *future* (vv. 25 – 29)

The highlight of the prayer came in 2 Samuel 7:19, after David had protested in verse 18 that he was personally unworthy of so singularly great an honor. In effect he asked, "What is so unique about me? And what is so special about my family?" The answer he expected was "Nothing!" He obviously felt that the blessing of God was incomparably greater than anything he deserved. Then he added in verse 19*a* his further amazement: "And as if this [present blessing on me and my family] were not enough in your sight, O Sovereign LORD, you have also spoken about the future of the house of your servant."

Immediately, in verse 19*b* came the words: *w^{e}z'ōt tôrat hā'ādām* ("And this is the law for men"). What type of sentence did these words form? Was it an interrogative sentence (as in the NIV) or an exclamation? Given the context and the parallel forms of *w^{e}z'ōt tôrat* plus a genitive in the Old Testament,[20] it must be an ejaculatory type of sentence. Nothing else would fit the sequence as it joined with verses 20ff. (as the TNIV agrees).

What then was the "this"? The antecedent will have to be the *substance* of the oracle and not the manner or way in which these great words came to David. The point was not that David was questioning, "Is this your usual manner or custom in addressing men like myself?" Such an interpretation would make two mistakes: (1) it would prefer to view the words as a question; and more seriously, (2) it would insist on translating the word *tôrâh* ("law") with such entirely anomalous meanings as "custom," "manner," "usual way of dealing with," or "estate" as do the Authorized Version, the New American Standard Bible, the New International Version, and the New English Bible.[21] However, these English words translate such Hebrew words as *hōq*, *mišpāṭ*, and *gôrāl*.

20. See Kaiser, "Blessing of David," 311.

21. However, the English Standard Version got it right: "and this is instruction for mankind, O Lord GOD!" Bruce K. Waltke in *An Old Testament Theology* (Grand Rapids: Zondervan, 2007), 692, comments, "Walt Kaiser plausibly interprets *tôrat hā'ādām* (2 Sam. 7:19) in David's response to the covenant by 'a charter for humanity' that impacts all nations."

As Willis J. Beecher concluded, "'This' ought logically to mean, from the context, the revelation spoken of in the passage concerning 'the seed' of Abraham, Israel, and David, who is to exist and reign forever, Jehovah's son, Jehovah's king, Jehovah's channel of Blessing to all nations."[22]

C. F. D. Erdmann likewise urged that "It must be the *content* of the Lord's words about the future of his house that moves him,... not the fact *that* the Lord condescends to him ... but *what* He has now *spoken* to him.... This is the divine *torah* or prescription for poor human creatures."[23]

How then should *tôrâh* be understood? Usually *tôrâh* means "teaching"; it comes from the verbal root *yārâh*, "to direct," "teach," "instruct." Out of 220 examples of this noun in the Old Testament, only in 17 cases is anything other than the law of God indicated.[24]

Tôrat hā'ādām ("law of the man") cannot be translated "the law of *Adam*" since there is no reference to Adam, or to a covenant being made with him, appearing elsewhere in the Davidic era. Nor can it be rendered "the law of *the Man*," that is, the Lord God, since such a usage would be unknown up to this era. None of these translations will do.

Since the "this" of 2 Samuel 7:19*b* refers to *content* of the promise traced so patiently in the words of Nathan, and since that promise was knowingly extended to "all the nations of the earth" as early as in the patriarchal revelations, we conclude that the best translation is "This is the charter for humanity." Henri Cazelles[25] may have put his finger on the exact cognate expression when in 1958 he pointed to the Akkadian term, *tērit nîse*. As he translated the Akkadian phrase, it was an oracle: "*qui fixe le destin des hommes*" or "the decree concerning humanity in general."

Precisely so in our passage! With the realization that he had just been granted an everlasting dynasty, dominion, and kingdom, David blurted out in uncontainable joy: "And this is the charter for all humanity, O LORD God!"[26] Thus the ancient promise-plan of God would continue, only now it would involve a king and a kingdom. Such a blessing would also involve the future of all humanity.

A Promised Kingdom

Six times David's kingdom had been declared eternal (2Sa 7:13, 16, 24, 25, 26, 29). But was this gift to David "a blank check of unlimited validity"?[27] M. Tsevat, along with a

22. Willis J. Beecher, "Three Notes," *Journal of Biblical Literature* 8 (1887): 138.

23. C. F. D. Erdmann, *The Books of Samuel*, in J. P. Lange, *A Commentary on the Holy Scriptures* (New York: Scribner, Armstrong & Co., 1877), 3:434.

24. See Kaiser, "Blessing of David," 313, nn. 48, 49, for documentation.

25. Henri Cazelles, "Review of Roland deVaux's *Les Institutiones de L'ancien Testament*," *Vetus Testamentum* 8 (1958): 322; idem, "Shiloh, the Customary Laws and the Return of the Ancient Kings," *Proclamation and Presence*, John T. Durham and J. R. Porter, eds. (Richmond: John Knox Press, 1970), 250.

26. For a treatment of the parallel 1 Chronicles 17:17, which has three dissimilarities, see Kaiser, "Blessing of David," 315–16.

27. Matitiahu Tsevat, "The Steadfast House: What was David Promised in 2 Samuel 7:11*b*–16?" *Hebrew Union College Annual* 34 (1963): 73.

host of other commentators, cannot accept this claim of irrevocability or unconditionally as part of the original passage. Rather, they prefer to treat as normative the theme of conditionality, which stressed the "if" clause and the necessity of loyalty and fidelity as found in 2 Samuel 7:14–15; 1 Kings 2:4; 8:25; 9:4–5; Psalms 89:31–38[30–37]; 132:11–12.

Yet David himself reflected on this same promise in 2 Samuel 23:5 and called it an "everlasting covenant" (*bᵉrît ʿôlām*). His exact words were: "Has he not made with me an everlasting covenant, arranged and secured in every detail?"[28] The same thought is repeated by David in the royal psalm (21:6–7[7–8]), where he rejoiced that God had "made him most blessed forever" and that the "covenantal love of the Most High [to David] would not be moved."

Psalm 89:28–37 [29–38] also commented on the immutability of this eternal covenant. It would endure "forever" (28, 29, 36, 37, Eng.): "As the days of heaven" (29), "as the sun" (36) and "moon" (37). God "will not violate, nor alter the word that is gone out of [his] lips" (34); he has "sworn by [his] holiness; [he] will not lie to David" (35)!

Nevertheless, the argument for conditionality still rages. Could not this covenant be broken (*pārar*)? Indeed, even though the Abrahamic covenant was also "everlasting" (Ge 17:7, 13, 19), yet "the uncircumcised man ... has broken [it]" (v. 14). Even the later "everlasting covenant" would be broken by the inhabitants of the earth (Isa 24:5), and an adulterous Israel despised "the oath of God" (the covenant) "to the extent of breaking (*lᵉhāpēr*) the everlasting covenant" (Eze 16:59, 63).[29]

The solution to these apparent breakings, frustrations, and invalidations of the covenant was the same as it was for the "if" clauses that concerned Tsevat and others: "If your sons keep my covenant and the statutes I teach them, then their sons will sit on your throne for ever and ever" (Ps. 132:12; cf. 2 Sa 7:14*b*–15; 1Ki 2:4; 8:25; 9:4–5; Ps. 89:30–33 [Eng.]). The "breaking" or conditionality can only refer to *personal* and *individual* invalidation of the benefits of the covenant, but it cannot affect the *transmission* of the promise to the lineal descendants. That is why God would staunchly affirm his fidelity and the perpetuity of the covenant to David in spite of succeeding rascals who would appear in his lineage. For in that case, he "finds fault with *them*" but not with his Abrahamic-Davidic-new covenant (cf. Jer 31:32; Heb 8:8; emphasis mine).

This same state of affairs shows up from the new research on the promissory land grant treaties of the Hittites and neo-Assyrians. By linking the "royal grants" made to Abraham and David with the grants of "land" and "house" (dynasty) in Hittite-Syro-Palestinian politics, M. Weinfeld[30] has demonstrated that the unconditional

28. Ibid., 74, for this translation of "every detail."

29. For a review of the evidence and a contrary opinion, see Marten H. Woudstra, "The Everlasting Covenant in Ezekiel 16:59–63," *Calvin Theological Journal* 6 (1971): 27–28, 31–33.

30. M. Weinfeld, "Covenant of Grant," 189–96. Note his brilliant observations even on the alleged conditionality of the Mosaic covenant, 195.

gift was also explicitly protected against any subsequent sins made by the recipients' descendants. In these treaties the grant of "land" or dynasty may be delayed or individually forfeited; however, it must still be passed on to the next in line instead of being granted to someone outside the specified family. So it was in David's situation: rascals there may be, but the blessing would never be revoked from the family; thus it was an "everlasting covenant."[31]

The Ark and the Kingdom

Nothing was more intimately connected with the presence and power of Yahweh than the ark of the covenant. This could be seen especially in the "history of the ark" in 1 Samuel 4:1 – 7:2. But 2 Samuel 6 also stressed its importance for the kingdom to David, who was about to receive it as is detailed in the 2 Samuel 7. The introduction of the ark to Jerusalem, a politically neutral enclave near the border separating Judah and the northern tribes, was important to establishing the extent of the kingdom over all Israel. But such a connection between David, the kingdom, and what most were pleased to call the "cult" was not an argument for sacral kingship.[32] This can best be seen by first tracing the development of the narrative about the ark.

Exodus 25:10 – 22 records the proposal for building the ark, and Exodus 37:1 – 9 narrates its actual construction by Bezalel. During the wilderness wanderings, the ark of the covenant of the Lord went before Israel three day's journey to seek out resting places for the people (Nu 10:33 – 34). So important was this "box" (*'ᵃrôn*; cf. Joseph's "coffin" in Ge 50:26 and Jehoiada's "chest" for contributions in 2Ki 12:9ff. [10ff.] and 2Ch 24:8ff.) that the "Song of the Ark" equated its presence with Yahweh's presence:

> Whenever the ark set out, Moses said,
> "Rise up, O LORD!
>   May your enemies be scattered;
>   May your foes flee before you."
> Whenever it came to rest, he said,
> "Return, O LORD,
>   to the countless thousands of Israel." (Nu 10:35 – 36)

On the other hand, when Israel presumed to launch an attack on her own without the ark of the covenant being with her, she was soundly defeated (Nu 14:44). But when it accompanied Israel's march across the Jordan (Jos 3 – 4) and around Jericho (Jos 6),

31. See H. Neil Richardson, "The Last Words of David: Some Notes on II Samuel 23:1 – 7," *Journal of Biblical Literature* 90 (1971): 259, 263. Following F. M. Cross Jr. (although both "with some hesitation"), Richardson finds an epithet for El here in 2 Samuel 23 and translates it: "His covenant the Eternal has given me." But this is a most unlikely suggestion in light of the awkwardness of the expression and the absence of the divine name El as in Genesis 21:33.

32. For a refutation of sacral kingship, see Arthur E. Cundall, "Sacral Kingship — the Old Testament Background," *Vox Evangelica* 6 (1969): 31 – 41.

the nation was usually successful. Only Israel's own sinfulness could frustrate its effectiveness.

When the ark was removed from Shiloh and lost to the Philistines (1Sa 4 – 5), the only conclusion could be "Ichabod" — that is, that the glory of God had departed. But its presence was too powerful for the Philistines, so they transported it back to Beth Shemesh without any further judgment (1Sa 6) after a plague had visited every Philistine city where the ark had been placed in the interim. But Uzzah was rebuked when he impulsively lunged to catch the tottering ark as David began to bring the ark to Jerusalem (2Sa 6) on an unauthorized form of travel — a cart, rather than being carried on the shoulders of Levites. In this case, these men were aware of the prescribed method of treating the holiness of God. Thereby they stood under greater condemnation than the Philistines, who had touched the ark and had used a cart to transport it in ignorance (1Sa 6).

The apex of the ark narratives is 2 Samuel 6 and Psalm 132, where its function and significance are closely connected with the presence of Yahweh, for in von Rad's words, "Wherever the Ark is, Jahweh is always present."[33] But in what sense was the presence of God intended? Was the ark (1) a witness to that presence, (2) a guarantee of Yahweh's presence, (3) a pledge or earnest of his presence, (4) a domicile of the Deity, (5) identical with Yahweh, or (6) an extension and representation of his presence?[34] Basically, it was a *pledge* of God's presence, for that presence was not automatic, nor was it mechanical. It was so only where this presence was "grasped believingly"[35] as Israel found out quickly in 1 Samuel 4:1 – 7:2. Nor was this an instance of mere thing-holiness. The Lord was not content with either mere "thingliness" nor with mere inwardness. Both internal and external aspects were important.

Yahweh's enthronement was also associated with the ark and the place of atonement (*kappōret*). His very name was "Yahweh of Hosts who sits enthroned on the cherubim" (2Sa 6:2; cf. 1Sa 4:4; 2Ki 19:15; 1Ch 13:6). Marten Woudstra concludes that this name, when used of the ark, points to God's "omnipotence, majesty and glory."[36] It spoke at once of the nature of his condescension, the character of his indwelling, and the reality of his person.

Accordingly, David brought the ark into a tent-shrine in 2 Samuel 6:17 until he could build the temple. In so doing, he thereby moved to establish the kingdom given to him by God. The two topics, the ark and the Davidic kingdom, are the subjects of Psalm 132, which celebrates the "oath" sworn to David and the signal shout or song of the ark: "Arise, O Lord, and come to your resting place ... for the sake of David your servant" (132:8 – 10).

---

33. Gerhard von Rad, *Old Testament Theology* (London: Oliver and Boyd, 1962), 1:237.

34. For documentation see, Henton Davis, "The Ark of the Covenant," *Annual of the Swedish Theological Institute* 5 (1966 – 67): 43 – 47. Also see R. E. Clements, *God and the Temple* (Philadelphia: Fortress Press, 1965), 28 – 39, and Marten H. Woudstra, *The Ark of the Covenant from Conquest to Kingship* (Philadelphia: Presbyterian and Reformed Publishing House, 1965), 13 – 57.

35. The phrase is from Woudstra, *Ark of the Covenant*, 46.

36. Ibid., 77.

The Royal Psalms

The books of Samuel and a number of the psalms that have come to be labeled as Royal Psalms (or Psalms of Zion) [37] share many common ideas. They depict God as the sovereign ruler over the nation of Israel and the nations of the world as he rules from Zion (e.g., Pss 46 – 48; 65; 93; 96 – 99; 100). But just as significant is the fact that these psalms also view David as God's son, carrying out God's authority over those same nations (Pss 2, 45, 72). These psalms can also be put into a lineal sequence for the most part. Thus, Psalm 2 speaks of the inauguration of the anointed one; Psalm 62 speaks of his majesty and glory; Psalm 72 speaks of the scope of his reign; Psalm 89, of his humiliation; and Psalm 132, of the hope for the future.

The Royal Psalms and the Kingdom

The royal psalms are steeped in the ideology of the Davidic dynasty and presuppose the promise and oath made to him. They formed a unity centering on the Davidic king who, as Yahweh's son, resided in Zion, the chosen city; ruled over Yahweh's people; and was heir to the promise.

Psalm 2 contrasted the hostility of the nations directed at the Lord and his messiah over against God's answer to them in the form of the royal investiture of his son, the Davidic king:

> I have installed my King
> on Zion, my holy hill.
>
> I will proclaim the decree of the Lord:
>
> He said to me, "You are my Son!
> Today I have become your Father.
>
> Ask of me,
> and I will make the nations your inheritance
> and the ends of the earth your possession." (Ps 2:6 – 8)

Thus, as God's son, he claimed rule over the world. It was not the eternal continuance of David's *house* that was in view here, but the triumphant conclusion to the divinely established filial relationship of the *person* of the Davidite to God. This personal kingship was explained by Conrad von Orelli as follows:

> In these words [v. 7] He has acknowledged him as belonging most intimately to Himself, investing Him even with personal kingship to God. The "I have begotten thee" sug-

37. The earliest discussion of "Die Königspsalmen" (Royal Psalms) by Hermann Gunkel appeared in 1914. In 1933 Gunkel and Begrich published the most comprehensive study, *Einleitung in die Psalmen*, ed. J. Begrich (Göttingen: Vandenhoeck & Ruprecht, 1933), 140 – 71. See now Keith R. Crim, *The Royal Psalms* (Richmond: John Knox Press, 1962).

> gests still more strongly than the simple "My son art thou," that the Messianic king has received a higher life from above. The conferring of this dignity was bound in the speaker's case to a definite point of time. The "today" was his Messianic birthday, whether on this day he first entered outwardly on his office, or its inner greatness was then revealed to him by prophet's message or personal inspiration.[38]

Centuries later, Paul would mark that "today" in the life of the Messiah as the day of the resurrection (Ac 13:30 – 33). That was the day when he was "marked out" to be the Son of God with power (Ro 1:3 – 4).

In a beautiful combination of the Sinaitic theophany (vv. 7 – 15) and an invincible King David (vv. 31 – 46), Psalm 18 and its verbal parallel in 2 Samuel 22 picture the victory and triumph of David. As a result, God's name was lauded before the nations, and the covenant was kept forever (Ps 18:47 – 50).

Psalms 20 and 21 appear to be paired as petition (20:4) and answer (21:2). The prayer for victory of Psalm 20 was answered with joy and thanksgiving in the numerous blessings in Psalm 21. The enemy was so soundly defeated that the scale of events outstripped the power of any king and called once more for the Messiah (Ps 21:9*b* – 12).

The Davidite was addressed as "Elohim" in Psalm 45:6. The judges of Israel represented God and also were called "Elohim" in that the solemnity of coming before a judge was comparable to coming before God (Ex 21:6; 22:8, 9, 28; cf. Ps 82:1, 6). Yet Psalm 45:6 claimed even more than Exodus did for the judges:

> Your throne, O God, will last for ever and ever;
> a scepter of justice will be the scepter of your kingdom.

Thus not only was the office of the king identified with Deity, but the very person of the king and his dynasty would rule like God forever! (Note vv. 2, 16 – 17.) Just as the Davidite was addressed in Psalm 89:26 – 27 as God's "son," his "firstborn" and "the Highest" (*'elyôn*, "Most High" when applied to God), so his throne by metonymy was now called Elohim in Psalm 45. Thus, what God stood for in heaven, David was appointed to be as a symbol and pledge of God's kingdom on earth. Human language appeared to be on the brink of bursting all boundaries as it described this unique filial relationship of a man and God.

The Hebrew text refuses to be softened as most contemporary translations insist on doing (e.g., the RV, RSV, NEB, but not JB or NASB). Neither did the New Testament writers miss the impact of this verse in Hebrews 1:8 – 9.[39] The mystery of the passage is that the "God" whom the psalmist addressed is himself appointed by God!

---

38. Conrad von Orelli, *The Old Testament Prophecy of the Consummation of God's Kingdom Traced in Its Historical Development*, trans. J. J. Banks (Edinburgh: T & T Clark, 1889), 161.

39. See the fine classic, Oswald T. Allis, "Thy Throne, O God, Is For Ever and Ever," *Princeton Theological Review* 21 (1923): 236 – 66.

Psalm 72 emphasizes the righteousness, blessing, endlessness, and worldwide extent of the Davidic kingdom.[40] The words of 2 Samuel 23:1 – 7 seem to have prompted the psalmist, for Psalm 72:6 – 7 pictured the righteous king as both the sun and rain on his subjects. While they flourished, so did the boundlessness of the realm. The concluding royal blessing of verses 16 – 17 brings to mind the theology of Genesis and the blessings of Moses in Leviticus 26 and Deuteronomy 28.

The most detailed commentary on 2 Samuel 7 was to be found in another royal psalm, Psalm 89. After commenting at length on the Davidic covenant in verses 3 – 4 and 19 – 37, verses 38 – 51 lament the downfall of the monarchy and plead that God would continue to be faithful to his promise to David. Likewise, Psalm 101, another royal psalm, prays for guidance for God's chosen ruler.

The most-quoted psalm in the New Testament is Psalm 110. Here the psalmist combined priesthood and royalty in the Messiah. For just as the whole nation had been constituted a kingdom of priests, a holy nation, so now the Davidic monarch was made a priest-king after one named Melchizedek, whose history and life paralleled the earlier man of promise, Abraham. The conquering scepter in the hands of the new Davidite to come would resume the Balaamic prediction, that is, that his conquering rule would dash in pieces all his enemies.

As David no doubt paused one day to reflect on the great victory God had given to Abraham, when he took on four Mesopotamian kings and won (Ge 14), stopping only to pay tithes to Melchizedek, the priest of Salem (=Jerusalem?), on the way home, he too felt refreshed (Ps 110:7), as if he had drunk deeply from a cool brook. That same promise was his, and thus the outcome of his battles, kingdom, and dynasty were as much a foregone conclusion as they had been for Abraham.

Psalm 132 combines the bringing of the ark into Jerusalem with the oath sworn to David about his dynasty. Second Chronicles 6:41 – 42, which quotes verses 8 – 10 of Psalm 132, shows that this psalm was in use in Solomon's time at the dedication of his temple and that the ark had ended its long journey. Now the kingdom was indeed established by God, for the temple was complete and the earnest of God's presence was in Solomon's temple.

The last royal psalm is Psalm 144, which is substantially like Psalm 18. Having recalled God's pattern of deliverance, David sang a "new song" in the new age to come (Pss 96:1; 98:1; 149:1; cf. Rev 5:9; 14:3).

Whether these psalms depict, as H. J. Krause thought, a royal festival in Zion with a procession representing the entry of Yahweh into Jerusalem to commemorate the transfer of the ark is doubtful. Likewise, the same could be said of the Uppsala school and Sigmund Mowinckel with their "enthronement psalms," which are mistranslated to read "Yahweh has *become* king" (Pss 47, 93, 96 – 99) rather than the correct rendering "Yahweh reigns." Nevertheless, nothing substantial in these views affects the theology of these psalms.

40. See Roland E. Murphy, "A Study of Psalm 72(71)" (Ph.D. diss., Catholic University of America, 1948).

More significant is the fact that what happened to the king happened to the people. Their lives were totally bound up with his. When he acted in faithfulness and righteousness, prosperity and blessing were the result (Pss 18; 45:6–7; 101). But when the king was rejected, so were they. The king, then, became the channel of God's blessings and judgments. So it would be with the last David or the new David; only his realm would be boundless and his reign would be righteous, just, and full of every perfection.

1 Kings 1–11

First Kings 1–11 covers the golden age of Israel under King Solomon, David's successor. They detail how Yahweh fulfilled his promise to David as his son Solomon came to the throne of Judah, which stood for the rule and reign of the Messiah, who would occupy it in the future.

But Solomon's tolerance for other religions eventually led to the collapse of the golden days of Judah, and after Solomon's reign ended, the sin of Jeroboam in the north would be typified by his setting up the worship of the bull-calf in Bethel and Dan. Nevertheless, God was not peevish or vindictive, as the heretic Marcion would later claim; for rather than punishing Israel and Judah for their idolatry and disobedience, he gave the people more than they could ask for and more than they deserved by way of his grace and mercy (1Ki 3:10–14; cf. 2Ki 3:17–18). As the books of Kings continued, there would be more than sixty references to Jeroboam's calf-shrine. It would not be until 2 Kings 25 that God's judgment would come, and so the Babylonian exile would begin. But this long delay in the judgment of God will also leave the same offense that Jonah complained about as he preached that judgment would come in forty days only to find that the Ninevites repented and the judgment was delayed for more than a century. Why was God so merciful for so long to Israel and Judah, and why was he so longsuffering with the Ninevites?

The Succession Narrative and the Kingdom

As indicated earlier in this chapter, Leonhard Rost convinced most scholars that 2 Samuel 9–20 and 1 Kings 1–2 form a "court history," in which the first two chapters of 1 Kings proved the key for the whole work. It was held that Solomon succeeded David rather than his older brothers Amnon, Absalom, and Adonijah because, unlike his brothers, he did not imitate David's sin with Bathsheba.[41]

41. For some of the more important contributions to a huge bibliography, see Jared J. Jackson, "David's Throne: Patterns in the Succession Story," *Canadian Journal of Theology* 11 (1965): 183–95; R. N. Whybray, *The Succession Narrative* (Naperville: Allenson, 1968); James W. Flanagan, "Court History or Succession Document?" *Journal of Biblical Literature* 91 (1972): 172–81.

Such a narrow purpose for the inclusion of this section into Israel's oracles of God (i.e., the justification of Solomon's reign) was faulted by Jackson[42] since 1 Kings 3 – 11 went on to detail so much failure in the life of Solomon. (Could the "final editor" have been so careless and naïve?) And while the text in its internal design does bring out a "delineation of character," to use Jackson's fine phrase, there is more here than a mere moralizing on the character of David's family.

It is "theological historiography," as von Rad puts it, and the initial "operation of the Nathan prophecy."[43] Even though the anointed one became ensnared in his own lusts, embarrassed by revolts from his own family, and cursed by others, God's guarantee to the Davidic dynasty still held. It was not so much "how David maintained legitimate control over the kingdoms of Judah and Israel," as Flanagan argued with some interesting bracketing of the narratives,[44] but how Yahweh controlled human destiny for his own purpose. True enough, there were only three explicit statements of Yahweh's intervention:

> But the thing David had done displeased the LORD. (2Sa 11:27)

> She gave birth to a son, and they named him Solomon; the LORD loved him. (2Sa 12:24)

> For the LORD had determined to frustrate the good advice of Ahithophel in order to bring disaster on Absalom. (2Sa 17:14)

This last is possibly the pivot verse of the whole document. But as Ronald Hals demonstrated for the book of Ruth,[45] so here too, the theology of God's intervention was often more implicit than explicit. And it all revolved around God's plan for the throne and kingdom of David. In the midst of human tragedy and failure, God's purpose and promise still went onward.

---

42. Jackson, "David's Throne," 185.
43. Von Rad, *Theology*, 1:316.
44. J. W. Flanagan, "Court History," 173.
45. Ronald Hals, *Theology of the Book of Ruth* (Philadelphia: Fortress Press, 1969), 3 – 19.

Chapter 6

Life in the Promise: The Wisdom Era

Job, Proverbs, Ecclesiastes, Song of Songs (About 1070 – 931 BC)

Jewish and Protestant scholars usually regard only Job, Proverbs, Ecclesiastes, and Song of Solomon as wisdom books, while Catholic scholarship adds the extracanonical books of Ecclesiasticus (Ben Sirach) and the Wisdom of Solomon. All three groups also add to these books a number of psalms.

The Book of Job

While the literary contents of the book of Job seem to belong to the Wisdom literature of Israel's sapiential (i.e., "wisdom") period, according to the majority of scholars, it is best regarded as coming from the patriarchal period, as we have already argued in chapter 2. Nevertheless, the book of Job is in the form of a poetic dialogue that also has a narrative framework. As a result of this unusual combination of literary genres, a tension arises between the prose form of the introduction and epilogue and the poetical form of the body of the book.

Until the last quarter of the twentieth century, Job was predominantly classified as Wisdom literature. But then a strong voice of opposition arose claiming that Job was either utterly unique or it was in a lament genre, a form that was not firmly established until recently.[1] But as Westermann noted, the question of genre has not had a decisive effect on the interpretation of the book. Most exegetes proceed on the assumption that Job deals with a problem: the issue of suffering that has troubled most mortals — How do we reconcile the suffering of a just person with the existence of a just God?

In a similar sort of problem involving form and content, the criteria for distinguishing wisdom psalms in the book of Psalms may be divided into two categories: formal (literary

1. Claus Westermann, *The Structure of the Book of Job*, trans. Charles A. Muenchow (Philadelphia: Fortress, 1981), p. 1, n. 1 and pp. 13 – 14.

style) and thematic (content). Using the studies of Roland E. Murphy,[2] Sigmund Mowinckel,[3] and R. B. Y. Scott,[4] the following distinct styles of wisdom psalms may be assembled: (1) alphabetic structure, such as acrostic psalms; (2) numerical sayings (e.g., "three, yea four"); (3) "blessed" sayings (*'ašrê*); (4) "better" sayings; (5) comparisons, admonitions; (6) the address of father to son; (7) the use of wisdom vocabulary and turns of phrase; and (8) the employment of proverbs, similes, rhetorical questions, and words like "listen to me." Typical wisdom themes are: (1) the problem of retribution; (2) the division between the righteous and the wicked; (3) exhortations to trust personally in the Lord; (4) the fear of the Lord; and (5) the meditation on the written law of God as a source of delight.

Using both formal and thematic criteria, the following psalms may easily be classified as wisdom psalms: 1, 37, 49, and 112. To these may be added 32, 34, 111, 127, 128, and 133. If meditation on the law of God is also used, Psalms 119 and 19:7–14 may also be included. Perhaps Psalm 78, with its invitation to "give ear, my people, to my teaching" and its proverbial (*māšāl*) and riddle (*ḥîdôt*) forms (v. 2), also qualify it to be classed with the wisdom psalms. Thus we conclude that Psalms 1, 19*b*, 32, 34, 37, 49, 78, 111, 112, 119, 127, 128, and 133 belong in the wisdom category along with the four wisdom books.

In addition to the issues of form and content, there arise issues of possible ancient Near Eastern sources for some of the wisdom material in the Bible. In the past sixty years or so, most of the research in Wisdom literature has dealt with the relationship of Israel's sapiential writings to those of her Egyptian and Mesopotamian neighbors. However, another welcome development has come about. Some have undertaken the task of discovering the connections between wisdom and creation,[5] between wisdom and Deuteronomy,[6] and between wisdom and the prophets.[7]

Wisdom literature was indeed the recipient of theological legacies from Mosaic times and the prophetic history of the earlier prophets as well. The best case made for a clear connection between these eras (albeit in a reversed order of dependence for which we are arguing here) was Moshe Weinfeld's study of "The Wisdom Substrata in Deuteronomy and Deuteronomic Literature."[8]

---

2. Roland E. Murphy, "Psalms," *Jerome Biblical Commentary*, ed. Raymond E. Brown, Joseph A. Fitzmyer, and Roland E. Murphy (Englewood Cliffs, NJ: Prentice-Hall, 1968), 574; idem, "The Classification of Wisdom Psalms," *Vetus Testamentum Supplement* 9 (1963): 156–67.

3. Sigmund Mowinckel, "Psalms and Wisdom," *Vetus Testamentum Supplement* 3 (1955): 204–24.

4. R. B. Y. Scott, *The Way of Wisdom* (New York: Macmillan, 1971), 193–201.

5. Walther Zimmerli, "The Place and Limit of Wisdom in the Framework of the Old Testament Theology," *Scottish Journal of Theology* 17 (1964): 146–58.

6. Moshe Weinfeld, "The Wisdom Substrata in Deuteronomy and Deuteronomic Literature," *Deuteronomy and the Deuteronomic School* (Oxford: Clarendon Press, 1972), 244–74; see also Erhard Gerstenberger, "Covenant and Commandment," *Journal of Biblical Literature* 84 (1965): 38–51, esp. 48–51.

7. William McKane, *Prophets and Wise Men* (London: SCM, 1965).

8. Weinfeld, "Wisdom Substrata," 244–45. In our order, Deuteronomy is clearly a second millennium document exhibiting the same outline in its entirety as did the literary *Gattung* of Hittite vassal treaties. Cf. M. Kline, *Treaty of the Great King* (Grand Rapids: Eerdmans, 1962); Kenneth Kitchen, *Ancient Orient and Old Testament* (Downers Grove, IL: InterVarsity Press, 1964); R. K. Harrison, *Introduction to the Old Testament* (Grand Rapids: Eerdmans, 1969). Other scholars who believed that Deuteronomy influenced biblical wisdom are listed by Weinfeld, "Wisdom Substrata," 260, n. 4. He names among others, A. Robert, "Les attaches littéraires bibliques de Prov.

For Weinfeld, the presence of leaders and magistrates who were "capable men who fear God, trustworthy men who spurn ill-gotten gain" (Ex 18:21), "wise men of understanding and full of knowledge" (Dt 1:13 – 17; cf. Nu 11:11 – 30) corresponded well with the qualities demanded of leaders in Wisdom literature. Thus, in Proverbs 8:15 – 16 it was by wisdom that "kings reign and rulers decree what is just ... princes rule and nobles govern." Weinfeld noted that even the phraseology found in the appointment of the judges in Deuteronomy 1:9 – 18; 16:18 – 20, "to respect persons in judgment," is seen again only in Proverbs 24:23; 28:21.

Some of the principal parallels that Weinfeld listed for Deuteronomy and wisdom were as follows:

1. "You shall not add to the word which I command, nor take from it" (Dt 4:2; cf. 12:32 [13:1]).
   "All the word of God proves true.... Do not add to his words" (Pr 30:5 – 6).
2. "You shall not move your neighbor's landmarks" (Dt 19:14; cf. 27:17). "Move not the ancient landmark set up by your fathers" (Pr 22:28; cf. 23:10).
3. "You shall not have in your bag alternate weights (*'eben wā'āben*) ... alternate measures (*'êpâh w^{e}'êpâh*) ... [but] a full and just weight (*'eben š^{e}lēmāh*) you shall have. For all who ... act dishonestly are an abomination to the LORD[9] your God" Dt 25:13 – 16). "Alternate weights (*'eben wā'āben*) are an abomination to the LORD" (Pr 20:10, 23); "but a just weight (*'eben š^{e}lēmâh*) is His delight" (Pr 11:1).
4. "When you make a vow to the LORD your God, you shall not be slack to pay it" (Dt 23:21).
   "Do not be rash with your mouth ... when you make a vow to God.... Pay what you vow" (Ecc 5:2, 4).
5. "You shall not be partial in judgment" (Dt 1:17; cf. 16:19). "Partiality in judging is not good" (Pr 24:23; cf. 28:21).
6. "Justice and only justice you shall pursue that you may live" (Dt 16:20). "He who pursues justice ... will find life" (Pr 21:21; cf. 10:2; 11:4, 19; 12:28; 16:31).

These, of course, are only the beginning. But they do illustrate the point that wisdom was not cut off conceptually or theologically from materials that we have judged to be earlier than sapiential times. Wisdom's influence also extended beyond its day into the era of the prophets, both the Earlier Prophets (Joshua, Judges, Samuel, Kings) and the Latter Prophets (Isaiah, Jeremiah, Ezekiel, and the Twelve).

---

i-ix," *Revue Biblique* 43 (1934): 42 – 68, 172 – 204, 374 – 84; 44 (1935): 344 – 65, 502 – 25; O. E. Oesterley, *Wisdom of Egypt and the Old Testament* (London: Society for Promoting Christian Knowledge, 1927), 76ff.

9. According to Weinfeld, "Wisdom Substrata," 268, the expression "abomination to the LORD" appears four times in *Teaching of Amenemope* (14. 2 – 3; 13. 5 – 16; 15. 20 – 21; 18. 21 – 19). In Deuteronomy it appears at 7:25 – 26; 12:31; 17:1; 18:9 – 12; 22:5; 23:18; 24:4; 25:13 – 16; 27:15 and in Proverbs at 3:32; 11:1, 20; 12:22; 15:8 – 9, 26; 16:5; 17:15; 20:10, 23.

Regardless of how far or, for that matter, in what direction that influence spread, the key question is: What theological rubric or special term brought promise and law together with wisdom? We believe that concept was "the fear of God/Lord." This concept will be found repeatedly in Proverbs, often in Ecclesiastes, and at times in the wisdom psalms.

The Book of Proverbs

The book of Proverbs contains two collections of maxims (10:1 – 22:16 and 25:1 – 29:27) along with a beginning and an ending (chapters 1 – 9; 30; 31) that form almost formal teaching instructions, developing themes to "my son." Solomon is identified as the author of the 375 proverbial sayings in Proverbs 10:1 – 22:16. The proverbs in Proverbs 25:1 – 29:27 were collected by a group of assistants of King Hezekiah (729 – 699 BC), while Agur composed chapter 30 and Lemuel is credited with Proverbs 31:1 – 9.

According to Proverbs 1:1 – 7, the purpose of the book is "for gaining wisdom and instruction; for understanding words of insight; for receiving instruction in prudent behavior, doing what is right and just and fair; for giving prudence to those who are simple, knowledge and discretion to the young" (1:2 – 4). The theme of the book can be found in verse 7, "The fear of the Lord is the beginning of knowledge, but fools despise wisdom and instruction."

The Fear of the Lord

The fear of the Lord more than any other phrase linked the patriarchal "promise" with law and wisdom. Hans Walter Wolff argued the same point, at least for part of that revelation, based on his view of the sources, when he observed that "God's normative word from Mount Sinai to all Israel is directed towards the same goal that he had set for the patriarchs: fear of God, which produced obedience through trust in God's promise (Gen. 22)."[10]

Wolff goes on to trace through some of the patriarchal and Mosaic materials what he regarded as one of the dominant themes: "the fear of God." It appeared in the patriarchal era as the response of Abraham's believing faith in Genesis 22:12, when he willingly offered his son Isaac to God; in Joseph's believing response (Ge 42:18); and especially as the divinely approved quality of life evidenced in Job (1:1, 8 – 9; 2:3).

In the Mosaic era, the visibility of the fear of God increased. The midwives were among those who feared God (Ex 1:17). Accordingly, "the people multiplied and grew

10. Hans Walter Wolff, *The Vitality of Old Testament Traditions*, ed. Walter Brueggemann and Hans W. Wolff (Atlanta: John Knox Press, 1975), 75.

very strong" (v. 20), and the families of the midwives prospered — and again the text underscored the reason — "because they feared God" (v. 21). So did Israel fear God at the exodus (Ex 14:31); in fact, if that fear would remain ever before them, they would not sin (20:20). Since the Lord was Israel's God, she should always fear him (Lev 19:14, 32; 25:17, 36, 43) and thus live.

But it was the book of Deuteronomy that had made the fear of the Lord a focal point of concern (4:10; 5:26; 6:2, 13, 24; 8:6; 10:12, 20; 13:4; 14:23; 17:19; 28:58; 31:12 – 13). This fear was not a worked-up feeling of some numinous awe, but it was the result of hearing, learning, and responding to God's word (4:10; 8:6). In Deuteronomy, the fear of the Lord went hand in hand with "keeping his commands," "walking after him," "serving him," "loving him," and "cleaving to him" (cf. esp. 10:12 – 13; 13:5). Thus, to fear him was to love him, cleave to him, and to serve him (10:20; 13:4 – 5).

To fear Yahweh was to commit oneself to Yahweh in faith as did *some* of the Egyptians (Ex 9:20, 30; cf. the "mixed multitude" that left Egypt with Israel in 12:38). Had not Solomon also prayed for "all the peoples of the earth" who would come to "know [his] name and fear [him]" in 1 Kings 8:43?

However, one had to *learn* how to fear Yahweh (Dt 4:10; 14:23; 17:19; 31:12 – 13; Ps 34:11[12]). This fear was a guiding principle for every aspect of life and for "as long as one lives on the earth" (Dt 4:10; 5:26; 14:23; 31:13; Pr 23:17).[11] It included the believer's obedience, love, loyalty, and worship as R. N. Whybray concluded.[12] Thus Obadiah remarked to Elijah, "I, your servant, feared/worshiped Yahweh since my youth" (1Ki 18:12).

When we come to wisdom books and wisdom psalms, the fear of the Lord has become the essence of the knowledge and wisdom of God. Even though this phrase occurred just over two dozen times apart from the suffixial forms (such as "thy fear") or the verbal statements, its locations are all extremely strategic and often served the whole purpose for writing some of these books. In Proverbs 1:7 it functioned as the motto for the whole book, while in Ecclesiastes 12:13 – 14 it functioned as the total summation of the argument of the whole book (cf. also Ecc 7:18; 8:12). Likewise in Job 28:28 it dramatically climaxed the whole poem on wisdom, which in itself was located at the eye of the whole stormy debate. Rather than viewing Job 28 as an inserted interruption in the flow of the argument between Job and his friends, it should be seen as the writer's attempt to give his readers a revelatory perspective in the midst of so much talk that was devoid of divine wisdom. Thus in three of the four wisdom books, the fear of God/Lord is critically important to their understanding.

In addition to its appearance as the motto for the book of Proverbs, the "fear of the Lord" occurs thirteen more times in that book: 1:29; 2:5; 8:13; 9:10; 10:27; 14:26 – 27;

11. See Weinfeld's discussion of "the fear of God," in "Wisdom Substrata," 274 – 81; Gerhard von Rad, *Wisdom in Israel* (Nashville: Abingdon, 1972), 65 – 73; Bernard J. Bamberger, "Fear and Love of God in the Old Testament," *Hebrew Union College Annual* 6 (1929): 39 – 53.

12. R. N. Whybray, *Wisdom in Proverbs* (London: SCM, 1965), 96 – 97.

15:16, 33; 16:6; 19:23; 22:4; and 23:17. In addition to this, one should also consider the verbal forms in 3:7; 14:2; 24:21; and 31:30.

Such a fear was the "beginning" (*rē'šît*, Pr 1:7) of knowledge, the "first principle" (*t^{e}ḥillâh*, 9:10) of wisdom. When people were rightly related to God, then they were in a proper relationship to understand objects and the world itself.

When people feared the Lord, they also avoided evil (Ps 34:11, 14; Job 1:1, 8; 2:3; 28:28). Indeed, they hated evil (Pr 3:7; 16:6) and walked instead in uprightness (14:2) and not in wickedness (16:17). The results of this type of life were an increased life span (10:27), increased wealth and honor (22:4), and security and protection (14:26; 19:23). The connection of blessing and the quality of holy living with the fear of God was not accidental.

Believers who feared God were easily distinguished from their counterparts in the Psalms also. They were the committed and righteous persons in the congregation of the Lord (Ps 34:7, 9 [8, 10]; also in non-wisdom psalms like 25:12, 14; 33:18; 103:11, 13, 17; 145:19). They kept the law of God and meditated on it day and night (19:7 – 14; 112:1; 119:33 – 38, 57 – 64). They praised the name of Yahweh (22:22 – 23) and God's favor rested on them (33:18; 103:13; 147:11).

The writer of Ecclesiastes also joined in to make a similar point: God had so built human beings that apart from a personal knowledge of the living God (that is, a fearing of him), everything else would be vapid (Ecc 3:14). But it would go well for those who feared God (8:12), and they would come forth victorious, having taken hold of true wisdom while rejecting evil (7:18). Even the way they worshiped would reflect their God-fearing status (5:1 – 7). In fact, this was the wholeness and totality of men and women: they would fear God and keep his commandments. That was the whole purpose for writing the book of Ecclesiastes (12:13).

It may be said with confidence, then, that the fear of the Lord was the dominating concept and organizing theological principle in Wisdom literature. It was the response of faith to the divine word of promise and blessing just as it had functioned in the days of Abraham and Moses.

Yet there was much more here than just a response of faith, belief, obedience, and worship. It was the entrée into the understanding and enjoyment of the created realm.[13] One of God's blessings was his work of creation; this too was part of his work in history! True, it had no direct relation to the redemptive process in Israel, but it was nonetheless one of his words and works of blessing — in every sense of the term, a gracious gift to mankind. And the very wisdom by which he had formed the world originally, he offered to men and women as his wisdom. Without that wisdom, humanity was destitute of effective leadership and bankrupt in its appreciation or apprehension of God, humanity, and things; in fact, life itself became meaningless and devoid of satisfaction and joy. But when the fear of the Lord led the way, then life was a blessing from God.

13. Zimmerli, "Place and Limit," 146 – 58.

Life in the Lord

The connection between the fear of the Lord and life is explicitly affirmed in the following texts from Proverbs:

> The fear of the LORD adds length to life,
> but the years of the wicked are cut short. (10:27)
>
> The fear of the LORD is a fountain of life,
> turning a man from the snares of death. (14:27)
>
> The fear of the LORD leads to life;
> then one rests content, untouched by trouble. (19:23)
>
> Humility and the fear of the LORD
> bring wealth and honor and life. (22:4)

Just as Leviticus 18:5 had counseled all those whose God was the Lord, "Do these things and you shall live," so the wisdom books continued the theme. They point out that: (1) obedience is the "path [or way] to life" (Pr 2:19; 5:6; 10:17; 15:24); (2) the teaching of the wise and the fear of the Lord are a "fountain of life" (13:14; 14:27); and (3) wisdom, righteousness, and a gentle tongue each are a "tree of life" (3:18; 11:30; 13:12; 15:4).

That had been the message of the law of Moses. Since Israel had received God's grace and redemption, the people were urged to "observe" and "do" all of their new Lord's commands "so that [they] may live" (Dt 8:1). Such *life* was not just a materialistic thing, but it had spiritual roots and goals. Men and women could not *live* by bread alone but by every word that proceeded out of the mouth of God (v. 3). Thus Israel had set in front of them life and death: they were urged to choose life (30:15, 19). This they could do by loving the Lord their God, obeying his voice, and "hold[ing] fast to him, for the LORD [was their] life" (v. 20).

To solve the problem of Sinai's relationship to promise was to solve wisdom's relationship to promise.[14] As Roland E. Murphy observed, these wisdom themes of "the fear of the Lord," "justice," "understanding," and "honesty" would have been identified by the Jews of that era "with the moral ideals expressed in the Law."[15] Thus, putting one's personal trust in the promised one who was to come (as Abraham had done in Genesis 15) was equal to being among those who "feared the Lord." Included within this initial decision to commit oneself to the God who promised an heir (the

14. See provisionally Walter C. Kaiser Jr., "The Law of the Lord: Teaching the Paths of Life," *The Old Testament in Contemporary Preaching* (Grand Rapids: Baker Book House, 1973), 49–69, 118ff. Coert Rylaarsdam, *Revelation in Jewish Wisdom Literature* (Chicago: University of Chicago, 1946), 23, also pointed to the parents' instruction fastened around the neck (Pr 6:20–22; 7:3) as being similar to the function of the law as a guide in Deuteronomy 6:4–9; similarly, "the upright will live in the land [as an inheritance]" (Pr 2:21; 10:30; cf. Dt 4:21, 38; 15:4; 19:10; 21:23; 24:4; 25:19; 26:1). Alfred von Rohr Sauer incorrectly argued that wisdom and law were later joined together in Ezra; "Wisdom and Law in Old Testament Wisdom Literature," *Concordia Theological Monthly* 43 (1972): 607.

15. Roland E. Murphy, "The Kerygma of the Book of Proverbs," *Interpretation* 20 (1966): 12.

"seed"), an inheritance (the "land"), and a heritage ("in your seed all the nations of the earth shall be blessed") was the subsequent lifestyle of obedience to the word and commands of God. The result or fruit of this trust and obedience could be summed up in one word: life. By definition, then, to fear God was to turn away from evil and to choose the way of life. All pride, arrogance, perverted speech, and devious behavior were to be dropped from the life of the man who feared the Lord (Pr 3:7; 8:13; 14:2; 16:6; 23:17).

The Book of Ecclesiastes

All too frequently, negative evaluations are ascribed to the book of Ecclesiastes, such as "fatalistic," "cynical," "temporal," and "nihilistic." However, all of these judgments miss the stated purpose of the book that appears in Ecclesiastes 12:13 – 14:

> Now all has been heard;
> here is the conclusion of the matter:
> Fear God and keep his commandments,
> for this is the entirety [my transl.] of man.
> For God will bring every deed into judgment,
> including every hidden thing,
> whether it is good or evil.

Everything gets off on the wrong interpretive foot when *hebel* (of Ecc 1:2, 37, etc.) is rendered "vanity," "meaninglessness," or the like. Instead, *hebel* should be rendered "transitoriness."[16] All is transitory (or changing). Solomon's point is not that all of life is a zero or a big waste; instead, he pointed (in Ecc 3:11) to the fact that "[God] has made everything beautiful in its time. He has set eternity in the hearts of men; yet they cannot fathom what God has done from beginning to end." Thus, without beginning with the creator God as a proper start, life was a puzzle, with time and events ever changing all around us, leaving no reference point or guide unless it be the living God himself.

Integration of Life and Truth in the Lord

The greatest case ever made for the unity of all truth, both so-called secular and sacred, is to be found in the book of Ecclesiastes. Solomon's whole point of view was positive, not negative or merely naturalistic. Six times the theme of the fear of God appeared (3:14; 5:7; 7:18; 8:12 [2x], 13) before the grand finale to his whole argument climaxed in

16. See the fascinating work by Glenn Fobert, *Everything Is Mist: Ecclesiastes on Life in a Puzzling and Troubled Temporary World* (Belleville, Ont.: Guardian Books, 2003).

12:13: "Here is the conclusion of the matter: Fear God, and keep his commandments, for this is the [entirety (*kol hā'ādām*)] of every human being."

No one has given a more programmatic essay on this book than J. Stafford Wright.[17] In his view, Ecclesiastes 3:11 was one of the key verses:

> [God] has made everything beautiful in its time. He has also set eternity [*hā'ōlām*] in the hearts of men; yet they cannot fathom what God has done from beginning to end.

Humanity in and of itself, argued Canon Wright, was unable to put the pieces of the puzzle of life together — secular or sacred. Yet people hunger to know how to make it all fit because they have a God-created vacuum as large as eternity, craving satisfaction in that being which is made in the image of God. The "vanity of vanities" (or better: "transitoriness of transitoriness") of Ecclesiastes, then, was not that life was a bore, filled with futility, emptiness, or the frustrating conclusion that nothing was worth living for. No! Instead "vanity" (*hebel*)[18] was simply that life *in and of itself* could not supply the key to its own meaning, nor could it truly liberate the person. No one part of God's otherwise good universe could in and of itself provide any all-embracing solution that would integrate truth, learning, and living.

Only when one came to fear God did a person begin to perceive the unification of truth, learning, and living (cf. Ecc 7:14 and 8:14 as well). Life was deliberately sketched in such stark contrasts as life and death, joy and pain, poverty and wealth, so that every person might realize that apart from a relationship of a total commitment ("fearing" the Lord), nothing would ever make sense — nor could it ever!

The charges that the message of Ecclesiastes contained Epicureanism, atheism, and hedonism were met head-on by Otto Zöckler:

> In a time inclined to the abandonment of faith in God's holy and just government of the world, he [the writer of Ecclesiastes] clings to such a faith with a touching constancy, and defends the fact of the wise rule of the Eternal and Omnipotent God against all the frivolous scoffs of fools (ii. 26; iii. 20sq., v. l; v. 17 – 19; viii. 14; ix. 1 – 3; compare ii. 13; iv. 5; x. 2 sq.; x. 13, 14).... He is never weary of pointing out the righteous retributions of the future as a motive to the fear of God, the chief and all-comprehending virtue of the wise (iii. 14 – 17; v. 6; vi. 6, 10; viii. 12sq.; x. 9; xii. 13, 14) and of commending unwavering constancy in individual callings as the best prudence ... (compare ii. 10; iii. 22; v. 17, 18; viii. 15, etc.).[19]

17. J. Stafford Wright, "The Interpretation of Ecclesiastes," originally published in *Evangelical Quarterly* 18 (1946), 18 – 34, and reprinted in *Classical Evangelical Essays in Old Testament Interpretation*, ed. Walter Kaiser Jr. (Grand Rapids: Baker, 1972), 133 – 50.

18. Theophile J. Meek contends that "in this short book, *hebel* would seem to be used in at least five different senses: 'futile' (most frequent, e.g., 1:2); 'empty' (e.g., 6:12); 'sorry' (e.g., 6:4); 'senseless' (e.g., 8:14); and 'transient' (e.g., 11:10)." See his article, "Translating the Hebrew Bible," *Journal of Biblical Literature* 79 (1960): 331.

19. Otto Zöckler, *Proverbs of Solomon*, in J. P. Lange, *A Commentary on the Holy Scriptures* (New York: Scribner, Armstrong & Co., 1877), 10:17.

Once again the connection with the law was obvious: fearing God and keeping his commandments were closely linked together. The counsel given in this book was applied to the more practical situations of life, but its aim was to commend the same standard of righteousness commanded in the law of Moses. Its own contribution to the unfolding expansion of that same core of truth was that the fear of the Lord was both the inception and essence of a truly integrated life. There was no hard divorce between the secular and sacred, faith and knowledge, learning and believing, faith and culture.

Gerhard von Rad also rightly chastised those like William McKane who would apply an evolutionary pattern to wisdom by suggesting that earlier wisdom was at first fundamentally secular and then it was "baptized" and theologized into the Yahwistic religion. Said von Rad with reference to a passage such as Proverbs 16:7 – 12, where "experiences of the world" alternated with "experiences of Yahweh": "It would be madness to presuppose some kind of separation, as if in one case a man of objective perception were speaking and in the other a believer in Yahweh."[20] Von Rad had yielded somewhat, however, for while noticing the call of wisdom was always a divine call, even though it was uttered in a secular world and apart from the sacred, he stressed that this divine call did "not legitimate itself from the saving history, but from creation."[21] Thus he concluded that the wisdom teachers were not all interested in

> ... searching for a world order.... One can in no sense speak of a world order as really existing between God and man.... The teachers move in a dialectic which is fundamentally incapable of resolution, speaking on the one hand of valid rules and, on the other, of ad hoc divine actions.[22]

But this disclaimer rips wisdom away from the rest of the Old Testament and from its own stated objectives. For while it may be conceded that creation plays a greater role than previously in theology,[23] the biblical writer's interest in integrating all of this must simultaneously be acknowledged.

To introduce the topic of the integration of truth, fact, and understanding is to appeal to the unity of truth made possible by the one God who created a *UNI*-verse. Thus the doctrinal base for any norms of truth and character are grounded ultimately in a doctrine of creation and the person of the Creator. It must also respectfully be pointed out that wisdom has as much a place in history between God and Israel as does Mount Sinai and the Mosaic covenant. To have seen the place for one is to have found

20. Von Rad, *Wisdom in Israel*, 62. Cf. William McKane, *Prophets and Wise Men* (Naperville, IL: Allenson, 1965), 47. H. Carl Shank made some of the same criticism of such nature-grace dichotomies as are found in the commentaries of Leupold, Delitzsch, Hengstenberg, or Scofield's notes. See his article, "Qoheleth's World and Life View as Seen in His Recurring Phrases," *Westminster Theological Journal* 37 (1974): 57 – 73, esp. 60 – 65, where he proposes a faith-sight dichotomy instead.

21. Gerhard von Rad, *Old Testament Theology* (Edinburgh: Oliver and Boyd, 1962), 1:452.

22. Von Rad, *Wisdom in Israel*, 107.

23. See Zimmerli "Place and Limit," 146 – 58. "Wisdom thinks resolutely within the framework of a theology of creation," 148.

the function of the other. Israel, like all creatures here below, was to fear the one true God, Yahweh. The universal standards were to be those norms prescribed in the Law of God (Pss. 19; 119; Ecc 12:13) and those proverbs on "life," "knowledge," "understanding," and the "fear of God." Consequently, an adequate worldview and a full enjoyment of life were impossible apart from a recognition of the Creator, the same God who had spoken his commandments. Remember, this same priority of "fearing Yahweh" was exactly what Deuteronomy had required; only there it was a prerequisite to keeping the law and authentic living. Wisdom and law both reflected proper responses of the authentic believer in the promise.

Wisdom from the Lord

Real wisdom cannot exist apart from the source of wisdom; accordingly, it cannot be known or applied apart from "the fear of the Lord." Lawrence E. Toombs observed:

> Wisdom is to be found with God, and nowhere else; and unless the quest for wisdom brings a man to his knees in awe and reverence, knowing his own helplessness to make himself wise, wisdom remains for him a closed book.[24]

At least five passages in Proverbs associate wisdom with the fear of the Lord (1:7, 29; 2:5; 8:12 – 14; 15:33). The fear of the Lord makes a person delight in wisdom and instruction (1:7); receive counsel and reproof (1:29 – 30); and listen to wisdom, understanding, and the knowledge of God (2:1 – 6).

Undoubtedly, the key teaching passage on wisdom is Proverbs 8. This chapter may be outlined as follows:

- A. Wisdom's Excellence (Pr 8:1 – 21)
  1. In Her Appeal (vv. 1 – 3)
  2. In Her Truth (vv. 4 – 12)
  3. In Her Loves and Hatreds (vv. 13 – 16)
  4. In Her Gifts (vv. 17 – 21)
- B. Wisdom's Origins (Pr 8:22 – 31)
  1. Her Antemundane Existence (vv. 22 – 26)
  2. Her Active Participation in Creation (vv. 27 – 31)
- C. Wisdom's Blessings (Pr 8:32 – 36)
  1. Concluding Admonition (vv. 32 – 33)
  2. Promised Blessing (vv. 34 – 36)

Centrally located in this discussion is verse 13, with its assertion that "to fear the LORD is to hate evil: I hate pride and arrogance, and evil behavior and deceitful speech." But

24. Lawrence E. Toombs, "Old Testament Theology and the Wisdom Literature," *Journal of Bible and Religion* 23 (1952): 195.

McKane could not accept verse 13*a* as it stood. He repeated in his commentary on Proverbs[25] the argument he had developed in his *Prophets and Wise Men*,[26] that "the fear of Yahweh is not an original ingredient of old wisdom" but rather a "prophetic reinterpretation of wisdom" and "imposed" on the ancient sage to give it more of a Yahwistic flavor![27] In support of this attempt to reinterpret the Proverbs passage, it was asserted that Proverbs 8:12 – 14 was dependent on Isaiah 11:1 – 2, which spoke of a spirit (*rûaḥ*) of wisdom (*ḥokmâh*) and understanding (*bînâh*), a *rûaḥ* of counsel (*'eṣâh*) and power (*gᵉbûrâh*). But if Proverbs can be shown to be largely Solomonic,[28] and all evolutionary claims proved to be as unfounded, as we have argued above, then the wisdom made available to human beings and kings in Proverbs was the same wisdom with accompanying qualities that were to be found in prophetic descriptions of the messianic king who was to come.

According to Proverbs 8:12, wisdom was at home with prudence and easily guided it. Her intellectual power included all carefully thought out plans. She offered counsel, understanding, and the energy to carry out the duties conferred on kings, nobles, princes, and rulers of the earth.

Her temporal priority was stressed by the use of these ten words: The "beginning" of his work, *rēšît* (Pr 8:22); the "first" of his works of "old," *qedem ... mē'āz* (v. 22); "from eternity," *mē'ôlām* (v. 23); "at the first," *mēro'š* (v. 23); "from the beginning," *miqqadmê* (v. 23); "when there was not," *bᵉ'ên* (v. 24); "before the mountains were formed," *bᵉṭerem* (v. 25); "before" the hills, *lipnê* (v. 25); "or the first" of the dust ... was made, *wᵉrō'š* (v. 26). Three more verbs described the way she came into existence: the Lord "created me," *qānānî* (v. 22); "I was born," *nissaktî* (v. 23), or if from *nāsîk* ("prince"), "I was appointed"; and "I was brought forth," *ḥôlāltî* (v. 24).

Since Proverbs 8:22 – 31 was an expansion of Proverbs 3:19, which stated, "By wisdom [Yahweh] laid the earth's foundations; by understanding he set the heavens in place," the discussion on the term *'āmôn* in verse 30 need not be so difficult. Without revocalizing the text to *'āmûn* (qal passive participle of *'āman*, "to nurse," hence, "nurs-

25. William McKane, *Proverbs: A New Approach* (Philadelphia: Westminster Press, 1970), 348. He argues that verse 13*a* "interrupts the smooth transition from v. 12 to v. 14."

26. McKane, *Prophets and Wise Men*, 48f.

27. Norman Habel, "The Symbolism of Wisdom in Proverbs 1 – 9," *Interpretation* 26 (1972): 144, n. 24; 143 – 49, incorrectly argued for a similar but internal division between "old [empirical] wisdom materials" and "Yahwistic reinterpretations" as illustrated in Proverbs 2:1 – 19, where verses 9 – 11,12 – 15 illustrate the former, and verses 5 – 8, 16 – 19 the reinterpretive process. But the scheme appears to be thinly supported by exegesis and the pattern imposed and intruded over the text and text sequence without any evidence. It would appear that whereas biblical scholars have argued for decades that the historical position of Wisdom literature had to follow the assumed literary development of all other nations — poem, narrative, and wisdom (coming after the prophetic literature and more precisely after Ezekiel because of the predominant factor of elements like personal recompense), since 1924, with the discovery and publication of the ancient Egyptian wisdom texts, they have pretty much abandoned that view. Scholars are retreating to a new line of defense that allows for ancient "empirical wisdom sayings" to be placed first in chronological order but that also restricts theological wisdom sayings to much later prophetic-like reinterpretations. Such desperation tactics should be obvious to all who work with the ancient Near Eastern data and the Wisdom literature of the Bible.

28. See internal claims and such discussions as R. K. Harrison, *Introduction to the Old Testament* (Grand Rapids: Eerdmans, 1969), 1010 – 21; Gleason L. Archer Jr., *A Survey of Old Testament Introduction*, rev. ed. (Chicago: Moody Press, 1974), 465 – 74.

ling, child"), we may translate it "I was beside him, the *Master Craftsman*."[29] Wisdom then claimed to have been present at creation; indeed, she claimed to have functioned as one of the means by which Yahweh created the world. Therefore, *'āmôn* stood in apposition to the pronoun representing Yahweh; and wisdom appeared as one of the key character traits manifested in that creation.

All this suggested not a hypostatization (i.e., an individual entity "standing under" or associated with the divine being),[30] or a mythological[31] origin, for wisdom, but a metaphorical one. Consistent with this, Whybray concluded:

> The terms used to describe wisdom's origin are metaphorical, not mythological, and the single word which can be interpreted as speaking of her *activity* [*'āmôn*] at the creation does not essentially go beyond the statement of 3:19. Everything which is here said about her can be naturally interpreted as belonging properly to the poetical personification of an attribute of Yahweh.[32]

Thus the connection or association (not, however, the full equivalence) of "the fear of the Lord" with wisdom denoted the intrinsically religious nature of any and all wisdom. Once again we can see that arrogant humanity in and of itself could not, and never would, understand or receive prudent counsel. This had to begin with a personal relationship to the Lord, the essence of which continued to inform all of a person's thinking, living, and acting. Hence, just as the attribute of God's holiness supplied the yardstick or norm for Mosaic theology, so God's attribute of wisdom provided the norm for all who related to it in "the fear of Yahweh."

Eudaemonism and the Lord

Many of the wisdom sayings at first sight appear to betray a materialistic sort of base pragmatism; that is to say, they appear to inculcate eudaemonism, that is, moral obligations merely for the sake of the well-being or happiness of the person — a sort of health, wealth, and prosperity message, if you please. But such a "profit motive" interpretation misses the author's truth-intention in statements such as the following:

> The righteousness of the upright delivers them,
> but the unfaithful are trapped by evil desires. (Pr 11:6)
>
> Lazy hands make a man poor,
> but diligent hands bring wealth. (Pr 10:4)

29. So argues Mitchell Dahood, "Proverbs 8:22 – 31: Translation and Commentary," *Catholic Biblical Quarterly* 30 (1968): 518 – 19.

30. Helmer Ringgren, *Word and Wisdom: Studies in the Hypostatization of Divine Qualities and Functions in the Ancient Near East* (Lund: Hakan Ohlssons Boktryckeri, 1947).

31. See Dahood, "Proverbs 8:22 – 31," 521; W. F. Albright, "Some Canaanite-Phoenician Sources of Hebrew Wisdom," *Wisdom in Israel, Vetus Testamentum Supplement* 3 (Leiden: E. J. Brill, 1955), 1 – 15.

32. Whybray, *Wisdom*, 103.

Instead, the wise man was the one who observed a divine plan and order established in things. Thus prosperity and blessing were not sought as ends in themselves, as if the wise man were arbitrarily making success a new idol. On the contrary, in accordance with God's pronouncement of "good" in Genesis 1, the wise approved work, things, and righteousness itself as "good" and self-vindicating. Diligence, obedience to the laws of God, and honest labor were rewarded; but neither the goal nor the motive was to be found in the blessing and reward itself. Every event in life was embraced in the plan of God (Ecc 3:1 – 5:20). It was God who had made everything beautiful in its time (3:11), each with its own appointment. While "To mortals belong the plans of the heart," according to Proverbs 16:1, the answer is from the Lord, "for the LORD determines one's steps." Men and women may plan their ways, but it must be the Lord who gives the guidance that is needed (16:9; 19:21; 20:24; 21:2). It is ultimately not people who earn their own reward; it is God who requites[33] to every person according to his or her work (24:12) — and that based on the principles of his "good" work in creation and his character.

True, outwardly there appeared to be inequities, and the divine order was not always transparently obvious. But adversity or affliction were not always nor necessarily an evil (Ecc 7:1 – 15), just as prosperity and material success were not always or necessarily a good either (6:1 – 12). Moreover that divine order and purpose may often remain hidden and unknown even though good men such as Job sought to discover it. Only in Elihu's addresses did it become plain that God was using suffering as a teaching device (*mûsār*)[34] and as a method by which to "open Job's ears" (Job 33:16; 36:10, 15).

Meanwhile, the Preacher argued for the removal of discouragements which appeared to contravene the plan of God (Ecc 9:1 – 12:8). Even the so-called mundane aspects of life like eating, drinking, and enjoying the benefits of one's paycheck were described as "gifts" of God (2:24; 3:13; 5:18 – 20; 8:15; 9:9). Yet there was nothing inherently good in people that they should be capable on their own of enjoying themselves and their mundane existence apart from God (2:24; 3:12). The ability to be happy, blessed, and to enjoy even eating, drinking, riches, wealth, and one's own wife was in the divine order a gift from above.

THE SONG OF SONGS

In the Song of Songs, another wisdom book, Solomon is named either as the author or as one of the main characters at least seven times (1:1, 5; 3:7, 9, 11; 8:11, 12). It is a love song or a type of lyric idyll. Therefore, what Jesus, the Living Word, did for marriage

33. See the review of the recent literature on the idea of retribution in the OT with four aspects of retribution in the book of Deuteronomy by John G. Gammie, "The Theology of Retribution in the Book of Deuteronomy," *Catholic Biblical Quarterly* 32 (1970): 1 – 12.

34. Jim A. Sanders, "Suffering as Divine Discipline in the Old Testament and Post-Biblical Judaism," *Colgate Rochester Divinity School Bulletin* 28 (1955): 28 – 31.

by attending the wedding feast of Cana in John 2:1 – 11, here the written word does in giving more teaching of the sanctity, holiness, and joy of marriage. As such, Song of Songs completes what was begun in Genesis 2:23 – 25.

There are three main characters in this book, not just two: Solomon, the Shulamite maiden whom Solomon is trying to win as another prize in his growing harem, and the boyfriend whom the maiden really wishes to marry instead of marrying King Solomon (e.g., Solomon, with his "vineyard" of many is contrasted with the boyfriend who has just one "vineyard" in 8:11 – 12).

The purpose for including this book in the Bible is found in the statement in 8:6 – 7.

> Place me like a seal over your heart,
> like a seal on your arm;
> for love is as strong as death,
> its jealousy unyielding as the grave.
> It burns like blazing fire,
> like the very flame of the LORD [marginal reading].
> Many waters cannot quench love;
> rivers cannot wash it away.
> If one were to give
> all the wealth of his house for love,
> it would be utterly scorned.

In other words, Solomon loved and lost, yet he learned much truth about what God had intended in a theology of marriage and how happiness in this institution was not to be found in collecting wives (or husbands) as if they were a bunch of toys.

The Song of Solomon celebrated that gift of one's spouse by dedicating a whole book to that theme. Again, if Solomon is the author of this work (and so the text as we have it lays claim in 1:1; 8:12), then the entrée to this work can be made through another piece by the same writer: Proverbs 5:15 – 21. There, in the infrequently used figure of speech known as an allegory, Solomon, under the inspiration of the Holy Spirit, taught mortals about marital fidelity. He likened enjoyment of sexual love in the marriage bond to drinking water from one's own cistern and well:

> Drink water from your own cistern,
> running water from your own well.
> Should your springs overflow in the streets,
> your streams of water in the public squares?
> Let them be yours alone,
> never to be shared with strangers.
> May your fountain be blessed,
> and may you rejoice in the wife of your youth.
> A loving doe, a graceful deer —
> may her breasts satisfy you always,

may you ever be captivated by her love....
For a man's ways are in full view of the LORD,
and he examines all your paths. (Pr 5:15–19, 21)[35]

Thus, when Song of Solomon 4:12, 15 repeated,

You are a garden locked up, my sister, my bride,
you are a spring enclosed, a sealed fountain....
You are a garden fountain,
a well of flowing water....

it continued many of the same metaphors and theology found in Proverbs 5:15–23. But the purpose of the book was stated in Song of Solomon 8:6–7: Love was a "flame from Yah[weh]"; it could not be extinguished, exchanged, or tempted by other goods such as riches, position, or honor. Indeed, Solomon had tried to woo the Shulamite maiden away from her shepherd boyfriend back home, but it was all to no use. Solomon could keep his "vineyard of confusion" (my translation for Baal Hamon, "lord of confusion," v. 11), indeed, "his thousand" wives (v. 12). But as for the shepherd, he had his one very "own vineyard" (wife) for himself (v. 12). The book then was intended as a commentary on Genesis 2:24 and a manual on the blessing and reward of intimate married love, once Yahweh had lit the flame and given the capability of enjoyment. Otherwise, it could not be purchased for love nor money—as Solomon learned the hard way and wrote under divine direction.

Immortality and the Resurrection of the Body

And what teaching is there in the Old Testament of that good above all goods—immortality or even the resurrection of the body? No text made the point more clearly, nor was that text more hotly contested on textual or hermeneutical grounds than Job 19:23–27. Clearly, Job had lost all hope in this life (17:1, 11–16); thus, he cried out that he would be vindicated postmortem, if it appeared he could not be vindicated antemortem.

And did he believe that it would include a resurrection of his physical body? Job 19:26 is difficult:

And after my skin has been destroyed
yet in my flesh I will see God.

Does "in my flesh" mean *apart from* one's body or *from inside* one's body each hoped to see God? Let verse 27 decide: "I myself will see him with my own eyes—I, and not another."

35. For a fuller treatment of this passage, see Walter C. Kaiser in "True Marital Love in Proverbs 5:15–23 and the Interpretation of Song of Songs," in *The Way of Wisdom: Essays in Honor of Bruce K. Waltke*, ed. J. I. Packer and Sven Soderlund (Grand Rapids: Zondervan, 2000), 106–16.

Such exegesis is still greeted with deep resentment. The idea is too advanced, so it is claimed, for even the Solomonic era, much less the patriarchal times of Job, where it may correctly be located, as we argued earlier. Never mind, of course, ancient humanity's preoccupation with the question of death and immortality. Never mind that Egypt already had geared the whole economy of the state to meet this one question of personal corporeal existence after death. Forget also, if we can, the Babylonian myth of Adapa and the narrative about Enoch (Ge 5:24) in the pre-patriarchal era. But even if we discount all this hard evidence, then let Job 14:7 be faced:

> At least there is hope for a tree:
> If it is cut down, it will sprout again [*yaḥ^a^lîp*],
> and its new shoots will not fail.

Just as often around the base of a felled tree one shoot after another will spring up as a continuation of the otherwise previously dead tree, so it is with humankind in Job 14:14:

> If a man dies, will he live again?
> All days of my hard service
> I will wait for my renewal [sprouting, *ḥ^a^lîpātî*] to come.

There it is! Job 14:14 stated in terms analogous to what happened to felled trees! Very few commentators will connect the two verses, but the writer intended his audience to do so. He did it by using the same Hebrew root (*ḥlp*) in the same context in Job 14:7, 14.

Likewise, Ecclesiastes 3:17 argued that God would meet us as our judge in that future day of appointed judgment (cf. 12:14); for the spirit of man goes upward (note the *article* on the participle and not the interrogative) while the life of the beast goes into the ground (3:21 – 22). Accordingly, human beings had best do something while they have breath and do it to the glory of God. But any deed of any significance would have to begin in the atmosphere of trust in the promised divine order of things, that is to say, in the fear of God.

Excursus: Wisdom's Relationship to Torah

All too frequently, the wisdom sections of the Old Testament have been described as the Achilles' heel of almost all biblical theologies. Since it appears to lack any direct references to the history of Israel, the covenant, election, or any of the major themes of what preceded or followed in the progress of revelation, it was treated as the stepchild and as an outsider to the theological development of the Bible.

The custom in scholarly circles has been to declare that Proverbs, for instance, was originally a secular enterprise provoked by the need for governing the state.[36] Instead of ascribing to early Israelite wisdom the central focus of the "fear of the Lord/God," it was argued that the name Yahweh was introduced later into the secular texts to give them a more spiritual and religious tone.[37] For example, it was as if God had not declared any divine guidelines for the office of king (which, of course he had in Dt 17:14 – 20) or had not declared what was demanded of the state by way of justice, righteousness, and fairness. The reason the earlier Sinaitic covenant was not brought into play in these scholarly discussions, despite the large number of allusions to parts of the Torah, of course, was the tendency to late-date the law of Moses until after the era of the prophets in the fifth century (exile) and even later (postexilic).

The documentary theory (usually under the rubric of J, E, D, and P) dominated most of the nineteenth and twentieth centuries as a presumed given, even though in recent years it has shown signs of beginning to wane for lack of evidential support.[38] But it was clear that if the law of God came later, wisdom could not share any correspondences with it, thereby leaving it as an orphan set of texts in the Scriptures.

These issues, more than the obvious lack of any reference to any covenant or history of Israel, were responsible for challenging the possibility of any kind of a unified organization or single mind of God that connected with the rest of the biblical canon. Modern scholarship, contrary to the internal claims of the text, regarded Wisdom literature as alien to the general tenor of the Old Testament, especially to the law of God.

However, our contention is that in the promise-plan of God, there are a large number of correspondences between the Torah and Wisdom, especially in the

36. So argued McKane, *Prophets and Wise Men*, idem, *Proverbs: A New Approach*. McKane's view was thoroughly critiqued by Frederick M. Wilson, "Sacred and Profane? The Yahwehistic Redaction of Proverbs Reconsidered," in *The Listening Heart: Essays in Wisdom and the Psalms in Honor of Roland E. Murphy, O. Carm*, ed. Kenneth G. Hoglund et al., *Journal for the Study of the Old Testament Supplement* 58 (Sheffield: JSOT Press, 1987). See the especially thoughtful article by Richard L. Schultz, "Unity or Diversity in Wisdom Theology? A Canonical and Covenantal Perspective," *Tyndale Bulletin* 48 (1997): 271 – 306.

37. So Joseph Blenkinsopp, *Wisdom and Law in the Old Testament: The Ordering of Life in Israel and Early Judaism* (Oxford University Press, 1995); James Crenshaw, *Old Testament Wisdom: An Introduction* (Atlanta: John Knox, 1981), 92 – 93; and Claus Westermann, *Roots of Wisdom: The Oldest Proverbs of Israel and Other Peoples* (Philadelphia: Westminster, 1995).

38. The main stream of critical scholarship that espouses the Documentary Hypothesis argues for an exilic or postexilic date for the "D" (Deuteronomy) and the "P" (Priestly Law Codes) of the Pentateuch. This line of reasoning has been countered by showing that the structure of Deuteronomy follows a second millennium BC (ca. 1400) five-part pattern found in the Hittite Treaties of the Great King with Vassal Kings, which also come from mid-second-millennium documents. See Meredith Kline, *The Structure of Biblical Authority* (Eugene, OR: Wipf and Stock, 1989), 21 – 44, and Kenneth A. Kitchen, *On the Reliability of the Old Testament* (Grand Rapids: Eerdmans, 2003), 283 – 306.

book of Deuteronomy.[39] Though some, such as Moshe Weinfeld, have noted the connections between the wisdom materials and Deuteronomy with respect to such things as not moving the boundary markers to any property and not falsifying the system of weights and measurements, they fail to give priority of written appearance to the Mosaic laws (and therefore its prior part of Scripture to the wisdom materials) because of their commitment to the Documentary Hypothesis.[40] However, Deuteronomy 19:14 had already forbidden moving a neighbor's boundary marker before it later appeared in Proverbs 22:28 and 23:10 – 11. Likewise, Deuteronomy 24:13 – 16 had also warned against cheating on the scales and weights, later put in proverbial form in Proverbs 11:1; 20:10 and 20:23.

But there were numerous other laws from the Torah that found their way into the form of proverbs in the Wisdom literature. For instance, Tremper Longman, an evangelical writer, pointed to a number of correspondences, for instance, between the Decalogue (Ex 20:12 – 17) and Proverbs, even though he does not see a necessary or unifying relationship between Law and Wisdom.[41] He listed the following:

The 5th Commandment	Proverbs 1:8; 4:1; 10:1; 13:1
The 6th Commandment	Proverbs 1:10 – 12; 6:17
The 7th Commandment	Proverbs 2:16 – 19; 5; 6:20 – 35; 7
The 8th Commandment	Proverbs 1:13 – 14; 11:1
The 9th Commandment	Proverbs 3:30; 6:18 – 19; 10:8, 12, 17, 19
The 10th Commandment	Proverbs 16:18

One could add other parallels, such as the payment of vows made to God (Dt 23:22 – 24; Ecc 5:1 – 5; Pr 20:25). Notice, again as just an example, the warnings against evidences of partiality in the rulings of judges appear in both the Torah and later in Wisdom (Dt 1:17; 16:19; Pr 24:23).

The fact that Proverbs speaks of "righteousness," "good," and "evil," as if they were givens, with little or no assumed need for a definition in Proverbs, had two opposite effects.[42] It drove Gerhard von Rad to separate between secular and

39. See Walter C. Kaiser Jr., *Toward an Old Testament Theology* (Grand Rapids: Zondervan, 1978), 66 – 69; idem, *The Christian and the "Old" Testament* (Pasadena, CA: William Carey Press, 1998), 115 – 26.

40. Moshe Weinfeld, *Deuteronomy and the Deuteronomic School* (Oxford: Claredon, 1972), 365 – 67.

41. Tremper Longman III, *Proverbs*, Baker Commentary on the Old Testament (Grand Rapids: Baker, 2006), 82. Tremper does not accept the concept of a unifying theme for the theology of the Old Testament and therefore is reluctant to acknowledge how law and wisdom share mutual interests, despite the plethora of evidence from the text that he presents so well.

42. This observation came from Cole Hamilton, a student in my Old Testament Ethics class at Gordon-Conwell Theological Seminary.

sacred origins for Wisdom.[43] James Crenshaw, however, argued that at least for Proverbs 1–9, "the fear of the Lord" is used "in such a way as to almost suggest *the laws and statutes* which God had made known to Israel."[44] Crenshaw was on a better track to solving the way Wisdom relates to the whole of biblical theology than was von Rad.

The theme of "the fear of the Lord/God" is the point of connection between the earlier and later forms of the promise doctrine. In fact, this theme is also present in every one of the five books of the Pentateuch except the book of Numbers[45] (Gn 20:11; 22:12; 42:18; Ex 1:17, 21; 9:30; 14:31; 18:21; 20:20; Lev 19:14, 32; 25:17, 19, 36, 43; Dt 4:10; 5:26; 6:2, 13, 24; 8:6; 10:12, 20; 13:4; 14:23; 17:19; 25:18, 58; 31:12–13).

"The fear of the Lord" is the theme of the book of Proverbs (1:7) and, as we have argued in this chapter, a theme that occupies much of the book. The same theme appears in the book of Job (1:1, 8; 2:3; 28:28) as it also does in the book of Ecclesiastes 3:14; 5:1–7; 8:12; and especially in 12:13. Qoheleth summarized his whole book of Ecclesiastes by saying "fear God and keep his commandments" (12:13). Therefore, Qoheleth argued that the wisdom he was advocating in his book equated to a large degree with wisdom that could be found in the observance and obedience to the commandments of God. That is how Moses argued in Deuteronomy 6:2 as well—the fear of the Lord was best seen in keeping all God's decrees and commandments.

Accordingly, the main stream of sapiential studies has missed the mark when it isolated wisdom from the law of God, only to be faced with a further dilemma of relating wisdom to the rest of Old Testament biblical theology. Instead of presuming that the name "Yahweh" was an intrusion laid over a secular base for wisdom, as modern scholarship has tended to do all too often in the past, it is here recommended that the law of God found in the Torah be taken for granted as the basis for understanding the wisdom books of the Old Testament.

Therefore, the connection between the promise and wisdom was the same as the connection between the law and the promise. Wisdom frequently took the instruction given in Torah and popularized it by placing it in proverbial forms that were brief, memorable, and with a bit of a salty edge that condensed

43. Von Rad, *Wisdom in Israel*, 62–64; 74–96.

44. James Crenshaw, "Prolegomena" in *Studies in Ancient Israelite Wisdom*, ed. James Crenshaw (New York: Ktav Publishing House, 1976), 96.

45. Again, I am beholden to my student Cole Hamilton for this observation in his paper, "What Has Wisdom to Do with Law? An Examination of the Correspondences of the Ethics of Law and Wisdom," written for my Old Testament Ethics class.

the command into a witticism that could be carried in the memory of all who heard it. Without such wisdom sayings, men and women would have been left without an appreciation of God, man, and all things good and fair. But where the fear of the Lord/God paved the way, life could suddenly make sense and provide the satisfaction of knowing how then we should live.

Chapter 7

The Day of Promise: Prophets of the Ninth Century BC

Obadiah, Joel

Once David's "house" and Solomon's temple had both been established, the promise-plan of God had reached a provisional plateau in its development. Thus the exodus narrative, which declared Israel to be Yahweh's son, his own people, a kingdom of priests, and a holy nation, could now be continued and renewed in the further aspects of the promise-plan given to the Davidic seed: David would possess an everlasting dynasty, throne, and kingdom, all of which would be a "charter for humanity." God's future ruler was now visible in the line of David.

The Prophets and the Promise

The prophets could now turn their focus on God's worldwide plan and the kingdom of God. Alas, however, Israel's sin claimed a significant portion of the prophets' attention. Nevertheless, mingled with these words of judgment against the sin of the nation Israel along with the other nations were the bright prospects of God's everlasting kingdom as announced so long ago in the promise made to the Israelites at Sinai and to others along the way.

But this complication would bring out the genius of the promise doctrine. It had, as Willis J. Beecher noted, a twofold character: "It was a *standing prediction* of the time to come, and it was *an available religious doctrine* for the time being" (emphasis mine).[1]

Thus the prophetic promise was not a group of scattered predictions that only later made sense after Christ appeared and others had reinterpreted many of the old prophetic words. If the prophets merely had been prognosticating or foretelling the future, then the focus of their message would have fallen only on two things: (1) the word spoken before the event, and (2) the final fulfilling event itself. While this view of prophecy

1. Willis J. Beecher, *The Prophets and the Promise* (1905; reprint, Grand Rapids: Baker, 1975), 242.

may be proper and legitimate in itself, at least according to some students of prophecy, it fails to capture precisely the aspect that had captivated the hearts and minds of the Old Testament writers and saints the most. Again, Beecher best described what that difference was. For him, the word *promise* was to be preferred over mere *prediction*, because the promise of the prophets also embraced the *historical means* employed for keeping that purpose alive over the centuries while it awaited the final fulfillment: Thus, (1) the *promise* and (2) the *means* and (3) the *result* (all three aspects) were

> all in mind at once.... If the promise involved a series of results, we might connect any one in the series of the results with the predictive clause as a fulfilled prediction. So far our thinking would be correct. But if we permanently confined our thought only to this series of items in the fulfilled promise, we should be led to an inadequate and very likely a false idea of the promise and its fulfillment. To understand the predictive elements aright, we must see it in light of the other elements. Every fulfilled promise is a fulfilled prediction; but it is exceedingly important to look at it as part of the promise-plan and not as mere prediction.[2]

Of equal importance was the inseparable connection between the prophetic word and the history and geography in which that word was located. The prophets' messages were not heterogeneous and disconnected predictions, randomly announced throughout an otherwise dull drone of chastisements. Nor was prediction even the main feature of prophecy. Rather, the prophets were proclaimers of righteousness, preaching both law and promise, grace and judgment, to motivate the people to repentance and a life of obedience in the will and plan of God. Their predictions were often given as incentives to their contemporaries for holy living in that day, seeing that the future belonged to their God and to his righteous reign.

More was to be found in these predictions, of course, than novel glimpses of the future scattered as bits of candy to whet the appetite of a sensate or occult mentality that hungered to be the first to know what would be in tomorrow's headlines in the newspapers. Instead of any such whimsical purpose as this, the prophets often deliberately cast their words about the future in the phraseology and conceptual patterns of past events or prophecies. There was a deliberate borrowing and supplementing from the previous words of the Abrahamic-Davidic promise. Hence, for them the future was part of God's single, cumulative, ongoing promise from the past as well as a pointer to the future. Thus the so-called messianic passages in the writing prophets were mostly repetitions and supplements that carried homiletical and practical implications and amplifications on the promise as originally given to Abraham, Israel, or David. Accordingly, these predictions were not disconnected or scattered predictions but offshoots from the common stem of the promise doctrine.

2. Ibid., 376.

But some will surely object to the persistent inclusions in that single promise-plan about Israel's national career with its geographical holdings. To be sure, some Jewish and rationalistic scholars have concluded that since Israel's political career and geographical holdings occupied such an obvious emphasis in the promise predictions, this is all that was meant — that these predictions were simply the demographic and political aspirations of the nation Israel as envisioned by some of Israel's prophetic bards! Consequently, all other attempts to apply this promise to the church or to Jesus Christ were false and were beyond anything the prophets ever intended. However, such a conclusion fails to take the Old Testament itself seriously; nor is it fair to the historical realities.

At the same time, many Christian interpreters have erred in the same manner, only on the opposite side of the promise. They have denied that the promise had anything left in it for national Israel, now that the Christian era has arrived. However, Willis J. Beecher commented at the turn of the twentieth century:

> If the Christian interpreter persists in excluding the ethnical Israel from his conception of the fulfillment, or in regarding Israel's part in the matter as merely preparatory and not eternal, then he comes into conflict with the plain witness of both testaments [and we might now add since 1948 "with what appears to be the verdict of history as well"].... Rightly interpreted, the biblical statements include in the fulfillment both Israel, the race with whom the covenant is eternal, and also the personal Christ and his mission, with the whole spiritual Israel of the redeemed in all ages. The New Testament teaches this as Christian doctrine, for leading men to repentance and for edification; and the Old Testament teaches it as Messianic doctrine, for leading men to repentance and for edification.... The exclusive Jewish interpretation and the exclusive Christian interpretation are equally wrong. Each is correct in what it affirms, and incorrect in what it denies.[3]

The promise, then, was both national and cosmopolitan. Israel would yet receive what God had unconditionally promised: nationhood, a Davidic king, land, and wealth. But so would the nations of the earth receive the promised blessing in Abraham's seed. Indeed, the very ends of the earth would turn to the Lord (Ps 72:11, 17). Such cosmopolitan implications of this great promise would later be the subject of the Jerusalem Council in Acts 15, and Paul would make the whole topic part of his discussion of the redemptive and soteriological plan of God in Romans 9 – 11.

Therefore, we conclude that the promise of God in the prophets was a single unified plan, which was eternal in its scope and fulfillment even though there were climactic plateaus reached along the way in the history of its development. In its buildup, it was cumulative. In scope, it was both national and cosmopolitan as Israel and all tribes, peoples, and nations were linked by faith in a single program. Such a doctrine of Mes-

3. Ibid., 383.

siah and many of its accompanying features was, according to E. Jenni,[4] without any real counterpart in ancient Near Eastern literature or ideology.

The Promise in the Ninth Century

The division of the kingdom after the days of David and Solomon was the first in a series of crises Israel would face as a result of the corrosive effects of sin. Inexorably, the storm clouds of divine judgment would continue to gather as a host of prophetic seers pleaded with the northern ten tribes (also called "Ephraim," or often just "Israel" vis-à-vis Judah) and the two southern tribes (which included Benjamin and is most frequently called just plain "Judah" to represent both) to repent and abandon the ruinous course they had chosen. But as the nation continued adamant and resolute in its preference for evil, idolatry, and rebellion against God, the prophets declared with increasing definiteness that the people of God must once again experience the crucible of divine judgment before being delivered and finally allowed to fulfill their true destiny. Thus the present form of the divine institution of the nation had to be judged, but this would be followed by another new day, new servant, new covenant, and new triumph from God.

The first signal of this new development appeared in Elijah and Elisha (1 Kings 17 – 2 Kings 9), whose direct involvements into the political arena of the northern kingdom were more pronounced in their actions than in their speaking. In their persons, they symbolized two aspects of the divine power toward the people: Elijah's work featured the divine judicial power opposing a rebellious people who were set on bringing on themselves wholesale destruction; Elisha was the dispenser of divine blessing when people repented.[5] But the extended word of God soon came through a long line of writing prophets. Without pretending to claim finality, it may be cautiously argued with a reasonable degree of assurance that Obadiah and Joel were the first of these writing prophets.[6] And for both of them, a future "day of the Lord" (*yôm YHWH*) was the theme of their message. This day was signaled and foreshadowed by its partial presence already in the tragic events of Edom's malicious joy over witnessing her rival, Jerusalem, being humiliated by an invader (as told by Obadiah), and also in a devastating locust plague and drought (as told by Joel) in Israel.

But regardless of any *present* effects of that impending day, its final appearance would be a time of divine reckoning with Israel and all nations when the Lord personally returned and revealed his righteous character. It would be a time more marked by

4. E. Jenni, "Messiah," *Interpreter's Dictionary of the Bible* (Nashville: Abingdon, 1962), 3:361.

5. This symbolism I owe to Conrad von Orelli, *The Old Testament Prophecy of the Consummation of God's Kingdom Traced in Its Historical Development*, trans. J. J. Banks (Edinburgh: T & T Clark, 1889), 194.

6. For a discussion of the history of this dating, see Leslie Allen, *The Books of Joel, Obadiah, Jonah and Micah* (Grand Rapids: Eerdmans, 1976), 129 – 33. The detailed proofs set forth by Caspari in 1842 still seem to be preferable to a 587 BC or postexilic date. Thus the book may be placed in the reign of Jehoram (2 Chr 21:8 – 10, 16 – 17), 848 – 841 BC; cf. G. L. Archer Jr., *A Survey of Old Testament Introduction*, rev. ed. (Chicago: Moody Press, 1974), 299 – 303. See also David W. Baker et al., *Obadiah, Jonah and Micah* (Downers Grove, IL: InterVarsity Press, 1988).

its contents than by its length of time or duration. Like the "latter days" or "last age" (*'ahªrît hayyāmîm*), which began to be discussed in Genesis 49:1 and Numbers 24:14, the day of the Lord is that time of world judgment when God will make known his supremacy over all nations and even nature itself.[7] Yahweh will vindicate himself by his great works, which all people will recognize as divine in origin. Judgment will be universal, inescapable, and retributive.

The Book of Obadiah

Obadiah, with its twenty-one verses, is the shortest book in the Old Testament. Obadiah, along with Malachi, is identified only by his name, which some have taken in both cases to describe their mission rather than their identities: Obadiah, meaning "servant of the LORD" (which appears in 1Ki 14:18; 2Ki 17:23 as a title for a prophet), and Malachi, meaning "my messenger." While treated here as names for these prophets, a good case can be made for their being titles rather than names of the prophets.

Obadiah's message was a prophecy against Israel's eastern neighbor, Edom, who was descended from Esau (Ge 36). God's message to Edom dealt first of all with her pride over her geographical position, her wealth from taxing the trade routes that went by her nation, her alliances with many of these trading nations, and her attitude of self-sufficiency (Ob 2 – 9). Edom was also castigated for the violence she brought her brother "Jacob" (that is, Israel) and the way she stood aloof in the day of Israel's defeat and offered no help, thereby colluding with the enemy (Ob 10 – 14). Edom will be judged for what she has done, but Israel will be restored (Ob 15 – 21).

Edom and the Promise

For the first time in prophetic literature, we find the phrase "day of the LORD" in Obadiah. Because of Edom's pride (1 – 9) and her violent action against her brother Jacob (10 – 14), she would receive the same treatment as the heathen nations in that "day of the LORD" (15 – 21). Just as the Amalekites had represented the counterpoint to the kingdom of God by their savage rearguard action against the straggling, sick, and aged Israelites as they journeyed through the wilderness (Ex 17:8 – 15; Dt 25:17 – 19), so Edom also had come to represent the kingdom of human beings. Edom now was the "quintessence of heathenism"[8] (Ob 15 – 16; cf. Isa 34:2, 5 and Eze 35:14; 36:5). Marten Woudstra stated it clearly:

7. While the two expressions are never formally linked together, nor does "latter days" have the idea of judgment in it, Deuteronomy 31:17 – 18 does connect God's judgment with "that day" to come.

8. Patrick Fairbairn, *The Interpretation of Prophecy* (London: Banner of Truth Trust, 1964), 222.

> By divine command and approval this enmity [cf. Ge. 3:15] existed between the people of God and the nations, the latter viewed as representatives of the forces of unbelief.... A look at Ex. 23:22 ["I will be an enemy unto thine enemies"] should make it clear that this enmity was real....
>
> This accounts for the note of ultimate seriousness that runs through some of the Psalms, such as Ps. 137 and Ps. 139:21 – 22. In these Psalms the believing Israelite identifies himself with God's cause. That cause cannot triumph unless that which opposes it is brought low.[9]

In this case, to mock and rejoice over the "inheritance" of Yahweh, the house of Israel, and their hardships (e.g., Eze 35:15), was to mock and challenge Yahweh himself, for he had attached himself to one people and one country (Dt 4:33ff.) for the purpose of saving all. Besides, he was the Sovereign over all nations anyway (Dt 32:8, 9); hence, all jeering and degrading his work of blessing or judgment among Israel was strictly out of place. Thus Edom would not escape that imminent divine judgment that would also fall on all the nations.

However, in contrast to the destruction of these nations, there would be a remnant, a "group of escaped ones" (*p^e^lêṭâh*; cf. Joel 2:32 [3:5] and Isa 37:32, where it is parallel to the more common word for "remnant," *š^e^'ērît*), in Mount Zion (Ob 17), who would emerge victorious again under the impetus of the divine energy bestowed once more on them. Then Israel would again extend her rule over ancient Canaan and the territories surrounding it, including the Negeb, the Philistine country, Gilead in east-Jordan and Syria, and as far north as Zarephath in Lebanon — all this as promised to the patriarch Jacob and to Joseph (Ob 18 – 20). David and Solomon had partially ruled these lands, but had afterward lost them. However, they would all return in that day.

The method God would use to reestablish his rule would be through human "saviors" (*môšî'îm* — Ob 21) performing the office of "judging," "ruling" (*šōp^e^ṭîm*), just as they had in the days of the judges (Jdg 2:16, 18). Zion, that is, Jerusalem, would be their center, and "the kingdom would belong to the Lord" (Ob 21).

As for the fulfillment of this prophecy, Obadiah combined in one picture what history split into different times and events. Indeed, Judas Maccabaeus, John Hyrcanus, Alexander Janneaeus, and the Zealot opposition to the Roman rule later brought about the demise of the Edomites or Idumaeans.[10] But that was only a token pledge of the final triumph of God against all hostile kindred nations. Hence the day of the Lord ran throughout the history of the kingdom of God so that it occurred in each particular judgment as evidence of its complete fulfillment, which was near and approaching.

9. Marten Woudstra, "Edom and Israel in Ezekiel," *Calvin Theological Journal* 3 (1968): 24 – 25.

10. Flavius Josephus, *Antiquities of the Jews*, 12.8.1; 13.9.1; 13.15.4; *Wars of the Jews*, 4.9.7.

The Book of Joel

Given that (1) Joel is located between Hosea and Amos in the Hebrew canon of the Minor Prophets; (2) Judah's foes are the neighboring nations and not the later empires of Assyria, Babylon, or Persia; (3) over half of the seventy-three verses in the book are quoted elsewhere in the prophets; and (4) the book does not mention the name of any reigning king in Judah, it seems on balance best to place the time for the writing of this book in the days of Joash, king of Judah (835 – 796 BC), during his minority when the responsibility for ruling rested on the priests and elders.[11]

The book is written to explain the cataclysmic plague of locusts that hit the Judean countryside (Joel 1:2 – 4). However, it looked beyond this immediate circumstance to an eschatological "day of the Lord" when God would judge all the nations of the earth. The problem of the locust plague was further exacerbated by drought and fire (1:19 – 20). Accordingly, drunkards wept because there was no wine (1:5), priests mourned because there were no products for any sacrifices (1:9), and farmers despaired over the ruined harvests (1:11). It was high time for putting on sackcloth and fasting as the nation repented (1:13 – 14).

The day of the Lord offered no panacea and relief for the disobedient but rather was a day of awful destruction (Am 5:18). That future day of the Lord would be a day of darkness and gloom (Joel 2:30 – 31) and would involve the nations who had abused Israel (3:1 – 16).

Twice over Joel repeated, "Surely the LORD has done great things" (2:20, 21), thereby assuring all that God was still in charge of history and the elements of nature itself. The locusts had been God's messengers to alert a tone-deaf people that things had gone awry and it was high time to "rend [their] heart[s]" (2:13) and not merely their garments.

The allusions to the language of Joel in the New Testament are manifold, as illustrated by C. H. Dodd and David A. Hubbard:

1. The sound of the trumpet to announce that day (Joel 2:1; cf. 1Co 15:52; 1Th 4:16; Rev 8:6 – 11:19);
2. The use of the word "near" to signal how imminent the day was (Joel 1:15; 2:1; 3:14; cf. Mt 24:32; Mk 13:29; Jas 5:8);
3. Judgment on the Gentiles (Joel 3:1 – 14; cf. Mt 25:31 – 46);
4. The signs of the darkening of the sun and the stars (Joel 2:30 – 31; 3:15; cf. Lk 21:25; Rev 8:12);
5. The shaking of the heaven and the earth (Joel 3:16; cf. Heb 12:26);
6. The command to "put in the sickle, for the harvest is ripe" (Joel 3:13; cf. Mk 4:29);

11. See Walter C. Kaiser Jr., *A History of Israel: From the Bronze Age Through the Jewish Wars* (Nashville: Broadman and Holman, 1998), 336 – 37.

7. The comparison of the locusts to horses (Joel 2:4 – 5; cf. Rev 9:7, 9);
8. The prophecy of the coming of the Holy Spirit (Joel 2:28 – 32; cf. Ac 2:14 – 41); and
9. The invitation that "everyone who calls on the name of the Lord will be saved" as the foundation of the gospel promise (Joel 2:32; cf. Ac 2:21, 39).[12]

The Day of the Lord

The dreadful locust plague and the distressing drought were both harbingers of the great and terrible day of the Lord. Even though the time was late, there still was opportunity to repent. Yet it must be a heartfelt genuine sorrow for their sin and an about-face in life (Joel 2:12 – 13).

When the people responded with fasting, weeping, and prayer (2:15 – 17), "then the Lord was jealous for his land and took pity on his people"; the Lord answered their prayers (vv. 18 – 19).[13] Thus, with verse 18 the tone of this book reversed. Whereas judgment had prevailed from 1:1 – 2:17, now blessing and hope would dominate the remainder of the book. Such a change could be attributed to two reasons: (1) the Lord their God "was gracious and merciful, slow to anger, and abounding in steadfast love" (2:13*b*); and (2) the people repented by "tearing [their] hearts and not [their] garments" (v. 13*a*). In response to their repentance, God promised to bless them. The gifts of God fell into two groups: (1) the immediate blessing of a land that was once again productive (vv. 19 – 27), and (2) the promise of a future outpouring of the Spirit of God on all flesh (2:28 – 32 [3:1 – 5]). Blessing, then, was also to be part of the contents of that "day."

Meanwhile, the rest of the description of the day of the Lord was much like Obadiah's. It was "destruction from the Almighty" (1:15 – 16), "a day of darkness and gloom," "cloud and thick darkness" (2:2), an "exceedingly terrible" day; "who could bear it?" (v. 11).

But the day of the Lord was again more than judgment. It was a time of deliverance for all who would call on the name of the Lord (2:32), accompanied by cosmic signs heralding its arrival (vv. 30 – 31). And as already noted, it was characterized by the outpouring of the Spirit of God on all flesh (vv. 28 – 29).

The time set for the outpouring of the Spirit was left indefinite, "after this" (*'aḥ^{a}rê kēn*). Of course, the "after this" could refer back to 2:23*b*, where the former and latter rains would come "as before" (*bāri'šôn*); then somewhat later "after this" would the Spirit be poured out. Note, however, 2:29 [3:2] repeated the opening phrase of 2:28 ("I will pour out my Spirit") with just one slight change: "in those days" (*bayyāmîm hāhēmmâh*). Therefore, the eschatological meaning the apostle Peter gave to these

12. C. H. Dodd, *According to the Scriptures: The Sub-Structure of New Testament Theology* (London: James Nisbet, 1952), 62 – 64; David A. Hubbard, *Joel and Amos*, Tyndale Old Testament Commentary (Downers Grove, IL: InterVarsity Press, 1989), 38.

13. Despite an unexplained preference in many modern translations for a future tense for the four verbs in 2:18, there is little question (based on repeated and extensive usage of the same type of Hebrew constructions elsewhere) but that these must be rendered as past tense verbs.

verses on the day of Pentecost is to be found in 2:29 if it is not in 2:28. This outpouring could not have been in the immediate future, since verse 26 pictures a period of quiet prosperity preceding any world crisis introduced in verse 28.[14] When Peter quoted this passage on the day of Pentecost, he located this blessing "in the last days" (*en tais eschatais hēmerais*, Ac 2:17). Such a view of the duration of eschatological time beginning with the Christian era and stretching until the second advent is found in a number of New Testament passages (e.g., Heb 1:1 – 2; 1 Pe 1:20; 2 Pe 3:3). Furthermore, the same phenomena of having near and distant events, or multiple fulfillments, all being part of the single truth-intention of the author, appeared in Obadiah's vision of the day of the Lord with its more immediate victory over Edom and the distant total victory of the kingdom of God. Thus Pentecost was part of the day of the Lord. There would, however, be yet another final day — if not many in between — when God would pour out his Spirit like rain "on all flesh" (cf. Joel 2:23).

How extensive, then, would this supernatural blessing of the Spirit be? Usually when the Old Testament used "all flesh" (*kol bāśār*), it meant the whole of humankind (Ge 6:12 – 13; Ps 145:21 passim). In this present context, the phrase "your sons and your daughters," according to some, would definitely limit it to all Jews.[15] This is not altogether certain. What is certain is that difference of age (young and old), sex (sons and daughters), or position (servants or handmaidens, who most naturally would be Gentiles, not Jewish servants) would not affect the universality of this gift of the Spirit. Thus, what Moses had once mentioned as only a wishful ideal for every Israelite in Numbers 11:29 would now actually be realized. Israel would in that day not only serve the Lord as a kingdom of priests (Ex 19:6), but as prophets also. Undoubtedly, this benefit would be extended beyond the Jews, even as later on the apostle Paul saw its application in Romans 10:12 – 13 to all mankind.

Besides the downpour of God's Spirit on all flesh, heaven and earth would convulse with mighty signs similar to that great deliverance from Egypt when God sent the plagues of blood and fire (Ex 7:17; 9:24) and when he appeared on Mount Sinai in pillars of smoke (19:18). Thus the natural world would be brought into intimate connection with the judgment and salvation of God as he intervened in human history. The original judgment day of Joel 2:1 – 17, temporarily halted by Judah's repentance, must again appear in the future. But whoever would "call on the name of the Lord" during those days "would be delivered" (*yimmālēṭ*, "be slipped away"). In Mount Zion, the head of the kingdom of God, there would be "those who escape" (*pᵉlêṭâh*), "survivors" (*śᵉrîdîm*, 2:32 [3:5]). However, while nations escaped, Yahweh would judge and destroy

14. Von Orelli, *Old Testament Prophecy*, 205, n. 13.

15. As Allen, *Books of Joel, Obadiah, Jonah and Micah*, 98, n. 10 commented, the translation of JB and NEB, "all mankind," was therefore incorrect, hence the amazement in Acts 10:45 of a Gentile Pentecost. In Ezekiel 39:29 God had specifically promised to "pour out [his] Spirit on the house of Israel." But are not the two expressions different without being mutually exclusive of each other? It is interesting to note that Paul applied our passage to the universal call of the gospel in Romans 10:12 – 13.

all nations in the valley of Jehoshaphat (3:2 [4:2]), presumably all those who had not repented.

Again, there was an antecedent theology that had informed this doctrine of the day of the Lord (Ex 32:34; Dt 31:17 – 18, 29; cf. Ge 49:1; Nu 24:14; Dt 4:30). What had begun in Exodus 32:34 as a "day of my visiting" when "my angel" "will visit on them their sins" was now projected from that day in the nation Israel to the last age and involving all nations. The appointed "day of Yahweh's visiting" the sin of his people in judgment grew. It was not just "a day of his visiting," which might be any time of national chastisement; it was "*the* day of his visiting," one day that stood out as supreme when compared to other days. In that final conflict on the earth, King Yahweh would decisively defeat the assembled nations who rose up against the armies of God. Suddenly the sickle of judgment would begin to swing, and the reaping and treading of the winepress would commence. Heaven and earth would quake, and multitudes would charge into the battlefield of the valley of decision (Joel 3:13 – 4).

Joel 3:1 – 21 [4:1 – 21] became the classic passage for the rest of the Old Testament on God's final judgment on all nations. It also became the classic statement of the blessed result for the people of God. They would possess an exceedingly fertile land enriched with fountains of running water and dripping with wine and milk. And to climax it all, Yahweh would personally dwell in Zion.

This day of the Lord was repeatedly said to be "near" (*qārôb*, Ob 15; Joel 1:15; 2:1; 3:14; and later in Isa 13:6; Zep 1:7, 14; Eze 30:3 passim). Beecher cautioned:

> This representation is made by prophets who lived many generations apart, and therefore by prophets who knew that other prophets had made it generations before. Perhaps this indicates that the prophets thought of the day of Yahweh as generic, not an occasion which would occur once for all, but one which might be repeated as circumstances called for it.[16]

And, of course, that final time would be climactic and the sum of all the rest. Though the events of their own times fitted the pattern of God's future judgment, that final day was nevertheless immeasurably larger and more permanent in its salvific and judgmental effects.

16. Beecher, *Prophets*, 311; idem, "The Day of the Lord in Joel," *Homiletical Review* 18 (1889): 355 – 58; idem, "The Doctrine of the 'Day of the Lord' Before Joel's Time, *Homiletical Review* 18 (1889): 440 – 51; idem, "The Doctrine of the 'Day of the Lord in Obadiah and Amos," *Homiletical Review* 19 (1890): 157 – 60.

Chapter **8**

Servants of the Promise: Prophets of the Eighth Century BC

Amos, Hosea, Jonah, Micah, Isaiah

A flurry of prophetic activity was divinely inaugurated in the eighth century BC, mainly to warn the northern kingdom of an impending destruction if the nation did not repent and reverse her way of life. Unfortunately, except for minor responses such as Micah's preaching, which had a momentary effect on Judah (but not northern Israel) during Hezekiah's reign (Jer 26:18 – 19), the northern ten tribes plunged headlong into the destruction of her national existence and her capital. This eventually came in 722 BC as their capital, Samaria, fell shortly after Syria's leading city, Damascus, had fallen a decade previously in 732 BC.

Graciously, God provided as much as four decades of prophetic preaching prior to this calamity during the eighth century in hopes of avoiding this catastrophe, but it was all to no or little avail. Included in this group of proclaimers were Amos, Hosea, Jonah, Micah, and the greatest of them all, Isaiah. Some of them began their warnings and promises while the nation was still flushed with the success of Jeroboam II and the expanded territory, wealth, and luxury his reign had brought. The rich stalked the poor and favored the guilty of their own rank in the courts. And all alike lacked credibility when they tried to walk with *both* Baal and Yahweh. Religious practice became a cover for all sorts of sins — immorality, injustice, and lewdness. Judgment or repentance had to fall, or else God would no longer be credible.

The Book of Amos

The prophet Amos is the only person in the Bible with this name, which means something like "to bear" or "to place a load on." Amos did not begin as a prophet but was a breeder of sheep and goats of a special kind, known for their short legs and fine hair (Heb. *nōqēd*), and a dresser of sycamore trees. (If the fruit of a sycamore tree was nipped in the proper time, bitter fluid and insects would escape, rendering the fruit good, but only as a poor man's diet.) His hometown was Tekoa, a city six miles southeast of Bethlehem, overlooking the Dead Sea. Amos ministered during the reigns of Uzziah (792 – 740 BC) and Jeroboam II (793 – 753 BC), times of great wealth and luxury in Israel.

His book has one of the clearest outlines, easily followed by his repeated use of rhetorical clauses. In Amos's judgment messages on the surrounding nations as well as on Israel and Judah, he repeatedly used the formula "For three sins of ____, even for four, I will not turn back my wrath" (1:3 – 3:15). The atrocities listed in these six nations included extreme cruelty, slave trade, kidnapping, slaughter of women and children, and desecration of corpses — all violations in principle of the Noachic covenant.[1] Then came three messages of "Hear this word" (3:1 – 15; 4:1 – 13; 5:1 – 17), followed by two woes: "Woe to you" (5:18 – 27; 6:1 – 14). The book concluded with five visions in chapters 7 – 8 ("This is what the Sovereign LORD showed me"), with two interruptions in 7:10 – 17 by the priest of Bethel named Amaziah) and another in 8:1 – 3 ("Hear this"). There were also two theological interludes in 8:4 – 14 and 9:1 – 10. Finally, Amos prophesied the restoration of David's collapsing dynasty (9:11 – 15).

For such times as these, God had prepared this herdsman and a dresser of sycamore trees from the town Tekoa, in the "wild west" of Judah. This southerner was sent north sometime around 760 – 745 BC with an urgent message of judgment or of salvation if the people repented.

Judgment on the Nations along with Israel and Judah

The record of Amos's ministry, as already noted, was neatly laid out in three sections: (1) in 1:1 – 2:16 he thundered against Israel and her neighbors for their lack of righteousness toward one another and toward God himself; (2) in 3:1 – 6:14 he enjoined Israel to seek God (5:4, 6, 14) or get ready for a face-to-face showdown with him (4:12); and (3) in 7:1 – 9:15 he received five visions offering at first some escape, but then hardening to promise no way of escape except for God's eschatological offer of hope vis-à-vis the present certain doom.

Most clearly, Amos viewed God as Sovereign Lord over all the earth. Not only was he the deliverer of Israel from Egypt and the Amorites (2:9 – 10), but he had conducted the exodus of Philistines from Caphtor and the Syrians from Kir (9:7). These, together with the Ethiopians, had been uniquely favored by Yahweh. Consequently, all nations also had to meet his standard of righteousness. Each nation that failed to live up to that standard stood condemned, not by its own gods, but by the only one true God, Yahweh. The list of divine grievances against these nations was ticked off by Amos: barbarism in warfare by Damascus (1:3 – 5) and Ammon (vv. 13 – 15); slave raids and slave trad-

1. See Jeff Niehaus, "Amos," in *The Minor Prophets*, ed. Tom McComiskey (Grand Rapids: Baker, 1992), 340.

ing by Philistia (vv. 6 – 8) and Tyre (vv. 9 – 10); Edomite hostility against his brother Jacob (vv. 11 – 12); Moabite desecration of the bones of the pagan Edomite king (2:1 – 3); rejection of the law of God on the part of Judah (vv. 4 – 5); and moral deviations of the northern ten tribes (vv. 6 – 16). All nations needed to learn as quickly as possible that the norm set by the character and law of Yahweh marked the standards by which the righteous rule of God would judge all nations universally.

This Lord of history was a sovereign ruler by right of creation. In three hymns Amos celebrated the greatness of the one "who formed the mountains and created the wind and declared to man what his thoughts were" (Am 4:13; cf. 5:8 – 9; 9:5 – 6). Indeed, the Lord of Hosts was his name. Yet he was more than Creator. He also was the controller of history and the destinies of people. His use of famine, drought, blight, pestilence, and war could have a redemptive purpose if people would only listen; for even when they failed to listen to the *precept* of the word of his servants the prophets, perhaps they would listen to his *penalty* — imposed not in retribution for their sins so much as a device to capture their attention. Note the series of five penalties in Amos 4:6 – 11, falling like the toll of a funeral dirge one after the other, with the even sadder refrain after each blast of divine judgment, "Yet you did not return unto me, says the LORD" (4:6*b*, 8*b*, 9*b*, 10*b*, 11*b*). And then came the final and most devastating stroke of all: "Therefore ... prepare to meet your God, O Israel" (4:12). It was as if the referee had counted on the mat of the pinned wrestler, "One — two — three — four — five — You're out" — for that is what this "meeting" with God was: the end of the northern kingdom. Israel and Judah together had been warned that such was God's method of dealing with people and nations. They had been warned of such alternative prospects of compounded judgment, or blessing, depending on what their response was, as far back in the canon as Leviticus 26 and Deuteronomy 28. In fact, some of Amos's vocabulary was directly informed by these passages, as were many of his fellow prophets' expressions on this subject.[2]

The God Who Speaks

God did more than act in history: he spoke! And when he spoke, Amos was compelled to prophesy (3:8). The nexus between that reception of God's estimates, meanings, interpretations, or announcements and the prophet's proclamation of them was set forth in a series of cause and effect statements in 3:2 – 8. For example, could the trumpet blow in a city (like our air-raid siren) and the people not be afraid? Could two meet together (especially in a crowded place) except by appointment? Therefore, how could God speak and Amos not prophesy?

Repeatedly, Amos stressed Israel's remarkable position in history. When Amos reminded Israel, "You only have I known of all the families of the earth" (3:2), he was

2. See the fine discussion of this point by Douglas Stuart in his introduction to *Hosea — Jonah*, Word Biblical Commentary (Waco, TX: Word, 1987), xxxi–xliii.

not claiming favored status or a chauvinistic partisanship for Israel; he merely reminded them of God's election. The word to "know" in this covenantal context had nothing to do with recognition or acknowledgment of one's deeds; it had to do with God's gift of choice — an unmerited choice, as had been made plain in Deuteronomy 7:8 (and elsewhere), but a choice or an election for service, as Genesis 12:3 would always remind them and us.

Likewise, all supercilious indulgence in solemn assemblies, feasts, offerings, and melodies were offensive to God, who inspected the heart of the worshiper first. A more pertinent prerequisite to meaningful religious observances was righteousness and justice (5:21 – 24). Otherwise all religious practice was despised and rejected by Yahweh.

The Day of the Lord

In the same class belonged all the talk about longing for the day of the Lord as a panacea for all the present ills of society — as if Israel knew what she was talking about (5:18 – 20). For those who were not prepared for the day of the Lord, it was to be a day of darkness. To make it even more graphic, Amos could describe the unreality of these religious escapists. That day would be like a man who fled from a lion only to meet a bear; and when he had shrewdly escaped both of these disasters, he went into his house and leaned on the wall, only to be bitten by a serpent. That day was not to be fooled with or desired above all other days if people were not living and walking in the truth.

No less dangerous was the peril of complacency (6:1 – 8), with no compassion for the needs of others or concern for the threatening disaster about to fall on Samaria. While the prophet's prayer of intercession for Israel did rescue her from certain trouble on two occasions (7:1 – 3, 4 – 6), when the plumb line of righteousness was dropped alongside the nation, she was out of line morally (7:7 – 9), and national calamity was now a foregone conclusion (8:1 – 3; 9:1 – 4).

The Fallen House of David

Nevertheless, there was hope beyond this disaster of the fall of Samaria. With a grand theological climax to the book in 9:11 – 15, God promised to rebuild David's house/dynasty, which in its current dilapidated condition could only be likened to a "fallen booth" or "hut" (*sukkâh*). What was normally styled "the house (*bêt*) of David" (2Sa 7:5, 11; 1Ki 11:38; Isa 7:2, 13), or dynasty of David, would shortly be in a collapsed state with "breaches" and "ruins" in it. The Hebrew active participle stressed either its *present* state of collapse or that it already was a "falling" house, in a state of ruin, or a house "about to fall." Thus the dynasty of David would suffer, but God would bring it back from its ruined condition, for he had promised David that his was an eternal house.

The suffixes on the words in 9:11 have special interest for the theologian. C. F. Keil commented on this passage, that the feminine plural suffix on "breaches *thereof* (*pirṣêhen*) could only refer to the tragic division of the Davidic house (which symbolized the kingdom of God) into two kingdoms, north and south (cf. 6:2, "these kingdoms").[3] God would, however, "wall up their rents." Thus, even before Ezekiel (37:15–28) had pictured the unification of the ten northern tribes with the two southern tribes, Amos had envisioned the same result. The masculine singular suffix on "*his* ruins" (*h^{a}risōtāyw*) referred to David himself and not to the "hut," which is feminine.

Thus, under a new, coming David (the Messiah himself), the destroyed house of that promised line of David would rise from the ashes. God would also "rebuild her [*b^{e}nîtîhā*] as in the days of old." The suffix is feminine singular this time and naturally refers to the fallen hut that would be rebuilt. But the phrase "as in the days of old" clearly points back to the antecedent theology of 2 Samuel 7:11–12, 16, where God had promised that he would raise up David's seed after him and give him a throne, a dynasty, and a kingdom that would endure forever.

The interpretation of the Davidic promise in 2 Samuel 7 as a "charter for humanity" (2Sa 7:19) was repeated here by Amos (9:12): "That they may possess the remnant of Edom, even all nations who are called by my name." For many scholars, verse 12 is even more problematic than verse 11—especially with its allegedly offensive reference to "the remnant of Edom" (*š^{e}ērît ^{e}dôm*). Gerhard Hasel[4] noted that Amos employed the remnant theme in a threefold usage: (1) to counter the proud claim that all Israel was the remnant (3:12; 4:1–3; 5:3; 6:9–10; 9:1–4); (2) to describe a true remnant from Israel (5:4–6,15), an eschatological sense; and (3) to include the "remnant of Edom" along with the other neighboring nations as benefactors of the Davidic promise (9:12). It was this representative role of Edom, which we saw in Obadiah, that was singled out again here. For the epexegetical or appositional note in verse 12, "and/even all the nations/Gentiles who are called by my name," surprisingly did not cast Edom in the role of being vanquished by David's or Israel's military machine; rather, it speaks of its spiritual incorporation into the restored kingdom of David along with all those Gentiles who were likewise "called by his name."

The usage of the phrase "called by my name" in the Old Testament always placed each of the objects so designated under divine ownership.[5] What God or humanity named, they thereby owned and protected, whether they were cities (2Sa 12:28; Jer 25:29; Da 9:18–19), or men and women (Isa 4:1; Jer 14:9; 15:16; 2Ch 7:14). Thus, when Israel walked by faith, Moses promised, "All the peoples of the earth shall see that you are called by the name of the LORD" (Dt 28:10). But when they refused to believe, they were "like those who [were] not called by your name" (Isa 63:19). The phrase is thus very much like Joel 2:32 [3:5]: "All who call upon the name of the LORD."

3. Carl Friedrich Keil, *The Twelve Minor Prophets*, in C. F. Keil and F. Delitzsch, *Biblical Commentary on the Old Testament*, trans. James Martin (Grand Rapids: Eerdmans, 1949), 1:303.

4. Gerhard Hasel, *The Remnant* (Berrien Springs, MI: Andrews University Press, 1972), 393–94.

5. For a full study, see W. C. Kaiser Jr., "Name," *Zondervan Pictorial Encyclopedia of the Bible*, ed. M. C. Tenney (Grand Rapids: Zondervan, 1975), 4:360–70.

The verb "to take possession of" (*yîršû*) was likewise chosen because of the antecedent theology in Balaam's prophecy of Numbers 24:17 – 18 that had predicted that a "star" and a "scepter" would rise in Israel "to take possession of Edom ... while Israel did valiantly." This one from Jacob would exercise dominion over all, predicted Balaam, for his kingdom would spread over the representatives of the earthly kingdom present already in that early day: Moab, Sheth, Edom, Amalek, and Asshur. Yet does not Amos now add to the ancient divine revelation that God would by divine plan "take possession" of a righteous and believing "remnant" from all nations, including even bitter Edom? Thus, some believing Edomites, along with all others who called on the name of the Lord would, to use Paul's term, be "grafted" into Israel as part of the people of God.[6]

The Book of Hosea

Hosea, which means "salvation of Yahweh," was the son of Beeri. His prophecy contains many words that appear only once in the Old Testament (*hapax legomena*), with many other rare meanings to some of the more common words, along with some unusual grammatical constructions. Some of his verses are like self-contained sermons reflecting a wisdom style in their epigrammatical terseness.

It is unusual to have the life story of the prophet as part of his message, but since this life and marriage spoke so forcefully of God's broken relationship with his people Israel, his story forms the first three chapters of this book. The key to the rest of the book lies in Hosea 4:1, where the prophet bemoans the fact that there is: (1) no truth (*ᵉmet*), (2) no love (*ḥesed*), and (3) no knowledge of God (*daʿat ʾelōhîm*). These topics are treated in reverse order in the book itself: the lack of the knowledge of God (Hos 4:2 – 6:3), no loving-kindness (6:4 – 11:12), and no truthfulness (12:1 – 14:9). However, note that after each section of condemnation, there is a rosy-tinted prophecy of a better day coming in the mercy and grace of God (Hos 6:1 – 3; 11:1 – 11; 14:1 – 9). No wonder some have called the book of Hosea "the heart and holiness of God" or "the gospel of John in the Old Testament."

Freely Loving Israel

In no prophet is the love of God more clearly demarcated and illustrated than in Hosea. The prophet's marital experience was the key to both his ministry and his theology. It was a picture of the holiness of God righteously standing firm, while the heart of God tenderly loved that which was utterly abhorrent.

6. See Walter Kaiser Jr., "The Davidic Promise and the Inclusion of the Gentiles (Amos 9:1 – 15 and Acts 15:13 – 18): A Test Passage for Theological Systems," *Journal of the Evangelical Theological Society* 20 (1977): 97 – 111.

Hosea bore this message of the love of God in his life as well as in word. He had been commanded at the inception of his ministry to marry Gomer, Diblaim's daughter, for so the expression "go and take to yourself a woman" (1:2) meant.[7] Since her name and her father's name appear to lack any special meaning or significance in and of themselves, and since everything appears to be in strict narrative prose, I have rejected the allegorical or visionary interpretations of the prophet's marriage. Rather, in our understanding of the grammar of the passage, Gomer was not a harlot when Hosea married her, just as her unborn children were not "children of harlotry" until after they had been born and received a stigma on their name because of their mother's loose style of living. For the only children mentioned are those she bore to Hosea (note especially 1:3, "She bore him a son."); and since he named the children (1:4, 6, 9), they were in all probability their own children.

The construction of Hosea 1:2*b* has proven troublesome to many: "Go, take to yourself a wife of harlotry and children of harlotry." This can signify result rather than purpose, as it does in Isaiah 6:9 – 12 and Exodus 10:1; 11:10; 14:4. Thus it was a way of stating at once the divine command and the subsequent result and experience. And so it was in Hosea 2:2, 5, 7, that Gomer, like Israel, left the security of her marriage and chased after other lovers. That pattern of marital fidelity at first, followed by physical and spiritual promiscuity, was exactly what Jeremiah 2:2 would remind Israel of in a later time: "I remember your youth when you went [devotedly] after me in the wilderness."

The Days of Honeymoon in the Wilderness

Therefore God will once more "allure her … into the wilderness and speak tenderly to her" (Hos 2:14 [16]), even as Hosea was commanded by God, "Go, show love to your wife again, though she is loved by another and is an adulteress" (3:1). All this was simultaneously aimed at the physical and spiritual harlotry of Israel; for as God commanded, Hosea named his children Jezreel ("God will scatter"), Lo-ruhamah ("not pitied"), and Lo-ammi ("not my people"). Only the unyielding love of Yahweh could reverse the judgment of that generation, for there was a day coming when, in accordance with the ancient promise, the people would be as innumerable as the sand on the seashore (Hos 1:10 [2:1]; cf. Ge 22:17; 32:12). In that day Israel would "be sowed by God" (Jezreel) and be called "My people" (*'ammî*), "sons of the living God" (Hos 1:10 – 11 [2:1 – 2]; 2:23 [25]). This vocabulary is very reminiscent of the Mosaic revelation (Ex 4:22; 34:15 – 16; Dt 31:16), though more extensively developed by Hosea. Yahweh's love would remain true, in spite of Israel's unfaithfulness (3:1); for even after the appropriate discipline, she would be betrothed again to him (2:19 [21]). Such love went back to God's deliverance of the nation from Egypt (12:9 [10]; 13:4). The threat of symbolically returning her to Egypt (8:13; 9:3; 11:5) is another

7. See elsewhere: Ge 4:19; 6:2; 19:14; Ex 21:10; 34:16; 1Sa 25:43. Note also the figure of speech, zeugma, where one verb joins two objects while it strictly only goes with one of them: "Take to thee a wife … and children." Cf. Genesis 4:20: "Such as dwell in tents and cattle"; also in 1 Timothy 4:3.

reminder of the Mosaic warning in Deuteronomy 28:68. Nevertheless, his love will still triumph. Hosea presents Yahweh as a father watching his son take his first steps (11:1ff.), a physician helping Israel (7:1; 11:3; 14:4), and a shepherd (13:5).

The Grace of God

Thus there is a dual emphasis in Hosea: the righteousness of God, and the love of God. Because he is righteous (2:19 [21]; 10:12), people should "turn" (*šûb*) to the Lord (5:4; 6:1; 7:10; 11:5; 12:6 [7]; 14:2) and "seek" (*bāqaš* in 3:5; 5:6, 15; 7:10; also *šāḥar* in 5:15; *dāraš* in 10:12) him. Some of the most gracious calls to repentance in all Scripture are found in 6:1 – 3 and 14:1 – 3. Thus judgment could not have the last word; God's grace would: "Afterward the Israelites will return and seek the LORD and David their king … in the last days" (3:5). This would not be the deported Davidic king but the promised messianic descendant of David (2Sa 7; Am 9:11ff.).

God's *ḥesed*, which was the only word the prophet had to describe "the riches of God's grace in the heart of God,"[8] would be evident when he again betrothed Israel (2:19 [21]). Thus he would "keep covenant and covenantal love" as the older texts had promised (Dt 7:9, 12; 1 Ki 8:23; cf. later Ne 1:5; 9:32; Da 9:4; 2Ch 6:14). He would do this "because he loved your father, therefore, he chose their seed after them" (Dt 4:37). For her part, Israel owed the same "loyal love" (*ḥesed*) to Yahweh (Hos 4:1; 6:4, 6; 10:12; 12:6 [7]). This was one of the three important catchwords in God's "controversy" (*rîb*), or court case with Israel (4:1). She had no "truth" (*ᵉmet*), no "loving-kindness" or "loyal love" (*ḥesed*), and no "knowledge of God" (*daʿat ᵉlohîm*).

No Knowledge of God. Each of the three charges in 4:1 was then taken up in reverse order, and each section closed with a bright picture of a better future when God's love would break through the barrier of Israel's persistent sin. Their lack of the "knowledge of God" (4:1, 6; 5:4) was evident from their physical and spiritual harlotry. Usually the expression "knowledge of God" meant theology or doctrine; what Israel lacked was *respect* for the law of God—for example, five of the Ten Commandments are given as samples in 4:2. But it also referred to a personal experience (cf. 5:4; 6:2; 13:4) and relationship with the only true God.

Accordingly, God would "return to [his] place until they … sought [his] face" (5:15). The first section (4:2 – 5:15) ended with a beautiful promise in 6:1 – 3 of a day when God would heal the people after he had torn them. People would then know the Lord, for he would raise them up again.

No Loving Graciousness. The second charge of no *ḥesed* was proffered against them in 6:4 – 10:15, but the glowing promise of God's love in 11:1 – 11 concludes that section. Yahweh's heart *recoiled* within him when he thought of giving up the northern tribes

---

8. George Farr, "The Conquest of Grace in the Book of Hosea," *Zeitshcrift für alttestamentliche Wissenschaft* 70 (1958): 102.

(11:8; cf. Dt 29:23, where the same verb "to overthrow" is used of the cities of Sodom, Gomorrah, Admah, and Zeboim); and his compassion was deeply stirred.

No Truth. The third section in 11:12 [12:1] to 13:16 [14:1] took up the charge of a lack of "truth" (*ᵓᵉmet*) or "faithfulness" (*ᵓᵉmûnâh*) and ended with a magnificent appeal and promise in 14:1 – 9 [2 – 10]: God's words and free love would be all that Israel would need. The promised blessing would be restored if Israel would return to the Lord and offer the sacrifice of her lips:

> "I will ransom them from the power of the grave;
> I will redeem them from death.
> Where, O death, are your plagues?
> Where, O grave, is your destruction?" (Hos 13:14)

Thus God would redeem his people at last, for any changing of his mind on this point was unthinkable (13:14b).

The Book of Jonah

Jonah was a happier preacher when he spoke of the expansion of the kingdom of God (2Ki 14:25) than he was a messenger of good news to a people who had barbarically invaded Israel — the Assyrians, who had been a thorn in Israel's side for generations. Jonah was given a commission to alert these Gentiles, whom he regarded as savage criminals, about a forty-day period until the wrath of God would fall on them. But such an announcement, reasoned Jonah, risked the possibility that some, or perhaps many of them, would be converted and extended the same grace that God had given to Israel.

Jonah decided to ship himself out of the country and go in the opposite direction of the call of God — to Spain! However, God graciously brought him back — special delivery — in an astounding set of circumstances, so that Jonah became a "sign" in his own person, as Jesus would say (Mt 12:38 – 41; 16:1 – 4; Lk 11:29 – 32), of the grace and mercy of God to the Ninevites, as well as a sign of Jesus' burial for three days and three nights.[9] Here was a book in the Old Testament entirely devoted to extending the good news of the gospel to a hostile nation of Gentiles! Such was the promise-plan of God.

Mission to the Gentiles

Thus, God's grace was extended to the most hostile and aggressive of Israel's Gentile neighbors — the Assyrians. Surprisingly, they were even more responsive to God's

9. This statement of "three days and three nights" is a formulaic expression in which any part of any of the three units counted as a full day and night. Thus, in 1 Samuel 30:12 – 13, David catches up with an Egyptian servant who served in the Amalekite army but who had taken sick and was abandoned "three days and three nights" ago, for "today is the third day" (literal trans.).

messenger than was Israel, much to the chagrin of Jonah. He had enjoyed prophesying about the expansion of Israel's national borders (2Ki 14:25) during the reign of Jeroboam II (793 – 753 BC). But to announce God's judgment to Nineveh, a mere forty days hence, was to provide an opportunity for her repentance and for God's merciful reprieve of his judgment. This Jonah disliked with a passion.

The theology of the book of Jonah thus revolves around the extension of the grace of God to Gentiles.[10] It is another amplification of Genesis 12:3. Much of its teaching centered on the character of God as already revealed in Exodus 34:6. As Jonah was reminded in Jonah 4:2, the Lord is gracious, merciful, slow to anger, and abounding in grace (*ḥesed*). Yahweh is creator of all (1:9) and the ruler of all affairs of life, as shown by his control of the sea (v. 15) and in his special appointments of a great fish (v. 17), a plant (4:6), a worm (v. 7), and a sultry east wind (v. 8). His power was not limited at all; he was the judge of all the earth (Ge 18:25). He was the leading actor in this book; and his was the first word, according to Jonah 1:2, and the last word (4:11).

God's Grace to Nature, Nineveh, and the Nervous Prophet

Nineveh had cost the only living God no end of toil and effort; therefore, why should he not have pity on it, as Jonah had expressed his pity on a castor oil plant (*qîqāyôn*), which, by contrast, had cost Jonah no effort and no labor? The elliptical form of these two verses is even more graphic when viewed against the clear theology of the book: God will have Gentiles to share in his grace as well. Accordingly, as Jonah affirmed in his credal confession of 1:9: "I fear Yahweh," so the polytheistic mariners "feared the LORD exceedingly" and "offered a sacrifice to Yahweh and made vows" (1:16).

So did the Ninevites affirm God's sovereignty in 3:9, saying, "Who knows? God may yet repent and turn from his fierce anger." Nineveh was spared as Jonah himself had been delivered from drowning — the subject of his prayer of thanksgiving in Jonah 2, which was heavily laden with quotes from the Psalter.

Saving Gentiles was not new to the divine plan. God had been doing so for a long time now — as in the case of Melchizedek, the multitudes who left Egypt with the Israelites, and others such as Jethro, Rahab, Ruth, and those of their kind. They too were objects of God's mercy, even as Amos 9:7 had claimed. Now Nineveh could claim that same distinction.

The Book of Micah

The Judean prophet from Moresheth was named Micah, meaning "Who is like/or compares to?" His name seemed to embody the essence of his message as well, for the book

10. For a good overall evaluation of the book, see John H. Stek, "The Message of the Book of Jonah," *Calvin Theological Journal* 4 (1969): 23 – 50.

concluded with what could well be called the whole purpose for his writing this short prophecy. Micah 7:18 asked, "Who is a God like you, who pardons sin and forgives the transgression of the remnant of his inheritance?" This compassion and forgiveness of God were directly linked to the promise-plan of God offered to Jacob, Abraham, and their ancestors "in days long ago" (7:20).

Micah laid out his material in three sections, each marked by the rhetorical device of "Hear (*šimʿû*). O peoples" (1:2 – 2:11); "Listen (*šimʿû*), you leaders of Jacob" (3:1 – 12); and "Listen (*šimʿû*) to what the LORD says" (6:1 – 7:7). These oracles of judgment, however, were each followed with oracles of salvation and the blessing of God (2:12 – 13; 4:1 – 5:15; and 7:8 – 20). Thus, as with many of the other prophets of the Old Testament, Micah was a prophet of hope as well as of doom and judgment. Destruction would indeed come if there were no repentance, but a "remnant" would always remain (2:12; 4:7; 5:7 – 8). God's final word was not doom, but hope, deliverance, and a salvation as pledged in the promise-plan of God.

Ruler of Israel

Micah, like his contemporary Isaiah (e.g., Isa 40:18, 25), stressed God's incomparability. Yahweh was "the Lord of all the earth" (4:13); and this was evident, as with most of the prophets, in the dual combination of divine works: judgment and salvation.

In three messages — each beginning, as already noted, with "Hear" (*šimʿû*) (1:2; 3:1; 6:1) — Micah decried the sin of Israel and Jacob. Their sins ran the whole gamut of wickedness, including idolatry (1:7a), harlotry (v. 7b), greed (2:1 – 2), perversion of true doctrine and religion (2:6 – 9; 6:2 – 7), false prophets (3:5 – 6), the occult (v. 7), and presumption (vv. 9 – 11). They had repeatedly broken the Ten Commandments: the so-called second table (6:10 – 12) and the first table (vv. 13 – 15).

But God promised to intervene. The vocabulary of theophany, complete with the now-familiar themes of earthquake and fire, opened the prophecy in 1:2 – 4. Yahweh would come to destroy the northern kingdom and its capital, Samaria. This local intervention was the start of God's judgment, which always began at the house of God; but that same anger and wrath would also be worked on all "the nations that did not obey" him (5:15).

Messiah, the Breaker

Yet Micah was no more able to rest his case there than was any other prophet of judgment or doom. He too ended each of his three sections with those glimpses of bright hope that sparkled with the ancient threads of the promise. Thus Micah 2:12 – 13 was the first such word of hope. So sudden was this about-face that most cannot see how the same prophet could have shifted so quickly from his words of doom. But Leslie Allen[11] has shown how

11. Leslie Allen, *The Books of Joel, Obadiah, Jonah and Micah* (Grand Rapids: Eerdmans, 1976), 301.

similar this word was to one credited to Isaiah in 2 Kings 19:31. He also noted that the word "gate" in verse 13 harked back to "the gate of Jerusalem" in 1:12 and "the gate of my people" in verse 9. Therefore, it did fit the internal scheme and context of the writer.

Its meaning was twofold: Yahweh would regather his sheep, the "remnant of Israel," in some unspecified future day and lead them through the gate as their "Head" and "King." Three times in verse 12 Jacob and Israel were promised the same deliverance as they had experienced from Egypt (Ex 13:21; Dt 1:30, 33). "All of you," promised Micah, will be assembled and led by the "breaker" (*happōrēṣ*, the bellwether, the leading ram) through the gates of their enemies' cities. Just as Sennacherib's blockade of Hezekiah, confining him to the inside of Jerusalem, had been swept away suddenly in a most decisive way, so it would be on that wonderful day when King Yahweh led his people's procession in their new return.

The Mountain of the House of the Lord

The heart of Micah's message of hope was set in chapters 4 – 5. Here he moved in three stages. He first assured Jerusalem that in spite of the fact that it "would become a heap of ruins" (3:12), yet, as the prophet Isaiah would also say (Isa 2:2 – 4), "The mountain of the house of the LORD would be established as the top of the mountains" (Mic 4:1 – 5). The second stage (Mic 4:6 – 13), resembling Amos 9:11 – 15, assured Zion that she would ultimately triumph over all the nations, even though the "tower" of David would for a brief time lose its "former dominion" and "the daughter of Zion" would experience for a time the pangs of childbirth. But the grandest prediction saw all the travail of the years exchanged for a ruler named "Peace," who would be born in the little town of Bethlehem in fulfillment of the ancient promise (5:1 – 15).

These events would come to pass "in the latter days" (4:1), a phrase whose meaning already had been well established by antecedent theology: this was to be part of that future day of the Lord in the last times or the eschaton. Jerusalem itself would have its fortunes reversed. It would now be central in the thoughts, importance, and journeys of the nations. From that center would go out not only ethical and doctrinal teaching, but arbitration for all the nations as well (4:3*a*)! The result of Messiah's reign in Zion would be an unprecedented and uninterrupted era of peace and secure prosperity (vv. 3*b* – 4).

Again, Micah promised that a "remnant" would be regathered (4:7*a*) when the Lord would reign over them in Mount Zion (v. 7*b*). The "tower of the flock" (v. 8, *migdal ʿēder*), probably was a place near Jerusalem (Ge 35:21), about a mile from Bethlehem according to Jerome.[12] It therefore stood for David's birthplace by metonymy. The "hill" (4:8, *ʿōpel*), or Ophel, was the conventional name for the southeast slope of the temple hill in Jerusalem where King David had ruled. Both of these places would be restored

12. As quoted in Charles L. Feinberg, *Jonah, Micah, Nahum* (New York: American Board of Missions to Jews, 1951), 87. Others refer to the "sheep-tower" on the south end of the temple hill.

to their "former dominion" (v. 8). God was doing and watching over all these things, including the temporary demise of glory and the travail of the nation, according to his "plan" and "thoughts" (v. 12). In the end, Zion's military power would be as if she had an "iron horn" and her hoofs as bronze as she triumphed over her enemies (4:13; cf. Micah's probable namesake, Micah ben Imlah in 1 Ki 22:9).

From these pains of childbirth would come fruit. From Bethlehem or, according to its ancient name, Ephrathah (cf. Ruth 1:2), would come the Davidic "Ruler" (*môšēl*). As Conrad von Orelli commented:

> Out of Bethlehem, with scarcely the rank of a country-town, will come forth One whose name is here mysteriously suppressed, only the dignity that awaits him being mentioned.... Moreover, the next mysterious feature forms a significant contrast to the obscure birthplace of the Messiah: "His going forth from the gray foretime, from days immemorial." Does this only mean that His extraction is traceable to the earliest age, that He is thus of good race, as in fact (Ruth iv.11ff.) David's ancestors are traced back to Perez, son of Judah? Although it must be conceded that *'ôlām* in poetic-prophetic discourse has not always an unlimited range (cf. Amos ix.11), it would yield here a very tame sense, especially to the Hebrew, to think only of physical descent from Jesse the humble ancestor, or from Judah. The descent of every genuine Israelite even from Jacob-Abraham was understood as matters of course. Or does this weighty description, containing a twofold, far-reaching definition of time, teach the pre-temporal existence of the Messiah, so that we should have here as in John i.1ff., viii.58, an irrefutable testimony to Christ's pre-existence? The expressions *qedem*, *'ôlām*, and the general conceptions of the Israelites, are too little metaphysical to warrant such an inference. Moreover, strictly speaking, a premundane existence is not affirmed, but a coming from time immemorial. In Micah vii. 20, *qedem* is used in reference to the patriarchal promises. We therefore do most justice to the statement by taking it to mean that the future ruler from Bethlehem is he who has been in God's view in the development of things.... His beginnings are rooted in God's primeval redeeming plan.[13]

The scope of this new Davidic ruler's powers would be worldwide. He would defend Israel (5:5 – 6), enable them to overcome their enemies (vv. 7 – 9), and personally obliterate all weapons of warfare (vv. 10 – 15). The "Assyrian" of verse 5 is typical and representative of all of Israel's enemies in that future day when the nations shall attempt to deal once and for all with "the Jewish question." The result here is the same as that already traced in Joel 3. However, there will be adequate princes ("seven," even "eight," v. 5) to meet every onslaught from the enemy. The "remnant of Jacob" would be like dew and showers (v. 7), like a lion or a young lion (v. 8), a source of blessing for the righteous and conquest against the wicked.

13. Conrad von Orelli, *The Old Testament Prophecy of the Consummation of God's Kingdom Traced in Its Historical Development*, trans. J. J. Banks (Edinburgh: T & T Clark, 1889), 307 – 8.

What God required of people in the meantime (6:6) was (1) fair and just dealings with their fellow human beings, and (2) a diligent life of faith lived in close communion with God (v. 8). That was the epitome and quintessence of the law. Ceremonial exactitude as an end in itself was as despised by God as it was worthless to its participants.

The Conclusion to the Prophecy

Micah concluded his message with confident expectations for the future and prayers for Israel (7:7 – 20). "I will wait for the God of my salvation" (v. 7), he prayed in a hopeful psalm (vv. 7 – 10). And after praying for the accomplishment of God's purpose for his land and people (vv. 14 – 17; cf. vv. 11 – 13), he sang a hymn of praise to God (vv. 18 – 20) for his incomparable gift of forgiveness and for God's "steadfast love" (*ḥesed*) (v. 18), which again demonstrated just what he had sworn to their fathers, Jacob and Abraham.[14] Their sins and iniquities, not their persons, would be "cast into the depths of the sea" (v. 19). Micah's theology does indeed shout the question of Isaiah 40:18, 25, "To whom then will you liken God?"

The Book of Isaiah

Isaiah, the son of Amoz, has given us one of the most theological books of all the prophets. His name appears sixteen times in his book, and he appears frequently by name in 2 Kings and three other times in 2 Chronicles. His message began, he tells us, in the year that king Uzziah died (740 BC) and continued through the reigns of the Judean kings Jotham, Ahaz, and Hezekiah. It ended (according to tradition) when he was martyred during the reign of Manasseh (696 – 642 BC), giving Isaiah a ministry of almost sixty years.

The most characteristic phrase found throughout the whole book is "the Holy One of Israel," which appears thirteen times in chapters 1 – 39 and thirteen times in chapters 40 – 66. It is a phrase that expresses the moral character of God and reminds us of God's holiness in the tri-sanctus (i.e., the thrice holy One) song of Isaiah 6.

The times in which Isaiah preached, along with his fellow eighth-century prophets, were troublous times to say the least. These were the days of the Assyrian expansion to the west. In previous days, King Ahab had halted the Assyrian drive westward at the Battle of Qarqar in 854 BC, but now Tiglath-pileser III (nicknamed "Pul," 745 – 727 BC) invaded the Phoenicia coast and made King Rezin of Damascus and King Menahem of

14. The oath of God receives special treatment in Psalm 105:8 – 11. There and in all of its other occurrences (Ge 22:16; 26:3; 50:24; Ex 13:5, 11; 33:1; Num 11:12; 14:16, 23; 32:11; in Deuteronomy, Joshua, Judges, and Jeremiah 32:22) "the content of this oath is the gift of the land," according to James L. Mays, *Micah: A Commentary* (Philadelphia: Westminster Press, 1976), 168 – 69.

Samaria pay him tribute. Later, Shalmaneser V (726–722 BC) and Sargon II (721–705 BC) succeeded in conquering and carrying Samaria into captivity and introducing a mixed population into northern Israel.

Matters were not any easier for Judah, for she too felt the boot of Assyria as the tribute taxes increased and the nation's freedom was severely reduced. Such were the times in which Isaiah ministered.

The Promise-Theologian

Beyond all question, Isaiah was the greatest of all the Old Testament prophets, for his thought and doctrine covered as wide a range of subjects as did the length of his ministry. While his writing can be divided into two parts—with chapters 1–39 keyed mainly to *judgment* and chapters 40–66 primarily emphasizing *comfort*—the book stands as a unit with its own continuity features such as the unique and distinctive phrase "the Holy One of Israel."[15]

The second part of Isaiah's work is a veritable Old Testament biblical theology in itself. For Christians, it might well be called the "Old Testament book of Romans" or the "New Testament within the Old Testament." Its twenty-seven chapters cover the same scope as the twenty-seven books of the New Testament. Chapter 40 begins with the predicted voice of John the Baptist crying in the wilderness as do the Gospels: chapters 65–66 climax with the same picture as does the Apocalypse of John in Revelation 21–22 of the new heavens and the new earth. Sandwiched between these two end points is the midpoint, Isaiah 52:13–53:12, which is the greatest theological statement on the meaning of the nature of the atonement in all Scripture.

No less significant, however, is the first part of Isaiah's writing. Its successive "books," to use Franz Delitzsch's term for outlining the book of Isaiah, are the books of Hardening (chaps. 1–6), Immanuel (7–12), Nations (13–23), the Little Apocalypse (24–27; 34–35), the Chief Cornerstone and Woes (28–33), and Hezekiah (36–39).[16]

Isaiah can be called the theologian's theologian. And when the continuing promise-plan of God was being considered, Isaiah excelled both in his use of the antecedent theology of the Abrahamic-Mosaic-Davidic promise and in his new contributions and development of that doctrine.

The Holy One of Israel

At the heart of Isaiah's theology was his call in chapter 6. While worshiping in the temple, he was given a vision of the Lord exalted on his throne with his glory—the

15. Conservatives have pointed to some forty additional phrases or sentences that appear in both parts of Isaiah as evidence for its unity, see Gleason L. Archer Jr., *A Survey of Old Testament Introduction*, rev. ed. (Chicago: Moody Press, 1974), 345ff.

16. Franz Delitzsch, *The Prophecies of Isaiah*, in C. F. Keil and F. Delitzsch, *Biblical Commentary on the Old Testament*, trans. James Martin (Grand Rapids: Eerdmans, 1969), 1:v–vii; 2:v.

skirts of his garments — filling the temple. Then he heard the angelic attendants chant the superlative holiness of God as he saw the earth-filling glory of God.

This vision, with its anthropomorphic but highly theological language, is the key to Isaiah's theology. In these two central concepts, "holiness" and "glory," Isaiah had set before him the themes for his prophecy and ministry.

Yahweh was the thrice holy God whose uniqueness, separateness, and transcendence were so immediately apparent even to the prophet that he cried out, "Woe is me; for I am undone; because I am a man of unclean lips" (Isa 6:5). Like Moses of yesteryear, Isaiah learned that since the Lord God was holy, Israel should also be holy. God's holiness was to be seen in his moral perfection, his righteousness, and his pure conduct.

But not only was Isaiah unfit in comparison to the holiness of God, so also was Israel: "I dwell in the midst of a people of unclean lips" (v. 5). That was the point of placing chapters 1 – 5 before the call of Isaiah in chapter 6. It spelled out the necessity and the real need for Isaiah's message to Israel to either repent or face judgment. Israel, at this point of her existence, was more the rebel (1:2, 4), hypocrite (vv. 10 – 15), and contemptuous breaker of the commandments (5:8 – 23) than God's "holy nation" or his "kingly priests."

Yahweh was holy or distinct from his people in his being as well as in his morality. The idols, the "work of men's hands" (2:8, 20), were "nothings" and "nonentities" (*ᵉlîlîm*, 2:8, 18, 20 [2x]). Beside Yahweh there was none other. Such transcendence and majestic sovereignty made the teaching of God's incomparability one of Isaiah's grandest doctrines, especially in the oft-repeated question of Isaiah 40:18 and 25: "To whom then will you liken me?"

Thus God's judgment had to fall when a stubborn populace hardened its heart as a result of hearing Isaiah's ministry of this word of holiness (6:9 – 12) but declining to make any response. Apparently, too many in Judah had mistaken the royal theology with its unconditional promise to David as a blanket approval of everything they did. The people falsely assumed that God would never visit Zion with destruction — for in so doing, he would only devastate his own promise and his everlasting plan. Therefore, according to their reasoning, God was stuck with them, for better or for worse, and at the moment it was admittedly worse. But the surprise was to be theirs. Isaiah announced that he would preach "until the cities lie waste without inhabitant, and houses without men, and the land was utterly desolate, and the LORD [had] removed [the] men far away" (Isa 6:11 – 12).

Such talk sounded treasonous. It admittedly sounded like a rejection of the patriarchal promise about the land and the Mosaic election of a people. That is where the second motif of Isaiah's vision of the Lord in the temple played its part: the glory of God.

The Glory of God

God's glory would yet fill the whole earth. There would indeed be a remnant, called here "a tenth" (*ᵃśîrîyyâh*, 6:13), which would remain like a stump after the tree is felled. And "the holy seed was its stump," said Isaiah, with a triumphant and obvious backward glance at the Abrahamic and Edenic word about the "seed" of promise. This theme he developed in the Little Apocalypse of Isaiah 24 – 27 and in 40 – 66.

The glorious final state "at the end of the days" of God's plan would see Jerusalem exalted as the center of the nations and the center for instruction in the paths of the Lord (2:2 – 4; cf. the discussion in Micah). Zion would be the center from which God's newly reconstituted people would come after catastrophic judgment (30:15). Thus, fair interpreters who take this call chapter (Isa 6) seriously do not find the theme of triumph and glory to be any more of an intrusion or a detraction (and hence, according to some, evidence of another hand or source) than is the demand for holiness with its accompanying threat of judgment. The two are authentic motifs in Isaiah.

The Branch of Yahweh

Who is the "sprout" or "branch" (*ṣemaḥ*) of Isaiah 4:2 – 6? Very few doubt that the one who is afterward called "the Branch" is the Messiah. Nor do they doubt that later prophets directly depend on Isaiah 4:2 for that title. Those prophets who use this same title for the Messiah are

"Branch of Yahweh" (Isa 4:2)
"Branch of David" (Jer 23:5 – 6)
"The Branch, My Servant" (Zec 3:8)
"Branch, a man" (Zec 6:12)

In Isaiah 4:2 the "Branch of Yahweh"[17] is the Davidic dynasty according to its human ("fruit of the land") nature as well as its divine nature ("of Yahweh"). In this case, "Branch" would be an equivalent term for "Anointed" or "Holy One."

But many object that "Branch" was not yet a fixed designation for Messiah; besides, its parallelism with "the fruit of the land" (4:2) favored a reference to the sprouting forth of the land under the beneficent influence of Yahweh. However, as the following chapters of Isaiah show, Messiah was the Mediator of these benefits, and he was himself the greatest of all the benefits.

Is it any wonder, then, that the later prophets applied this title to the living personal source of all these gifts in the last days? Some of those gifts found already in this passage are (1) the promise of the fruitfulness of the land; (2) the certainty of a remnant of "survivors"; (3) the holiness of the remnant; (4) the cleansing and purification of the moral filth of the people; and (5) the radiant glory of the personal presence of Yahweh dwelling in Zion with his people forever. The "holy nation" of Exodus 19:6 would finally be completely realized, as would the permanent "dwelling" of Yahweh in their midst. Even the "cloud by day" and "fire by night" (4:5) were to be renewed. For just as they

17. See Walter C. Kaiser Jr., *The Messiah in the Old Testament* (Grand Rapids: Zondervan, 1995), 156–58, and David Baron, *Rays of Messiah's Glory: Christ in the Old Testament* (1886; reprint, Grand Rapids: Zondervan, 1952), 71–128.

were the visible proofs of God's presence in the wilderness (Ex 14:19ff.), so they would be a shade by day and illuminate the night to shield the city of God from all violence.

Immanuel

What the previous "Branch [or Sprout] of the LORD" passage left indefinite was now given personal shape and definition in the Immanuel prophecies of Isaiah 7 – 11. This word came against the background of the Syro-Ephraimitic War, in which Pekah, king of Israel, made an alliance with Rezin, king of Syria, to advance against Ahaz, king of Judah, with a view to installing the son of Tabeal as their puppet king on David's throne. This threat to Jerusalem and Judah was countered by Isaiah's invitation to Ahaz to "believe" God in order that Ahaz himself might "be believed," that is, established (7:9). In fact, God would validate his good offer in so improbable a situation by performing any sign (i.e., miracle) Ahaz might choose from Sheol or heaven; he had only to ask and God would oblige him.

But Ahaz, true unbeliever that he was, piously rejected Yahweh's offer of help with an oblique reference to Deuteronomy 6:16 about not tempting the Lord his God. The truth of the matter was that he expected little from Yahweh; moreover, he had probably already secretly sought the support of Tiglath-Pileser, king of Assyria (2Ki 16:7ff.). Nevertheless, the Lord gave a sign anyway: "The virgin will be with child and will give birth to a son, and will call him Immanuel" (7:14).

Now it is important to note several things: (1) the word *ʿalmâh* denotes a "virgin" in every case where its meaning can be determined;[18] (2) it has the definite article, "the virgin"; (3) the verb "to call" is second person feminine and not third person feminine; and (4) the wording of this verse made use of older biblical phraseology: at the birth of Ishmael (Ge 16:11); at the birth of Isaac (Ge 17:19); and at the birth of Samson (Jdg 13:5, 7). Thus, the sign given to Ahaz consisted in repeating to him the familiar phrases used in promising the birth of a son.

But this passage dealt with the birth of three children, all three being signs in Israel (8:17 – 18). Each of the three was introduced and then was later the subject of an expanded prophecy as follows:

1. Shear-Jashub — "remnant shall return" 7:3 → 10:20, 21, 22; 11:11, 16
2. Immanuel — "God with us" 7:14 → 8:8, 10
3. Maher-Shalal-Hash-Baz — "haste spoil, hurry prey" 8:1, 3, 4 → 10:2, 6

> In each of these passages we have the mention of a child born in fulfillment of the promise that had been made to David, to the effect that his seed should be eternal.... In the second half of his discourse on the three children, Isaiah thus reiterates the promise that

18. Besides this text, it appears in the account of Rebekah (Ge 24:43); the sister of Moses (Ex 2:8); in the phrase "the way of a man with a maid" (Pr 30:19); and in the plural in Psalm 68:25 [26]; Song of Solomon 1:3; 6:8; and the titles to Psalm 46 and 1 Chronicles 15:20.

> had been made to David, and insists upon it. He makes it the foundation of his rebuke to the people for their corruptions....
>
> Those who heard him understood that when Ahaz refused to ask the offered sign, the prophet repeated to him, in a new form, Jehovah's promise concerning the seed of David, and made that to be a sign that Jehovah would both keep his present pledge and punish Ahaz for his faithlessness. It may be doubted whether any of them had in mind the idea of just such a person as Jesus, to be born of a virgin, in some future century; but they had in mind some birth in the unending line of David which would render the truth, "God with us," especially significant.[19]

Furthermore, before this son, the most recent birth in the line of David, was able to understand right from wrong (7:16 – 17), a political revolution of major proportions would remove both Pekah and Rezin from power. But several other facts must be borne in mind if one is rightly to identify this "son." According to 8:8, 10, he is addressed as the prince of the land ("thy land, O Immanuel") and as the expected anointed one of David's house in 9:6 – 7 [5 – 6] ("There will be no end of the increase of his government and peace [as he rules] on the throne of David over his kingdom ... forevermore."). Also Isaiah, like his contemporary Micah, everywhere presupposes that a period of judgment must precede the glorious messianic age. Therefore, whatever this sign and birth is, it cannot be the completion of the "last days."

Who then was this child? His messianic dignity totally excludes the notion that he may have been Isaiah's son born to some maiden newly married to the prophet after Shear-Jashub's mother supposedly died. Still less likely is it a reference to any marriageable maiden or some particular ideal maiden present at the time of the proclamation of this prophecy, since the prophet has definitely said "*the* virgin." It is preferable to understand him to be a son of Ahaz himself, whose mother Abi, daughter of Zechariah, is mentioned in 2 Kings 18:2 — namely, it is his son Hezekiah. It is well known that this was the older Jewish interpretation, but it is also supposed that Hezekiah could not be the predicted "sign" of 7:14, since on present chronologies he must have already been nine years old at that time (about 734 BC). That last point is to be thoroughly studied before it is adopted. The chronology of Israel and Judah has been well secured with only one minor exception: a ten year difficulty in the rule of Hezekiah. Without arguing the point at this time, I would like to suggest that only Hezekiah meets all the demands of the text of Isaiah and yet demonstrates how he could be part and parcel of that climactic messianic person who would complete all that is predicted in this Immanuel prophecy. Only in this, the most recent installment in the Abrahamic-Davidic promise, could it be seen how God was still being "with" Israel in all his power and presence.[20]

19. Willis J. Beecher, "The Prophecy of the Virgin Mother: Isa. vii:14," *Homiletical Review* 17 (1889): 357 – 58.

20. Walter C. Kaiser Jr., "The Promise of Isaiah 7:14 and the Single-Meaning Hermeneutic," *Evangelical Journal* 6 (1988): 55 – 70.

In Isaiah 9:6, a series of descriptive epithets is given to this newborn son who is to climax the line of David. He is "wonderful counselor," "mighty God," "Father of eternity,"[21] and "Prince of Peace." These four names, represent, respectively, (1) the victory due to his wise plans and great skill in battle; (2) the conqueror who brings home a remnant (cf. 10:21); (3) the fatherly rule of Messiah and his divine attribute of eternality; and (4) the everlasting peaceful reign of Messiah. His government and the peace during his regime would know no boundaries, for he would establish his kingdom in justice and righteousness forevermore (Isa 9:7). Unique among the descriptions of peace that will be observed during that era is the picture of all nature at rest and devoid of hostility (11:6 – 9). Again, there is a graphic prediction of the restoration of both the north and south to the land "in that day" (vv. 10 – 16). And from the stump of David's father, Jesse, would come that "shoot," even a "branch" (*nēṣer*), upon whom the sevenfold gift of the Spirit of the Lord would rest as he ruled and reigned righteously and awesomely (vv. 1 – 5). The whole picture of the future person and work of the Messiah was cast in terms of the Davidic promise as a glowing encouragement for Israel.[22]

The Lord of History

Yahweh's purpose and plan embraced the whole earth with all its nations. Nations rose and fell in accordance with that plan (Isa 14:24 – 27). But when national pride became exalted and motivated by imperialistic aggression, these nations were reminded quickly that they could not continue on ruthlessly. Even when they were the God-ordained instruments of judgment aimed at Israel, they were not to burn, kill, and destroy at will whomever they wished; for in that case, Yahweh would again remind them that they were merely his axes in their hands. The axe must not pretend that it was equal to the one who chops with it any more than the saw was greater than the one who sawed with it (Isa 10:15). So Assyria would learn that she served at the pleasure of the living God and not her own.

The prophecies concerning some ten nations were compiled in Isaiah 13 – 23. The most amazing of all is Isaiah 19. It is a burden message against Egypt wherein the Lord himself would bring judgment on Egypt's government (vv. 2 – 4), economy (vv. 5 – 10), and wisdom (vv. 11 – 13). As if to underline the source of these judgments, verse 14 again stresses that it was Yahweh who had mixed a spirit of confusion in Egypt.

However, there was to be another "day," part of that grand future "day." "In that day," Judah would terrify Egypt according to the plan of the Lord Almighty (19:16 – 17). And a harsh ruler would oppress his own Egyptian subjects (v. 20), but Yahweh would miraculously deliver Egypt so that she, along with Israel and Assyria, should be "thirds" together in worshiping the Lord and in inheriting from the Lord (vv. 24 – 25). Thus, even though the Lord would smite Egypt, he would heal her by sending a judge or "savior" as

21. It is not "Father of booty," which does not match the permanent attribute of "Prince of Peace"; rather, the Hebrew *ʾᵃbîʿad* is "Father of Eternity" as *ʿad* means in Genesis 49:26, Isaiah 57:15, and Habakkuk 3:6.

22. For further development of this theme, see Kaiser, *The Messiah in the Old Testament*, 148–67.

he had done for Israel in the period of the judges. Then Egypt would worship the living God along with Israel (vv. 18 – 19, 21 – 22).

As Yahweh had dealt with Samaria and Damascus in the Syro-Ephraimitic War, so would he deal with all nations. He alone would be sovereign in spite of all their supposed sovereignty. He would also finally triumph over them all. This process of shaking the nations is dramatically told in the "Little Apocalypse" of Isaiah 24 – 27.

The Chief Cornerstone

Proud Samaria was still standing when the prophecy of Isaiah 28 announcing the end of this "fading flower" of Ephraim was uttered. Yet there was a rebuke for Jerusalem also, for as in chapter 7, Judah had turned to Assyria instead of to the Lord for help. The word of the prophets was disregarded as so much trivia, for the people fancied themselves quite secure against death and Sheol. But they too were doomed. Their lies and deceit would shelter nothing: they would be caught in the overwhelming flood.

Meanwhile, Adonai, the sovereign Lord, was laying in Zion a foundation stone. The basic passage that informed the theology of this text was Genesis 49:24, where the "mighty one of Jacob" was called the "stone of Israel." Likewise, Deuteronomy 32:4 had identified God as a rock (*ṣûr*), and Isaiah 8:14 identified God as both a rock and stone. In contrast to the shaky shelter offered by lies, the stone stood firm and immovable.

Ever since the Davidic dynasty had been inaugurated, this stone had lain in Zion. It was therefore a "stone of testing," for men would be tested by it. Whereas in Isaiah 8:14 the Lord himself is called a Stone of Stumbling and a Rock of Offense, here the stone was his revelation and work in the world. That stone would be fixed in location and precious in value so that all who believed in him would not be restless. They would be quiet and relaxed in contrast to the excited, agitated, and false refuge previously offered by their lies.

It had been said of Abraham that he "believed" (*he'ᵉmîn*, Ge 15:6) and God added it up to him for "righteousness" (*ṣᵉdāqâh*). That faith was a full inward surrender to the Lord; it was a trust in the divine promise that was later repeated to the other patriarchs and to David, Solomon, and their line. The divine promise was the object and content of their faith. Isaiah's demand for faith appeared for the first time using the verb *he'ᵉmîn* in 7:9, and thereafter was used in 11:5 and 28:16. It was a believing trust, regarding God as a steadfast object of trust. The stem *bāṭaḥ* is used of belief in God in Isaiah 30:15, but it is also used of false confidence in Isaiah 30:12; 31:1; 32:9 – 11. Other great words of faith or belief in Isaiah are "hope" (*qiwwâh*, 8:17; 40:31); "wait for" (*ḥikkûh*, 8:17; 30:18); and "rest" (*nûaḥ*, 28:12 [2x]; 30:15).

Short Theology of the Old Testament

One of the most remarkable sections of all the Old Testament is Isaiah 40 – 66. In its general plan, it is laid out in three enneads — that is, sets of nine chapters: 40 – 48,

49 – 57, and 58 – 66. In each of these three sets of nine messages, the focus is directed to the particular aspect of the person and work of God. It is as close to being a systematic statement of Old Testament theology as is the book of Romans in the New Testament. Its majestic movement begins with the announcement of the coming person and work of John the Baptist and spins to the dizzy heights of the suffering and triumphant Servant of the Lord by the time the middle of the second ennead is reached. But this climax is again superseded by the concluding message on the new heavens and the new earth.

In each of the three sections there is a central figure. In Isaiah 40 – 48 the key figure is a hero who would come from the east to redeem Israel from captivity, namely, Cyrus. The revelation of this hero, coming as it did in the middle of the addresses (44:28 – 45:10), served as a bold challenge to the idols or deities embraced in that day to do likewise for the people. However, their inability to speak anything about the future could only lead to one conclusion: Yahweh was indeed the only God, and they were nothing at all.

In Isaiah 49 – 57 the central figure is the "Servant of the LORD," who combined in his person all the people Israel, the prophet and prophetic institution, and the Messiah in his role as the Servant of the Lord. Again, the climactic description and his most important work were located at the middle point of this ennead: 52:13 – 53:12. The salvation effected by this servant had both objective and subjective aspects (54:1 – 56:9); indeed, its final and concluding work would involve the glorification of all nature.

The third ennead, 58 – 66, triumphantly announces the dawning of a new day of salvation for nature, nations, and individuals. At the center of this ennead was a new principle of life — the Spirit-filled Messiah (61:1 – 63:6) who bore the powers and dignities of the prophetic, priestly, and kingly officers.

Thus in each successive ennead another aspect of the Godhead and God's work was celebrated. In order, the emphases fell on the persons of the triune God: Father, "Servant" (Son), and Holy Spirit. In work, they were: (1) Creator — Lord of history, (2) Redeemer, and (3) Sovereign Ruler over all in the eschaton. The five major forces in Isaiah's message were God, the people of Israel, the event of salvation, the prophet, and the word of God. Finally, this message even has several distinctive stylistic features. It has a plethora of divine self-asseverations, such as "I am the first and the last" or "I am Yahweh"; a long series of participial phrases after the formula "Thus says the LORD" or "I am the LORD," which continue on to detail his special character; and a profuse number of appositional words appearing after the names of Yahweh or Israel as well as a great abundance of verbs to describe Yahweh's work of judgment or salvation. Such is the style of this most magnificent section of the Old Testament. But let us treat each of these enneads in turn to examine that theology more closely.

1. *The God of All (Isa 40 – 48).* The theme of Isaiah's call to the work of God returns in this section as the holiness and righteousness of God are praised repeatedly. God

is “the Holy One” (40:25; 41:14, 16, 20; 43:3, 14; 47:4; 48:17; and in the later sections in 49:7 [2x]; 54:5; 55:5). He also is righteous (*ṣedeq*), that is, straight, right, and faithful to a norm, his own nature and character. His righteousness could best be seen in his work of salvation, for the prophet often joined his righteousness and his performance of the covenant promise together (e.g., 41:2; 42:6 – 7; 46:12 – 13; note later 51:1, 5, 6, 8; 54:10; 55:3; 62:1 – 2). Only of God could it be said, “He is [in the] right” (41:26) or he is “a righteous God and Savior” (45:21), who declares “what is right” (v. 19) and who brings people near to his righteousness (46:13).

His nature is especially to be seen in his singleness and self-sufficiency. In Isaiah’s famous set of six variations on the formula of self-predication, he set forth the incomparability[23] of Yahweh: Beside him there was no other God (44:6, 8; 45:5 – 6, 21). Thus the question remained: “To whom then will you liken me?” (40:18, 25; 46:5). The forms of self-predication[24] are:

“I am Yahweh” or “I am Yahweh your God”
(41:13; 42:6, 8; 43:3, 11; 45:5, 6, 18)

“I am the first and I am the last”
(41:4; 44:6; 48:12)

“I am He”
(41:4; 43:10, 25; 46:4; 48:12)

“I am God”
(43:13; 46:9)

“I am your God”
(41:10)

But God’s works were likewise enumerated in this first ennead. He was Creator, Kinsman-Redeemer, Lord of history, King of all, and Discloser of the future.

Repeatedly Isaiah stressed the fact that God had “created” (*bārā’*); “made” (*‘āśâh* or *pā’al*); “spread out” (*nāṭâh*); “stretched out” (*rāqā‘*); “established” (*kûn*); and “founded” (*yāsad*) the heavens and the earth. In this vocabulary, so reminiscent of Genesis 1 – 2, he established God’s ability to create as part of his credentials as rightful Lord of humanity’s present history and final destiny (40:15, 17, 23 – 34; 42:5; 43:1 – 7; and later 54:15 – 16).

Yahweh was also a Kinsman-Redeemer (*gô’ēl*) just as Boaz acted toward Ruth. The verb to “redeem” (*gā’al*) and its derivatives appear twenty-two times. Here Isaiah used the motif of the exodus as his source (cf. Ex 6:6; 15:13; Isa 45:15, 21). Involved in this

23. For an excellent study on this concept, see C. J. Labuschagne, *The Incomparability of Yahweh in the Old Testament* (Leiden: E. J. Brill, 1966), esp. 111 – 12, 123ff., 142 – 53.

24. See the discussion by Morgan L. Phillips, “Divine Self-Predication in Deutero-Isaiah,” *Biblical Research* 16 (1971): 32 – 51.

redemption were (1) physical redemption from bondage (43:5 – 7; 45:13; 48:20; and later 49:9, 11, 14; 52:2 – 3; 55:12 – 13); (2) inward, personal, and spiritual redemption with the removal of personal sin for Israel (43:25; 44:22; 54:8) and for the Gentiles (45:20 – 23; 49:6; 51:4 – 5); and (3) the eschatological redemption when Jerusalem and the land were rebuilt (40:9 – 10; 43:20; 44:26; 45:13; 49:16 – 17; 51:3; 52:1, 9; 53:11 – 12). Yahweh was a Kinsman-Redeemer without equal.[25]

Yahweh was in charge of history itself, and the nations did not frighten him at all (40:15, 17). In fact, foreign leaders were raised up to do his bidding in history (as aptly illustrated by Cyrus in 41:1 – 4); and they were ransomed or conquered on his authority (43:3 – 14; 44:24 – 45:8; 47:5 – 9). No wonder he was called "King" on four occasions. He was "King of Jacob" (41:21); "your King," O Israel (43:15); "King of Israel" (44:6); and as 52:7 summarized, "Your God is King." Isaiah also used the additional royal titles of "Shepherd" (40:9 – 11), "Witness," "Commandment-Giver," and "Leader" in Isaiah 55:3.[26]

One more word must be added before leaving the theology of this ennead: Yahweh was the discloser of the future. Before things happened, the prophet was told about them.[27] The challenge to the gods, who were poor rivals and actually nonentities at best, was to declare what was to come to pass in the future, be it good or bad. The most graphic of all the divine predictions by Yahweh was the naming of Cyrus and two of his greatest works for Israel some three centuries before they took place (44:28). On such works as these Isaiah rested his case. Yahweh was God of gods, Lord of lords, King of kings and beyond all comparison. He was the God of all.

2. *The Savior of All (Isa 49 – 57).* Two words would summarize the second plank in this, Isaiah's mini-theology book (chaps. 40 – 66): *servant* and *salvation*. But it was the figure of the "Servant of the Lord" that captured the limelight in this section.

The advances in the portrayal of this corporate figure of "servant" are already observable in the use of the singular form twenty times in Isaiah 40 – 53 and in the plural form ten times in Isaiah 54 – 66.[28] That the servant is a collective term as well as an individual one representing the whole group, can be seen in two sets of data: (1) the servant is "all Israel" in twelve out of the twenty singular references[29] and (2) the four great Servant Songs: Isaiah 42:1 – 7; 49:1 – 6; 50:4 – 9; and 52:13 – 53:12, all present the servant as an individual who ministers to Israel. Therein lies one of the greatest puzzles for those scholars who reject the corporate solidarity of the servant: he was the one who represented all Israel, yet he was the nation Israel as well.

25. See F. Holmgren, *The Concept of Yahweh as Gô'el in Second Isaiah* (Ph.D. diss., Union Theological Seminary, New York: University Microfilms, 1963). Also Carroll Stuhlmueller, *Creative Redemption in Deutero-Isaiah* (Rome: Biblical Institute Press, 1970).

26. Carroll Stuhlmueller, "Yahweh-King and Deutero-Isaiah," *Biblical Research* 11 (1970): 32 – 45.

27. Isaiah 41:22 – 23, 26; 42:9; 43:9 – 10; 44:7 – 8; 46:10 – 11; 48:5

28. Isaiah 54:17; 56:6; 63:17; 65:8 – 9, 13 [3x], 14 – 15; 66:14.

29. Isaiah 41:8 – 10; 43:8 – 13; 43:14 – 44:5; 44:6 – 8, 21 – 23; 44:24 – 45:13; 48:1, 7, 10 – 12, 17.

Israel, the servant, is the "seed of Abraham," the patriarchal "friend" of God (41:8). "Abraham ... was called and blessed" when "he was but one" and was subsequently "made ... many" (51:2; cf. 63:16). Now God had already called Abraham his servant in Genesis 26:24, and so had Moses referred to Abraham, Isaac, and Jacob as servants of the Lord (Ex 32:13; Dt 9:27). In fact, all Israel was regarded as his servants in Leviticus 25:42, 55. Thus the seed was still the center of God's blessings (43:5; 44:3; 45:19, 25; 48:19; 53:10; 54:3; 59:21; 61:9). "The seed shall be known among the nations ... that they are a seed whom Yahweh has blessed" (65:9, 23; 66:22). That seed was God's "servant," or, as it regularly appears in Isaiah 54–66, his "servants." As John Bright noted, "The figure of the Servant oscillates between the individual and the group.... He is the coming Redeemer of the true Israel who in his suffering makes the fulfillment of Israel's task possible; he is the central actor in the "new thing" that is about to take place."[30]

In the four Servant Songs, many of the individual's titles or descriptions are matched by identical ascriptions made of Israel in the Isaianic poems, for example:[31]

An Individual		**All Israel**
42:1	"my chosen"	41:8–9
49:3	"my servant"	44:21
49:6	"a light to the nations"	42:6; 51:4
49:1	"called me from the womb"	44:2, 24; 43:1
49:1	"named my name"	43:1*b*

Yet, striking as this evidence might be, the "servant" of these songs has the task and mission "to bring Israel back" and "to gather" Israel to himself, "to raise up the tribes of Jacob and restore the preserved of Israel" (49:5–6). Therefore, the Servant of the Lord cannot be totally equated with Israel as the servant in all respects.

The apparent ambivalence is the same type of oscillation found in all the collective terms previously observed in the promise doctrine. They were inclusive of all Israel, but they were simultaneously focused on one representative who depicted the fortunes of the whole group for both that present time and the climactic future. The connection was to be found, not in some psychological theory of personality, but in the "everlasting covenant," even the "sure loyal love for David" (Isa 55:3; 61:8; cf. 2Sa 7).[32] The Servant of the Lord was the messianic person in the Davidic line then as well as that last new David who was to come and who was known as the Seed, the Holy One (*ḥāsîd*), the Branch, and so on.

The second ennead also detailed the salvation won by the Servant. In a real turn of events, the prophet Isaiah had God take the cup of his wrath from Israel's lips and put it to her oppressor's mouth instead (51:22–23; cf. the seventh-century prophet Nahum

30. John Bright, *Kingdom of God* (Nashville: Abingdon, 1953), 150ff.

31. Ibid.

32. Walter C. Kaiser, "The Unfailing Kindnesses Promised to David: Isiah 55:3," *Journal for the Study of the Old Testament* 45 (1989): 91–98.

[1:11 – 14]). Furthermore, a new exodus and redemption were envisaged for the future (52:1 – 6). This was "good news" (*m^ebaśśēr*) to Zion (v. 7). Then all the ends of the earth would see God's salvation (52:9 – 10; cf. 40:9).

This Servant who would personally rule, a fact that would startle all the kings of the earth (52:15), would also be the One who would suffer on behalf of all humanity so as to make God's atonement available. The first advent of this Servant would amaze many (vv. 13 – 14), but his second advent would catch the breath of even the kings of the earth (52:15) — therein lay the mystery of the Servant. His rejection followed: people would reject his message (53:1), his person (v. 2), and his mission (v. 3). But his vicarious suffering would effect an atonement between God and humanity (vv. 4 – 6); and though he would submit to suffering (v. 7), death (v. 8), and burial (v. 9), he would subsequently be exalted and richly rewarded (vv. 10 – 12). On the Servant of the Lord, then, was laid the iniquity of all humanity. Such was the rejection of the Servant/Messiah.

The result of the Servant's suffering was that the "seed" would "possess the nations"; for their tent would be enlarged, the ropes lengthened, and the pegs driven in deeper (54:2 – 3). Yahweh would then be "the God of the whole earth" (54:5; 49:6). Thus, as "it was in the days of Noah," so it would be when Yahweh returned to "gather Israel" and to extend his "steadfast love" (*ḥesed*) and "covenant of peace" (54:5, 9 – 10). Meanwhile, the free offer of salvation was extended to all nations through David's son (55:3 – 5; cf. 55:1 – 2, 6 – 9; 49:6; and the NT comment in Ac 13:45 – 49; 26:22 – 23).

3. *The End of All History (Isa 58 – 66).* The inauguration of the eschaton was sharply demarcated by the ending of the "former things"[33] (41:22; 42:9; 43:9, 18; 44:8; 46:9; 48:3) and the introduction of God's "new thing." There would be a "new" sincere repentance (58 – 59), a "new" Jerusalem (60), and a "new" heavens and "new" earth (65:17 – 25; 66:10 – 24; cf. 2 Peter 3:13; Rev. 21:1 – 4).

This would be the era of the Holy Spirit, according to 63:7 – 14. A call would go forth for a new Moses to lead a new exodus (vv. 11 – 14) and give them that "rest" (*nûaḥ*) promised long ago to Joshua. As the Servant was empowered by God's Spirit (42:1), so was this "anointed" person. Indeed, he was equated with the Servant in Isaiah 61:1: "The Spirit of the Lord God is on me because the Lord has anointed me." There he described the joy of his mission (vv. 1 – 3) and the content of his message (vv. 4 – 9), including

1. "You shall be called priests of the Lord and ministers of our God" (v. 6; cf. Ex 19:6)
2. The "everlasting covenant" will be carried out (v. 8)
3. Their "seed" would be known among the nations as those whom God had truly blessed (v. 9)

33. C. R. North, "The Former Things and the 'New Things' in Deutero-Isaiah," *Studies in Old Testament Prophecy*, ed. H. H. Rowley (Edinburgh: T & T Clark, 1950), 111 – 26.

Even the equipment and character of this Spirit-filled messianic Servant were noted in 61:10 – 11: "For he has clothed me with the garments of salvation and arrayed me in a robe of righteousness, as a bridegroom adorns his head like a priest ... so the Sovereign LORD will make righteousness and praise spring up before all the nations."

The Redeemer would come in the last day "for the sake of Zion" (Isa 59:20). He would be dressed as a warrior (59:15*b* – 19) and would wage war on all evil and sin, especially that type of hypocritical lifestyle described in Isaiah 57 – 59:15*a*. He would be invested with God's words and his Spirit (59:21). Then Jerusalem would experience violence no longer, for the Lord of glory would be her greatest asset (60). The wealth of the nations would pour into Jerusalem as all humanity arrived to praise the Lord (60:4 – 16). Then the exalted city of Jerusalem would be at peace forever, and the presence of the Lord of everlasting light would make the need for the sun or moon obsolete (vv. 17 – 22).

While the "day of vengeance" (63:4 – 6) and "year of redemption" brought judgment on the nations when God trampled down the nations in his winepress, even as Obadiah and Joel had proclaimed, God's irrevocable purpose for a rebuilt city of Jerusalem, which would be inhabited by the "holy people" of God, would be realized (62). Even though the clothes of the Hero were sprinkled with the blood of the winepress (63:1 – 6; cf. Isa 34; Joel 3:9 – 16; and later Zec 14; Eze 38 – 39), he would be vindicated as this era drew to a close and the new one began.

Part of that renewed — for so the word "new" should be understood here — world to come, where righteousness dwelt, included new heavens and new earth. Once again, Isaiah's paradisiacal pictures of peace in nature came to the fore (cf. Isa 11 and 65:17 – 25; 66:10 – 23). Death would be abolished (Isa 25:8), and the everlasting worldwide rule and reign of the new and final Davidic king would begin. Only the judgment of eternal torment on the wicked and finally unrepentant interrupted this picture, for they were perpetually in agony and forever apart from God.

So Isaiah ended his magnificent shorter theology. His dependence on antecedent theology was evident at almost every turn. While relating the "servant" to the earlier teaching about the "seed" (Isa 41:8; 43:5; 44:3; 45:19, 25; 48:19; 53:10; 54:3; 59:21; 61:9; 65:9, 23; 66:22) and to the "covenant" already given (Isa 42:6; 49:8; 54:10; 55:3; 56:4, 6; 59:21; 61:8), not to mention "Abraham" (41:8; 51:2; 63:16) or "Jacob" (41:21; 44:5; 49:26; 60:16) or "David" and the "everlasting covenant" (55:3; 61:8), Isaiah carefully systematized to a large degree the total plan, person, and work of God in the short scope of twenty-seven chapters. No wonder his theology has so profoundly affected people over the centuries.

Chapter 9

Renewal of the Promise: Prophets of the Seventh Century

Nahum, Zephaniah, Habakkuk, Jeremiah

The seventh century marked one of the most critical periods in the history of the nation of Israel, for the southern two tribes were tottering on the threshold of national destruction and the long-predicted Babylonian captivity. Already, Judah's sister nation of the ten northern tribes had met disaster in the previous century after refusing to repent of her sin, despite the battery of prophets who were graciously sent to warn her of the impending danger. Especially disastrous was the northern kingdom's introduction of idolatrous calf worship and its accompanying forms of apostasy. Finally, in 722 BC, Samaria fell to the Assyrian invaders (2Ki 17); the end came suddenly, and the land was quiet again.

But Judah was none the wiser for her sister nation's lesson. She too plunged headlong into disaster, courting God's judgment at every turn, with very few reprieves of justice and goodness toward God or people.

Once again God sent prophets, this time to warn Judah. Their theme was the imminent divine judgment. Nahum warned of God's judgment on Nineveh because of that city's wickedness and her ruthless destruction of Samaria in 722 BC, which had exceeded the method and extent of the divinely authorized judgment on Samaria. At the same time, Zephaniah reintroduced the message of Joel and Obadiah; however, for him the day of the Lord was both a day of worldwide judgment and a day when Judah would be punished. In that same time period, Habakkuk's message carried God's rebuke for Judah's sin and Babylon's haughty excess in administering that rebuke. But the greatest of all these spokesmen for God was Jeremiah. No prophet agonized more over the announcement of the bitter words of impending judgment than he did. Yet to Jeremiah was also given a most surprising word about another future day when God would fulfill his ancient promise made to the fathers and David. Thus, as remarkable as the times were, so were the words of the prophets. Instead of concluding that the old promise-plan had now failed and God's everlasting plan had been prematurely but permanently terminated, they projected its continuity on into the future.

The Book of Nahum

Apart from the opening verse of this prophet, Nahum (meaning "comfort") is unknown to us from any other sources. Even the location of his home, Elkosh, is uncertain; there are some four separate candidates for the location of this city.

The main subject of Nahum's prophecy is the destruction of Nineveh, a subject encountered more than a century ago in the book of Jonah, where the Ninevites found mercy and forgiveness. This time it would be different, however, for Nahum's prophecy fell between the sack of Thebes (Heb. *No-Amon* in Na 3:8 – 10) in 663 BC and the anticipated fall of Nineveh, the capital of the once proud and victorious Assyria that had captured Samaria in 722 BC. However, Nineveh fell to the Babylonians in 612 BC.

Mission to the Gentiles Revisited

Nahum's prophecy was the complement to Jonah, for whereas Jonah's message resulted in a celebration of God's mercy, Nahum's words marked the relentless march of the judgment of God against all sinners worldwide, including Nineveh. Jonah 3:10 had focused on God as merciful and forgiving, but Nahum 3:1 – 8 now demonstrated God's judicial wrath against all wickedness.

Nevertheless, even in this book of judgment Yahweh's mercy was not altogether absent. Triumphantly, Nahum announced that Yahweh was "slow to anger" (1:3*a*), "good," and "a stronghold in the day of trouble" (v. 7). Thus, while he will not overlook or absolve the wicked (v. 3*b*), neither is he without love and forgiveness.

The Zeal of Yahweh

"A zealous God [*'ēl qannô'* — or, less appropriately, "jealous" God] ... is Yahweh," began Nahum in a simple, but formidable, introduction to his book (1:2 – 6). Popular misconceptions about this adjective *qannô'* or the related noun *qin'âh* must not be attached to Nahum's meaning,[1] such as a God who was otherwise suspicious, distrustful, and fearful of rivalry. When used of God, however, God's zeal denoted: (1) that attribute which demanded exclusive devotion (Ex 20:5; 34:14; Dt 4:24; 5:9; 6:15); (2) that attitude of anger directed against all who persisted in opposing him (Nu 25:11; Dt 29:20; Ps 79:5; Eze 5:13; 16:38, 42; 25:11; Zep 1:18); and (3) the energy he expended in vindicating his

1. Walter A. Maier has provided the main substance of our definition in *The Book of Nahum* (St. Louis: Concordia Publishing House, 1959), 149 – 50. His defense of Nahum's doctrines on 70 – 87 is excellent and unmatched in other works on Nahum.

people (2 Ki 19:31; Isa 9:7; 37:32; Joel 2:18; Zec 1:14; 8:2). Thus his zeal was the forerunner of his vindication or impending punishment (Dt 4:24; Jos 24:19). He was the Judge, the "Vindicator" (*nōqēm*,[2] not "Avenger"); for after years of affliction meted out by the Assyrians, Yahweh would move to vindicate his people. Even the Assyrians would be forced to recognize the universal sovereignty of the Lord.

The Sins of Nineveh That Merited Judgment

Three types of transgression committed by Assyria are mentioned. The first, in Nahum 1:11, is probably a reference to Sennacherib's unsuccessful attack on Jerusalem (2Ki 18), when his generals taunted God's covenant people, the Judeans, with slurs on the impotency of Yahweh (2Ki 18:22ff.). This transgression was the same type of religious fault committed by the Pharaoh of the exodus. The second set of sins is in 3:1 — the blood guilt of Nineveh as she conducted some of the most murderous and brutal wars known to the ancient Near East.[3] Furthermore, she was filled with deception and lies; she could not be counted on in any of her dealings. Even her plunder was a ready witness against her as she disregarded the property rights of others. The third set of sins appears in 3:4 and consisted of a harlotry, which in this case was the sale of nations, wherein diplomats bickered over the fate of other nations. Thus we can see that Nahum was no proud nationalist who evidenced a contemptuous disdain for the heathen.

On the contrary, one of his complaints was that Nineveh sold "*nations* by her prostitution and peoples by her witchcraft" (Na 3:4b), so that her sins passed "endless[ly]" over to all nations (3:19). Moreover, when Nineveh's fall came, it would be a relief as well as a warning to other *nations*, for the Lord said, "I will show the nations your nakedness and the *kingdoms* your shame" (v. 5). All of Nineveh's robbery, plunder, harlotry, murder, and warmongering, in addition to being basic sins, were also against Yahweh and his plan for the nations (1:11).

A word of blessing or promise was also to be found in Nahum. God still knew those who took refuge in him, and he would be their "refuge" in the day of trouble (Na 1:7). In fact, F. C. Fensham,[4] following the lead of W. L. Moran, identified the word "good" (*ṭôb*) as a covenant term in Nahum 1:7. And following the study of H. W. Wolff on Hosea and Herbert B. Huffmon on Near Eastern materials, Fensham also connected the word "to know" (*yādaʿ*) with the covenant God had made between himself and his people (v. 7). Thus, while God's enemies would suffer the heat of his anger (vv. 6, 8), his own covenant people would be safe in his stronghold.

2. George Mendenhall, "The 'Vengeance' of Yahweh," *The Tenth Generation* (Baltimore: Johns Hopkins University Press, 1973), 69–104.

3. See the boasts of Ashurbanipal and Shalmaneser as collected in D. D. Luckenbill, *Ancient Records of Assyria and Babylon*, 1:146–48, 213; 2:319, 304, as quoted in Hobart Freeman, *Nahum, Zephaniah, and Habakkuk* (Chicago: Moody Press, 1973), 36–38.

4. F. C. Fensham, "Legal Activities of the Lord According to Nahum," *Biblical Essays: Proceedings of the Twelfth Meeting of "Die ou-Testamentiese Werkgemeenskap in Suid-Africa,"* ed. A. H. van Zyl (Potchefstroom, 1969), 18.

The Good News

The "good news" (m^e*baśśēr*) that Nineveh was to be destroyed (Na 1:15 [2:1]) was a reminder of God's justice and faithfulness, even as it had been in the parallel wording of Isaiah 52:7. Even as the tables had been turned on someone who had gone out from Nineveh (Sennacherib) and had planned and spoken evil against Yahweh and his covenant people only to find that matters had turned out differently, so the cup of affliction had been taken from Israel and had been given to the afflicting nations in Isaiah 51:22 – 23. Isaiah 52:10 – 13 went on to point to the universal work of God's salvation and to his Servant who would be his instrument by which his total reign over all humanity would be effected. But so did Nahum 2:1 – 2 [2 – 3] place the "good news" about Nineveh's destruction along with Yahweh's work of restoring "the splendor of Jacob and the splendor of Israel." The whole of Israel ("Jacob" and "Israel") would be "restored" (*šûb*), while those who had stripped and plundered her vine branches (cf. Ps 80:8 – 16) would go down in defeat.

The Book of Zephaniah

The genealogy of the prophet Zephaniah was surprisingly extended back for five generations, apparently to reach Hezekiah, King Josiah's grandfather (Zep 1:1). If that Hezekiah was indeed the thirteenth king of Judah, then he was the last reformer Judah had seen until the next reformer arrived on the scene, the young King Josiah (640 – 609 BC), who ruled in the days of the ministry of Zephaniah.

The "day of the Lord" was the all-consuming theme of Zephaniah's message. Earlier, Joel (ch. 2), Obadiah (vv. 15 – 21), Amos (5:18 – 20; 8:9 – 14) and Isaiah (2, 14, 24), had already treated this theme, but Zephaniah made it the major part of his message.

The Day of the Lord

Zephaniah, as already noted, ministered during the days of that remarkable king, Josiah (1:1). Abruptly, he commenced his prophecy with an announcement of a universal judgment over all the "ground" (v. 2) and "mankind" (v. 3). The terms and scope of this impending divine judgment were precisely those given by God prior to the Noachic flood (Ge 6:7). The day of the Lord was "at hand" (Zep 1:7). It would be "the day of Yahweh's sacrifice" (v. 7), "the great day of Yahweh," "the day of Yahweh's wrath," "a day of terror and distress," "a day of desolation and destruction," "a day of darkness and gloom," "a day of clouds and smoke," "a day of trumpet blast and battle alarm" (vv. 14 – 16).

While many earlier prophets had already spoken of this day, it was left to Zephaniah alone to emphasize more strenuously than all of them the universality of its judgment while also, surprisingly, predicting the conversion of the nations as one of its fruits.

Therefore, he urged, "Be still before Yahweh, Lord [of all]! For the day of the LORD is near." Zephaniah intoned that on that day, "The LORD has prepared a sacrifice; he has consecrated those he has invited" (1:7). Isaiah 13:3 had already alluded to that sacrificial feast and to the guests who were the wild foes whom the Lord would summon against his people. Judgment would begin against Judah first (Zep 1:4), for so judgment always begins at the house of God. It would be a divine rebuke for Judah's introduction of the worship of Baal, the celestial bodies, and Milcom (vv. 4–6).

The Call to Seek Yahweh

Instead, Judah should "seek" (*biqqēš*) and "inquire of" (*dāraš*) Yahweh (1:6). That seeking could be defined: it was an attitude of humility (*ᵃnāwâh*), which turned back to trust Yahweh and drew near to him (2:3; 3:12). Such humble people of the land observed and did the commands of Yahweh, for the will of God was their own (2:3). They also were known as those who "feared" him and accepted "discipline" (*mûsār*) in Zephaniah 3:7.[5]

All three of these terms linked the prophet's message to the Wisdom literature: the humble, the God-fearers, and those who accepted correction. They would be part of that future "remnant" (*šᵉʾērît*, 2:7, 9; cf. 3:13) or "flock" (*ṣôʾn*, 2:6) who would enjoy the promised blessing of God after Yahweh had triumphed over the nations.

Beyond the terrible and dreadful day of the Lord, Zephaniah saw a new era dawning. The gods of the earth would vanish; and from the distant countries of the earth ("isles," meaning those countries surrounding the Mediterranean Sea), all would pray to Yahweh (2:11). Such pedagogical significance to the judgment of the nations had been previously taught in Isaiah 24–27. Now "all of them in their own lands" (Zep 2:11), where they were at home, would pay homage to the Lord.

As Kapelrud summarized the order of the promises,[6] they were as follows: (1) believers would be hidden on the day of wrath (2:3); (2) the remnant would settle down peacefully along the seacoast (v. 7); (3) Israel would have her revenge on her enemies (v. 9); (4) foreigners would call on the name of the Lord (v. 9); (5) shame and wickedness would have come to an end and cease forever (vv. 11–13). These promises were followed with a final and triumphant shout: "The LORD, the King of Israel, is with you; never again will you fear any harm" (3:15).

The purification of the language ("lip") of the nations previously defiled by the names of strange gods was much as Isaiah had promised to Ethiopia (Isa 18:7) and Egypt (Isa 19:18). Then the poor and humble would rejoice as Isaiah had promised (Isa 29:19) and as Conrad von Orelli so aptly cautioned:

> If Zephaniah has not spoken of the human mediator of the days of redemption, who was to spring from David's stem, he bears witness all the more powerfully to the divine aim, which even the Messiah must serve, viz., the future blessed rule of God, which according

5. See the fine discussion of Zephaniah's terminology in Arvid S. Kapelrud, *The Message of the Prophet Zephaniah* (Oslo: Universitetsforlaget, 1975), 55–102.

6. Ibid., 91.

> to him also will have its centre on Zion, while dispensing life and blessing throughout the world. . . . The range of the divine plan, the universality of the judgment which must subserve that plan, [and] the universality of the redemption arrived at, are dwelt on by Zephaniah with special emphasis. . . . His visions move around the summits of Isaiah's prophecy, illuminating them from fuller consciousness of the range they command.[7]

The Book of Habakkuk

Unfortunately, nothing is known about the person Habakkuk. An apocryphal text, Bel and the Dragon, calls him a Levite who assisted Daniel in his times of need, but few (if any) put any historical value in this allusion. His book, however, was written toward the end of the seventh century BC, just as the Babylonian power was gearing up to be the dominant force in the Near East. The book seems to predate the fall of the Assyrian capital of Nineveh in 612 BC as well as preceding the complete destruction of the Assyrian empire in 605 BC.

The center of Habakkuk's message is to be found in that famous statement that "the righteous will live by his faith" (Hab 2:4). This theme is reechoed in the New Testament in Galatians 3:11; Romans 1:17; and Hebrews 10:38.

The Just Shall Live by Faith

If Zephaniah stressed humility and poverty of spirit as prerequisites for entering into the benefits of the company of the believing, Habakkuk demanded "faith" as the most indispensable prerequisite. But these are all part of the same picture. Whereas Zephaniah stressed Judah's idolatry and religious syncretism, Habakkuk was alarmed by the increase of lawlessness, injustice, wickedness, and rebellion. So sensitive was his own heart to these things that he cried to God for relief; either he must be changed or the people's sin had to be dealt with in judgment (1:2 – 4).

The divine solution was as straightforward as it was disturbing to this prophet: the Babylonians would invade Judah and punish her for her sin (1:5 – 11). This only increased the agony of the prophet, for how could God use a more wicked agent to punish a less wicked people (vv. 12 – 17)?

The answer to that last question was delayed until the fivefold woe was completed in 2:6 – 20. Here Habakkuk reminded Babylon, as Assyria had already been warned in Isaiah 10, that God is the one who wielded the ax of judgment, even though it was in the hands of an Assyria or Babylon; therefore, nations should be especially careful what method and what persons they involved in their warfare.

7. Conrad von Orelli, *The Old Testament Prophecy of the Consummation of God's Kingdom Traced in Its Historical Development*, trans. J. J. Banks (Edinburgh: T & T Clark, 1889), 322.

No wonder Habakkuk called his message a "burden" (*maśśā'*, 1:1). *Maśśā'* occurs 67 times in the Old Testament,[8] probably being derived from the root *nś'*, "to lift." The first reference in which this word was used of a prophecy whose contents were described is in 2 Kings 9:25 – 26. There Jehu reminded Bidkar, his officer, how the Lord had uttered this *maśśā'* against Ahab, his father: "Yesterday I saw the blood of Naboth and the blood of his sons, declares the Lord, and I will surely make you pay for it on this plot of ground, declares the Lord." Jehu referred to Elijah's prophecy in 1 Kings 21:19, 29 as a "burden." Thus *maśśā'* could be nothing less than God's "sentence" (as the *Jerusalem Bible* correctly translated it) passed on Ahab and his son for murdering Naboth in order to get his vineyard.

In Isaiah, nine of eleven oracles against foreign nations were designated *maśśā'* (Isa 13:1; 14:28; 15:1; 17:1; 19:1; 21:1, 11, 13; 23:1). Nahum (1:1) and Habbakuk (1:1) both had categorized their messages by this name (cf. later Jer 23:33 – 40 for the people's mocking use of *maśśā'*, and Zec 9 and 12). These prophecies all emphasized the grave and solemn note in their contents. The modern versions translate *maśśā* as an "utterance" or "oracle," but they miss the awesome aspect of the Hebrew, which carries more the idea of a "verdict" or "sentence" in addition to being a declaration from the Living God. Habakkuk obtained God's verdict for Judah's sin and for Babylon's excessive cruelty in carrying out the divinely decreed judgment on Judah.

Nevertheless, there was more than divine judgment, even in a *maśśā'*. The central oracle found in Habakkuk 2:4 was a word of hope and salvation. The importance of this remarkable word was indicated by the directions that were given along with this verdict to the effect that it was to be engraved on stone tables in plain letters so that all who passed could easily read it (2:2). It was to bear witness in the latter days, after it had come to pass, that God was true to his word.

But this word did not move to a ready condemnation of Babylon as Habakkuk might have expected. In a way, that had already been given in Habakkuk 1:11: "guilty people, whose own strength is their god." What needed to be shown to Judah, Habakkuk, and future generations was the striking contrast between the character of the wicked and the righteous people of God. To point to one's character was in effect to determine one's final destiny.

Habakkuk 2:4*a* described the character of Babylon: "See, he is puffed up; his desires are not upright." Babylon's inflated opinion of itself and its accomplishments were the very opposite of Zephaniah's humble, poor-in-spirit believer. In contrast to the arrogance and conceit of the kingdom of wickedness came the description of the believer in verse 4b: "But the righteous will live by their faith." Thus, the righteous "will not die," even as

8. See J. A. Naudé, "*Maśśā'* in the Old Testament with Special Reference to the Prophets," *Biblical Essays*, 91 – 100 (1969). Note also the study by P. A. H. de Boer, "The Meaning of *Maśśā'*," *Oudtestamentische Studiën* (Leiden: E. J. Brill, 1948), 214ff. Also, Walter C. Kaiser Jr., "*Maśśā*," in *Theological Wordbook of the Old Testament*, 2 vos., ed. R. Laird Harris, Gleason L. Archer Jr., and Bruce K. Waltke (Chicago: Moody Press, 1980), 2: 601–2.

Habakkuk 1:12b had promised, but they "will live" (2:4) despite the horror of the impending judgment.

What did living "by their faith" (*beʾmûnātô*) mean to Habakkuk and his hearers?[9] When used of physical things, it meant "firmness" (Ex 17:12), but in the moral realm it meant "moral firmness" or "trustworthiness," as in daily living or commerce (Pr 12:17). It also meant, when used of God, that his fidelity to his word could be trusted (Dt 32:4). But in Habakkuk 2:4, faith was simply an unwavering trust in God's word. In contrast to the overbearing disposition of the wicked, the believer, like Abraham in Genesis 15:6 and Isaiah in Isaiah 28:16; 30:15, put an immovable confidence in the God who had promised his salvation and the coming Man of promise. It was a steadfast, undivided surrender to Yahweh, "a childlike, humble and sincere trust in the credibility of the divine message of salvation."[10]

Therefore, despite Babylon's aspirations of empire building, another power would possess the earth: "for the earth will be filled with knowledge of the glory of the LORD as the waters cover the sea" (Hab 2:14). This is a clear use of the older Isaiah 11:9 with slight changes.

With this bold announcement, Habakkuk prayed that the triumphant advent of God would come soon. Whatever had to take place by way of judgment under the hands of the Babylonians, he prayed that it would have an advantageous effect on God's work, and that the ancient promise-plan would be renewed and thus mercy would be interspersed with the wrath that also had to come.

Then, borrowing language from God's appearance on Sinai (3:3ff.) and his victory under Joshua when the sun ceased its shining and the moon was rebuked during a hailstorm (Jos 10:12–14), Habakkuk portrayed another theophany yet to come. He was frankly frightened by the awesomeness of God's glory as it appeared on this "day of trouble"; yet his joy was grounded in the same Lord in whom he had learned to put his trust and faith. God's salvation of his people (3:13) would include the salvation of his Messiah, who would "crush the head [that is, the kingdom or dynasty] of the wicked" (3:13). Because the kingdom of the ungodly had been crushed, it no longer would be able to protect its inhabitants. But the redemption of God's people was assured. With that the prophet was confident and full of joy (3:16, 18–19).

The Book of Jeremiah

Jeremiah received his call to be a prophet to the nations (Jer 1:5) apparently while he was still a young man in the village of Anathoth, just a mile or two north of Jerusalem,

9. I am indebted to von Orelli, *Old Testament Prophecy*, 325, for this analysis of the word *ʾmûnâh*.

10. Ibid., 326.

in the year 627 BC. His ministry would cover some of the most tempestuous years in ancient Near Eastern political history as it extended from 627 down to the 570s BC.

The political crisis was stirred up by the westward and southern spread of the Babylonian empire. Jeremiah would see in his early ministry the reform movements of King Josiah of Judah, including the finding of the book of the law of God in 622 BC. But things really took a turn for the worse when young King Josiah (only 39 years of age) was struck down in 609 BC at the Megiddo Pass while trying to deter Pharaoh Necho from going to enter the Assyrian-Babylonian fray.

Thus, from 609 BC until the fall of Jerusalem in 587 BC, this prophet pleaded with the nation of Judah to repent of its sins and turn back to the Lord — but to no avail. Babylon conquered the city of Jerusalem in 587 BC, and shortly thereafter the small remnant that remained carted Jeremiah off to Egypt after he had warned them that this was not God's will. The prophet apparently died in Egypt sometime in the 570s BC.

The Word of the Lord

Jeremiah was the prophet of the "word of the LORD" (1:2). According to J. G. S. S. Thomson, Jeremiah used "Thus says the LORD" or similar phrases 157 times out of the total of 349 times such phrases are used in the Old Testament.[11]

"Now, I [God] have put my words in your mouth" (1:9; 5:14), Jeremiah would report as the basis of his authority to speak for God. But if pressed further on the mechanics of this reception of divine revelation, he would describe how he not only spoke but also wrote at God's command (36:1 – 2). Baruch, Jeremiah's secretary, volunteered that the prophet was *in the habit of* dictating (36:18, Heb. imperfect) while Baruch was writing (active participle) it down. This took place over a long period of time. What Baruch wrote was "from [Jeremiah's] mouth," and what Jeremiah spoke was from the Lord.

That word was more than an objective revelation spoken for the benefit of others. It was food for the prophet's own soul (15:16; cf. 1:4ff.), the "joy and rejoicing of his heart." On the other hand, the word of the Lord became a reproach to him (20:8), for the ministry of that word often seemed to be fruitless (v. 7ff.), without any good results. Nevertheless, an inner compulsion drove Jeremiah to persist even when he was determined to cease from speaking in the name of the Lord. God put that word in his heart, and it burnt like a fire in his bones until it was released. Most of Jeremiah's so-called confessions (11:18 – 23; 12:1 – 6; 15:10 – 20; 17:14 – 18; 18:18 – 23; 20:7 – 11) were conflicts such as this one. In his personal communion with God, he laid bare the depths of his own agony of soul as he cried out "violence and destruction" (20:8), and the people mocked him in response. Jeremiah pleaded his case before the Lord and sought God's vindication.

---

11. James G. S. S. Thomson, *The Old Testament View of Revelation* (Grand Rapids: Eerdmans, 1960), 60 – 61.

Jeremiah's prophecies can be divided into three parts, not including an introductory call chapter and a concluding historical chapter: (1) his early messages to Judah (2 – 24); (2) his prophecies of judgment and comfort (25 – 45); and (3) his messages to the nations (46 – 51). Each had its own distinctive contribution to the theology of the Old Testament.

The Vanity of External Religion

In his celebrated Temple Gate Message (Jer 7 – 10; cf. 26), Jeremiah demonstrated both his style and the essence of his call to prophesy in Judah. As the people made their way into the house of God, Jeremiah announced three main propositions: (1) attendance at the house of God was no substitute for real repentance (7:4 – 15); (2) observance of religious rituals was no substitute for obedience to the Lord (7:21 – 29); and (3) possession of the word of God was no substitute for responding to what that word said (8:8 – 12).

The people had come to place an unholy confidence in the outward form of the ceremonial law and the theocracy. They felt they were impervious to any threatened judgment of God as they rallied around the slogan "The temple of the LORD, the temple of the LORD, the temple of the LORD" (7:4). It was as if they were using God's temple as a rabbit's foot charm for good luck. God could not and would not storm his own sanctuary and dwelling place — so Judah thought! Where would God go if he deserted the temple? In the meantime, Judah continued to steal, murder, commit adultery, swear falsely, burn incense to Baal, and walk after other gods — only to then stand brazenly in the presence of God and say, "We are safe — safe [in order] to do all these detestable things!" (v. 10).

On the contrary, Judah would see, cried Jeremiah. It was not that God looked for sacrifice so much as an obedience that preceded and accompanied that sacrifice. He had not spoken "for the sake of" (*ʿal divrê*) burnt offerings per se, but for the same thing Moses had emphasized in Deuteronomy: "Walk in all the ways I command you, that it may go well with you" (Jer 7:22 – 23; cf. Dt 5:33).

Likewise, that word from God should have made Judah blush, but instead she turned it into a salve to superficially heal the hurt of that people (8:11). There was an outright rejection of that word. But all these charades would take Judah nowhere. The emptiness of such heartless, noncommittal religion would lead straight to the day of God's wrath against Judah and ultimately against the nations.

Jerusalem, the Throne of Yahweh

In a most astonishing prediction, Jeremiah made the following announcement in 3:16 – 17:

> "In those days, when your numbers have increased greatly in the land," declares the LORD, "men will no longer say, 'The ark of the covenant of the LORD.'" It will never enter their minds or be remembered; it will not be missed, nor will another one be made. At that time they will call Jerusalem The Throne of the LORD, and all nations will gather in

Jerusalem to honor the name of the LORD. No longer will they follow the stubbornness of their evil hearts."

The ancient blessings of Genesis 1:28 were still remembered as God's promise-plan drew to a conclusion in that final day. Amazingly, no longer would that most central object of all in Israel's worship be significant, nor would it even come into anyone's mind; for God's presence would no longer need a symbol when he himself was plainly discernible.

In saying this, Jeremiah clearly passed sentence on the ceremonial institutions of the Mosaic legislation, which at the beginning had been given with a built-in obsolescence. They were only modeled after the real, which existed apart from these temporary copies of it. Repeatedly, Moses had been warned that the tabernacle was to be built after a "pattern" (Ex 25:9, 40; 26:30; 27:8) or "plan" shown to him in the mountain. Jeremiah here added to that idea by declaring that they would one day be needed no longer. Instead of God's symbolic enthronement between the cherubim, he would be enthroned in Jerusalem. For a declaration of inwardness, immediacy of access to God, and self-revelation of God, this word could not be surpassed.

The nations would then be drawn to the glory of God (3:17; cf. Isa 2:2 – 3; Mic 4:1 – 2), and the stubborn heart of Judah and Israel would have been dealt with and changed by a work yet to be described in Jeremiah.

Yahweh Our Righteousness

The "righteous Branch," already announced in Isaiah 4:2, was the same Davidite foreseen in Jeremiah 23:5 – 7 and 33:14 – 22. The special name given to this messianic "Branch" or "Sprout" (*ṣemaḥ*) was "Yahweh our righteousness" (YHWH *ṣidqēnû*), a name that was reminiscent of Isaiah's Immanuel, "God is with us."

This name was shared with Jerusalem since it was to be Yahweh's throne. Thus the rule and reign of this final new Davidite would be in the interests of righteousness. He would proceed wisely, and the righteousness of the people of God would be grounded, not in any outward institution, law, or action, but in Yahweh's character. In that day Yahweh would establish and protect the righteousness of his people.

Especially significant in Jeremiah 33:14 – 22 was the work of the "Branch," which would be the culmination of several ancient promises: (1) the Noachic covenant on the perpetuity of the seasons; (2) the Abrahamic covenant on the innumerable seed; (3) the covenant with Phinehas on the perpetuity of the priesthood; and (4) the Davidic covenant on the everlasting reign of his seed. In every case these had been declared "everlasting" or "eternal," and so they were in Jeremiah's projections.

The New Covenant

The heart of Old Testament theology and of the message of Jeremiah was his teaching on the new covenant in Jeremiah 31:31 – 34. Set in the context of the "Book of Comfort" (chaps. 30 – 33), the message of Jeremiah rose to the lofty peaks of an earlier Isaiah (Isa 40 – 66). Especially significant were the six strophes of chapters 30 – 31: (1) 30:1 – 11, the great distress of Jacob in the day of the Lord; (2) 30:12 – 31:6, the healing of Israel's incurable wound; (3) 31:7 – 14, God's firstborn restored to the land; (4) 31:15 – 22, Rachel weeping for her children in exile; (5) 31:23 – 34, the new covenant; and (6) 31:35 – 40, the inviolable covenant given to Israel.[12] Note that the whole context, chapters 30 – 33, meticulously connected this new covenant strophe with the restoration of the Jewish nation.

It is the fifth of these six strophes that constituted the largest teaching passage on the problem of continuity and discontinuity between the Old and New Testaments. Yet it is at precisely this point that the biblical theologian's perplexity rises to its greatest height: Why call this a "*new* covenant," since most of the content of this covenant is but a repetition of those promises already known from the Abrahamic-Davidic covenants?

What, then, were the essentially new items that were "not like" (Jer 31:32) and "no longer" similar to the old covenant (v. 34 [2x])?

1. *Its Name.* This is the only place in the Old Testament where the expression "new covenant" (31:31) occurs; however, it would appear that the concept was much more widespread. Based on similar content and contexts, the following expressions may be equated with the new covenant: the "everlasting covenant" in seven passages (Isa 24:5; 55:3; 61:8; Jer 32:40; 50:5; and later in Eze 16:60; 37:26); a "new heart" and a "new spirit" in three or four texts (Jer 32:39 [LXX]; and later in Eze 11:19; 18:31; 36:26); a "covenant of peace" in three passages (Isa 54:10; and later in Eze 34:25; 37:26); and "a covenant" or "my covenant," placed in the context of "in that day" in three passages (Isa 42:6; 49:8; 59:21; see also Hos 2:18 – 20). That makes a total of sixteen or seventeen major passages on the "new covenant."

Still, Jeremiah 31:31 – 34 was the *locus classicus* on the subject, as may be seen from several lines of evidence. It was this passage that stimulated Origen to name the last twenty-seven books of the Bible "the New Testament."[13] But it was also the largest piece of text to be quoted *in extenso* in the New Testament — in Hebrews 8:8 – 12 and partially repeated in Hebrews 10:16 – 17. Furthermore, it was the subject of nine other New Testament texts: four dealing with the Lord's Supper (Mt 26:28; Mk 14:24; Lk 22:20; 1 Co 11:25); two Pauline references to "ministers of the new covenant" and the future forgiveness of Israel's sins (2 Co 3:6; Ro 11:27); and three additional references in Hebrews (9:15; 10:16; 12:24; cf. the two large teaching passages mentioned above).

2. *Its Contrasts.* Jeremiah 31:32 explicitly contrasted this new covenant with an old covenant made with Israel during the era of the exodus. Repeatedly, Jeremiah had stressed

---

12. This outline was suggested by Charles A. Briggs, *Messianic Prophecy* (New York: Scribner's, 1889), 246 – 47. Essentially the same outline is given by George H. Cramer, "Messianic Hope in Jeremiah," *Bibliotheca Sacra* (1958): 237 – 46.

13. T. H. Home, *Introduction to the Critical Study and Knowledge of the Holy Scriptures* (New York: R. Carter and Brothers, 1858), 1:37. See also Geerhardus Vos, *Biblical Theology* (Grand Rapids: Eerdmans, 1954), 321. Albertus Pieters had the same assessment in *The Seed of Abraham* (Grand Rapids: Eerdmans, 1950), 61.

this type of antithesis in his message: "People will no longer say ... but ... not like this ... but this" (Jer 3:16; 23:7 – 8; 31:29; cf. 16:14 – 15). Thus Jeremiah was attempting to revise the warped values and religious crutches that people had used in his day. Ezekiel later used the same formula — "You will no longer [say]" (18:2 – 4) — to introduce current maxims used by the people as a form of oath or religious declaration, maxims that need correction due to an exaggerated emphasis on only one aspect of the whole teaching.[14]

The truth of the matter was that Jeremiah found no fault with the Sinaitic covenant. Both Jeremiah and the later writer of Hebrews were emphatic in their assessment of where the trouble with the covenant made in Moses' day was to be found. The problem was with the *people*, not with the covenant-making God or with the moral law or promises reaffirmed from the patriarchs and included in that old covenant. The text of Jeremiah 31:32 explicitly points the finger when it says, "because they broke my covenant, though I was a husband to them." So also did Hebrews 8:8 – 9: "But God found fault *with the people* ... because they did not remain faithful to [his] covenant" (emphasis mine).

The verb *hēpērû* ("they brake") was not unique to the Sinaitic or obligatory types of covenants, as opposed to Abrahamic-Davidic promissory types, for the same verb occurred in the Abrahamic covenant (Ge 17:14, "Any uncircumcised male ... will be cut off from his people; he has broken [*hēpar*] my covenant").[15] Even the eternal and irrevocable covenant of David contained some qualifications that provided for *individual* invalidation, frustration, or destruction of the benefits of that covenant (1 Ch 22:13; 28:7; Ps 132:12), but that would not halt the transmission of that covenant in the plan of God to its destined end. Indeed, Jeremiah 31:35 – 37 had argued that the stars would drop out of the sky and the planets spin out of their orbits before God would abandon his total pledge to the nation of Israel.

3. *Its Continuity.* The structure for Jeremiah 31:31 – 34 was best analyzed by Bernhard W. Anderson.[16] The expression *n*ᵉ*'ūm YHWH* ("declares the LORD") appeared four times: twice in the first section, indicating its beginning (v. 31a) and its conclusion (v. 32b); and twice in the second section, again marking its beginning (v. 33a) and its end (v. 34b). In the second section (v. 34), there were also two climactic *kî* ("indeed") clauses (31:34b, 34c).

When the items of continuity found in the new covenant are tabulated in this passage, they are: (1) the same covenant-making God, "my covenant"; (2) the same law, "my

14. Also note Ezekiel 12:22; cf. 12:27 and Jeremiah 12:23. For a discussion with different conclusions, see Moshe Weinfeld, "Jeremiah and the Spiritual Metamorphosis of Israel," *Zeitschrift für alttestamentliche Wissenschaft* 88 (1976): 17 – 55.

15. Note the crucial importance made between conditional and unconditional covenants in Charles Ryrie, *Dispensationalism Today* (Chicago: Moody Press, 1965), 52 – 61, and the strong disavowal in O. T. Allis, *Prophecy and the Church* (Philadelphia: Presbyterian and Reformed Publishing House, 1945), 31 – 48. See D. F. Payne, "The Everlasting Covenant," *Tyndale Bulletin* 7 – 8 (1961): 10 – 17: "A New Covenant? Yes, but only the unimportant details of the 'Old' were obsolescent, and even the author of Hebrews apparently could not quite bring himself to call the Old Covenant 'obsolete.'"

16. Bernhard W. Anderson, "The New Covenant and the Old," *The Old Testament and Christian Faith*, ed. Bernhard W. Anderson (New York: Harper and Row, 1963), 230 n. 11.

torah" (not a different one than the one given at Sinai); (3) the same divine fellowship promised in the ancient tripartite formula, "I will be their God"; (4) the same "seed" and "people," "they will be my people"; and (5) the same forgiveness, "I will forgive their wickedness."

Even the features of inwardness, fellowship, individualism, and forgiveness had been either hinted at, or fully known, in the covenant made with the ancestors. Deuteronomy 6:6 – 7, 10:12, and 30:6 had urged that Israel place the words of the Sinaitic law upon her heart. Indeed, Psalms 37:31 and 40:8 claimed this was so for some already: "Thy law is within my heart." The Lord's forgiveness was also celebrated in that oft-repeated formula: "The LORD, the LORD, the compassionate and gracious God, slow to anger, abounding in love and faithfulness, maintaining love to thousands, and forgiving wickedness, rebellion and sin" (Ex 34:6 – 7; Nu 14:18; Dt 5:9 – 10; Ps 86:15; Joel 2:13; Jnh 4:2; and later Ne 9:17, 31). In fact, he removed transgression "as far as the east is from the west" (Ps 103:8 – 12).

Thus the word "new" in this context would mean the "renewed" or "restored" covenant (cf. Akk. *edêšu*, "to restore" ruined temples, altars, or cities; Heb. *ḥodeš*, connected with the new moon; and Ugar. *ḥadaṯ*, "to renew the moon"). We conclude, then, that this covenant was the old Abrahamic-Davidic promise renewed and enlarged.

4. *Its New Features.* There were items of discontinuity as well. If we were to use all seventeen passages noted above, some of the new features would be: (1) a universal knowledge of God (Jer 31:34); (2) a universal peace in nature and the absence of military hardware (Isa 2:4; Hos 2:18; Eze 34:25; 37:26); (3) a universal material prosperity (Isa 61:8; Hos 2:22; Jer 32:41; Eze 34:26 – 27); (4) a sanctuary lasting forever in the midst of Israel (Eze 37:26, 28); and (5) a universal possession of the Spirit of God (Joel 2:28 – 32).

In this list, the new covenant transcends all previous announcements of the blessings of God. Thus the new is more comprehensive, more effective, more spiritual, and more glorious than the old — in fact, so much so that *in comparison* it would appear totally unlike the old. Yet in truth, it was nothing less than the progress of revelation in the ancient but ever-renewing promise-plan of God.

The "new" began with the "old" promise made to Abraham, Moses, and David; and its renewal perpetuated all those promises and more.

5. *Its Addressees.* Just as the Abrahamic and Davidic promises were made directly with each of these men, so the new covenant was made with all "the house of Israel and the whole house of Judah." Now if this address of Jeremiah 31:31 appears too restricted and therefore of limited usage in pre-Christian times, then it can also be said that the same restrictions applied to the Abrahamic and Davidic promises.

But therein lay the solution for all of these passages, for the "seed" that would benefit from the Abrahamic and Davidic promises included all believers of all ages. So also were the benefits of the new covenant applicable to all believers for the same reasons.

George N. H. Peters demonstrated that "we have decided references to ... [a] renewed Abrahamic covenant, conjoined with the Davidic [as] being a distinguishing characteristic of, and fundamental to, the Messianic period, e.g., Micah 7:19–20; Ezekiel 16:60–63; Isaiah 55:3."[17]

It need only be noted that the new covenant also was part of that messianic era! Here, then, was a new footing for an old stalemate. The new covenant was indeed addressed to a revived national Israel of the future; but nonetheless, by virtue of its specific linkage with the Abrahamic and Davidic promise-plan of God contained in them all, it was proper to speak of a Gentile participation both at that time and in the future. The Gentiles would be adopted and grafted into God's covenant with national Israel.[18]

The seventh century was the greatest moment of impending destruction for the nation; yet in the midst of the faithful warnings of God's servants came one of the most spectacular series of promises of hope.

17. George N. H. Peters, *The Theocratic Kingdom* (Grand Rapids: Kregel, 1957), 1:322. See also Francis Goode, "God's Better Covenant with Israel in the Latter Day," *The Better Covenant*, 5th London ed. (Philadelphia: Smith, English & Co., 1868), 239–71.

18. For further discussion of the New Testament implications, see W. C. Kaiser Jr., "The Old Promise and the New Covenant," *Journal of the Evangelical Theological Society* 15 (1972): 11–23.

Chapter 10

The Kingdom of the Promise: The Exilic Prophets

Ezekiel, Daniel

The worst had happened. Jerusalem had fallen in 587 BC, and the greater part of her citizens had entered a seventy-year captivity in Babylon. Now the ominous notes of threatening would soon come to a conclusion, and the new emphasis of the prophetic theology would be the deliverance and new birth of God's people Israel.

Jeremiah's younger contemporary Ezekiel had been deported with King Jehoiachin in 597 BC, about a decade prior to Jerusalem's fall to Babylon. From that place of exile, he continued to warn Judah in the first section of his book (Eze 3:22 – 24:27). In his meticulously dated prophecies, he turned to warn the nations during the dark hours of Jerusalem's siege and fall (Eze 25 – 32). (Note that the prediction of the fall in 24:21 – 23 and the report of its happening in 33:21 bracket the messages to the nations.) Thereafter, the oracles of hope and promise take over in Ezekiel 33 – 48. With the old Davidic order at an end, there was only one place to go: to the new David, the Messiah, his throne, and his kingdom. This became the sustaining hope for a people who had lost every outward symbol of hope; it was also the all-consuming focus of Ezekiel and Daniel.

The Book of Ezekiel

The prophet Ezekiel was the son of Buzi, a priest of the family of Zadok (Eze 1:3). Like Jeremiah and Zechariah, Ezekiel combined the offices of priest and prophet in one person.

While there is much discussion as to his exact age at the time he was carried off into exile in Babylon, it is most probable that he was about twenty-five years of age at the time. This is assumed from Ezekiel 1:1, which begins, "In the thirtieth year," which appears to be a reference to the time of his call to a prophetic ministry. That year is linked in the next verse with "the fifth year of the exile of King Jehoiachin"

(1:2), who was taken captive at the same time, 597 BC, making the fifth year to be 592 BC.

Ezekiel's prophecies, in one of the best-dated books of the Bible, range from 592 to 571 BC. After describing his call and commissioning in Ezekiel 1 – 3, chapters 4 – 24 contain prophecies against Judah and its capital, Jerusalem, followed by chapters 25 – 34 with prophecies against the foreign nations, and concluding with God's word about the restoration of Judah and Jerusalem in the final day, chapters 33 – 48.

The Good Shepherd's Reign

Ezekiel, a priest by descent, was called to be a watchman for Israel. His ministry was filled with some of the most exotic of all symbolic actions performed by the prophets. He was fond of allegories and parables, and he used them more freely than his colleagues. In his hands, the use of apocalyptic language received new impetus, especially in the third section of his work. But above all, it was his inaugural vision that explained the theme of his work: the glory of God.

Ezekiel's language was often repetitive in style. One of the most frequent phrases was "that you might know that I am the LORD." This phrase appeared fifty-four times, not including eighteen more expansions of the same phrase. God's holiness was also set off in contrast to Israel's sinfulness, especially in the parable of the foundling (16:1 – 63), the parable of the two sisters (23:1 – 49), and the historical review of 20:1 – 31 with its repeated phrase "I acted for the sake of my name, that it should not be profaned in the sight of the nations among whom they dwell" (20:9, 14, 22).

But right from the beginning, Ezekiel made it plain that in spite of Israel's deep sin, Yahweh would remember his covenant with that nation exactly as he had pledged to do in the days of her youth (Eze 16:60):

> Yet I will remember the covenant I made with you in the days of your youth, and I will establish [*hēqîm*: (1) to set up what does not yet stand, or (2) to cause to stand, ratify, stabilize, resuscitate what is already there] an everlasting covenant with you.

In this case, *hēqîm*, "to establish" is best understood by meaning number two: it was a ratification of what was already there. Naturally, it will be necessary to judge the nation for her sin as verse 59 noted:

> I will deal with you as you deserve, because you have despised my oath by breaking [*l^e^hāpēr*, the *l^e^* of attendant circumstances] the covenant.

But the promise and its blessings would continue!

The Glory of Yahweh

Dominating every scene and word of the book of Ezekiel is the throne of God (Eze 1:4 – 28). The vision of this throne constituted Ezekiel's call as he sat by the "river" Chebar; and its magnificence was sufficient to assure the prophet that like that heavenly chariot of God's throne, which could easily bring his presence east, west, north, or south, so would that same presence of God be with him.

The scene was much like that which John would experience on the isle of Patmos as he wrote the book of Revelation (4 – 5). For Ezekiel there was a crystal platform holding a sapphire throne with the one enthroned having the "likeness" and "appearance of a man" (1:26). The platform was supported by four living creatures, which in turn were associated with wheels that apparently were much like modern desk furniture wheels; they were able to turn in any direction without the need of a steering mechanism. All this was punctuated with the flash of lightning, the roar of thunder, and the rainbow of color surrounding the whole scene. Obviously, the central figure was none other than the Holy One enthroned — an awesome personage whose appearance radiated fire and brightness.

As for the meaning of it all, Ezekiel was told it was "the appearance of the likeness of glory of the LORD" (1:28*b*). The connection between fire and the presence of the Lord was well known in Israel. Moses had experienced it in his call at the burning bush; Israel in the wilderness saw the pillar of fire; Elijah on Mount Carmel experienced the powerful consuming presence of God; in fact, only Daniel (7:9ff.) would describe in detail his meeting with the "Ancient of days." But one thing was certain, the sheer weight, or gravity (*kābēd*) of his presence evoked an attitude of worship from Ezekiel (1:28*b*), for he felt he was in the immediate presence of God. This meeting with Yahweh would comfort and direct the prophet as well as give shape to his whole message. God would triumph despite Israel's most tragic failure. His promise would not die; it would go on.

God's presence would continue to be with his prophet, his promise, the remnant, and his kingdom to come; but his presence would leave its place of residence where he had dwelt since the days of Israel's wandering. When Ezekiel was transported in a vision to the temple in Jerusalem (8:2 – 4) and there witnessed firsthand the horrible sins of Judah done right in the house of God, it was clear that God's glory could stay there no longer. There were such unspeakable absurdities as "the image of jealousy" (perhaps goddess Asherah poles, cf. 2Ch 33:7, 15) erected in the temple (8:3b); animal worship (vv. 7 – 13); women weeping in sympathetic magic for Tammuz, the Sumerian god of vegetation (vv. 14 – 15); and worship of the sun (vv. 16 – 18).

The only possible sequel to such confusion was that of Ezekiel 10:18: "Then the glory of the LORD departed from over the threshold of the temple." Indeed, for Judah, her government, her religious pretense, and her religious institutions, it was Ichabod: "The glory had departed"!

Yahweh the Sanctuary

During those days of exile, Yahweh himself would be the real temple of the true believers:

> "Although I sent them far away among the nations and scattered them among the countries, yet for a little while I have been a sanctuary for them in countries where they have gone." (Eze 11:16)

Yahweh himself, people would learn, was more important than buildings and all the trappings. What was more, he would one day restore the people to the land, bringing them from every country to which they had been dispersed (11:17). Only in that future day all the old abominations would have been removed and a new inner capacity would be implanted in the people — the inner self would be so changed that Ezekiel could only refer to it as a "new spirit," "an undivided heart," and a "heart of flesh" (11:19). Such was the old vision of Isaiah 4:2 – 6 and Jeremiah 30 – 31.

The New Davidic Kingdom

Ezekiel 17 is an allegory of the cedar of Lebanon (that is, David's house) with an indictment of the last Davidite, Zedekiah, who relied on Egypt rather than Yahweh. But all was not lost, for this history concluded in 17:22 – 24 with the promise of a sprig, a tender shoot from the top of this majestic cedar tree, which would grow to overtake all the other trees (kingdoms).

The Babylonian eagle would carry away the crown of the cedar tree into captivity, but God would exalt the lowly. Once more Yahweh would break off another twig, this time from the transplanted sprig, and this new piece of cedar he would replant on the mountain heights of Israel. There, what would only appear to be insignificant would grow into a powerful tree under which all the birds of heaven would seek shelter. To that new tree, all the kingdoms of earth would come and acknowledge their inferiority and its superiority.

Once again, the theme of God's new World Ruler coming from humble origins was the point (cf. Isa 7:14ff.; 9:6ff.; 11:1ff.; Mic 4:1ff.). While Zerubbabel was the next Davidic person to govern, and he was transplanted from Babylonian exile back to Zion, he clearly did not exhaust the universal terms of this passage.

The remnant would inherit all the ancient promises given to David and Abraham. And God's kingdom would triumph over all the nations; in fact, under the umbrella of that kingdom would dwell all sorts of nations (or, as the oriental figure of speech loved to put it, all the birds of heaven and beasts of every type would seek its shelter).

The Rightful King

One last installment in the developing doctrine of promise is to be found in the first section of Ezekiel (21:26 – 27 [31 – 32]). As the prophet unleashed his message of destruction against Jerusalem, the temple, and the land of Israel (cf. Eze 20:45 – 21:17), he was instructed to mark the crossroads where the advancing king of Babylon would need to determine whether he was going to take the road southeast to the Ammonites or the road to Jerusalem. Even though Nebuchadnezzar would use divination (belomancy, necromancy, and hepatoscopy, 21:21), Yahweh had already determined that the lot would be for him to proceed to Jerusalem (v. 22)!

As for the wicked Davidic prince, Zedekiah, he should remove his "crown" (*miṣnepet*) and the high priest his "mitre" (tiara or turban, *ᵃṭārâh*, cf. Ex 28:4, 37, 39; 29:6; 39:28, 31;

Lev 8:9; 16:4). For the kingdom and the priesthood, as experienced up to that point in Israel's history, would be abolished and would suffer an interruption for a time. They would remain in ruins until the advent of one appointed by Yahweh reclaimed them (*'ad bô' ᵃšer lô hammišpāṭ*, "until he comes whose right it is," 21:27 [32]).

This passage is remarkably similar to Genesis 49:10 and its cryptic use of "Shiloh." No doubt Ezekiel deliberately harked back to the messianic promise given to Judah as her only hope in her hour of tragedy. When David and Aaron's lines had failed to carry out their divine mission, then the earnests of the promise must cease until the One to whom the kingship and priesthood *together* belonged would claim them. When he appeared, then crown and mitre would be given to this new and final King-Priest, the Messiah.

Meanwhile, the Messiah's counterpart continued to manifest himself in a series of anti-messiahs. There was the king of Babylon in Isaiah 14:12ff., and now the king of Tyre in Ezekiel 28:11ff. Each message was addressed not so much to a historical figure but to one who epitomized the final representative (Antichrist) of the Serpent's seed as promised in Genesis 3:15. History was not a contest between mere mortals; it was simultaneously a supernatural battle for dominion,[1] and Satan had his own succession of tyrants corresponding to God's Davidite line of successors as well as his climactic person, the tyrant of all tyrants.

The Good Shepherd

If any passage was at the heart of Ezekiel's contribution to the ongoing promise, it was Ezekiel 34:11 – 31. "I myself will search for my sheep, ... I will shepherd the flock with justice." No doubt this passage served as a background for Jesus' message on the Good Shepherd in John 10.

The picture of the shepherd, of course, points to the benevolent Ruler who can be trusted in the leadership role. Coming, as it does, on the heels of the fall of Jerusalem, it was good news indeed to learn that there was some leader who would gather the smitten and scattered nation. This same figure of the tender shepherd appears in Psalms 78:52 – 53; 79:13; 80:1; Isaiah 40:11; 49:9 – 10; Jeremiah 31:10; and later in Zechariah 11.

Relief for this battered flock was promised in an eschatological era, in "a day of clouds and thick darkness" (34:12; cf. Joel 2:2; Zep 1:15). Then Yahweh would destroy the oppressors ("fat and strong ones") who had pounced on the weak (34:16).

Just as Jeremiah 30:9 had pointed to a new David to come, so now Ezekiel 34:23 – 24 promised:

> I will place over them one shepherd, my servant David, and he will tend them; he will tend them and be their shepherd. I the LORD will be their God, and my servant David will be prince among them. I the LORD have spoken.

1. Anthony Williams, "The Mythological Background to Ezekiel 28:12 – 19," *Biblical Theology Bulletin* 6 (1976): 49 – 61.

The themes are very familiar by now. God's Servant is that representative person promised to head up the whole group known as the "seed" of Abraham, Isaac, Jacob, and David. Part of the tripartite formula appears here as well: "I will be their God."

This too was a piece of the old promise doctrine (note 34:30 for a fuller repetition of the formula). And when God pointed to David, the prediction of an everlasting dynasty, kingdom, and throne came easily to mind once again. Ezekiel loved to call that future Davidic king a "prince" (*nāśî'*). In fact, twenty out of his thirty-eight usages of this word "prince" refer to a coming Davidic king, the Messiah.

As if to make sure readers and listeners connected this new word about the Good Shepherd with the old promise, Ezekiel was instructed to call this promise about a future Davidic "prince" and its paradisiacal effects on nature, God's "covenant of peace" (34:25). That is only an alternative name for the new covenant, for its banishment of wild beasts and picture of safety, fertility, and productivity are similar to what Isaiah (11:6–9) and other prophets hoped for (Hos 2:22; Joel 3:18; Am 9:13–14; and later Zec 8:12). The "peace" of that covenant is the restored *harmony* that exists in a world where things *work* as they were meant to operate without the negative intrusions or wasteful disappointment.

The New Cleansing and New Birth

A passage that comes close to matching the majesty and scope of Jeremiah's new covenant passage is Ezekiel 36:25–35. Here Ezekiel promised that Yahweh, "for the sake of [his] holy name" ("not for [Israel's] sake," 36:22a, 32a; cf. 36:22b, 32b), would vindicate Israel by regathering them to their own land from all the countries where they had been dispersed. Thus "through" Israel all the nations of the earth would acknowledge that God had performed what he had promised, and thus his holy reputation and character would remain untarnished.

But that was not the half of it. More importantly, those who came under the new covenant by personal belief would experience what Conrad von Orelli has clearly stated as

> cleansing or justifying (ver. 25), and positive *new-birth* through the Spirit of God (vv. 26ff.) in consequence of which the people will henceforth be able and willing to keep the divine commands.... The Lord himself must sprinkle this impure people.... The human heart, the source of all volition and inclination (Deut. xxx.6), of all desire and effort, is unfit for God's service (Gen. viii.21), as Israel's whole history shows.... God will give His accepted people a new heart, related to the former one as flesh to stone, i.e., instead of a heart hard, stubborn, unreceptive, one sensitive to God's word and will, receptive to all good or as Jeremiah says, like a soft table on which God can write His holy law. And the new Spirit that is to fill these receptive hearts will be God's Spirit, who impels to the keeping of divine commands.... Every individual member of it is *born again* of water and spirit.... Although the outward bliss, which is the fruit of

> this inner work of grace, is presented under O.T. limitation (xxxvi.28f.), the act of grace itself, from which the peace with God springs, is seen with divine clearness.[2]

No wonder Jesus marveled that Nicodemus did not know about the new birth and the work of the Holy Spirit (Jn 3:10). As a teacher of the Jews, he should have been familiar with this passage and therefore the teaching on this subject. Men and women could be cleansed by the same Lord who, by the gift of the Spirit, would perform a heart transplant in them and give them a new birth. Related activities of the Spirit have already been enumerated in Joel 2:28 – 32 and Isaiah 42:1; 44:3; 59:21. Then a purified people would dwell once again in a purified land, like the garden of Eden (Eze 36:35), where the Edenic blessing would once again reign unchallenged (vv. 37 – 38).

A Reunited, Restored Israel

It is most likely that the valley where Ezekiel received his vision of the dry bones in Ezekiel 37:1 was the same place where he received his first revelation of the imminent destruction of Jerusalem (3:22). If so, the book would be bracketed in a rather unique way.

The scattered dry bones were the whole house of Israel (37:11) to whom Ezekiel was given the frustrating command to "prophesy" (v. 4). As he obeyed, the miracle of reassembly took place through the medium of the preached word of God and the powerful work of God. But these people, even though they had been restored, were still not revived; they were dead! Therefore Ezekiel was told to "prophesy" again, and breath and life came into those who had been slain (37:9).

The teaching was expressly given by Ezekiel in 37:12 – 14:

> My people, I am going to open your graves and bring you up from them; I will bring you back to the land of Israel.... I will put my Spirit in you and you will live, and I will settle you in your own land.

Thus, as Adam had the breath of life breathed into his nostrils and he became "alive," so would a restored Israel. This chapter, then, does not deal with the doctrine of the personal bodily resurrection but with national resurrection.

Moreover, the two separated brethren, the ten northern tribes of Joseph or Ephraim and the two southern tribes of Judah and Benjamin, would be reunited under a new David in that day of national resurrection, according to Ezekiel 37:15 – 28. In that passage Ezekiel was told to join the two sticks, marked Judah and Joseph, respectively, into *one* stick (vv. 16 – 19). Then they will once again, for the first time since 931 BC, be "*one* nation" (v. 22a), under "*one* king" (v. 22b), with "*one* God" (v. 23), and "*one* shepherd." "My servant David will be king over them" (v. 24), and this state will last "forever"

2. Conrad von Orelli, *The Old Testament Prophecy of the Consummation of God's Kingdom Traced in Its Historical Development*, trans. J. J. Banks (Edinburgh: T & T Clark, 1889), 322 (italics his).

(v. 25) as part of God's "everlasting covenant" (v. 26). Yahweh's "dwelling place will be with them" (cf. the "rest" and "place" themes of the prophetic history of Joshua's era): "I will be their God and they shall be my people. Then the nations will know that I the LORD make Israel holy, when my sanctuary is among them forever" (vv. 27 – 28).

With that keynote theme, Ezekiel proceeded to give a detailed description of the restored land of Israel after he had treated the battle with Gog and Magog in chapters 38 – 39. In that land a new temple would again be the dominating piece of architecture. From this temple would issue a stream or river of life that increased in depth and power as it made its way to the sea formerly known as the Dead Sea (cf. Ps 46:4 – 5; Isa 33:13 – 24; Joel 3:9 – 21). Along its banks were the trees of life yielding their healing leaves and monthly fruits in a restored paradise picture of the new Jerusalem.

But is Ezekiel 40 – 48 merely an ideal, symbolic description or a prophetic reality? Perhaps each of these categories is a little too simplistic for the depth of idea here. In our view, there is to be a real relocated temple in the midst of the land. There worship of the living God will continue as described here under those concomitant features of worship known in the day Ezekiel was writing. (Compare this to how the prophets described the armaments of future eschatological battles in terms of the implements of war known to that day: bow and arrows, spears and horses.)

Certainly, when Ezekiel described the river of life and the fruit, he was moving more to apocalyptic terminology such as we later meet in John's Apocalypse. But the reality of a restored heaven and restored earth — named "THE LORD IS THERE" (Eze 48:35) in the New Jerusalem of Israel — is secure. The conclusion of Ezekiel's prophecy, then, is an expansion and further elaboration of Isaiah 65 and 66, which speak of the new heavens and the new earth. Only here the accent falls on the Lord tabernacling in the midst of his worshiping people, wherein nature is healed and restored to its original design and productivity.

The Book of Daniel

Daniel, meaning "God is my judge," was an exilic statesman and a mediator of the divine revelation for Israel and the nations. Born into an unidentified family of nobility in Judah sometime just prior to Josiah's reformation in 622 BC, he was taken by Nebuchadnezzar along with the first captives from Judah to Babylon in 605 BC.

Daniel was a hostage, serving to prove Judah's good faith toward Babylon's continued mastery over Judah. So in the third year of King Jehoiakim (Da 1:1, 3), he and his three friends (Hananiah, Mishael, and Azariah), were put into a three-year course in Babylon in preparation for some type of royal service (Da 1:4, 5).

The theme of this book could well be represented in Daniel 2:44:

> In the time of those [Gentile] kings, the God of heaven will set up a kingdom that will never be destroyed, nor will it be left to another people. It will crush all those kingdoms and bring them to an end, but it will itself endure forever.

Thus, God's sovereignty is seen in the abiding kingdom that God will eventually set up after the last of human empires and its leaders come to a decisive end, as determined by God himself.

Daniel prefers to use the more general name for God, *'elohim*, restricting his use of the personal name of Yahweh (= LORD) to his prayer in Daniel 9. In this way, Daniel made the point that this Lord was not just the God of the Jews, but he is God over all the nations. Accordingly, he is called the "Most Holy [God]" (4:17; 5:18), the "God of gods" (2:47), and the "Lord of kings" (2:47). God is in charge of all of history, and he controls it so that it terminates in the conclusion he has determined for history and not one chosen by any human rulers for their own benefit.

The Promised Kingdom's Success

The theology of Daniel is clearly set forth in antithesis to the successive kingdoms of humankind. In contrast to these kingdoms is the abiding but finally triumphant kingdom of God that is central to Daniel's message. Daniel, another exile along with Ezekiel,[3] looked beyond the catastrophe of Jerusalem's collapse and the present demise of the Davidic line to that abiding promised kingdom of God that would triumph over all the presently observed obstacles.

The Stone and the Kingdom of God

The dream of Nebuchadnezzar recorded in Daniel 2 set the stage for this prophecy. There a colossal image was described, which was composed of four decreasingly valuable metals. The statue is characterized by increasing weakness and division as one proceeds from head to toes. This image represented the human alternative to that "Stone" which fell on the feet of the colossus and crushed the whole image to pieces. After this, the "Stone" became a great kingdom that filled the whole earth. The "Stone" called to mind Isaiah's "Cornerstone" (Isa 28:16), while the metals of the statue were clearly identified as the four kingdoms, beginning with Babylon, followed by the split dominion of Medo-Persia, Graeco-Macedonia, and the Roman or Western empires.

The interpretation to this royal dream given in Daniel 2:44 was crystal clear: In the future God will set up a kingdom that will never be destroyed, that will endure forever.

3. We do not hesitate to defend the case for a sixth-century Daniel. This date, though extremely unpopular with biblical scholars, must still be pressed on evidential, not doctrinal, grounds. See the arguments of my colleague Gleason L. Archer Jr., *A Survey of Old Testament Introduction*, rev. ed. (Chicago: Moody Press, 1974), 377 – 403, and the bibliography he cites there.

The Ancient of Days

The parallel of Nebuchadnezzar's dream (Daniel 2) is Daniel's own vision in chapter 7. Again there were four kingdoms; and Nebuchadnezzar's head of gold, identified as Babylon in chapter 2, was represented here as Daniel's "lion" (7:4). The earthly monarch's silver breast and arms in Daniel 2 here seem to be aligned with Daniel's "bear" (v. 5), later identified as the ram with two horns in Daniel 8:20 — no less than Media and Persia. The belly and thighs of brass or copper in Daniel 2 become, in Daniel 7:6, a leopard with four heads and four wings. This is the same as Daniel's rough goat that grew four little horns in Daniel 8:21 – 22, which was Alexander the Great of Greece and the four generals who succeeded him. Nebuchadnezzar's iron-and-clay-legged image become a terrible and indescribably horrible beast in Daniel 7:7. This was a picture of a western or Roman empire, which finally was divided among ten kings plus a boastful antichrist (vv. 24 – 25) who would subdue three of the ten kings and shout against the Most High and wear out the saints of God for a designated period of time until God's everlasting kingdom would arrive (vv. 25b – 27).

In Daniel 7, the same four world empires appeared, only this time in succession out of the storm-laden sea. But again, when their time had expired and the ruler coming from among the ten horns of the fourth beast had done his worst against the God of heaven and his saints, the "Ancient of Days" approached in judgment. Said Daniel in verses 13 and 14:

> In my vision at night I looked, and there before me was one like a son of man, coming with the clouds of heaven. He approached the Ancient of Days and was led into his presence. He was given authority, glory and sovereign power; all peoples, nations and men of every language worshiped him. His dominion is an everlasting dominion that will not pass away, and his kingdom is one that will never be destroyed.

In contrast to the beastly nature of human empires, a *human* Mediator came from the Most High God, whose countenance and person immediately called to mind Ezekiel's and Isaiah's visions. Thus the coming Messiah would not only be the true David, but he would also be the true Son of Man,[4] combining in his person the high calling of humanity and the position reserved alone for God. His heavenly origin was stressed in that he would come "with the clouds of heaven" (7:13, which is more explicit than the falling stone of 2:34), and his divinity was underscored by the abiding and indestructible kingdom and dominion that was given to him (7:14).

Those world powers, governed by that mixture of savage, sensuous, and self-serving impulses, grim with distorted features, horns, teeth, and carnivorous appetites, would now confront God's judgment as the Ancient of Days took his seat in the heavenly court.

---

4. See E. J. Young, "Daniel's Vision of the Son of Man," in *The Law and the Prophets*, ed. J. Skilton (Nutley, NJ: Presbyterian and Reformed, 1974), 425 – 51.

His garments were sparkling white and pure as snow, his hair was like pure wool, and his throne was like a fiery mass of flames. The judgment was in accordance with what was written in the books (7:10), and the judgment thrones were set up on earth (v. 9). The retinue of the Ancient of Days was enormous: ten thousand times ten thousand served him and stood before him (cf. the heavenly retinue of the judge in Zec 14:5).

The Saints of the Most High

The "saints of the Most High" (7:18, 22, 27 in the Aramaic phrase, *qaddîšê 'elyônîn*),[5] to whom the kingdom and dominion were given after the judgment of nations, were in the same line of descent as the "holy nation" (*gôy qādôš*, Ex 19:6), or the "holy people" (*'am qādôš*, Dt 7:6; 26:19) of the Mosaic era, or the "seed" promised to Eve and the patriarchs. Israel had been promised a great kingdom already in the Old Testament (Nu 24:7; Isa 60:12; Mic 4:8), and this kingdom was to be ruled by the coming Davidic king. It was of more than passing interest that "the saints" belonged to God (note the possessive genitive) and that they formed a remnant even as Isaiah had spoken of a "holy seed" (*zera' qōdēš*, Isa 6:13)[6] that would remain after the repeated destructions.

The Seventy Weeks

The future of Jerusalem and the nation of Israel were outlined for Daniel as he realized that the seventy years of captivity prophesied by Jeremiah (29:10) were almost over. That future involved seventy sevens or weeks (Da 9:20 – 27) arranged in three groups: (1) one set of seven weeks, (2) another of sixty-two weeks, and (3) a final set of one week. Hence 70 weeks, forming 490 years were to be divided into 49, 434, and 7 years, respectively. The purpose of this further extension of time before the awaited consummation set in was described in the six infinitives of verse 24:

To finish transgression
To put an end to sin
To atone for wickedness
To bring in everlasting righteousness
To seal up vision and prophecy
To anoint the most holy [place/person]

The order of events before the full redemption arrived included the complete deliverance from sin and guilt, the conclusion of prophetic activity, and the introduction of the righteous kingdom with its anointed sanctuary in Zion as predicted in Ezekiel 40 – 48, Zechariah 3:9 – 10, and their predecessors.

5. For the most recent defenders of the Israelite view and for the massive bibliography, see Vern S. Poythress, "The Holy Ones of the Most High in Daniel vii," *Vetus Testamentum* 26 (1976): 208 – 13; and Gerhard F. Hasel, "The Identity of the Saints of the Most High in Daniel 7," *Biblica* 56 (1976): 173 – 92.

6. A fact noticed by G. Hasel, "Identity of the Saints," 191.

Most commentators agree that the 490 years began with the decree of Artaxerxes, in his twentieth year of reign in 445 BC (Ne 2:1 – 8),[7] which allowed the city of Jerusalem to be rebuilt, and the years continued through 483 of those 490 announced, until the first advent of Messiah. But commentators differ widely on whether there is a gap of undetermined length between the first 69 weeks or 483 years and the last week of 7 years, or whether that week also did not expire during the first Christian century — during the persecution of the early church as symbolized by Stephen's martyrdom. The former position (the "gap" interpretation) points to the temporal notation of "*after* the sixty-two weeks [period]" (9:26) and the cutting off of Messiah (approx. AD 30) and the destruction of the temple (AD 70) as indicators of nonsequential timing in an otherwise linear stream previous to this time; whereas the latter group tends to equate the "anointed one" and the "prince" of verse 26, and to argue for the completion of the seventieth week during the first century AD.

In my view, the "Anointed One" (*māšîaḥ*, 9:26), "the princely, kingly, Anointed One" (*māšîaḥ nāgîd*, v. 25) is the same one as the "Son of man" in 7:13, who will return to earth in triumph after he has suffered death on earth.

The Little Boastful Horn

Over against God's holy remnant in the final day will stand "another horn," "a little one" (7:8), "ruler/prince" (9:26b – 27), or "king" who will "do as he pleases," "magnify himself above every god," and "will say unheard-of things against the God of gods" (11:36).

Just as the king of Babylon in Isaiah 14 and the king of Tyre in Ezekiel 28 functioned as surrogates for the final, coming evil one in his challenge against God and his people, so Daniel envisioned the appearance of one who turned out to be Antiochus (Epiphanes) IV. His desecration of the altar of the sanctuary by offering on it a pig (11:31) and his breaking of his covenant were an essential part of what that final Antichrist, the one who was to come as the "beast" (Rev 13), the "man of sin" (2Th 2), or the "little horn" and "prince" of Daniel, would do. This did not mean that Daniel was undecided between a historical or eschatological personage for his meaning. Rather, the meaning was one and only one throughout.

As the later Antiochian school of interpretation explained it by their principle of "Theoria," the prophet was given a vision of the future in which he saw not only the final fulfillment as the conclusion to the word he uttered, but he also often saw and spoke of one or more of the intervening *means* and connecting personages, who were so in tune with one or more aspects of that final fulfillment that they became

7. The word for "decree" is literally "word." According to a paper read by Dr. Allan MacRae at the 1976 annual meeting of the Evangelical Theological Society, that "word" was the one given by Jeremiah. Thus, he would favor two gaps of unspecified duration between the seventh week and sixty-two weeks, and between the sixty-ninth and seventieth week, respectively.

a collective or corporate part of the single prediction. The apostle John similarly described his understanding of this person: "The antichrist is coming, even now many antichrists have come" (1Jn 2:18). Together they embodied a whole "seed" (Ge 3:15) of "the Serpent"; however, they did from time to time have their representatives who were only earnests and harbingers of the final Antichrist, even as each chosen child of the successive patriarchs and reigning Davidites were representatives yet one with the single meaning about the true Seed, Servant, and David who was to come.

The Future Resurrection

"At that time ... a time of distress such as has not happened from the beginning of nations until then," God would deliver his people and introduce his everlasting kingdom (Da 12:1). The projected completion of the promise with its kingdom, throne, and reign would come to fruition.

As in Isaiah 26:19, God would restore that godly band of believers to life by means of a bodily resurrection of the dead. One class would enjoy eternal life, for their names were written in the book (12:1 – 2). The other class would be resurrected to eternal shame and contempt — that is, their doom (cf. Isa 24:22; 66:24). Job had been assured that just as a tree would sprout again even if it were cut down, so would a person live again (Job 14:7, 14). In fact, he longed for the opportunity to look on his Redeemer with his own eyes even after the worms had destroyed his body (19:25 – 27).

Thus, as the colossus of human attempts to tyrannize people came to an end with the irruption of the kingdom of God and his King according to the ancient but renewed promise, there appeared one final all-powerful king who was the summation of all the power and kingdoms of humanity, the anti-messiah. But God's Messiah would easily vanquish that evil one, introduce his kingdom, and give that new righteous and everlasting dominion to his "holy ones," many of whom he would resurrect bodily from the dust of the earth; and they would shine as stars forevermore.

Chapter 11

The Triumph of the Promise: Postexilic Times

Haggai, Zechariah, Malachi
Chronicles, Ezra, Nehemiah, Esther

With the divinely predicted yet nevertheless surprising permission of the Persian King Cyrus, a small portion of the exiled nation returned to Jerusalem under a representative of David's royal house, Governor Zerubbabel, and the High Priest Joshua. But everywhere the persistent reminders of their abysmal defeat under the Babylonians were all too evident.

Even when they strove to lay again the foundations of that most important symbol of the presence of God, their sanctuary, discouragement took its toll. The whole project came to a complete stop for sixteen long years (Ezr 4:24). Everything was wrong: they lacked the means, then the inclination, and finally even the will, to build the temple; their every attempt met with constant opposition both from within the small group and from the outside (Ezr 3:12 – 13; 4:1 – 22). So it would have remained had not God graciously sent the prophets Haggai and Zechariah (Ezr 5:1).

The Book of Haggai

Haggai, along with Zechariah, was one of the two prophets God used to stir up the exiles who had returned from Babylon. The famous Cyrus Cylinder recorded how the Persian conqueror of Babylon gave permission in 539 BC for the exiled population of Babylon to go free and to return to their own countries. Thus, in 538 BC a small group of Jews (not quite 50,000) made the 900-mile journey back to Jerusalem and immediately began to lay the foundations for their temple in 537 BC. However, such a strong dissention arose that the project had to be abandoned, and for the next sixteen years the footers of the foundations stood incomplete and without any evidence of completion.

In 520 BC, however, God sent Haggai and Zechariah to stir up the people to once again take up this abandoned task to the glory of God. This, then, became the occasion for Haggai's four messages. There are only two other brief references to Haggai, one in Ezra 5:1 and the other in Ezra 6:14.

The House of God

The theological problem of this period was simply this: Where was the activity and presence of God to be found amidst the lethargy of God's people toward spiritual things? Certainly, it did not lie in the dilapidated political state of Israel or in the destroyed temple. Thus the circumstances of life had forced people to enlarge their thinking to focus on the internal promise of God while its external fortunes seemed to flounder.

But those sixteen years of indifference toward the construction of the house of God had proven costly not only to Israel's spiritual development but also in her recent material reverses. How could there be any material progress when there was no corresponding spiritual development and growth?

In 520 BC, Haggai met the people's flippant excuse that the "time" was inopportune (a way of really blaming God for not having prospered them more so that they could erect the temple) by asking the people to apply the same logic to their own luxuriant dwellings (1:2 – 4). How was it, the prophet probed, that they had been able to build their own homes if the economy, the times, and the international political situation had been so adverse?

In fact, so bothersome had the fact that the temple lay in "ruins" (*ḥārēb*, 1:4) become to Yahweh that he had called for a "drought" (*ḥōreb*, v. 11) on their crops (notice the word play). Once again, where the *precept* of God had not been heeded, then the *penalty* of God was used to capture the people's attention. Thus the small group of returnees were sowing more but harvesting less, eating and drinking more but enjoying it less, wearing more but feeling its warming effects less, and earning more but able to buy less and less (v. 6). This was what they should take to heart and consider carefully (Hag 1:5, 7; cf. 2:15, 18). Not every single or isolated reverse was to be interpreted as an evidence of the discipline of God against the nation. But when these calamities began to come to them in a series and increased so much in severity that the prestige and well-being of the whole nation was affected, then that nation should know that it was the hand of God and that it was high time that men and women should return to him. This principle was first announced in Leviticus 26:3 – 33 and used in most of the prophets, especially Amos 4:6 – 12.

Amazingly, the people responded and "obeyed" the word of the Lord and the voice of Haggai the prophet (1:12). God added his ancient name and his promise of his presence with the words: "I am with you" (1:13; 2:4) as his Spirit stirred up the leadership and the people to work on the house of the Lord (1:14).

The proof that God still dwelt with Israel, according to the ancient promise given in connection with the tabernacle (Ex 29:45 – 46) and the tripartite formula, was to be seen in the fact that he made his Spirit abide among them (Hag 2:5). Furthermore, the small beginnings of that second temple were directly connected with the fortunes, glory, and honor to be received in the future temple of God described by Ezekiel and others; for Haggai pointedly asked in 2:3, "Who of you is left who saw the glory of *this* house [the second temple] in its former glory [Solomon's temple]?" Then he boldly proclaimed, "'I will shake all nations, and what is desired by all nations will come, and I will fill *this* house with glory,' says the LORD Almighty" (2:7). All three temples of the past and future were one and the same as they participated in the glory and splendor of the universal acknowledgment accorded to the temple of Yahweh in that final day. Indeed, the nations would pour their wealth into that house in recognition of Yahweh's sovereignty as had been envisioned by Isaiah 54:11–14; 60; Jeremiah 3:14–18; and Ezekiel 40–48. Thus, no one was to despise the day of small things begun in the name, power, and plan of God.

The Coming Cosmic Shakeup

But before such a day could come, there would be a worldwide convulsion in the physical, political, and social realms (2:6, 21–22). This accorded well with the by-now-familiar prophetic theme of the "day of the Lord." The judgments of God and his undisputed triumph were described by Haggai in terms used of past conquests when God had acted decisively for Israel—for example, at the Red Sea when "the horses and their riders will fall," or in Gideon's deliverance when everyone fell by the "sword of his brother" (2:22). So Yahweh would shake the heavens and the earth and "overturn" (cf. Sodom and Gomorrah) the throne of kingdoms and destroy the power of the kingdoms of the nations (2:22).[1]

God's Signet Ring

The significance of this shake-up for David's royal house became clear in 2:23 when Haggai declared that "on that day" Yahweh would take Zerubbabel, a Davidite, God's "Servant," and make him a "signet ring" (*ḥôtām*). Therefore, the overthrow of the kingdoms was in order to exalt the coming Davidic person. Thus Zerubbabel, the current heir to the throne of David, had in his office and person a value that would be raised to an exceptionally glorious status when the projected worldwide catastrophe catapulted all competing empires into their final termination.

This "signet ring" was the seal of authority that had been taken abruptly from Jehoiachin (also named Jeconiah and Coniah) in Jeremiah 22:24, for God had rejected his leadership. The use of seals in marking property and documents was well known in the ancient Near East; therefore, the signet ring was no doubt the royal insignia that was used in authorizations and authentications of the power and prestige of that government (cf. SS 8:6; Ecc 17:22). This new Davidite will be God's sign to the world that he intended to continue to fulfill his ancient promise-plan. The "mercies of David" were

1. For further explanation of this characteristic in prophecy, see Walter C. Kaiser Jr., *Back toward the Future: Hints for Interpretating Biblical Prophecy* (1989; reprint, Eugene, OR: Wipf and Stock, 2003), 51–60.

"sure" or "unchangeable" (Isa 55:3). Even his title of "My Servant" was more than polite court language. On the lips of Yahweh, it was a transparent reference to that corporate entity, but final single individual, who embodied the whole group as announced in the eighth century by Isaiah (e.g., Isa 42:1).

The Book of Zechariah

Zechariah (meaning "Yahweh has remembered") was the son of Berechiah and the grandson of Iddo (Zec 1:1), who prophesied to the returned exilic remnant of Judah in the years 520 – 518 BC (Zec 1:1; 7:1). As a contemporary of Joshua the high priest, and Zerubbabel the governor (Ezr 5:1, 2; Zec 3:1; 4:6; 6:11), Zechariah preached the need for repentance and a return to the Lord God if this returned remnant hoped to count on the presence, power, and glory of God.

The heart of his message, as it was also the heart of the eight night visions given to Zechariah, was to be found in Zechariah 4:6: " 'Not by might nor by power, but by my Spirit,' says the Lord Almighty."

The Call to Repentance

With eight night visions (1:7 – 6:8) and two burden messages (9 – 11; 12 – 14), the priest-prophet Zechariah traced the growth of God's kingdom from its humble beginnings to its triumphant victory over every opposing force. Working hand in hand with the prophet Haggai, Zechariah delivered the most intense call to repentance ever given by any Old Testament prophet (Zec 1:1 – 6) in November, 520 BC. The evil that had overtaken (*hiśśîgû*, v. 6) the nation in the catastrophe of 587 BC and the seventy years of exile were exactly what Moses had warned with the very same vocabulary in Deuteronomy 28:15, 45.

Eight Night Visions

In the mutually complementary eight visions, Zechariah received a whole picture as God's answer to those who questioned the validity of the old promise-plan of God and the future of Zion. In the first vision, the report of the four horsemen was disheartening, for the nations of the earth remained at ease and comfort (1:11), despite the repeated threats of imminent destruction. But by the time of the eighth vision, the four chariots had completed their work of carrying out the judgment of God in every direction (6:1 – 8). How this was to be done was detailed in the second vision, where the four horns (1:18 – 21 [2:1 – 4]), the same, no doubt, as Daniel's four successive world powers, were humbled and broken off by each of the successive four smiths raised up by God.

While judgment was to be ordered upon the nations, Jerusalem was to experience a rebuilding, enlargement, and exaltation (2:1ff. [2:5ff.]): "And I myself will be a wall of fire around it, declares the LORD, and I will be its glory within" (2:5 [9]; cf. Isa 60:19; Rev 21:23); and "'I am coming, and I will live among you,' declares the LORD. 'Many nations will be joined with the LORD in that day and will become my people. I will live among you and you will know that the LORD Almighty has sent me to you'" (2:10 – 11 [14 – 15]).

My Servant-Branch, the Stone

The outward establishment of the city of God as the personal residence of Yahweh must be preceded by a divine work of inner cleansing. For in Zechariah's fourth vision, he saw the High Priest Joshua wearing dung-spattered clothes and standing in the presence of the angel of the Lord with the accusations of Satan being hurled at him. For the accuser, the Lord ordered silence; but for the besmirched High Priest Joshua, he ordered the removal of his filthy garments and the new clothing of rich clean apparel. The guilt of the whole nation was resting on the high priest, and thus it had made them all unclean (cf. Hag 2:11 – 14). But it also promised the reestablishment of the office of high priest after a long interruption (Zec 3:7). God will remove the sin of the land "in a single day" (v. 9), promised the Lord. Thus Joshua, as representative of that "kingdom of priests" (Ex 19:6), was a "sign" (*môpēt*, 3:8).

It was a "wonder" that the high priesthood even existed after the long interruption of the exile; yet it too was a sign of the future. The advent of God's true and only adequate representative was the Messiah, who here was called by three titles.

The "Branch" (or "Sprout") of 3:8 and 6:12 was another proper name for the last Davidite, who would arise out of obscurity, already known from Isaiah 4:2 and Jeremiah 23:5 – 6. The fact that he appears as the "Servant" in connection with the priesthood cannot be a mere coincidence. It is here made plain that the "Branch" or "Servant" will not only be David's successor but also Joshua's. As Isaiah had declared that the Servant would give his life as an atonement for others and thereby remove their sin and iniquity, so Zechariah 3:9 also promised that the Messiah would do so in "a single day."

But if the "Servant-Branch" represented Messiah's first advent, then the "Stone," as in Daniel 2:34 – 35, represented Messiah's second advent. Thus in the fuller passage of Zechariah 6:9 – 15, Zechariah was directed to make "crowns" from silver and gold brought to the returnees from the nationals in Babylon. This event summarized the eight night visions and their scope in one act — princely gifts coming from the far-off nations in Babylon were but a harbinger and precursor of the wealth of the nations that would pour into Jerusalem when Messiah the Branch was received as King of Kings and Lord of Lords. These gifts were made into a crown for the King-Priest, the "Man" whose name was "Branch," who would "build the temple of the LORD," "sit and rule on his throne," and "be a Priest on his throne" (6:12 – 13). The same Lord who helped complete the building of that second temple would rule as Priest and King — both offices in one Person! Numerous peoples would come to seek the Lord resident in Jerusalem in that day, and ten people would cling to the skirts of one Jew, saying, "Let us go with you, because we have heard that God is with you." This was the prospect outlined by Zechariah in 8:20 – 23.

The same Priest-King was the theme of Psalm 110, only there he was a conquering king, whereas here in Zechariah 6 he is enthroned in peaceful dominion.

The King of Humility and Righteousness

As Zechariah began the first of his two burden messages, he predicted the victorious progress of one we would come to know by the name of Alexander the Great (Zec 9:1 – 8). The theme was already set: a judgment was coming in which God would destroy the Gentile world powers that had also held sway over Israel. Israel's true King was coming, and his inauguration into office would be symbolized by his riding on the donkey (9:9, cf. Jdg 5:10; 10:4; 12:14).

His character was "righteous," the same description used by Isaiah (9:7; 11:4 – 5; 32:1). Yet he had also brought "salvation" and was therefore characterized as one who freely gave out the grace of God to others. He was "gentle," "and riding on a donkey," the symbol of one who was being invested with the rule and reign of a king (1Ki 1:38). This was Israel's new king. He was meek, and yet he was also to be victorious over all; he would destroy the implements of war (Zec 9:10*a*), and yet he would reign in peace over the whole earth (v. 10*b*). The latter picture was identical with that of Isaiah 9:1 – 7; 11:1 – 9; and Micah 5:2 – 5. "His rule will extend from sea to sea and from the [Euphrates] River to the ends of the earth" as Psalm 72:8 had proclaimed (cf. Zec 9:10*b*).

Yet even after Israel had been restored to her land after the Babylonian exile, the prospect of a regathered, reunified nation still appeared in Zechariah 10:9 – 12. The importance of this passage and its late postexilic date of 518 BC should not be lost by those who interpret the promise of the land spiritually or as a temporal blessing, which according to this alternate interpretation declared that the land had been forfeited by a rebellious nation due to her failure to keep her part of what they have labeled a conditional and a bilateral covenant. This text argues against that view. The hope of a return to the land that had been promised to the patriarchs now burned brighter, despite the fact that Israel had become more and more scattered.

The Smitten Shepherd

Israel had had evil rulers (shepherds) who had taken advantage of their flock, but the Good Shepherd was at first accepted and then rejected and sold for thirty pieces of silver (Zec 11:7 – 14). As long as he ruled them in the past, he had used two staves named "delight" and "union" (*noʿam, ḥôblîm*); but when these two staves were broken, the power that this brother-kingdom wielded in God's name was snapped and disrupted. Thus the Lord was often dismissed from this nation — indeed, at times even by his Davidic representative. Then, as a reward, or even as their estimate of his service, they weighed out the sum paid for a slave (Ex 21:32): thirty pieces of silver! Thus the Shepherd became the Martyr-Shepherd (Zec 13:7 – 9) for the sheep who had rejected his leadership.

But in another section (Zec 12:10 – 13:1), the people would mourn for the One they had pierced as one mourned for his only son. The Shepherd was not personally deserving of this suffering, but he suffered on behalf of the sins of his people.

But the Spirit would be poured out on the people in that day, along with the divine Spirit of grace and supplication, with true penitence of heart and genuine sorrow for rejection of the Messiah. And as Ezekiel had predicted that the Spirit of God would give the knowledge of Yahweh and of the Savior, so that same Spirit would open conviction and repentance in the hearts of Israel.

That Final Day of Victory

One decisive battle remained yet to be fought by Yahweh. In that day, he would bring the nations of the earth together as they attempted to deal decisively and conclusively with the "Jewish question" (Zec 14:1 – 2). But that was the very day selected by the Lord of Hosts in which he would go forth and fight against those nations (v. 3). With simultaneous great convulsions in nature, the Lord of Glory will descend with clouds of heaven (Da 7:13), along with all his saints (Zec 14:5), and plant his feet on the Mount of Olives (vv. 4 – 5). Then history and the first aspect of the grand plan of God's salvific promise would be wrapped up in the most decisive triumph ever witnessed on planet earth. He also would remain victor over all peoples, nations, and nature (v. 9ff.). Holiness to the Lord would be the dominant motif from that day onward (v. 20ff.) as the wealth of the nations would be gathered in worship of the present King, the promised "Seed" of the woman Eve, Abraham, Isaac, Jacob, and David (v. 14ff.). Seventeen times in this second "burden" message of Zechariah 12 – 14, Zechariah had proclaimed, "In that day"; and twenty-two times he had pointed to "Jerusalem" and thirteen times to the "nations." These statistics alone can correctly identify the time, themes, and participants stressed in these chapters: it would be earth's finest hour as her Creator, Redeemer, and now-Ruling King returned to complete what he had promised to do so long ago.

The Book of Malachi

It is often debated whether the name Malachi, meaning "my messenger," is a name or a title. While slightly more favorable evidence points to the fact that it was his name, it is more important to note that Malachi ministered some time after the exile, for already the service to God had become perfunctory and lacked real integrity. However, since he makes no reference to Ezra or Nehemiah in his book, his writing should probably be placed prior to the 445 BC reforms of both of those men. That would mean a time of approximately 450 BC.

The prophet opened his message with a categorical assertion, saying, "I have loved you, says the LORD" (Mal 1:2). Add to this Malachi 3:6, "I the LORD do not change," and it is possible to claim that the theme of this book is the "unchanging love of God for his people."[2]

God's Messenger of the Covenant

One more time a prophet sent from God, now late in the fifth century, answered the incredulous and blasphemous taunts of a people immersed in their own miseries as they complained, "Where is the God of justice?" (Mal 2:17).

Malachi's response was simple: "The Lord you are seeking will come" (3:1). However, before he would come, Yahweh would send a forerunner to prepare the way ahead of him (v. 1), just as Isaiah had predicted (40:1ff.), for it was necessary that humanity be morally prepared for such an advent. But when the messenger of the covenant (*mala'k habb^{e}rît*, 3:1) would come to his temple, he would be none other than the promised Messiah, for the day of his coming was also the day of the Lord so frequently mentioned by the prophets (v. 2).

"The Lord" (*hā'ādôn*, note the article and singular form) will come to "his temple" (Mal 3:1); thus, he was Yahweh (cf. Isa 1:24; 3:1; 10:16, 33). This "angel [or messenger] of the covenant" was the mediator through whom the Lord himself would take up his abode in his temple. This renewed residence in the temple was partially realized in God's gracious presence in the temple as a built-in response to the preaching of Haggai and Zechariah, and thus ended the self-imposed absence of the glory of God mentioned in Ezekiel 11:23.

But Malachi now also saw a personal abode of this "angel of the covenant" (Mal 3:1), the coming Messiah, in his temple. Furthermore, so intense was his presence that it would contain a dreadful danger for all sinners. "Who can endure the day of his coming?" asked Malachi, "Who can stand when he appears?" (3:2). Accordingly, this was but a repetition of the promise made at the time of the exodus: Yahweh would signally manifest himself in the person of the theophanic angel. That is what he had promised in Exodus 23:20–21: "See, I am sending an angel ahead of you ... since my Name is in him" (cf. Ex 32:34; 33:2).

Hence, Malachi's generation, like the eighth-century audience of Amos (Am 5:18, 20), was mistaken in longing for the day of the Lord as if that day would be a cure-all for an unprepared people. The presence of the Lord could only mean that they would all be consumed, for his holiness and their stiff-necked ways could not mix (cf. Ex 33:3).

2. See Walter C. Kaiser Jr., *Malachi: God's Unchanging Love* (1984); reprint, idem, *The Preacher's Commentary*, vol. 23, ed. Lloyd J. Ogilvie (Nashville: Thomas Nelson, 1992), 449–513.

It was necessary that people be sifted as in a furnace, or as by soap, so that the filth or dross of sin could be purged. Such a judgment would fall particularly on the priests (Mal 3:3), who would need to be cleansed before they could be used in his service.

The forerunner is first presented as a "messenger" (Mal 3:1) and then as "Elijah the prophet" (4:5). Probably we are not to think of Elijah the Tishbite, a fact sometimes encouraged by Elijah's translation into heaven without experiencing death. But after the analogy of that new or second David, so there was to be a new or second Elijah. He would be a man who would come in the "spirit and power" of Elijah, even as Jesus pointed to John the Baptist and said that he was Elijah, for he had come in the "spirit and power of Elijah" (Mt 11:14; 17:11; Lk 1:17). Thus the work of the second Elijah was also to turn the hearts of the fathers to the children and the children to the fathers in reconciliation. Mortals must voluntarily dedicate themselves wholeheartedly to the Lord, for if they would not do so, then he would be forced ultimately and finally to come and visit the earth with a "curse" (*ḥērem*, 4:6 [3:24]). This "curse" was a "ban" or an "involuntary dedication" of everything to the Lord, by which he finally took everything, which rightfully belonged to him in any case, as a rebuke for steadfast resistance to giving any part to him.

But Malachi was certain that all would not end in gloom and despair:

> "My name will be great among the nations, from the rising to the setting of the sun. In every place incense and pure offerings will be brought to my name, because my name will be great among the nations," says the Lord Almighty. (Mal 1:11)

Yahweh's success was as extensive geographically as was the circuit of the sun, and his places of worship were to be located, not just in Jerusalem but "in every place" around the globe where men and women would offer "pure offerings" — in other words, worship untainted by soiled hands or hearts. God's name would be "great" and highly exalted among the Gentile nations of the world. Thus, the Mosaic discussion of "place" and offerings is climaxed by a universality of the gospel and a purity of worship unknown in history past or present, but surely a real part of the future.

The Books of Chronicles, Ezra, Nehemiah, and Esther

The books of Chronicles are known in Hebrew as *dibrê hayyāmim*, literally, "happenings of the days," which title occurs only once in Chronicles itself (1Ch 27:24), but thirty-two times in the books of Kings, once in Nehemiah (12:23), and twice in Esther (6:1; 10:2).

The most likely author of the books of Chronicles is Ezra, who is listed as a scribe in Ezra 7:6. The Talmudic tradition of *Baba Bathra* (15a) identified Ezra as the author as well. Since Ezra returned to Jerusalem in 457 BC, and spiritual and moral laxity had set in after the temple was rebuilt in 520 – 516 BC, it is a pretty good guess that the best time for Ezra to remind his people of their spiritual and national roots would have been in the times while Nehemiah served as governor in his first return in 445 BC and again in 432 BC.

Two driving purposes seem to provide the writer of Chronicles with the reason for his composition of these books: (1) to trace the line of David all the way back to Adam and focus on that reign in its military supremacy and his vital interest in worship, and (2) to take the programmatic statement of 2 Chronicles 7:14 ("If my people, who are called by my name, will humble themselves and pray and seek my face and turn from their wicked ways, then will I hear from heaven and will forgive their sin and heal their land") as a basis for the five recorded revivals in the history of Judah. Those revivals, along with the catch-phrases from the programmatic statement of 2 Chronicles 7:14 were:[3]

"Humble [yourselves]"	2Ch 11 – 12	King Rehoboam
"Seek my face"	2Ch 14 – 16	King Asa
"Pray"	2Ch 17 – 20	King Jehoshaphat
"Turn from their wicked ways"	2Ch 29 – 32	King Hezekiah
"Humble [yourselves]"	2Ch 34 – 35	King Josiah

These revivals of the past became the basis for urging a change in the lives of the nation in the postexilic days as well as for the distant and foreseeable future.

The books of Ezra-Nehemiah were originally regarded by the Jews as a single work. Furthermore, the opening verses of this work, when compared to the closing verses of Chronicles, demonstrate that Ezra-Nehemiah continued the history of the books of Chronicles, for the verbal repetitions are obvious. Thus, Ezra is said to be the author of this joint work as well as the books of Chronicles.

The center of this work focuses on the restoration and reformation of the community of God. But in an even larger sense, it focuses on the Lord who was still sovereignly and graciously working on behalf of his people. Thus, when the wall around Jerusalem was rebuilt by Nehemiah, all their enemies "lost their self-confidence, because they realized that this work had been done with the help of our God" (Ne 6:16).

Likewise, while the book of Esther is ostensibly written to explain the origin of the Feast of Purim, its greater purpose is to trace the divine hand of providence in the assorted details of life. King Ahasuerus is to be equated with King Xerxes I (486 – 465 BC).

The book of Esther begins in Susa, the winter palace of the Persian kings, in the third year of King Xerxes (483 BC). Esther won the contest, which featured the search

3. Walter C. Kaiser Jr., *Revive Us Again: Your Wakeup Call for Spiritual Renewal* (Ross-shire, Scotland: Christian Focus Publishers, 2001).

for a new queen to replace Queen Vashti, who had refused to appear before drunken revelers. Esther was a Jewish orphan who lived in Susa with her older cousin, Mordecai. Her Hebrew name was Hadassah (Est 2:7), meaning "myrtle."[4]

The heart of the message of Esther's book is found in Mordecai's message to Esther in 4:13 – 14:

> Do not think that because you are in the king's house you alone of all the Jews will escape. For if you remain silent at this time, relief and deliverance for the Jews will arise from another place, but you and your father's family will perish. And who knows but that you have come to royal position for such a time as this?

The Kingdom Is the Lord's

At the end of Israel's long historical climb from nonexistence into nationhood and from destruction into a weakened state in the postexilic period, the Chronicler (perhaps one or more writers of Ezra, Nehemiah, Esther, 1 and 2 Chronicles) selected those historical events and words from the Davidic and Solomonic kingdom that could be used to project the image of the anticipated eschatological consummation of the promise in the new David. His awaited reign would be the climax to the old promise, and this prospect would rekindle hope amid the encircling gloom of the meager growth during the postexilic period.

The People of the Promise

The Chronicler had a vision of a reunited Israel in a future day with its capital at Jerusalem along the lines of the glorious days of David and Solomon. The expression "all Israel" appeared forty-one times in Chronicles and eight times in Ezra-Nehemiah, besides such additional phrases as "all the house of Israel" or "all the tribes of Israel." This "all Israel" theme definitely underscored the prophets' description of the future reunification of the divided kingdom into one united kingdom (e.g., Isa 11:13; Hos 1:11 [2:2]; Jer 3:18; Eze 37:15).

The people would be God's people, a united congregation (*'ēdâh*) of Israel as they lived, loved, and worshiped Yahweh with a "whole [or perfect] heart" (*lēbāb šālēm*). This expression occurs nine times in Chronicles out of a total of thirty times in the whole Old Testament, but altogether there are thirty references in Chronicles to "heart" in the sense of right or wrong relationship. As Hanani the prophet said to King Asa:

> For the eyes of the LORD range throughout the earth to strengthen those whose hearts are fully committed to him. (2 Ch 16:9)

4. For further detail, see Walter C. Kaiser Jr. *A History of Israel From the Bronze Age Through the Jewish Wars* (Nashville: Broadman and Holman, 1998), 434 – 37. See also J. Stafford Wright, "The Historicity of Esther," in *New Perspectives of the Old Testament*, ed. J. Barton Payne (Waco, TX: Word, 1970), 37 – 47.

Life in the Promise

The Torah or law of God was the standard by which the people of God received their instruction. Thirty-one times the Chronicler referred to the name of Moses as compared to twelve times in Samuel-Kings; and almost forty times Torah was used in Chronicles as compared to a mere twelve times in Samuel-Kings. Fourteen times the law was designated "the Torah of the Lord," or "of God" or "of the Lord God."[5]

In Nehemiah 8 there is an account of how Ezra brought the Word of God with him and read it to the people as they listened intently (vv. 8–9), for as he read, Ezra "gave the sense" (v. 8, *śôm śekel*). Thus, as King Jehoshaphat had earlier sent out a group of men to instruct the people of Judah from the Torah of the Lord (2Ch 17:9), so now had Ezra in these postexilic times:

> For Ezra had devoted himself to the study and observance of the Law of the LORD, and to teaching its decrees and laws in Israel. (Ez 7:10)

Just as Solomon had been promised the blessing of the benefits of God's unconditional promise to the house of David "if" he was careful to observe all that the Lord had commanded Moses (1Ch 22:12; 28:7), so "all Israel" was urged to walk with their "whole heart" in accordance with all that God had commanded in the law of Moses. That would be the pathway of life and blessing. The eternal plan of God was an essential part of this balance between divine sovereignty and human responsibility.

While it is true that the Chronicler more frequently than not stressed the aspect of divine agency in human events in contrast to the parallel account in Samuel-Kings (which focused on the human agency), there was a message in the book that emphasized both aspects of divine sovereignty and human responsibility. In cases where people were clearly at fault, God still allowed the cause or situation to stand, "for this thing is done of me," said Yahweh. For example, in the case of Rehoboam's rejection of the sagacious advice to cut taxes, he refused and thereby split the kingdom, "for this turn of events was from God, to fulfill the word the LORD had spoken to Jeroboam son of Nebat through Ahijah the Shilonite" (2Ch 10:15; cf. 11:4).[6]

This dual presentation of the events of Israel's history during the postexilic days also led to the technique of indirect references to God in writing such histories as the book

---

5. These statistics come from Jacob M. Myers, "The Theology of the Chronicler," *1 Chronicles*, Anchor Bible (Garden City, NY: Doubleday, 1974), lxxviii ff. The bibliography on the Chronicler's theology continues to grow. Some of the older contributions with good bibliography are Roddy L. Braun, "The Message of Chronicles: Rally Round the Temple," *Concordia Theological Monthly* 42 (1971): 502–14; P. Ackroyd, "The Theology of the Chronicler," *Lexington Theological Quarterly* 8 (1973): 108–16; Phillip Roberts, "An Evaluation of the Chronicler's Theology of Eschatology Based on Synoptic Studies Between Samuel-Kings and Chronicles," (M.A. thesis, Trinity Evangelical Divinity School, 1974); John Goldingay, "The Chronicler as a Theologian," *Biblical Theology Bulletin* 5 (1975): 99–126; H. G. M. Williamson, "The Accession of Solomon in the Books of Chronicles," *Vetus Testamentum* 26 (1976): 351–61.

6. For additional passages, see 1 Chronicles 10:13; 11:9; 21:7; 2 Chronicles 12:2; 13:18; 14:11–12; 16:7; 17:3, 5; 18:31; 20:30; 21:10; 22:7; 24:18, 24; 25:20; 26:5, 7, 20; 27:6.

of Esther. Ronald M. Hals[7] made an excellent case for God's all-causality, even though his name was absent: the oblique but telling references to "another quarter" (*māqôm a' ḥēr*, Est 4:14), the passive form in Esther 9:22, "the month when their sorrow was *turned* into joy and their mourning into a day of celebration," and the timely coincidences (?) of the king's insomnia (6:1), or the reading of Mordecai's earlier favors done for the king (v. 2). Even the question "Who knows?" of Esther 4:14*b* is not one of despair or frustration but a rhetorical device that has its own answer for any who reflect with any care on what was happening.[8]

The Kingdom of the Promise

God's promise to David was repeated in 1 Chronicles 17:14. "I will set him over my house and my kingdom forever." So David blessed Yahweh in his prayer of thanksgiving for the freewill gifts so abundantly and generously provided by Israel in response to the need for a temple to be built by Solomon.

> Yours, O LORD, is the greatness and the power,
>   and the glory and the majesty and the splendor,
>   for everything in heaven and earth is yours.
> Yours, O LORD is the kingdom;
>   you are exalted as head over all.
> Wealth and honor come from you;
>   you are the ruler of all things.
> In your hands are strength and power
>   to exalt and to give strength to all. (1Ch 29:11 – 12)

This "kingdom of Yahweh," which was "in the hands of David's descendants" (2Ch 13:8) belonged to the Lord. The king of Israel was merely God's vicegerent who owed his office to God and who symbolically continued that reign as an earnest of God's triumphal occupation of that throne. Thus, to aid the sagging spirits of a downtrodden people, the Chronicler revived the image of the kingdom at the height of its greatest power in order to set forth the glories of Messiah's kingdom.

The focus on the temple, the ordinances connected with the temple, and the emphasis on music and prayer in times of revival and worship were a fitting doxology to the one to whom the kingdom belonged and whose reign had already begun in the lives of all believers, but was yet to have its total sway over heaven and earth. That ancient prophetic word of promise had not failed, nor would it.

This message had a larger audience in mind than the Israelites themselves, for the total purpose of the genealogical lists in 1 Chronicles 1 – 9 was not satisfied when it served

7. Ronald M. Hals, "Comparison with the Book of Esther," in *The Theology of the Book of Ruth* (Philadelphia: Fortress Press, 1969), 47 – 53.

8. Few have interacted with the creative suggestions of Canon J. Stafford Wright, "The Historicity of the Book of Esther," in *New Perspectives on the Old Testament*, ed. J. Barton Payne (Waco, TX: Word Books, 1979), 37–47.

merely to authenticate those uncertain about their lineage and who wished to be included in the priesthood of Zerubbabel's day. It also exhibited the connection of the nation with the whole human race and thus addressed all descendants of "Adam." The word was not as direct as Genesis 12:3, "In your seed [Abraham] all the nations of the earth shall be blessed." However, the inference of the genealogy and the explicit claim of the promise made with David as unfolded in the kingdom theology of the Chronicler made it clear that all humanity was affected by the enormity of God's eschatological work.

Part 2

A Biblical Theology of the New Testament

Introduction

The Arrival of the Promise: Jesus the Messiah

About 6 BC – about AD 6

To begin a New Testament theology is to start in space and time where the divine author began, that is, with five main characters, all of whom were given the privilege of introducing God's new advances in his promise-plan: John the Baptist; his father, Zechariah; the Virgin Mary; the elderly Simeon; and the prophetess Anna. However, while each played a part in announcing that which was new, they also connected that newness with what God had already given as fulfillments and assurances for the future in the Old Testament.

The lines of continuity with God's past work in the history of Israel were just as strong as the promises of God's new works of fulfillment, though these new revelations marked off some strains of discontinuity as well. Together, these five witnesses form the bridge from the Old to the New Testament while simultaneously signaling that God was about to do a new work that would show the progress of revelation beyond the frontiers set in the older Testament.

John the Baptist: The Call to Repentance and Preparation for the Kingdom of God

The record of John the Baptist[1] found in all four Gospels amounts to 194 verses: 47 are found in Matthew, 28 in Mark, 85 in Luke, and 34 in John's gospel.[2] This amount of exposure to the life and ministry of the forerunner of the Messiah is amazing when seventeen of the twenty-seven books of the New Testament all have a smaller total number of verses allotted to them than the combined coverage for John the Baptist in

1. Two of the more recent books on John the Baptist include: Serjius Bulgakov, *The Friend of the Bridegroom: On the Orthodox Veneration of the Forerunner*, trans. Boris Jakim (Grand Rapids: Eerdmans, 2003), and Catherine M. Murphy, *John the Baptist: Prophet of Purity for a New Age* (Collegeville, MN: Liturgical Press, 2003).

2. The passages that speak of John are: Mt 3:1 – 16; 11:1 – 19; 14:1 – 12; 16:14; 17:12 – 13; Mk 1:2 – 10, 14 – 15; 6:14 – 29; 8:28; 9:11 – 13; Lk 1:5 – 25, 57 – 80; 3:1 – 22; 7:18 – 35; 9:7 – 9, 19; 20:4 – 6; John 1:6 – 8, 15 – 37; 3:23 – 30; 5:33 – 35; and 10:40 – 41.

the Gospels.[3] Surely, this indicates something of the significance and importance of the message and work of the Baptizer.

Of all these verses, however, only about thirty record his words, with hardly more than half of them as distinct or separate utterances, while the others are parallels or duplicate sayings found in the other gospel writers. But add to this the amazing statistic that of these eighteen or twenty distinctive verses, there are more than fifty allusions or references to Old Testament statements, either in substance or form or both. Even more startling is the fact that more than forty of these fifty quotes and allusions are from three Old Testament prophets: Isaiah, Malachi, and Jeremiah.[4]

There can be little doubt that John the Baptist lived and breathed the message of the Old Testament and saw his ministry as being directly linked to that of the Old. In this way, John formed the real bridge across the imaginary divide that many incorrectly make between the two Testaments. In fact, even the names "Old Testament" and "New Testament" come from the time of the church father Origen (ca. AD 185 to ca. 254) and not from the Scriptures themselves! The worst page in most Bible translations is the blank sheet of paper between the two Testaments. If it were simply to indicate that there exists a space of almost four hundred years from Malachi to Matthew, then a similar piece of blank paper should be put for approximately the same period of time between Genesis and Exodus for the same reason. But a blank sheet was not inserted after Genesis, so why should one be placed after Malachi?

Add to these 194 verses from the Gospels another seven allusions to John the Baptist in the book of Acts (1:4 – 5; 1:21 – 22; 10:36 – 39; 11:15 – 16; 13:24 – 25; 18:24 – 26; 19:1 – 7),[5] and together they form our earliest testimonies to John, all arguably from the first century AD alone, with one external work, Josephus's *Antiquities of the Jews* (18:116 – 19), written around AD 93.[6]

Just as striking as John's use of the Old Testament is the abruptness with which John is introduced, as if the gospel writer had wanted to emphasize John's relationship to the prophet Elijah, who appears in just such an abrupt way in 1 Kings 17:1.[7] John bursts on a scene that had apparently had no prophetic ministry for almost four hundred years. Then, all of a sudden, there he was: a voice crying out in the desert, declaring that people must get ready and repent by asking for forgiveness, for the Messiah was now

3. These books (and the number of verses) are as follows: Galatians (149); Ephesians (151); Philippians (104); Colossians (94); 1 Thessalonians (89); 2 Thessalonians (47); 1 Timothy (113); 2 Timothy (83); Titus (46); Philemon (25); James (107); 1 Peter (104); 2 Peter (61); 1 John (105); 2 John (13); 3 John (14); and Jude (25).

4. The statistics for these 194 verses are from J. Elder Cumming, *John: The Baptist, Forerunner and Martyr* (London: Marshall Brothers, n.d.), 104 – 5.

5. The references to the book of Acts are discussed in Murphy, *John the Baptist*, 9 – 13.

6. John is referred to in the Koran (3:39; 6:85; 19:1 – 15; 21:89 – 90) as Yahya' and presented as a prophet, but this witness is from around AD 600. There are other apocryphal so-called Gnostic and Ebionite Gospels, but they do not come from the first century either. See *The New Testament Apocrypha*, vol. 1, ed. Wilhelm Schneemelcher, trans. R. M. Wilson (Louisville, KY: Westminster/John Knox, 1992).

7. Cumming, *John: The Baptist*, 34.

about to come. Catherine M. Murphy is dramatic in her wording: "John the Baptist inaugurates the good news of God's kingdom like a champagne bottle shattered against the hull of a new ship."[8] John launched, as it were, what would later be called the days of "the age to come" (Heb 6:5 NRSV) or "the last days" (Heb 1:1 NIV).

Although John was out in the desolate area of the desert, great crowds came out to hear him, despite the fact that he was not saying popular words that would please the culture of that day. He had no political agenda, nor was he campaigning against Rome or any other societal force. Representatives from every walk and station in life made their way out into the desert to hear one who only claimed to be a forerunner of the One who was coming. The arrival of this royal personage that he proclaimed, who would come from the line of David, called for a moral and spiritual preparation: it was time for all mortals to repent and to produce the fruit of the repentance in righteous and justice in every aspect of life.

But what a time to arrive on the scene in Israel! It had been centuries since God had spoken by a prophet. Who would show those desert-bound listeners the meaning of the events that surrounded them? And how would the end of the oppression that Judah was experiencing from the Gentiles happen, especially the oppression inflicted on them by the imperial armies of Rome? True, there were a few small political and military rebellions against Rome, but what were these against so strong an empire? Other movements, like that of the remote Qumran community, isolated from the main society down by the Dead Sea, focused on new meanings to Old Testament Scriptures. However, their main emphasis was more of a legalistic one, despite their use of a new form of "pesher interpretation" of the prophets' message that gave contemporary values to prophecies about kingdoms that had long since ceased to exist, with little or no canonical basis for such new equations with the names of nations or the leaders found in the text. The Dead Sea community had withdrawn to the desert basically to study the law of God and to await the coming of the kingdom of God. The imperial eagle on the top of the occupying Roman Legion's standards was a strong enough witness that the Jewish people were far from being free. God's answer to all these longings for change and relief was to send a man named John, who called for repentance, because the kingdom of God was about to commence.

Luke alone gives the account of John's earlier life: he was indeed the son of Zechariah, a priest in the rotation of Abijah, and of Elizabeth, of the family of Aaron (1:5 – 6), who was a relative (probably not a "cousin" as some translations say) of the Virgin Mary (1:35), who paid Elizabeth a three-month visit immediately before the birth of John six months later (1:56). John's proper Hebrew name was Johanan, a name given under divine direction (1:13), despite opposition by their neighbors and relatives (1:58 – 63), who wanted to name John after his father, Zechariah. John was born in an unnamed "city of Judah," which was

8. Murphy, *John the Baptist*, 1.

situated in "the hill country." He was Jesus' senior by six months (Luke 1:36–37, cf. 2:6); but most importantly, he was the predicted forerunner of Jesus the Messiah.

Little is known of John's early childhood, but what is told relates solely to his spiritual growth. The announcing angel, Gabriel, declared, "He will be filled with the Holy Spirit even from birth" (Lk 1:15). Even in these times before the New Testament era, John enjoyed the presence and ministry of the Holy Spirit, starting from his birth! This is startling, for to this present day many do not think of the Holy Spirit's presence in the Old Testament as being a norm for those who believed. But be that as it may, John was "filled with the Holy Spirit!"

As a result of this divine blessing, an angel told Zechariah, "Many of the people of Israel will he bring back to the Lord their God" (Lk 1:16). Moreover, his ministry would be "in the spirit and power of Elijah" (Lk 1:17*a*), with the same result as that also mentioned in Malachi (4:6): he would "turn the hearts of the fathers to their children and the disobedient to the wisdom of the righteous — to make ready a people prepared for the Lord" (Lk 1:17*b*). There was a moral and spiritual preparation that was necessary if men and women were going to enjoy the results of the long-awaited promise of God. The coming of the Messiah was certain and sure, but the participants were only validated by their preparation for that coming.

The Preaching of the Gospel of Promise by John

The essence of the message of this stern man of the desert, according to Matthew 3:2 was this: "Repent, for the kingdom of heaven has come near." Both parts of this message were equally important: (1) repentance (Grk. *metanoia*, literally, "a change of mind") was necessary; and (2) the promised messianic kingdom that was soon to appear as it had never been seen before.

Repentance, which normally has the primary emphasis of sorrow for sin, along with a genuine change of one's heart and mind, is better rendered in Western thought as "conversion,"[9] for it called for a basic turning around — that is, a reversing of one's direction. John not only called for godly sorrow and a reversal of direction, heading back toward God rather than toward one's own self or self-interests, but he also called for the accompanying evidence that showed production of "fruit in keeping with repentance" (Mt 3:8).

When the crowd asked, "What should we do then?" (Lk 3:10), John did not pull any punches. Tax collectors should not collect more than they were required to collect; soldiers should be satisfied with their pay and stop extorting money and accusing people falsely; and Pharisees and Sadducees were to put away their pride and their love of recognition, evidenced in their loving to have the preeminence for their teaching the law and receiving the reverence of the people. Moreover, the one owning two

9. As George E. Ladd correctly suggested, *A Theology of the New Testament* (Grand Rapids: Eerdmans, 1974), 38–39.

coats should share with the one who had none. If they all genuinely repented and reversed their habit of life, they would be prepared for the Messiah and his kingdom. John's call influenced all strata of society, much as the prophets of old had called for in their preaching. His call for conversion did not stop there, but he went on to issue a cry for proof of that sincerity by exhibiting real social, ethical, and moral changes in the heart and life as well. This change and turning to God was not merely a change in opinions or a change of beliefs; it had to be accompanied by works and practical conduct as well.

At the center of John's proclamation was anticipation of the arrival of the Messiah. No one was to confuse John with the one he was announcing and the one for whom he was to prepare the way. While it is true that the fourth gospel differs from the synoptic presentation of John, the difference is not such that a harmonization of the two cannot be adequately explained. In fact, the gospel of John presupposes the events of the Synoptic Gospels. This is shown by the fact that John 1:32 – 33 notes that the baptism of Jesus had already taken place and also by the fact that the priests and Levites wanted to know by what authority he did what he was doing. So the gospel of John's narrative about John begins a little later than where the other three gospel writers began.

In John's gospel, the Coming One is presented as the Lamb of God who takes away the sin of the world (Jn 1:29). The best chronology that shows how the Synoptics and the gospel of John fit together is the one that has the fourth gospel showing that John the Baptist pointed to Jesus on the banks of the Jordan (1:15 – 36) *after* the forty days of temptation. Here it was that John the Baptist was led by the Holy Spirit to see a new feature in his message: Jesus also came to be the sin-bearer of the world. It might well be that the Baptizer had meditated over texts such as Isaiah 53 during his sojourn in the desert. His twice-repeated emphasis on the fact that Jesus "surpassed" (Grk. *emprosthen*) him may indeed have indicated that he understood this as referring to the *preexistence* of Jesus as the "Son of God" (or, as I would translate *emprosthen*, that the Messiah "was before him") — a temporal reference ("before him"), instead of the comparative one ("surpassed me"), would be more in keeping with the thirty-one other instances of *emprosthen* with a similar meaning. In only two instances have translators taken the word to mean "higher rank" or the equivalent in this context. "A man/One who comes after me was *before* me, for he [always] was/existed" (Jn 1:15, 30). The evangelist John, the writer of the gospel, probably meant by *emprosthen*, then, that Jesus was the preexistent one. But if that is so, why then did the Baptist say, "I myself did not know him"? (Jn 1:31). When the Nazarene first presented himself to the Baptist (Mt 3:13), John declined to baptize Jesus, sensing his own unworthiness. However, when the Baptist saw the sign of the Holy Spirit coming down on Jesus, he knew immediately that this was the Son of God (Jn 1:34), even as he had been forewarned that this sign would confirm the Messiah's identity and deity.

John the Baptizer recognized another feature of the message of the gospel: that judgment would also accompany the coming of Christ. This judgment would not fall on the Gentiles only, as the Talmud had limited the effect of the judgment,[10] for repentance, or conversion, according to John the Baptist and the gospel itself, was a necessary prerequisite for *all* who would enter the kingdom of heaven. To claim descent from Abraham would not be sufficient for salvation, nor would it be enough to gain entrance into the kingdom of God (Mt 3:9). Every worthless and empty tree that did not bear fruit had to be cut down and thrown into the fire — hence there was not only a baptism of the Spirit, but of fire as well (Mt 3:7 – 8). Judgment was just as important a feature of the promise as was the good news. This note of judgment had to be struck right at the beginning of the announcement of these things so that the Messiah would be presented not only as the Savior and the way of salvation, but also as the means of punishment for all unrepentant sinners. The gospel is not only good news; it is also the announcement of bad news for those who refuse to hear God's call and refuse to repent and to produce the evidential fruit along with that repentance.

The Baptism of John

In addition to the spoken message that John the Baptist brought, there was the great symbol of his ministry implanted in his title, "the Baptist." Baptism was not new to the Jewish nation, however, for long before New Testament times, Gentile proselytes to Judaism were being baptized. Proselytes understood that in doing so they renounced their past and sought shelter under the wings of the Shekinah. Others have pointed to other possible sources for understanding John's baptism. The Mosaic law prescribed a number of washings for the Jews (Lev 11 – 15; Nu 19), but these were ethical rites and ones that could be separated (which some, no doubt, did) from any moral or spiritual conditions put on the recipients. Another possible source for John's baptismal rite was the messianic lustrations foretold by the prophets Jeremiah (33:8), Ezekiel (36:25 – 26) and Zechariah (13:1). God would open up a fountain for the cleansing of all sin and uncleanness and grant a new heart and a new spirit within mortals. John took these messianic promises and pointed to the coming Messiah as the only one who could fulfill them. John's baptism was one of preparation, yet it was even more a baptism of promise: the promise of the kingdom and the promise of the coming of the king himself. The Baptizer baptized with water, but when the Messiah came, he would baptize them with the Holy Spirit and with fire (Mt 3:11).

The baptism of Jesus is mentioned in all three Synoptics (Mt 3:13 – 15; Mk 1:9 – 10; Lk 3:21). This baptism took place at Bethany on the other side of the Jordan (Jn 1:28). Jesus'

10. Jerusalem *Ta'anit.* 64*a*, as quoted by Alfred Edersheim, *The Life and Times of Jesus the Messiah* (Grand Rapids: Eerdmans, 1953), 1:271.

baptism is not directly mentioned in the fourth gospel; however, the fourth evangelist refers to the descent of the Holy Spirit on Jesus as a dove (Jn 1:32–35), the authenticating sign that Jesus was indeed the promised Messiah who also was the Son of God. This descent of the Holy Spirit on Jesus at the baptism ties the Synoptics' picture of Jesus' baptism with the picture in the gospel of John. Before he baptized Jesus, the forerunner of the Messiah did not also know that Jesus was indeed the "Son of God." For John to gain such an understanding, the heavens had to open and the Holy Spirit descend upon him, much as Peter later experienced in another setting (Mt 16:13–20) later on.

John did have a preliminary Old Testament knowledge and expectation about a number of things concerning the Messiah, but in the progress of revelation, more would need to be added to his understanding. Indeed, the same Lord who sent him also told him that the one on whom he saw the Spirit descending in the form of a dove would be the Son of God. But this sign exceeded all he had ever known prior to this. If all four Gospels refer to the same incident, which is how we understand them, John's instruction in the knowledge of the Messiah increases at this point; Jesus is not only the expected Messiah, but he is the Son of God as well.

The forerunner's testimony that this was the Son of God (Jn 1:34) fully anticipates, as we have just indicated, the apostle Peter's confession at Caesarea Philippi (Mt 16:16). Neither John the Baptist nor Peter made this confession by their own wits, wisdom, or rational powers (for "flesh and blood" did not reveal this to them), but by the communicating work of the Holy Spirit. But for John the Baptist, what he was enabled to see by the Holy Spirit was no meager grace. It became one of the great boundary markers between the Old and New Testaments, while simultaneously uniting them in the person and message of the forerunner. As Jesus (Mt 11:13) later commented, "For all the Prophets and the Law prophesied until John." John was both a boundary marker and a bridge between the Testaments. The distinctiveness of the Testaments is affirmed, while at the same time their unity is praised by our Lord in the person and ministry of John the Baptist.

Not only was John the Baptist the forerunner of Christ, but he also chose and prepared disciples for the Messiah. When the Baptist pointed to Jesus as the Lamb of God who takes away the sin of the world, two of John's disciples left him and immediately followed Jesus (Jn 1:37). John's own testimony became the firstfruits of the harvest that was to come in the church. He is truly the boundary marker and the signal for the unity of the Old and New Testaments.

John's Imprisonment and Death

According to the Synoptics, the arrest and execution of the Baptist was due to Herodias's hatred of what John was saying against her (Mt 14:3–12; Mk 6:17–29; Lk 3:19–20). The Roman tetrarch, Herod, had taken Herodias, his sister-in-law, from his brother to be his own wife, contrary to the Mosaic law (Lev 18:16; 20:21). Josephus, on the other hand, claimed that Herod put John to death because he "feared lest the great influence John had over the people might put it in his power and inclination to raise a rebellion; for they seemed ready to do anything he should advise."[11]

However, these two explanations may not be far apart, for although John's death was principally due to Herodias's intransigent hatred of John, Herod may have felt later on that this was not as adequate an explanation for the Jews of that day — especially for such a popular person as John — and thus added the political reasons. Josephus made it all sound more politically correct to direct the attention away from Herod's weak acquiescence to his wife's demands. John the Baptist could hardly have qualified as a political revolutionary: he, who was born into a priestly family, probably also of modest means. No doubt he would ordinarily have stepped into the priestly honors and its rotations with the easiness that was part of his birthright as the eldest son, but he chose instead to retreat to the desert to reflect and to meditate on spiritual things. He was anything but an activist; rather, he was more of an ascetic, who, like the Essenes, had grieved over the prevailing luxury and corruption of his day. His retreat to the wilderness made a statement about his disapproval of society as he found it and his decision to make a clean break with it and with the superficial piety that was prevalent among the Pharisees. But more than that, John was "set apart" for the office of a prophet (Lk 1:14 – 17, 76 – 78), just as the prophet Elijah had been.

That John sent his disciples to ask Jesus whether or not he was the Messiah seems strange in light of all we have seen of John in the Gospels and the testimony John himself gave that Jesus was the Messiah. Some say John sent his disciples, not because his own faith was wavering, but for the sake of his disciples: he wanted them to hear firsthand from Jesus' lips just who he was. But another, simpler explanation seems to fit best: that true to human nature, depression struck the forerunner in his prison confinement. He who had been accustomed to freedom in the desert and wide open spaces was now confined to a dreary prison. This, along with his own great disappointment over the delay in Jesus' announcement of his kingdom and the swift exercise of his power, may have filled him with doubt and the fear that he may have made a mistake.

Whatever doubts John may have had, his faith was still in Jesus, for he still went right to Jesus, rather than taking an alternative path for a resolution of his problems. The Bridegroom (as John called Jesus in John 3:28 – 29) sent back reports of what was happening as one miracle of healing after another took place, and as the invasion of the kingdom of God into Satan's stronghold was seen when demons fled at the rebuke of his voice. This was accompanied by a strong word of encouragement: "Blessed is the man who does not fall away because of me" (Mt 11:6). The Castle of Macchaerus, once a fortress and a palace but now a prison on the eastern shores of the Dead Sea, became

11. Flavius Josephus, *Antiquities of the Jews*, 18:116 – 19.

the place where John ended his earthly pilgrimage.[12] The forerunner had completed his calling: the one he had announced must now take up the work of the gospel.

Jesus' Estimate of John the Baptist

Jesus declared that John was "a lamp that burned and gave light" (Jn 5:35); indeed, he was much "more than a prophet" (Mt 11:9). He was one who, as Messiah's forerunner, had come in the spirit and power of Elijah to restore all things. Indeed, "Among those born of women there has not risen anyone greater than John the Baptist" (Mt 11:11), declared Jesus. John the Baptist is our best transition from the older days of the promise to the realizations that would now take place. Despite the fact that he did not perform any miracles, John's voice trumpeted the call for conversion and influenced large numbers of people as he marked the boundary with the old and formed a bridge to the new part of the single plan of God.

Zechariah: A Speechless One Gives His Benediction

Zechariah the priest, who had been speechless for nine months because of his unbelief over the angel Gabriel's announcement of the coming birth of John (Lk 1:11 – 18), suddenly had his tongue loosened (1:57 – 66) as he poured out his praise to God in a hymn known today as the "Benedictus" (Lk 1:67 – 79). The hymn is so named because it begins with, "Praise be to the Lord, the God of Israel" (Lk 1:68a), rendered in the Latin Vulgate as "*Benedictus Dominus Deus Israel.*" Commentators have detected some thirty-three allusions to or quotations from the Old Testament in this hymn, once again showing how each of these five individuals was both a bridge over and a marker of the boundaries between the Testaments. This is indeed a song of praise to God for the way God had worked to raise up the messianic "sunrise" in the coming of Jesus' birth. Surely, that is how the older Testament closed in Malachi 4:2, with its promise that "the sun of righteousness will rise with healing in its wings." "And you," continued the prophet Malachi, "will go out and leap like calves released from the stall" (cf. Lk 1:78).

"This song," summarizes R. Kent Hughes, "is an ecstatic chain of praise from beginning to end — first, praise to God for keeping his promise to David (the Davidic Covenant) [Lk 1:68 – 71]; second, praise to God for keeping his promise to Abraham (the Abrahamic Covenant) [vv. 72 – 74]; third, praise to God for keeping his promise to Zechariah in giving him his son John, the forerunner [vv. 76 – 77]; and fourth, praise to God for the coming of 'the rising sun' [vv. 78 – 79]."[13]

As far as Zechariah was concerned, the completion of the promise of God was as good as done, for he puts his verbs in the prophetic past tense. This coming one was "a horn of salvation," a metaphor used in the Old Testament to symbolize power and

12. Flavius Josephus. *Antiquities of the Jews*, 18:v.1, 2. Also Pliny, *ist. Nat.* v. xvi. 72.

13. R. Kent Hughes, *Luke: That You May Know the Truth* (Wheaton, IL: Crossway Books, 1998), 1:74.

strength, for when a strong animal such as a buffalo or an ox tosses or lifts up its horns, it is ready to begin its deadly charge (cf. Dt 33:17; Ps 148:14). A horn of salvation had been promised through the dynasty of David in 2 Samuel 7:11 – 19 and Isaiah 9:6 – 7. That horn would mean redemption and a ransoming of the people of God in the One coming from David's line as well as deliverance from their enemies on earth (Rev 19:1 – 16).

The "mercy" God would show, as already noted, would come in direct fulfillment of the promise God had made with Abraham in Genesis 12:1 – 3 and Genesis 22:16 – 18, so that by two proofs, in which it was impossible for God to lie — in other words, both by his *word* and by his *oath*, all of us might have a wonderful confidence (Heb 6:13 – 20) that the future belonged to Messiah and that it was secure. So Zechariah praised God for his ancient word offered in his "holy covenant" and for the "oath he swore to our father Abraham" (Lk 1:72 – 73).

It is difficult to express the overwhelming joy of Zechariah and Elizabeth as they gazed on their newborn son John. Not only did this birth take away any stigma that barrenness might have brought, but this boy would "be called a prophet of the Most High." He would go on to prepare the way for the Lord, "to give his people the knowledge of salvation through the forgiveness of their sins" (1:76 – 77). Imagine a personal, inward experience of salvation that would immediately grant "the forgiveness of sins"! The one who would forgive those sins was the same one John was born to announce and to be his forerunner (cf. Mt 1:21).

Zechariah's song of benediction ends with the promise of the "rising sun," a word rendered in the older King James Version text and Christmas carols as the "Daystar." It would be as the light of a new morning breaking over the horizon and dispelling the gloom of darkness that had settled as a shroud over all creation. Indeed, Jesus is the "morning star" who rises in our hearts (2 Pet 1:19). He is "the Root and the Offspring of David, and the bright Morning Star" (Rev 22:16), "the light of the world" (Jn 8:12). All who trust him will "shine like the sun in the kingdom of their father" (Mt 13:43).

For all who are living in "darkness" (an emblem of alienation from God) and the "shadow of death" (because such continued alienation eventually leads to perdition) the "rising sun" will shine on us from heaven "to guide our feet in the path of peace" (Lk 1:79). What a benediction and what a bridge between the Testaments is Zechariah's "Benedictus"!

Mary's Song: God's Mercy to Abraham

A song such as Mary's, had Herod heard her words, would have troubled him to no end, especially the lines: "[God] has brought down rulers from their thrones but has lifted up the humble" (Lk 1:52) and he "has sent the rich away empty" (v. 53). But Mary's song is more than a mere canticle of praise to God for being mindful of her low station in life; it is rather a thanksgiving to God for not only giving to her a son, but a son who would be in the line of David and who would establish his throne and kingdom that would last forever.

Mary may have come from the backwater streets of Nazareth, but despite her youth (somewhere between thirteen and sixteen years old, some speculate), she knew the songs of Hannah, Deborah, and David. These were the songs she no doubt had sung at the festivals in Jerusalem, along with the psalms sung at the daily offering of the morning and evening sacrifices.

Now that Mary was legally engaged to Joseph, she still had some months to go before the wedding could take place (a year-long engagement period was usual). But Joseph and Mary were considered husband and wife even though they had not, nor would they have, had sexual relations until the marriage ceremony. But nothing would have prepared her for God's gracious surprise and the special favor that was to come to her.

The message from the angel Gabriel was "Greetings, you who are highly favored! The Lord is with you" (Lk 1:28). Mary wondered, what could this sort of greeting signify? But when she was told that she would conceive a child who would be "called the Son of the Most High," and who would sit on "the throne of his father Jacob forever," with a "kingdom [that would] never end" (Lk 1:31 – 33), she asked, "How can this be … since I am a virgin?" (Lk 1:34). Her response was not one of doubt, it seems, but rather one of involuntary declaration of amazement.

The angel answered, "The Holy Spirit will come on you, and the power of the Most High will overshadow you. So the holy one to be born will be called the Son of God" (Lk 1:35).

Amazingly, Mary responded, "I am the Lord's servant.… May it be to me according to your word" (Lk 1:38). Mary must instinctively have known that this would cause her a lot of trouble — suspicion, rumor, and castigation by all her friends, neighbors, and possibly even by Joseph. The penalty for adultery (for engagement carried the same legal status as marriage in that day) was stoning (Dt 22:23 – 24), or at the very least, the drinking of the "bitter waters" in cases in dispute by a jealous partner (Nu 5:11 – 31).

So why did Mary concede and respond with "May it be to me as you have said?" Could such news as this be "good news?" There was only one way she could have said those words so willingly: she knew that the God of Israel was a merciful God who would be her help in this trying time.

The song God gave to her also helps us to know how God fortified her and gave her a deep contentment in the promised work of her heavenly Father. This song is called the "Magnificat" because the first line in the Latin Vulgate begins with: *Magnificat anima mea Dominum*, "My soul glorifies [magnifies] the Lord" (Lk 1:46). The tone of Mary's hymn is one of deep inner quietness, whereas Elizabeth greeted her "in a loud voice" (Lk 1:42):

> Blessed are you among women, and blessed is the child you will bear! But why am I so favored, that the mother of my Lord should come to me? As soon as the sound of your greeting reached my ears, the baby in my womb [John the Baptist] leaped for joy. Blessed is she who has believed that what the Lord has said to her will be accomplished. (Lk 1:42 – 44)

No longer was Mary simply Elizabeth's relative; she was now "the mother of my Lord." Perhaps she had heard from Zechariah the promises God had made about their son, John, and his role in preparing the way for Mary's son, the Messiah. Their joy at giving birth to the forerunner, whose task was to prepare the way for the Messiah, quickly brought to mind a score of Old Testament promises about both of their sons. So Mary stayed with Elizabeth for three months, perhaps awaiting the birth of John (Lk 1:56), and then returned home to Nazareth.

Mary's song has some similarities to Hannah's song in 1 Samuel 2:1 – 10, but there is also a marked difference between the two. Hannah's words are words of personal triumph and marked by cries of vindication over her rival in a polygamous marriage, while Mary's words are marked by a deep humility of spirit. Moreover, Mary's words are grounded as much on the Psalms as on parts of Hannah's song.

Generations following Mary would not only call her blessed because she was the mother of the Son of God but also because of the great things God had done (Lk 1:49). Mary celebrates the display in her life of three great divine attributes: God's power, his holiness, and his mercy (Lk 1:48*b* – 50). Despite her low position in society and humble rank among her contemporaries, she rejoices for herself and all those like her who are on the margins of society but can now begin to see that the promised victory of Messiah would answer their questions about where is God and why has he allowed things to go on as they have with the proud, the greedy, and the rich looking out only for themselves.

By this merciful act of a birth of the promised one in the line of David, rulers will already have been put on notice that their days are numbered, soon to end ignominiously. Likewise, the rich will be sent away empty, as God will, with the birth of this son, begin to act to finally bring an end to the heavy taxation that Herod and Rome foisted on the heads of the humble, hungry, and the poor and to set up a kingdom that will never cease.

Just as God helped his "servant" (Lk 1:54; cf. Isa 41:8) Israel by "remembering" them in the days of their Egyptian bondage (Ex 2:23 – 25), so he had once again remembered "to be merciful to Abraham and his descendants forever, even as he said to our fathers" (Lk 1:54 – 55).

The promise-keeping God alone was to be magnified and praised, for what had been foretold was even now coming to pass in ways that amazed and startled all who heard and saw these happenings.

Simeon: Now Ready for His Departure

Once again it is Luke who lets us see what took place behind the scenes in advance of the ministry of the New Testament writers, as Luke 2:25 – 35 introduces us to the elderly Simeon. As F. Godet wisely observed, "In times of spiritual degeneracy, when an official clergy no longer cultivates anything but the form of religion, its spirit retires amongst the obscurer members of the religious community, and creates for itself unofficial organs, often from the lowest classes. Simeon and Anna [Lk 2:36 – 38] are representatives of this spontaneous priesthood."[14]

This "righteous and devout" man, Simeon, "was waiting for the consolation of Israel" (Lk 2:25). The word "consolation" shows up in verbal forms in the Septuagint translation of Isaiah 40:1 — "Comfort, comfort my people" — and in the messianic prophecies that follow in Isaiah 40 – 53.

Simeon's expectation was that Israel's days of warfare and chastisement would soon be over and God would step in to comfort his people with his promised appearance and deliverance. But this comfort was not restricted to Israel only. Based on verses in Isaiah such as 42:6 or 49:6, he saw a day coming when the light of God's salvation would shine to the ends of the earth as well.

At the presentation of Jesus by his parents in the temple, Simeon takes up the infant Jesus in his arms and proclaims his famous song, remembered in the Latin Vulgate translation as "Nunc Dimittis," "Now dismiss" or "Let your servant depart in peace, for my eyes have seen your salvation" (Lk 2:29 – 30). This is a most amazing scene, for the God of the whole universe, now in diapers or the like, is gathered up in the arms of Simeon, who had expected a day like this when the Messiah would appear. Now that Simeon has seen that day, he announces that he is ready to die, for the rest is but a footnote to history; it will all take place as God had promised. Previously, it had been revealed to him, once again by the ministry of the Holy Spirit, "that he would not die before he had seen the Lord's Christ" (Lk 2:26). That same Holy Spirit "moved" him to go into the temple courts just at the very moment that Jesus' parents were bringing Jesus to the temple "to do for him what the custom of the Law required."

Three rites were required of all Israelites following a boy's birth: circumcision on the eighth day (Lk 2:21), an additional thirty-three days of purification for the mother (Lev 12), and the presentation of a firstborn (Ex 13:2; Nu 8:16; 18:15 – 16). The day Simeon intercepted them in the temple was the third of these three rites. The very humble offering that Jesus' parents made, "a pair of doves or two pigeons" (Lev 12: 8), indicates that they were at the poverty level financially. Nevertheless, they were chosen by God for high privilege indeed.

Simeon met the parents as they faithfully fulfilled what had been required of them in the law (Lk 2:23 – 24). Though they were at the bridge to the new day of revelation, Joseph and Mary still kept to the exact letter of the law that had been prescribed for them in the Old Testament. The link between the two Testaments was once again made.

This man held in his hands the Savior of the whole world! God had allowed him to see not just a part of his salvation: Christ alone was all that this fallen world needed.

14. F. Godet, *A Commentary on the Gospel of St. Luke*, 5th ed., trans. E. W. Shalders (Edinburgh: T & T Clark, 1870), 1:137.

What God had done was not done in a corner, but it had been "prepared in the sight of all people" (Lk 2:31). Moreover, it had relevance not just for the Jewish people, but Messiah was to be "a light for revelation to the Gentiles" as well as "for glory to your people Israel" (Lk 2:32). Whether this meeting between Simeon, Jesus, and his parents took place in the court of the Gentiles or not, we cannot say for sure, but the Gentiles were placed first in his affirmation, and then followed the promises such as appeared earlier in Isaiah 42:6; 49:6; and 60:3. Did Simeon also realize, as the apostle Paul would later say, that the full salvation of the Jews would only come after the Jews had been provoked to jealousy (Rom 10:19; 11:25–26)? Again, it is impossible to say for sure.

Simeon completes his witness to the Messiah by blessing Joseph and Mary. But then he adds one final word to Mary: "This child is destined to cause the falling and rising of many in Israel, and to be a sign that will be spoken against, so that the thoughts of many hearts will be revealed. And a sword will pierce your own soul too" (Lk 2:34–35). The Greek text begins with *idou*, "Behold," which usually announces a revelation of an unexpected truth. The "falling" and "rising of many" speaks to the opposition caused by the general unbelief of many of Jesus' own countrymen. Thus, in the midst of the joy of being the "mother of [her] Lord," there would also appear the mischief of bitter tears as she watched her son suffer on the cross. The sheer hatred of the Messiah would pierce the very heart of Mary as the hidden hostile thoughts many had toward God came out despite the sophistry of pharisaical piety and ritual.

Nevertheless, Simeon knew all would be well, for he (and the whole world) had seen what had been promised. He had held in his own arms the God of the whole universe; he was ready to depart. God would complete his promise-plan as he had anciently and was now presently assured in the sight of all the people.

Anna: Among Those Waiting for God's Redemption

The prophetess Anna was the daughter of Phanuel, from the tribe of Asher (Lk 2:36). Although married for seven years, she had been a widow for eighty-four years, or, as others count it, she had lived up to this point for eighty-four years. If the eighty-four years date from the days she began her widowhood (as I surmise is the better reading), and she was married somewhere around the age of fifteen, she would have been 106 at this point, which is not impossible. This was the day she too, along with Simeon, had waited to enjoy.

Regardless of how old she was, Anna had spent her days in the temple of God, fasting and offering supplications to her Lord. Some have suggested that she probably would not have been allowed to stay overnight in the temple; nevertheless, her worship of God continued day and night. However, most translators understand Luke to say that she "never left the temple" (Lk 2:7*b*). If so, some unusual provision must have been made for her to stay in or by the temple.

Anna was a devout and saintly woman who, like Deborah and Huldah of Old Testament fame, enjoyed the prophetic gift. She, along with an unnamed group, "were [among those who were] looking forward to the redemption of Jerusalem" (Lk 2:38). That group of believers had read the promises of comfort and hope concerning the Messiah and the promise-plan God offered in the Old Testament. While this group no doubt represented a minority of the Jewish people as a whole, a remnant had taken God at his word and expected that God would act just as he had promised.

In the providence of God, Anna approached Jesus' parents at the very moment that Simeon was pronouncing his "Nunc Dimittis," and she too blessed the baby Jesus and spoke unrecorded words about who this child was and what he would do. All of what was said, however, was a direct vindication of the promised redemption that was to come to Jerusalem and the whole earth.

Conclusion

Five persons of enormous import set the boundaries between the two Testaments, acting as a bridge that could prepare us for the new revelation of God. Their grounding, however, was thoroughly in the *Torah* (Law), the *Nebi'im* (Prophets), and the *Kethubim* (Writings) of the *Tanak* (Old Testament). God's promise-plan would not go dead; instead, it would burst out like the dawn of a new day to announce that the old word had come to new life. The Messiah and his kingdom would inaugurate a series of events that would end, as the rest of the revelation would go on to say, in a fantastic triumph in that future day of the Lord. The nations could fret all they wanted, but God had installed his King with an investiture (Ps 2) that signaled an end to all other competitors. The evangelist Luke has prepared us for the next part of the study of biblical theology as we examine the twenty-seven new additions to the thirty-nine previous revelations of God.

Chapter 12

The Promise-Plan and the Law of God

James, Galatians (About AD 45 – 48)

Few areas of biblical theology are more difficult and engender more heat than the relationship of the gospel of promise to the law of God. However, the problem seems to rest more with the way we in contemporary times understand how the law in the Old Testament related to the promise of the gospel than with the way the gospel relates to the law in the New Testament.

The law of God, understood as that part of it that dealt with the ceremonies and rituals carried out by the priests in the tabernacle and in the temple, was fulfilled, of course, in Jesus' death and atonement and therefore was obsolete for all who followed our Lord. In fact, Moses himself was cautioned at the time that those ceremonies were revealed to him in the Sinaitic code that there was a built-in obsolescence related to them (Ex 25:8, 40), for they were merely a "copy" or "model/pattern" of the real, which remained in heaven until Christ came and fulfilled the entire part of that legislation. When that happened, those parts of the law that were only a "shadow" or "copy" of the real would become antiquated and would be superseded by the coming of the real in Christ himself.

However, the moral law and the Old Testament ethic, which Jesus also taught, remained. It is this law that we are concerned with as the church takes its first steps into Christian maturity. But under no circumstances, in either Testament, was the law to be used, either hypothetically or in reality, as a way of gaining eternal life. It was confusion of this point that caused so much difficulty, especially during the early days of the church in the first Christian century.

But just as assuredly, we can assert that few matters in the Bible are more central and include so many of the core teachings as does the promise-plan of God. That is the theme that will be highlighted in our working through the biblical theology of the New Testament as it was in the Old Testament.

James: The Perfect Law of God

Perhaps the earliest book in the New Testament collection is the book whose author identified himself by the name of "Jacob" (from which we get our name James).[1] He was the brother — i.e., the half brother — of our Lord and served the church in Jerusalem as one of its key leaders.

While there is very little certainty about the date when this book was written, the best explanation for the date allows for some time to elapse between James's teaching (2:14 – 26) and Paul's on justification, while still making it prior to the actual face-to-face meeting of these two leaders at the Jerusalem Council (Acts 15), which took place sometime between AD 48 and 50. This would place James's letter "sometime in the early or middle 40s,"[2] making it one of the earliest New Testament writings, if not the earliest.

Good cases have been made for the traditional Jacobean (i.e., "James") authorship of this book. Despite the mention of three other men named James in the New Testament,[3] it is best to regard this James as the (half) brother of our Lord Jesus (Gal 1:19). Since he is mentioned first in Mark 6:3 and Matthew 13:55 among the brothers of Jesus, he was no doubt the oldest of his brothers. The apostle Paul (1Co 15:7) mentioned that Christ appeared to James after Jesus rose from the grave. Later, in Galatians 1:19, we see James among the apostles at Jerusalem; and in Galatians 2:9 he is regarded as one of the "pillars" of the church along with Peter and John, who wished Paul and Barnabas Godspeed as they set out on their mission to the Gentiles.

The literary style of the epistle of James is bold and vigorous. W. Montgomery described it this way:

> The author plunges into his subject with a bold-paradox, and his short, decisive sentences fall like hammer-strokes. He constantly employs the imperative, and makes much use of the rhetorical question. His rebukes contain some of the sharpest invective in the NT (4:1 – 4; 5:1 – 6), and he knows when irony will serve him best (2:19). He piles up metaphor upon metaphor until the impression becomes irresistible (3:3 – 12) and multiplies attributes with the same effect of emphasis (e.g., 'earthly, sensual, devilish' [3:15; cf. 1:4, 8, 19]). Like most vigorous writers, he delights in antithesis (cf. 1:9f., 22, 25; 3:5; 4:7). In his illustrations he uses direct speech with dramatic effect ('sit thou here in a good place,' etc. [2:3; cf. 2:16; 4:13]).[4]

---

1. Joseph B. Mayor, *The Epistle of St. James*, 3rd ed. (Grand Rapids: Zondervan, 1954 [1913]), i.

2. D. A. Carson and Douglas J. Moo, *An Introduction to the New Testament*, 2nd ed. (Grand Rapids: Zondervan, 2005), 627.

3. James the son of Zebedee, brother of John, one of the Twelve (Mk 1:19); James the son of Alphaeus, also one of the Twelve (Mk 3:18), who may also appear as "James the younger" (Mk 15:40); and James the father of Judas (Lk 6:16). But each of these is different from James, "the Lord's brother" (Gal 1:19), one of the early pillars in the Jerusalem church (Acts 12:17; 15:13; 21:18).

4. W. Montgomery, "James, Epistle of," in *Dictionary of the Apostolic Church*, ed. James Hastings (Edinburgh: T & T Clark, 1915), 1:629.

James's purpose in writing is to protest the prevailing worldliness of the Jewish Christians, who are all too easily caught up in what the culture was practicing at the time — to the neglect of the law of God. James assumed he was writing to persons of faith in the Lord Jesus Christ (2:1). He wanted them to know that the perfect law of liberty had set them free from the yoke of bondage (1:25; 2:12). However, these believers were mixed among those who blasphemed the name of Christ and persecuted the believers (2:6 – 7). While most of them were poor (2:5), the few who were rich in their midst (1:10) were in danger of apostasy because of their pride, covetousness, and worldliness (4:3 – 6, 13 – 16).

Although the main story line of the gospel is assumed in the book of James, it is just as clear that he also knows and adheres to the ancient promise-plan of God. For example, in 2:5, he speaks of the "kingdom [God] promised those who love him." Moreover, without using the technical terms for the promise, it is just as clear that James's theology was saturated in the teaching of the Old Testament.

The Jewish nationality of those addressed in this book can be underscored by the address found in 1:1 "to the twelve tribes scattered among the nations." This address to the "twelve tribes" is to be taken in the literal sense because: (1) Abraham was called their "ancestor"[5] (2:21); (2) the readers addressed in this book show that they were acquainted with the stories of Job, Elijah, and the prophets (5:11, 17 – 18); (3) the reference to the phrase "Lord of sabaoth" is one Jewish persons would know (5:4 KJV); (4) the use of the term "synagogue" for the place of meeting for the Christians shows a very early period in the history of the Jewish-Christian relations (2:2); and (5) the high value placed on the law of God also underscores their Jewish heritage.

Even though the letter of James is brief, its five chapters show an amazing acquaintance with the Old Testament. J. B. Mayor, one of the great commentators on James, found references or allusions to twenty-two Old Testament books in this little book.[6]

The Theology of James

So random and, at first impression, so scattered are the themes found here that the book of James seems to have no more organization than some parts of the book of Proverbs. Some, such as Martin Dibelius, fault the book for being without a theology.[7] But this is hardly the case, for while the style in James is very similar to that of Proverbs, today we are slowly discovering that both books have more organization and theology than was previously recognized by most scholars.

5. Just as the apostle Paul called his Galatian believing audience the children of Abraham.

6. Mayor, *Epistle of St. James*, cx – cxvi. They include Genesis, Exodus, Leviticus, Numbers, Deuteronomy, Joshua, 1 Kings, Job, Psalms, Proverbs, Ecclesiastes, Isaiah, Jeremiah, Ezekiel, Daniel, Hosea, Joel, Amos, Jonah, Micah, Zechariah, and Malachi.

7. Martin Dibelius, *James: A Commentary on the Epistle of James*, ed. Helmut Koester, trans. Michael A. Williams, Hermeneia (Philadelphia: Fortress, 1976), 21, as cited by Buist M. Fanning, "A Theology of James," in *A Biblical Theology of the New Testament*, ed. Roy B. Zuck (Chicago: Moody Press, 1994), 17.

It is also true that James does not explicitly mention the incarnation, cross, or resurrection of Jesus and says very little about the Holy Spirit (though James 4:5 is debated). It makes no direct reference to the doctrines of the church and gives only a brief reference to the Lord's second coming (e.g., Jas 5:7). However, he seems to group his ideas around three or four key themes: trials and temptations (1:2 – 15; 5:7 – 11); concern for the poor and the needy (2:1 – 26); the bridling of the tongue and the need for wisdom (1:19 – 27; 3:1 – 18); and the necessity of living a life of practical holiness (4:1 – 5:6).[8]

Especially controversial is the relation of faith and works as compared with the teaching of the apostle Paul in Galatians (3:11 – 14) and Romans (3:28; 4:2). At the heart of this debate is the text in James 2:14 – 26. What makes this text even more problematic is the translation given to it by the King James Version in verse 14: "Can faith save him?" Put that way, it seems like a challenge is being offered to the teaching that salvation is by faith alone, as set forth in Ephesians 2:8. But there is no conflict here, as shown in the way the Revised Version and the New English Bible render verse 14, "Can *that* faith save him?" or as the Revised Standard Version puts it, "Can *his* faith save him?" and as the New International Version states it: "Can *such* faith save him?" The issue was not the doctrine of salvation or the doctrine of faith, as taught by the apostle Paul, but the substitution of a *spurious* faith that exposed itself for what it was by the way it reacted to human needs of others or by being a mere intellectualizing of "faith," which ended up being no different than the faith possessed by demons (v. 18). Actually, the devil and his demons are quite kosher in their theology; however, despite the fact that they can give orthodox answers to all questions of theology, they nevertheless have refused to believe in and commit themselves to Christ.

Accordingly, rather than describing true faith, which consisted of faith in the Lord Jesus Christ (Jas 2:1), James was dealing with a "faith" that was a mere resemblance of true faith but that ended up being an empty profession, lacking the vitality of living faith that committed oneself wholeheartedly to Christ.[9] Some fail to recognize that James 2:18 includes both an objection and the writer's reply. Thus, by "faith" James means those who make a mere profession that is of their own construction, but it is not the same as the faith Abraham and Rahab had (2:20 – 26). So the proper relationship between faith and works is that true faith is complemented by supporting evidences of

8. Montgomery, "James," 629, suggests that James's style is one where the emphatic word of one sentence becomes the "catch-word" (*leitmotif*) for the next. Thus "joy" in v. 1 becomes the key-word for "joy" in v. 2, and "perfect" and "lacking nothing" in v. 4 becomes the key-word for "lack" wisdom in v. 5, while "ask" in v. 6 is developed up to v. 8, etc.

9. Zane C. Hodges, *The Gospel Under Siege: A Study on Faith and Works*, 2nd ed. (Dallas, TX: Redencion Viva, 1992), set forth a vigorous denial that the salvation spoken of here was our eternal salvation. He was opposed by John F. MacArthur Jr., "Faith According to the Apostle James," *Journal of the Evangelical Theological Society* 33 (1990): 13 – 34 and several others.

its reality and by the way it shows itself in the habits of the heart and its lifestyle. As J. A. Motyer put it so nicely:

> What are the primary works of faith? They are the works of Abraham and Rahab. And is it not wonderful how the Word of God brings these two together: a man and a woman, a Jew and a Gentile, a man of great sanctity in his walk with God, and a woman of great uncleanness? This shows us that these works of faith are for all the people of God and none can make excuse.[10]

It is also important to realize that James and Paul are using the word "justify" (Gr. *dikaioō*) in two different ways. Paul is using "justify" to speak of the declaration of our righteousness, whereas James is using it as the demonstration or vindication of our righteousness. Both senses of the word are found in the biblical text, so one must follow what the writer meant by his use of the word rather than letting other writers and passages import their meanings into the text.

In Paul's use of the word "justify," he focuses on the initial announcement of our being declared just and righteous before God; in James's use of that same word, he focuses instead on the vindication of that status before God both now in this present age and in the coming judgment in the last day. James's emphasis, then, was that a faith without works was dead. Paul's emphasis was that salvation is by faith alone and not by works of any kind.

James and the Law of God

Despite all that has been said so far in protest about whether or not there is a theology in the book of James, it is not uncommon for some believers to be puzzled, if not downright bewildered, over the contents of this letter. Martin Luther, for example, was not a fan of the book; his accusations that it is an "epistle of straw" and that it is chaotic in its organization are well known.

Luke T. Johnson has proposed that James may have used the Septuagint (LXX) version of Leviticus 19:12 – 18 as his text for the remarks in his book.[11] As Johnson observes, James 2:8 is a direct quote from the LXX version of Leviticus 19:18*c* ("Love your neighbor as yourself"). Yet Johnson notes that James has also placed this citation in the same contextual setting as it had been originally placed in Leviticus, that is, that of showing no partiality when rendering a judgment (Jas 2:9; cf. Lev 19:15).

But even more illuminating is that, according to Johnson, there are six other thematic or verbal allusions in James to this part of the law of Moses that is generally called the "Holiness Code" (Lev 18 – 20):

10. J. A. Motyer, *The Tests of Faith* (London: Inter-Varsity Press, 1970), 58.

11. Luke T. Johnson, "The Use of Leviticus 19 in the Letter of James," *Journal of Biblical Literature* 101 (1982): 391 – 401.

Leviticus 19:12–18	*The Book of James*
19:12 "Do not swear falsely by my name and so profane the name of your God."	5:12 "do not swear … or you will be condemned."
19:13 "Do not hold back the wages of a hired man overnight."	5:4 "Look, the wages you failed to pay the workmen who mowed your fields are crying out against you."
19:14 "Do not curse the deaf or put a stumbling block in front of the blind."	(No parallel.)
19:15 "Do not show partiality."	2:1 "Don't show favoritism."
19:16 "Do not go about spreading slander among your people."	4:11 "Brothers, do not slander one another."
19:17 "Rebuke your neighbor frankly so you will not share in his guilt."	5:20 "Whoever turns a sinner from the error of his way will save him from death and cover over a multitude of sins."
19:18*a* "Do not seek revenge or bear a grudge against one of your people."	5:9 "Don't grumble against each other, brothers."
19:18*b* "Love your neighbor as yourself."	2:8 "Love your neighbor as yourself."

It is most astonishing that a text from the heart of a book containing much of the ceremonial law along with the Holiness Code (Lev 18–20) should become the basis for such practical, ethical, and moral nurturing in the New Testament as is found in the book of James. It is almost as if James were giving an expository sermon based on this text from the Mosaic law. Only verse 14 from Leviticus 19:12–18 is without any parallel in James.

Four of the six parallels are fairly certain; only two (Lev 19:17 and 19:18*a*) are less likely. Moreover, as Johnson further noted, the apodictic commands of Leviticus 19:11, "Do not steal, do not lie," and "do not deceive one another," which reflect the contents of the Ten Commandments, as does Leviticus 19:12 (about not profaning the name of the Lord), form the context for using this passage in James. In fact, the thought of the Decalogue runs parallel with the substance of Leviticus 19:12–18, as does James 3:13–4:10.

James called the command to "love your neighbor as yourself" "the royal law found in Scripture" (2:8). Therefore, rather than avoiding or disregarding the law, James argues that a fulfilling of it in its practical implications was carrying out what the Scriptures required! Surprising as it may seem, James appears to link the "royal law" of love for one's neighbor with the warning in James 2:9 about being guilty of being a "lawbreaker." His use of the Greek correlatives, *mentoi* in verse 8 with *de* in verse 9 ("If... But") reinforces this linkage between the two verses.

Believers have a legitimate obligation to render obedience to both the moral law and the holiness laws (but *not* for their salvation), for this is how they can show that the faith they possess is genuine. Johnson concludes:

> Keeping the law of love involves observing the commandments explicated in the Decalogue (2:11) and Lev. 19:12 – 18 in their entirety....
>
> For James, Lev. 19:12 – 18 provides an accurate explication of the law of love which should be obtained in the Church.[12]

There is no opposition, then, between the gospel found in God's promise-plan and his moral law, as we have also seen in the discussion of the law in the Old Testament. The point is that one must use the law properly; it must not (and is not, nor was it ever devised to) become an alternate route to eternal life. The apostle Paul came to the same conclusion, for he pronounced the Old Testament law "holy, righteous and good" (Ro 7:12); in fact, the law was "spiritual" (Ro 7:14), but it is we who must "use it properly" (1Ti 1:8).

The solution to the alleged law/gospel dichotomy is "the obedience of faith" (Ro 1:5; 16:26), a concept that Paul uses in the book of Romans as an *inclusio* that brackets the beginning and the end of his great epistle on salvation. Genuine faith can be expressed by lovingly showing obedience to all that God has taught us.

Love is an essential part of the ethic of both the Old and New Testaments, but it is not a *how* word, for it will in itself never tell us *what* we should do — for example, the content of our ethic. It only helps us in providing a *manner* for whatever it is we are going to do: we must do it with love. This means that if we do not know what it is that we must do in order to be obedient, we must go back to the Decalogue and the Holiness Law to find the substance for that which we are going to express with love.

Galatians: The Observance of the Law

If, as many scholars believe, the South Galatian theory[13] is correct in locating the message of this book in the southern part of Asia Minor, and if Paul wrote this letter just prior to the Jerusalem Council around AD 48 – 50, then this letter must be placed

12. Ibid., 400.

13. A theory developed by William M. Ramsay more than anyone else. See his *The Church in the Roman Empire* (London: Hodder & Stoughton, 1893), 10 – 11.

somewhere around AD 48 and is the first of the numerous letters sent by the apostle Paul to the missionary churches he established.[14]

"Galatia" seemed to be the only name Paul had available to designate the churches of Antioch, Lystra, Iconium, and Derbe, unless there were some churches we do not know about in the central plateau and the northern part of Asia Minor, or present-day Turkey. Traditionally, Galatia had been the name reserved to point to the Greek-speaking people who settled the central plateau of Asia Minor populated by the Celtic tribes of the Gauls from the third century BC onward. But in broader parlance, Galatia at times represented the southern part of the country as well. Thus the question became: Did Paul use an imperial standpoint and only refer to the Roman divisions of the empire, or did he employ territorial names — which are not always the same names as those of the Roman provinces — and point to the central plateau and the northern parts of that country? Most say the former and not the latter. The answer to this question will determine the date for this letter.

Galatians and the Promise

Few chapters in the New Testament have so many references and such a strong emphasis on the "promise" as does the third chapter of Galatians. Indeed, the whole "blessing" that was to come through Abraham to the Gentiles was called the "promise of the Spirit" (Gal 3:14). These were "the promises ... spoken to Abraham and to his seed ... meaning one person, who is Christ" (Gal 3:16), Paul explained. Since this declaration from God came 430 years before the law, it simply was impossible to set aside "the promise" God had already made (3:17). The "inheritance" of this divine decree could not and did not rest on the law, but on "a promise" (3:18), so that is why it could not be overridden or supplanted by the law or anything else. Accordingly, the law could not be, and was not, opposed to "the promises of God" (3:21). In this way, the whole world was locked up to sin precisely so that "what was promised" might come through faith (3:22), making not only the son of the free woman, Sarah, an heir (4:23), but all who belong to Christ, whether Jew or Gentile, slave or free, male or female, a part of Abraham's seed and heirs with Isaac (3:29).

Galatians and the Judaizers

The apostle Paul began this letter with an immediate emphasis on his apostolic authority, which would lead nicely into the subject at hand and the accusations his opponents were raising. The "churches in Galatia" (1:2), to whom this epistle is addressed, are the ones who owed their new Christian lives to the preaching of Paul (1:8). Originally, Paul was

14. The problem with the term "Galatians" is whether it refers to ethnic Galatians in the north or to the Roman designation of the province of Galatia, which was made up of various races. Galatia traditionally referred to the north inhabited by the Gauls, but which of the two uses did Paul intend when he referred to Galatia?

headed for a different destination, but illness led him or detained him, so that is how the gospel came to these churches instead (4:13). During that time, Paul had been warmly welcomed by the Galatian people (4:14), indeed, as "an angel from God" (4:14). As a result, they believed the gospel and were baptized (3:26 – 27). With such a great beginning to their Christian lives (5:7), they had enjoyed the gift of God's Holy Spirit (3:3 – 5).

However, something happened to disrupt this progress. It seems that "some people," who appear to have been Judaizers, opposed Paul (1:7; 3:1; 5:10) and challenged his apostolic authority, along with the adequacy of the gospel he proclaimed. These persons so disturbed these churches that a great confusion arose amongst them.

What caused all this trouble?

First, they denied the apostolic authority of Paul. When Paul first heard of the defection of the Galatians, he was unable to come to them for some unstated reason (4:20), so he sent this letter to deny the insinuations of his accusers and to show them the awful consequences of the positions they were about to take.

Paul is quick to assert that the gospel he preached was from no human source but was revealed to him directly by the Lord Jesus (1:11 – 14). Nor was he taught this gospel by other apostles, for he did not meet with them until some time after his conversion (1:15 – 17). Finally, he did visit Jerusalem later, but he talked only briefly with Peter and James. In fact, he was there for such a brief time that most believers in Jerusalem probably could not recognize him by sight (1:18 – 24).

Fourteen years later, Paul visited Jerusalem again and demonstrated his freedom with regard to the Law by refusing to circumcise Titus (2:1 – 5). Moreover, his independence from the other apostles was further demonstrated when he had to publicly rebuke Peter for his strange behavior in refusing to eat with the Gentiles (contrary to what he had been doing up to that point) because some of the Jewish brethren had just then come into town (2:11 – 14).

But there was a second accusation against Paul: that the gospel he preached was insufficient because he denied that salvation could be attained through works.[15] Paul was scandalized by the effect such accusations had on those to whom he had introduced freedom in Christ. In fact, it was as if someone had put the evil eye on them, bewitching them, and thus had perverted the gospel (3:1 – 5). Mortals were justified by faith (Gal 2:16 [2x]; 3:8, 11, 24) and "in Christ" (2:17), not by obedience to the law (2:16 [3x]; 3:11).

15. E. P. Sanders, in *Paul and Palestinian Judaism* (Philadelphia: Fortress Press, 1977), created quite a stir by rejecting the idea that the Jews of Paul's day argued that keeping the law would merit salvation. Sanders said that in "Covenantal Nomism," Jews were saved by being a member of the covenant community. Keeping the law only guaranteed one's remaining in the community. See also Sanders, *Paul, the Law, and the Jewish People* (Philadelphia: Fortress Press, 1985), esp. 27. The difference between the Jewish people and the Christians, said Sanders, was that Christians accepted Jesus as Messiah; the Jews did not. Their differences did not turn on justification but on the Messiah. For a partial refutation, see Robert H. Gundry, "Grace, Works, and Staying Saved in Paul," *Biblica* 66 (1985): 1 – 38, and Frank Thielman, *From Plight to Solution: A Jewish Framework for Understanding Paul's View of the Law in Galatians and Romans*, Supplementum — *Novum Testamentum* 61 (Leiden: Brill, 1989).

The contrast could not have been clearer, despite what some modern studies are now trying to advocate (see n. 15).

The Promise of the Gospel and the Law

The gospel was given "in advance to Abraham." This gospel, according to Genesis 12:3, claimed that "all nations will be blessed through you" (Gal 3:8). Thus, Abraham was "pre-evangelized" with a word that Paul clearly labeled as the "good news": "The promises were spoken to Abraham and to his seed. Scripture does not say 'and to seeds,' meaning many people, but 'and to your seed,' meaning one person, who is Christ" (Gal 3:16). Paul's gospel, as it turns out, was no different than what God had originally given for persons to be saved in the Old Testament. So why was he being charged with introducing a deficient plan of salvation? The answer is that Paul was not introducing something that was brand-new! God's promise-plan was the same original plan still being advocated here by Paul.

How, then, could the argument be correct that if the Gentiles wished to become part of the family of Abraham (Gal 3:29), as well as part of the family of God, they must first be circumcised and promise to keep the whole of the Mosaic law (Gal 4:10, 21; 5:2; 6:12)? The promise of the good news had been given to Abraham 430 years before the law came. Moreover, if one is to argue that salvation could only come as a result of obedience to the law, then Christ died for no good reason (Gal 3:21 – 22). Such an offer was never part of the law, nor did it appear anywhere else in the revelation of God to humanity. It was a later invention that many had confused with what the law itself taught.

"O foolish Galatians, do not be tricked into turning away from salvation by faith, or by trying to achieve it by the works of the law" was Paul's plea (3:1 – 8 paraphrased). It is the gospel that brings blessing; the law brings a curse (3:10 – 18). The law develops our sense of sin when we see ourselves over against that to which God has called us. In that sense, the law points us to a state of bondage, but now that we are no longer children, but fully matured persons, we can be one with Christ through faith in him and thus come to our full freedom as children and heirs of God (3:19 – 4:11). All these points can be put into an allegory, Paul summarized, in an attempt to use the Jewish way of reasoning that was prominent in his day,[16] in which Hagar represents bondage to the law; and Isaac, the child of promise, represents the promised seed of Abraham and of Christ. Can't you Galatians see, Paul cries, that "we are not children of the slave woman, but of the free woman" (4:31)?

Paul and his opponents did not differ over the nature of righteousness; they differed over the way to attain that righteousness. The picture behind the word "righteous" (Gr.

16. Paul's argument in Galatians 4:24 is that "all these things" (literal rendering) can be put into an allegorical or figurative way of speaking. He is not thereby giving us an exegesis of the Genesis text, but instead he is accommodating his audience's way of speaking to get his point across. See Robert J. Kepple, "An Analysis of Antiochene Exegesis of Galatians 4:24 – 26," *Westminster Theological Journal* 39 (1976 – 77): 239 – 49.

dikaios; Heb. *ṣaddiq*) was one where two litigants faced a judge, and the judge pronounced one of them to be "in the right." Used here, "righteousness" meant one who was in right relationship with God and in a state of acceptance with God. And there was only one way to get into the relationship and that state of acceptance: it was by faith in the Messiah, the one promised to the patriarchs, David, and his line. This promise was fulfilled in the birth of Jesus of Nazareth.

Paul put his finger on the key weakness in the opponents' argument: they took no account of the inborn depravity that was part of the human nature. Mortals cannot save themselves because they have a depraved nature that sins. Therefore, to search for justification by works was a lost cause. The law could not help; all it could do is show what the divine commands were and then pass sentence on us for failing to live up to God's standard (2:16; 3:12 – 13).

But thanks be to God! The promise God made millennia ago has been fulfilled by Jesus, the true seed of Abraham (3:9, 17, 29). The promise of God was an unconditional covenant; the law was conditional. The law was spoken through human and angelic mediators (3:19); the promise to Abraham came directly from God (3:18). The two were not on the same playing field. Surely, the law had a purpose to fulfill in that it led us to Christ. But whatever other purposes were to be found in the law, serving as a means of salvation was not one of them.

It would appear that in light of the Qumran document called the *Miqsat Maʿase ha-Torah*, which uses the same phrase Paul used, the "works of the law/obedience to the law," that this phrase is used at Qumran and in later Rabbinic Judaism to refer to what was known as the *halakah*.[17] The *halakah* was an interpretation of the law of Moses that demanded obedience to the law as a basis for acceptance into the membership of the people of God. It would appear this is the law the Judaizers had in mind as they appealed to it for their authority. But this was to appeal to what they had "heard it was said," rather than appealing to the word of God in Scripture. The Greek term *nomos*, "law," was not an exact equivalent translation for Hebrew *torah*, which meant "instruction" or "direction," but it was also used to refer to legalism, the law of tradition as well as to the Torah of Moses given by God.

The Torah never stated that one of the purposes of the law was to be a means of salvation. To argue that such was the law's purpose was to forfeit the freedom offered in Christ, and it further was to be made slaves out of the present generation, just as Israel once had been in Egypt (2:4).

Paul carefully grounded his message to the Galatians on Scriptures found in the Old Testament. For example: he cited Genesis 15:6 in Galatians 3:6; Genesis 12:3 in Galatians 3:8; Deuteronomy 27:26 in Galatians 3:10; Habakkuk 2:4 in Galatians 3:11;

17. Roy E. Ciampa, "Galatians," in *New Dictionary of Biblical Theology*, ed. T. Desmon Alexander and Brian S. Rosner (Downers Grove, IL: InterVarsity Press, 2000), 313.

Leviticus 18:5 in Galatians 3:12; Deuteronomy 21:23 in Galatians 3:13; Genesis 12:7 in Galatians 3:16; Isaiah 54:1 in Galatians 4:27; Genesis 21:10 in Galatians 4:30; Leviticus 19:18 in Galatians 5:14.[18] It is clear what law he was talking about all along.

Galatians is a brief letter, but one of enormous importance. While the promise does not contradict the law, since both come from our Lord, it certainly preceded the law by some four centuries. And the law, while not given for the purpose of saving individuals, still set forth God's standard of holiness.

Excursus: The Promise of Gentile Inclusion and the Law in the Old Testament and Paul

The gospel given to Abraham in Genesis 12:3, namely, that "all the peoples on earth will be blessed through you," clearly opened the offer of the good news to every person on earth. This promise of God was repeated in slightly different forms in Genesis 18:18; 22:18; 26:4; and 28:14. Thus the scope envisioned for this Abrahamic promise was "all nations" (Heb., *kol gôyim*), which the Greek Septuagint rendered in Genesis 18:18; 22:1; and 26:4 as *panta ta ethnē*, "all the nations." The word for "nations" (Heb. *goyim*) is also the word for "Gentiles." This means that the message of the Old Testament was not exclusively for the Jewish people but was intended to be a message for the nations and the Gentiles as well.

But that had been the case since the pre-patriarchal age of Genesis 1 – 11. Before God had called a Jewish nation into being, the offer of the good news was to all the nations, for all this was prior to calling Abraham. God did personalize that call, and it came through Abraham. But he and his people were only to serve as the channels through which that word was to come to the whole world.

As evidence for this Gentile extension of the gospel, one need only refer to Melchizedek of Genesis 14, a "king of Salem" and a "priest of God Most High" (Ge 14:18). Where, when, and how this man became a believer, the text does not even give us a hint, but Abraham gave him one-tenth of the booty he had taken in his victory over the four kings from Mesopotamia. The fact that Melchizedek received these gifts as unto the Lord showed he was in some type of personal relationship with Yahweh.

18. Ibid., 314. Also idem, *The Presence and Function of Scripture in Galatians 1 and 2* (Tübingen: Mohr Siebeck, 1998).

There was also Jethro, a "priest of Midian" (Ex 18:1), who met Moses as he returned from the exodus in Egypt. Instantly, he offered praise of Yahweh, a name always used as the personal name of God, for what God had done for Israel (Ex 18:10 – 11). Then Jethro brought a burnt offering and other sacrifices to the Lord as Aaron and all the elders of Israel broke bread together with him in fellowship with the Lord. Surely, he too was regarded as one in the faith with Moses and the elders.

To the names of Melchizedek and Jethro we can add the name of Balaam, son of Beor, who lived in Upper Mesopotamia near the Euphrates River (Nu 22:5) and who gave evidence of having a prophetic gift from God even though he was a Gentile. On four separate occasions he delivered the word of God, even though he came to a bitter end in an apparent attempt to placate his Moabite host (Nu 31:8). Whether he was an actual believer, we cannot say, but he at least demonstrated the fact that Yahweh was known well enough by a Gentile to be the oracle through whom God sent his message about the Messiah, whose arrival would be preceded by his star (Nu 24:17).

No less important was Rahab the prostitute, whose testimony gave evidence of her faith as well (Jos 2:9 – 11; Heb 11:31; Jas 2:25). Her confession was that "Yahweh is God," but how much of that confession also had as the object of her faith precisely this coming Man of promise — that is, the Messiah — is not definitively stated. But how else could she have made it into the "hall of faith" chapter in Hebrews 11? An identical case can be made for Ruth, the Moabitess. She too had come to take refuge under the wings of the God of Israel (Ru 2:12).

The most dramatic case of a Gentile conversion was that of the Syrian army commander Naaman (2 Kings 5:1 – 19). At the advice of a captured Israelite girl, he went to the prophet Elisha in Israel to be cured of his leprosy and became a true worshiper of Yahweh (2Ki 5:15 – 19).

Add to these Gentile witnesses the book of Psalms, which is full of missionary preaching. George Peters counted more than 175 references in the Psalms to the fact that the gospel is for all the nations of the world.[19] The Psalms to which Peters called special attention for this emphasis were Psalms 2, 33, 66, 72, 117, and 145. I would add to these the great Psalms 67, 96, and 100.

Other parts of the Old Testament carry missiological implications. Chief among them would be the book of Jonah, addressed to that great city of Nineveh, the capital of Assyria. Despite their brutal treatment of Israel in warfare, God

19. George Peters, *A Biblical Theology of Missions* (Chicago: Moody Press, 1972), 115 – 16.

wanted that nation to also have an opportunity to repent. And that is exactly what that people did. But Jonah was not the only prophet who carried this same message to the Gentiles, even though he was more than reluctant throughout the whole venture. There were others as well. The prophet Joel saw a time when "all flesh" (2:28) would experience a downpour of the Holy Spirit.

In the eighth century BC, the prophet Amos saw a day when the house of David, which was in a present state of collapse, would be restored "so that they may possess the remnant of Edom, and all the nations that bear my name" (Am 9:11 – 12). The Septuagint and one Dead Sea Scroll reading of this same text had it that "the remnant of *men* [not: "Edom"] and the nations that bear my name may *seek* [not: "possess"] the LORD." The words for "Edom" and "men" are spelled with the same Hebrew consonants and thus could easily be confused. Either reading can be accepted, for the later reading seems to result in the same meaning intended by the reference to "Edom" and Israel's "possession" of it, that is, that Edom stood as the symbol of all the Gentile nations and their capture would be a spiritual one as the Gentiles "sought" the Lord as their own Lord and Savior.

We will return to this passage a little later. But first let us briefly mention the large number of chapters devoted to the Gentile nations in Isaiah 13 – 23, Jeremiah 46 – 51, Ezekiel 25 – 32, and Amos 1 – 2. Add to this the pictures given to us in Micah 4:1 – 5 of a future day when all the nations will flood into Jerusalem to worship the Lord. Zechariah 2:11 and 8:20 – 23 affirm the same vision. Jonah was hardly alone in his witness to the worldwide aspect of this promise-plan and gospel of God.[20]

It is little wonder, then, that the apostle Paul, in his trial before Felix, said, "I believe everything that agrees with the Law and that is written in the Prophets" (Ac 24:14). Paul's mission was decisively one of going to the Gentiles, for it was at Antioch of Pisidia that Paul announced his decision to turn exclusively to the Gentiles in his missionary preaching (Ac 13:46). He supported this decision with a quotation from Isaiah 49:6, "I will also make you a light for the Gentiles, that you may bring my salvation to the ends of the earth."

The universality of that mission was also the theme of the book of Acts, as Acts 1:8 demonstrates: "But you will receive power when the Holy Spirit comes on you; and you will be my witnesses in Jerusalem, and in all Judea and Samaria, and to the ends of the earth." In his two-volume history of Luke-Acts, Luke, the physician who traveled with the apostle Paul, made the conversion of Cornelius (Acts 10:1 – 11:18) the centerpiece of Paul's justification for preach-

20. For a fuller discussion of these and other similar points, see Walter C. Kaiser Jr., *Mission in the Old Testament: Israel as a Light to the Nations* (Grand Rapids: Baker, 2000).

ing the gospel to the Gentiles. Paul's authority for going to the Gentiles, of course, was anchored in God's long-term plan of reaching out with the gospel to Gentiles in the Old Testament. But it was also clear that God had sent Paul to open up this field as it had never been opened before.

However, this part of the plan of God was not understood or appreciated by all, especially the Jewish converts. As a result, a fight broke out at the Jerusalem Council, led by those believers who belonged to the Pharisee party. The controversy had a two-pronged charge to it: (1) these Gentiles cannot be part of the believing community until they are circumcised as the law of Moses required, and (2) they must also be required to keep the law of Moses (Ac 15:5). What were the Jewish believers in Jesus going to do with all these Gentiles that were coming to faith in Christ, and why weren't they being required to obey Moses' law? Wasn't circumcision the sign of the covenant? Was not the law of Moses given by God for our obedience?

In a separate meeting of the apostles and elders, it was pointed out that God had "some time ago ... made a choice among you that the Gentiles might hear from my lips the message of the gospel and believe" (Ac 15:7). There was to be no distinction between the Jew and Gentile believer (Ac 15:8 – 9). Both were saved only by the "grace of our Lord Jesus" (Acts 15:11).

In a meeting that followed with the whole assembly, Paul and Barnabas tried to quiet the troubled waters by describing instances of God's miraculous work among the Gentiles. This was followed by Peter's testimony, no doubt about his culturally wrenching experience of being in Cornelius's house and seeing how the Holy Spirit fell on these Gentiles just as it had fallen on Jewish believers.

But apparently none of these experiential speeches moved the divided house until James, the half brother of our Lord and leader of the Jerusalem assembly, got up and pointed the assembly back to the Scripture of Amos 9:9 – 15. This work of God among the Gentiles was part of God's restoration and rebuilding the old dynasty (that is, house) of David that had been in a state of collapsing. The Davidic covenant, argued James, included the promise that the Gentiles would be among those who sought the Lord.[21] It was James's judgment, then, that the believers should not make it difficult for the Gentiles who were turning to God (Ac 15:19 – 21). Because Moses was continually being preached since earliest times in every city and was being read in every synagogue on every Sabbath, there was little need to add more, except four

21. Walter C. Kaiser Jr., "The Davidic Promise and the Inclusion of the Gentiles (Amos 9: 9 – 15 and Acts 15:13 – 18): A Test Passage for Theological Systems," *Journal of the Evangelical Theological Society* 20 (1977): 97 – 111.

commands to the Gentiles: (1) abstain from food offered to idols, (2) abstain from sexual immorality, (3) abstain from meat of strangled animals, and (4) abstain from [eating] blood.

The strongest case that the apostle Paul made for going to the Gentiles with the gospel is found in Romans 15:8 – 12. This passage was the climax to the whole outline of salvation that Paul laid down in the book of Romans. He strung five Old Testament texts together (2Sa 22:50; Ps 18:49; Dt 32:43; Ps 117:1; and Isa 11:10) to demonstrate that this outreach to the Gentiles was at the heart of the promise-plan of God. Rather than seeing the Gentile mission as an add-on, Paul decisively argued that it had always been an essential part of what God wanted to do.

The plan of God is as global in its extent as it is broad ethnically, geographically, culturally, and personally. Men, women, the young and the old, the employed and the employers — no one was to be left out. All were to come by grace through faith. And obey they must, but it would be an "obedience of faith" (Ro 1:5; 16:26).

Chapter 13

The Promise-Plan and the Mission of the Church

1 and 2 Thessalonians, 1 and 2 Corinthians, Romans (The AD 50s)

God called the man who set out to "destroy the church" (Ac 8:3) to be the one he would divinely use to build and establish that body of Christ from one end of the Mediterranean to the other. Not only did Paul build that church, but in the providence of God he was also called to write a dozen or so letters to those missionary churches. Early on, these letters were placed alongside the "other Scriptures," that is, the Old Testament (2Pe 3:16), even during the days of the formation of the New Testament.

The first six letters Paul wrote were all composed within approximately a ten-year period from about AD 48 to 58. In the previous chapter we looked at the first epistle he wrote, Galatians, written sometime between AD 45 and 48 and addressed to the churches in the southern part of Asia Minor at Antioch, Iconium, Lystra, and Derbe, soon after his first missionary journey to those sites (Ac 13 – 14).

On Paul's second missionary journey, he composed two more letters addressed to the new group of believers at Thessalonica, namely, 1 and 2 Thessalonians. Both of these letters were probably written from Corinth, with the first coming in AD 51, and the second either that same year or early in 52.

Finally, on the third missionary journey, the apostle directed three more letters to new churches. First Corinthians was written in the last year of his three-year stay in Ephesus (Ac 20:31), during the spring of AD 56. The Corinthian church was just about four years old at the time and needed a lot of pastoral advice and teaching. Later, in the fall of that same year, he wrote 2 Corinthians. Some claim that 2 Corinthians 10 – 13 was not a part of that second letter but belonged to a lost letter referred to in 2 Corinthians 2:4 — a letter that made the Corinthians sorrowful and caused them to grieve. But the description in 2:4 does not match the firm hand that Paul exhibited in that section of 2 Corinthians.

The final letter of the first six Pauline epistles is the book of Romans, written probably in the fall of AD 57, and sent to a church Paul did not found — the only exception in this list of six churches. Perhaps it was because he was not the founding pastor of the

Roman church that he felt it necessary to give the most structured theological presentation of the doctrine of salvation found in any of his writings.

1 and 2 Thessalonians: The Coming of the Lord

Thessalonica had the distinction of being among the first cities on the continent of Europe to be evangelized by Paul, Silas, and Timothy. It was Paul's Macedonian vision (Ac 16:9 – 10) that had moved these missionaries to travel to this region, for if Paul had traveled to northern Asia Minor, to Bithynia, as he at first had purposed, the gospel might well have gone in an eastward direction first (perhaps with the good news heading into Russia and China) instead of going west; and the first part of the American continent to be settled and hear the gospel could well have been the western rather than the eastern coast of the United States. That Macedonian vision was a critical moment in the history of the gospel and the world.[1]

The three missionaries sailed to the port of Neapolis and then went to the Roman colony of Philippi, where they stayed for several days (Ac 16:11 – 12). After preaching and being jailed at Philippi, they passed on to Amphipolis and Apollonia before coming to Thessalonica, about one hundred miles south of Philippi. Here they stayed for some three weeks, preaching every Sabbath day in the synagogue that Jesus is the Messiah/Christ (Ac 17:1 – 4). Paul, Silas, and Timothy had to make a hasty exit from Thessalonica, whereupon they went to nearby Berea, where Paul left Silas and Timothy as he left for Athens before going on to Corinth.

The young church at Thessalonica quickly encountered some problems, which came to Paul as he was at Corinth. So stiff had been the opposition to Paul's preaching there that he had to flee, as already mentioned, to nearby Berea (Ac 17:5 – 10); so it seemed best, for the moment, that he not personally return. However, he answered their questions in the letter we call 2 Thessalonians, which he sent by the hand of Timothy, whom Paul had sent back to Thessalonica to find out how the believers were doing (1Th 3:5 – 6). In that second letter, Paul hoped to quell some of the misunderstandings and to counter the false teaching that had accumulated already in this new congregation.

Thessalonica was a port city on the Aegean Sea and on the Egnatian Way, a Roman road that linked Rome and Byzantium. Between these two avenues of travel and commerce, this capital city, one of the four capitals in each of the four divisions of Macedonia, was one of the wealthiest and most populous cities in Macedonia, with some 200,000 persons. It is to this new body of believers that Paul now addresses his teaching, with special emphasis and instruction on the second coming of our Lord.

1. I first heard this idea from my seminary teacher, Dr. Merrill C. Tenney. He also included it in his book *New Testament Survey, Revised Edition*, ed. Walter M. Dunnett (Grand Rapids: Eerdmans, 1991), 279 – 80.

Theology of the Second Coming

Over against the nearby Mount Olympus, with all of its heathen gods and goddesses, not to mention its Greek penchant for philosophical abstractions for any kind of god, Paul announced that God was "the [only] living and true God" (1Th 1:9). Moreover, Jesus was "his Son from heaven, whom [God] raised from the dead" (1Th 1:10). The picture of the full Trinity was completed within that same first paragraph of 1 Thessalonians, as the gospel Paul preached came "not simply with words but also with power, with the Holy Spirit, and with deep conviction" (1Th 1:5). The triune God was not a philosophical idea, a dead idol of wood or stone, or even "the force." On the contrary, he was a living reality that had influenced the Thessalonians, as witnessed by the evidence of the physical resurrection of Jesus from the dead and the powerful and deep conviction they had experienced in their own hearts and lives as Paul announced the words of the gospel in their midst. So significant was the doctrine of the resurrection in all of its forms that practically every chapter in Thessalonians ends with a reference to it in some form.

But it was Paul's teaching about the doctrine of the Lord's victorious second coming that had aroused so much interest when Paul had been with them for three short weeks. While neither 1 or 2 Thessalonians purports to give a complete description of this future event that will climax human history, these letters allow us to see some of the points Paul raised and the practical questions that his teaching had aroused. Thus, the teaching of 1 Thessalonians is directed toward answering this question: How will those who have already died as believers take part in this parousia, the second coming of Jesus?

This teaching comes to its highest expression in 1 Thessalonians 4:13 – 5:10. First of all, Paul assured them, there was no reason to fret, like those who have no hope, over those who had died already when the parousia still had not yet occurred. The same Lord who had already raised our Lord Jesus from the grave — just as he had promised in his plan that stretched back into the Old Testament — is the God who will also raise up from the grave all who believe. The believing dead will not have a disadvantage compared to those who are still living at that time, because the dead in Christ will rise first, followed by those who are still alive and trusting in Jesus. The knowledge and assurance of Jesus' resurrection became the pledge for the resurrection of his followers (1Th 4:15; 5:10).

Here, then, is how it will happen: "For the Lord himself will come down from heaven, with a loud command, with the voice of the archangel and with the trumpet call of God" (1Th 4:16). The dead in Christ will rise first, followed by those who are alive; together we "will be caught up ... with them in the clouds to meet the Lord in the air" (1Th 4:17).

All of this is not fanciful or wishful thinking, for Paul claims to be telling them this "according to the Lord's word" (1Th 4:15). It is not certain whether Paul means that what he taught here was derived from actual sayings of Jesus recorded in the Gospels (e.g., Mt 24:30 – 31; Jn 6:39) or some direct personal revelation he had from the Lord Jesus. Regardless of which it is, the language, concepts, and terms are very familiar to Old Testament and Jewish Apocalyptic literature. The words: "with a loud command/ shout" (Gr. *keleusma*), "with the voice of an archangel" (Gr. *phonē archangelou*), and "with the trumpet call of God" (Gr. *salpingi theou*), are connected with theophanies in the Old Testament when the Lord appeared in some direct manner to his people (e.g., Ex 19:16; Zec 9:14). Thus it should not be a surprise that some of these same terms should describe the coming of our Lord in the parousia.

In the promise-plan of God, Daniel 7:13 mentioned how the Lord would come down from the clouds of heaven to receive the kingdom the Father would hand over to him (cf. Mt 24:30; 26:64). Moreover, Daniel 12:1 – 2 had also noted there would be a resurrection at the end of the age in which some were raised to everlasting life and others to everlasting shame. But there was no parallel concept for the snatching up of the living in clouds as first announced in 1 Thessalonians 4:17. This is the first appearance of this aspect of the doctrine of the second coming in the progress of revelation.

The Time of the Parousia

Some have mistakenly taken the twice-repeated statement "we who are still alive" (Gr. *hēmeis hoi zōntes hoi perileipomenoi*), to imply that Paul expected to see the parousia in his own lifetime. But that thought contradicts what he and others teach in other passages, that "about times and dates we do not need to write to you, for you know very well that the day of the Lord will come like a thief in the night" (1Th 5:1 – 2). Probably when Paul said "we" in verses 15 and 17, he did not intend to include himself in that group necessarily, but only to say that those who are living and who survive to that day were the ones he was referring to.

"The day of the Lord" was another one of those specifications that belonged to the promise-plan of God. We have already encountered this Old Testament terminology that spoke of a future day of God's coming when he would exercise both his deliverance and his judgment (e.g., Joel 1:15; 3:14; Zep 1:14 – 18; 3:8 – 20). Repeatedly, the Old Testament prophets had associated this "day of the Lord" with the time when God would bless some and settle accounts with others. It would occur at the end of this age, which had already been overlapped by the age to come since the day when Christ made his first advent and rose victoriously from the grave.

The Signs of the End of the Age and the Second Coming

The second letter to the Thessalonians supplements what Paul had taught both when he was present in Thessalonica and when he wrote his first letter. Whereas the first letter answered what will happen in the parousia to those believers who are already dead, the second letter dealt more with the hysteria that had been created by the false notion that the Lord's second coming was so close that everyone could stop whatever they were doing and just do nothing until that event took place. Paul halted this idea by saying that believers must not "become easily unsettled" or "alarmed" (2Th 2:2). Thus, while both letters focus on these eschatological events, they treat different aspects of the same subject.

Certain things must happen prior to the coming of the Lord, Paul went on to say in 2 Thessalonians. First, there will be a "rebellion," or "an apostasy" (Gr. *hē apostasia*, 2Th 2:3). Mortals will revolt and fall away from righteousness, from all good, and from what is moral and right. This will be followed by the appearance of "the man of lawlessness/sin" (Gr. *ho anthrōpos tēs anomias*, 2Th 2:3). This person appears to be the culmination of all evil and matches the description of the Antichrist (a name found in 1 Jn 2:18 – 20). It is a borrowed description also assigned to Antiochus Epiphanes in Daniel 11:36 – 39, as one of those who came in the same line as Antichrist but only exhibited some of the aspects seen in the one who would finally appear. This final person will claim divinity and take his seat in the temple, displaying a series of signs and wonders to deceive as many as possible (2Th 2:4). Another allusion to this same teaching can be seen in Mark 13:14, where the personal character of "the abomination that causes desolation" seems to be indicated by the Greek masculine participle *hestēkota*, a further allusion to Daniel 9:27; 11:31; 12:11.

The "mystery of lawlessness" or "the secret power of lawlessness" (2Th 2:7), of which the above-mentioned things will be the climax, is already operating in the life and times of the world in which the church at Thessalonica exists. However, in this present time there is a damper on this evil (Gr. *ho katechōn*, 2Th 2:7) or some hindering influence (Gr. *to katechōn*, 2Th 2:6) that is holding back the full exercise and development of evil in all its viciousness. This influence or person must first be removed before the Antichrist can be revealed. Many link this restrainer with the Holy Spirit, but it is difficult to say with certainty if that is correct because of the two Greek grammatical forms that exhibit both a masculine participle and a neuter form.

The Contribution of the Thessalonian Epistles

These two letters to the Thessalonians exhibit samples of what must have been earlier forms of Paul's messages to the missional church. Some compare these letters to his early preaching at Lystra (Ac 14:15 – 17) and Athens (Ac 17:22 – 31). The style is straightforward and direct. These letters also show Paul's pastoral side and his gentleness toward new converts. He is patient with all sorts of silliness and with the difficulties the people got themselves into by listening to wrong teachers. Paul never gave up on his converts; instead, he longed for his children to develop the faith to make spiritual progress.

Finally, we see Paul as a man whose heart and soul were saturated with the teaching of the Old Testament. The eschatological ideas from the Hebrew Scriptures were so much ingrained in his thinking that he seemed to breathe the very air of the old promise with its focus on the Messiah, his resurrection, and his final triumph as the kingdom was handed over to him by the Father.

1 and 2 Corinthians: Fixing the Disorders in the Church

The promise-plan of God contained a large number of specifications that surrounded the doctrine of the Messiah and the gospel. For example, as the plan began in Genesis, we saw that it included words of judgment as well as good news. So in Paul's letters to the church at Corinth, it was also necessary to correct problems as well as deviations from the teaching of Jesus, his cross, and his resurrection. Nevertheless, out of the good news of the gospel had come a body of believers who were united by the same power that first brought the gospel into their lives. All threats to that unity had to be addressed, and that is what we gain from the study of the biblical theology of the two books of Corinthians.

Corinth, the commercial capital of Greece, was situated on the north-south, east-west crossroads for shipping and commerce. It was on the southern side of a narrow isthmus that joined together the Peloponnesus to the mainland of Greece. The city existed under the shadow of an enormous rock outcropping, more than 1,800 feet above sea level, named Acrocorinth. It had functioned as a fortress and later as a site for the worship of Aphrodite.

With a harbor on the east side of the isthmus, called Cenchreae, and another harbor on the west side, named Lechaeum, merchants going to and from Spain, Italy, Sicily, Asia Minor, Syria, Phoenicia, and Egypt usually elected to transship their cargoes (for larger vessels) across the five mile isthmus or to haul the smaller vessels across the land from sea to sea on a five-mile tramway, rather than attempt to circumnavigate the stormy Cape Malea. Thus, Corinth was "the bridge of the sea," and "the gate of the Peloponnesus." No wonder it was known for its wealth, opulence, and prosperity, given all the trade that flowed through its portals.

The Roman Lucius Mummius totally decimated Corinth in 146 BC, but Julius Caesar refounded and resettled Corinth with Roman veterans and freepersons around 44 BC. It quickly regained its old stature in the eyes of the merchants, traders, and business people. Anthony Thiselton,[2] following Ben Witherington,[3] showed how the Roman system of patronage led not only to fame and easy fortunes but also to a sense of self-

2. Anthony Thiselton, "I Corinthians," in *New Dictionary of Biblical Theology*, ed. T. Desmond Alexander and Brian S. Rosner (Downers Grove, IL: InterVarsity Press, 2000), 296.

3. Ben Witherington III, *Conflict and Community in Corinth* (Grand Rapids: Eerdmans, 1995), 8, 20, 24.

promotion that had permeated every level of society and had developed itself almost to an art form among the populace. The patrons used their influence to help their clients make the proper contacts, and in turn, the client was to respond by making sure folks knew how well-connected his patron was. For self-promoting, socially ambitious persons, Paul brought the cross of Jesus Christ, which hit right at the heart of such manipulative self-promoting and self-esteeming personalities. Even as the Corinthians would have regarded the cross as "folly" (1Co 1:18), God in his wisdom cut across all their categories and exposed them for what they really were: nothing.

Because the Isthmian games were established around the sanctuary of Poseidon and held thereafter every five years, Corinth claimed the honor for being the center of Hellenic life (Strabo, VIII.22). With such high dependency on the sea, one would think that Poseidon would be the god of choice in that city, but the Corinthian Aphrodite (probably the same as the Phoenician Astarte) took top ascendancy as more than one thousand hierodules daily ministered vices seldom found at other shrines in Greece. "To live like a Corinthian" (Gr. *Corinthiazesthai*) became a synonym for abandoning one's self to immorality and profligacy.

Into this den of iniquity, commerce, and art traveled the apostle Paul in AD 51. Four years later, while in Ephesus during the third year of his third missionary journey, he would write 1 Corinthians in the spring of AD 56, followed by a second letter perhaps in the fall of that same year. But so full of pastoral problems was this mission church that we are given, as a result, a doctrine of the church and teaching about its ministry as well.

The Church and the Christian Ministry

Paul's metaphor of choice to talk about the church was the "body and its members" (1Co 12). Every person was a necessary part of that body, so one part could not vaunt itself over the others. The whole point of Paul's metaphor was the *unity* of the body and the accountability of each part to one another.

It was the same lesson about unity that the apostle had used to rebuff the factions that had arisen in the body at Corinth (1Co 1:10 – 17). To have some claiming to be of the party of Paul, others of the party of Apollos, or some of the party of Cephas, and still others claiming to be of the party of Christ did not make for Christian unity. Could Christ be divided? Were they baptized into the names of these mortals? (1Co 1:13).

The splits represented by these various parties do not seem to represent doctrinal divisions, for in that case Paul would have addressed those doctrinal aberrations. But there is no word about such potential heresy. Instead, it seems to be more a matter of boasting about prestigious personalities and rallying to them rather maintaining the unity of the body in the midst of their diversity.

Paul is anxious to steer away from those who serve as apostles and ministers at the expense of lifting up the Lord himself, who is the source of life and growth in the church (1Co 3:5 – 9). It is wrong for the parties to promote Paul, Apollos, or Cephas — those who ministered the things of God to them. But at the same time, the Corinthians should be careful not to place a low view on the ministry, for these are "God's coworkers," purposely put there for cultivating "God's field" and "God's building," which they were tending as ones called to serve his church (1Co 3:9).

Even the fact that one is an apostle is not a basis for calling attention to oneself or asking for pride of place. It is true, of course, that Paul did urge the church to "imitate me" (Gr. *mimētēs*, 1Co 4:16; 11:1), but the full formula was that they were to do so only as Paul imitated the Savior (1Th 1:6; Eph 5:1). Paul described his so-called rights as an apostle in 1 Corinthians 9:1–23. The result of any imitation of Paul as an apostle was the concern that each person showed for the other and not for one's own self, the Achilles' heel of the Corinthian mentality. Thus, believers were called to forego what each might consider their rights so that the whole body might be built up as the church of Jesus Christ.

First Corinthians 12:12–30 developed the metaphor of the body to its fullest. This body, of course, has many parts, but it still forms one body, showing that there is unity even in this amount of diversity. Moreover, we have all been baptized into one body by the one Spirit (1Co 12:13). This teaching was not up for discussion or adoption; it was true as a result of the powerful working of the Holy Spirit.

That is why all silly comparisons are beside the point. Individual members must not start the game of one-upmanship where members "gifted" in one area are considered by others to be of greater importance than those with gifts judged to be lower in a spiritual pecking order. Neither should those who view themselves as "strong" push their point of view over on what they consider the "weak." The same rule goes for the self-styled "wise," "influential," or anyone who wishes to advance some other form of superiority. Single-gifted individuals who wish to make their gift the new norm for the whole group are reductionistic and overly simplistic in their view of the body. Paul taught that the whole body had need of every one of the gifts that God had distributed among all members in order for the church to be the body — complete as God had intended it to be.

This love and concern for each other is illustrated in the issue of taking another believer to law (1Co 6:1–11) as well as a willingness to exercise church discipline for the case of incest (1Co 5:1–5). The body must restore such a person in either case after that one has repented and shown a desire for holiness once again. The offended (and offending) believer ought to be able to take these matters to church rather than asking the secular world to judge them. If one member of the body was hurting, then the whole body was hurting as a result. The damage must be repaired, but it must be done in truth and love.

In typical Corinthian hubris, objections to such teaching can be heard in 1 Corinthians 6:12, "Everything is permissible for me" (repeated twice) and 1 Corinthians 10:23, "Everything is permissible" (repeated twice). Flushed with their new freedom in Christ, some Corinthians began to confuse freedom with anarchy. Paul did not deny their freedom in Christ, but he immediately qualified it with the reminder that "not everything is beneficial," for we must "not be mastered by anything" (1Co 6:12), and "not everything is constructive" (1 Cor 10:23). Consequently, the believers' freedom is not one of autonomy or acting in any way they choose to act since they are secure in Christ. Such talk violates the fact that we belong to a body and we are no longer our own, but are servants of Christ and part of the whole church (1Co 6:17; 9:9 – 23; 10:31 – 33).

The principle of being concerned for the welfare of the other person was further illustrated in the long discussion of marriage (1Co 7:1 – 40) and in the issue of food sacrificed to idols (1Co 8:1 – 13). On the marriage issue, Paul's principle was that each one should retain the place in life the Lord assigned to him and to which God had called him (1Co 7:17). Paul chose celibacy because "the time is short" (1Co 7:29) and because he wanted to give "undivided attention to the Lord" (1Co 7:35). On the food bought at the markets that had come from the temples of idols, Paul consistently urged that the exercise of their freedom should not become "a stumbling block for the weak" (1Co 8:9). Love "builds up," whereas flaunting one's knowledge "puffs up" (1Co 8:1).

The concern for the body and its unity dominated Paul's first letter to the Corinthians. But even when Paul turned to describing the gifts of the Holy Spirit in chapters 12 – 14 of 1 Corinthians, he still stressed that all these gifts were given "for the common good" (1Co 12:7), not for raising up one member at the expense of the other.

The Gifts of the Holy Spirit

Even though there is a wide variety in the number and types of gifts given to individual believers, they all come from the same Holy Spirit (1Co 12:4). There should therefore be no rivalry or feelings of superiority or inferiority in the body over who got what or who was better than someone else because their gift was thought to be more esteemed or valued by the group. Instead, one should "eagerly desire the greater gifts" (1Co 12:31), identified immediately in 1 Corinthians 13 as "love."

Paul especially singled out the gifts that related to speech: speaking in tongues and the gift of prophecy (1Co 14). These gifts, if shared publicly, had to be rendered intelligible for the whole body (14:13 – 17). The one who interpreted the tongue seemed to be a different person from the one who uttered the tongue in order to have any apologetic value for the unbeliever who might be in the worship service (14:8, 22).

Services had to be conducted in an orderly manner. One might have a hymn, another a word of instruction, a tongue, or an interpretation (14:26), but they were to proceed one at a time, "for God is not a God of disorder but of peace" (14:33).

It appears that a further question came to Paul about women speaking in the services. Or to put the question another way: Would it be better if women who wanted to say something in church waited until they could ask their husbands at home (14:34 – 35)? Paul's response is brief and in line with what he has been trying to teach about the whole body respecting and loving each other, regardless of their station in life, their gifts, their gender, or how wise, weak, or strong they were. He replied laconically, "Did the word of God originate with you? Or are you the only people it has reached?" (14:36).

The Greek particle *ē* that begins that quote might be translated: "Huh, did the word of God originate with you?" And the Greek word for "the only people" is *monous*, a masculine plural, as if Paul said, "Or are you *men the only ones* it has reached?"

Regardless of how this very brief statement is taken, Paul wanted it to be a demonstration of the love for the unity of the body. However, he has one more issue to raise before he finishes this first letter: the resurrection.

The Credibility of the Resurrection

The tendency for self-sufficient persons is to live only for the present. But the church must always remember that it was because of the cross of Christ that she exists. So all of this takes us back to the essence of the gospel (15:1 – 2), which was at the heart and soul of what Paul preached to them. It was a matter of "first importance" (14:3) that Paul's message be received as in accordance with what the Old Testament had taught: that "Christ died for our sins according to the Scriptures, that he was buried, [and] that he was raised on the third day according to the Scriptures" (15:3 – 4).

The credibility of Christ's resurrection is strengthened by the large number of witnesses to his postresurrection appearances, many of whom were still alive in AD 56 as this letter was being written. Everything they stood for or hoped for depended on the reality of the resurrection. If Jesus had not come back from the dead, everything the church taught and lived for was in vain, and all believers were still in their sin. But thanks be to God, the faith of the Corinthians was not in vain, for God raised him from the grave.

This Jesus thereby became the "firstfruits" (that is, the first piece of ripe fruit on the tree that was the promise of all the other fruit on the branches, 15:20) of all who would later be resurrected from the grave. However, each was to come in one of three "turns," squads, or platoons (Gr. *tagmati*, a military term, 15:23*a*). The three squads or companies were as follows: first, there was the resurrection of Jesus (15:23*b*); after that (Gr. twin particles, *epeita … eita*, "then … then") those who belonged to him when he came (15:23*c*); followed finally by "Then the end will come" (15:24*a*). It is clear that everyone can be resurrected, for the text prefaced these three groups with the promise that "all will be made alive" (15:22*b*), but that did not mean all would be redeemed and saved. Some theologians have incorrectly taught a universal salvation for all mortals from this text. But that is not what is taught here. In fact, the twin particles that seem to go together all the time in Greek depict a definite time separation between the resurrection of believers (presumably at the second advent) and the resurrection of all the rest of the dead, presumably at the judgment. So everyone will be raised from the dead, but only some to everlasting life with the rest to everlasting torment at the final judgment of God.

Nevertheless, some will still ask, "How are the dead raised?" (15:35*b*). Paul answers quickly: by dying. Just as any seed must first die before it is going to live, so mortals must first die. They also are raised by the power of God. Those are the two answers to the question of how dead people are resurrected.

The questioner persists: "With what kind of body will they come?" (15:35*c*). Just as adroitly, Paul responds: With the same kind of body as the seed that was sown, except what was perishable and mortal will now be imperishable and immortal. No one expects cabbages to grow from corn seed; you only get cabbages. That is how it is with our bodies as well. Therefore, the members of the body of Christ should be immovable (despite current fads, trends of theology, and the national and international affairs), always abounding in the work of the Lord, since that work in Christ's church will not be lost or empty. That is also why it is worthwhile supporting that work with the collection that is to be taken on the first day of every week (16:1 – 2). Christ's church is part of that everlasting plan that will not pass away.

The Ministers of Christ's Church

Second Corinthians, written shortly after 1 Corinthians in the fall of AD 56, generally is viewed as consisting of three parts: chapters 1 – 7, in the main, exalt in the majesty of the ministry; 8 – 9 deal with the collection for the poor in Jerusalem; and 10 – 13 is a polemic against some "super-apostles" who were challenging Paul's authority and message.

We owe 2 Corinthians 1 – 7, on the supreme joy that is to be found in ministering in Christ's church, to Paul's temporary dejection over what seemed to be taking place in the church at Corinth. The history that led up to this point included the following: (1) Paul stayed for eighteen months after founding the church at Corinth (Ac 18:1 – 17); (2) he wrote a letter to the church at Corinth, which is probably lost; (3) members of the house of Chloe reported to Paul about some quarrels in the church (1Co 1:11); (4) Paul may have sent Timothy to them at this point (1Co 4:17; 16:10); (5) a committee arrived with questions for Paul (1Co 7:1); and (6) Paul seems to have sent Titus to Corinth with the letter of 1 Corinthians, but he worried that he had been too stern in the letter. If Paul had indeed sent Titus, he could not stand the anxiety. As he awaited the results of that letter, Paul grew more and more apprehensive. But when Titus finally arrived with the good news of how the Corinthians had responded (2Co 7:5 – 16), his rebound was as high as had been his depression.[4] The "pressure" (Gr. *epistasis*) and the "anxiety" (Gr. *merimna*; 2Co 11:28) for the work at Corinth, and the other churches, was on the apostle daily. In fact, so heavy was this burden over Corinth that he had lost some of his appetite for the work (2Co 2:13).

That all changed with the coming of Titus and his good report. Paul now had a new outlook and a reinvigorated appreciation for the ministry. It was like marching in God's triumphal procession, rather than the Roman victory celebration after which his words were modeled. Just as the Romans sent their incense machines down the streets alongside of the parade, so Paul was leaving a trail of the aroma of the perfume of Christ, but

4. A. T. Robinson, *Glory of the Ministry* (1911; reprint, Grand Rapids: Baker, 1967), 36 – 37.

it was the smell of death to those who were perishing (2:15). In no sense was Paul, as God's minister, "huckstering" or "peddling" the word of God (2:17). The effectiveness of his ministry could be seen in the commendations that come from others (3:1 – 3). His readiness for ministry came from God and not from any natural ability (3:4 – 6). Thus, he did not lose heart (4:1, 16), for while any proficiencies that the minister might have is like a treasure stored in a clay jar, what is seen by those to whom he ministers is that the "all-surpassing power is from God and not from us" (4:7).

So Paul sets his sights on what is as yet unseen, as he describes what takes place immediately upon a believer's death in 5:1 – 10. The intermediate state takes place immediately after the death of a mortal and lasts until the second advent of Christ. This teaching finds its fullest description in this passage. To be absent from the body is to be personally, actually, and really present immediately with the Lord.

What kept Paul and all ministers going were the four constraints of the ministry, which he laid out in this same context (5:14): (1) "We make it our goal to please him" (5:9); (2) "We try to persuade men" knowing how great is the terror of the Lord (5:11); (3) "From now on we regard no one from a worldly point of view" (5:16), for all racial, political, economic, sociological, or educational barriers are torn down; and (4) "We are therefore Christ's ambassadors, as though God were making his appeal through us" (5:20).

It is for these reasons that "we commend ourselves in every way" (6:4). Suffering and troubles there were aplenty (6:4*b* – 10; 11:23 – 29), but the God of all comfort has seen to all of that (1:3 – 11; 7:5 – 16).

The Grace of Giving in the Church

Paul wanted the church to "excel in [the] grace of giving" along with the other areas they were growing in as believers (8:7). This would be a practical expression of their love for Christ and for one another. Despite the extreme poverty of the believers in Macedonia, they had given most generously for the poor at Jerusalem, a model for all the other churches to follow. Paul did not make this an optional grace, but urged that all at Corinth excel in it beginning immediately.

The best model for urging this experience was the grace found in our Lord Jesus Christ and his "indescribable gift" of himself (8:8 – 9; 9:15). Thus, the law of the harvest illustrates the results of our own giving: sow bountifully and a good return harvest can be expected (9:6 – 9). After all, it is God who can make all grace to abound to all who would follow him in this area of giving (9:8, a verse that has five "alls"). Giving was not outside of the opportunities and the specifications of the promise.

The False Quest for Super-Spirituality

So different are the final four chapters of 2 Corinthians that most hold that they may not belong to the same letter as chapters 1 – 9. But they do belong, even though Paul rebuked the unscrupulousness of the false teachers, whom he had tagged as being the "*huper*-men"[5] or "super-apostles" who placed themselves in a class above Paul. Actually, they were outsiders who needed to give their own self-commendations (3:1; 10:12). These "super-apostles" (11:5) were "masquerading as apostles of Christ," but they were "deceitful workmen" (11:13) and ministers "for Satan" (11:14). In addition to this, they were money-hungry, charging Paul with not being a real apostle since he refused any payment from any church (11:7, 9; 12:13 – 18). Even more disturbing was the fact that they taught a somewhat different Jesus, a different Spirit, and a very different gospel. Their arguments raised "proud obstacles" (10:5), which led to their "putting on airs" (11:20), sporting a kind of deeper spiritual life in their wrongful quest for more.

Paul's answer was to teach the Corinthians to surrender to Christ alone (10:1 – 6), to boast in Christ alone (10:13 – 18), and to be united/married to Christ alone (11:1 – 6).

The principle the Lord taught Paul in this situation was this: "My grace is sufficient for you, for my power is made perfect in weakness" (12:9). Here was a grace that was greater than boasting (12:1), greater than even revelations of a man (that is, Paul) who went from here to eternity and back again (12:2 – 6), and a grace that was greater than any weakness (12:7 – 10).

For all who demanded "proof" or "documentation" that God was speaking through Paul, rather than through these "*huper*-men," the apostle offered a faith that is made powerful in our weakness (13:4 – 5), a faith that could stand self-examination (13:5 – 6), and a faith that would result in personal maturation (13:7 – 9).

The church, the body of Christ, would endure, not because it members and ministers were so strong and spiritual, but because of the love that bound them together and the power of the presence of the Living Christ and the ministry of the Holy Spirit. All of this was included in the promise of the gospel, and that is what made all the suffering, stress, and anxiety placed on God's ministers and his body more than worthwhile. It was the power of the gospel in full demonstration.

Romans: Righteousness from God in the Gospel

No one knows how and when the church at Rome began. The most common view is that it was started by people who had been converted and received the outpouring of the Holy Spirit on the day of Pentecost before returning to Rome to start a group of believers. Even though Paul had never been to Rome (and therefore was not the founder

5. The Greek *huper* is used in this section as much as we today would use "super," as in "supermen" — for so they mistakenly regarded themselves.

of this church) he wrote in about AD 57 to this church on his third missionary journey from the port city of Cenchrea, near Corinth. Perhaps he had heard about some of the issues in the church from his friends, Priscilla and Aquila, and decided to write to tell them of his plans to travel on to Spain, perhaps after briefly visiting Rome. Most of Paul's epistles seem to be prompted by some type of special difficulties in the churches he is writing to. In this case, Paul may also have perhaps heard about a potential division of the church of Jewish believers and Gentile believers (14:1 – 15:3). The "strong" and the "weak" of chapters 14 and 15 are identified by some scholars with distinct parties that are supposed to have stirred up the church at Rome. But the evidence for such a conclusion is not clear, and Romans 15:14 seems to discredit such a notion. Rather, his purpose simply was to impart a spiritual gift (1:11; 15:14) and perhaps to prepare them for his stopover on the way to Spain.

No matter how it was that Paul got into writing to the Roman church, he ended up giving us one of the grandest statements of the gospel that we have in Scripture. While Romans is not a book that gives a complete systematic theology covering all the points of Christian doctrine (nor was it intended to be such), it surely focuses on the gospel as the righteousness of God that comes by faith. Once more we are following the path of the promise-plan of God, which had the gospel as one of its core doctrines ever since Genesis 12:3 (cf. Gal 3:8).

Paul taught five hours a day, six days a week, for a full two years in Ephesus, according to a marginal note in one manuscript on Acts 19:10. If so, that would amount to some 3,120 hours of instruction, which is equal to a full three-year seminary education in our day. If this was his pattern in Asia Minor, it could well be that Romans is an outline of what he taught in those places where he stayed for a longer period of time.

The Gospel as the Righteousness of God

Paul announced his theme right from the beginning: "I am not ashamed of the gospel, because it is the power of God that brings salvation to everyone who believes: first for the Jew, then for the Gentile. For in the gospel a righteousness from God is revealed — a righteousness that is by faith from first to last, just as it is written: 'The righteous will live by faith'" (1:16 – 17). One could not talk about soteriology, much less eschatology (later in Romans 9 – 11) without broaching the subject of Jew-Gentile. That subject was an essential part of the good news of salvation.

Paul's appeal for authority once again went to the Old Testament — to Habakkuk 2:4, to be specific. The basis for all that Paul would write would be exactly what had been shown programmatically to exist in the ancient promise-plan of God: "The righteous will live by faith."

This was the very same gospel that God "promised beforehand through his prophets in the Holy Scriptures," that is, the Old Testament (Ro 1:2). Paul uses the word "gospel" six times in that first chapter (vv. 1, 2, 9, 15, 16, and 17). This gospel focused on God's "son," in the line of David, but also clearly marked him out (Gr. *horizō*)[6] to be the Son of God with power by his resurrection from the dead (1:4). There was no nonsense here about a "Christ-less Christianity," as some would have it. Paul had encapsulated a full Christology in twenty-eight Greek words and forty-one English words in verses 3 – 4!

Accordingly, the problem Paul set out to teach on is this: How can mere mortals be just and righteous before God, both inwardly and externally? It was a question asked long before Paul (e.g., Job 9:2). Externally, there is the issue of escape from the day of wrath and the judgment of God (Ro 2:5; 5:9), but even more importantly there is also the need for peace with God in one's inner being.

However, before Paul could give a solution to this problem, he had to address the sinful condition of all mortals (1:18 – 3:20). It did not matter whether one was a Jew or a Gentile, all men and women were caught in the web of sin's power. God's righteousness had been revealed from heaven against all the godlessness and wickedness of mortals (1:18). One after another, the pagan was condemned (1:18 – 32), as was the moralist (2:1 – 16), the religionist (2:17 – 3:8), and finally, in summary, the whole world (3:9 – 20). Sin had brought the wrath of God against all mortals.

The "wrath of God" is a subject that many contemporary teachers and ministers tend to avoid today, but in the Old Testament there are more than twenty words in nearly six hundred key passages that deal with the topic of God's wrath. In the New Testament there are two main Greek words for wrath, *thumos* and *orgē*, both depicting a coming judgment that continues to mount up until finally God's patience can no longer justify his refraining from acting. Paul refers to God's wrath ten times in Romans (1:18; 2:5, 8; 3:5; 4:15; 5:9; 9:22; 12:19; and 13:4 – 5). While this is not a sudden flailing out in a petulant anger, there is nevertheless a firmness here and a hatred for all that stands in opposition to all God is and what he stands for.

God is angry because mortals have suppressed even what little truth they know about God. Despite the fact that God's eternal power and divine nature has been clearly shown to all through the natural world itself (1:19 – 20), men and women have refused to acknowledge it. As a result, their minds have been darkened (1:21), their hearts have become foolish (1:21 – 22), and substitutes for the true religion have been invented (1:23). As a result, God has abandoned their culture to its own degradation, shameful lusts, and depraved mind-sets (1:24 – 32). In the catalog of vices listed here (1:29 – 31) there is perhaps a glimpse of hell, for all of them tend to surface in one or another person on the slippery slope away from God, even in this life.

It is no different for the moral or virtuous person as well (2:1 – 16). God can cut through all their excuses and rationalizations as he judges according to the truth, as mortals

6. The same Greek word had been used in Acts 10:42; 17:31 to speak of Christ's being "appointed" as judge over the living and the dead.

deserved, in proportionate ways, and according to their deeds. This type of person is just as sinful and therefore blameworthy as the pagan described in the previous chapter.

The religionists (2:17 – 3:8) try to avoid this universal condemnation by cataloging assets: the law of God, the special relationship enjoyed by the Jewish nation, the knowledge of God's will, the divine endowment to approve what is superior and to serve as a light for those in the dark, an instructor for the foolish, and a teacher for spiritual infants. While these assets are real in principle, Paul's point is that knowledge is not enough; God looks at the heart rather than just the external appearance. It will do no good to appeal to circumcision as a way to get out from under this universal condemnation, for circumcision as a sign of the covenant is only useful if it is accompanied by a heart relationship and the appropriate evidence of an inward change.

Mortals can be put "in-the-right" with God, not by their own machinations and strivings, but only by the work of Jesus on the cross. Romans 3:21 – 26 is an extremely important statement of how people can be declared righteous as a free gift of God by faith. For those who have no righteousness, God will provide his own righteousness. But this gift does not come out of the blue with no one paying for it: Christ died in our place and provided for our redemption. The gift is available through simple faith and trust in the Lord Jesus Christ.

In Romans 3:24 – 25, Paul taught that people can be "justified freely by his grace through the redemption that came by Jesus Christ. God presented him as a sacrifice of atonement, through faith in his blood." Three Greek words are at the heart of Paul's theology: (1) *dikaioō*, "to justify," which is built on the same root as the word "righteous" (*dikaios*) and "righteousness" (*dikaiosunē*); (2) *hilastērion*, "sacrifice as an atonement, or propitiation"; and (3) *apolutrōsis*, "redemption, a losing or setting free by the payment of a price."

George E. Ladd nicely summarized the teaching on the first word of this group in Greek:

> The importance of justification in Paul's theological thinking has been debated. While Paul used the verb "to forgive" (*aphiēmi*) only once (Rom 4:7), the noun (*aphesis*) twice (Eph 1:7; Col 1:14), and another verb "to forgive" (*charizomai*) twice (Eph 4:32; Col 2:13), he used the verb "to justify" (*dikaioō*) fourteen times, and righteousness (*dikaiosunē*) fifty-two times. It is, however, a fact that these terms are concentrated in Romans and Galatians. Thus the verb "to justify" is found outside of Galatians and Romans only in I Corinthians 6:11 and Titus 3:7.[7]

Justification is not equal to a pardon, for in a pardon only the debt/penalty is excused, a negative concept. In justification, however, there is full acceptance, a posi-

7. George Eldon Ladd, *A Theology of the New Testament* (Grand Rapids: Eerdmans, 1974), 437 – 38.

tive concept. Nor is justification similar to amnesty, where one is pardoned without principle. In amnesty, one simply decides to overlook and forget all the wrongdoing, declining to raise the issue, or to care for the debt or the penalty. But in justification we are *declared righteous*, not "made" righteous; it is an acquittal of a forensic type similar to what a judge would issue from the bench. In this case the judge who issues the declaration is the same one who also personally cared for the debt and removed the wrath of God that accompanied our guilt.

The channel of that justification is faith (3:25 – 26), but not a faith in faith, as if it too were another type of work, or even a state of mind; it is simply a means and a channel for justification. Faith is mentioned three times in this paragraph (3:22, 25, 26); the object of this faith is Christ, the content of this faith is the work of Christ on the cross, and the extent of this faith is a trust and commitment of the will to Christ as well.

No less significant is the other word in Romans 3:25, rendered by the NIV as "sacrifice of atonement." It too has been a center of controversy, for it translates the Greek *hilastērion*, "propitiation" (cf. 1Jn 2:2; 4:10; Heb 2:17), which meant that the wrath of God had been turned away and thus appeased. But this traditional rendering is opposed by some current scholars, who prefer to render it instead as "expiation,"[8] meaning that we cover over or wipe away our guilt and sins. However, the same word, *hilastērion*, is used in the Greek translation of the Old Testament (the Septuagint) to render the word for the "mercy seat" in the tabernacle, where the blood of the sacrificed animal was sprinkled. It is clear, of course, that the blood of animals did not take away sins (Heb 10:1 – 2), nor did the Old Testament anywhere teach that it did. But the principle spoken of here in Romans is the same as that in the tabernacle: God's wrath against sin demands that a life be substituted for our lives if we are to be forgiven and go free by his grace. Thus, what was symbolized in the "mercy seat" of the tabernacle and the temple as well as on the Day of Atonement (Lev 16), Jesus fulfilled by giving his life in place of ours at the very place where God draws near to us for our redemption.

From the world of commerce came a third Greek word important to the teaching of righteousness and justification in Romans 3:24: "redemption" (Gr. *apolutrōsis*). It referred to buying or selling (often a slave) in order to set that one free. This did not make God a mercenary, but Christ by his own death on the cross bought us from the slavery of our sin by paying for it with his life on the cross. The Hebrew word *kôphēr* spoke of the same process in which mortals were ransomed or delivered by means of a substitute. Never did the Hebrew verbal form of this noun mean "to cover," except in its exclusive use with Noah's ark in Genesis 6 – 8, where it was used of a covering or caulking of the ark with pitch to make it watertight.

8. This rendering can be found in the RSV, in the NEB, and from scholars such as C. H. Dodd. The Council of Trent (1545 – 64) said justification takes place at baptism. The baptized were not only cleansed from their sins, but they were simultaneously infused with a new supernatural righteousness.

Now all of this was not new, for in Romans 4:1 – 25 Paul showed that Abraham was similarly "justified," but not by his works. Rather, it happened just as "the Scriptures say" (4:3): "Abraham believed God and it was credited to him as righteousness" (Ge 15:6). This did not mean that Abraham became a theist, one who now believed in God for the first time — and that was all that happened! No, it meant that he put his faith in the coming Man of promise, his own "seed," which God had just disclosed to him in Genesis 15:1 – 5. The object of his faith was in principle the same as it ever was or ever will be: the Messiah himself. On that basis, God declared Abraham righteous.

No less similar was the experience of David (4:6 – 8); he too was justified, for that is why he said in Psalm 32:1 – 2,

> Blessed is he
> whose transgressions are forgiven,
> whose sins are covered.
> Blessed is the man
> whose sin the Lord does not count against him.

If some are thinking that God gave this declaration to Abraham because he was circumcised or because he obeyed the law, think again: Abraham was justified before the institution of circumcision and long before the law was given by Moses (Ro 4:9 – 25). The continuity between the Old and New Testaments on this point could not be clearer.

The Power of the Gospel in its Present and Future Effects

The second major section of the book of Romans builds on the results of the first four chapters, which showed how mortals could be declared to be right with God by faith in the atoning work of Christ on the cross. In one long sentence (in the Greek) in Romans 5:1 – 2, Paul shows that nothing is able to separate believers from the love of God in Christ Jesus because of the hope one has in the glory of God. Instead of moving on to the topic of sanctification, as many presume, Paul moves from justification to glorification, as he also does in Romans 8:30.

The first benefit of justification is peace with God, in which grace we now stand (Ro 5:1 – 2). Because of this standing, we can bear up under suffering (5:3 – 5), for suffering produces perseverance, and perseverance produces "character" (Gr. *dokimē*, similar to our word "documentation"), and character produces hope, a word not of tentativeness but of full certainty.

Christ has reversed the effects of Adam's sin and provided life eternal for all who believe (5:12 – 21). Despite this fact, there is still the problem of daily sin, the flesh, and death itself that must be conquered by the same power of Christ that introduced us into being righteous with God (Ro 6:1 – 7:25).

However, the Holy Spirit is at work in our mortal bodies to help life in the realm and power of the Spirit (8:1 – 13). Do not fret: God will not abandon what he has begun (8:14 – 39).

The Promise-Plan of God and the Nation of Israel

Paul began in Romans 1:16 with the Jew and the Gentile; both must now come in for special consideration in chapters 9 – 11. Some have tended to treat these chapters as an intercalation, a parenthetical insertion, or even a disruption in his discourse on salvation, but these chapters are central to the continued argument he is making about how Jew and Gentile can be reconciled to God.

Here was the troubling question: "Did God reject his [own] people?" (11:1). It is not a question about Israel, first of all; it is a question about God. The answer is no, for the promises of God are "irrevocable" (11:29). But whatever rejection may appear to be the case, in any event it is temporary. God will not forget his word, and his word cannot fail (9:6). Long ago, God chose Isaac, not Ishmael; God chose Jacob, not Esau (9:7 – 12).

Well, in that case, "Is God unjust?" (9:14). Hardly; the marvel is that God had mercy on anybody, especially at the time of the golden calf (9:14 – 18; see Ex 32 – 34), out of which context this allusion is taken. The present rejection of Israel is neither absolute nor unqualified.

That still leaves another question: "Then why does God still blame us?" (9:19). If his choice is a sovereign one, and it is, fine; but how can he still hold those who are not chosen responsible for not accepting him? Paul's response is this: in God's "choosing to show his wrath and make his power known, [he] bore with great patience the objects of his wrath — prepared for destruction" (9:22). The Greek verb *katērtismena*, "prepared," is one where the passive and middle[9] voices fall together in the Greek language, thus it could be translated, "were prepared for destruction" (passive form of the verb) or "they prepared themselves for destruction" (reflexive form). I think the reflexive idea of the middle voice is the correct choice here.

However, God has not forgotten his ancient promise to Israel about the land and about the gospel. Paul's prayer was that Israel still might come to repentance and faith (10:1). In the meantime, "a hardening in part" (11:25) has come over Israel, but when the "full number of the Gentiles" (11:12, 25) has been reached, Israel will be saved (11:26) and grafted back as separate branches into the olive tree from which they had been taken.

During this interim, believing Gentiles have been grafted into the olive tree that had its roots and trunk in the patriarchal promises and the people of Israel, while many of the Jewish people had been cut out of the tree because of unbelief. The church does not have an independent existence or genesis on its own, as if it had no roots and no history, for in that case it would be devoid of all association, rootage, or previous contacts. Its nourishment and sustenance comes from the promise roots embedded in the words given to the patriarchs and to the nation of Israel.

9. Whereas English has only the active and passive voices, Greek has a middle voice that is reflexive in nature. However, its spelling in some forms ends up being spelled the same way as the passive so that only context distinguishes one from the other.

The Practical Outworking of the Gospel

Having received so great a salvation, believers will want to give themselves wholly to the service of God similar to the whole burnt offerings of Leviticus 1 (Ro 12:1). The venues for service are manifold (12:3 – 8), but at the heart of them all is love (12:9 – 21).

Such service also meant respecting the legitimate claims of government (13:1 – 7) and the rights of those who at certain points had a weaker conscience than the strong did on those same points (14:1 – 15:8). In the midst of all this talk about Jew and Gentile, and the long assurance that God is not yet finished with the Jewish nation, Paul shares his intent to reach the Gentiles all the way out to Spain, after stopping to see the believers in Rome (15:8 – 29).

Paul asked for prayer as he carried the collection for the poor in Jerusalem (15:30 – 33). He concluded by greeting a long list of individuals who had given him help along the way, with a surprising number of women among them (16:1 – 27), including Phoebe, who served Christ in the church at Cenchrea, near Corinth.

Thus the letters to these five mission churches during the decade roughly of the AD 50s set the ethical, moral, theological, and practical grounds for much that was to follow in Christ's church. But always at the heart of the message, and the motivation for all that ensued, was the promise-plan of God.

Chapter 14

The Promise-Plan and Paul's Prison Epistles

Colossians, Philemon, Ephesians, Philippians (Early AD 60s)

Four of Paul's letters are called his Prison Epistles: Colossians, Philemon, Ephesians, and Philippians. Most believe these letters were written somewhere around AD 60, when Paul was imprisoned under house arrest in Rome (Ac 28:16); however, some would place these letters at a time when Paul was also held at Caesarea for two years in AD 57 – 59 (Ac 23:33; 24:27), while a few others hold out for Ephesus as the place of his confinement (in which case the date for these books would be earlier, around AD 58).

In 2 Corinthians 11:23, Paul noted that he had been in prison "more frequently" than not. In fact, Clement of Rome[1] gave the total number of Paul's imprisonments as seven. He was indeed a real bond servant for Christ!

But what appears to tip the scales in favor of a Roman imprisonment are the references to the praetorium, or palace guard (Php 1:13), which was located, of course, in Rome, and Paul's reference to "those who belong to Caesar's household" (Php 4:22). Therefore, I lean toward favoring a Roman jail as the base from which these four letters were written.

Colossians: The Primacy of Jesus and New Life in Christ

Colossae was the name of the ancient Phrygian city one hundred miles east of Ephesus on the south bank of the Lycus River, which in turn ran into the Meander River. Situated on the lower end of a narrow glen some ten miles long, Colossae was one of

1. See 1 Clement 5:6, as cited by D. A. Carson and Douglas J. Moo, *Introduction to the New Testament*, 2nd ed. (Grand Rapids: Zondervan, 2005), 503.

three sister cities (Laodicea and Hierapolis being the other two), which all received the gospel at about the same time (Col 4:13). Laodicea was ten miles downstream in the Lycus Valley. Fronted on the north side of its valley, high up on a plateau, was the other city of Hierapolis. From the numerous hot streams in Hierapolis, which were heavily saturated with a form of alum that flowed down over the side of that city's hill, the snow-white incrustations gave (and still do to this day) the impression of an enormous frozen ice-falls. These three merchant towns on the trade route from Rome to the east were well situated, but Colossae had already started to decline, whereas the other two cities were still prospering.

The churches in these three sister cities were not founded by the apostle Paul, who was prevented on his second missionary journey from going into Asia (Ac 16:6). In fact, later Paul purposely avoided going that way on his third missionary tour in order not to build on anyone else's foundation (Ac 18:23; 19:1). Instead, these three churches were probably founded by Epaphras, a native of Colossae (Col 1:7; 4:2, 13). Epaphras no doubt met Paul (and may have been converted by him) while the apostle was at Ephesus. Luke tells us that the two years Paul lectured at the lecture hall of Tyrannus in Ephesus, "all the Jews and Greeks who lived in the province of Asia heard the word of God" (Ac 19:10). Epaphras surely was one of those whom Paul discipled.

The Gospel, the Word of Truth

The good news, which began certainly with the promise delivered to Abraham, was here firmly equated with the "word of truth" (Col 1:5). As such, it was "the word of [from or about] God in its fullness" (1:25), indeed, the very "word of [from or about] Christ" (3:16). This word from the gospel also had a "mystery" aspect to it: it had "been kept hidden for ages and generations, but [was] now [being] disclosed to the saints" (1:26). The mystery was Christ himself (2:2), and the truth of Christ's indwelling of the Colossian Gentiles and all other believers (1:27). Therefore, believers were instructed to be on their guard: "See to it that no one takes you captive through hollow and deceptive philosophy, which depends on human tradition and the basic principles of this world rather than on Christ" (2:8). Similarly, human rules and prohibitions, such as "Do not handle! Do not taste! Do not touch!" (2:21) were not part of this powerful gospel of Christ. Traditions of mortals had to be sharply distinguished from the word of God.

That truth also included a "hope" (1:5*a*, metonymy for "an inheritance"), which God had "stored up for you in heaven" (1:5). This good news involved, among other things, the inclusion of the Gentiles as the "people of God" (1:27; Ge 12:3; Isa 42:1 – 4). That certainly rang true with the earliest expression of the content of the gospel.

The Supremacy of Christ

Few words summarize Paul's theology of the Messiah better than the famous hymn of Colossians 1:15 – 20. Christ's dual work as Creator (1:15 – 17) and Redeemer (1:18 – 20) were lifted high in this hymn to make the case that Christ was supreme. This hymn, in part, had some clear roots in the wisdom materials of the Old Testament (Ge 1:1; Prov 8:22; Job 28:23 – 28; Pss 95:6 – 7; 100:3) and in some of Judaism's apocryphal works as well (Wisdom of Solomon 7:22 – 27 and Ecclesiasticus 24).[2]

Christ's supremacy in creation was set forth by phrases such as "the image of the invisible God," "the firstborn of all creation" (1:15), and in the description of his work, "for by him all things were created: things visible and invisible" (1:16).

The word "firstborn," one of the key terms in the promise-plan of God, had its roots in Exodus 4:22 (see also Heb 1:6; Rev 1:5). There Israel was called "my son, my firstborn," referring to the primacy of the coming Messiah through Israel. Likewise, the word had roots in the promise to David in Psalm 89:27: "my firstborn," which Messiah also was the harbinger of all the "firstborn ones" (that is, believers, Heb 12:23; note the plural here) and the "firstborn from among the dead" (Col 1:18).

This title, "firstborn," stressed the Son's preeminence in *rank* as well as his priority to all the created order; it did not mean the Son was the first object of God's creation, made before God created the world. The fact that "firstborn" means "first in rank," "first in preeminence," and not "first in chronology" can be shown by the fact that Jacob (later called Israel) was the second child born to his parents, yet he is called "firstborn" in Exodus 4:22, as was David in Psalm 89:27 (the eighth child, not the first), the forerunner of Messiah. Likewise, Ephraim, who was Joseph's second son, was called his "firstborn" in Jeremiah 31:9, whereas Manasseh preceded Ephraim in the birth order. To say Jesus was the first one/object that God created before he created the world was to fall back into the Arian heresy, still propagated in our day by the Jehovah Witnesses, who claim that Jesus is not as eternal as the Father is and thus not fully divine in the same way that God the Father is.

Christ exceeds all wisdom, for he was the eternally uncreated person who incarnated and embodied all of the attributes of God. Not only did he make everything in heaven and on earth, but he also continues to sustain everything as well ("in him all things hold together," 1:17). He is the ruler of the kingdom to which his saints belong, thus, he has supremacy over everything (1:18).

But Christ is also the Redeemer of his body the church (1:18*a*). He functions as its "head" and its "originator" (1:18*b*), the one blazing the trail for the believer's resurrection to immortality (1:18*c*). While the power of his redemptive work extends to all creation, human and otherwise, the focus of that power is on reconciling sinners to himself through his death and work on the cross (1:20). Thus he is both the Mediator and the Provider of peace for all who are reconciled to him. This group of reconciled persons forms his "body" (1:18), for which body Paul now labors to "fill up in my flesh what is

2. See Darrell L. Bock, "A Theology of Paul's Prison Epistles," in *A Biblical Theology of the New Testament*, ed. Roy B. Zuck (Chicago: Moody Press, 1994), 302.

still lacking in regard to Christ's afflictions" (1:24). Moreover, Christ is also indwelling this body of believers (the great "mystery," 1:26 – 27), so that those who are redeemed no longer live for themselves, but for Christ (3:1 – 17).

New Life in Christ

A new humanity has been formed as a result of persons being "renewed in knowledge in the image of [their] Creator" (3:10) and redeemed by his blood. As Murray Harris put it:

> In the OT the call to humans to be holy was based on God's own holiness and his gracious intervention to save his people. "I am the LORD who brought you up out of Egypt to be your God; therefore, be holy, because I am holy (Lev 11:45; cf. 11:44; 19:2; 20:7, 26). In a similar way, at the heart of Pauline ethics (and the NT ethics in general) is the relationship between theological proclamation and moral exhortation, between affirmation and appeal, between the indicative and the imperative: "you are ... therefore be!" "You have died (*apethanete*)" (3:3, NRSV), "Put to death, therefore (*nekrōsate oun*)" (3:5).[3]

Prior to coming to Christ, "the old self" (3:9) with all its evil practices, was the habit and style of life of all mortals. But that is all over now, for believers are told to shed that old self just like one would take off a pair of old clothes. Now there is a new self, which has left behind all the old ways and habits of life. Old ethnic, racial, and social distinctions are now passé, because a transformation has taken place. Moreover, believers have been raised with Christ (3:1); accordingly, their minds and hearts are set on "things above" and "not on earthly things" (3:1, 2). These are now new persons in Christ Jesus.

Now that believers belong to Christ as his "chosen people, holy and dearly beloved" (3:12), the call is to clothe themselves with "compassion, kindness, humility, gentleness, and patience, bearing with each other and forgiving whatever grievances [each] may have against one another" (3:12*b* – 13). Christology was not merely of cognitive value; it was to result in an ethic of love and the transformation of a new self after the image of the one who created and redeemed us.

The Colossian Heresy

There is a hint of a problem in Colossians 2:4, 8, 16 – 23, but because Paul is so cryptic in his reference to whatever was troubling them, it is not clear what the problem was exactly. For the most part, the Colossian church was sound, for Paul praised how "orderly" they were and how firm was their faith in Christ (2:5). Apparently, then, Paul did not wish to make a major issue out of what must have been a minor distraction to

---

3. Murray J. Harris, "Colossians," in *New Dictionary of Biblical Theology*, ed. T. Desmond Alexander and Brian S. Rosner (Downers Grove, IL: InterVarsity Press, 2000), 324.

them. Paul tended to be somewhat more subtle and proximate as to what the troubles were, for these Colossians were well taught, so there was less fear that they might be tempted to slide over into one or more of these issues.

Whether the heresy exposed here was Hellenistic or Jewish in nature cannot be settled for certain either. Perhaps it was a little of both — an eclectic assortment of ideas, but it was much too early to find here any settled second-Christian-century form of gnosticism. Even "the fullness" (Gr. *to plērōma*) of the Godhead (1:19) does not appear to have the later technical sense it would accumulate in gnosticism in the next centuries. In any case, scholars have suggested that later gnostics derived their usage from Paul and not the other way around.

Whoever they were, these cultic and self-implied "deeper life" persons focused on observing the Sabbaths, new moon celebrations, and other religious festivals (2:16). These items suggest a Jewish flavor, but there also were hints of ascetic practices and appeal to heavenly mediatory spirits or angels, which strikes one as being more Hellenistic, for no Jew would worship angels (2:18).

Darrell Bock notes that there was a movement in Judaism known as "*Merkabah* mysticism," an allusion to the prophet Ezekiel's vision (Eze 1, 10). Thus, the teaching of some was that one must prepare with days of fasting in order to get ready for a chariot journey similar to Ezekiel's into the heavens to see God.[4] But this too is only a suggestion; we do not know if this was one of the teachings Paul was quietly trying to quell.

It was, however, a "deceptive philosophy" (2:8) that had "fine-sounding arguments" (2:4) and must have claimed it had the revelation of secret or mystery wisdom and knowledge (2:2, 3). In addition, it seemed to have stressed special rules of asceticism (2:21), along with all its other peculiarities.

Rather than refuting these disturbing tendencies and thereby giving them free press, Paul went beyond all speculative assertions and announced that Christ is God's "firstborn" and goal of all creation (1:15 – 17). This pre-existent Man from heaven is the One who will also indwell all who believe. Yes, there are angels in the world, ones by which even the law came (Dt 33:2, LXX), thus the objection is not to angelology itself, but to a misplaced emphasis on the subject. Paul will refer positively to angels (Ro 8:38; 1Co 2:6 – 8; 6:2; 11:10; 15:24; Gal 1:8), but there was also the tradition of bad angels (Job 4:18; 15:15; Ps 82:1 – 2).

Some have noted that there are forty-six words used in Colossians that are not used elsewhere by the apostle Paul,[5] but that is only if one takes only the four great works (such as Romans, 1 and 2 Corinthians, and Galatians) of Paul as being normative. Moreover, the majority of those forty-six words are used in connection with the Colossian heresy

4. Bock, "A Theology of Paul's Prison Epistles," 305, gives an extensive bibliography of Jewish sources.

5. L. W. Grensted, "Colossians, Epistle to the," in *Dictionary of the Apostolic Church*, ed. James Hastings et al. (Edinburgh: T & T Clark, 1915), 1:231.

and Paul's refutation of the same. Only eleven of these words are used by no other New Testament writer. Furthermore, it must be remembered that Paul was now in Rome; one could expect that he enlarged his vocabulary by all his new associations.

Others note that there is a close association of Colossians with Ephesians, for the structure of the two is very similar, except for the special warnings about the Colossian heresy. But there too, it must be observed that Ephesians has a second thanksgiving and prayer (Eph 1:15 – 23; 3:14 – 21) that is not found in Colossians. There are also some very close verbal parallels going for several verses between the two letters. But this would only suggest that both letters come from the same person (Paul), or that one letter has been deliberately styled after the other one.

The gospel that Paul preached is "bearing fruit and growing throughout the whole world" (1:6). This is the same word that Abraham announced in Genesis 12:3 (Gal 3:8). The Messiah is also called God's "firstborn" (1:18), a name first announced in the earliest forms of the promise-plan in Exodus 4:22 – 23. Thus, the plan continues to build as it progresses through time.

Philemon: The Fellowship Found in the Gospel

Philemon is a private letter to a slave owner by the same name, who probably lived in the city of Colossae, in the Roman province of Asia Minor, present-day Turkey. He had been won to Christ through Paul's ministry during the apostle's long stay at Ephesus (Ac 19:26). "Apphia" (Phm 2) was no doubt his wife and "Archippus" (Phm 2) might have been his son, who possibly later served as the pastor of the church that met in Philemon's house (Col 4:17).

Philemon's slave was Onesimus (Phm 10), who ran away from his master and who, as a result, faced the death penalty under Roman law. This, then, was the occasion for the letter. Slavery, of course, was rampant in the first Christian century. Paul, a Roman citizen, did not pause to condemn slavery in this letter, but neither did he condone it. Instead, Paul's ethics were grounded in the law of Moses, which included a provision, at least for a Jewish person placed in bondage to another Jewish person, that he or she could be held for no more than six years or until the year of Jubilee came (Ex 21:2 – 13). However, if the master, in the interim, had caused an injury that resulted in the slave's death, it was a capital offense and demanded capital punishment of the owner (Ex 21:12). Also, if he punished the slave and as a result left an impairment or mark of any kind, the slave automatically won his or her freedom immediately, and whatever collateral was owed was rescinded forthwith as the slave went free (Ex 21:26 – 27). The prophet Jeremiah had warned that permanent slavery of some of the Jews would earn God's disfavor and be one of the reasons for the coming exile to Babylon (Jer 34:8 – 24).

All of this provided the apostle with his ethical base as he dealt with this social and pastoral problem.

When this letter was written, Paul was in prison (Phm 9), but not all agree that it was written during his first Roman imprisonment. Some prefer Paul's Caesarean imprisonment for the following reasons: (1) a runaway slave would first go to a city nearby, such as Caesarea; (2) the apostle had also asked that a guest room be prepared for him when he visited Colossae, which would imply it was near enough to take advantage of it (Phm 22); and finally, (3) Paul had reason to expect an early release from his Caesarean imprisonment, but not his Roman one.

But an internment at Rome (as the site from which this letter was written) still seems preferable for Onesimus, because it would be easier to hide in Rome with all the slaves there. Also the money Onesimus had stolen from Philemon would probably have been large enough to get to Rome, while he probably would not have needed as much if he only wanted to get to Caesarea.[6]

A Theology of Fellowship

In the New Humanity that God had brought together in his body, the church, all sorts of economic, social, political, and racial barriers had to be broken down. There was a "fellowship" (Gr. *koinōnia*, Phm 6, 17) that counted for more than just a tolerance of those who were different. This unity in Christ gave a new status to each member of the body that defied all the cultural norms of that age (and every age since). It provided for a full fellowship and partnership in the ancient gospel set forth long ago in the promise-plan of God.

Paul stated his purpose for writing this letter in Philemon 6, but that verse is syntactically difficult to render. Surely this "fellowship" refers to a participation in Christ that allows believers to get involved with each other in ways of sharing they never would have dreamed of doing before becoming believers. Darrell Bock paraphrased verse 6, Paul's prayer that Philemon's "participation involved with [his] faith would become effective to the point of understanding and practicing the good that sharing in Christ mean[t]."[7] Learning is good, but it would just as well be demonstrating what this fellowship meant.

A Theology of Forgiveness

Fellowship, in the case at hand, would mean Philemon's forgiveness of Onesimus, a full reconciliation between the two, and a harmony among all who met in the church in Philemon's house.

6. John W. Robbins, *Christianity and Slavery* (Unicoi, TN: Trinity Foundation, 2007). Robbins focuses on verse 16, "no longer a slave," and convincingly argues that "the only sense in which Paul can be understood as urging Philemon to free Onesimus is the purely formal, legal sense. Morally, Onesimus is no longer a slave. Paul is teaching Philemon, the church in his house, and us some of the social implications of Christianity, in which no man is naturally a slave ..." (42).

7. Bock, "Theology of Paul's Prison Epistles," 307.

Onesimus, though a fugitive from justice, had somehow met Paul in Rome and had been led to the Lord by Paul. As a spiritual son, he had become most "beneficial" or "useful," a play of the meaning of Onesimus's name (v. 11), to the apostle during his confinement in Rome. Even though Paul could have continued to benefit from Onesimus's services, he felt it best not to do so without Philemon's permission. Therefore, he was sending him back to Colossae (vv. 12 – 14), no longer a slave, but "a dear brother"; indeed, "a brother in the Lord" (v. 16). Here indeed was a real test of how effective this "fellowship" in the gospel was. Could a truly forgiven domestic take a place right alongside of his master in the worship and life of the church?

Paul's point was direct: "If, therefore, you have fellowship with me" (v. 17, my translation), "welcome him as you would welcome me." Philemon must forgive this thief and runaway slave just as Christ forgave each person. Paul knew that Onesimus had done Philemon wrong and that he owed him as well. That was never in dispute by Paul or by Onesimus. But how would Philemon react to his financial loss and to this awful breach of culture and society?

Paul makes an offer to Philemon, which as legal tender is as good as a check would be today. Adolph Deissmann[8] some years ago showed from the Greek papyri of that era (which were closer to the Koiné Greek of the New Testament than classical Greek) that these words of Paul in verses 18 – 19 could have been "cashed in" by Philemon for all that Paul was worth, had he had a mind to do so. In fact, Paul signed what was in effect a virtual "check," when he said, "I, Paul, am writing this with my own hand. I will pay it back" (v. 19). It was tantamount to being a signature and a bank draft that was fully negotiable!

However, lest Philemon take Paul up on his offer too quickly to reimburse Philemon, Paul reminded Philemon that he owed Paul as well, for Paul had led him to the Lord and apparently had instructed him as well. Perhaps it was time for Paul to reap some "benefit" or "usefulness" (another play of Onesimus's name) from Philemon in the Lord as well. It was a little crafty of Paul to do this, but it was a fair reminder of how so many are indebted to so many others for all that one has in Christ.

Paul, however, preferred real actions demonstrating true *koinōnia* in place of any money, for that would "refresh [his] heart in Christ" (v. 20) more than any offers of cash reimbursement would.

This is the way God's new society would work. It would never let social stratification or any other social, economic, political, or educational distinctions be employed to either allow or disallow fellowship in the body. Our Lord had paid too dearly for the ripping down of all of these barriers. No one held a trump card over anyone else in the

8. Adolph Deissmann, *Light from the Ancient East* (London: Doran, 1927), 330–32.

gospel. Christ's death and resurrection were meant to transform all these relationships with a whole new order of living, thinking, and worshiping together.

Accordingly, it appears that Philemon did forgive his newly converted slave, but he also received him as a full brother in Christ. Had Philemon not received Onesimus as Paul had hoped, no doubt a second letter would have followed this one, but no such letter is attested. No doubt they sang, prayed, and listened to the word of God together in that house church at Colossae on an equal level with the master of the house — the same house in which Onesimus must have continued to serve.

Ephesians: The Mystery of God

Paul, while still in his Roman prison (Eph 3:1; 4:1; 6:20), identified himself as the writer of this letter "to the saints in Ephesus" (1:1*b*). However, there exists a good deal of evidence that this letter had originally been intended to be a circular letter to be shared with a number of congregations throughout the whole province of Asia, of which Ephesus was the capital. The reason for claiming this was a circular letter is that some of the better Greek manuscripts lack the phrase "in Ephesus" (1:1*b*). Another reason is the lack of personal references, especially in Ephesians 1:15 and 3:2, where it seems Paul merely heard about those who would receive this letter but apparently had never personally met them. Since Paul spent three years teaching in Ephesus, it would seem that he would mention several there by name as his habit was in his other letters.

The town of Ephesus lay at the head of a gulf approximately in the middle of the western coast of Asia Minor. It was situated on the left bank of the Cayster River at the foot of the surrounding hills that sloped down to the river. Originally the river reached the city gates, but due to gradual silting up of the river, Ephesus is now more than six miles from the sea. In the meantime, the river's silting action has also raised the level of some of the land.

The archaeological ruins of this much excavated city are some of the most dramatic and most extensive in that whole region. There is little doubt that it was a flourishing city with a population of 200,000 to 300,000 inhabitants in Paul's day. Its most famous ruin is that of the temple of Artemis/Diana, which made the site both famous and the occasion for the famous clash between the silversmiths of Artemis, who stirred up the whole city to riot, and the apostle Paul (Ac 19:23 – 41).

The letter was sent by the hand of Tychicus (Eph 6:21), who had accompanied Paul on part of his third missionary journey. He also was the messenger of two other letters written at this same time and addressed to the same district: Colossians and Philemon (note also that Col 4:7 – 9 also mentions Onesimus, who is at the center of the Philemon letter).

Different from most of Paul's other thirteen (or fourteen) writings, Ephesians lacks a special or urgent issue or purpose stated in the letter (in Colossians and Philippians, the only other exceptions, there is only a hint of a problem). There are no rivals, opponents, or identifiable heresies looming on the horizon in this book. It would appear that the Judaizing teachers such as Paul confronted in Galatia are now in the past, and the troubles at Colossae are history as well. Again, only faint traces of some of these battles may be heard (perhaps in Eph 2:11, 14, 17). Thus, the letter addressed, in the main, Gentile converts and the unity of the church. Especially significant was Paul's focus on the "mystery of Christ."

The Mystery of Christ

With the danger from Judaizing teachers becoming less of a threat and the growth in the number of Gentiles in the body of Christ, there was now the danger that the Gentiles would despise the Jewish believers in their midst (Eph 2:11 – 15). However, Christ was the source of peace (2:14), not merely of an inner quietude for each individual but for racial reconciliation between Jews and Gentiles. In this new body of believers, Christ not only made men and women right with himself, but just as importantly, they were made right with each other despite previous racial, religious, or ethnic barriers.

Karl Marx popularized the word *alienation* (*apellotriomenoi*, "separated," in Eph 4:18, or "excluded" in Eph 2:12), which he took from the German theologian Ludwig Feuerbach. Marx and Feuerbach used the term *alienation* for men and women who were disaffected and cut off from enjoying what they had produced and from the political seat of power. But the Bible analyzed it differently: men and women were cut off from God (Eph 4:18; Col 1:21) and from the "covenants of promise" (Eph 2:12). Deep-seated hostilities had divided Jew and Gentile so that a fivefold alienation took place. All Gentiles were Christless, stateless, promiseless, hopeless, and Godless (2:12). Gentiles were those who were "far away/once far off" (2:13), a phrase used in Isaiah 49:1; 57:19, and Acts 2:39 to describe the Gentiles. But now in Christ's salvation, the Gentiles "have been brought near" (2:13*b*), just as Israel had been described as being "near" to God in Deuteronomy 4:7 and Psalm 148:14. Because of this nearness, there was "access to the Father by one Spirit" (2:18). The old "dividing wall of hostility" (2:14) symbolized in Herod's temple by a five-foot-thick wall that separated the court of the Gentiles from the rest of the temple, contained this inscription in Greek:

> No foreigner may enter within the barrier and enclosure around the temple. Anyone caught doing so will have himself to blame for his ensuing death.[9]

9. A Greek version of this inscription (which also may have appeared in Latin) can be seen in the Istanbul Archaeological Museum in Turkey.

But Jesus destroyed the wall of demarcation that had been set up in the temple. Instead, he created a whole new humanity made up of Jews and Gentiles who were united into one body with full citizenship granted to both as believers (2:19 – 22). Now all who believed, regardless of ethnic descent, were "fellow citizens" of the kingdom of God (2:19), part of God's everlasting family (2:19*b*), and part of God's building/temple, whose foundation was the teaching of the apostles and prophets (2:20 – 22).

Paul went on to write, as he had in Colossians, about the "mystery made known to me by revelation" (3:3). In English, a "mystery" is something that is puzzling, mostly obscure, possibly inexplicable, and incomprehensible. In the Greek New Testament it has a different sense, for it is a secret, to be sure, but it is an *open* secret that is no longer closely guarded or kept under wraps. Nor was it similar to the heathen Greek mystery religions that claimed esoteric secrets that they shared only with the elite.

For Paul this "mystery" was not one shared only with the spiritually elite, who were given special access to the truth to which no one else had entrée, but this biblical mystery involved words that were openly shared with the whole church, even if some of it was partially hidden from human knowledge and understanding in former days.

So what was the big truth to be more fully disclosed now? It was the "mystery of Christ" (3:4), "which was not made known to men in other generations *as it has now* been revealed by the Spirit to God's holy apostles and prophets" (3:5, emphasis added).

In Colossians Paul had stressed that the "mystery" was that the Messiah would indwell believing Gentiles ("Christ in you," Col 1:26 – 27), but here in Ephesians, Paul will stress how much Jew and Gentile believers will share and own in common: they will be "co-heirs" (Gr. *synklēronoma*), "co-members" (Gr. *syssōma*) of the body, "co-sharers/partakers" (Gr. *symmetocha*) of the same promise-plan of God (3:6) — all three of these nouns were prefaced with the Greek *syn*, "together," or "with." Thus the mystery was not about the church itself, or that the Gentiles would be part of that church, for the incorporation of Gentiles into the "people of God" had long been part of the promise-plan of God (see Ge 12:3; 2Sa 7:19; Ps 2:8; Isa 42:6; 49:6; and Am 9:11 – 12). But what that mystery did involve were certain details and principles connected with the inclusion of the Gentiles into the body of Christ. In Ephesians 3:6 Paul spelled out that there was a new partnership, a new sharing, and a new commonality in the whole body, with the Gentiles being fellow heirs of the blessing and grace of God, fellow members of the same body, and fellow partakers of the same promises that God had given to Eve, Abraham, Isaac, Jacob, David, and all who followed in the "seed of Abraham" (Gal 3:29).

Paul's emphasis was that what had been revealed earlier was not revealed "as [it had] now [Gr. *hōs nyn*] been revealed by the Spirit . . ." (Eph 3:5). Paul had already spelled out a further understanding of this "mystery" in Romans 16:25 – 26. There the mystery was the "proclamation of Jesus Christ" (v. 25), which preaching of Paul's was in accord with what had been known from "the prophetic writings" (v. 26) of the Old Testament. But again, the point was that it had not been *to the degree* that it was now being announced to that day and generation. This mystery had roots that went all the way back to the Old Testament promise-plan of God, but there were also *aspects* of this mystery that were *brand-new* as well. No wonder, then, that Paul affirmed in his preaching: "I believe everything that agrees with the Law and that is written in the Prophets" (Ac 24:14) and "I have the same hope in God ... that there will be a resurrection of both the righteous and the wicked" (24:15). Moreover, Paul went on to declare in his defense before King Agrippa this: "I am saying nothing beyond what the prophets and Moses said would happen — that the Christ would suffer and, as the first to rise from the dead, would proclaim light to his own people and to the Gentiles" (Ac 26:22*b* – 23).

In all of Paul's discussion of "mystery," he ends up virtually equating mystery and gospel, for the mystery is the truth revealed to Paul, which truth is also the gospel that was to be proclaimed. Already in Romans 1:2, Paul had made the point that the gospel was the same as what God "promised beforehand through his prophets in the Holy Scriptures." Again in Galatians 3:8, "Scriptures foresaw that God would justify the Gentiles by faith, and announced the gospel in advance to Abraham." The essence of the gospel that was given to Abraham was this: "All nations will be blessed through you." And right in line with that argument was the one given by the writer of Hebrews. There he argued that just as the gospel was being preached to those to whom the letter of Hebrews was addressed, so it had likewise been preached to all those who died during the wilderness journey from Egypt, for the same gospel was preached to them as well (Heb 3:12 – 4:2).

The purpose of this revelation of the mystery that was at the heart of Paul's preaching was to make "the unsearchable riches of Christ" (Eph 3:8) available to the Gentiles and the church of God. In fact, the contents of the first three chapters of Ephesians as the "Wealth or Riches of Christ" (Eph 1 – 3) were followed by the "Walk with Christ" (Eph 4 – 6:9), and finally by the "Warfare for Christ" (Eph 6:10 – 20). The wealth and riches that believers have in Christ include the resurrection from the dead of all believers, being seated with Christ in the heavenly realm, reconciliation with God and with one another, access to the Father through the Son, full membership in God's kingdom, and assurance of being part of the household of God. In this way the church has become the demonstration of the manifold (Gr. *polypoikilos*, "many-colored," "many-splendored," [and we could add, multicultural, multiracial, multisocially tiered, and multigenerational]) wisdom of God (3:10). Here was the eternal purpose of God now being actualized by our Lord Jesus.

The Church and the Holy Spirit

The book of Ephesians also laid a great amount of emphasis on the Holy Spirit as the "Promised One" (1:13), who was at the heart of the church (1:13; 2:18; 3:5, 16; 4:3, 4, 30; 5:18; 6:17). As the Ephesian and Asian believers came to faith, the Holy Spirit marked them with a "seal" (1:13), and thus the Holy Spirit became the "earnest" (or "down payment," Gr. *arrabōn*, a word still used in modern Greece today to refer to an "engagement ring," which acts as sort of a down payment on the fact that the suitor will come back and marry the woman). Accordingly, the Holy Spirit in the life of a believer, Paul taught, was God's "engagement ring" that he would complete his work of saving men and women all the way up to the day of their resurrection.

The Holy Spirit was also the means by which we have access to the Father (2:18 – 22). Moreover, he was the source of the unity of all believers (4:3), past and present, near and distant, ethnically and culturally similar or not. Since God declared that this unity already existed, all believers were commanded to take special pains to go the extra mile in recognizing this unity despite differences that often tend to separate groups in the modern church.

This "unity of the Spirit" did not mean that a "unity of the faith/doctrine" also existed (4:13), for all believers were on their way to that goal, but few if any had fully attained to it yet. Unity in doctrine and belief were not as easily achieved, but they must also remain a goal, even while believers are in different stages of arriving at that goal.

This did not mean that some unfortunate members of the body were without a "gift/grace" from Christ. On the contrary, "to each one of us grace has been given as Christ apportioned it" (4:7). To demonstrate that truth, Paul appealed to Psalm 68:18, where God came down on Mount Sinai and chose the Levites to be his ministers at the altar for the work of the ministry, because they were the only ones who stepped forward when Moses asked, "Whoever is for the Lord, come to me" (Ex 32:26). In the same way, Paul reasoned, inasmuch as grace has been given to every last believer, while he at the same time took some mortals as his captives for the work of the ministry, just as he had taken the Levites at the time of the golden calf debacle. This is why Jesus was able to return to the Father, for God the Father went up and left Moses and the Levites to serve in Exodus 32 – 34, which is exactly what Psalm 68 celebrates as well. It is this same Lord who distributed gifts of apostle, prophet, evangelist, pastor, and teacher; however, it was done specifically to prepare persons for the work of the ministry so they could build up the body and keep all growing up in Christ until we all come to the "whole measure of the fullness of Christ," (4:13), no longer spiritual babies, shaken by every deceitful doctrine of false teachers that came down the road, but mature in Christ (4:14). How can this be done? It can be done by "speaking the truth in love" (4:15).

The ministry of the Holy Spirit in one's personal spiritual development is set forth in Ephesians 5:15 – 21.[10] Rather than living in the darkness (5:8 – 14), it was high time to wake up and be careful how one lived (5:14 – 15). Opportunities were to be grabbed

10. Walter C. Kaiser Jr., "The Holy Spirit's Ministry in Personal Spiritual Development: Ephesians 5:15 – 21," in *The Spirit and Spirituality: Essays in Honor of Russell P. Spittler*, ed. Wonsuk Ma and Robert P. Menzies (London: T & T Clark, 2004), 62 – 68.

up as one had to understand what the will of the Lord was (5:16 – 17). Instead of being inebriated with wine, believers were to keep on being filled with the Holy Spirit (5:18). There followed, then, five Greek participles that described how one might be filled up with the Holy Spirit continually (5:19 – 21): (1) by "speak[ing] to one another in psalms, hymns and spiritual songs"; (2 and 3) by "sing[ing] and mak[ing] music in [one's own] heart to the Lord"; (4) by "always giving thanks to God the Father for everything, in the name of our Lord Jesus Christ"; and (5) by "submit[ing] to one another out of reverence for Christ." This is how God's new body grew and matured spiritually.

Paul extended this call to serve others into every area of life. It influenced marital, family, and master-servant relationships. This was a body, and it was to live by the power given from God by his Holy Spirit that produced new selves and a new love for one another.

The Armor of God

Paul concluded this threefold emphasis on the wealth, walk, and warfare of the believer by showing how believers were to be equipped to resist all the assaults of the enemy in spiritual warfare (6:10 – 20). God had supplied the equipment that was needed both defensively and offensively. There was a battle to be won, for ours would be a frequent confrontation with evil; it would not be a contest in the flesh, but one that was conducted in heavenly realms.

This full armor included the belt of truth, the breastplate of righteousness, feet outfitted with the readiness that came from the gospel of peace, and the helmet of salvation. Nothing was provided for the back, so retreat was unthinkable. The offensive weapons were the sword of the Spirit, which is the word of God, and prayer for all the saints and for Paul's delivery of the "mystery of the gospel" (6:19).

Paul, writing in Ephesians, wanted to see God's new humanity working and functioning in the power and blessing of God. All barriers were to be erased immediately, and Christ was to be exalted above everything else, for nothing else rivaled him or the riches he wanted to give to all who walked with him.

The health of the body of Christ was strong and growing by the day. Its focus was clearly that shown for us in the life, obedience, death, and resurrection of Christ.

The "mystery" that was attached to the gospel was only one of degree, for it was in full accord with the meaning and scope of the promise-plan of God announced long ago to the patriarchs and the prophets of the Old Testament.

Therefore, the church was to equip itself with the full armor of God and to live a lifestyle that was in accord with all the wealth and riches already possessed by every believer in Christ.

The fellowship enjoyed by the body was one that broke down every form of any known barriers to believers. By this means, they were to act much differently than the standards held by the societies of that day and any forthcoming day as well.

Philippians: Imitation of Christ

Philippi, located on the Egnatian Way, which connected all the eastern provinces of the Roman Empire, became the first major European city Paul visited after he had come from Asia Minor across the Aegean Sea in response to his Macedonia vision (Ac 16:11 – 40). Little light is shed on how the church was begun there, for this letter makes no reference to its founding, since the letter came later when Paul was imprisoned in Rome in AD 60.

Philippi was located in the eastern part of Macedonia (ten miles inland from the Aegean Sea) and was founded by Philip of Macedonia, the father of Alexander the Great. It lies on a spur of the Pangaean Mountain range, which also separated the city from its seaport, Neapolis. Originally called Crenides, it was named for the many "springs" that watered its rather large green plains. In 168 BC, the Romans subdued that part of the country and subdivided it into four districts, thereby breaking its national unity.

The Christian faith probably first came to Philippi sometime late in the year AD 50 as the apostle Paul responded to the appeal of the man of Macedonia he saw in his vision. Paul does not appear to have found a synagogue in that city, for it was more of a military colony and probably had less commercial attractions for the Jewish Diaspora. However, he did find a place of prayer (Gr. *proseuchē*) on a Sabbath day, outside the city, alongside of the Gangites (modern Angitis) River (Ac 16:13, 16), where some women were meeting. Paul's first European convert was a proselyte named Lydia, "a seller in purple cloth from the city of Thyatira," Asia Minor (Ac 16:14).

Another Philippian woman who showed interest in the gospel was a soothsayer who did "fortune-telling" and so bothered Paul and Silas with ranting and raving about who they were that Paul commanded the evil spirit to come out of her. When her owners saw their profits were going up in smoke, they stirred up the whole city on trumped-up religious charges, which landed the two missionaries in jail with beatings — an illegal punishment for Roman citizens. The magistrates were thereby liable to being degraded and counted unfit to ever hold office again (Ac 16:37), should these beatings of Roman citizens be discovered.

Five years later, in the autumn of AD 55, Paul revisited Macedonia and this city. In the spring of the following year, on his way back to Jerusalem, he celebrated the Passover in that city with the believers again (Ac 20:6).

Paul wrote this letter from prison (Php 1:7, 13, 17), though he did not say in what city he was imprisoned. Even though Paul had been held in a prison at Caesarea for two years (Ac 23:33; 24:27), the references to the "Praetorium" (1:13) implies the palace guard at Rome, as does his reference to the greetings that were sent from all "those who belong to Caesar's household" (4:22).

The prominence of women, who composed Paul's first audience in this city and who were among his first converts, is also seen in his mention of two ladies, Euodia and Syntyche (4:2 – 3), who were out of sorts with each other and who needed to be reconciled.

Paul's purposes in writing this letter, for there were several, were to acknowledge the monetary help this church had sent by the hand of Epaphroditus "to take care of my needs" (2:25; 4:14 – 18); to report on how ill Epaphroditus was (2:29 – 30), but that he was now restored to good health (2:27); to report on Paul's own circumstances (1:12 – 18); to plead for peace and unity between the two fighting women (4:2 – 3); and to commend Timothy to them, as he prepared to visit them (2:19 – 24). But at the heart of everything Paul wanted to say to them was his call to them to imitate Christ (2:5 – 11). The contents of this letter, in which the centrality of Christ was set forth so prominently, could be summarized as follows: chapter 1—Christ our Life; chapter 2—Christ our Example; chapter 3—Christ our Goal; and chapter 4—Christ our Supply (easily remembered by the acronym LEGS).

The Imitation of Christ

There can be no doubt that Jesus Christ is central to the whole tone and argument of the book of Philippians. Nor can there be any doubt that the hymn found in Philippians 2:6 – 11 is both the high point and the chief emphasis that the apostle was trying to make with these most responsive recipients of the message Paul had preached.

While the hymn in Philippians 2:6 – 11 is rightfully one of the most famous parts of Pauline theology, it is also one of the most debated pieces of text he wrote, probably because so much is at stake in the centrality of who Christ was and is to the believing community. So rhythmical is its structure and its thought and so carefully stated is it, that many suspect that Paul borrowed it from a previously existing composition. But no convincing arguments seem to sustain that point of view.

This passage began as Paul dealt with the problem of rivalry that was leading to disunity (2:1 – 4). Paul called for a "like-minded[ness]" that exemplified love and oneness in spirit and purpose (2:2). Rather than being preoccupied with their own interests, believers ought to demonstrate the same kind of humility and altruism that Jesus demonstrated (2:4 – 5). That led to this magnificent statement, often called the "kenosis passage" because of the key word (Gr. *ekenōsen*) found in Philippians 2:7: Jesus "made himself nothing" (TEV) "emptied himself" (NRSV).

The incarnation of our Lord is remarkable, especially when it is remembered how Jesus was in his very own nature no less than God himself (2:6*a*). But this high status and the full equality that he enjoyed with God before the incarnation were not something he insisted upon or that he exploited as an excuse to avoid going to earth to live and die for the salvation of mortals (2:6*b*).

Accordingly, the One who was on the same level of authority with God the Father in his pre-existent state of full and eternal deity, "made himself nothing" or "emptied himself." But did that mean that he gave up all (or any of) his being and authority as part of the Godhead, as the Wesley hymn so infelicitously put it in the hymn, "And Can It Be," that he "emptied himself of all but love"? Hardly, for there was more on that cross of Jesus than just "love"! It was the Son of God who was fully God and fully human. Therefore, what Christ yielded up was not his being, status, authority as God, or anything like that, but as A. H. Strong put it,[11] Jesus gave up the "*independent* exercise of the divine attributes" and his will to the Father, saying, "Not my will, but yours be done." He could have done a million other things, but what he did was to obey the will of the Father.

The contrast, then, was to set before our eyes Jesus' position of supreme authority and the person he enjoyed being prior to his incarnation, with the way in which he became a human being and plumbed the depths of suffering as he bore our sins in obedience to God. Yes, he was "obedient to death — even death on a cross!" (2:8*b*). John Milton had this text in mind when he wrote:

> That glorious Form, that Light unsufferable,
> And that far-beaming blaze of Majesty,
> Wherewith He wont at Heav'n's high Councel-Table,
> To sit the midst of Trinal Unity,
> He laid aside; and here with us to be,
> Forsook the courts of everlasting Day,
> And chose with us a darksome House of mortal Clay.
>
> *(On the Morning of Christ's Nativity, 8 – 14)*

For this, God has highly exalted him and given him a name that surpasses all other names (2:9 – 10). Here, then, is the depiction of the exalted Christ, now in glory with the Father.

That was the model Paul set before the scrapping and feuding Euodia and Syntyche. They and all other believers needed a whole new mind-set and attitude (2:5) that would imitate how Christ acted and lived. This is the kind of relationship Christ wanted his body, the church, to have.

The Faith of the Gospel

Paul wanted to make sure that nothing that happened to him or to the Philippians would affect the cause of Christ, or the gospel (1:27 – 30; 3:1 – 4:9). The point was that all were to live in a manner that showed the worth and the value of the gospel. This gospel was the heart and soul of all they together stood for in Christ. Together, not individually, they were to show a communal *esprit de corps*, for the body they belonged to was not just the earthly group that met at Philippi; it was a heavenly community to which they also belonged.

11. A. H. Strong, *Systematic Theology* (1907; reprint, Grand Rapids: Revell, n.d.), 702 – 3.

Fidelity to the gospel was imperative. Nothing would detract from that gospel more than those personal antagonisms with one another. Nor should they let Paul's status as a prisoner be understood as a defeat for the gospel and its power; instead, it would only serve "to advance the gospel" (1:12). All types of pessimism must, therefore, be rejected. His imprisonment had given fresh incentive to others to act with boldness; Paul's chains would not bind the gospel, nor would it ever do so (1:16 – 18). What the apostle wanted was to see the love of each one increasing more and more so that they could discern what was best and pure all the way up until the day of Christ's second coming (1:9 – 10).

Philippians, the epistle so filled with joy, laid out the goal of the prize for which all believers are called: "to press on to take hold of that for which Christ Jesus took hold of me" (3:12 – 14). Paul described a Christology with heavenly calling in the gospel.

Chapter 15

The Promise-Plan and the Kingdom of God

The Gospels of Matthew and Mark (AD 63 – 65)

It has become an almost universal practice of modern scholars since the end of the eighteenth century to call the first three gospels, Matthew, Mark, and Luke, the Synoptic Gospels, according to the name given them by the German biblical scholar, J. J. Griesbach in 1774. The adjective "synoptic" comes from the Greek *synopsis*, which meant "seeing together." The three gospels were said to look alike because their structure, content, and tone were very similar to each other in contrast to the gospel of John.

From the days of Tatian, in the second Christian century, to our own day, numerous attempts have been made to put the Gospels in the form of a harmony by taking the three (or at times four) accounts of the life of Christ and arranging them in parallel columns in order to present the complete story of Jesus in chronological order. Tatian's harmony was called the *Diatessaron* (Gr. *to dia tessarōn*, "the one by means of four").

While Matthew, Mark, and Luke relate almost exclusively (except for their accounts of the closing scenes) to Jesus' Galilean ministry, John confines himself to Judah, with Jesus' ministry in Jerusalem during his periodic visits.

A biblical theology is not the place to answer key questions posed by historical criticism: How did the Gospels come into being in the scriptural corpus? How are they to be understood as literary genre? Of course, they were dependent on the prompting and work of the Holy Spirit, but why is it that there are so many similarities along with some significant differences? Were the three writers in personal contact with each other, perhaps at Antioch, or did they have access to written documents for a good part of their material which they used with the permission of the Spirit of God? All of these questions are worthy of further research and discussion, but our focus will be on the purpose of each book as each had its own plan and purpose for writing.

Our study of the progress of revelation will begin with Mark's and Matthew's gospels. Later we will consider Luke's gospel as part of a two-volume study in Luke-Acts, and finally, we will study John's gospel, which will come at the end of the first Christian century along with John's other writings.

The Gospel of Mark: Jesus as a Ransom for Many

The gospel that now carries Mark's name is of course anonymous, but the very early testimony of Papias, bishop of Hierapolis in Asia Minor, left us this statement in about AD 125, which was recorded in Eusebius's *History of the Church* in 325:

> And the presbyter used to say this, "Mark became Peter's interpreter and wrote accurately all that he remembered, not, indeed, in order, of the things said or done by the Lord. For he had not heard the Lord, nor had he followed him, but later on, as I said, followed Peter, who used to give teaching as necessity demanded, but not making, as it were, an arrangement of the Lord's oracles, so that Mark did nothing wrong in writing down single points as he remembered them. For to one thing he gave attention, to leave out nothing of what he had heard and to make no false statements in them.[1]

Here, then, was a very early witness to the fact that the content and order of this gospel's material was actually that of the apostle Peter, who had witnessed firsthand what Mark later reported. In fact, the outline of events in Mark closely matched the outline of Peter's sermon to Cornelius at Caesarea (Ac 10:34–43). Justin Martyr, in around AD 150, also taught that Mark wrote down Peter's recollection of the events he had witnessed as he followed Jesus.

Mark, the writer of this gospel is no doubt the John Mark[2] whose name appears ten times[3] in the New Testament. In Colossians 4:10 Mark is called the cousin of Barnabas. John was his Jewish/Hebrew name, and Mark/Marcus was his Latin/Roman name.

Mark met Barnabas and Paul in the Antioch church in AD 46 and then accompanied them on their first missionary journey. However, when he suddenly left Paul and Barnabas on that journey, Paul lost confidence in him (Ac 15:37–39). Later, Mark joined Barnabas on Cyprus. By AD 60–62 Mark had regained the apostle Paul's trust in him, for Paul complimented him as a fellow worker (Col 4:10–11; Phm 24). Not only did Mark assist Paul and Barnabas, but later he was seen assisting Peter in "Babylon" (1Pe 5:13). After that, Paul asked Mark to come to Rome to help him while he was in prison (2Ti 4:11).

---

1. This quotation of *Historia Ecclesiastica* 3.39.15 is from Kirsopp Lake's translation in *Eusebius: Ecclesiastical History*, vol. 1 (Cambridge, MA: Harvard University Press, 1926), 297.
2. See Martin Hengel, *Studies in the Gospel of Mark* (London: SCM, 1985), 45–52.
3. Acts 12:12, 25; 13:5, 13; 15:37; Col 4:10; 2Ti 4:11; Phm 24; 1Pe 5:13. Some add Mark 14:51, 52, about the youth who fled at the arrest of Jesus with only a loin cloth, though no name is given.

Christ's Life as a Ransom

Ever since the day when the Passover was instituted and the time when the Day of Atonement began, there was the expectation that God would fulfill his promise-plan by somehow giving his Son as a "ransom for many" (Mk 10:45). Therein lay the purpose of this gospel of Mark and the ancient promise-plan. None of the gospels were meant in and of themselves to be biographies of the life of Christ; instead, each gospel was more like a tract that contained a special message leading its hearers and readers to come to a special decision about this promised one, the Lord Jesus.

In Mark 10:45, Mark disclosed his purpose in writing his book:

> For even the Son of Man [Jesus] did not come to be served, but to serve, and to give his life as a ransom for many.

Mark placed his purpose statement at the very heart of his gospel, which had the effect of dividing his gospel into two parts. In the first half of the book, Jesus' servanthood was stressed; the second part, which followed Mark 10:45, showed how he moved relentlessly on to the events of that Passion Week — namely, his death, burial, and resurrection as he completed the sacrifice by which he would offer up his life as an atonement and a ransom for mortals.

Prior to the modern era, the gospel of Mark was regarded by many as being comparatively unimportant when compared to the other gospels. Especially when compared to the other two Synoptic Gospels, Mark was much shorter in length, and it contained only about ten percent of the story of Jesus not found in Matthew or Luke. However, much has changed in recent years, and Mark is now regarded as the first of the New Testament gospels to be written and the heart of the story told by the other two evangelists.

Mark is the only gospel to call itself a "gospel" (Mk 1:1, "The beginning of the gospel about Jesus Christ, the Son of God"). This does not mean that Mark gave what we today regard as a biography of the life of Jesus, for he gives us no information on the birth of Jesus (in contrast to Matthew and Luke), Jesus' upbringing, or our Lord's personality, appearance, habits, and the like. Instead, Mark focused on Jesus' public ministry and how it affected others. Mark devoted a large part of his gospel to the miracle stories of Jesus, thus emphasizing his power and authority over disease, nature, sickness, and sin.[4]

Even the events of his ministry are not in a chronological order, but instead center around certain themes. Thus, while the first half of Mark's gospel focuses on the ministry of Jesus, especially in his healing miracles, all this seems to be a rather long introduction to the passion narrative, which is at the heart of what Mark is getting to. Repeatedly, Jesus foretold his coming death and resurrection (Mk 8:31; 9:31; 10:33 – 34).

4. Mark 1:21 – 28, 29 – 31, 32 – 34, 40 – 45; 2:1 – 12; 3:1 – 6, 7 – 12; 4:35 – 41; 5:1 – 20, 21 – 43; 6:35 – 44, 47 – 52, 53 – 56; 7:24 – 30, 31 – 37; 8:1 – 10, 22 – 26; 9:1 – 12, 14 – 29.

Thus, the same gospel that opened by identifying Jesus as the "Son of God" (1:1) concluded with the testimony of the Roman centurion watching Jesus die on the cross and saying these words: "Surely this man was the Son of God!" (15:39) — a wonderful *inclusio*.

Unlike Matthew and Luke, who regularly quote from the Old Testament, Mark rarely does so (except, e.g., in Mark 4:12; 7:6 – 7, 10; 8:18). But his allusions to the Old Testament are numerous.[5] For example, in the passion narrative, Mark 15:24 alludes to Psalm 22:18 in the casting of lots and the dividing of Jesus' garments at the foot of the cross. Again in Mark 15:29, the ridicule poured out on Jesus by the rabble-rousing crowds that watched as he hung on the cross is a clear allusion to Psalm 22:6 – 7.

The word "ransom" (Gr. *lytron*) is found only here (10:45) and in Matthew 20:28. It was usually connected in that day with the price paid for freed slaves or for those taken hostage. But in this case, Christ gave his life in exchange for the release of others; his life was substituted for their lives. That was the whole purpose in Christ's coming to this earth, argued Mark. But that also is what had been part of the promise God had signaled to Israel years ago. The metaphors for redemption in the Old Testament include the exodus from Egypt and the redemption of slaves (Heb. *pādâh*, "to redeem, to ransom," and *gā'al*, "to redeem, to serve as [a kinsman-] redeemer"). These two Hebrew verbal concepts are represented in the New Testament as Greek *lytroō*, "to redeem or to ransom," and *agorazō*, "to buy," in such expressions as "to buy *back*" or "to buy *in place of*."

The psalmist had taught, of course, that "No one can redeem the life of another or give to God a sufficient ransom for him" (Ps 49:7), but that principle did not include the Son of Man, whom Paul would later describe as the "one mediator between God and man, the man Christ Jesus, who gave his life [literally, "himself"] as a ransom [Gr. *antilytron*] for all" (1Ti 2:5 – 6).

What bewildered many during the days of our Lord on earth was the combination of his great *authority* over sin and disease and demonic powers along with the constant evidence of his *humiliation*. This led a scholar, William Wrede,[6] in 1901 to propose the much-discussed theory of the "Messianic Secret" in Mark. The question posed in this so-called secret was why Mark gave so much attention (as did the other gospels, e.g., Mt 16:20; Lk 8:56) to the theme that Jesus did not want his disciples to publicize who he was? What was the reason for this constant request?

But the answer to this dilemma is found in Mark 10:45. Jesus did not come (in his first advent) to be the king over all the universe; he came in his first advent to give his life a ransom in place of all humanity. There could be no mistaking Jesus' purpose and mission; it was a crucial distinction that must be understood.

5. For a good example of Mark's use of allusions, see Craig A. Evans, "Mark," in *New Dictionary of Biblical Theology*, ed. T. Desmond Alexander and Brian S. Rosner (Downers Grove, IL: InterVarsity Press, 2000), 269 – 70, where he lists ten Old Testament allusions in the transfiguration narrative in Mark 9:2 – 8.

6. This work is now available in English: William Wrede, *The Messianic Secret*, trans. J. C. G. Grieg (Greenwood, SC: Attic, 1971).

The Kingdom of God

Mark began his gospel by quoting Jesus' proclamation: "The time has come. The kingdom of God is near. Repent and believe the good news" (1:15). Mark places this kingdom in direct opposition to Satan and his emissaries. There could be nothing less than all-out war between the two kingdoms, but Mark 3:23 – 29 comforts us with the assurance that Jesus is the stronger of the two in this contest and that he will one day tie up Satan (3:27), bind him, and cast him into the lake of burning sulfur (Rev 20:10). Jesus will plunder Satan's house and the evil spirits will likewise cower before him, as they already have begun to do during his earthly ministry (Mk 1:24, 34; 3:11; 5:6 – 10; 9:20, 25).

Surely these works of Jesus were evidences that his rule and reign had power and authority that reached from heaven even to the depths of hell itself. That was "good news" indeed, but that is what made Jesus' humiliation so puzzling as well.

This kingdom of God was so different from what persons living in the Roman Empire had experienced. Instead of a usurpation of power by force and might, the "secret of the kingdom" (4:11) was contained in the parable of the sower. It would begin and grow as the seed of the word of God was sown and multiplied. Not all of it would reap the same benefits, for it depended on how prepared the soil of the hearts of men and women were. But from such inauspicious beginnings as these would finally emerge a kingdom that would never pass away.

Participation in this rule and reign of God would not depend on any kind of special citizenry status such as Rome granted, or on any other human capabilities and works such as the rich young ruler wanted to bring to Jesus (10:17 – 31). If keeping the Ten Commandments would not guarantee entrance into God's salvation (10:26), what would? inquired the rich young ruler. Jesus' answer was that he should go and sell all that he had and give it to the poor. This was too much for the young man, for he had great riches. Jesus gave a special test for one whom he knew put other things before his complete trust in Jesus. When the disciples objected, saying "Who then can be saved?" Jesus reminded them that while things were impossible from a human standpoint, "all things are possible with God" (10:27). Trusting Jesus' ransom for us would work, but everything else was worthless as far as getting into God's heaven or becoming a part of the kingdom of God. That is why Jesus once again, for the third time, returned to the announcement of his coming death and resurrection in Mark 10:32 – 34.

The kind of kingdom Jesus was pointing to was lost on James and John, if not to all the others as well (10:35 – 45). They just didn't get it! Instead, James and John put in reservations for places of honor in the seating arrangement in the kingdom. But instead of having their visions for exaltation confirmed, the theme of humiliation was restated by Jesus. Only God could do what these men were requesting. Besides, "whoever wants to become great among you must be your servant, and whoever wants to be first must be slave of all" (10:43 – 44), for that is how the Son of Man himself came!

Yes, there was a kingdom over which Jesus would reign supreme, for remember, this "Son of Man" was also the "son of David" (10:47, 48). The story of the healing of blind Bartimaeus (who was calling out for the "son of David" to heal him) recalled the promised throne, dynasty, and kingdom promised to David in the promise-plan set forth in 2 Samuel 7:16 – 19. Mark's allusion to Jesus as "the son of David" as his central point for including that healing of Bartimaeus is followed immediately with the narrative of the triumphal entry into Jerusalem by Jesus. There the crowds shouted, "Blessed is the coming kingdom of our father David" (11:10). Once again, Jesus was the long-expected one from the line of David, the one to whom the kingdom with all its authority and power were given long ago.

But when will this kingdom come in all of its fullness? If Jesus is that king and he is now here in our midst, they must have reasoned, what is the holdup? Mark will answer that there must first come "days of distress unequaled from the beginning" (13:19). Only after that will mortals "see the Son of Man coming in clouds with great power and glory" (13:26; 14:62). Then the enigma of the relationship between Christ's humiliation and his ruling authority will become clear.

Jesus himself is the "good news" in Mark's gospel. There is no doubt that Jesus is the true Son of God, fully divine, and with all power in heaven and on earth. Yet Mark wanted us to see the human side of Jesus, one who got angry at the stubborn refusal of the religious leaders and the populace to see God's power as he healed the man's shriveled hand (3:5), was "indignant" when his disciples tried to rebuke those who brought their little children to the Lord (10:14), and was exasperated ("sighed deeply") when the Pharisees came to test him and to ask for a sign from heaven (8:12). But on the other hand, Jesus "looked at [the rich young ruler] and loved him" (10:21), even in his awkward attempts to gain salvation by keeping the commandments.

It is the words of the Roman centurion that Mark leaves with us and that continue to ring in our minds as the point he wanted all his readers to arrive at: "Surely this man was the Son of God" (15:39).

The Gospel of Matthew: The Kingdom of God

The writer of this gospel does not identify himself in the book, but it has traditionally been ascribed to Levi, son of Alphaeus (Mt 9:9; Mk 2:14; Lk 5:29), though Matthew may have been his other name, since it was not uncommon in Galilee for a man to have two names.

If Levi indeed is the writer, then he is the one who was called by Jesus while sitting at his tollbooth. This tollbooth would have been on the trade route road north of the Sea of Galilee, leading from Damascus to Acre on the Mediterranean Sea. It was the road that marked the boundary between the territories of Philip the Tetrarch and Herod Antipas. Matthew's task was to inspect the goods that came down that road and to levy a toll. Thus, this Jew was an employee of Herod, which involved breaking the Sabbath and seeing that the Roman's coffers were getting full for both Herod and Caesar, not to mention his own pockets.

The fourth-century church historian Eusebius quoted Papias's statement (ca. AD 125) that Matthew was the writer of this gospel and that he wrote it in Hebrew (Aramaic?) language.[7] And from the subject matter of the gospel, it can be said that Matthew wrote it mainly for Jewish believers.

The structure for Matthew's gospel is seen by many to center around the fivefold rhetorical formula that is unique to Matthew, namely, "And it happened, when Jesus had finished saying ..." These five formulaic colophons appear in Matthew 7:28; 11:1; 13:53; 19:1; and 26:1. Accordingly, Matthew had five central teaching blocks (which some unwisely attempt to make parallel to the five books of Moses or to some kind of new Torah), prefaced by a Prologue in Matthew 1:1 — 4:25 and an Epilogue in Matthew 26:2 — 28:20. The five teaching blocks are:

I. The Ethics of the Kingdom (5:1 – 7:28)
II. The Authority of the Kingdom (8:1 – 11:1)
III. The Program of the Kingdom (11:2 – 13:53)
IV. The Reaction of the King to His Opposition (13:54 – 19:2)
V. The Future of the Kingdom (19:3 – 26:1)

The Messiah from David

Jesus is quickly established in this gospel as one who is legally descended from David and Abraham (Mt 1:1). While the Davidic monarchy had been lost as it went into the Babylonian exile, it reemerged in Jesus, who was born as "king of the Jews" (2:2). That was how he entered Jerusalem on Palm Sunday (21:5); and that was how he suffered at his crucifixion: "THIS IS JESUS, KING OF THE JEWS" (27:37, 42). But that would not be the end of it, for one day he would "sit on his glorious throne" (25:31) to judge the nations.

Had not King David, by the inspiration of the Holy Spirit, recognized that the Man of Promise, who would be born in his line, was the one David called his own "Lord"? (22:44; Ps 110:1)? Thus, while he truly was the son of David, Jesus was nonetheless the Son of God. The evidence for this was not only in his supernatural birth but also in the fact that it all had taken place as divinely foreordained (1:22). True, there had been women in that line with some questionable history (Tamar, Rahab, Ruth, and Bathsheba, 1:3, 5, 6), but in the divine providence, God used them to open up the invitation of salvation to Gentiles, if not also to stop those who were murmuring and whose tongues were clucking over the virgin birth of Jesus. They could look into their own closets and backgrounds as well for legacies that were not all top of the line if they wanted to demean the birth of Jesus!

7. Eusebius, *Historia Ecclesiastica* 3.24.26; 39.16. His Greek is extremely hard to translate, though the general tenor is clear.

Had not the Spirit of God come from heaven at Jesus' baptism and declared: "This is my Son, whom I love; with him I am well pleased" (3:17; cf. 12:18)? Was it not true as well that God had "committed to [Jesus] ... all things" (11:27), along with "all power" (28:18)?

Many of the events of Jesus' life, even the minutest details, had been foretold in the unfolding promise-plan of God in the Old Testament. For example, time and again Matthew appealed to the Old Testament to vindicate his claim that this Jesus was the very one that the Old Testament had predicted would come:

The Promise-Prediction	*The Matthean Fulfillment*
The place of Jesus' birth — Mic 5:2	Mt 2:6
He would be born of a virgin — Isa 7:14	Mt 1:18
The flight to Egypt — Hos 11:1	Mt 2:13
Massacre of the infants — Jer 31:15	Mt 2:17
Settlement in Nazareth — Isa 11:1(?)	Mt 2:23
Heralded by John — Isa 40:3	Mt 3:3
Ministry in Galilee — Isa 9:1–2	Mt 4:14–16
Healing the sick — Isa 42:1–4	Mt 12:17–21
Entry into Jerusalem — Zec 9:9	Mt 21:5
Jesus' betrayal — Ps 41:9	Mt 26:24

More is said in Matthew about Christ as the one who fulfilled the promises of God than is said of Jesus' own works, for Matthew was interested in the Messiah's embodiment of all that had been foretold in the Scriptures. However, a good deal could be said of Jesus' works as well, for so mighty was this Son of God that he could heal by merely speaking the word (Mt 8:8), and the cure came without the intervention of medicine or anything else (see 9:22; 15:28; 17:18). He also had control over the forces of nature (8:26–27). Even the demons of hell were submissive to his authority and power (8:28–34).

But even more convincing was the fact that he had power to forgive sin (9:1–8) and to raise the dead (9:25). Even his miracles of multiplication pointed to his deity, for he fed the masses with a few loaves and a few fishes (14:13–21; 15:32–39). Jesus' supernatural power showed him to be the long-expected Messiah, who was born according to the promise-plan made to Abraham and David.

The Kingdom of God

Matthew used the term "kingdom of heaven" thirty-three times and "kingdom of God" only four times (12:28; 19:24; 21:31, 43), whereas Mark and Luke used "kingdom of God" exclusively. Why this is so is not known for sure, but since Matthew was writing for a Jewish audience, it may have involved his sensitivity to the avoidance of the name of God, lest one misuse God's name inadvertently. Note, however, the synonymous use of "kingdom of heaven" equals the "kingdom of God" in Matthew 19:23 – 24.

Matthew made a point of saying that this is how Jesus began his ministry, for as he began his preaching in Capernaum, by the Sea of Galilee, it is said, "From that time on Jesus began to preach: 'Repent, for the kingdom of heaven is near'" (4:17). Wherever Jesus went, he taught this good news that the kingdom of heaven was at hand.

The English word for "kingdom" generally points to a physical or spatial realm, incorporating both people and land. However, this is just one of the aspects of the kingdom in both the Old and New Testaments. Kingdom can also designate the rule and reign of a potentate in its more dynamic sense, rather than just his realm.

Now if the term "kingdom of God" is seen to possess both the spiritual and political aspects, how is it that it also is given a temporal duality? For example, those living in the Old Testament times seemed already to be participants in the kingdom of God. Likewise Psalm 145:10 – 12 claimed:

> All you have made will praise you, O LORD;
> your saints will extol you.
> They will tell of the glory of your kingdom
> and speak of your might,
> so that all men may know of your mighty acts
> and the glorious splendor of your kingdom.

This indicates that the kingdom of God was already a present reality in some sense of the term. The same could be said for Psalm 103:19, where God's kingdom was said to rule over all, even in that day.

Other texts, however, carried a future concept of the kingdom. For example, Daniel 7:13 – 14 indicated that the Son of Man will come with clouds from heaven and be given a "kingdom ... which will not be destroyed," with a rule over all peoples, nations, and persons of every language. Isaiah also foretold that the coming Messiah would one day sit and rule from David's throne as he reigned over his kingdom forever (Isa 9:7).

But all of this raised a problem, for if the kingdom of God existed prior to the ministry of Jesus and John the Baptist, what was it that they were announcing that was different from what had been experienced so far?

First of all, the kingdom of God was used in a way that described all the blessings of God enjoyed in one's salvation. Thus, when the rich young ruler wanted to receive "eternal life" (19:16), he stumbled over the fact that such a gift could not be earned. After he left, Jesus remarked on how hard it was for a rich person to enter the "kingdom of heaven" — it was like threading a camel through the eye of a needle.[8] In the same way,

8. Incidentally, this probably does not refer to unloading a camel to get it through one of the Jerusalem gates. Jesus was having fun: imagine licking a camel's nose first, as we invariably do when we go to put thread through the eye of a needle, and then pushing the camel through the small needle hole, especially when we get to the first or second hump on the camel: it's hard!

in the parable of the sower, the understanding of the truth of the gospel was like "the knowledge of the secrets of the kingdom of heaven" (13:11). For those who heard it and received this "message about the kingdom" (13:19) were saved.

Nevertheless, there was something in this kingdom that was near and was about to happen. What was it? Jesus declared, "If I drive out demons by the Spirit of God, then the kingdom of God has come upon you" (12:28). The verb here, *ephthasen*, "has come," is an aorist tense, which signifies that something has already happened as a result of Jesus' invasion into the kingdom of Satan. Anyway, this would also accord with what John the Baptist had announced, namely, that the kingdom of God was close or near by (Gr. *ēngiken*, 3:2). This meant that what had begun as a spiritual rule and reign in the hearts of believers would one day extend in every nook and cranny of the universe, without any pockets of resistance or any economic or political opposition. What had begun as a spiritual manifestation in the hearts of believing mortals, and what had once been seen as the Lord of All Creation finished his work, would one day be completed as the last part of the plan of salvation saw its completion, following the death, resurrection, and ascension of Christ.

We conclude that the kingdom of God had indeed a new initiation, involving some special beginnings. When Jesus' ministry began to affect the demon world during his earthly ministry, a new episode in the progress of the kingdom of God had taken place. But there is also some flexibility here, for these evidences of the kingdom of God are but tokens of what the final and full reign of God will be (13:43). After Jesus' ascension, he would come with the clouds of heaven (16:27 – 28) as his angels would gather up the elect (24:31). The Lord would sit on his throne (16:28; 19:28; 25:31). Accordingly, just as in later New Testament teaching there is both a "now" and a "not yet" aspect to what scholars call an "inaugurated eschatology," so also there is with the doctrine of the kingdom of God. Jesus announced both the kingdom's incipient arrival and its future fulsome appearance.

When would all that was future happen? Only God the Father knew the exact time and season (24:30). But when it did take place, the twelve disciples would sit on twelve thrones, judging the tribes of Israel (19:28). In the meantime, Jesus must (Gr. *dei*, "it is necessary," 16:21) suffer and die, and be raised from the dead. All of his disciples were to preach the good news about the coming reign of God (10:7; 24:14).

The Law and the Kingdom

Matthew is unique among the gospels in his discussion of the law. He records Jesus as saying:

> Do not think that I have come to abolish the Law or the Prophets; I have not come to abolish them but to fulfill them. I tell you the truth, until heaven and earth disappear, not the smallest letter, not the least stroke of a pen, will by any means disappear from the Law until everything is accomplished. Anyone who breaks one of the least of these

> commandments and teaches others to do the same will be called least in the kingdom of heaven, but whoever practices and teaches these commands will be called great in the kingdom of heaven. (Mt 5:17 – 19)

In Matthew's gospel, aimed at a Jewish audience, it would be important to get Jesus' attitude toward the law of Moses. He straightaway declared that neither he nor his mission was to be understood as one that would abolish the law; on the contrary, his purpose was to fulfill it. Teaching otherwise would be detrimental to one's status in the kingdom. It is also significant to note that observing the commandments is part of what it meant to be in the kingdom of heaven!

Some believe that what Jesus had in mind was not the law as given originally through Moses, but the law as reinterpreted by the Messiah. But the antitheses described in Matthew 5:21 – 48 ("You have heard it said… But I tell you …," vv. 21 – 22, 27 – 28, 31 – 32, 33 – 34, 38 – 39, 43 – 44) were not given in order to place Jesus over against what Moses had said. Jesus was correcting the *oral* traditions that had accumulated around the law ("You have heard it said"). He did not say, as all too many presume, something like, "It is written, but I now correct that by saying…."

This can be shown to be the correct meaning by looking at Matthew 5:43: "You have heard that it was said, 'Love your neighbor and hate your enemy.'" However, nowhere in the Old Testament did anyone ever say, "Hate your enemy." That was part of oral tradition, but it was not part of the Scriptures. For some years now, I have offered my students a monetary prize if anyone can find the second part of that quote anywhere in the Old Testament. So far no one has claimed the prize.

The same was true for the law that said "Eye for eye, and tooth for tooth" (5:38). In Exodus 21:24, this law was a principle, functioning like a rule of thumb that was given to the "judges" (Ex 21:1 [Heb. *mišpāṭîm*, "judgments"]; 22:8, 9) that they must make the punishment fit the crime (for example, bumper for bumper in a fender-bender car accident, and no more, such as trying to get next year's tuition for it too). Nevertheless, despite what the guiding principles were for the judges, Jesus urged those who had suffered an injustice to avoid all forms of retribution. This would not have been an unusual understanding of these matters in either Testament.

The Jewish Christian community was in about the same practical dilemma in Matthew's day as the messianic Jewish synagogues are today. To what extent are many of these Jewish practices simply expressions of an ethnic heritage, and to what extent do many of them make unintended statements, advocating forms of Judaism instead? The Jews of Matthew's day seem to have observed temple worship (5:23 – 24), almsgiving (6:2 – 4), fasting (6:16 – 18), and Sabbath observance (24:20); they also paid temple taxes (17:24 – 27). But in no case did any of these practices amount to working for or earning one's salvation, for if any were done out of a perfunctory ritualism that lacked any evidence of the heart, it all amounted to just so much showy external routines.

Jesus followed the six antitheses just noted in Matthew between the Old Testament teaching and the oral tradition of that day with a discourse on three areas in a believer's private life: giving (6:1 – 4), prayer (6:5 – 15), and fasting (6:16 – 17). Once again his admonitions were: "Be careful" (6:1), "Do not be like them" (6:8), and "Do not look somber" (6:16).

Israel, the Church, and the Kingdom

The most difficult portion of the book of Matthew concerns the limitation of Jesus and the disciples' mission to the Jewish people. In Matthew 10:5 – 6, Jesus instructed the twelve in one episode: "Do not go among the Gentiles or enter any town of the Samaritans. Go rather to the lost sheep of Israel." In a second episode, a Canaanite woman cried out for mercy to our Lord (Mt 15:21 – 28). When the disciples urged Jesus to send her away, he responded, "I was sent only to the lost sheep of Israel" (v. 24).

Surprisingly enough, however, Matthew also recorded how Jesus simultaneously affirmed a Gentile mission to "all the nations" (24:14). This mission was part of the final instructions Jesus left for all his disciples (28:19). There were other Gentiles in Matthew's gospel that clearly anticipated this outreach. For example, there were the Magi who came in search of the newborn Messiah (2:1 – 12). There was also the centurion, whose faith even startled our Lord, for he said: "I tell you the truth, I have not found anyone in Israel with such great faith" (8:10). Last, Matthew 12:21 quotes Isaiah 42:4 (LXX): "In his name, the nations [Gentiles] will put their hope."

So it is not that Matthew's gospel is so exclusively Jewish in its orientation and prejudice that there is no room for any Gentile offer of the gospel; instead, while the Jewish mission is given precedence, the Gentile mission is not neglected either. Why, then, do we find this emphasis in Matthew? Donald Hagner responds:

> The answer is that Matthew is eager to underline the fulfillment brought by Jesus as in the first instance the manifestation of God's *covenantal faithfulness to Israel.* Far from being disloyal to the faith of the patriarchs and the hope of Israel, Jesus comes precisely to fulfill it and to fulfill it for the Jews exclusively. Only subsequently would the Gentiles be part of the fulfillment (cf. Paul's perspective in Rom. 1:16).[9]

This is a somewhat helpful comment, but the Gentile mission had been announced as early as Genesis 1 – 11 and stated straightforwardly to Abraham in Genesis 12:3, "All peoples on earth will be blessed through you."

Nevertheless, three parables indicate that Israel's privileged position was not to be taken for granted, for while the promise of God was secure, those who would not participate in that promise by faith were not secure. There was always a difference between *transmitting* the promise from one generation to another and personally *participating*

9. D. A. Hagner, "Matthew," in *The New Dictionary of Biblical Theology*, ed. T. Desmond Alexander and Brian S. Rosner (Downers Grove, IL: InterVarsity Press, 2000), 263.

in that promise by faith, thereby enjoying the benefits of those promises. Thus, in the parable of the two sons, the one who promised his father that he would go and work in the vineyard but then did not do so was a picture of the unbelief of the Jewish leadership. In their place, Jesus declared that "the tax collectors and the prostitutes are entering the kingdom of God ahead of you" (21:31).

In the second parable, the parable of the tenants (21:33 – 43), those working in the vineyard not only refused to share any of the fruit with the owner of the vineyard, but they mauled and killed the servants sent to collect the rent, and finally the owner's own son. What will the owner do with these wretches? "He will rent the vineyard to other tenants, who will give him his share of the crop at harvest time" (21:41). The allusion to God sending his own Son, Jesus, and the way that the Jewish people treated him is too transparent to miss.

The third parable was about the wedding banquet (22:1 – 10). When the wedding was ready, those invited paid no attention to the invitation, so the king gave the orders to go out into the city and "invite to the banquet anyone you find" (22:9). For the third time in these parables, the Jewish people had turned down their privileged position as recipients of the promise-plan of God.

To whom would the promises come if Israel, by and large, had missed the time when she too could have participated in them by faith? Some answer too quickly that the church and the believing Gentiles were now the recipients of all the promises formerly made with the patriarchs and the Davidic line. This unfair conclusion is sometimes called a "Replacement Theology," "Displacement Theology," or "Supersessionism." To argue that God was now forever finished with Israel would be reading too much into these statements of Matthew. In no sense was God finished with Israel, for in the Pauline letter to the Romans, Paul argues that what God had promised to Israel long ago was still "irrevocable" (Ro 11:29). This should in no way give aid and comfort to any of the modern (or ancient) forms of anti-Semitism. But it did open up a new advance for the Gentile believing community as God introduced his church, where both Israel and all the believing from the nations found their identity and unity.

The Promise and the Church

Matthew is the only gospel that mentions the word "church" (Gr. *ekklesia*). This word for the body of believers appeared for the first time in Matthew's gospel after Peter's marvelous confession that Jesus was the Messiah (16:18). In response to the question "Who do you say I am?" (16:15), Peter responded with "You are the Christ [Messiah], the Son of the living God" (16:16). Jesus promised to "build my church, and the gates of Hades will not overcome it" (16:18b). Come what may, the church would go on, for our Lord guaranteed it.

The second reference to the church came in Matthew 18:17, where a brother was instructed on what procedures to follow if he was found to be in some fault. As a last resort, the unsettled matter was to be taken to the "church" (18:17), whose opinion must be respected and followed or else the person would be disciplined. Matthew, then, led the way for seeing this body as God's continuing instrument for following him and for reconciling any and all breaches of conduct, problems of ethnicity, or the like.

In sum, while Mark is the model for the basic story of Jesus, he nevertheless also focused on the fact that Jesus came to give his life as a ransom for many. Matthew, on the other hand, is the gospel of fulfillment. It is also the gospel of the kingdom of God and God's new ecclesiastical provision for gathering the group of believers together for their mutual growth and magnification of the name of God. His gospel integrated law and gospel and prepared the world for the introduction of his church.

Chapter 16

The Promise-Plan and the Promise of the Holy Spirit

The Two-Volume History of Luke-Acts (Early to Mid 60s)

Luke-Acts makes up some 27 percent of the total New Testament, according to Darrell Bock.[1] In fact, Luke itself is the longest book in the New Testament. Moreover, it is Luke, the physician, more than anyone else, who tells the whole story of Jesus, one that began with his birth and carried it continuously on into the birth of the church, followed in the main by the ministries of Peter and Paul.

Luke wrote this two-volume history to "most excellent Theophilus" (Lk 1:3) "so that you may know the certainty of the things you have been taught" (1:4). Since the church was undergoing persecution at that time, as reported in the book of Acts, many, like Theophilus, may have wondered if the promise-plan of God was still in force. Luke-Acts was a work dedicated to assure Theophilus and all like him that no amount of persecution could be interpreted as a sign of God's judgment or a sign that the promise-plan of God had failed.

Theophilus is presented as a person of some rank and class, for the title "most excellent" is also applied to two governors: "most excellent Felix" (Ac 24:3) and "most excellent Festus" (Ac 26:25). Theophilus means "lover of God," which some have taken in a symbolic way, saying this book is addressed to godly people in every place. But it is best to regard him as a real person, perhaps Luke's patron, who also may have paid for the costs of publishing this two-volume set dedicated to him.

Luke too was probably a Gentile Christian, for in Colossians 4:10 – 14 Paul addressed Aristarchus, Mark, and Jesus-Justus as "the only Jews among my fellow workers," but then added later "our dear friend Luke, the doctor" (4:14). This seems to place Luke outside the Jewish workers and to categorize him as a Gentile worker. To be sure, all who have wrestled with the opening paragraph in Luke 1:1 – 4 will attest to the fact that it

1. Darrell L. Bock, "A Theology of Luke-Acts," in *A Biblical Theology of the New Testament*, ed. R. B. Zuck (Chicago: Moody, 1994), 87. He commented that of the 7,947 verses in the New Testament, Luke-Acts comprised 2,157. In comparison, he also noted that all the Pauline Epistles only had 2,032 verses and all the Johannine writings had only 1,407.

is in the classical Greek style and not the easier-going Koiné Greek usually represented in the rest of the New Testament. This surely indicated that he was a person of some intellectual polish and academic achievement.

In four sections in the book of Acts, Luke used the first person plural pronoun "we" (Ac 16:10 – 17; 20:5 – 16; 21:1 – 18; and 27:1 – 28:16) that tended to suggest he was an eyewitness traveling with the apostle Paul to many of the events and situations he was describing. These references, along with the identical appearance of the first person plural pronoun in the opening verses of Luke's gospel (only this time it is "us"), helped later readers to know both that Luke showed a personal interest in his readers and that it was the work of a reporter who was also an eyewitness to many of the things he spoke about.

At the center of that promise-plan that Luke portrayed were two foci: Jesus and the church he was building. What had been inaugurated in the life and ministry of Jesus was now continuing to be fulfilled through the church. These two parts, Jesus and the church, would both be brought to their planned consummation when Jesus returned again (Ac 3:17 – 26).

The two-volume history of Luke-Acts was written sometime in the early to mid – 60s AD. Since the last event in the book of Acts was the imprisonment of Paul in Rome, which most say took place in AD 62, this would seem to set the terminus ad quem, since Luke does not take the story of the church (or of the apostle Paul) any further, despite the astounding events of the fall of Jerusalem in AD 70 and Paul's release from the Roman prison. However, there are a number of scholars who place the book's writing in the 80s because it is suggested that Luke knew about the fall of Jerusalem in AD 70, as might be noted in Luke 19:41 – 44.[2] But if that is the correct interpretation of this Olivet Discourse passage, why did Luke stop where he did in Acts and not discuss this most tragic event more directly? So the early to mid 60s date seems to be the best date for the Lucan gospel and the book of Acts.

The Promise-Plan of God

Given the fact that Luke set out to supply Theophilus with an "orderly account" of "everything from the beginning" (1:3), it will come as no surprise that his two-volume work focuses on God's carrying out his plan as set forth in that ancient promise. Already in our introduction, we have seen how that promise-plan began with John the Baptist's fulfilling what had been prophesied about his task as a forerunner in the prophets Isaiah and Malachi. No less significant were the accomplishments of the ancient promise in John the Baptist's father, Zechariah; the elderly Simeon; and the prophetess Anna

2. For example, Kirsopp Lake, "Acts of the Apostles," in *Dictionary of the Apostolic Church*, ed. James Hastings (Edinburgh: T & T Clark, 1915), 1:20, who said "The most, therefore, that can be said is that [it] raises a slight presumption in favour of a date later than AD 70"; Joseph Fitzmyer, *The Gospel According to Luke I—IX*, Anchor Bible (Garden City, NY: Doubleday, 1981), 35 – 39, also argues for the 80s.

in Luke's opening chapters (Lk 1:14 – 17; 31 – 35; 68 – 75; 2:34).[3] Moreover, right in the middle of the two-volume Luke-Acts, Jesus bore testimony that "everything must be fulfilled that is written about me in the Law of Moses, the Prophets, and the Psalms" (Lk 24:44*b*). But all too many were still slow to discern that this was precisely what God had revealed previously in the Old Testament. That was why the Lord had to scold Cleopas and his companion for being so obtuse. Jesus rebuked them, saying:

> "How foolish you are, and how slow of heart to believe all that the prophets have spoken! Did not the Christ have to suffer these things and then enter his glory?" And beginning with Moses and the Prophets, he explained to them what was said in all the Scriptures concerning himself." (Lk 24:25 – 27)

It was right in front of their eyes all this time, but Cleopas and his friend, along with many others in the Old Testament and in the first Christian century, missed the promise-plan of God — just as many continue to miss it today!

But that same picture continues in the book of Acts, where the outpouring of the Holy Spirit is witnessed (Ac 2:17 – 21) just as the prophet Joel had promised in the plan of God (Joel 2:28 – 32). The story went on in Acts 3:22 – 26, which described Jesus as the promised "prophet" announced in Deuteronomy 18:15, 18, 19. That same theme continued when Luke used Paul's speech at Antioch of Pisidia to show that Jesus was the Promised One in the line of David, the Son of God — indeed, the Holy One, who would rise again from the dead as predicted in Isaiah 55:3; Psalms 2:7 and 16:10. In fact, Luke maintained the line of this argument on the promise-plan of God to the end of the book of Acts, where Paul declared:

> "I am saying nothing beyond what the prophets and Moses said would happen — that the Christ would suffer and, as the first to rise from the dead, would proclaim light to his own people and to the Gentiles." (Ac 26:22*b* – 23)

The Design and Necessity of the Program of God

All that Jesus had done and all that he would do was done according to divine necessity and to God's everlasting plan. Darrell Bock laid out for us this sense of divinely guided planning when he commented:

> Perhaps no theme underscores divine design more than the Lucan "it is necessary" (*dei*) theme. This Greek word is used [101][4] times in the New Testament, of which 40 are in Luke-Acts. The references cover a wide variety of topics. Christ *must* [*dei*] be in his Father's house (Luke 2:49). He *must* preach the kingdom (4:43). He *must* heal women tormented by Satan (13:16). In looking at the events associated with his death or

3. See the discussion on these points above in "Introduction: The Beginnings of New Testament Theology."

4. Originally, he said here "99 times," but he corrected that to "101 times" in his article on "Luke" in the *New Dictionary of Biblical Theology*, ed. T. Desmond Alexander and Brian S. Rosner (Downers Grove, IL: InterVarsity Press, 2000), 274.

> his return, certain things *must* precede the end (21:9). A Passover lamb *must* be sacrificed.... The Son of Man or the Christ *must* suffer....[5]

Luke used the verb "must" or "it is necessary" (*dei*) some eighteen times in his gospel and twenty-two times in Acts. Only John comes close to this total in his gospel with ten times in the rest of the New Testament.[6] All of this indicated that none of the events of Christ's life or in the life of the church were haphazard or were just thrown together as they went along. There was a divine urgency, an absolute necessity, and a divine guidance that had long existed and was now being put into place.

The greatest of these divine necessities was the absolute requirement that Jesus go to the cross to suffer (Lk 9:22; 17:25; 24:7, 26, 44; Ac 17:3). If Scripture were to be fulfilled (Ac 1:16), then Jesus must bring to completion what God had begun in the older promises. It was imperative that Jesus "be numbered with the transgressors" (Lk 22:37), even as Isaiah 53:12 had predicted, for this was at the heart of Luke's theology. Jesus had to "press on today and tomorrow and the next day — for surely no prophet can die outside of Jerusalem!" (Lk 13:32).

When Jesus was "handed over" to the rulers of Israel and the Roman court, Luke quoted the apostle Peter as saying that it happened "by God's deliberate plan [*boylē*] and foreknowledge [*prognōsei*]" (Ac 2:23). "Indeed Herod and Pontius Pilate met together with the Gentiles and the people of Israel ... [and] they did what [God's] power and will [*hē boylē*, 'the plan'] had decided beforehand [*proōrisen*] should happen" (4:27 – 28). Moreover, "the people of Jerusalem and their rulers did not recognize Jesus, yet in condemning him they fulfilled [*eplērōsan*] the words of the Prophets that are read every Sabbath" (13:27). Thus, "What God promised [*epangelian genomenēn*] our fathers [Abraham, Isaac, Jacob, and David], he has fulfilled [*ekpeplēroken*] for us, their children, by raising up Jesus.... For when David had served God's purpose [*tē tou theou boylē*, 'the plan of God'] in his own generation, he fell asleep; he was buried with his fathers and his body decayed. But the one whom God raised from the dead did not see decay" (13:32*b* – 33, 36 – 37). God's sovereignty over people (Ac 17:26), and the events of history and the church even up to the last day (17:31), showed he was in charge all the way and was working out all things according to his plan and sovereign design. That same note was found in many other passages, such as Acts 24:14 – 15 and 26:22 – 23.

Jesus' role in fulfilling the promise God had made was the heart of his plan and was the keynote Luke sounded as he began his gospel: "Many have undertaken to draw up an account of the things that have been fulfilled [*peplērophorēmenōn*] among us" (Lk 1:1). This same idea was continued in the prologue to Acts, where the disciples raised

5. Bock, "Theology of Luke-Acts," 94.
6. Leon Morris, *New Testament Theology* (Grand Rapids: Zondervan, 1986), 173.

the question of how God would finish his plan and in what times and what season (Ac 1:6 – 7). But Jesus replied that the matter of time was not part of the plan that could be disclosed. However, there was more than enough data on the promises of God for the church to reflect on.

The Geographical and Historical Timeline of Luke-Acts

There is a geographical progression and a real sense of history in the timeline that Luke used to set out the various facts and events in the life of Jesus and the church. First, after the infancy narratives and the ministry of John the Baptist (Lk 1:1 to 4:13), the focus fell on Jesus' Galilean ministry (Lk 4:14 – 9:50). From that point onward, Luke, in contradistinction to the other two gospel writers, repeatedly emphasized that Jesus was headed to Jerusalem (Lk 9:51; 13:33; 17:11; 18:31). Thus the journey to Jerusalem was highlighted in Luke 9:51 – 19:44, which then flowed into the passion, resurrection, and ascension narratives in Luke 19:45 – 24:53.

In like manner, Luke had a geographical progression for the church in the book of Acts, as laid out in Acts 1:8. The movement was from Jerusalem to Judea, on to Samaria, and then to the ends of the earth. Therefore, Acts 1:1 – 6:7 described the witness of the apostles in Jerusalem, followed by their witness to all Judea and Samaria in Acts 6:8 to 9:31. As the church's witness moved to feature the Gentiles (Ac 9:32 – 28:31), the progress of the church's witness went all the way to Rome, the symbol of moving out from Jerusalem to the ends of all the earth, as shown by the extent of the Roman Empire in those days.

Not all are happy with this emphasis and attention given to geography and history. For example, Hans Conzelmann identified Luke 16:16 ("The Law and the Prophets were proclaimed until John. Since that time, the good news of the kingdom of God is being preached, and people are forcing their way into it") as "the key to the topography of redemptive history."[7] Conzelmann was correct, of course, to see how meaningful history is to God's plan of salvation. And in many ways, John the Baptist did form a watershed of some major significance. His arrangement was to see the period of Israel lasting up to Luke 16:16, followed by the period of Jesus' ministry, without reference to his life, and then the period since the ascension.

Conzelmann, unfortunately, refused to take the geographical references in Luke seriously, for he argued that they functioned only in a symbolic way, but not with any connection with reality. However, Conzelmann's point of view ran counter to what Luke claimed he wanted to do. His references to geography and the historical events connected with it, he argued in his preface, were to help Theophilus and all who followed him have the assurance and knowledge of the certainty that all of this was not

7. Hans Conzelmann, *The Theology of St. Luke* (London: Faber and Faber, 1960), 23, as cited by D. A. Carson, Douglas Moo, and Leon Morris, *An Introduction to the New Testament* (Grand Rapids: Zondervan, 1992), 123.

done in a corner, but right out where all the world could see the progress of the gospel and the plan of God.

It is now time to see how the promise-plan of God was enunciated in Luke-Acts, so we turn to the development of his theology. Not all see Luke as a theologian; Vincent Taylor, for example, claimed Luke was "not primarily a theologian."[8] Others, however, saw Luke as a "master theologian," and as "one of the three major New Testament theologians" (Paul and John being the other two).[9]

The Promise of the Holy Spirit

One of the major emphases in Luke-Acts is the coming of the promised Holy Spirit from the time of John the Baptist onwards. Leon Morris stated:

> Luke has a good deal to say about the Holy Spirit. He uses the word *pneuma* ["Spirit"] 36 times in his Gospel and 70 times in Acts, the latter number being the most in any New Testament book (1 Corinthians with 40 is next; but Paul's total of 146 exceeds that of Luke [106]).[10]

As the book of Acts began, Jesus instructed the disciples not to leave Jerusalem, "but wait for the gift my Father *promised*" (1:4, emphasis mine). He went on to speak of the baptism of John, but then he explained what that promised gift was: "in a few days you will be baptized with the Holy Spirit" (1:5*b*). Obviously, Jesus was referring to the event of Pentecost, when the Holy Spirit was poured out on all who believed only a few days after he spoke (2:33).

Whereas other religions spoke of a divine spirit being given perhaps to a few leaders and the like, here was the Spirit being effusively given, like a tropical downpour of rain, but given to all believers. Nor was the reality of the experience of the Holy Spirit seen simply by ecstatic actions and behavior; instead, the presence of the Holy Spirit was seen best in the "fruit" produced in the lives of these believers. This had to be a revolutionary thought in the history of the religions of the world.

But even prior to Pentecost, the Holy Spirit had been seen working in the lives of believers. An angel from God announced to John the Baptist's father, Zechariah, that he would have a son, to be named John, who would be "*filled* with the Holy Spirit from birth" (Lk 1:15). When Mary was approached by Gabriel, he explained that she, though a virgin, would conceive a baby by the "power of the Most High" as the Holy Spirit came upon her (1:35). Later, when Mary went to visit her pregnant relative Elizabeth, the latter "was *filled* with the Holy Spirit" (1:41), as was John the Baptist's father, Zechariah, "*filled* with the Holy Spirit [as he] prophesied" (1:67). But even if these men and women were examples of special infillings of the Holy Spirit for the special situations

8. Vincent Taylor, "Luke," *IDB*, ed. George A. Buttrick and Keith R. Crim (Nashville: Abingdon, 1976), 3:181.

9. J. Christian Beker, *Paul the Apostle* (Edinburgh: T & T Clark, 1980), 162; and James D. G. Dunn, *ExpT* 84 (1972–73): 3.

10. Morris, *New Testament Theology*, 191.

presented at that time, other cases, such as that of Simeon, look more like a permanent state of the abiding presence of the Holy Spirit: "The Holy Spirit was upon [Simeon]" (2:25) as he was "moved by the Spirit" (2:27) to take up the baby Jesus in his arms. He declared he had seen the salvation God had promised long ago; he was therefore ready now to die, for the rest of all that God was going to do would be history, so sure was he of the promises of God (2:29 – 32). Amazingly, the Holy Spirit had "revealed to him ... that he would not die before he had seen the Lord's Christ" (2:26). That assurance had to be linked with a prior understanding of what he had read and heard in the Old Testament Scriptures!

The Spirit was not any less real and present in the rest of the story. If John baptized with water, Jesus would baptize them with the Holy Spirit (Lk 3:16). Thus, when John baptized Jesus, the Holy Spirit came down upon Jesus in the form of a dove (3:22). But if the descent of the Holy Spirit marked the beginning of Jesus' earthly ministry, so did the baptism of the Holy Spirit mark the beginning of the ministry of the church at Pentecost (Ac 1:4 – 5; 2:4, 33). The two parts of Luke's history, therefore, are both parallel and according to the plan of God.

Luke likewise stressed that in Jesus' temptation by the devil, Jesus was "full of the Holy Spirit" (Lk 4:1*a*). Moreover, Jesus was "led by the Spirit in the desert" (4:1*b*), where Satan tried to offer another sort of messiah and another nonbiblical type of kingdom — all to no avail. When the temptation was all over, Jesus "returned to Galilee in the power of the Spirit" (4:14). He went to the synagogue in Nazareth on the Sabbath day and opened to the text in Isaiah 61:1 – 2, which began with "The Spirit of the LORD is on me, because he has anointed me to preach good news to the poor" (4:16 – 19). Even though this fact is not directly commented on throughout the next years of Jesus' ministry, we may assume that the power of the Holy Spirit was constantly evident, even as Luke 10:21 did explicitly mention: "At that time [i.e., at the time of the return and report of the seventy-two disciples who were sent out by the Lord], Jesus, full of joy through the Holy Spirit," praised God for the effective way the kingdom of God was invading, with great success, the kingdom of the Evil One. For those who would ask of their Father in heaven, he would give them the Holy Spirit as well (10:31).

The church begins in Acts 2:4 as they "were all filled with the Holy Spirit." That identical clause was used to describe what Peter and John experienced before the Sanhedrin (4:8), and what the believers experienced as they were praying for Peter and John's release (4:31) — in fact, "the place where they were meeting was shaken" as they "were all filled with the Holy Spirit."

Later, Ananias was sent to meet the blinded and stricken Saul, who had been on his way to Damascus with letters for taking believers as prisoners. Ananias was to grant Saul, later called Paul, the restoration of his sight, and he was told to see that Saul was "filled with the Holy Spirit" (9:17). This is what happened to Saul as he ministered on Cyprus and confronted Elymas the sorcerer: he was "filled with the Holy Spirit" (13:9).

In a similar way, the new disciples of Iconium and the surrounding region were likewise "filled with joy and with the Holy Spirit" (13:52).

Along with the verb "*filled*" seems to be the parallel expression "*full* of the Holy Spirit" in Acts 6:3, 5; 7:55; and 11:24, or the "*coming*" of the Holy Spirit on the disciples (1:8; 19:6), his "*falling*" on them (10:44; 11:15) or his being "*poured out*" on the people (2:17 – 18; 10:45) or his being "*given*" to them in Acts 8:18; 15:8.

There is much more of the Spirit's work in Luke-Acts, but few could deny that even before Jesus' birth, the presence of the Spirit was evident in the lives of many, as that presence was in the exciting early days of the life of the church. Surely some, as Stephen observed, had "always resist[ed] the Holy Spirit," just as their fathers had (Ac 7:51), while others, like Ananias and Sapphira, had lied to the Holy Spirit (Ac 5:1 – 11). This couple were guilty not only of lying by saying the price of the land was less than what they actually received, but they "agreed to put the Spirit of the Lord to the test" (5:9), and thus they exhibited an attitude that refused to treat the Spirit as holy, separate, and distinct. One must not treat the Holy Spirit in a trite way by demeaning him, for all who do so, and who thereby blaspheme him, will not be forgiven (Lk 12:10).

The Cross, Resurrection, and Ascension of Jesus

Few chapters stress the work of Jesus as the "righteous sufferer" more than Luke 23. Here Luke employed the psalms of lament from the Old Testament, especially Psalms 22:18 and 31:5.[11] Luke focuses on Jesus' innocence throughout this whole chapter (Lk 23:14 – 15, 20, 22, 47).

The same theme continues on into the messages of the book of Acts. In Acts 2:23 – 24, Peter preaches that Jesus "was handed over to you by God's deliberate plan and foreknowledge; and you, with the help of wicked men, put him to death by nailing him to the cross. But God raised him up from the dead, freeing him from the agony of death." Three times, Luke mentions that Jesus was "killed by hanging him on a tree" (Ac 5:30; 10:39; 13:29), a clear allusion to Deuteronomy 21:23, "Anyone who is hung on a tree is under God's curse." This is the curse that God bore in our place.

It is the cross of Christ, then, that makes it possible for our Lord to extend his forgiveness of sin to all who will accept him. The church has been "bought with his own blood" (Ac 20:28). But death could not keep its prey, for Christ arose from the grave (Ac 2:24; 3:15; 4:10; 5:30 – 31; 17:31). Herein lies Luke's great argument and God's vindication that the One who suffered was no less than the Son of God, whom the Father raised up from the dead once again.

Luke is the only New Testament writer that describes the ascension of Jesus into heaven to sit at the right hand of God the Father (Lk 24:50 – 53; Ac 1:6 – 11). There our

11. See Bock, "Theology of Luke-Acts," 15, for the idea expressed here.

Lord remains until he returns to be the judge of the living and the dead (Ac 1:11; 3:21; 10:42; and 17:31). All of this happened to fulfill what had been promised in the plan of God announced in the Old Testament.

The Theologian of Repentance

If one is ever to identify a mission and purpose statement in Luke, perhaps Luke 5:30 – 32, along with Luke 19:10, function best as summing up Luke's presentation of that mission: "I have come not to call the righteous, but sinners to repentance" (5:32); and, "For the Son of Man came to seek and to save what was lost" (19:10). Even though these mission statements parallel in part statements in the other Synoptics — Matthew 9:13 and Mark 2:17 — neither of the other two gospels mention the concept of "repentance"; this is indeed distinctive to Luke and the theology he sets forth here.

Bock shows that there are "three portraits of repentance" in Luke that form the proper response one can make to the message of the good news. They are "repent," "turn," and "believe" (i.e., to have "faith"). All three are best highlighted in perhaps two of Luke's best descriptions of Jesus' works mentioned in this gospel: one in which Jesus is likened to a physician who calls those who are spiritually sick and impotent back to himself (Lk 5:30 – 32), and the other in the well-known parable of the prodigal son (Lk 15:11 – 32).[12]

The first response, "to repent" (*metanoeō*), involved a change in one's thinking but also a change of one's will and direction. This concept of repentance had Old Testament roots, of course, for Jesus had declared that the men of Nineveh would "stand up at the judgment" in the final day to condemn the generation he was ministering to in Israel, for those in Nineveh had "repented at the preaching of Jonah," but those who had witnessed the miracles of Jesus and had heard his words proclaimed still had not yet repented for the most part (Lk 11:32). The point here was not to try to figure out, as some apparently were trying to do, why Pilate had been allowed by God to mingle the blood of the Galileans with their sacrifices, for "unless you repent, you too will all perish" (Lk 13:3). The same went for those trying to sort out the problem of evil in the collapse of the tower in Siloam (13:5). But for anyone who did repent, there was joy in heaven "in the presence of the angels of God" (15:10).

However, repentance could not be forced on those who did not respond to the evidence they had available to them. That is why it was no use sending someone back from Hades to warn the rich man's five brothers (16:19 – 31). Jesus remarked, "If they do not listen to Moses and the Prophets, they will not be convinced even if someone rises from the dead" (v. 31). Jesus was willing to let the case for the salvation of the rich man's five brothers rest on their trusting the message found in the Old Testament as the basis for their repentance!

---

12. Ibid., 130 – 34.

Luke gave four very graphic pictures of repentance: (1) Jesus as the Great Physician (5:31 – 32); (2) the story of the prodigal son (15:11 – 31); (3) the parable of the tax collector who cried out, "God, have mercy on me, a sinner" (18:9 – 14); and (4) Jesus' summary of his whole mission, that "repentance and forgiveness of sins will be preached in my name to all nations, beginning at Jerusalem" (24:47).[13] Repentance was a key part of Luke's theology and our Lord's call for action.

The second response called for was "to turn" [*epistrepho*] back to God. In the Old Testament, this word "to turn, to return" (Heb. *šûb*), summarized the emphasis and the heart of the message of all sixteen writing prophets. Thus, according to the prophet Zechariah, almost the last in the line of writing prophets, the summary of the essence of the message of all fourteen prophets who had preceded him could be epitomized in this word: "This is what the LORD Almighty says, 'Return [*šûb*] to me,' declares the LORD Almighty, 'and I will return to you' " (Zec 1:3).

Surprisingly, the word "turn" or "return" is fairly uncommon in Luke's gospel. For example, John the Baptist's task was "to turn" Israel back to their Lord (1:17), just as Jesus prayed that when Peter had "turned back" to the Lord (22:32), he was to strengthen his brothers. The other use of "turn" does not deal with salvation, but with one who seeks forgiveness of another, "turning" to him seven times (17:4).

But in Acts, the call for a "turning" back to God became a major part of Luke's emphasis. For example, in Acts 3:19, Peter called his listeners in Solomon's colonnade to "Repent, then, and *turn* to God, so that your sins may be wiped out, that times of refreshing may come from the Lord" (Ac 3:19). In Lydda and Sharon, Peter saw many who "*turned* to the Lord" (9:35) as did those in Antioch who heard the words of life from men of Cyprus and Cyrene: "The Lord's hand was with them, and a great number of people believed and *turned* to the Lord" (11:19 – 21). The apostle Paul likewise urged the idolaters of Lystra and Derbe "to *turn* from these worthless things to the living God" (14:8 – 18). That is why it was reported at the Jerusalem Council that the Gentiles were "*turning* to God" (15:19). Paul explained the same message to King Agrippa as he related how God had called him to "*turn* [many] from darkness to light, and from the power of Satan to God" (26:18). Even under guard at Rome in a rented home, Paul repeated the call given to the prophet Isaiah some seven centuries previously, that if men and women would "*turn*," then God would "heal them" (28:27). The call to "turn back" to God was central in the Lucan theology of the book of Acts, for it said that repentance must involve a basic change in one's direction away from sin and toward the Savior.

The third response was "faith," which Luke-Acts presented in two terms: "faith" (*pistis*) and "to believe" (*pisteuō*). Luke used the noun "faith" twenty-six times in his two-volume history and the verb "to believe" forty-six times. Simply put, faith involved putting one's

13. As suggested by Bock in "Luke," *New Dictionary of Biblical Theology*, 277 – 78. In his "Theology of Luke-Acts," 131 – 32, he listed only three such "portraits" of repentance.

full trust in another; but here, especially where salvation was concerned, it meant putting one's complete trust in Jesus himself. Thus, by faith the centurion (Lk 7:9), the woman who anointed Jesus' feet (7:47 – 50), the Samaritan leper (17:19), and the blind man (18:42) all put themselves totally in the hands of the Lord Jesus, who alone could save them.

So closely allied was the Christian movement to this call for "faith" that the whole Christian walk was known as "the faith" (Ac 6:7; 13:8; 14:22; 16:5). Those who believed were called "believers" (5:14; 15:5; a participial form of the verb "to believe").

Faith, of course, had to have an object, and that object was none other than Christ himself (20:21; 24:24; 26:18). But in addition, belief was simultaneously expressed in the message (4:4), the gospel (8:12 – 13), the Old Testament promise (24:14), and the prophets (24:14). Believers were numbered among those from Berea (17:12), Athens (17:34), Corinth (18:8), Ephesus (19:18), and the Gentiles in general (21:25), not to leave out the Jewish people (21:20).

The Theology of Discipleship

Repentance was not to be a halfhearted response to the gospel; it had to involve a major overhaul of a person's whole orientation to life. In fact, so prominent was this feature that Christianity began to be labeled as "the Way" (Ac 9:2; 19:9, 23; 22:4; 24:14, 22) or even as "the Way of the Lord" (18:25) or "the Way of God" (18:26). It was a whole new way of thinking, acting, and living. How this term "the Way" began, and where it came from, is not exactly known, but the Christians used it to describe themselves in the earliest days of the faith. To be sure, the Old Testament had often talked about "walking in the way of righteousness" (e.g., Pr 8:22) and the like, but it cannot be said for certain that something such as this triggered the name the Christians gave to themselves. Clearly, however, there was a path and an approved style of life expected from believers that was distinctive and separate from all that was around them.

Luke's emphasis was on the fact that one must respond wholeheartedly to the gospel; it could not be a wishy-washy affair. While, along with the other Synoptic Gospels, he records Jesus' call to Simon Peter and his brothers James and John, Luke uniquely adds that they "left everything" (Lk 5:11). Likewise, when Jesus called Levi, also known as Matthew, to become his disciple, only Luke records that Matthew also "left everything" (Lk 5:28). And for others who wished to become Jesus' disciples, Matthew and Luke both relate how Jesus warned that foxes and birds have places where they can return, but not the Son of Man (Mt 8:18 – 22). However, Luke goes a step further and says that to the one who wanted to return to say good-bye to his family, Jesus warned, "No one who puts his hand to the plow and looks back is fit for service in the kingdom of God" (Lk 9:62).

A would-be disciple must think things over first before choosing to follow Jesus, just as Luke stressed in the two parables he gave in 14:28 – 33 of the builder who constructed a tower before he added up what it would cost and the king who started off to war without figuring what it too would cost. There is a cost to discipleship. It involved taking up one's cross "daily" (a word Luke stressed exclusive of the other gospels, 9:23). Discipleship involved real discipline and a commitment that brooked no rivals in place of the Lord himself.

So strong was the loyalty demanded by our Lord of his disciples that the priority he demanded on the one hand was put over against the demands from one's own family or closest relatives on the other hand. While Jesus did not encourage any outright hatred of those relations (for had he not given instructions to the contrary in the Decalogue?), yet family and relatives were to be "loved less" in comparison of one's love to God (Lk 14:25 – 33; Mt 10:37 – 38). So strong must our love for God be that "the best of earthly loves [would] seem like hatred in comparison."[14]

Women, the Poor, and the Disreputable

Luke had a special love and concern for those who were treated as the outcasts of society. He focused on them with special care and prominence.

Women, along with widows, were given special treatment in Luke's gospel, it would seem. This was revolutionary when compared to every other sector of society in the ancient world. For example, the rabbis simply would not teach women; they felt it was sin to do so. Rabbi Eliezer taught: "If any man gives his daughter a knowledge of the Law, it is as if he taught her lechery."[15] Nor were the Greeks and the Romans any more open to women's participation in society. Generally, unless they were from a few well-off families, no woman in either Greece or Rome could transact business without the presence of a male guarantor.[16] They were forbidden in those cultures even to go to the theatre. Meanwhile, men in the synagogue prayed an old prayer: "Blessed art thou, O Lord ... who hast not made me a woman."[17]

When that picture is put over against the one of Mary sitting at the feet of Jesus learning despite Martha's protest about her not helping with the preparation of the meal, the situation is all the more startling. Add to all of this the even more shocking statement of Jesus that Mary had chosen "what is better, and it will not be taken away from her" (Lk 10:42), and one can see how revolutionary was our Lord's approach to teaching women.

But there is more. Consider Jesus' entourage that consisted of Mary Magdalene, Joanna, Susanna (8:1 – 3); "These women were helping to support [Jesus and the Twelve] out of their own means" (8:3). Moreover, the infancy narratives of Jesus included Elizabeth, Mary, and the prophetess Anna (1:46 – 55; 2:38).

Jesus even took time to care for the widow of Nain, who had just lost her only son, whom Jesus raised to life. Jesus' comforting words to her were: "Don't cry" (7:13). Then

14. Morris, *New Testament Theology*, 197.

15. R. Eliezer as quoted from *Mishnah*, Sotah 3:4, as cited in Morris, *New Testament Theology*, 202.

16. M. Cary and T. J. Haarhoof, *Life and Thought in the Greek and Roman World* (London, 1961), 142, as cited by Morris, *New Testament Theology*, 202 – 3 n. 1.

17. Morris, *New Testament Theology*, 203.

there was the sinful woman who anointed Jesus' feet and wiped them with her hair (7:36 – 50). Why would Luke, much less Jesus, take time to focus on these women when everyone else passed over them as if they did not exist? But such is the message of the gospel.

Luke reports some instances of Jesus' contact with women that the other evangelists did not record. For example, in one of his discourses, Jesus referred to the widow of Zarephath, who saved the prophet Elijah (Lk 4:26). Luke alone noted that it was the women who followed Jesus as he was taken to be crucified (23:27 – 31). He is also alone in telling the parables of the woman who lost a coin (15:8 – 10) and of the widow who kept pestering the unjust judge until she got a fair hearing of her case (18:1 – 5).

In the book of Acts, women continue to play a major role. The apostles were assembled in Jerusalem "along with the women" including Mary, the mother of Jesus (Ac 1:14). At Pentecost, the Holy Spirit fell on the women as well as the men, for that is what Joel had prophesied (Ac 2:17 – 18; Joel 2:28 – 32). As the church grew, "more and more men and women" believed (5:14), and as at Samaria, "they were baptized, both men and women" (8:14). Nor were women exempt from the persecutions that Saul, and those in Jerusalem, carried out on the new believers, for "[Saul had formerly] dragged off men *and women*, and put them in prison" (8:3; emphasis mine, cf. 9:2; 22:4). On the other hand, there was also opposition from "God-fearing women of high standing" (13:50), who stirred up persecution against Paul and Barnabas.

But among those females who did believe were Tabitha, also called Dorcas (9:36); Mary, John Mark's mother, who used her house as a gathering place for believers (12:12); and the slave girl in that house called Rhoda (12:13 – 17). Since there does not appear to be a synagogue at Philippi, the work began at the riverside outside of town, where a number of women had gathered among whom was Lydia, a seller of purple from the city in Asia Minor called Thyatira (16:14 – 15; cf. Rev 2:18 – 29). As the group grew, Luke noted next at Thessalonica that "not a few prominent women" believed (17:4). The same was true of what happened at Berea, where again "a number of prominent Greek women" believed (17:12). The gospel was successful both among females and among the upper class, in addition to its general outreach into all of society.

There were also the accounts of individual women such as Timothy's mother, whom we meet at Lystra (16:1). In Athens we meet "a woman named Damaris" (17:34) and a most impressive woman teacher named Priscilla, who gave instruction to Apollos (18:2, 18, 26). Philip, one of the seven deacons, had "four unmarried daughters who prophesied" (21:9). Wives and children were also among those who came out from Tyre to say goodbye to the apostle Paul as he boarded ship to go to Jerusalem (21:5). In addition to all of these, there are reports of other women in Luke's history, such as Candace, queen of the Ethiopians (8:27); Drusilla, wife of Felix the governor (24:24); and Bernice, wife of King Agrippa (25:13, 23; 26:30).

As for the "poor," Luke used the word *ptōchos*, "poor" some ten times, whereas Matthew and Mark used it only five times each. Luke also used *plousios*, "rich" or "wealthy," eleven times, while Matthew used it three times and Mark only twice. Luke warned against wealth and a fascination with possessions for their own sake in texts such as Luke 8:14; 12:13–21; 16:1–15, 19–31; and 18:18–25. Yet he also left room for a positive use of money in Luke 8:1–3; 19:1–10; 21:1–4. It is not as if Luke called for a complete divestiture of all wealth, for even though Zacchaeus gave away half of his possessions to the poor, he still had the other half left (Lk 19:8). The point is that goods and wealth were not to be hoarded and used selfishly.

For those who have been forced by circumstances into being poor, Jesus' beatitude "Blessed are the poor" (Lk 6:20) was not to be understood as a benediction on poverty. The words to the "poor," in this case, were meant to be an encouragement for those who did not add up what they possessed and valued, as unbelievers added things up, in order to determine worth and values. Instead, the poor may have been very short on what is regarded as wealth but vastly more blessed in Christ. In the Old Testament, the "poor" were often those who piously followed what Scripture taught. More to be pitied were those who trusted in riches (Pr 11:28) than those who were poor. Jesus, in his first sermon at Nazareth, read from Isaiah 61:1–2, where God had appointed him "to preach the good news *to the poor*" as well as to the prisoners, the blind, and the oppressed (Lk 4:18–19, emphasis mine). That piece of evidence was specifically used as the climactic proof that was to be given to John the Baptist that Jesus was the Messiah: tell John, he said, that "the good news is proclaimed *to the poor*" (7:22).

All that being said, the wealthy are warned that they have already received their reward and comfort (6:24). Surely, wealth had at many times made it easier, speaking hyperbolically, for a camel to go through the eye of a needle than for a rich man to enter the kingdom of God (18:25). Riches can complicate one's coming to Christ, but they also were not an unconquerable factor.

Finally, Luke favors the underdog, or at least those who are considered disreputable by society at large. Thus, the message of Jesus' birth amazingly came first to shepherds (2:8–20). So low were shepherds on the social scale that they were not allowed by Jewish law to give evidence in a court of law (Talmud, *Sanhedrin* 25b). Their wandering habits cast suspicion on them as being possible thieves and as nonobservant about the ceremonial law. In this same class were tax collectors, whom Luke mentions ten out of the twenty-one times they are found in the New Testament. Even Matthew, himself a tax collector, only had eight references to this class.

Luke noted that it was a sinful woman who anointed and wiped Jesus' feet (7:37–50). He also repeated many of Jesus' parables that use people who were on the margins of society to show that the gospel was for them as well (7:41–42; 12:13–21; 15:11–32; 16:1–12; 18:1–8).[18] Luke wanted to make sure that the mission of Jesus was shown to be exactly what it was in reality: "The Son of Man came to seek and to save what was lost" (19:10).

18. This list is from Morris, *New Testament Theology*, 211.

The Kingdom of God

Jesus brought the kingdom of God "near" (Lk 10:9) as well as in the future (17:22 – 37). When Satan's kingdom had received a good beating at the hands of the seventy-two who had been sent out by Jesus (10:18 – 19), then one could be certain that God's reign had already put in a real appearance (11:20 – 23). In the Old Testament, the "day of the Lord" also had both a near and a distant aspect to it. Since God's kingdom was an important component of the day of the Lord, it is not surprising that "kingdom of God" enjoyed the same dual aspects in its definition.

Luke used the concept of the "kingdom of God" some thirty-two times in his gospel and another six times in Acts. Leon Morris observed that Luke's presentation of the kingdom fitted very nicely with his parallel emphasis on "power" (*dynamis*), which he used fifteen times in the gospel and ten times in Acts. The next highest use of the concept of "power" in the New Testament is 1 Corinthians with a use of fifteen times. In addition, the verb *dynamai*, "I am able, can," appears twenty-six times in the gospel and twenty-one times in Acts. The next closest frequency in usage is John, who uses the verb thirty-six times.[19] Clearly, God is supreme in his present and coming reign.

The essence of Jesus' ministry is stated in Luke 4:43, "I must preach the good news of the kingdom of God." There was a divine necessity in Jesus' mission, but there also was an equating of the gospel with the news about the kingdom as well. That same duality could be seen in Paul's summary of his ministry as he bid farewell to the elders at Ephesus:

> I have declared to both Jews and Greeks that they must turn to God in *repentance* and have *faith* in our Lord Jesus Christ.... I consider my life worth nothing to me, if only I may finish the race and complete the task the Lord Jesus has given to me — the task of testifying to the *good news* of God's grace. Now I know that none of you among whom I have gone about preaching the *kingdom* will ever see me again.... I am innocent of the blood of all men.... For I have not hesitated to proclaim to you the whole will of God. (Ac 20:21, 24, 25 – 27, emphasis mine)

Paul, too, linked the preaching of the kingdom with the gospel message of repentance and faith in Christ. The future rule and reign of God was not to be ripped away from the present work of the gospel in their midst.

It is no wonder, then, that our Lord taught that "the kingdom of God does not come with your careful observation, nor will people say, 'Here it is,' or 'There it is,' because the kingdom of God is within you [*entos hymōn*]" (Lk 17:21). While the meaning of "within you/among you/in the midst of you" is disputed, it referred to Jesus' person being present with the men and women of that first Christian century. Other texts in the New Testament will teach that the kingdom is spiritual and inward (e.g., Ro 14:17),

19. Ibid., 146 n. 6.

but here Jesus wanted us to see that he himself was the present embodiment of the coming reign of God.

There was a future aspect to his kingdom, a time when all rule and all authority would be his without challenge or opposition. Jesus pointed to that future aspect in the Passover he celebrated with his disciples in Luke 22:16. There he said, "For I tell you I will not eat it again until it finds fulfillment in the kingdom of God." Thus, the Passover, which celebrated Israel's deliverance from Egypt, pointed forward typologically to an even greater deliverance that would come in that final day when God's kingdom arrived in full.

That future day would come dramatically with cosmic disturbances, as alluded to in the teaching of the day of the Lord (Lk 21:25 – 27; cf. Joel 2:30 – 31; Hag 2:6, 21; Isa 24:19). As the Son of David, Jesus would rule on the throne of David on earth, as had been prophesied by the Virgin Mary in her song, by John the Baptist's father, Zechariah, and later, by John the Baptist himself (Lk 1:32 – 33, 46 – 55, 69 – 75).

In the forty days between the resurrection and the ascension, Jesus "spoke about the kingdom of God" (Ac 1:3). This theme we see embodied in the preaching of the early church as Philip the evangelist ministered in Samaria "preach[ing] the good news of the kingdom of God" (Ac 8:12). Even to the end of the book of Acts, Paul worked "from morning till evening ... explain[ing] and declar[ing] to them the kingdom of God and try[ing] to convince them about Jesus from the Law of Moses and from the Prophets" (Ac 28:23).

Since Luke-Acts represents close to one-third of the whole New Testament, it is difficult to summarize his teaching in just one chapter. But I have tried to capture those emphases that are key to understanding the contribution Luke made to the ongoing promise-plan of God. Luke wrote so that a full assurance and a full certainty of what God had done in Christ could be known by all. He was certain about the fact that all that took place in the life of Christ and his church was born of necessity in the long-range plan and purpose of God. Luke emphasized the promise of the Holy Spirit, by which God in Christ would carry out the work of building his church. And he also stressed repentance and faith in Christ.

Chapter 17

The Promise-Plan and the Purity of Life and Doctrine

1 and 2 Peter, Jude (About AD 64 – 65)

The books of first and second Peter and Jude (along with Hebrews, James, 1, 2, and 3 John, and Revelation) belong to that group of texts in the New Testament known as the "Catholic Epistles" or the "General Epistles." The reason for this description is that they are not addressed to a particular church, but are apparently addressed to the church universal, that is to say, to the church at large. All three books have a good number of references to the Old Testament and treat those texts as the grounds and the foundation for what God was now adding in the progress of revelation.

1 Peter: The Suffering of Believers

Given the important role Peter played both during the lifetime of Jesus and in the preaching of the early days of the church (Acts 2 – 5), it is not surprising that two books of the New Testament should come from his hand. First Peter claims to have been written by "Peter, an apostle of Jesus Christ" (1Pe 1:1). He refers to himself as a "fellow elder" (1Pe 5:1) and "a witness of Christ's sufferings" (5:1).

The New Testament gives us four different names for Peter: "Peter," "Simon," "Symeon," and "Cephas." The best known of all was "Peter," appearing some 124 times in the New Testament.[1] "Simon," appearing by itself as a name, occurred eighteen times; while "Cephas" was used uniformly by Paul (1Co 1:12; 3:22; 9:5; 15:5; Gal 1:18; 2:9, 11, 14). His name appeared as "Symeon" only twice: in Acts 15:14 and again 2 Peter 1:1. Of the four names, Peter and Simon are Greek, while Symeon and Cephas are Semitic in

1. Shirley Jackson Case, "Peter," in *Dictionary of the Apostolic Church*, ed. James Hastings (Edinburgh: T & T Clark, 1918): 2:191. The statistics: 20 times in Matthew, 18 times in Mark, 15 times in Luke, 16 times in John, 52 times in Acts, twice in Galatians, and once in 1 Peter.

origin. Among the Jews in Hellenistic times, Hebrew names were usually supplanted with Greek names as a concession to the culture of that day.

The addressees of this letter were recent converts to Christianity throughout the Roman provinces of Pontus, Galatia, Cappadocia, Asia, and Bithynia; all in Asia Minor, which is present-day Turkey. These believers were facing some type of persecution and suffering in Asia Minor, but what kind of suffering they actually faced depended in part on the time this persecution actually happened.

There are three possible times in the life of the early church when this could have been happening: (1) in the latter part of Nero's reign (AD 54 – 68); (2) a time under the Emperor Domitian (81 – 96); and (3) in the time of Tatian (98 – 117). The Neronian date appears to be the best time for the suffering that is alluded to in this book, even though we possess less data about what was going on by way of persecution in Asia Minor at this time than we do for the persecutions that were simultaneously happening in Rome.

Tacitus wrote in his *Annals* (xv. 44) sometime around AD 115 that Nero had blamed the Christians for setting the great fire of AD 64 in Rome in order to steer the blame away from himself. Tacitus did not believe the Christians did it, but he still regarded the Christians as malefactors who deserved the severest of punishments. Suetonius, who wrote about five years later (*Nero,* 16) agreed that Nero brutally punished this new and mischievous superstition, but said the great fire in Rome was not the occasion for his action. Clement of Rome (*ad. Cor.* 5 – 7), writing in about AD 95, also seems to put the beginning of the Christian persecutions coming sometime at or shortly after the great fire in AD 64. Clement traced the believers' troubles to "envy" and some type of popular animosity. Tacitus decided the Christians were "hated for their enormities," but whatever they were, he did not list them!

The Christians saw their troubles as suffering for the name of Christ, but the trouble that had begun in Rome spread until it apparently reached into the east and affected the believers in Asia Minor. Of course, Christians would not have looked kindly on the Roman customs of deifying the Caesars and sacrificing to the gods and goddesses of the Roman culture, thus they were targets for hatred that could break out anywhere in the Roman Empire.

First Peter records the provenance of this letter in a cryptogram by saying, "She who is in Babylon sends greetings" (5:13). The place he was referring to had to be Rome, for "Babylon" was a coded symbolic way to refer to that city as the place of extreme immorality, godlessness, luxury, and anti-God sentiments. It must be remembered that if this was a time of agitation against Christians and persecution against them, then one had to communicate in a very covert way so as not to attract unnecessary attention. Thus, Peter wrote the letter to those in Asia Minor from Rome sometime around AD 64 – 65.

Peter's Purpose

This letter had as its most central aim to comfort and encourage believers who were facing opposition and even persecution. In order to support these hurting persons, Peter turned their attention to that future day when God would send Jesus in his final day of judgment. If the central purpose of this letter is to be found in a single, all-encompassing verse, 1 Peter 4:19 might well be that text:

> So then, those who suffer according to God's will should commit themselves to their faithful Creator and continue to do good.

In this one verse, the themes of *suffering* ("those who suffer") and the theme of putting one's whole *trust* in God ("according to God's will") along with the third theme of *obedience* ("commit themselves to their faithful Creator and ... do [what is] good"), are all found together.[2] Hence, herein lay the purpose of Peter in writing this brief letter.

In the meantime, despite the aim of Rome's rulers, this persecution was nevertheless perfecting the salvation of the believers. Believers were "kept in heaven" and were "shielded by God" "through faith" in a "salvation ... ready to be revealed in the last time" (1:5). Therefore, though they were "refined by fire" (1:7), they were to "set [their] hope fully on the grace to be given when Jesus Christ [was] revealed" (1:13). Thus, 1 Peter 1:3 – 12 praised God for the certainty of his salvation that would come, notwithstanding some temporary persecution.

Peter returned to this theme of bearing up under persecution in 1 Peter 3:8 – 5:11. Surely, the Lord knew that it had been their zeal for righteousness that had brought on them much of their current suffering, but in this regard they were just following in the footprints left by Christ, who also innocently suffered for us (4:1). Therefore, whenever their enemies faced them with trumped-up charges and persecuted them because of their faith in Christ, they were not to be surprised (4:12 – 13). They thereby participated in Christ's sufferings (4:13); moreover, they were not at all to be ashamed (4:16).

For those pagan critics who were charging them with all sorts of antisocial and anti-Roman conduct, they were to have a ready answer (3:15). They were to "revere Christ as Lord" in their hearts (3:15) rather than acknowledge Caesar or anyone else as their "Lord." However, any kind of response to those who questioned them for the reason of the "hope" they possessed, had to be done with "gentleness and respect" (3:15), even if those who were asking such questions were pagans!

While no evidence seemed to suggest that the trials and persecutions had yet involved imprisonment or martyrdom, there does seem to be, not far beneath the surface, general hostility, false accusations, suspicions, verbal assaults, and perhaps occasional physical beatings. Peter used words for suffering sixteen times out of fifty-seven New Testament occurrences.[3] But those in Asia Minor were to be encouraged and comforted by the fact that Jesus also had suffered innocently (2:21 – 25) so that his gift of

2. Following Wayne Grudem, *1 Peter,* Tyndale New Testament Commentaries, ed. Leon Morris (Leicester, UK: InterVarsity Press, 1988), 39.

3. Buist M. Fanning, "A Theology of Peter and Jude," in *A Biblical Theology of the New Testament,* ed. Roy B. Zuck (Chicago: Moody, 1994), 451.

salvation could be offered to all. Since our Lord did not take things into his own hands and retaliate when he was falsely accused and abused, but rather left it up to God to right things in the final day as he acted as the final Judge, so believers had in that action a pattern for their own present situation.

Edward G. Selwyn commented that the trials that beset the readers of 1 Peter were not those of the organized type and those that occurred on a universal scale, but were instead more of the sporadic and random types. He pointed to three specific passages where the suffering was being experienced, as discussed in 1 Peter 1:6; 3:13 – 17; and 4:12 – 19. On the first text in 1 Peter 1:6, he observed:

> The Christians are suffering trials (*peirasmoi*) of various kinds (*poikiloi*). The choice of terms is significant. The specific term *diogmos* ["persecution"] does not occur in 1 Peter, nor does *thlipsis* ["oppression"], which is often associated with it in NT *peirasmos,* though it is commonly the result of some evil intent, is a general term, and the plural is therefore very appropriately joined here with *poikiloi*.... They are difficulties and sorrows ... caused by opposition, and they are means by which God tests (*dokimazei*) the mettle of men's faith.[4]

On the text in 3:13 – 17, Selwyn merely noted that we are called to suffer "for righteousness sake" (14) and "for doing good" (17). But in 4:12 – 19, there are more definite allusions. Here, he explained,

> A state of *pyrōsis* ["fiery ordeal"] exists, calculated to cause alarm (verse 12); but this word itself involves a metaphor which is most easily explained by reference to the "testing by fire" already mentioned in 1:7.... The difficulty turns on the degree in which we regard the trials referred to in the earlier passages as contingent rather than actual.... The general ordeal (*pyrōsis*) lay in the complete lack of security which exposed the Christians at any moment, and in any part of the empire (v. 9), to slander, defamation of character, boycott, mob violence, and even perhaps in some cases death: they were, or at any time or place might be, hated of all men for Christ's sake; society was inhospitable and the world unjust.[5]

It must always be noted that the suffering Peter refers to is a distinctively Christian phenomenon. There are two unique features to such suffering: (1) it is undeserved (2:19, 20; 3:17); and (2) it is ordained by God (3:17). Even though this suffering was also illustrated by Christ's suffering and had many similarities in principle, Christ's sufferings were distinctive both in character and in consequence. In his suffering, Christ bore the penalty that rightfully belonged to us. Moreover, his suffering resulted in an immediate triumph over death and evil as he was raised from the grave. In the case of the believers in Asia Minor, the suffering seemed to be more protracted.

4. Edward Gordon Selwyn, *The First Epistle of St. Peter* (London: Macmillan, 1955), 53.

5. Ibid., 54.

The Old Testament prophets were enabled by the Holy Spirit to foresee both Christ's sufferings and the resultant glory, even if they did not see or know the time or the particular circumstances that would surround Messiah's passion (1Pe 1:9 – 12).[6] Therefore, even as Christ's sufferings were earthly sufferings, yet they proved to be extremely well worth it as he entered into glory with the task completed. Consequently, our suffering is very temporary on the scale of eternity, but the results are far-reaching, with heavenly consequences.

The Call for Purity and Holiness of Life

Believers are called to "Be holy, because [the Lord is] holy" (1:16). That same call had been issued in the Mosaic law (e.g., Lev 11:44 – 45; 19:2; 20:7), which also said, "Be holy, because I the Lord your God am holy." This call for purity and distinctiveness was to be in evidence in all that they did (1Pe 1:15). This could be described as "doing good" (2:15, 20; 3:13, 17), or doing "what is right" (3:6), and "turn[ing] from evil," and "seek[ing] peace" (3:11). Herein was the "will of God" (2:15; 4:2).

The readers of Peter's letter were also characterized as those who were obedient (*hypakoēs*) to their Heavenly Father (1:14). He used the same word in 1:2 and again in 1:22. In fact, it was through obeying that Peter's readers had "purified" themselves (1:22). These believers were not to "conform" (*syschēmatizesthe*), a word used only here and in Romans 12:2, "to the evil desires [they] had when [they] lived in ignorance" (1:14). The days of ignorance had passed, and now it was time to let one's character and lifestyle be molded by the power that resided in their hearts since they had become believers (1:14). They were now a new race, who had come to the "living Stone" (2:4). As a result, believers themselves had become "living stones" (2:5), built into a "spiritual house," and a "holy priesthood" that now offered to God acceptable sacrifices through Jesus Christ (2:5).

Once again, the Old Testament had said as much when, in Isaiah 28:16, it said that a "chosen and precious cornerstone" had been laid in Zion so that all "who trust in him will never be put to shame." Thus, "the stone the builders rejected [had] become the capstone," according to another Old Testament passage (Ps 118:22). Peter used one more "stone" passage, Isaiah 8:14, to lock in the point. The promise-plan of God had correctly predicted what God would do.

6. The RSV, NASB, and the ESV all render the Greek *eis tina ē poion kairon* as "what *person* or what time" (emphasis mine) the Spirit of Christ in the Old Testament prophets was indicating when they spoke of the Messiah. Wayne Grudem's commentary had a long note contending earnestly for the fact that the Old Testament prophets did not know the *person* they were speaking about. He argued that *poios* could not mean "what kind of," but only meant "what?" Therefore it would be redundant to have *tina* mean "what?" also. Instead, argues Grudem, it meant "what *person*?" as in the RSV, NASB, and ESV (*1 Peter*, 74 – 75). But if that argument is correct, then why does the text go on to say that the Holy Spirit revealed five things to them: (1) the Old Testament prophets were talking about the Messiah/Christ; (2) they knew he would have to suffer; (3) they knew he would be glorified; (4) they knew he would be glorified after he had suffered; and finally, (5) they knew they were not just ministering for themselves but also to following generations such as those of Peter's day?

However, just as Israel had been called to be "a kingdom of priests and a holy nation, a people belonging to God" (Ex 19:5 – 6), so now Peter declared that the believers in Asia Minor would be the same — all who once had not been a people were now the people of God, Peter affirmed (vv. 9 – 10), as he again alluded to the Old Testament in Hosea 2:23.

The Gospel Preached to Those Who Are Dead

First Peter 4:6 argues, "For this is the reason the gospel was preached even to *those who are now* dead, so that they might be judged according to human standards in regard to the body, but live according to God in regard to the spirit" (emphasis mine). The Greek text merely had "the gospel was preached to the dead," but the NIV, while being more paraphrastic in this situation, probably helped most readers of this text sense its proper meaning.

The antecedent of "this" in verse 6 referred back to the subject of the previous sentence, that is, the final judgment. Thus, in light of the *coming* final judgment, the gospel was preached to many who are now no longer with us but who had believed while still alive on earth. However, since they now had died, and since Christ's salvation had never been previously offered to rescue people from physical death, it could be said that the gospel had been preached to those *who were now dead.* So while death will come to all mortals in the flesh, the gospel was given so that we could live with God.

Peter used another expression that can also be misunderstood at first: "[Christ] went and preached to the spirits in prison" (3:19). Certainly this was not to offer the departed dead a second chance to respond to the gospel. In an excursus that follows this chapter, I will argue that "the spirits in prison" refer to unrighteous mortals who had had the gospel preached to them in the days of Noah, *while the ark was being prepared,* as Christ himself went, through the preaching of Noah (2Pe 2:5; Noah is called a "preacher of righteousness") during those 120 years, presumably during the ark construction, although none seemed to have repented. Surely, this was a warning for the generation of Peter's day, just as it is a warning to us. But note that the call for salvation was just as real in Noah's day as it is in ours. That is why they were held accountable in the plan of God, which offer of salvation through repentance matches that known in the New Testament times.

2 Peter and Jude: The Condemnation of False Teachers

Second Peter shares many close parallels with the letter of Jude; in fact, all of Jude except the first three and last seven verses is principally found in 2 Peter. The problem faced by both writers was the presence of false teachers and heretics set on subverting the faith of believers.

Jude would have preferred to have written about "the salvation we share" (v. 3), but instead he "had to write and urge [them] to contend for the faith that was once for all entrusted to the saints" (v. 3*b*).

Likewise, Peter's chief purpose for writing was to combat false teachers who had apparently made the Christian teaching of liberty a license to do as they pleased. Moreover, they had dismissed the idea of an impending judgment of God as proclaimed by the previous generation of believers.

Demonstrating the Certainty of Our Salvation

In 2 Peter 1:3 – 21, the writer made the point that God gave to believers his very own "divine power," so that we have "everything we need for life and godliness" (1:3). In addition to this, God has also given "very great and precious promises" so that through these words from the older, and now newer Scriptures, believers might be able to "participate in the divine nature and escape the corruption in the world caused by evil desires" (1:4).

The expression "participate in the divine nature" is unique to Peter, and he does not pause to explain. It does not equate to a divinization of a person, but rather to a sharing of the divine nature by the indwelling of God's Spirit in us, as John later explained. It is a gift from God and not something earned as a right or by merit.

It is for this reason that believers should be diligent to cultivate the virtues listed in verses 5 – 11: faith, goodness, knowledge, self-control, perseverance, godliness, brotherly kindness, and love. Possession of these virtues in increasing measure will prevent Christian growth from being stunted and ineffective (1:8). Practicing these virtues would prevent a fall, as some of the false teachers had experienced (1:10).

Refutation of False Teachers

Peter never identified these scoundrels, for he was not going to give them any free advertising for their views. It was clear, however, that whatever they thought and said was extremely serious, for they were "denying the sovereign Lord who bought them" (2:1). Precisely how they denied Christ and his work on the cross was not described by Peter, but certainly the way they lived was at complete odds with a genuine commitment to Christ.

Believers needed to be reminded of the ethical dimensions of the call of God, for "even though [they] know them, and are firmly established in the truth," it is appropriate that their memories be refreshed as long as they are mere mortals (1:12 – 14). False teachers prey on those who are unstable in doctrine, ethics, and morals (2:14). Peter concluded his letter in 2 Peter 3:17 with an admonition that summarized the purpose of his writing, couching it in a negative form:

> Therefore, dear friends, since you already know this, be on your guard so that you may not be carried away by the error of lawless men and fall from your secure position.

Jude made the same plea; however, he put it in more positive terms:

> But you, dear friends, build yourselves up in your most holy faith and pray in the Holy Spirit. Keep yourselves in God's love as you wait for the mercy of our Lord Jesus Christ to bring you to eternal life. (vv. 20 – 21)

Jude added the same desire in that famous benediction with which he concluded his book:

> To him who is able to keep you from falling and to present you before his glorious presence without fault and with great joy.... (v. 24)

The false teachers had rejected the doctrine of the second coming of our Lord by scoffing, "Where is this 'coming' he promised?" (2Pe 3:4*a*). They counted heavily on an improper use of the law of uniformitarianism, wrongly applied here to the field of eschatology, when they said, "Ever since our ancestors died, everything goes on as it has since the beginning of creation" (3:4*b*).

The false teachers' lifestyle was despicable. They had thrown off all restraint (2Pe 2:10 – 12). To this they had added a licentious way of living, which they now tried to persuade others to follow in the name of full liberty (2:13 – 18). In so doing, they had become captives and slaves to licentiousness and were therefore worse off than they had been in the Christian community (2:19 – 22).

Six Eschatological Events

Contrary to the nay-saying of these false teachers, God would not retract what he had said would take place in the future. This could be seen in the following six affirmations about an apocalyptic eschatology that remained sure and certain.[7]

First, Jesus will return just as the prophets of the Old Testament had promised and as the apostles of that day had also taught (2Pe 3:1 – 4). Had not Jesus' glorification on the Mount of Transfiguration adumbrated exactly this same promise (1:16 – 18)? Second, a final judgment accompanied with fire had also been prefigured in the judgment by water, which God had brought on the earth in Noah's day (3:5 – 7). Third, if these heretics thought that things linked with the future were moving too slowly, then they could think again, for God's measurement of time was and is much different than our own (3:8 – 10, 15): "With the Lord a day is like a thousand years, and a thousand

7. I am beholden to Peter H. David's article, "2 Peter," in *New Dictionary of Biblical Theology*, 350, for the essential idea of these six points.

years are like a day" (3:8). Fourth, the heavens and the elements in the universe are all too transitory (3:10), but God promised a renewed heaven and earth (Isa 65:17 – 25) in that final day. Fifth, given the transitory nature of this life, we had better find a fixed position from which to gain a more stable understanding of both the present and the future (3:11), which was, of course, the word of God in the ancient plan of God in the Old Testament. Sixth, and finally, living holy and godly lives will actually "speed [the] coming" of the "day of God" (3:12). Therefore, the licentious lifestyles of these false teachers further extended the time that they felt already was too long delayed.

The Role of Scripture

The word of the Old Testament prophets had likewise warned of the very things that the heretics were now rejecting (1:19). One had to recall that "no prophecy of Scripture came about by the prophet's own interpretation of things. For prophecy never had its origin in the human will, but prophets, though human, spoke from God as they were carried along (*pheromenoi*) by the Holy Spirit" (1:20 – 21). So opposition to the teachings of the Old Testament prophets and the more recent apostles was opposition directed at God himself, who gave the records of these coming events in the first place.

Peter placed Paul's letters in the category of "Scripture," along with the authoritative writings of the Old Testament (3:15 – 16). True, not everything found in Paul's letters was equally understandable, but if one intended to distort them, then it would be to his or her own destruction.

While both Jude and 2 Peter draw on the same Old Testament accounts for their teaching on the certainty of the coming judgment, Jude alluded to an account in an apocryphal book known as the Assumption of Moses (Jude 9) and from another such book called 1 Enoch (Jude 14 – 15). There is no problem with including a quotation from a noncanonical book; the apostle Paul does the same in Acts 17:28; 1 Corinthians 15:33; and Titus 1:12. The question is whether Jude presented them as authoritative or merely used them to reinforce his idea from other contemporaries. The latter seems to be preferable, since Jude does not urge these texts upon his readers as authoritative as he did with the prophets and the apostles. Moreover, it is doubtful that the believers in Asia Minor knew 1 Enoch that well, for the reference could just as easily have been to his appearance in the Genesis genealogy of Genesis 5.

In another text that draws on the Old Testament (1Pe 1:10 – 12), as I have already shown in note 6 above, the prophets promised the coming of Messiah and described what some of his works would be. They knew at least five facts: (1) that they were pointing to the Messiah, (2) that Messiah would suffer, (3) that he would be glorified, (4) that the order of these last two events had already been determined, for it was the glory that should follow, and (5) that they were not only ministering to their day but also to the audience of Peter's day — that is, the church. What they did not know were: (1) the exact time, and (2) the circumstances that would surround that event of his first coming.

The Duty of Believers

Given that all of this present world must be destroyed, men and women ought to live holy and godly lives (3:11 – 18*a*). They must not misinterpret any seeming delay in the plan of God, nor must they pervert the doctrine of Christian liberty, especially as written by the apostle Paul (3:15 – 16). Instead, they were to grow in the knowledge and grace of our Lord Jesus Christ (3:18).

Excursus: Did Jesus Descend into Hell to Preach? (1 Peter 3:18-20)*

In light of this text and others in the New Testament, it is often asked whether that part of the Apostle's Creed that says, "He suffered under Pontius Pilate, was crucified, dead and buried, *he descended into hell,* the third day he rose again from the dead" is reflected in a text such as 1 Peter 3:19, where "[Christ] went and preached to the spirits in prison." The questions raised are these: Who were those "spirits in prison"? What did Christ preach? When did he preach? And what does Noah have to do with all of this?

The most common interpretation, I suppose, is that the spirits in prison in 1 Peter 3:19 are the evil angels who "were disobedient in the days of Noah" in that they came down and had sexual relations with the women on earth, thus producing a race of giants in the days of the flood (Gen 6:1 – 4).[8] It is true, of course, that 2 Peter 2:4 and Jude 6 speak of those angels that fell and landed in hell. But the word "spirits" (*pneumata*) can refer to either angelic spirits, both good and bad (Mt 8:16; Heb 1:14), or they can refer to the spirits of people who have already died and passed on (Ecc 12:7; Mt 27:50; Lk 23:46; Jn 19:30; Ac 7:59; 1Co 5:5; Heb 12:23).[9] We will argue for this second meaning in the discussion that follows. The imprisonment of these mortal spirits tends to emphasize the binding power and control that sin has over their lives, and thus they live in a prison of their own sin.

This interpretation was that "the spirits in prison" are the unbelieving dead who are now confined to hell after a life of rejecting the gospel. Some have

*I am beholden to Wayne Grudem, *1 Peter,* 203 – 39, for the general outline of the discussion found in this excursus. He, in turn, mentions the fine data supplied in the outstanding commentary by Selwyn, *The First Epistle of St. Peter,* 197 – 202, and W. J. Dalton, *Christ's Proclamation to the Spirits* (Rome: Pontifical Biblical Institute, 1965), 135 – 201, even though both Selwyn and Dalton have views that are different from Grudem's and mine.

8. See our comments on this text in chapter 1 in this book.

9. Grudem, *1 Peter,* 158, cites Selwyn and Dalton to the effect that this same dual usage can be found in the extrabiblical literature, where they counted 25 uses of *pneuma* to angelic spirits and 17 to human spirits.

argued that the word "spirits" is used absolutely, without any further definition or specification in the context. But that is not quite true, for 1 Peter 3:19 does give further definition to these "spirits" by saying that they were the ones "in prison" and also those who "disobeyed in the days of Noah" at the time "when God waited patiently ... while the ark was being built."

But the question then arises, "Yes, but were these spirits already incarcerated at the time that the preaching happened, or did the preaching take place prior to their incarceration?" This text can be understood to say that these "spirits" are now in hell, but they were once alive on earth at the time that the preaching took place. In brief, Peter spoke of the present incarcerated situation of those "spirits," even as he described a prior action of preaching that had already taken place while they had been alive in the days of Noah. The same type of speaking is held by most commentators for 1 Peter 4:6, which says, "the gospel was preached [even to those who are now] dead ..." (the material we have bracketed are words added by the NIV translators to give the sense of the verse, as mentioned above). Thus, while the words "spirits in prison" can mean either angelic or human spirits, we opt for human spirits because of the context in which these words are located. As has been said, it must be decided if the preaching was to those in hell at that time, or to those who are now in hell but who heard the word preached to them prior to arriving in hell. I conclude that they heard the preaching while they were still living.

The narrative in Genesis 6:5 – 13 makes it clear that God was upset with the sin of human beings, who adamantly disobeyed the words preached to them through the lips of Noah while he was building the ark. Noah's words, Peter teaches, were as good as Christ himself going and preaching to them. When God saw the level of their sin, God was sorry that he had made mortals, not that he had made angels (Ge 6:6, 13). That is why God brought a flood on the earth and not a flood in heaven. His wrath was aroused because of human corruption and their sin in society.

Later, in 2 Peter 2:5, Noah is described as "a preacher of righteousness." Likewise, Jesus used the illustration of the days of Noah, describing the people of that ancient day who refused to listen to any talk about an impending judgment and thus were overwhelmed in the flood (Mt 24:37 – 39; Lk 17:26 – 27). That same sort of hardness of heart about another coming judgment on the earth in the final day of the Lord will once again be just as adamantly rebuffed and mocked as it was in Noah's day, Jesus asserted (Mt 24:37).

Nevertheless, some will continue to protest: "Isn't God waiting for these spirits in prison to repent, for what else would seem to be the point of the patience of God?" First of all, that could not apply to angels, for nowhere does Scripture call angels to repentance. The fallen angels of 2 Peter 2:4 and Jude 6 are not given a chance to repent either then, now, or in the future. However, God was patient, it appears, for the 120 years mentioned in Genesis 6:3, while the ark was being built. As neighbors, friends, and relatives came to see Noah working on a monstrosity that was supposed to float out in the middle of nowhere, so it seemed, they heard over and over again the message that he literally hammered home: they must repent or they too would perish. This idea seemed so preposterous that it demanded little more action on their part than to openly scoff at such an event that was supposed to take place so far away from water that would lift that huge heap of wood into a floating vessel!

The most astounding part of this word about Noah's being a herald and proclaimer of righteousness was that Christ was active and working in and through Noah, even in this Old Testament setting. The word to "preach/proclaim" is *kērysso,* which can mean "to proclaim," without specifying the content, whether it be a proclamation of repentance or of condemnation. Probably it was a proclamation of both, for 2 Peter 2:5, which links *kēryx,* "preacher," with "righteousness" certainly also makes it a message of repentance as well.

Amazingly enough, Peter teaches that the "spirit of Christ" was active in the Old Testament, even as early as the days of Noah. Some may object to Christ's going (*poreutheis*) at the time of the Old Testament, but this objection overlooks the fact that God is often depicted in the Old Testament as "going" to one place or another (Ge 3:8; 11:7; 18:21). Christ is even depicted as accompanying Israel as they traveled through the wilderness (1Co 10:4).

If this is the correct interpretation, then why does the Apostles' Creed say that Christ "descended into hell/hades"? The answer is that the sixty-five times that *sheol* appears in the Old Testament, it uniformly means "the grave." There are other words for the doctrine of hell in both Testaments, but this was not one of them.

Why, then, did it appear in the Apostles' Creed? Actually, it did not appear in the earliest form of the creed, which originated in about the fourth Christian century, but it came later in about the sixth century. Apparently, the words in some of the early creeds said "he suffered under Pontius Pilate, was crucified, dead and buried, and rose the third day." Other creeds used the poetic words "he descended into hades," instead of "he was buried." Ultimately, the two were blended with the "hades" reading being used in apposition to the "grave." Moreover, this text in 1 Peter 3:18 – 20 does not, in any case, support the concept anyway.

Chapter 18

The Promise-Plan and Letters to Pastors

1 and 2 Timothy and Titus (About AD 62 – 67)

Both of the epistles that bear Timothy's name and the one to Titus have been grouped together under the label of the "Pastoral Epistles." This title was first given, as far as can be determined, by D. N. Berdot in 1703, followed by Paul Anton in 1726.[1] Today this eighteenth-century term is almost universally accepted, or at least used as a handy designator, for these three books. Most will also point out, however, that the title is not quite accurate, for the letters do not deal so much with pastoral duties and responsibilities as they are addressed to individuals who have the responsibilities of the pastorate. Even though the three epistles are routinely considered together, it is not as if they each deal with the same topic of the ministry. First Timothy has a fair amount on the topic of the pastor and some of the responsibilities, but Second Timothy and Titus are more personal and have almost nothing to say on that subject. What the three letters do have in common is that all three call for opposition to the false teaching that was challenging the church or that could bring great difficulties.

These books claim to have been written by the apostle Paul (1Ti 1:1; 2Ti 1:1; Tit 1:1), but many scholars deny Pauline authorship, usually preferring to credit these books to a pseudepigraphical author who wrote sometime in the second century, pretending to be Paul writing to two of his colleagues! But more than adequate arguments have been supplied in favor of Pauline authorship, so that is what is presumed here.[2]

The assumption is that Paul was released from his imprisonment in Rome. The chronology of his life from that moment onward is not too certain, but there are strong

1. D. A. Carson and Douglas J. Moo, *An Introduction to the New Testament*, 2nd ed. (Grand Rapids: Zondervan, 2005), 554.

2. For some defense of Pauline authorship, see Donald Guthrie, *The Pastoral Epistles* (Grand Rapids: Eerdmans, 1957); C. Spicq, *Saint Paul: Les Epitres Pastorals*, 4th ed. (Paris: Gabalda, 1969); D. Edmond Hiebert, *Titus and Philemon*, Everyman's Bible Commentary (Chicago: Moody, 1957); and T. D. Lea and H. P. Griffin Jr., *1, 2 Timothy, Titus*, New American Commentary (Nashville: Broadman, 1992); Carson, Moo, and Morris, *Introduction to the New Testament*, 367 – 71. For those opposing Pauline authorship, see P. N. Harrison, "Important Hypotheses Considered; III: The Authorship for the Pastoral Epistles," *Expository Times* 67 (1955): 77 – 81; A. T. Hanson, *The Pastoral Epistles*, New Century Bible (Grand Rapids: Eerdmans, 1982).

indications that Paul was able to go to Spain, which he may have done immediately after his release. Since it has been traditionally held that Paul was martyred under the Emperor Nero, who died in AD 68, Paul's death is placed around AD 67. That is the year Eusebius assigns to Paul's death, which if correct, then puts the writing of the three Pastorals somewhere between 62 and 67.

1 Timothy: Conduct in the Household of God

Timothy was born at Lystra, in Phrygia of Asia Minor (Ac 16:1 – 3). His father was a Greek, but his mother, Eunice, and grandmother, Lois, seemed to be godly Jewish women (2Ti 1:5; 3:14, 15) from whom he learned much of the Hebrew Scriptures (Ac 16:2). It is not possible to say under whose leadership, or when, Timothy was converted to Christianity. Some want to say it was during Paul's first missionary journey and preaching in Lystra, but there is no direct evidence to support that view. Paul did call him a "true son in the faith" (1Ti 1:2; cf. Ac 14:6, 19), if that can be taken to indicate that Paul was the one who led him to Christ.

The apostle Paul, on his second missionary journey, identified this believer in Lystra, whom he recognized as a good candidate for learning and helping him in the ministry. So he eventually had the elders set Timothy apart for the work of evangelism (Ac 16:3; 2Ti 1:6 – 7). Then Paul took Timothy along with him and his fellow worker Silas, as he went on in his second missionary journey, where together they evangelized Philippi and Thessalonica. Timothy appears to have escaped imprisonment in Philippi, but later he stayed on in Thessalonica, as he also remained at Berea with Silas to give further instruction as Paul went on to Athens. He later joined Paul at Corinth.

Timothy's two chief centers of operation became Macedonia and Ephesus (Ac 19:21 – 22; Php 2:19 – 20; 2Ti 1:15, 18; 4:13). In ecclesiastical tradition, Timothy is called the first bishop of Ephesus by Eusebius (*Hist. Eccl.*, 3.4.5), and in the fifth century source *Acta Timothei*, it is also said that he was made bishop of Ephesus by Paul during the reign of Emperor Nero. He was reputed to be the friend of the apostle John and was finally martyred on January 22 under Nerva, when Peregrinus was proconsul of Asia. Paul and Timothy had a long friendship, for he is mentioned in eight of Paul's other epistles (1Th 1:1; 3:2, 6; 2Th 1:1; 1Co 4:17; 16:10; 2Co 1:1, 19; Php 1:1; 2:19; Ro 16:21, Phm 1:1; Col 1:1) as well as in 1 and 2 Timothy. Timothy is also mentioned in Hebrews 13:23 as one who had just been released, apparently from prison.

The Purpose of 1 Timothy

Paul wrote the following to Timothy:

> Although I hope to come to you soon, I am writing you these instructions so that, if I am delayed, you will know how people ought to conduct themselves in God's household, which is the church of the living God, the pillar and foundation of the truth. (1Ti 3:14 – 15)

In Paul's view, the church was the primary vehicle that God would use to accomplish his work before coming again. Jesus had promised as much, when in Matthew 16:18 – 20, he did not even give the gates of hell a chance of having a victory over the church he promised to build.

As successor to the old theocracy in Israel, the church was declared to be the household of God, to which God had committed his word (1Ti 3:15; 2Ti 2:19; 3:14 – 17). The church must keep that divine truth in all its purity, with soundness of doctrine, remaining evangelistic in heart and action, and practicing purity in life and suitability in organization for optimum effectiveness.

Injury to its fellowship or apostasy from its source of truth would bring the greatest damage to this household of God (1Ti 1:20; 3:6 – 7). Therefore, the purpose of this letter was to prepare Timothy with confidence in the gospel he would preach and for giving close attention to the establishing and the functioning of the church.

The Church of the Living God

What appears to be an early creed of the church is stated in 1 Timothy 3:16:

> Beyond all question, the mystery of godliness is great:
>
> He appeared in a body,
> was vindicated by the Spirit,
> was seen by angels,
> was preached among the nations,
> was believed on in the world,
> was taken up into glory.

This creed is nicely explained by R. A. Falconer:

> In 1 Tim. the Church, the house in which God dwells, takes a place of great importance as the organized body which guarantees the truth. This truth is a healthy doctrine, but in 1 Tim. 3:16 it is also equivalent of "the mystery of godliness," and is set forth in a hymn which contains the salient features of the historic manifestation of Jesus Christ, what we might term an outline "gospel." The hymn seems most simply interpreted as referring to the Incarnation; the recognition of Divine Sonship in the Baptism, Temptation, Transfiguration; the revelation of the historic Jesus to the heavenly world, as e.g. to the celestial choir at His birth, the Transfiguration, Gethsemane (Lk 22:43), the Resurrection (Lk 24:4, 5); ... the preaching to the Gentiles; the founding of the Church in the world; and the culmination of His triumph in the Ascension.[3]

3. R. A. Falconer, "Timothy and Titus, Epistles," in *Dictionary of the Apostolic Church* (Edinburgh: T & T Clark, 1918), 2:589 – 90.

There are, in fact, three pairs of opposite thoughts in this hymn or early doctrinal saying in 1 Timothy 3:16. It went from the "flesh" (of the incarnation) to the "Spirit," in which Jesus was shown to be in the right; from "angels" to the preaching among the Gentile "nations"; and from the "world" (in which he was believed) back up to "glory" (where he ascended).

It is difficult to capture exactly what Paul is intending to do with Timothy since, as Donald Guthrie observed, Paul had had personal contact with both Timothy and Titus very recently.[4] After spending so much time with Paul, one would think that much of what Paul had to say in these letters about the work of the church and watchfulness for false teaching and false teachers would have been ingrained in both of these men already. So why were these letters so necessary if that is a true reading of the situation?

Two responses could be made to this important question. First, it appears that Timothy in particular was somewhat timid. This seems to be borne out when Paul sent him to the difficult situation in Corinth. Timothy was not made of the same stern stuff that Titus apparently was, so Paul sent Titus to follow up on Timothy's visit (2Cor 2:13; 7:5 – 7). It may well be the case, therefore, that Paul wrote the two letters to Timothy to counteract his timid nature. A second reason may have been to give both Timothy and Titus's leadership backup support with the authority of his own apostleship. There is evidence in Timothy's letters that some were inclined to demean and look down on Timothy, either because of his age or his inexperience.

At the heart of Paul's instruction to Timothy in this first letter was the teaching on the "house of God/God's household" (1Ti 3:15). Whereas that term had been associated in the past with the material temple with its furniture and services in the minds of some — yet even there Moses had been faithful in all God's house (Nu 12:7) — what made the house of God distinctive was not the buildings but the people. No wonder, then, that the writer of Hebrews drew a parallel between Moses, who was faithful in God's house, and Christ, who was likewise faithful in that house. But Hebrews 3:6 went on to say, "And we are his house, if we hold on to our courage and the hope of which we boast." First Peter 2:5 made the same point that believers were "a spiritual house"; thus, there was a living union with the living Christ, for such is God's house!

So long as a church abides in her living Lord, she is not dead. The living God is the source of the church's life and hope as well as the fountainhead of the truth it shares. While God does not personally descend from heaven each day, nor does he send his angels to proclaim his truth, he had indicated the ministry of the church; and her pastors' task was to support, maintain, and proclaim the truth. Nothing more can or need be added to the church to increase her influence, respect, greatness, or effectiveness.

4. Donald Guthrie, "Pastoral Epistles," in *The Zondervan Pictorial Encyclopedia of the Bible* (Grand Rapids: Zondervan, 1975), 4:615.

The church of the living God must be the "pillar and foundation [ground] of the truth" (1Ti 3:15); all else was secondary, including recognition, success, and particular methods and strategies. What makes a palace different from all other houses is not just the architecture but the fact that the king is resident. In like manner, that is what makes the church special: Christ is resident!

One God and One Mediator

First Timothy 2:5–6 taught that "there is one God and one mediator between God and human beings, Christ Jesus, himself human, who gave himself as a ransom for all people." The term "mediator" (*mesitēs*) described the work of a negotiator who served as a go-between for two parties who were at enmity with each other. Since all men and women found themselves as slaves to sin and at enmity with God, there was a desperate need for a mediator. In the gracious provision of God's grace and his salvation, Jesus was the only one who could actually fill that role. Since he was fully human as well as fully God, he, by his death and resurrection, could be the only mediator between God and mortals.

Moreover, to the question of what God will look like when we see him in heaven, this passage teaches that he has forever assumed the humanity that was part of his incarnation. Our text teaches that he is right now in heaven as the "human" Christ Jesus. This second Adam is surely separate and distinct from the first Adam, for Jesus now heads up a whole new humanity. This accords well with what the men of Galilee were told as they stood gazing up into heaven watching our Lord ascend to the Father. The angels asked: "Men of Galilee, ... why do you stand here looking into the sky? This same Jesus, who has been taken from you into heaven, will come back *in the same way* you have seen him go into heaven" (Ac 1:11, emphasis mine).

The word "ransom" (*antilytron*) in 1 Timothy 2:6 depicted the price that our Lord paid to free captive mortals under the bondage of sin and guilt. The preposition *hyper*, "for," emphasized all the more the substitutionary aspect of the work of Christ. Thus the death of Christ is *sufficient* for all, but it actually is *efficient* only for those who believe, for that is what 1 Timothy 4:10 said: he is "the Savior of all people, and especially of those who believe."

The Christian Life

While the apostle Paul taught very similar things in Philippians 4:8–9, here he goes even further and also uses some of the Hellenistic vocabulary to emphasize his model for wholesome Christian living. For those who respond positively to the preaching of the gospel, God raises up faith, a pure heart, a good conscience, and a moral life that can be evidenced in love, patience, righteousness, and piety, even under the duress of suffering (1Ti 1:5; 4:10–12; 6:11). In these cases, the word has fallen on the good soil and has sprung up, as the parable of the sower expresses it in the Gospels. But that soil must be cultivated and stirred up so that true "godliness" (*eusebeia*) will show itself in good works. Paul used this term ten times in 1 Timothy (2:2, 10; 3:16; 4:7, 8; 5:4; 6:3, 5, 6, 11).[5] This piety of life, or "godliness," is demonstrated when one lives out of a life of faith in love and service to others. Instructed in sound doctrine, the believer denies all worldly lusts and lives an "upright and godly life," showing "self-control" in all things (Tit 2:12).

If one exercises godliness, then the evidence for "self-control" (*sōphrosynē*) will follow and be another evidence of a real Christian life. Ten of the sixteen uses of this noun in the New Testament are found in the Pastoral Epistles. Self-control is particularly urged for those who are in their youth, as well as being one of the best adornments for pious women (1Ti 2:9; Tit 2:5, 6, 12).

Another term that the Pastorals seem to share with Hellenistic culture is the concept of "discipline" (*paideia, paideuō*). It is used four times in the Pastorals, but only three other times in Paul's other letters. It is used seven times in Hebrews and twice in Acts, where it describes the education of a child. In fact, this term expressed the essence of Greek learning and is today often contrasted with the Berlin university model, which stressed research rather than character building in the educational process.

Closely related to "discipline" is the word "exercise" (*gymnazein*), as seen, for example, in 1 Timothy 4:7. One can almost hear our English word *gymnasium* as the background for this word. What good would result from mentally assenting to these teachings about the Christian life without exercise in them? Training in righteousness is as necessary as are physical training and exercise.

But the most important term in these Pastoral Epistles is the word "teaching" (*didaskalia*), which occurs fifteen times. This teaching is often qualified with words such as "good" (*kalē*) or "healthy" (*hygiainoysē*; cf. English "hygiene"). The centrality of biblical and doctrinal teaching is never far from Paul's lips and instructions. In fact, "teaching" almost rises to the equivalence of "the faith" itself in 1 Timothy 6:1, 3 and Titus 2:19. This is what must be taught and exercised daily, for otherwise the growth in Christian things cannot be automatic or merely assumed; it must be practiced daily as a discipline, a spiritual workout, a routine of godliness and of self-control. While the classical culture did offer parallels to some of these same terms and concepts, the Greeks saw it as the basis for a well-ordered and harmonious life in which one's practice of an ascetic lifestyle was often mixed with ecstatic worship of idols of gods and goddesses. Here, however, the Christian life had a supernatural source in the living God, who alone was the source of faith, godliness, and life (2Ti 1:13; 3:12).

The Holy Spirit

Some complain that whereas the Holy Spirit was so central in the earlier Pauline letters — where he often argued that the indwelling Holy Spirit produced the fruit

5. R. A. Falconer, *Timothy and Titus*, 590, noted that the term *eusebeia* is used twice in 2 Timothy and twice in Titus. Outside the Pastorals, the term is found most frequently in Acts in connection with the phrase "God-fearers" (*hoi sebomenoi ton theon, hoi phoboumenoi ton theon*), proselytes who have converted.

of the Christian life — in the Pastorals all that seems to have changed. However, despite the fact that there are only five references to the Holy Spirit in the Pastorals (1Ti 3:16; 4:1; 2Ti 1:7, 14; Tit 3:5), nevertheless the Spirit's role is just as central as it was in Paul's earlier letters.

In 1 Timothy 3:16, as we have already seen above, the Spirit *vindicated* Jesus' resurrection. In 1 Timothy 4:1, the Spirit *warned* that apostasy would afflict the church in the latter days, something that was already happening in Paul's day. Second Timothy 1:7 argued that the Spirit was the *enabler* for ministry; otherwise the spirit of "timidity" (*deilias*), which may have been what Paul worried about in Timothy's character, would take over. But God meant for a "spirit of power, of love and of self-discipline" to be the hallmark of his servants. Likewise, 2 Timothy 1:14 called for the Holy Spirit to be the one *preserving* the message of the gospel. Of course, that did not absolve Timothy from his work of "guarding" the faith (2Ti 1:13), but he and the Holy Spirit were to work together to *preserve* what God had given. Finally, in Titus 3:5 the Holy Spirit is present in the work of *regeneration and renewal.*

Therefore, the charge that there is a difference between Paul's earlier emphasis on the work of the Holy Spirit in the Christian life and that found in the Pastorals is not convincing. What the indwelling Holy Spirit is said earlier to have produced as *fruit* in the life, here in the Pastorals is characterized as discipline, exercise, teaching, godliness, and self-control — all meant to *prune* the moral life so that more fruit is possible.

Instructions for Men and Women

One of the most fiercely debated passages in the New Testament is 1 Timothy 2:8 – 15. Paul had urged that both men and women were to lead in prayer at the worship services, but each was to be careful of a different potential fault. When men "lift up holy hands in prayer," they are to do so without "anger or disputing" — that is, they are to avoid leading in public prayer while inwardly gritting their teeth over some slight or an offense someone has committed against them. Women, however, were to lead in public prayer "in the same way" (*hōsaytōs*) that men were, but women often naïvely tended to forget that God had made them beautiful creatures, therefore they were to dress for that situation of leading in public prayer in a modest way that was appropriate for women who were professing (or "proclaiming") godliness (*epangellomenais theosebeian*).

The shocker in this passage came in verse 11: "Let the women learn" (*gynē … manthanetō*) commanded Paul (a third person imperative form, for which English does not have a command form, as it does for the second person pronoun, and an idea that was unthinkable for the Greeks, Romans, and Jews of that day in any case). The very notion that women were to be taught would have caused a storm of protest in Paul's day. No one taught women — except the Christians! But this learning was to be done with an attitude and demeanor of quietness and with full submission. In the meantime, women were not to teach or to exercise authority over men. The reason for this restriction followed in verses 13–14 with the word "for" (*yar*): for God "formed" (*plassō*, "to form," "to shape," either educationally, spiritually, or creatively) Adam first. Rather than this "forming" referring, as many think, to the "orders of creation"—for which Paul would no doubt have used his primary word for "to create," *ktizō*—that is, Adam was "created" first and then Eve—it seemed to be the "orders of education." Adam was (educationally) shaped or taught first, and only then was Eve taught.

A second reason followed, which was that Adam was not the one who was "tricked/deceived," but it was the woman who was "thoroughly deceived" (*exapatētheisa*), apparently because she had not had a chance to be fully taught yet, as had Adam, who had walked and talked with God in the garden prior to the formation of Eve. It is possible to trick someone best when they have not yet been taught. Nevertheless, before anyone starts accusing women of being more liable to sin, God declared that he had chosen a woman for the most special event in the plan of God. Women would be rescued, because it was a woman that God chose, and not a man, to bear the Christ child (2:15).

The Characteristics of a Departure from the Truth

The apostle Paul used a series of words to describe the marks of one who had left the truth in which he had been brought up. As Paul began his letter in 1 Timothy 1:3, he urged Timothy to stay in Ephesus to "command certain men not to teach false doctrines any longer." These teachers majored in "myths" and "endless genealogies" (1:4). They also taught "false doctrines" that did not "agree to the sound instruction of our Lord Jesus Christ," nor did it agree with teaching in godliness (6:3). They were "conceited and understood nothing" as they reveled in "quarrels about words" that had the effect of ending in "envy, strife, malicious talk, evil suspicions and constant friction between men of corrupt mind, who have been robbed of the truth and who think that godliness is a means to financial gain" (6:4–5).

What marked these persons as false teachers? Mark L. Bailey listed four characteristics.[6] First, they were "wandering" about (*astocheō*, 1Ti 1:6). Instead of being on target, they had shot wide of the mark that solid teaching would have served them.[7] They were vagabonds as far as the truth was concerned. The second characteristic could be seen in the fact that they had "rejected" (*apōtheō*) the faith and a good conscience (1:19). The result was that they had made "shipwreck" of their faith, as Hymaneus and Alexander were outstanding examples (1:20).

In addition to being wanderers and rejectors of the truth, they also were "abandoning" the faith, as they "apostatized" (*apostēsontai*) in 4:1. Paul called these men "hypocritical liars," who had no conscience, or if they did, those consciences were "seared" over "as with a hot iron" (4:2). They tried to get people to refuse to get married and to abstain from

6. Mark L. Bailey, "A Theology of Paul's Pastoral Epistles," in *A Biblical Theology of the New Testament*, ed. R. B. Zuck (Chicago: Moody, 1994), 337–38.

7. Ibid., 337, citing Lea and Griffin, *1, 2 Timothy, Titus*, 69.

certain foods (4:3). But they were following "things taught by demons" and "deceiving spirits" (4:1). This was spiritual and moral apostasy in its fullest expression.

Finally, these vagabond, truth-rejecting traitors to the faith were robbing other people of the truth (6:5). This had left them bankrupt and destitute of the truth. What was left to them, after they had abandoned the truth, were myths that they repeated or had invented for themselves. How dangerous it is to chuck the truth and to try to find adequate substitutes!

2 Timothy: Godlessness in the Last Days

Many refer to this epistle as Paul's "swan song," for in 2 Timothy 4:6, Paul wrote that his departure from this life was close. Therefore, he wanted to strengthen the hand of his fellow worker, Timothy, as best he could before the day for his death arrived. Accordingly, Paul had summed up his ministry by saying:

> For I am already being poured out like a drink offering, and the time has come for my departure. I have fought the good fight, I have finished the race, I have kept the faith. Now there is in store for me the crown of righteousness, which the Lord and righteous Judge, will award to me on that day — and not only to me, but also to all who have longed for his appearing. (2Ti 4:6 – 8)

The Purpose for Writing 2 Timothy

Second Timothy 1:6 – 7 seems to set forth Paul's purpose for this letter very nicely:

> I remind you to fan into flame the gift of God, which is in you through the laying on of my hands. For God did not give us a spirit of timidity, but a spirit of power, of love and of self-discipline.

Some would rather point to 2 Timothy 4:6, but that verse sums up Paul's life and states the reason he was so anxious that Timothy and Titus get on with the work. Though Timothy had been molded by Paul's teaching (2Ti 3:10 – 11), there might have been just a tinge of concern in Paul's mind that Timothy may have slipped and grown a little lax in his duties (1Ti 1:18; 4:11 – 16; 6:3 – 16). Timothy seems to have been thought timid (2Ti 1:7), and perhaps he shrank from suffering (2:3). Nothing can be asserted for sure, but why would Paul insist on warning him so specifically at each of these points if he did not feel something might possibly develop in Timothy's character in these areas?

Better to be fortified and to have been warned in advance than to suffer the sting of falling and bring reproach on the ministry. Therefore, Paul reminded him of his ordination and the power of God that was within him. That is why this letter is so filled with personal references. Timothy was to be one of Paul's successors in the proclamation of the gospel. His strength and help was to come from the grace of the Lord Jesus Christ who had also called him and set him aside for this purpose (2Ti 2:1 – 12).

A Trustworthy Saying

The Pastorals have a number of "sayings" that rise, on some accounts, to the level of early creedal statements. The one in 2 Timothy 2:11 – 13 summarized the salvation that is available to the elect (2:10). Here follows a series of "if" and "then" clauses in which the *protasis* of each of four statements is the action expected of the believer, followed in the *apodosis* by the way Christ will respond. The first two (2:11 – 12a) are positive, but the second two (2:12*b* – 13) expects a possible negative experience.

> If we died with him,
> we will also live with him;
> if we endure,
> we will also reign with him.
> If we disown him,
> he will also disown us;
> if we are faithless,
> he will remain faithful,
> for he cannot disown himself.

The first conditional statement about dying with Christ assures us that we will also live with him. The second one assures us that enduring for Christ's sake will result in reigning with him. In the third condition, any disowning of Christ will result in his disowning us. However, even if we are unfaithful, Christ will remain faithful, for he cannot and will not deny himself. This latter reference seems to be to temporary lapses in the life of the believer. That condition was much different from the third one, which appeared to be about one who never even had a genuine relationship to Christ. That one Christ would disown.

The Authority and Use of Scripture

One of the strongest statements on the authority and use of the Old Testament Scriptures is found in 2 Timothy 3:15 – 16.[8] Timothy had known these texts "from infancy," began Paul, so he was not pointing out anything new or original.

This ancient plan of God, Paul urged, was still "useful." It could "make [one] wise for salvation through faith in Christ Jesus" (3:15). Those same Old Testament Scriptures were "useful" (*ōphelimos*) for "teaching" (*didaskalia*), "rebuking" (*elegmos*), "correcting" (*epanorthōsin*), and "training (*paidea*) in righteousness" (3:16). This is the most definitive statement in the New Testament on how the Old Testament is to be used and what roles it

8. See my extended discussion of this text in Walter C. Kaiser Jr., *Toward Rediscovering the Old Testament* (Grand Rapids: Zondervan, 1987), 26 – 32.

must play in the life of believers. Only by following the words recorded in this older Testament could the man or woman of God be completely equipped for every good work (3:17).

Titus: The Grace of God

Paul addressed this letter (which has only 46 verses) to Titus, who seems to have been born in Antioch or its vicinity and who was converted to Christianity perhaps through the ministry of the apostle himself (Tit 1:4).

Crete, the field to which Paul took Titus, seemed to be one of the hardest fields to evangelize (1:12 – 13). One of the largest islands in the Mediterranean Sea, Crete, which lies about 60 miles south of Greece, stretches some 150 to 160 miles in length and varies from 7 to 35 miles in width. Though most of its territory is taken up with mountain ranges, its valleys are fertile and the climate is usually mild. Its economy, based on agriculture and trading, seems to have been fairly prosperous; however, with prosperity came excess, including avarice, mendacity, drunkenness, and laziness. Paul quoted one of the Greek poets named Epimenides, who in his hexameter wrote, "Cretans are always liars, evil brutes, lazy gluttons" (1:12).[9] The Greeks coined a special word for the kind of talk and conduct of the Cretans: to *krētizein*; indeed, Plato declared that to out-Cretan a Cretan was to outwit a knave.

It is not known at what time the church was planted on the island of Crete, but it may well have been on a missionary trip after Paul's first imprisonment in AD 62. As Paul left Crete, Titus remained to "straighten out what was left unfinished and appoint elders in every town" (1:5).

The Purpose for Writing to Titus

Paul wrote to Titus with these instructions:

> These, then, are the things you should teach. Encourage and rebuke with all authority. Do not let anyone despise you. (Tit 2:15)

And again:

> I want you to stress these things, so that those who have trusted in God may be careful to devote themselves to doing what is good. These things are excellent and profitable for everyone. (Tit 3:8)

Even if Titus had been instructed by word of mouth by Paul previously, he wanted to strengthen Titus's hand so that he could deal with the Cretans from a position of authority and apostolic blessing.

9. The biblical text, as indicated in the NIV and other translations, uses *prophētēs* ("prophets"), not *poiētēs* ("poets"), possibly because the Cretans ascribed several fulfilled predictions to the highly esteemed Epimenides.

The Grace of God That Brings Salvation

Titus 2:11 – 15 has to be one of the most memorable passages in this book. It is also one of three texts that point to the "appearances" of God's grace. The first "appearance" (*epiphainō* in its verbal form and *epiphaneia* in its noun form; cf. English "epiphany") was in our Lord's incarnation (1Ti 3:16; 2Ti 1:10; Tit 2:11). Our Lord appeared on earth in a human body. The second epiphany, which has appeared to all, is the "grace of God" (Tit 2:11; 3:4 – 5). This grace from God came in "the kindness and love of God" (Tit 3:4). The third appearance will be the return of Christ a second time (1Ti 6:14; 2Ti 4:1, 8; Tit 2:13). This epiphany is very much like the other word Paul used, *parousia*. But in 2 Thessalonians 2:8, Paul used both terms, *epiphaneia* and *parousia*.[10]

However, the text we wish to focus on is Titus 2:11 – 15. This grace of God brought five wonderful blessings to all men and women who would avail themselves of his kindness and love. First of all, it brought *salvation*. The gift of God's saving grace is no small gift indeed. Secondly, it brought us *solid teaching*. That instruction had both a negative and a positive aspect: it taught us how to say no to "ungodliness," and "worldly passions." But God's grace also educated us in how to live self-controlled, upright, and godly lives (2:12). God's grace did not just gift us at the time of salvation, but it stayed with us on into the rest of our lives as we entered our growth period in Christ as well. Thirdly, God's grace has also given to us an *expectation*, for we now "wait for the blessed hope," which is "the glorious appearing of our Lord Jesus Christ" (2:13). God's grace continues to minister to us all the way up until the time when we see our Lord face-to-face. Fourthly, this grace has also given us an *acceptance*, in that he "gave himself for us to redeem us from all wickedness and to purify for himself a people that are his very own, eager to do what is good" (2:14). Finally, that same grace of God has given to us an *impetus* to "teach" these things, to "encourage," and "rebuke with all authority," letting no one despise us in so doing (2:15). What a wonderful grace of God!

Even though these letters are very personal in their address to Timothy and Titus, the teachings on how to behave in the household of God, the fact that Jesus has forever remained in his human form and works as our mediator, and the warnings about departing from the truth, all make these books further contributions on God's everlasting promise-plan.

There is much to avoid in the coming godlessness of the last days, but there are even stronger reasons to place one's confidence in the living God, who is greater than all the invasions of the kingdom of the Evil One. Moreover, God has given us the Scriptures so that we may be fortified for every eventuality.

In the end, it is the grace of God that continues to be the mainstay of all who trust in Christ. His grace not only brought us our salvation, but it also continues to educate us and to give us a hope and expectation that is beyond all that one could expect or imagine.

10. I am indebted to Mark L. Bailey for these three stages set forth in "Theology of Paul's Pastoral Epistles," 344 – 45.

Chapter 19

The Promise-Plan and the Supremacy of Jesus

Hebrews (About AD 65)

Of all the New Testament books classified as "epistles," the epistle to the Hebrews is in many ways more similar to a full treatise than to a typical letter. It does not have in common with other New Testament epistles an opening salutation that names the writer and the addressees to whom it was sent. It does, however, conclude with typical epistolary features such as a benediction, some personal remarks, and a farewell (Heb 13:20 – 25). There is little doubt that the writer of this letter had some very specific persons in mind though, for he sprinkled throughout his writing a number of strong exhortations that were specifically directed to his readers and some current issues they were facing (e.g., 2:1 – 4; 3:12 – 14; 4:1, 11 – 14; 5:11 – 6:12; 10:19 – 12:29).

A sustained theological argument goes through the whole letter, causing some to conjecture that perhaps the work was originally a homily, or even a series of homilies that were later gathered together and presented as an anonymous letter. Who can say, given our present shortage of evidence? Nevertheless, it still has the feel of a real letter with numerous personal touches, as seen in the constant exhortations and the closure of the letter.

The Author of Hebrews

Origen's famous remark, "But who wrote the epistle God only knows certainly" (*tis de ho grapsas tēn epistolēn to men alēthes theos oiden*),[1] was originally applied only to the amanuensis or to the translator of this work. But since then, other scholars have found the words helpful in expressing their views, not just on the identity of the amanuensis but also to the mystery of who was the actual author of the book.

The Eastern Church, leaning on Clement of Alexandria and Origen, credited this book to the apostle Paul — as did an early-third-century papyrus text called "P46."

1. Origen as quoted by Eusebius, *Hist. Eccl.*, 6.25.13.

But the Western Church was not so sure. They felt that the Greek of Hebrews was too polished for Paul. Their preference was to suggest that Paul wrote the book in Hebrew and then his traveling companion and doctor, Luke, put it into polished Greek. They also explained the lack of a Pauline superscription with the explanation that Paul deliberately left this out so as not to prejudice his Jewish readers, for whom he intended it, by the strong biases they may have had for such an argument coming from Paul. Nevertheless, Pauline authorship of the book was not accepted by the Western churches until the latter part of the fourth century AD. Some also have suggested Barnabas as the author, and even the name of Priscilla has been suggested. We just do not know!

The Provenance and Date of Hebrews

Just as we are uncertain about the author, we are even less sure about where this book originated geographically. All commentators focus on Hebrews 13:24: "Those from Italy send you their greetings." But this note can be rendered in several ways: these persons may be a group of Italian believers who have left Italy and now send their greetings back home to their native land, or it can refer to those in Italy who send their greetings to a place that is unspecified, where the letter was being sent.

Even if we knew who the author was, it probably would not help much, for like Paul, that author could have been on the move geographically as well. So the question of location is left open too.

Since the persons addressed in this letter appear to belong to the second generation of believers (Heb 2:3), this letter could not have been written before AD 50, and probably not before AD 60. A terminus ad quem can be set from the references in the church father Clement, whom almost no one dates later than AD 96. In 1 Clement 36:1 – 6 there are a number of quotations from the letter to the Hebrews. That would leave a range for dating this epistle from AD 50 or 60 to AD 96. However, the writer makes no reference to the fall of Jerusalem in AD 70, which would have strengthened his statement that the old covenant "will soon disappear" (8:13). If the absence of an allusion to the fall of Jerusalem is recognized, then this would place it sometime before AD 70, which we surmise would be approximately AD 65.

The Purpose for Writing Hebrews

The writer seems to have a dual purpose in mind as he writes: a need to be pastoral for those who needed special prompting to be faithful by not deserting their faith in Christ, and a need to set forth the teaching on the supremacy and finality of Jesus Christ.

There are both negative and positive aspects in this purpose: negatively, to warn and to prevent his readers from turning back into their pre-Christian state by developing "a sinful, unbelieving heart that turns away from the living God" (Heb 3:12; cf. 3:6, 14; 4:14; 10:23); and positively, to encourage readers "to go on to maturity," leaving behind "the elementary teachings about Christ" (6:1). It would appear that some were having second thoughts about their conversion to Christ. Could it be that they had really missed God's plan and in following Christ had abandoned their own roots as found in Abraham, Moses, and David?

To counter these improper feelings and views, the writer of Hebrews used the Old Testament as his most important source, directly quoting it thirty-five times and making many allusions to Old Testament teachings, persons, events, and doctrines. The writer of Hebrews also used the word "promise" (*epangelia*) more than anyone else in the New Testament — a total of fourteen times. Only Galatians, with its ten references to "promise," came at all close to the number found in Hebrews. For example, the writer can focus on the one promise of "entering [God's] rest" in Hebrew 4:1, or refer to the multiple specifications in that single promise-plan of God by using the plural form, "promises" (note the Greek of 6:12). Thus, what the writer was arguing for in the supremacy of Christ was merely the fulfillment of God's ancient promises in his unified plan.

There are three main centers to the writer's argument: (1) Christ offers a *better priesthood* than operated previously in the Old Testament (with Ps 110:4 as the central Old Testament text for Heb 7:1 – 28; 10:19 – 22); (2) Christ offers a *better sacrifice* than seen in the Old Testament (with Ps 40:6 – 8 as the central text for Heb 8:8 – 13; 9:15 – 22); and (3) Christ offers a *better covenant* than seen before (with Jer 31:31 – 34 as the central text for Heb 8:7 – 13; 10:15 – 18).

Therefore, the central theme in Hebrews is Christ. He is supreme over the angels (Heb 1), over Moses (3:1 – 6), over Joshua (4:9), and over Melchizedek (7). But all of this is not so innovative that it had no roots or anticipations in the revelation of God up to this point. On the contrary, it happened exactly as it had been predicted in the promise-plan of God.

The writer used the term "better" (*kreitton*) thirteen times in Hebrews (1:4; 7:7, 19, 22; 8:6 (2x); 9:23; 10:34; 11:16, 35, 40; and 12:24) supplemented by *kreisson* in 6:9. Other terms and expressions are used to make the same point (e.g., 2:2 – 4; 3:3 – 6; 5:4 – 10; 10:27 – 28; and 12:25), but the superiority of what Jesus introduced was the theme of the book. Truly, this book wants to show that something more and better had arrived with Christ. But the contrast was not so strong that it entirely *superseded* the old; rather, usually it just *supplemented* it, unless the old had a built-in warning of an obsolescence that would pertain if the actual and the real, to which these "patterns" and "copies" pointed, finally arrived and thereby rendered the copies obsolete.

The Supremacy of Jesus as the Son of God

This second generation of Hebrew believers needed to know that just as God had spoken in the past to their ancestors through the prophets, using different ways and means at different times, so he now continued to communicate to all of us in these "last days" through his Son Jesus (Heb 1:1 – 2). This theme has given rise to what some in theology have called "the finality of Jesus Christ in all of history."[2] To substantiate this high claim, the writer made seven declarations about the Son (1:3 – 4):

1. Jesus is the Heir of all things.
2. Jesus is the Creator who made the universe.
3. Jesus is the Radiance of God's glory.
4. Jesus is the Exact Representation of God's being.
5. Jesus is the Sustainer of all things.
6. Jesus is the Priest who provided purification for sins.
7. Jesus is the King who sat down on his throne in his place of honor.

The Son's superiority is further demonstrated in six more arguments backed up by eight Old Testament anticipations of these very events (1:5 – 13):

1. Jesus is perpetually related to the Father as his Son (1:5), as predicted in Psalm 2:7 and in 2 Samuel 7:14; 1 Chronicles 17:13. That was the promise God had given to David — that God would be a Father to the coming Son, and the one ultimately born in that line would be God's own Son.
2. Jesus would be worshiped by the angels when the Father brought his "firstborn" into the world as David's heir. That was what the ancient promise had called for in Psalm 97:7 and Deuteronomy 32:43 (as this Deuteronomy passage reads in the text of the Dead Sea Scrolls and the Septuagint).
3. Jesus would have a reign as the coming Messiah that would last forever, and he would have righteousness as his scepter, as confirmed by Psalm 45:6 – 7.
4. Jesus will roll up the heavens and the earth like a robe or a change of garments, but he will remain the same forever even as Psalm 102:25 – 26 had promised.
5. Jesus now sits enthroned at the Father's right hand with his enemies functioning as his footstool, as predicted by Psalm 110:1.
6. Jesus is the divine Son of God. Repeatedly, the Old Testament had announced that this would be the exact title and dignity he would possess. Jesus' deity was evidenced over and over again by the predictions of the Old Testament and by his very person and works. But for the writer of Hebrews, none of the evidences was more convincing and more authoritative than the promises issued long before his birth.

The Supremacy of Jesus as True Man

As the deity of Christ is argued for in Hebrews 1:1 – 2:4, so the humanity of Christ is argued for in Hebrews 2:5 – 18. As one who was fully human, our Lord is described as

2. This was the title of Robert Speer's famous book, *The Finality of Jesus Christ* (Westwood, NJ: Fleming H. Revell, 1933).

someone who belonged to the tribe of Judah (7:14), endured opposition from sinful mortals (12:3), and was put to death outside of Jerusalem (13:12).

But what was the Father's purpose in Jesus' humanity and in his showing such solidarity with human beings? Once again, the writer appeals to the ancient promise of God, this time in Psalm 8:4. God did not put this world in subjection to angels, but rather to created men and women. By subjecting everything under the feet of humans, God left nothing outside of humanity's managerial oversight and accountability. This did not give license for mortals to plunder, destroy, and trample anything and everything on earth so long as there was a profit to be gained or for some other selfish reason, however.

God's plan for humanity was spoiled temporarily, but it would not be permanently foiled. Currently, we do not see everything in subjection to mortals as originally provided for by God, but what we do see is that sin has now entered the world and the task, given by God to men and women, has been subverted. However, "We do see Jesus" (2:9), whom God has sent to do what men and women failed to do because of their fall into sin. Jesus is one giant step forward for humanity, for the immortal God took on flesh and blood and became what neither angels nor people were, nor could be, without the intervention of God. He tasted death so that all human beings might be brought back to God.

Jesus' death on the cross was the second giant step forward for humanity. Hebrews 2 argued that there were eight distinct purposes for the death, burial, and resurrection of our Lord. Neither Jewish nor Gentile believers were to be offended by the cross; instead, they were to take note of what had been provided (2:9 – 18):

1. Jesus tasted death for "everyone" (2:9) so that mortals could live forever with God. Reconciliation to God could only take place if a perfect life of a perfect God-man provided for the release of sinners.
2. Jesus was designated "the author (*archēgos*) of their salvation, which salvation he made perfect through suffering (2:10). Jesus was the forerunner, the pathfinder and pioneer of our faith. He was not made "perfect" in the philosophical sense or in an abstract perfection, but in the sense that he was made fully adequate for the task for which he had been called by the Father. The same Greek words are used in the Septuagint in connection with ordaining and consecrating priests for service (Ex 29:9, 29, 33; Lev 8:33; 21:10).
3. Jesus made all who believe part of the same family (2:11 – 13), thereby setting them apart and sanctifying all who trust in him. If Jesus was not ashamed of mortals, then how is it that mortals are embarrassed by the cross? As a man, Jesus got hungry (Mt 4:2) and grew tired (Jn 4:6), thirsty (Jn 19:28), and sorrowful over the loss of a friend (Jn 11:35). Jesus is the head of a new humanity (Ps 22:22; "Go ... tell my brothers").

4. Jesus had to "destroy [the devil] who holds the power of death" (2:14). 1 John 3:8 taught the same doctrine: "The reason the Son of God appeared was to destroy the devil's work." That is why the "last enemy" to be destroyed by our Lord is death (1Cor 15:26).
5. Jesus died to "free those who all their lives were held in slavery by their fear of death" (2:14). The Messiah not only abolished death by his dying and rising again from the dead, but he also brought life and immortality to light as well (1Ti 1:10). Death still has a sting, but it no longer has any legitimate hold over any believer.
6. Jesus accomplished our salvation in order to take hold of us as Abraham's descendants (2:16). In the same manner that God the Father "took hold of" (*epilambanetai*) the hands of the Israelites to lead them out of Egypt (Heb 8:9), so God will do the same for all believers, now counted to be Abraham's seed (Gal 3:29).
7. Jesus thereby became a merciful and faithful High Priest in the service of God (2:17). Jesus had to "become" a human. He was under no obligation to provide salvation for mortals except that which he imposed on himself. He did not have to die for men and women, but once he started on that road, there was no stopping. He removed sin by offering himself as a vicarious substitute.
8. Jesus' suffering will help those who are tempted because he too was tempted (2:18). Why should believers yield to temptation when help is readily available?

These, then, are the eight purposes for our Lord's humanity and for his atonement for all. This text of Hebrews 2:9 – 18 is one of the finest teaching blocks on the purposes of the atonement.

The Supremacy of Jesus to Moses

Hebrews 3:1 – 4:13 acts almost as an interlude in the writer's argumentation. Even as the writer is anxious to get to his discussion of the one who purifies mortals from sin (1:3) and state how our high priest, Jesus, is now in heaven (4:14), he needs to apply what has been learned thus far in Hebrews 1 – 2.

Jesus, whom believers confess, is the "apostle" — that is, God's ambassador — as well as the high priest (3:1) of the Christian faith. He was faithful in all that the Father had given him to do, but so too was Moses "faithful in all God's house" (3:2) as Numbers 12:6 – 7 showed, where in contradistinction to all other prophets, God spoke with Moses directly and not in enigmatic ways. Nevertheless, "Jesus was found worthy of greater honor than Moses," (Heb 3:3*a*), just as the builder of a house deserves more credit than the house itself (3:3*b*). That house, of course, is made up of all believers (3:6).

But despite Moses' faithfulness, he lost his temper in public in the fortieth year of the wilderness wanderings (Nu 20:9 – 10). He thereby failed to set God forth in the eyes of the people as distinct and holy. Therefore, rather than focusing on Moses, the focus now ought to be on Jesus (3:1). Jesus exceeds Moses in every respect, despite the huge honor and place God gave Moses in the Old Testament.

What should be avoided at all costs is any acting or disobedience such as was evidenced by those in the wilderness, who hardened their hearts against God and his grace and were thereby refused entrance into the "rest" of God (as the writer quotes Ps 95:7 – 11; Heb 3:7 – 19). For those who have become (Gr. perfect tense, a past state that now continued to exist) partners with God on the basis of belief could be sure that what will happen in the future depended on what the believer has already become as a partner with God. Hardened hearts and rebellious spirits were and still are evidences of unbelief. However, the same gospel announced in the New Testament had been preached to those who rejected it in the wilderness (4:2, 6). That gospel message was united with the same message that had been given in Genesis 12:3 to Abraham and was explained in Galatians 3:8 as being the same one still being announced in the New Testament.

What, then, was the "rest" of God? It was what had been promised by Moses with regard to the land of Canaan, yet it remained the identical rest that was still being offered up to this very day (4:1). To be sure, part of that "rest" was physical — that is, the promised land offered to Israel in the land of Canaan (3:11) — but the other part was spiritual, which included a cessation of work, into which God himself entered after six days of creation, as well as the eternal peace and presence of God, which would last on into the eternal state. Similar to the many predictions of the future, there was both a "now" aspect and a "then" significance to the doctrine of rest.[3]

The Supremacy of the Priesthood of Jesus

There are three qualities one must have to be a high priest: (1) he is appointed and called by God (5:4); (2) he is compassionate and "able to deal gently with those who are ignorant and are going astray" (5:2); and (3) he is one with the people, for he represents the people "in matters relating to God" (5:1, 7). Jesus exhibited all three.

Jesus' experience in Gethsemane is vividly depicted in Hebrews 5:7. The fact that Jesus was divine gave him no special treatment or magical pass from the reality of the suffering he experienced. In fact, it was through his sufferings that "he learned obedience" (5:8). Nothing in this text claims, or even implies, that Jesus was in any way imperfect or deficient in any area. There is another type of perfection, however, that is the result of actually having suffered — one that is altogether different from a readiness to suffer. This perfection is one that has completely carried out the purpose for which

3. For more details on this theme and passage, see Walter C. Kaiser Jr., "The Promise Theme and the Theology of Rest," *Bibliotheca Sacra* 130 (1973): 135 – 50, and slightly revised in idem, "Experiencing the Old Testament 'Rest' of God: Hebrews 3:1 – 4:10," in *The Uses of the Old Testament in the New* (Chicago: Moody Press, 1985; reprint, Eugene, OR: Wipf and Stock, 2002), 153 – 75.

one (or something) was designed. Thus, Jesus was perfectly fitted by God to carry out the task of being the Savior of all men. The Greeks loved to connect the concept of "learned" (*emathen*) with "suffered" (*epathen*), for with them learning came from suffering (note the presence of assonance as well).

The priesthood of Jesus was not like the priesthood of Levi or the high priesthood of Aaron, for Jesus descended from the tribe of Judah and not Levi and Aaron. Instead, as far as his high priestly office was concerned, he was in the line of Melchizedek. In this way it was superior to the Aaronic priesthood, even though this teaching will not be easy for those brought up in that Levitical system God gave to Moses.

Melchizedek was a priest and a king in Salem (probably Jerusalem). In Genesis 14 he met Abraham as he was returning from the conquest of the four Mesopotamian kings who had carted off Abraham's nephew, Lot, along with the captives of the five cities of the Jordan Plain. We actually know very little about Melchizedek. For example, we do not know when he was born, when he died, or who his parents were. He had no genealogy. It is as if he had no beginning or end to his days; therefore, he seems to remain a priest forever. We only know that Abraham paid tithes to him and that Melchizedek blessed Abraham — and not the other way around, where the greater usually blesses the lesser. It is for that reason that Psalm 110:4 said of Messiah, "You are a priest forever in the order of Melchizedek."

Accordingly, four arguments champion the thesis that the ceremonial law, with its ministry from the line of Aaron, is now finished and has completed its service as intended by God. First, Jesus "remains a priest forever" (7:1 – 10, esp. vs. 3). Secondly, a change in the high priesthood signals a change in the law (7:11 – 17). If perfection had been attained under the Aaronic priesthood, there would have been no room for another line of priests. However, a change was necessary. Moreover, such a priesthood could not be on the basis of some kind of regulations about ancestry. Instead, it is "on the basis of the power of an indestructible life" (7:16). Thirdly, Jesus' investiture guarantees a better covenant (7:18 – 22), which covenant, as found in Hebrews 8 and 10, will be discussed later. Fourthly, an uninterrupted priesthood is far superior because it will never be upset by death, for he lives forever (7:23 – 28).

This priesthood of Jesus has five essential qualities: it is "holy," it is "blameless," it is "pure," it is "set apart from sinners," and it is "exalted above the heavens" (7:26). This too marks it off from what was experienced under the Aaronic line of priests.

The Supremacy of Jesus' Sacrifice to All Previous Sacrifices

Five new realities in the life and work of Jesus have replaced the former service of sacrifices under the older times of the Mosaic ceremonial law, argued the writer of Hebrews in chapter 10. These five new realities were:

1. God's law pointed to the good things that were to come in Christ (10:1 – 4). What had been given previously had an accompanying warning, that all of what the tabernacle and its service represented was made only after the "pattern" or

"copy" (*tabnît*, Ex 25:9, 40) of the real, which remained in heaven. That is why they were only a "shadow" (*skia*, Heb 10:1) of what Jesus would make real.[4]

2. Jesus gave his body as the only effective sacrifice that could accomplish the will of God (10:5 – 10). This was in accord with what the psalmist had promised in Psalm 40:6, 9. Messiah had come to do God's "will" (that "will" occurs four times, in 10:7, 9, 10, 36).
3. Jesus sat down at the right hand of God after offering the one great sacrifice for all sin for all time, and he now awaits the moment defined by the Father for the final vanquishing of all enemies (10:11 – 14). Every single priest stood to serve in the older dispensation, but our Lord sat down, for all that needed to be done was now complete. By this one sacrifice, Jesus had made perfect forever those who are in the process of being sanctified (10:14).
4. The Holy Spirit had testified in the older covenant that this new order that Jesus introduced was coming (10:15 – 18). Now the law of God will be grafted onto the hearts of men and women.
5. Jesus' stunning sacrifice calls forth the triad of faith, hope, and love (10:19 – 25). Men and women can now draw near to God with full assurance of faith and with the confidence won by Christ's blood and death on the cross. Accordingly, believers must have unflinching hope (10:23) in Christ for today and all the tomorrows. That is why believers must work to spur each other on to love and good deeds (10:24).

Christ was indeed "a merciful and faithful high priest in the service of God" (2:17). The major emphasis of Hebrews was that Jesus made one offering of himself once for all (7:27). So important was this fact of a single, final act, that Hebrews stresses it by repeating it over and over again. In 9:26, "he has appeared once for all at the end of the ages to do away with sin by the sacrifice of himself." Again in 9:28, "Christ was sacrificed once to take away the sins of many people." In 10:12, this sacrifice was for "all time one sacrifice for sins." And in 10:18, "there is no longer any sacrifice for sin."

The problem with the Levitical sacrifices was that "it is impossible for the blood of bulls and goats to take away sins" (10:4); but neither had the law of Moses promised that the sacrifices would have had that kind of efficacy. These sacrifices merely pointed to the work of Christ that would come in the future; until then, the word of God applied to the heart of a genuinely repentant sacrificer was proleptically beneficial in anticipation of Christ's death. The picture of sacrifice of the animals pointed to the need for a vicarious

4. On the basis of this distinction between heavenly realities and earthly copies, some have argued that the writer betrays an indebtedness to a Platonic cosmology. Plato argued that the perfect "idea" was in heaven and what we see on earth is merely an imperfect representation of the heavenly prototype. However, it is the Old Testament, and not Plato or Greek philosophy, that informs the writer's theology. Usually this kind of real form and copy dualism gives rise to allegorical types of interpretation, but that too is far from the purview of the writer of Hebrews.

substitute who would give up its life for the life of the one who had sinned. But the problem was these sacrifices had to be repeated over and over again, and the lives yielded up in death were the lives of animals and not that of a perfect man who was also God.

The Supremacy of a New Way in Christ to Approach God

In Hebrews 9 the writer contrasts two ways of approaching God: (1) through the sacrifices of the old tabernacle and temple, or (2) through Christ's atoning sacrifice that completed the task once for all. There were some severe limitations to the old covenant's system of worship. Even though that was the system God had devised until he provided a new order, it still was an "earthly sanctuary" and a "man-made sanctuary" (9:24). And in that sanctuary there was a "second curtain" (9:3), behind which was the room called the Holy of Holies.

The point is this: the way into the Holy of Holies was barred, closed, and cut off as long as that tabernacle or temple stood with its second curtain or veil. That divine design of the curtain was to indicate that the new way of entry into the Holy of Holies had not yet been provided — that is, not until Christ had come.

The old sacrifices, rituals, washings, and gifts were unable to make the worshiper clean in conscience or to remove guilt. It was not as if the Israelites could not be forgiven of their sins when they brought their sacrifices in faith and repentance. But those sacrifices were only tokens and signs pointing away from themselves to something better. They were not efficacious in and of themselves. But Christ, through his blood, obtained eternal redemption (9:12) of those transgressions for those who were under the covenant of Moses. Christ was offered up in order to "bear [*anenegkein*] sin" (9:28; Isa 53). This greater cleansing power was "so that [the cleansed] may serve the living God" (9:14).

All of this is fine, but this new relationship and provision of a new way of entry needed to involve the death of Christ. Why? some ask. Because no covenant is operative until death occurs. It was Leviticus 17:11 that taught that "the life is in the blood," and that it was "the blood that makes atonement." Forgiveness is not cheap; it always is a costly affair. God and mortals cannot be put "at-one" unless there is a deliverance by a substitute. This cannot be a cover-up job. In order to be *subjectively* efficacious (a sense of inward cleanness and riddance of guilt), there must be an *objective* efficaciousness (in the death of Christ). Under the old covenant, those who were forgiven experienced *subjective* efficaciousness, but that all awaited Christ's death that made it all *objectively* possible.

The Supremacy of the New Covenant to the Old Covenant

If God was the author of the old Sinaitic covenant, what was so wrong with it? Certainly the problem was not with the covenant-maker, God. What was wrong then?

The Sinai covenant had two problems: (1) the law's ceremonial aspects were only "copies," "patterns," or "shadows" of the real that was to come; and (2) the main problem was with the people, for they "broke" God's covenant (Jer 31:32; Heb 8:8).

Some have argued that it was the Lord's intent to replace the old with a new covenant, but if that were true in every respect, then why does the new covenant repeat almost three-fourths of what had been in the Abrahamic-Davidic covenants? Rather than *superseding* the covenants of promise that had preceded it, it affirmed them as well as *supplemented* them. It would be wrong to think that just because the sacrificial system had been replaced therefore the whole law, including the moral law of the Decalogue (Ex 20; Dt 5) and the Holiness Code (Lev 18 – 20), had likewise been superseded and replaced.[5]

The Supremacy of the Age to Come

Despite its emphasis on the supremacy of Christ and the salvation he provided, the writer included a future dimension to his theology. There is a "world to come" (2:5); therefore, the Christian hope kept recurring in this letter (3:6; 6:11, 18; 7:29; 10:23; 11:1). Out of the promise of God has come the certainty of a sure hope for the future. Indeed, the promise of entering God's future rest still remains open (4:3).

There is a "day approaching" (10:25) in which God will "once more ... shake not only the earth, but also the heavens" (12:26; cf. Hag 2:6). In connection with this whole complex of future events, the glorified Christ will appear once more for all at the end of the age (9:26). This "day" is certainly the "day of Yahweh" spoken of so frequently by the prophets (e.g., Amos 5:18; Isa 2:12) in God's promise-plan.

That day will also include a resurrection of the dead (6:2; 11:35), a giving account for what was and what was not done in this life (13:17), and a future judgment (6:2; 10:27, 31; 12:23). Thus, even though the "last days" have already begun (1:2), this is only the "now" aspect of the "not yet" that is to come.

The Response to So Great a Salvation

Hebrews 11 is one of the best-known chapters in the epistle to the Hebrews because of its "Hall of Faith." But these Old Testament and intertestamental men and women are not included because of some quality they exhibit. On the contrary, they are there simply because of their faith and belief. It is not only a faith that was completed in the past; it is a faith that looks more so to the future. In fact, it is through faith and steadfastness that we inherit the promises of God (6:12), otherwise we will never enter into his promised rest (4:5 – 6).

5. The argument that the whole law had been "replaced" and "superseded" is illustrated by Buist M. Fanning, "A Theology of Hebrews," in *A Biblical Theology of the New Testament*, ed. R. B. Zuck (Chicago, Moody, 1994), 198 – 403. He further says, "The point is not that the sacrificial system and the priesthood alone are set aside, while the law itself is retained. Nor is it that the cultic or ceremonial aspects of the law were abrogated. This sort of limitation is never given.... This can be seen in the parenthetical comments of 7:11, 18 – 19 and 10:8." However, we respond that it is in those very contexts that the priesthood and the sacrifices are being singled out for special mention!

Conclusion

Hebrews has made a great case for the finality and the supremacy of Jesus Christ. No thing or person even comes close to matching who he is and what he has done as One who was greater than Moses and greater than Aaron, and is the Mediator of the new covenant.

Excursus: Warnings against Defiantly Rejecting the Knowledge of the Truth

Two of the most famous, and perhaps the most feared, of all the warnings in Hebrews occur in Hebrews 6:4 – 6 and 10:26 – 31. They seem to speak of a certain impossibility of restoring some people back to Christ after they had "once been enlightened, who have tasted the heavenly gift, who have shared in the Holy Spirit ... [and who have fallen away]" (6:4 – 6). All too frequently, genuine believers with sensitive consciences have read these warnings with little or no attention to their contexts, and have concluded that either they have already, or will someday, commit this apparently irreversible, or unpardonable sin and therefore lose their salvation. But what needs to be remembered once again is the central point: there is a Great High Priest who represents mortals in the service of God (5:1 – 6:3, resumed again in 8:1).

The goal for all believers is set out in Hebrews 6:12: the goal of maturation by imitating the right person — Jesus. The maturity or perfection spoken of in Hebrews 5:14 or 6:1 does not refer to complete knowledge or perfect behavior; it looks for an achievement of a certain level of growing up in the Christian faith. Pythagoras divided his students into the "learners" (*hoi manthanontes*) and the "mature" (*hoi teleioi*). Philo used three divisions: "Beginners" (*hoi archomenoi*), "making progress" (*hoi prokoptontes*) and those "reaching maturity" (*hoi teleiomenoi*).

In a similar manner, this text urged all believers to press on to "perfection," meaning that Jewish believers in particular should leave behind the earthly sanctuary of the Sinaitic legislation, with all its lights, vestments, altars, lavers, and the like, in the worship of God. However, some were faltering; they seemed to be troubled over questions like: What about Aaron's high priesthood? What about the sacrifices offered at the temple? To these questions and others like them, the writer of Hebrews 6:9 was convinced of "better things in [their] case." However, those who were sitting on the fence, hovering between two opinions, had to be warned of the extreme seriousness of these issues.

So what about the "impossibility" (6:4) issue? What was impossible? Was it impossible for God to forgive sin? No! Was it impossible to forgive those who have never repented and did not plan ever to do so? Yes! Was it impossible to forgive one who at some point in their Christian life grew cold and worldly, but who turned back to God in repentance? No!

But those who were being described in Hebrews 6:4–9 were also once "enlightened." Was that not equal to being converted? No! For the same word is used in John 1:9 to describe everyone who comes into the world as being "enlightened." But once our eyes have seen the light, it is difficult to shut out that knowledge that we have.

Yet these persons also "tasted of the heavenly gift" and "shared in the Holy Spirit" (6:4). Does that not go a long way beyond a mere sampling of spiritual things in an introductory way? Not necessarily, for while they have understood the freeness of God's gift and have had the convicting work of the Holy Spirit operating on their lives so that they know the goodness of God and have caught a vision as to who he is, yet it is also true that they have turned back, despite all of that prevenient grace of God (a grace that gives the knowledge of sin, a knowledge of the gospel, and the convicting work of the Holy Spirit). These impossible cases are just like those who likewise heard in John 8:31–58. When they discovered what Jesus was really teaching and what he stood for, when they suddenly realized that, then they no longer followed him.

This passage, then, does not contradict what many other New Testament passages have said about the eternal security of the believer (e.g., Jn 6:37; 10:28). Neither is this case a purely hypothetical one. But if the case spoken of here is actually something that could never happen to the true believer, then why talk about it at all?

The reason we talk about it is that it can happen in a particular way or sense. Recall Acts 8:13, where Simon Magus is said to have believed and been baptized, yet Peter severely rebuked him by saying, "Your heart is not right before God ... you are full of bitterness and captive to sin" (Acts 8:21–23). Simon Magus was in real trouble, for he seemed to have had a fake conversion. There is the parallel to our case.

Consequently, the writer of Hebrews is saying, "It is hard to get those who have been exposed far enough in the faith and who know what it is all about to change their minds to accept Christ after they have *repeatedly* rejected the prompting of the Spirit of God" (my paraphrase). They have had a real knowledge of sin, a good understanding of what the gospel is, and the convicting work of the Holy Spirit, yet they have so often turned their backs on all of it that no longer does it seem like a real option for them to believe. In fact, the writer follows up his description of this tragic situation with an illustration in 6:7 – 8. Some soils and ground, for example, are refreshed and moistened by a rain so that they produce an excellent crop. Other ground only produces thorns and weeds when it is given the advantage of the same rain. Would the solution, then, be to send more rain? Hardly. Therefore, so it is once a person's eyes have been really opened and then they have turned back and rejected all that was shown to them. So what will it be? Will we go on to maturity or will we turn back to our own folly?

The identical issue reappeared in Hebrews 10:26 – 31. Once again, there was the case of the person who "deliberately [kept] on sinning after [he had] received the knowledge of the truth" (10:26). This could not be a person who had previously believed, for a Christian does not make it a habit or a practice to constantly sin (1Jn 3:6 – 10). True believers do sin, but they do not, and cannot, *persist* in it; they must confess their sin and ask for God's help.

So what is left for those who turn their backs on the knowledge of the truth? Just "a fearful expectation of judgment and of raging fire that will consume the enemies of God" (10:27). "No sacrifice for sin is left" (10:26) either. What these God-rejecting persons are doing is "trampl[ing] the Son of God underfoot" and "treat[ing] as an unholy thing the blood of the covenant that sanctified them," in addition to "insult[ing] the Spirit of grace" (10:29). What they have done is similar to what the Old Testament calls "sinning with a high hand" (Nu 15:30 – 31; Dt 17:12). It is a sin that takes God on with an audacity that cannot be imagined when one considers who God is. Everything of who God is in his person, his office, his authority, and his offer of free grace is thrown back in the face of God. Such demeaning and detracting from the blood of Christ is dangerous in the extreme. "Insult[ing]" (*enybrisas*) the Holy Spirit of God by contemptuously describing the truth and veracity of the Holy Spirit's testimony to Jesus is another indication of how serious things have gotten for these persons. These individuals are worthy indeed of the eternal punishment measured out to them, especially when one compares how rejection of the law of Moses called for temporal punishment.

These two passages (as supplemented by similar warnings in 2:1 – 4; 3:6 – 4:13; and 12:12 – 29) are some of the most impressive warnings in the whole Bible. Yet the solution is not to focus on the negative consequences that will come to those who apostatize, but it is rather to hold firm with confidence in God to the calling each has in Christ Jesus our Lord. We need to be faithful and to run the race of life with endurance (10:36; 12:1 – 3) with eyes fixed, not on the circumstances or on ourselves, but on "Jesus, the author and perfecter of our faith" (12:2).

Chapter 20

The Promise-Plan and the Gospel of the Kingdom

The Gospel of John; 1, 2, 3 John; Revelation (About AD 85 – 95)

John, the disciple who "testifie[d] to these things and who wrote them down" (Jn 21:24), designated himself as "the disciple whom Jesus loved" in John 21:20 and in four other texts (Jn 13:23; 19:26; 20:2; 21:7). Indeed, he was that disciple who reclined next to Jesus (13:23). This had to be either Peter, James, or John; yet it could not have been Peter since John 21:20 said that Peter looked back and saw the one "Jesus loved." It could not have been James either, since he was martyred too early to be the writer of the gospel or of the three epistles and the book of Revelation, which came much later than his death (Ac 12:1 – 2) in AD 62.

John may have been a disciple of John the Baptist (Jn 1:35) at first. It is not known how long he was with this preacher out in the wilderness by the Jordan River, but when Jesus returned to the Jordan after his temptation, John met Jesus, apparently for the first time. John recalled this event years later, even the very hour it took place, for he said it was about four o'clock in the afternoon (1:36 – 40) when he heard the Baptist say, "Look, the Lamb of God!" (1:36) when he was introduced to Jesus.

John came from Galilee, possibly from the city of Bethsaida. His father, Zebedee, was a fisherman by trade, but perhaps he was a man of some means (Mk 1:20). John's mother was Salome (cf. Mt 27:56 with Mk 15:40; 16:1). After meeting Jesus, John accompanied him the next day as he went to Galilee, where he was present at the marriage ceremony at Cana (Jn 2:1 – 11). John may have gone home for a time to help out with the fishing business, but when John the Baptist was imprisoned, this seemed to have signaled that it was time for Jesus to give a call for his disciples to enter full-time into the work. Thus it was that Jesus appeared at the lakeside to call John, and so began a long involvement in the ministry of the gospel (Mt 4:18 – 22; Mk 1:16 – 20; Lk 5:1 – 11) from that day, in around AD 27, until about the middle of the 90s.

The Gospel of John

The Purpose of John's Gospel

The theological emphasis of all five of John's books was supremely about Jesus. The best way to show this is to note, with Leon Morris, that John's gospel used the name "Jesus" 237 times, while Matthew, with the next highest frequency of use in the New Testament, had only 150; Luke had 89; and Mark, 81. In all of the Pauline correspondence, Paul used "Jesus" only 213 times, with the book of Romans having the most, 37 references to Jesus' name.[1] John's passion, then, was to tell the world about Jesus.

John made his purpose explicit in John 20:31: "But these are written that you may believe that Jesus is the Christ, the Son of God, and that by believing you may have life in his name." Thus, John wrote with a strong evangelistic purpose. Jesus was indeed the Son of God, the promised Messiah that the Law and the Prophets had foretold.

In the first half of his narrative (1:19 – 12:50), he set forth a strong case for Jesus' messiahship by means of seven selected "signs" or miracles that Jesus performed. They were:

1. Changing water into wine — 2:1 – 11
2. Healing a man's son — 4:46 – 54
3. Healing a lame man — 5:1 – 9
4. Multiplying the bread and fish — 6:1 – 15
5. Walking on water — 6:16 – 21
6. Healing a blind man — 9:1 – 7
7. Raising Lazarus from the dead — 11:38 – 44

Along with these signs, John included seven "I am" sayings of Jesus, most of which went along with the narrative that described the seven sign miracles:

1. I am the bread of life — 6:35, 41, 48, 51
2. I am the light of the world — 8:12; 9:15
3. I am the door for the sheep — 10:7, 9
4. I am the good shepherd — 10:11, 14
5. I am the resurrection and the life — 11:25
6. I am the way, the truth, and the life — 14:6
7. I am the true vine — 15:1, 5

The second half of the gospel (13:1 – 20:31) began with Jesus' Farewell Discourse to his disciples in the upper room (Jn 13 – 17). Here the Master Teacher prepared his men for continuing ministry in the church. This discourse was followed by the Passion Narrative in 18 – 19, where our Lord's death was presented as the atonement for sin. This,

1. Leon Morris, "The Gospel of John, the Doctrine of Christ," in *New Testament Theology* (Grand Rapids: Zondervan, 1986), 225.

in turn, was followed by Jesus' resurrection appearances in chapter 20, concluding with an epilogue in 21:1 – 25.

Jesus Is the Word (Logos)

Four times in John's prologue (1:1 – 18), he calls Jesus the "Word" (1:1 [3x], 14). The *logos* was a familiar philosophical concept for most educated people of that day, but John's gospel was not a philosophical treatise by any stretch of the imagination. While the Jewish culture did not share exactly the same concept as was found in Hellenistic culture, it did have the concept of creation of the world by the spoken "word" (*dabar*) of God (Ge 1 and Ps 33:6, 9). That word also functioned almost on its own in that repeated formula found so frequently not only in creation but in the formula of the call of the prophets, such as "the word of the LORD came ..." (Hos 1:1; Jer 1:2, 4; Eze 1:3).

There also was what amounted to almost a personification of the "wisdom" in Proverbs 8:22 – 30 and of the "law" in Isaiah 2:3 and Micah 4:2, which approximated the way *logos* functioned. Another practice within the Jewish community had a bearing on this subject as well. The name of God was usually not pronounced as one read from the Tanak (Old Testament). Instead of reading aloud the name of "Yahweh," they would substitute "Adonai," "Lord," or at other times the reader would just say "the Word" (Aramaic *memra*).[2] This was done to avoid taking God's name in vain (the third commandment of the Decalogue).

John placed the "Word" (*logos*) "in the beginning," when the Word was "with God" and the Word "was God" (1:1). Ten times over, the creation narrative of Genesis 1 repeated, "And God said...." This affirmed the full deity of the Son, yet it showed there was a relationship between the two persons, that is, between God and the Word, which two were not to be confused or thought to be interchangeable, for God the Father was God, just as Jesus was God too.

It was also through that spoken word that God created the world, for without him nothing was made that now appears. The second person of the Trinity, Jesus, was present at creation as the agent of that work as well.

But the Word also bore a relationship to humanity, for John 1:14 declared that "The Word became flesh and made his dwelling among us." In Jesus' humiliation, he took on human form in his incarnation.

Jesus Is the Christ, the Messiah

John is the only one of the four gospel writers who actually used the Aramaic/Hebrew word for Messiah (*messias*, 1:41; 4:25), simultaneously giving its Greek translation as

2. See M. McNamara, "The Logos of the Fourth Gospel and *Memra* of the Palestinian Targum, Ex. 12:42," *Expository Times* 79 (1967 – 68): 115 – 17.

Christos. But his argument that Jesus fulfills the promise of the coming Seed of the woman and the seed of Abraham, Isaac, Jacob, and David is continuous.

The whole point of John's writing was to demonstrate that Jesus was the Christ/ Messiah (20:31). That is why this theme ran through his whole gospel, but especially the first half. It began with John the Baptist denying that he was "the Christ" (1:20), but declaring that the one everyone was asking about, the Messiah, was already in their midst (1:26). That set the stage for Philip, who told Nathanael, "We have found the one Moses wrote about in the Law, and about whom the prophets also wrote — Jesus of Nazareth, the son of Joseph" (1:45). Jesus was the one the Old Testament was pointing to in its predictions and promises. When Jesus told Nathanael that he saw him under the fig tree even before Philip invited him to come see Jesus, Nathanael concluded, "Rabbi, you [an emphatic pronoun] are the Son of God; you [again, in the emphatic position] are the King of Israel" (1:49). Nathanael certainly was a fast learner!

In the second chapter of John, Jesus cleared out the temple and drove the traders outside. This action must have brought to mind Psalm 69:9, "Zeal for [God's] house consumes me [i.e., the Messiah]," as well as Malachi 3:1, "Then suddenly the Lord you are seeking will come to his temple; the messenger of the covenant, whom you desire." That "messenger" was none other than the expected Messiah.

After talking with Nicodemus (John 3), Jesus returned to the countryside where John the Baptist was. The Baptist repeated again, "I am not the Christ but am sent ahead of him" (3:28). Jesus was the expected Bridegroom (3:29); the Baptist was only his best man. But there was no question in the Baptist's mind that Jesus was the Messiah.

The case for Jesus as the Messiah continued into John 4 with the woman at the well, who confessed, "'I know that Messiah' (called Christ) 'is coming. When he comes, he will explain everything to us'" (4:25). John recorded Jesus as saying to this, "I, who speak to you — am he," that is, the long-awaited Messiah of the Old Testament promises (4:26). After Jesus surprised her by revealing that she had had five husbands and was now living with someone who was not her husband, she left the well and her water jug and hurried back to tell the townsfolk, "Come, see a man who told me everything I ever did. Could this be the Christ?" (4:29). John wanted that question to linger in the mind of his readers, for that was the central question of his gospel.

After Jesus healed the man at the pool of Bethesda (John 5), he responded to those who violently rejected his claim to be equal with God: "If you believed Moses, you would believe me, for he wrote about me" (5:46). In the same way, John used the feeding of the five thousand to make the point that just as God had sent manna down from heaven to feed the Israelites in the wilderness for forty years, so Jesus was "the bread of God" that "comes down from heaven and gives life to the world" (6:33).

At the Feast of Tabernacles in John 7, it was widely rumored that perhaps the Jewish authorities had come to the conclusion that Jesus indeed must have been the Christ (7:26), for he was speaking publicly with no arrest in sight. The rulers of that day thought they knew where Jesus came from (Nazareth), but even in this they had not done their homework, for he had been born in Bethlehem, where it had been predicted that the Messiah would be born (7:41 – 42).

When Jesus proclaimed that he was the "light of the world" (8:12) — since the rabbis had taught that "Light is the name of the Messiah"[3] — Jesus was giving another proof that he was the Messiah. But by now the authorities had had enough of such claims. When Jesus healed the man born blind (John 9), and the authorities interrogated the man's parents, the parents refused to say what was already so obvious: this was something only the Messiah could do. Instead, they spoke out of fear, claiming they had no idea how their son suddenly was able to see. "The Jews had decided that anyone who acknowledged Jesus was the Christ would be put out of the synagogue" (9:22). Nevertheless, the rulers persisted in their attempts to trap Jesus publicly.

Once again, at the Feast of Dedication (John 10), the Jewish leaders pretended to be earnest inquirers: "How long will you keep us in suspense? If you are the Christ, tell us plainly" (10:24). But Jesus retorted, "I did tell you, but you do not believe" (10:25).

John gathers other witnesses, such as Martha, to testify about Jesus the Messiah. As Jesus was dining with Mary, Martha, and Lazarus, after Lazarus had been raised from the dead, Martha, who usually worried more about all the meal preparations, instead this time boldly announced, "Yes, Lord, I believe [Greek perfect tense, indicating an action that began in the past but continued to remain settled] that you are the Christ, the Son of God, who was come into the world" (11:27). John used her confession in his epistle, for it matched his purpose statement in 20:31 very closely.[4]

As Jesus began to prepare the crowds for his imminent death, the crowd protested with a confused question: "We have heard from the Law that the Christ will remain forever, so how can you say, 'The Son of Man must be lifted up?' " (12:34). This proved, once again, that a little theology can be a dangerous thing. God is immortal, which is correct, of course. But there were some within Judaism who understood that the Messiah must also first die.[5] And that is what the prophets had taught as well (Isa 53:1; 1Pe 1:10 – 12).

By now the point is clear: in every chapter in which John portrayed Jesus' public ministry, the disciple repeated over and over again that Jesus was indeed the Messiah. Moreover, in John's epistles, when there was open denial that Jesus was the Messiah, John once again set forth the case to counter their arguments (1Jn 2:22; 4:3; 2Jn 7). In another three cases in the book of Revelation, the name Jesus was combined with Christ to make the same point (Rev 1:1, 2, 5). It must also be noted that in close relation with the term Messiah was another title, "King of Israel" (Jn 1:49; 12:13). The Messiah was the anticipated heir to the throne of David and the Sovereign over all.

3. Cited by Morris, "Gospel of John," 230 n. 13, from John B. Lightfoot, *A Commentary on the New Testament from the Talmud and Hebraica* (Grand Rapids: Zondervan, 1979), 330.

4. Morris, "Gospel of John," 231.

5. Ibid., 232. Morris cites *1 Enoch* 49:1; 62:14.

Jesus Is the Son of Man and the Son of God

The Synoptic Gospels use the title "Son of Man" more prominently than does John; however, this title does appear in John 1:51; 3:13 – 14; 5:27; 6:27, 53, 62; 8:28; 12:23, 34; 13:31. The source of this title was Daniel 7:13, where the Son of Man "came with the clouds of heaven" (thereby pointing to the fact that his origin was from heaven). Yet Jesus was fully human, especially as signaled by his incarnation. The title "Son of Man" was used exclusively by our Lord and was never used by his disciples or those around him.

The Son of Man sayings of Jesus can be placed into three separate groups of texts: (1) of the Son of Man ministering on earth, (2) of the Son of Man in his humiliation and death on the cross, and (3) the Son of Man coming in power and great glory.[6]

John is distinctive in emphasizing Jesus as the Son of God throughout his *whole ministry*, beginning even with the confession of John the Baptist (Jn 1:34, 49). While the Synoptic Gospels seem to wait until the disciples grasp this truth sometime near the middle of Jesus' ministry (see, e.g., Mk 8:29), John links Jesus' messiahship with the fact that he is also the Son of God in his purpose statement (20:31) and tracks it from the very beginning of his work.

To strengthen this claim, John used the Greek word *monogenēs*, rendered "only-begotten" in the King James, with the meaning, his "unique" son. The stem of this Greek noun does not come from the verb "to beget" (*gennaō*), but from the verb "to become, to happen" (*ginomai*). Jesus had a unique relationship to the Father that was distinctive and unmatched by anyone else. Jesus is called "uniquely God," who is in the bosom of the Father: he has made him known" (1:18).[7] God the Father sent his "unique Son" into the world to provide salvation for all (3:16). Those who do not believe "in the name of God's one and only/unique Son" (3:18), stand condemned and will not see life eternal.

Though all who believe may become "children of God" or even "sons of God," John wanted to show that Jesus is the only one in his class, unique in every respect.

Jesus Is the Lamb of God

John the Baptist twice refers to Jesus as "The Lamb of God" in John's gospel (1:29 and 36). Later, in the book of Revelation, John will use the "lamb" concept a total of twenty-seven times.[8]

The Greek word for "lamb" in John's gospel is *amnos*, which is the word the Greek Septuagint used to translate Isaiah 53:7. In John 1:29, the apostle followed the title by saying, "who takes away the sin of the world." Thus the metaphor of the "Lamb of God" carried a redemptive message with it, even an allusion to the Passover lamb. It was

6. George E. Ladd, *A Theology of the New Testament* (Grand Rapids: Eerdmans, 1974), 244 – 45.

7. Many early and excellent Greek manuscripts read *monogenes theos* rather than *monogenēs hyios*, but the probability lies with the former and not the latter reading.

8. Revelation 5:6, 8, 12 – 13; 6:1, 16; 7:9 – 10, 14, 17; 12:11; 13:8; 14:1, 4, 10; 15:3; 17:14; 19:7, 9; 21:9, 14, 22 – 23, 27; 22:1, 3.

no coincidence that the bones of the Passover lamb were not to be broken (Ex 12:22) just as not a bone in Jesus' body was broken, which John saw as another fulfillment of prophecy (Jn 19:36).

In the Apocalypse, however, a different Greek word for "lamb," *arnion*, was used. There existed in Jewish apocalyptic literature the symbol of a conquering lamb who would take on the evil of this world.[9] But the lamb in Revelation already had been offered up and now is "standing in the center of the throne" (Rev 5:6). The sacrifice by the Son had been completed, and the lamb stands triumphant though still carrying the marks in his body bearing witness to the fact that he had been slain but now is alive again (5:6).

The Witness of and to Jesus

Another term in John's distinctive vocabulary is the word "witness" (*martyria*), which occurs nineteen times as a noun (whereas it appears in Mark only three times, in Luke once, and not at all in Matthew), and thirty-three times as a verb (while Matthew and Luke use it only once, and Mark not at all).[10] Especially in the first part of the gospel, the concept of witness or witnessing is never far from his thinking.

It is the person and claims of Christ that are the center of this witness. Especially significant is the witness of the Father (5:31), though Christ could witness to himself and that witness would be valid (8:14). The reason Christ said that if he witnessed to himself it would not be valid (5:31) was because of a Jewish law that invalidated one's testimony to one's self.[11] Perhaps the basis for this tradition was Deuteronomy 19:15, where two or more witnesses were needed to establish a point in court cases. However, Jesus, being the Son of God, could testify on his own behalf and that testimony would be true. In John 8:14 Jesus lays claim to having full knowledge of everything past, present, and future. Also, the Holy Spirit bore witness to the Son (Jn 15:26; 1Jn 5:6).

The first to bear witness to Jesus among mortals was John the Baptist, who "came as a witness" (Jn 1:7) and "came only as a witness to the light" (1:8), which of course was Jesus. Indeed, this was John's "testimony" (1:19): he clearly affirmed that he himself was not the Christ (1:20), but he was merely the voice proclaiming that there was one greater than he who would succeed him immediately. Likewise, the disciples were called upon as witnesses for Christ, for they had been with the Lord from the beginning (15:27). The evangelist himself, writer of this gospel, bore his testimony to Christ "so that you also may believe" (18:35). His testimony is true (21:24).

As has been argued all along in this biblical theology, the Old Testament Scriptures bear witness to Jesus as well (5:39, 40). There was nothing haphazard about the person,

9. See W. Hal Harris, "A Theology of John's Writings," in *A Biblical Theology of the New Testament*, ed. R. B. Zuck (Chicago: Moody, 1994), 193, for the Jewish sources.

10. Morris, "Gospel of John," 238.

11. Ibid., 240 n. 17: "The rabbis said things like, 'None may be believed when he testifies of himself.... None may testify of himself' " (*Mishnah*, Ketub. 2:9).

works, and happenings in the life of Christ, for it all happened according to God's eternal plan.

Finally, even Jesus' works testified as to who he was and where he came from (10:35; 14:11). The witness that converged on Jesus as the promised Messiah came from every avenue that it possibly could to lead the readers of John's five books to the truth.

God the Holy Spirit

The evangelist begins his teaching on the Holy Spirit in his gospel with the descent of the Spirit on Jesus at the baptism of John the Baptist (1:32 – 34). This was the predicted "sign" that the Baptist was looking for as the Spirit came and "remain[ed]" on Jesus (1:33). But it was in Jesus' interview with Nicodemus in John 3 that we saw the argument for the regenerating power of the Holy Spirit. Jesus led Nicodemus directly into the key issue: "No one can see the kingdom of God," Jesus reminded him, "unless he is born again" (3:3). This confused Nicodemus, for what did being "born again" mean? Jesus further explained that it meant being "born of water and the Spirit" (3:5). He was alluding to the Old Testament passage in Ezekiel 36:25 – 27. Water referred to the cleansing from all impurities and the Spirit referred to the internal work of God's Holy Spirit.

Nicodemus was stymied. He had never heard of such things, to which Jesus remarked, "You are Israel's teacher, and do you not understand these things?" (3:10). Jesus must have wondered where Nicodemus had gone to yeshiva and why they had not instructed him better in the Word of God. Nicodemus should have known that the new birth came about, even in the Old Testament, by the regenerating work of the Holy Spirit and by the new birth.

It was the Father who gave the Son the Spirit so that he might confer it on those whom he wished (3:34). That may have been exactly what was fulfilled when, in John 20:22 – 23, Jesus "breathed on [his disciples] and said, 'Receive the Holy Spirit.'" The disciples had bestowed on them the same power of the Holy Spirit that Jesus had received as he was baptized by John the Baptist. Since most do not think there were two separate gifts of the Spirit, and since the Spirit did not come, according to many, until Pentecost, Jesus must have been acting out a promissory parable that anticipated the actual later coming of the Holy Spirit *in state* and *in a visible way* at Pentecost. However, what took place at Jesus' baptism was indeed separate from what happened on the day of Pentecost.

John 7:39 is even more difficult to understand in light of the Holy Spirit's presence and work in the Old Testament, for "up to that time the Spirit had not yet been given, since Jesus had not yet been glorified," yet the disciples had already begun their ministries and they were not waiting until Pentecost to begin their witness. Jesus had announced on the last day of the Feast of Tabernacles, "If anyone is thirsty, let him come to me and drink. Whoever believes in me, as the Scripture has said, streams of living water will flow from within him" (7:37 – 38). The living water, most agree, is the

Holy Spirit, but who or what is the source of this water? Most prefer to say the source is Christ, as John 4:14; 6:35; and Revelation 22:17 depict it.

The Greek literally reads in John 7:39, "It was not yet Spirit." The word "given," which is usually supplied here, is not present in the Greek text. However, persons like Elizabeth and Zechariah had already been described in Luke 1:41, 67 as being "filled with the Holy Spirit." Also, when Jesus sent out the Twelve, he assured them: "It will not be you speaking, but the Spirit of your Father speaking through you" (Mt 10:20; cf. Lk 11:13; 12:12). Therefore, John was apparently saying the manifestations of the times of the Holy Spirit had not yet been seen in some special way, nor would they be, until Jesus went to be with the Father.

In John 14:16, Jesus promised that he would send "another counselor" (*allon paraklēton*), who was the Holy Spirit. The Greek word *paraklētos*, transliterated as "Paraclete," is most difficult to translate. Many English translations prefer to say "Comforter," but he also is a "Defender," a "Helper," and a "Mediator," the latter idea paralleling the Hebrew term *mēlîṣ* in Job 33:23, which was used of the coming Messiah. Certainly, it had the idea of advocacy and instruction combined in this name of the Paraclete.

Some of the most significant teaching on the person of the Holy Spirit is found in Jesus' teaching in the upper room at Jesus' Farewell Discourse (Jn 13:31 – 16:33). John marks the upper room discourse with a sevenfold repetition of phrases similar to "All this I have spoken while I was with you":

1. "All this I have spoken while I was with you" (14:25)
2. "I have told you this, so that my joy may be in you, and that your joy may be complete" (15:11)
3. "All this I have told you, so that you will not go astray" (16:1)
4. "I have told you this, so that when the time comes you will remember that I warned you" (16:4)
5. "Because I have said these things, you are filled with grief" (16:6)
6. "Though I have been speaking figuratively, a time is coming when I will no longer use this kind of language" (16:25)
7. "I have told you these things so that in me you may have peace" (16:33)

In this farewell address, Jesus promised his disciples that he would send more revelation of himself by the Holy Spirit. They could expect what we now call the New Testament to be delivered to them by the ministry of the Spirit. For example, in John 14:25 – 27, the Holy Spirit would bring to the writers of the New Testament "everything I have said to you [disciples]" (14:26). This, in part, is the answer to the Synoptic Problem of how four gospel writers could have replicated what Jesus did and said so many years prior to their writing it down.

Again, in John 15:26 – 27, the Holy Spirit would come from the Father to testify about Jesus. These disciples had to bear witness to him, for they had "been with [him] from the beginning" (15:27). Here is a great clue that Jesus is not talking about all believers, for we have not been with him from the beginning. But since the Spirit was called the "Spirit of truth," (15:26), therefore his witness in giving this new section of the Bible could be trusted.

Finally, in John 16:12 – 15, Jesus summarized his whole discourse by saying he had much more to say and to teach these twelve disciples, but it would be more than they could bear at that time (16:12). But the Spirit, who again is announced as the "Spirit of truth," would guide them into all truth. He would not speak on his own, but he would say only what he has heard. Part of that teaching would be about "what is yet to come" (16:13), that is, matters of eschatology. Jesus said, "The Spirit will take from what is mine and make it known to you" (16:15). This was no doubt the theology about the doctrine of God.

The point is that much of this upper room discourse was aimed at those disciples who would be called by God to add to the Old Testament the new Scriptures.[12] The promise to lead into all truth was not addressed to the whole body of Christ at this time, but it was to speak of the distinctive work of writing the New Testament canon of Scripture that our Lord was commissioning his disciples to carry out. To be sure, there is a similar but not identical promise in 1 John 2:20 – 21: "But you have an anointing from the Holy One, and all of you know the truth. I do not write to you because you do not know the truth, but because you do know it and because no lie comes from the truth."[13]

The most interesting text in this regard is found in John 14:17, "The world cannot accept [the Spirit of truth] for it neither sees him nor knows him. But you know him, for he lives with [*para*] you and will be [or *and is*] in you." Some very good early manuscripts read the present tense, "*is* in you," rather than "*will* be in you." The two Greek forms of *estai* and *estin* are very easily confused. But B. F. Westcott correctly observed that "the present tense appears to be less like a correction."[14] Furthermore, John 14:17 had already said that the Holy Spirit was "with" the Old Testament believer, thus the present tense made more sense in that context.

What then was so new about the Holy Spirit? As George Smeaton so wisely observed, Pentecost was necessary, for the Holy Spirit "must have a coming in state, in a solemn and visible manner, accompanied with visible effects as well as Christ had [at Calvary] and whereof all the Jews should be, and were, witnesses."[15]

---

12. Some will object to portions of the upper room discourse being directed solely (or mainly) to the disciples who would later write portions of the New Testament. The argument many use to back up the fact that the discourse was for all believers is to say, "Then the Great Commission was only addressed to the disciples as well!" However, that argument will not support this thesis either, for the Great Commission does go on to say, "And surely I am with you always, even to the very end of the age" (Mt 28:20), which if it is addressed only to the disciples would make them extremely old today!

13. See further discussion on these matters in Walter C. Kaiser, "What Was the OT Believer's Experience of the Holy Spirit?" in *Toward Rediscovering the Old Testament* (Grand Rapids: Zondervan, 1987), 135 – 41. Idem, "The Baptism in the Holy Spirit as the Promise of the Father: A Reformed Perspective," in *Perspectives on Spirit Baptism: Five Views*, ed. Chad Owen Brand (Nashville: Broadman and Holman, 2004), 15 – 46.

14. B. F. Westcott, *The Gospel According to St. John* (1881; reprint, Grand Rapids: Eerdmans, 1967), 206.

15. George Smeaton, *The Doctrine of the Holy Spirit*, 2nd ed. (Edinburgh: T & T Clark, 1889), 49.

1, 2, 3 John: Love for the Brethren

The epistles of John carry the same basic themes and message found in John's gospel, though with some distinctives. So aphoristic are many of John's thoughts in these letters that they resist most of the usual suggested structures.

First John has an introduction in 1:1 – 4 and a summary in 5:13 – 21. In between these two bookends lies the main body, which features an ethical theme, "God is light; in him there is no darkness at all" (1:5), and a christological theme, "Who is the liar? It is the man who denies that Jesus is the Christ" (2:22). Jesus is that Man of promise who has existed from the very beginning.

The Test for Fellowship: Faith in Jesus

The "last hour" had arrived (2:18), and many antichrists had already come as harbingers of the final Antichrist who was yet to come (2:18 – 19). All falsehood culminated in the denial of the messiahship of Jesus (2:18 – 28). But those who believe are to hold steadily what they have been told from the beginning. Those who do so will not be ashamed when Jesus comes again (2:28).

Loving the Brethren Is a Sign We Love God

The major evidence of righteousness is love for the brethren (2:29 – 3:24). Already believers are the "children of God" (an alternate designation for the "people of God" used elsewhere in the promise-plan), but what they will become has not yet appeared (3:2). First John 3:2 is one of the best texts to show what is meant by "inaugurated eschatology": "*Now* we are the children of God, and what we will be has *not yet* been made known" (emphasis mine). Even though part of the single prediction of the future already has an immediate fulfillment, often with a multiple number of fulfillments in the future, the "now" and the "not yet" are bonded together as one in the total work of God. I have repeatedly pointed to this same phenomenon earlier in the promise-plan, especially in the prophets' concept of the "day of the Lord."

Hatred by the world should not surprise God's children (3:13 – 18), for that is how some naturally react in the presence of good. But it is the example of Christ that teaches us what love really is and how we should manifest it to others.

Handling False Teachers

Instead of directly confronting those who were teaching falsehood, John chose the route of exhorting and encouraging. However, we do get small glimpses of who these problem persons might have been. In 1 John 2:19, there were those who seceded from the believing group. Chances are that these were Judaizers. Perhaps this is why John insisted on the confession that Jesus is the Messiah (2:22; cf. 4:2; 5:6), indeed, the Man of promise.

While there is no clear or sustained evidence of a fully developed gnosticism this early in the first century, there may be hints of it, such as the reference to *sperma autou*, "his [God's] seed" in 3:9. Some think that is a side reference to the system soon to be made popular by Basilides, a Gnostic who taught during the reign of Emperor Hadrian (AD 117 – 38). John stressed that "God is light" (1:5), which may again be an allusion to the emerging gnostic claim that the *pneymatikon*, "spiritual" insights, are superior to any obligations to the law of God.

Docetism does not appear to be far in the background either, for the docetists tried to subvert the reality of the incarnation. They wanted to say that Jesus only "appeared," or "seemed" to be "the Word made flesh," but he never was human at all. But again, no real traces of docetism are clearly found in the text.

The first epistle of John concludes with a strong ethical chapter (4) and a strong christological chapter (5). The epistle ends with the question: How can we know that we have eternal life? (5:13 – 17). Verses 18 – 21 end with a triple "We know": (1) that "anyone born of God does not continue to sin"; (2) that "we are the children of God and that the whole world is under the control of the evil one"; and (3) that "the Son of God has come and has given us understanding, so that we may know him who is true."

The other two epistles, 2 and 3 John, are very brief, but their similarity of style, vocabulary, ideas, and general structure leave few questions, if any, in our minds that the writer and source of these letters is the same as the writer of 1 John and the gospel of John.

The purpose of the second letter is to give advice to a young church or a family about how and to whom this group should give hospitality to those allegedly from other churches. There are two tests that are to be administered: (1) Do these new folk walk in love? and (2) Do they confess that Jesus came in the flesh and was fully human?

The contents of the third letter of John also deal with this question of offering hospitality to traveling missionaries and teachers. It is affirmed that offering hospitality is a Christian virtue. However, the writer warns, be careful of Diotrephes, "who loves to come first" and who "will have nothing to do with us" (v. 9). His malicious gossip about John and others must be stopped.

Revelation: The Apocalypse of John

The writer of Revelation described himself as God's "servant, John" (Rev 1:1). When he wrote this book, he was on the island of Patmos (1:9), which is a small island some sixty miles southwest of the city of Ephesus in the Aegean Sea. John associated himself with seven churches in the Roman province of Asia Minor (present-day southwest Turkey).

There is a strong unity to this book, even though it is saturated with almost four hundred allusions to the Old Testament — especially to Daniel, Ezekiel, Isaiah, Jeremiah, and Joel — at the rate of some twenty allusions per chapter and almost one allusion in each verse. While this book shares many of the features of apocalyptic material, and while he actually calls this book the "Revelation [*apokalypsis*] of Jesus Christ" (1:1), John himself labeled his book as a prophecy several times (1:3; 22:7, 10). Thus, John used the apocalyptic format to give to us "the word of God" (1:2) as a prophecy.

The Purpose of Revelation

The central theme of this book is Christ crucified, risen, and ascended into glory (1:1; 1:17 – 18; 5:6, 12 – 13). The whole substance of John's prophecy is the "testimony of Jesus," which "is the spirit of prophecy" (19:10; cf. 1:1 – 3). The age to come is imminent, and those who will inherit it are the true worshipers of God and the Lamb of God, Jesus Christ (1:5 – 8; 7:9 – 17).

Jesus Is Lord Over All

For those who were tired of being pushed around by the Romans and who may have been in danger of being disillusioned as believers, John wants to assure them that what they see happening is only part of the picture. God has a purpose that he is working out in history, which will result in the reign of God over every principality and prince in the world.

Jesus is the "firstborn from the dead and the ruler of the kings of the earth" (1:5). The vision of him (1:12 – 18) sets the stage for understanding the whole book, for it is not just about events present and future; Christ dominates the whole book. In fact, the throne scene in chapters 4 – 5 must be referred to over and over again as the book is read and as one asks the questions about where is history going. Jesus is "the first and the last." He is "the Living One," who was dead but is alive forever. And he holds "the keys of death and Hades" (1:17 – 18). He is "the Son of David" (2:18), the one "who holds the key of David" (3:7), the "ruler of God's creation" (3:14), "the Lion of the tribe of Judah, the root of David" (5:5), and "the Lamb, looking as if it had been slain" (5:6). Almost all of these royal and conquering themes resonate with the presentation of the Messiah and the promise-plan, especially in the Prophets.

The Triumph of the Kingdom of God

God is sovereign over all other powers and dominions. In the end, "the kingdom of the world has become the kingdom of our Lord and of his Christ, and he will reign for ever and ever" (11:15). The forces and powers he will defeat come in many shapes, but each will be vanquished: "The great dragon was hurled down — that ancient serpent called the devil or Satan, who leads the whole world astray" (12:9). Included in God's final cleanup are the beast that came out of the sea and his sidekick, who came out of the earth (13:1, 11), the unclean spirits (16:13; 18:2), demons (9:20; 18:2), spirits of demons

(16:14), and the devil's angels (12:9) along with that "great harlot" (17:1) and "Babylon the great" (17:5; 18:2). Evil may be strong, but God is stronger, and he will finally triumph gloriously.

Worship in Revelation

The verb to "worship" (*proskyneō*) is used twenty-four times in this book out of a total fifty-nine in the complete New Testament. While most of the worship is in heaven (e.g., 4:10; 7:11), this is a model for those on earth. False worship, of course, should be avoided, for evil deities are also worshiped in this book (13:4; 14:11). Worship must be given, not to an angel, but to God alone (19:10; 22:8 – 9). Worship is also prescribed for the first day of the week, Sunday (Rev 1:10).

John is one of the most graphic writers of the Bible. But he is also one who cannot stress enough the need to confess and believe that Jesus has appeared in the flesh and that he is the Son of God as well as the Son of Man.

Excursus A: Is Satan Bound *Before* or *After* the Second Coming of Christ?

Revelation 20:1 – 3 describes how an angel came down from heaven with a key to the abyss and a great chain. "He seized the dragon, that ancient serpent, who is the devil, or Satan, and bound him [*edesēn*] for a thousand years" (20:2). He was then thrown "into the Abyss, and locked and sealed it over him, to keep him from deceiving the nations anymore until the thousand years were ended. After that, he must be set free for a short time" (20:3).

It is agreed by most interpreters that the second coming of Christ has already been introduced in Revelation 19:11 – 16. If the book of Revelation is generally organized in a chronological way, then the events described in Revelation 20 come *after* the second advent of our Lord.

It is also true that the binding of Satan began as Jesus began casting out demons, for when the Pharisees charged Jesus with casting out demons by the power of Beelzebub, Jesus rejected that accusation. Instead, he asked, "How can anyone enter a strong man's house and carry off his possessions unless he first ties up [*dēsē*] the strong man?" (Mt 12:29). The same Greek word (*deō*) that is used of binding the "strong man" in Matthew 12:29 is used for binding Satan in Revelation 20:2.[16] This binding that Jesus spoke

16. Anthony A. Hoekema, *The Bible and the Future* (Grand Rapids: Eerdmans, 1979), 223 – 38, esp. 228 – 29.

of is different from the binding John speaks of in Revelation 20:2, however. As George Ladd commented, "The former meant the breaking of the power of Satan that individual men and women might be delivered from his control. The latter binding [in Revelation 20:2] meant that he should deceive the nations no more."[17]

The same arguments would apply to Jesus' response as the seventy-two returned from their preaching mission in Luke 10:17 – 18. Jesus said, "I saw Satan fall like lightning from heaven." And in yet another passage, John 12:31 – 32, the same "now" aspect, of the "not yet" part of inaugurated eschatology, is operating. Again, Jesus said, "Now is the time for judgment of this world; now the prince of this world will be driven out [*ekblēthēsetai*]" — indeed, the same root (*ballō*) is the word used in Revelation 20:3, "He threw him [*ebalen*] into the Abyss."

It is agreed, then, that all through the gospel age in which we are now living, our God is short-circuiting and curtailing the influence and work of Satan over the lives of individuals by the power of the word of God. But in the Apocalypse of John, Satan's work is more than curtailed; it is halted and stopped cold in its tracks! Moreover, Satan's work on the *nations* is demolished in the Apocalypse. One more difference between Christ's invasion of the kingdom of evil during the gospel age and the final day: the scene in Revelation 20:1 begins with "an angel coming down out of heaven" to initiate the action against Satan. The work in the gospel age takes place on earth.

Therefore, what Jesus talked about is indeed an integral part of that final triumph over Satan and evil, but the whole of that action is "not yet," but awaits that glorious day of the second coming. Revelation 19 – 20 is portrayed as being continuous in much the same way as is the general line of the argument for the whole book. Thus, the destruction of the beast, then the false prophet (19:20 – 21), followed by the destruction of the power of death itself with the one who had the power of death — namely, the devil himself — complete God's conquest of that evil triumvirate. Thus, chapter 20 is not a recapitulation of the previous chapter(s); it moves to the next and final step in the plan of God.

17. George Eldon Ladd, "An Historic Premillennial Response," in *The Meaning of the Millennium: Four Views*, ed. Robert G. Clouse (Downers Grove, IL: InterVarsity Press, 1977), 189.

Excursus B: Are There Two Resurrections or Just One, and If Two, Is One Spiritual and the Other Physical?

The second issue in this philosophy of history passage of Revelation 20:1 – 10 is the meaning of the verb rendered "they came to life [*ezēsan*] and reigned [*ebasileusan*] with Christ a thousand years" (Rev 20:4). George Ladd argued that *zaō*, "to come to life," "is never used in the New Testament of life after death, *except in resurrection.* The word can be used of coming to life spiritually (Jn 5:25) — indeed, Paul describes life in terms of resurrection and ascension with Christ (Eph 2:6). But it is never used of the soul living on after the death of the body [as Hoekema argued]."[18]

So, are there two resurrections in Revelation 20:4 – 5, and are they both physical? Once again, Ladd comments,

> What does it mean "to live"? The entire interpretation of the passage hinges upon the question of whether the first *ezēsan* and the *ezēsan* of the rest of the dead mean the same thing, namely, bodily resurrection. What is the "first resurrection"? Is it literal, a resurrection of the body, or spiritual, a resurrection of the soul? If we can find the answer to this question, we have the key to the solution of the millennial question in this passage.[19]

Now, it is true that the New Testament does teach a type of spiritual resurrection, as we have already noticed, especially in Ephesians 2:1 – 6 and John 5:25 – 29. That point is not in contention here. But where the issue is joined is this: can these passages provide a basis for interpreting one or both of the resurrections in Revelation 20:4 – 5?

John 5:25 – 29 has the best chance of providing a real analogy to the text in the Apocalypse. It reads:

> I tell you the truth, whoever hears my word and believes him who sent me has eternal life and will not be condemned; he has crossed over from death to life. I tell you the truth, a time is coming and has now come when the dead will hear the voice of the Son of God and those who hear will live [*zēsousin*].... Do not be amazed at this, for a time is coming when all who are in their graves will hear his

18. Ibid., 190 (emphasis his).

19. Ibid., 35.

> voice and come out [*ekporeysontai*] — those who have done good will rise to live, and those who have done evil will rise to be condemned. (Jn 5:24 – 25, 28 – 29)

Ladd, however, points out some real differences between this passage in John's gospel and in his Apocalypse. He argues that the gospel context supplied its own clues for the spiritual interpretation. Concerning the first group, who "live," the "time ... has now [already] come." But the second group "are in their graves" (v. 28). They are physically, not spiritually dead. Moreover, the dead will be raised, some to live and others to be condemned.[20]

But there are no similar contextual clues in Revelation 20. The same word for "coming to life" is used of both resurrections. The most natural meaning of the passage, then, is to give both verbs (*zaō*) the same sense. Ladd observed,

> If, in a passage where *two resurrections* are mentioned, where certain *psychai ezēsan* at the first, and the rest of the *nekroi ezēsan* only at the end of a specified period after the first, — if in such a passage the first resurrection may be understood to mean *spiritual* rising with Christ; while the second means literal rising from the grave; — then there is an end of all significance in language, and Scripture is wiped out as a definite testimony to anything.[21]

We conclude, then, that the "thousand years" spoken of here come *after* the second coming of Christ. And both resurrections are physical, serving as boundaries to the thousand years. Hoekema argued consistently, but contrary to the line of thought taken here, that neither of the two resurrections were bodily resurrections, but few have followed him in this judgment. For him, there is "nothing about an earthly reign of Christ.... Rather, it describes the reigning with Christ in heaven, between their death and Christ's second coming, of the souls of deceased believers. It also describes the binding of Satan during the present age in such a way that he cannot prevent the spread of the gospel."[22]

As with all prophecy, Jesus said, "I am telling you now before it happens, so that when it does happen you will believe that I am He" (Jn 13:19). This implies two principles that are relevant to this very complex issue we have just discussed: (1) history is the final interpreter of prophecy; and (2) prophecy is not about our being right or wrong, but about Jesus being correct in what he declared the future to be like.

20. Ibid., 36.

21. Ibid., 37 – 38 (emphasis his).

22. Hoekema, *The Bible and the Future*, 232 – 38. On page 233 Hoekema concludes, "We therefore understand the word *ezēsan* (lived, or came to life) in verse 4 as describing the fact that the souls of believers who have died are now living with Christ in heaven and sharing his reign."

Epilogue

As we have argued throughout this work, there is no finer summary of the connection that exists between the Old and New Testaments than that given by Willis J. Beecher in his Stone Lectures delivered at Princeton just after the turn of this century:

> The proposition that the Old Testament contains a large number of predictions concerning the Messiah to come, and that these are fulfilled in Jesus Christ, may be Scriptural in substance, but it is hardly so in form. The Bible offers very few predictions save in the form of promises or threatenings. It differs from the systemized theologies in its [refusal to disconnect] prediction from promise or threatening ... [and] in emphasizing one promise rather than many predictions. This is the prevailing note in both testaments — a multitude of specifications unfolding a single promise, the promise serving as a central religious doctrine.
>
> This biblical generalization of the matter may be thus formulated: *God gave a promise to Abraham, and through him to all mankind; a promise eternally fulfilled and fulfilling in the history of Israel; and chiefly fulfilled in Jesus Christ, he being that which is principal in the history of Israel* (italics his).[1]

The New Testament Catchword for the Old Testament

The New Testament writers named this single plan or development the "promise" (*epangelia*). About forty passages may be cited from almost every part of the New Testament that contain this word "promise" as the quintessence of the Old Testament teaching. Moreover, there is only *one* promise; it is a single plan. Paul, standing before Agrippa in court, affirmed:

> And now I stand to be judged for the hope of *the promise* made of God to our fathers; unto which our twelve tribe nation ... hopes to attain. (Ac 26:6 – 7, my translation)

Paul's confidence, then, rested on a single promise, not a prediction or a number of scattered prognostications. It was a definite singular plan of God to benefit one man and through him to bless the whole world.

This one promise can be identified as that which was given to Abraham and repeated to Isaac, Jacob, and David. The writer of Hebrews said that God "made his promise to Abraham" and that Abraham, "after waiting patiently, received what was

1. Willis J. Beecher, *The Prophets and the Promise* (1905; reprint ed., Grand Rapids: Baker Book House, 1975), 178.

promised" (Heb 6:13 – 15). Further, Isaac and Jacob were "heirs with him [Abraham] of the same promise" (11:9). "Yet none of them received what had been promised. God had planned something better for us so that only together with us would they be made perfect" (11:39 – 40).

Rather than posing a contradiction, the text distinguishes between receiving the *word* of promise, its partial samples of the total fulfillment, and receiving the climactic *fulfillment* itself in all its aspects. Obviously, they did not receive that last aspect in most instances, but they did have the promise itself, along with an earnest of it as well: they "received the promises," "not what was promised" (vv. 33, 39). Likewise, Paul identified the promise made to Abraham and his descendants as the one that rested on grace and "guaranteed to all his offspring" that "they would be heir of the world" (Ro 4:13, 16).

The single promise was made up of many specifications; thus it was possible for the New Testament writers to speak of promises, using the plural. Oftentimes the writer used the article with the plural: "The promises [given] to the fathers" (Ro 15:8 – 9; cf. 9:4); "inherit the promises" (Heb 6:12); or Abraham who had "the promises" (Heb 7:6; cf. 11:13, 17). But the use of the plural did not weaken the concept of a single all-embracing doctrine of promise that included threatening and blessing, Israel and the nations, Messiah and all the believing community of all times; rather, it pointed to its multifaceted nature and breadth of scope.

For the New Testament writers, this one promise of God epitomized all that God had begun to do and say in the Old Testament and that he continued doing in their own era. Among the variant features embraced by this single promise were the word of the blessing of the gospel for Gentiles (Gal 3:8, 14, 29; Eph 1:13; 2:12; 3:6 – 7); the doctrine of the resurrection from the dead (Ac 26:6 – 8; 2Ti 1:1; Heb 9:15; 10:36; 2Pe 3:4, 9; 1Jn 2:24 – 25); the promise of the Holy Spirit in a new fullness (Lk 24:49; Ac 2:33 – 39; Gal 3:14); the doctrine of redemption from sin and its consequences (Ro 4:2 – 5, 9 – 10; Jas 2:21 – 23); and the greatest of all, the promise of Jesus the Messiah (Lk 1:69 – 70, 72 – 73; Ac 2:38 – 39; 3:25 – 26; 7:2, 17 – 18; 13:23, 32 – 33; Gal 3:12).

The promise was continually fulfilled in the Old Testament, yet it awaited some climactic fulfillments in connection with the two advents of the Servant-Messiah. Still, the promise went on beyond these two advents and remained eternally operative and irrevocable (Gal 3:15 – 18; Heb 6:13, 17 – 18). The generation of the first-century believers, according to Hebrews 6:18 (note the "*we*" and "*us*"), were given the same two unshakable and immutable signs that the promise was just as unchangeable and irrevocable for them (and hence the succeeding generations) as it was for the patriarch: the divine word of promise (Ge 12; 15), and the divine oath (Ge 22). God thereby bound himself eternally.

The very phraseology adopted by the New Testament writers likewise showed a strong predilection on their part to employ the identical technical terms and metaphors used in the Old Testament. For example, there are numerous references to my Son, my

Holy One, Servant, Elect or Chosen One, Messiah, Kingdom, Branch, Shoot, Lamp of David, Seed, Root of Jesse, Horn, Lion, Star, among others.[2] In their view, they were contributing to one continuous doctrine.

The Unity of the Old Testament and the New Testament

Cheap and facile contrasts between the two Testaments are as abundant as they are wrongheaded.[3] Marcion's well-known attempt to excise the Old Testament from the church's canon was a clear failure. Unfortunately, as Marcion himself recognized all too well, such a move must also carry with it the necessary corollary that a good part of the New Testament text be likewise excised, since it too often pictured God in much the same way and used much of the Old Testament doctrine and Jewish culture. To greater or lesser degrees, others followed Marcion's lead. For Schleiermacher, Harnack, Kierkegaard, and the younger Delitzsch, the Old Testament was a waste or just a pagan religion.

Nor was Origen's solution to the problem of the amount of continuity or discontinuity between the Testaments any better. His way out of the problem was to change the obvious meaning of many Old Testament passages into allegories. In *De Principus* 4:9, he proposed this remedy:

> Now the reason for the erroneous apprehension of all these points ... is no other than this, that holy Scripture is not understood by them according to its spiritual, but according to its literal meaning.... All narrative portions, relating either to the marriages or to the begetting of the children, or to battles of different kinds, or to any other histories whatever, what else can they be supposed to be, save the forms of hidden and sacred things.

In our own times, David Leslie Baker has attempted to classify the modern solutions to the problem of the relationship between the two Testaments.[4] Basically, Baker found three different solutions: (1) Arnold A. van Ruler and Kornelis H. Miskotte represented a solution in which the Old Testament was the essential and real Bible, with the New Testament being its sequel or merely its glossary of terms. (2) On the other hand, Rudolf Bultmann and Friedrich Baumgartel took the New Testament as the church's essential Bible and they regarded the Old Testament as its non-Christian presupposition or preliminary witness. (3) Finally, Baker grouped a variety of solutions under the rubric

2. For a detailed list of the Davidic references in the New Testament, see Dennis Duling, "The Promises to David and Their Entrance into Christianity—Nailing Down a Likely Hypothesis," *New Testament Studies* 20 (1974): 55–77.

3. Robert Gordis, *Judaism in a Christian World* (New York: McGraw-Hill, 1966), 136–37, quotes Claude G. Montefiore's brilliant response to such contrived contrasts (*Synoptic Gospels*, 2:326) by giving a series of contrived retrogressions from the Old to the New Testament as a proper rebuttal to those who painfully and artificially do the opposite.

4. David L. Baker, "The Theological Problem of the Relationship Between the Old Testament and the New Testament: A Study of Some Modern Solutions" (Ph.D. diss., University of Sheffield, August 1975); published as *Two Testaments: One Bible* (Downers Grove, IL: InterVarsity Press, 1976).

"biblical solutions," including Wilhelm Vischer's *christological approach*, where *every* Old Testament text pointed to some aspect of Christ's person, work, or ministry; the *typological approach*, where the Old Testament was investigated for its historical and theological similarities or correspondences to the New Testament; and the *salvation-history approach*, in which the Old Testament was "actualized" in the New Testament. Others within this grouping suggested a continuous tension along the lines of continuity and discontinuity between the Testaments, for example, Th. C. Vriezen, H. H. Rowley, C. H. Dodd, John Bright, and Brevard S. Childs.

Our solution does not appear to fit easily into any single one of these three categories. The imposition of external grids over the biblical materials must always be rejected. Thus the selection of one part of the canon over the other is just as arbitrary and deduced *ab extra* as is the application of some such principle as a christological, typological, or salvation-history approach. Where the text as it now exists does not validate such an organizing principle, it is to be laid aside in favor of one that can be inductively validated. The object of the discipline of biblical theology is to discern what flow of continuity, if any, the writers betrayed in their works. Were they aware of any antecedent contributions to their subject or related subjects? And did they ever indicate that these could be grouped together or were to be differentiated from what the people of previous generations had been told?

The evidence already culled from the Old Testament canon clearly argues that these writers strongly believed that they were part of a single tradition. But by the same token, New Testament connections were more than historical-chronological continuities, textual citations of previous writers, or shared ethnic and cultural heritages. The connection of subject matter and terminology was even more obvious and pointed than those of history, literature, and culture. It would be impossible to describe the message of a New Testament writer without referring to the seed, the people of God, the kingdom of God, the blessing of God to all nations, the day of the Lord, and so forth. Moreover, these shared subjects gave way to shared vocabulary that tended to become technical terms because of their frequent appearance at critical junctures in the argument.

Additionally, history had a certain compelling force within it, for as the writers of the Gospels frequently expressed it, the Messiah "must" (*dei*)[5] suffer and then rise gloriously. Likewise, the apostles took comfort in times of persecution against the early church that this was nothing more or less than what had been foretold by the Old Testament writers and the antipathy that had already occurred against God's Anointed (Ac 4:25–30). It was all predestined in the "plan" of God, to use the word of Peter and John.

This was not a "casual" and "free" use of the Old Testament. In contradistinction to most modern assessments of the New Testament use of the Old Testament, the writers

5. Mark 8:31; and see especially our discussion in chapter 16, e.g., Luke 17:25; 22:37; 24:7, 26; Acts 17:3. See W. Grundmann, "*Dei*," in *Theological Dictionary of the New Testament*, ed. Gerhard Kittel, trans. G. W. Bromiley (Grand Rapids: Eerdmans, 1965), 2:21ff.

appealed to the Old Testament in a very sober and measured way. On rare occasions, they did refer to the Old Testament only for illustrative purposes (e.g., "which things [*hatina*] can be put in another way [*allēgoroumena*]," Gal 4:24). But when they cited the Old Testament for doctrine or in disquisition aimed at impressing the Jewish part of their audiences with the obvious continuities in this new religion, they had better not have been wide of the mark established by the original truth-intention of the Old Testament writers, nor were they in our view.

The Better Covenant

The key to understanding the "better covenant" of Hebrews 8:6 is to observe the equation made between the Abrahamic promise (Heb 6:13; 7:19, 22) and the new covenant (8:6 – 13). Since the Mosaic covenant was the first to be completely actualized and experienced by the nation, the Abrahamic is not the first according to that writer's numbering. The Mosaic covenant did have its faults (v. 7), but it was not because of any inadequacies on the part of the covenant-making God or the subject matter of that word from God. Rather, many of the provisions had a deliberately built-in planned obsolescence. This was indicated from the beginning when the ceremonial and civil institutions were expressly called "copies" or "patterns" made after the real (Ex 25:9, 40; Heb 9:23). Many were temporary teaching devices until the "surety" of the "better covenant" arrived (Heb 7:22). The superiority came from the progress of revelation and not from the errors or deliberate misinformation of the former covenants.

Of course, the Sinaitic or Mosaic covenant was, as we have argued above, an outgrowth of the Abrahamic covenant; yet many of its provisions were merely preparatory. Thus, when God *renewed* the ancient patriarchal promise, which continued to appear in the Sinaitic and Davidic promises, nothing was deleted, abrogated, jettisoned, or replaced except that which was clearly so delimited from its first appearance. Therefore Jesus, by his death, renewed the covenant, but he did not thereby institute an entirely "new" covenant.

Our contention is not that the new covenant only fulfilled the spiritual promises made to Abraham's seed. True, the middle wall of partition had been broken down between believing Jews and Gentiles (Eph 2:13 – 18), but this again did not imply or explicitly teach that national identities or promises were likewise obviated any more than maleness and femaleness were dropped. Paul's claim is that Gentile believers have been "grafted into" the Jewish olive tree (Ro 11:17 – 25)[6] and made "fellow-heirs of the same body and partakers of his *promise* in Christ by the gospel" (Eph 3:6, emphasis mine). Since "salvation is of the Jews" (Jn 4:22), and since there is only one sheepfold, one Shepherd, and yet "other sheep that are not of this sheep pen" (Jn 10:16), it should not be too surprising to see the New Testament writers add to the emerging thesis of

6. See the superb analysis of this passage by Bruce Corley, "The Jews, the Future, and God: Romans 9 – 11," *Southwestern Journal of Theology* 19 (1976): 42 – 56.

the Old Testament that there is just one people of God and one program of God even though there are several aspects to that single people and single program.

Paul made the Gentile believers part of the "household of God" (Eph 2:19) and part of "Abraham's seed" (Gal 3:16 – 19). Furthermore, he called them "heirs" according to the promise (Gal 3:19), which "inheritance" was part of "the hope of their calling" (Eph 1:18) and part of the "eternal inheritance" given to Abraham (Heb 9:15). Thus Gentiles, who were "excluded from citizenship in Israel" (Eph 2:12) and "foreigners and strangers" (v. 19) to "the covenants of the promise" (v. 12), have been made to share in part of the blessing of God to Israel.

In the midst of this unity of the "people of God" and the "household of faith" there yet remains an expectation of a future inheritance, which will also conclude God's promise with a revived nation of Israel, the kingdom of God, and the renewed heavens and earth. It is evident that Gentiles in this present time share already in some of the benefits of the age to come; yet the greater part of that same unified plan still awaits a future and everlasting fulfillment.

Appendix A

Chronological Charts on the Dates of the Books of the Bible

I.

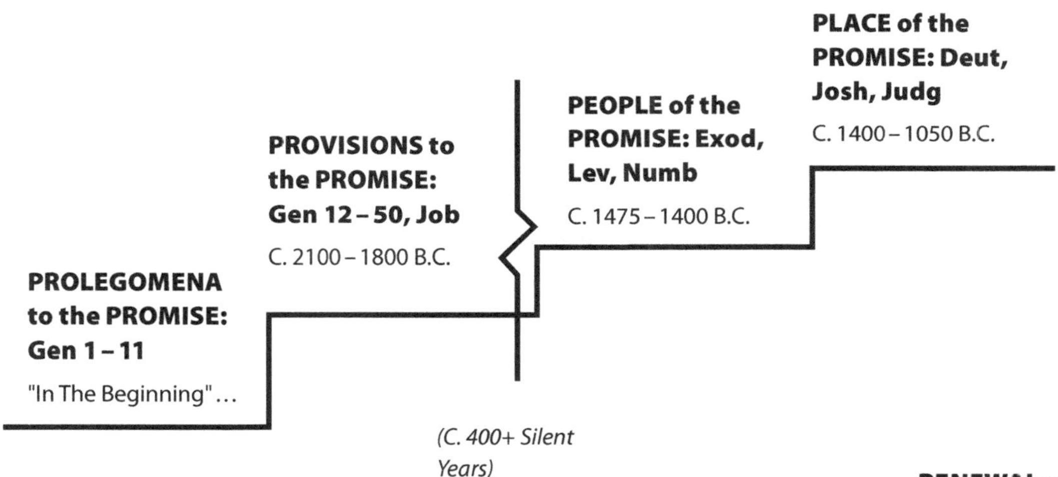

II.

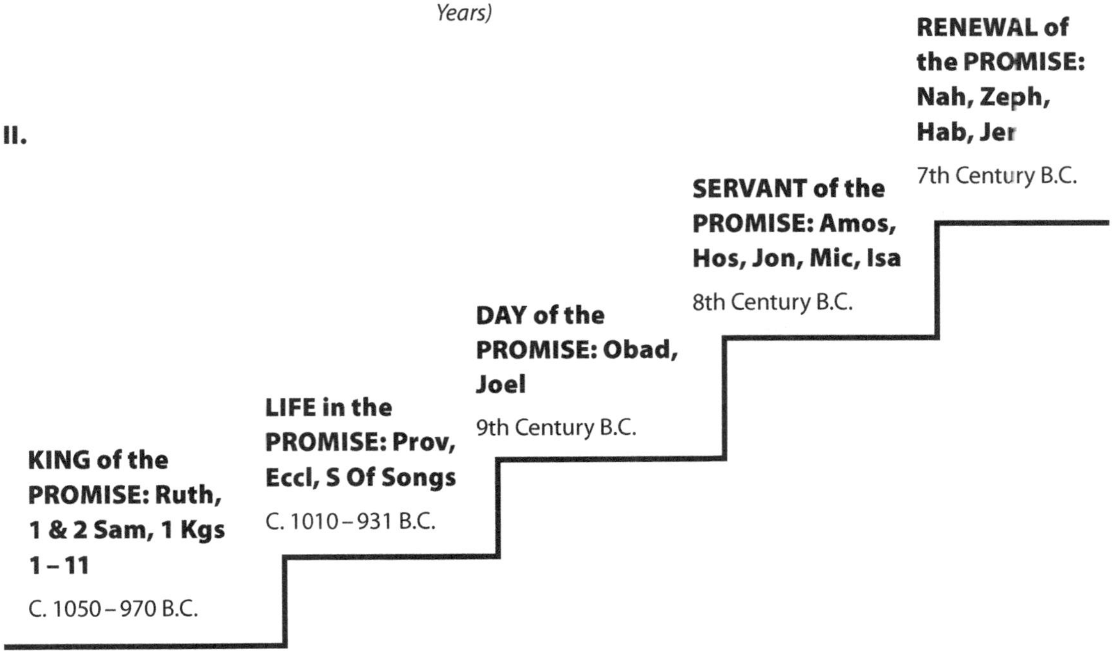

III.

KINGDOM of the PROMISE: Ezek, Dan
6th Century B.C.

TRIUMPH of the PROMISE: Hag, Zech, Mal, Chron, Ezra, Neh, Esther
5th Century B.C.

(C. 400 Years Silence)

ARRIVAL of the PROMISE: John the Bapt, Zech, Mary, Simeon, Anna
C. 6 B.C.–6 A.D..

PROMISE and the LAW of GOD: Jam, Gal
C. A.D. 46–48

IV.

PROMISE and the MISSION of the CHURCH: Thess, 1 & 2 Cor, Rom
A.D. 50'S

PROMISE and PAUL'S PRISON EPISTLES: Col, Philem, Eph, Phil
Early A.D. 60'S

PROMISE and the KINGDOM of GOD: Matt, Mark
A.D. 63–64

V.

PROMISE and the PROMISED HOLY SPIRIT: Luke-Acts
A.D. 60–65

PROMISE and PURITY of LIFE and DOCTINE 1 & 2 Peter, Jude
C. A.D. 64–65

PROMISE and the PASTORAL LETTERS: 1 & 2 Tim, Titus
C. A.D. 62–67

VI.

PROMISE and the SUPREMACY OF JESUS: Hebrews
C. A.D. 65

PROMISE and the GOSPEL of the KINGDOM: John, 1 & 2 & 3 John, Rev
C. A.D. 85–95

Appendix B

Biblical Frequency of the Word *Epangelia*, "Promise"

Percentage of All Occurrences in Each Book of the NT

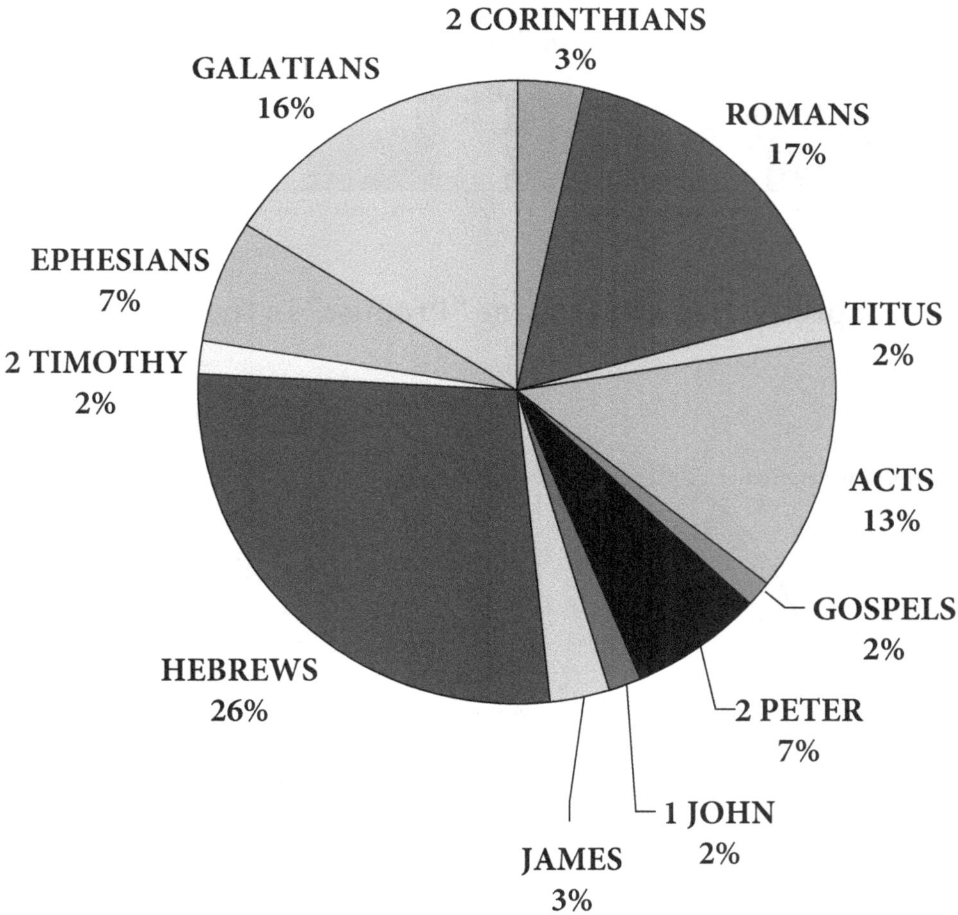

Occurrences of "Promise" in the NT

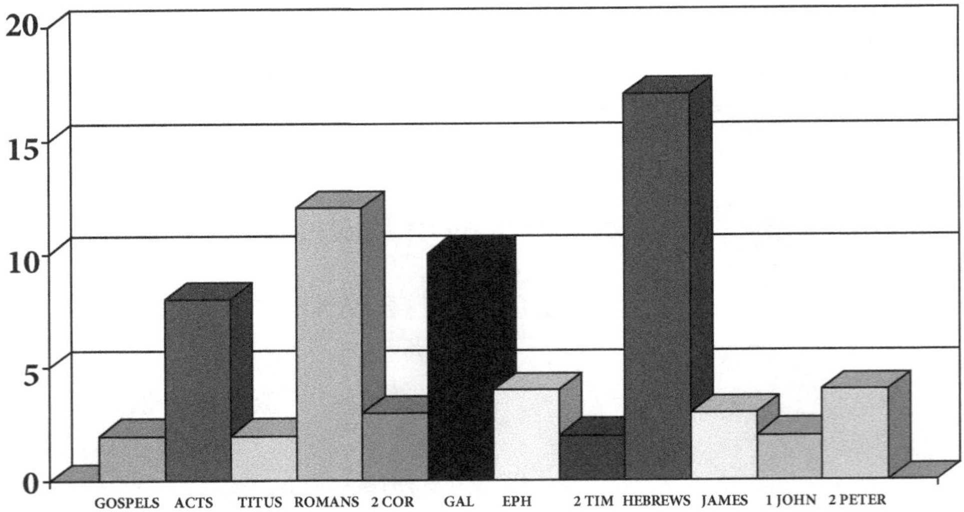

Specific Items in the One "Promise" in the NT

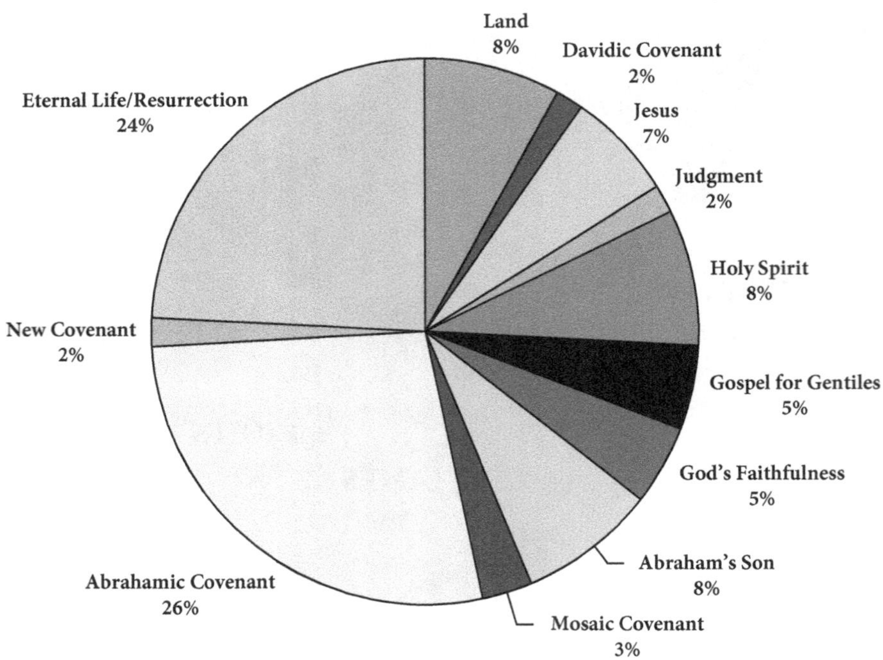

Categories of "Promise" Occurrences

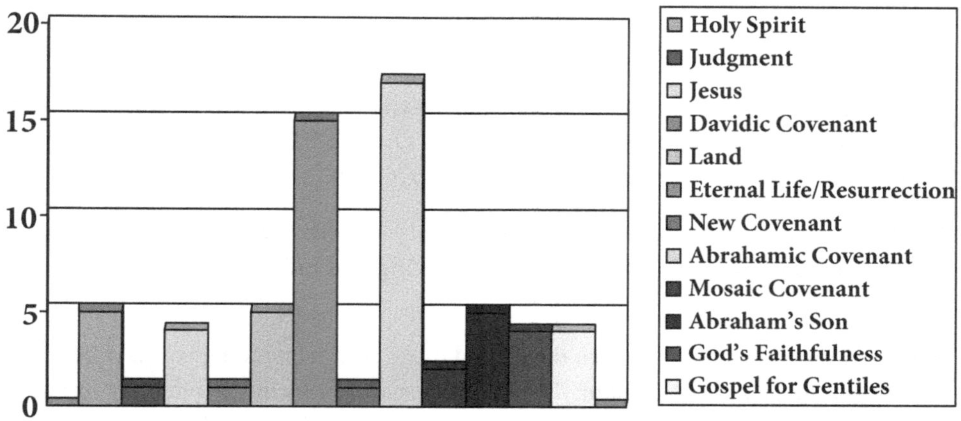

Number of References to the Promise in the NT

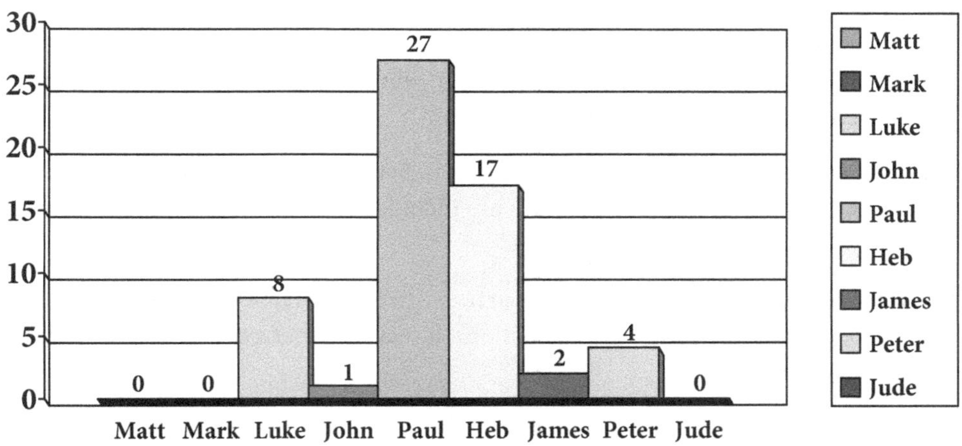

Glossary

Abrahamic covenant. The agreement or contract that God initiated with Abraham in Genesis 12:1 – 3; reiterated in Genesis 13:14 – 17; 15; 17; 22:15 – 18. It was also later confirmed to Isaac (Ge 26:3 – 5, 24) and Jacob (Ge 28:13 – 15; 35:9 – 12).

Advent, first and second. The "coming or arrival" of Jesus the Messiah to redeem all humanity back to God (first advent) and as King and Judge of the nations (second advent).

Allegory. A metaphor that has been developed into a story conveying truths other than what the surface story is about. The only three allegories in the Bible are Jotham's parable (Jdg 9:7 – 15), the allegory on marital fidelity (Pr 5:15 – 23), and the Sarah and Hagar allegory (Gal 4:21 – 31).

Amillennialism. The view that the kingdom promises made to Israel in the Old Testament are fulfilled spiritually rather than literally in the New Testament church. Christ will return literally and physically, but there is no one-thousand-year (millennial) reign on earth in connection with that return.

Antichrist. The final world ruler who opposes God, his Son Jesus, and believers at the end of the ages, setting up worship to himself as his final insult to God (1 Jn 2:18, 22; 4:3; 2 Jn 7).

Apocalypse (apocalypsis). A term from the Greek, meaning "to uncover" or "to reveal," occurring also as the title of the book of Revelation. As a literary genre it usually refers to the form of Daniel and Revelation, which has dreams, an expectation of the end of the ages, and extensive symbolism.

Corporate solidarity. The frequent oscillation in Scripture between the one who represents the many and the many who are included in the one, as in the messianic terms "Seed" or "Servant of the Lord."

Covenant. An agreement involving two parties — in Scripture, between God and mankind, between mortals, or between nations. It may be either a conditional or unconditional covenant.

Covenantal theology. A system of theology that received creedal status in the Westminster Confession and Catechisms (1643 – 49) and were amplified by Johannes Cocceius (1603 – 69). God abrogated the covenant of works made with Adam and

Eve and graciously gave a covenant of redemption that was divided into a time of law and a time of grace.

Davidic covenant. The agreement made by God with King David, who stood as the representative head of the Davidic line or dynasty (2 Sa 7:11 – 19; 1Ch 17:10 – 17), that included a kingdom, a throne, and a dynasty.

Day of the Lord/Yahweh. A common biblical term (Heb. *yom YHWH*) that is used in both testaments to describe the deliverance/salvation and the judgment of God at the end of the age.

Dispensationalism. The system of theology, beginning in the nineteenth century, that states that God revealed his word in several administrations or stewardships (Gr. *oikonomeo*). When he tested the people under that form of the word, the people failed, so he judged them and offered a new word of revelation. Israel is always to be kept separate from the church, and the earthly and heavenly programs of God must be kept separate as well. See *Progessive Dispensationalism* and *Ultradispensationalism.*

Eschatology. The study of "last things" in the Bible. The rabbis distinguished between "this age" (Heb. *ha-'olam hazeh*) and "the age to come" (Heb. *ha-'olam habba*), a distinction that also appears in the New Testament Greek as pairs some thirty times.

Inaugurated eschatology. A concept often contained within one biblical prophecy for both a near and a distant fulfillment — i.e., a "now" and a "not yet" aspect to the single idea contained in the prediction. Thus, "now are we the sons of God, yet it does not appear what we shall be"; or the "antichrist will come," yet already "many antichrists have come."

Kingdom of God/Kingdom of heaven. Two expressions used synonymously to refer to the rule and reign of God that began with his casting out of demons during his earthly ministry and continues on into the eternal state.

Masoretes/Masoretic text. Medieval Jewish textual scholars who analyzed the Hebrew Bible and developed the Tiberian pointing system of vowels for the Ben Asher text that is the basis for the modern editions of the Masoretic Hebrew text of the Bible (Codex Leningradensis).

Messianic secret. A view initiated by William Wrede in 1901 that attempts to explain why Jesus did not want his disciples to publicize who he was.

Midrash. A type of early rabbinic interpretation characterized by fanciful and whimsical explanations of the biblical text that generally ignored the grammatical-historical context of the Scriptures being interpreted.

Millennium. The biblical view that Jesus will return a second time to rule and reign on earth for one thousand years, during which time Satan will be bound but then briefly released at the end of those years before he is finally judged and cast into the Lake of Fire (Rev 20:2 – 7) and history ends and becomes eternity.

Moderate dispensationalism. See *Ultradispensationalism.*

Mystery. A part of the revelation of God that has been revealed, but not to the degree it is now being announced more recently (Ro 16:25 – 26; Eph 3: 5).

New covenant. The agreement made with the house of Israel and the house of Judah that renewed the Abrahamic and Davidic agreements while also enlarging them to include new elements.

People of God. The term for the continuity found in both testaments to describe all who have believed in the coming Man of Promise/Messiah and thus are the spiritual "seed of Abraham."

Pesher. A method of interpretation especially popularized by the Dead Sea Community (Essenes?) that emphasizes contemporizing biblical prophecy and the supernatural illumination of the interpreter.

Postmillennialism. The view that God's kingdom of righteousness and peace would be brought to earth by the triumphant progress of Christianity and the power of the church in world affairs.

Premillennialism. The view that God completes in historic times his promise of regathering Israel to the land he promised them and that he rules and reigns on earth with all his resurrected saints of all ages for a thousand years while Satan is bound for most of that time.

Progressive dispensationalism. A view that began with a study group in 1986 at the annual meeting of the Evangelical Theological Society, which announced this term at its 1991 meeting. Generally it argues that there is one people of God (with distinguishable aspects such as Israel and the church) and one program of God (with various aspects such as the spiritual and material).

Replacement theology/Supersessionism. The argument that because of Israel's failure to obey the covenant, all the promises originally made out to Israel were given over to the church.

Ultradispensationalism. The view that holds that the church, the body of Christ, began with the apostle Paul after the events described at the end of the book of Acts. *Moderate Dispensationalism* sees the church beginning with the conversion of the apostle Paul in Acts 9. All Scripture that precedes these starting points may be read by us today, but the biblical mail addressed to us really begins at these points.

Bibliography

Alexander, D. "The Old Testament View of Life After Death." *Themelios* 11 (1986): 41 – 46.

Anderson, B. W., ed. *The Old Testament and the Christian*. New York: Harper & Row, 1969.

Babb, O. J. *The Theology of the Old Testament*. New York: Abingdon-Cokesbury, 1949.

Baker, D. L. *Two Testaments: One Bible*. Downers Grove, IL: InterVarsity Press, 1976.

Barth, C. *God with Us: A Theological Introduction to the Old Testament*. Edited and translated by G. W. Bromiley. Grand Rapids: Eerdmans, 1991.

Barton, J. "Understanding Old Testament Ethics." *Journal of Theological Studies* 9 (1978): 44 – 64.

Becker, J. *Messianic Expectations in the Old Testament*. Philadelphia: Fortress, 1980.

Beckwith, R. T. *The Old Testament Canon of the New Testament Church and Its Background in Early Judaism*. London: SPCK, 1985.

Betz, O. "Biblical Theology, History of," in *The Interpreter's Dictionary of the Bible*. Edited by G. A. Buttrick. 4 vols. Nashville: Abingdon, 1962. 1:432 – 37.

Birch, B. C. "Tradition, Canon, and Biblical Theology." *Horizons in Biblical Theology* 2 (1980): 113 – 25.

Birch, B. C., and L. L. Rasmussen. *Bible and Ethics in the Christian Life*. Minneapolis: Augsburg, 1976.

Birkeland, H. "The Belief in the Resurrection of the Dead in the Old Testament." *Studia Theologica* 68 (1949): 60 – 78.

Bornemann, R. "Toward a Biblical Theology," in *The Promise and Practice of Biblical Theology*. Edited by J. Reumann. Minneapolis: Fortress, 1991.

Briggs, C. A. *Messianic Prophecy: The Prediction of the Fulfillment of Redemption through the Messiah*. 1889. Reprint, Peabody, MA: Hendrickson, 1988.

Bright, J. *The Kingdom of God: The Biblical Concept and Its Meaning for the Church*. Nashville: Abingdon-Cokesbury, 1953.

_________. *The Authority of the Old Testament*. Nashville: Abingdon, 1967.

Bruce, F. F. *The New Testament Development of Old Testament Themes*. Grand Rapids: Eerdmans, 1969.

Brueggemann, W. *The Land*. Philadelphia: Fortress, 1977.

________. *Old Testament Theology: Essays on Structure, Theme and Text*. Edited by P. D. Miller Jr. Philadelphia: Fortress, 1992.

_________. *Theology of the Old Testament: Testimony, Dispute, Advocacy*. Minneapolis: Fortress, 1997.

Bultmann, R. *Theology of the New Testament*. Vol. 1. New York: Scribner, 1955.

Burrows, M. *An Outline of Biblical Theology*. Philadelphia: Westminster, 1946.

________. "The Task of Biblical Theology." *Journal of Bible and Religion* 14 (1946): 13 – 15.

Cahill, L. S. "The New Testament and Ethics: Communities of Social Change." *Interpretation* 44 (1990): 383 – 95.

Cazelles, H. "The Unity of the Bible and the People of God." *Scripture* 18 (1966): 1 – 10.

Chapman, C. *Whose Promised Land?* Oxford: Lion, 1992.

Charlesworth, J. H., ed. *The Messiah: Developments in Earliest Judaism and Christianity*. Minneapolis: Fortress, 1992.

Childs, B. S. *Biblical Theology in Crisis*. Philadelphia: Westminster, 1970.

________. *The New Testament as Canon*. London: SCM Press, 1984.

_______. *Biblical Theology of the Old and New Testaments: Theological Reflection on the Christian Bible*. Minneapolis: Fortress, 1992.

Christensen, D. L. "The Center of the First Testament within the Canonical Process." *Biblical Theology Bulletin* 23 (1993): 48 – 53.

Clements, R. E. *Old Testament Theology.* London: Marshall, 1978.

________. "The Messianic Hope in the Old Testament." *Journal for the Study of the Old Testament* 43 (1989): 319.

________. *Wisdom in Theology.* Minneapolis: Augsburg, 1990.

Clines, D. J. A. *The Theme of the Pentateuch.* Journal for the Study of the Old Testament Supplement Series 10. Sheffield, UK: JSOT Press, 1986.

Clouse, R. G., ed. *The Meaning of the Millennium: Four Views.* Downers Grove, IL: InterVarsity Press, 1977.

Clowney, E. P. "A Biblical Theology of Prayer," in *Teach Us to Pray: Prayer in the Bible and the World.* Edited by D. A. Carson. Exeter, UK: Paternoster, 1990. 136 – 73.

Collins, J. J. "Is a Critical Biblical Theology Possible?" in *The Hebrew Bible and Its Interpreters.* Edited by W. H. Propp et al. Winona Lake, IN: Eisenbrauns, 1990. 1 – 17.

Conzelmann, H. "Wisdom in the New Testament," in *The Interpreter's Dictionary of the Bible: Supplementary Volume.* Edited by K. Crim. Nashville: Abingdon, 1976. 956 – 60.

Craigie, P. *The Problem of War in the Old Testament.* Grand Rapids: Eerdmans, 1978.

Crenshaw, J. L. *Old Testament Wisdom.* Atlanta: John Knox, 1981.

Cullmann, O. *Christ and Time.* 2nd ed. London: SCM Press, 1962.

Davidson, A. B. *The Theology of the Old Testament.* Edited by S. D. F. Salmond. Edinburgh: T & T Clark, 1904.

Davies, W. D. *The Gospel and the Land: Early Christianity and Jewish Territorial Doctrine.* Berkeley: University of California Press, 1974.

Dearman, J. A. "The Problem of War in the Old Testament: War, Peace and Justice." *Austin Seminary Bulletin* 99 (1983): 5 – 14.

Dentan, R. C. *Preface to Old Testament Theology.* Rev. ed. New York: Seabury, 1963.

Deutsch, R. "The Biblical Concept of the 'People of God.'" *Southeast Asia Journal of Theology* 13 (1972): 4 – 12.

DeVaux, R. "Is It Possible to Write a 'Theology of the Old Testament'?" in *The Bible and the Ancient Near East.* London: Darton, Longman & Todd, 1971.

Dodd, C. H. *According to the Scriptures.* London: James Nisbet, 1952.

Duling, D. C. "Kingdom of God, Kingdom of Heaven," in *Anchor Bible Dictionary.* Edited by D. N. Freedman. 6 vols. New York: Doubleday, 1992. 4:49 – 69.

Dumbrell, W. J. *Covenant and Creation: A Theology of Old Testament Covenants.* Nashville: Thomas Nelson, 1984.

Dunn, J. D. G. *Jesus, Paul and the Law: Studies in Mark and Galatians.* London: SPCK, 1990.

Dunn, J. D. G., and J. P. Mackay. *New Testament Theology in Dialogue.* London: SPCK, 1987.

Dyrness, W. *Themes in Old Testament Theology.* Downers Grove, IL: InterVarsity Press, 1979.

Ebeling, G. *Word and Faith.* Philadelphia: Fortress, 1963.

Eichrodt, W. *Theology of the Old Testament.* 2 vols. Philadelphia: Westminster, 1961, 1967.

Eissfeldt, O. "The Promise of Grace to David in Isaiah 55:1 – 5," in *Israel's Prophetic Heritage.* Edited by B. W. Anderson. New York: Harper & Row, 1962. 196 – 207.

________. "The History of Israelite-Jewish Religion and Old Testament Theology," in *The Flowering of Old Testament Theology: A Reader in Twentieth-Century Old Testament Theology, 1930 – 1990.* Edited by B. C. Ollenburger, E. A. Martens, and G. F. Hasel. Winona Lake, IN: Eisenbrauns, 1992.

Ellisen, S. A. *Who Owns the Land?* Portland, OR: Multnomah Press, 1991.

Fretheim, T. E. *The Suffering of God: An Old Testament Perspective.* Philadelphia: Fortress, 1984.

Fuller, D. P. "The Importance of a Unity of the Bible," in *Studies in Old Testament Theology.* Edited by R. L. Hubbard et al. Dallas: Word, 1992.

Gabler, J. P. "An Oration on the Proper Distinction Between Biblical and Dogmatic Theology and the Specific Objectives of Each," in *The Flowering of Old Testament Theology: A Reader in Twentieth-*

Century Old Testament Theology, 1930 – 1990. Edited by B. C. Ollenburger, E. A. Martens, and G. F. Hasel. Winona Lake, IN: Eisenbrauns, 1992.

Gammie, J. G. *Holiness in Israel*. Overtures to Biblical Theology. Minneapolis: Fortress, 1980.

Gese, H. "Tradition and Biblical Theology," in *Tradition and Theology in the Old Testament*. Edited by D. A. Knight. London: SPCK, 1977.

Goldingay, J. *Theological Diversity and the Authority of the Old Testament*. Grand Rapids: Eerdmans, 1987.

_________. *Old Testament Theology: Israel's Gospel*. Vol. 1. Downers Gove, IL: InterVarsity Press, 2003.

_________. *Old Testament Theology: Israel's Promise*. Vol. 2. Downers Grove, IL: InterVarsity Press, 2007.

Goldsworthy, G. *According to Plan: The Unfolding Revelation of God in the Bible*. Leicester, UK: Inter-Varsity Press, 1991.

Goshen-Gottstein, M. "Tanakh Theology: The Religion of the Old Testament and the Place of Jewish Biblical Theology," in *Ancient Israelite Religion*. Edited by P. D. Miller Jr. et al. Philadelphia: Fortress, 1987.

Gowan, D. E. *Eschatology in the Old Testament*. Philadelphia: Fortress, 1986.

_________. *Theology of Exodus: Biblical Theology in the Form of a Commentary*. Louisville: Westminster, 1994.

Guthrie, D. *New Testament Theology*. Downers Grove, IL: InterVarsity Press, 1981.

Hals, R. M. *The Theology of the Book of Ruth*. Facet Books Biblical Series 23. Philadelphia: Fortress, 1969.

Hagner, D. A. "Biblical Theology and Preaching." *Expository Times* 96 (1985): 137 – 41.

Hammershaimb, E. "On the Ethics of the Old Testament Prophets." Supplements to *Vetus Testamentum* 7 (1990): 75 – 101.

Hanson, P. D. "The Responsibility of Biblical Theology to Communities of Faith." *Theology Today* 37 (1980): 35 – 50.

_________. *The Diversity of Scripture: A Theological Interpretation*. Philadelphia: Fortress, 1982.

Harrington, W. *The Path of Biblical Theology*. Dublin: Gill & Macmillan, 1973.

Harvey, J. "The New Diachronic Biblical Theology of the Old Testament." *Biblical Theology Bulletin* 1 (1971): 5 – 29.

Hasel, G. F. *The Remnant: The History and Theology of the Remnant Idea from Genesis to Isaiah*. Berrien Springs, MI: Andrews University Press, 1972.

_________. *Old Testament Theology: Basic Issues in the Current Debate*. 4th ed. Grand Rapids: Eerdmans, 1988.

Hayes, J. H., and F. Prussner. *Old Testament Theology: Its History and Development*. Atlanta: John Knox, 1984.

Hays, R. B. *The Moral Vision of the New Testament: A Contemporary Introduction to New Testament Ethics*. San Francisco: Harper, 1987.

Heinisch, P. *Theology of the Old Testament*. Collegeville, MN: Liturgical Press, 1955.

Hillers, D. R. *Covenant: The History of a Biblical Idea*. Baltimore: Johns Hopkins University Press, 1969.

Hoegenhaven, J. *Problems and Prospects of Old Testament Theology*. Sheffield, UK: Sheffield Academic Press, 1988.

Houlden, J. L. *Ethics of the New Testament*. Harmondsworth, UK: Penguin Books, 1973.

House, P. R. *Old Testament Theology*. Downers Grove, IL: InterVarsity Press, 1998.

Howard, G. E. "Christ the End of the Law: The Meaning of Romans 10:4ff." *Journal of Biblical Literature* 88 (1969): 331 – 37.

Hubbard, D. A. "Hope in the Old Testament." *Tyndale Bulletin* 34 (1983): 33 – 59.

Hubbard, R. L., et al. *Studies in the Old Testament*. Dallas: Word, 1992.

Jacob, E. *The Theology of the Old Testament*. New York: Harper & Row, 1958.

Janzen, W. *Old Testament Ethics: A Paradigmatic Approach*. Louisville: Westminster, 1994.

Jermias, J. *Jesus' Promise to the Nations*. London: SCM Press, 1958.

_________. *New Testament Theology, Part I*. London: SCM Press, 1971.

Kaiser, W. C., Jr. "Leviticus and Paul: Do This and You Shall Live (Eternally?)." *Journal of the Evangelical Theological Society* 14 (1971): 19–28.

________. "The Promise Theme and the Theology of Rest." *Bibliotheca Sacra* 130 (1973): 135–50.

________. "The Blessing of David: The Charter for Humanity," in *The Law and the Prophets: Oswald T. Allis Festschrift*. Edited by J. Skilton. Philadelphia: Presbyterian and Reformed, 1974. 298–318.

________. "The Center of Old Testament Theology: The Promise." *Themelios* 10 (1974): 1–10.

________. "The Weightier and Lighter Matters of the Law: Moses, Jesus, and Paul," in *Current Issues in Biblical and Patristic Interpretation: Studies in Honor of Merrill C. Tenney*. Edited by G. F. Hawthorne. Grand Rapids: Eerdmans, 1975. 176–92.

________. "Wisdom Theology and the Centre of Old Testament Theology." *Evangelical Quarterly* 50 (1978): 132–46.

________. *Toward an Old Testament Theology*. Grand Rapids: Zondervan, 1978.

________. "The Old Promise and the New Covenant," in *The Bible and Its Literary Milieu*. Edited by J. Maier and V. Tollers. Grand Rapids: Eerdmans, 1979. 106–20.

________. "The Promise of God and the Outpouring of the Holy Spirit: Joel 2:28-32 and Acts 2:16-21," in *The Living and Active Word of God: Essays in Honor of Samuel J. Schultz*. Edited by M. Inch and R. Youngblood. Winona Lake, IN: Eisenbrauns, 1982. 109–22.

________. *Toward Old Testament Ethics*. Grand Rapids: Zondervan, 1983.

________. "Israel as the People of God," in *The People of God: Essays on the Believer's Church: Essays in Honor of James Leo Garrett Jr.* Edited by P. Basden and D. S. Dockery. Nashville: Broadman, 1991. 99–108.

________. *The Messiah in the Old Testament*. Grand Rapids: Zondervan, 1995.

Käsemann, E. "The Problem of a New Testament Theology." *New Testament Studies* 19 (1973): 235–45.

Kaminsky, J. S. *Corporate Responsibility in the Hebrew Bible*. Journal for the Study of the Old Testament Supplement Series 196. Sheffield, UK: JSOT Press, 1986.

Klein, G. "The Biblical Understanding of 'The Kingdom of God.'" *Union Seminary Quarterly Review* 38 (1983): 193–201.

Knierim, R. P. "The Task of Old Testament Theology." *Horizons in Biblical Theology* 6 (1984): 25–57.

_______. *The Task of Old Testament Theology: Substance, Method and Cases*. Grand Rapids: Eerdmans, 1995.

Knight, G. A. F. *A Christian Theology of the Old Testament*. Richmond: John Knox, 1959.

Koehler, L. *Old Testament Theology*. Translated by A. S. Todd. Philadelphia: Westminster, 1957.

Kraftchick, S. J., et al., eds. *Biblical Theology: Problems and Perspectives*. Nashville: Abingdon, 1995.

Kraus, H.-J. *The People of God in the Old Testament*. New York: Association Press, 1958.

Ladd, G. E. *A Theology of the New Testament*. Grand Rapids: Eerdmans, 1993.

Lemke, W. E. "Is Old Testament Theology an Essentially Christian Theological Discipline?" *Horizons in Biblical Theology* 11 (1989): 59–71.

Levenson, J. D. "Why Jews Are Not Interested in Biblical Theology," in *Judaic Perspectives on Ancient Israel*. Edited by J. Neusner et al. Philadelphia: Fortress, 1987. 281–307.

Lewis, J. P. "What Do We Mean by Jabneh?" *Journal of Bible and Religion* 32 (1964): 125–32.

Lindars, B. "The Bible and Christian Ethics." *Theology Today* 76 (1973): 180–89.

Long, E. L. "The Use of the Bible in Christian Ethics: A Look at Basic Options." *Interpretation* 19 (1965): 149–62.

March, W. E. *Israel and the Politics of Land: A Theological Case Study*. Louisville: Westminster/John Knox, 1994.

Marks, J. H. "God's Holy People." *Theology Today* 29 (1972): 22–33.

Marshall, I. H. "The Hope of a New Age: The Kingdom of God in the New Testament." *Themelios* 11 (1985): 5–15.

Martens, E. *God's Design: A Focus on Old Testament Theology*. Grand Rapids: Baker, 1981.

________. "Embracing the Law: A Biblical Theological Perspective." *Bulletin for Biblical Research* 2 (1992): 1–28.

May, P. "Towards a Biblical Theology of Missions." *International Journal of Theology* 8 (1959): 21 – 28.
McComiskey, T. E. *The Covenants of Promise: A Theology of the Old Testament Covenants.* Grand Rapids: Baker, 1985.
McConville, G. *Law and Theology in Deuteronomy.* Journal for the Study of the Old Testament Supplement Series 33. Sheffield, UK: JSOT Press, 1984.
McKenzie, J. L. *A Theology of the Old Testament.* Garden City, NY: Doubleday, 1974.
McLelland, J. C. "Covenant Theology — A Reevaluation." *Canadian Journal of Theology* 3 (1957): 182 – 88.
Mendenhall, G. E. "Covenant," in *The Interpreter's Dictionary of the Bible.* Edited by G. A. Buttrick. 4 vols. Nashville: Abingdon, 1962. 1:714 – 23.
Miller, P. D. "The Gift of God: The Deuteronomic Theology of the Land." *Interpretation* 29 (1969): 451 – 61.
________. "The Place of the Decalogue in the Old Testament and Its Law." *Interpretation* 43 (1989): 229 – 42.
Montgomery, J. W. "Wisdom as Gift: The Wisdom Concept in Relation to Biblical Messianism." *Interpretation* 16 (1962): 43 – 57.
Moo, D. J. "Jesus and the Authority of the Mosaic Law." *Journal for the Study of the New Testament* 20 (1984): 3 – 49.
Morgan, R. "New Testament Theology," in *Biblical Theology: Problems and Perspectives.* Edited by S. J. Kraftchick et al. Nashville: Abingdon, 1995. 104 – 30.
Morris, L. "The Biblical Use of Blood." *Journal of Theological Studies* 3 (1952): 216 – 27.
________. *New Testament Theology.* Grand Rapids: Zondervan, 1986.
Mowvley, H. "The Concept and Content of 'Blessing' in the Old Testament." *The Bible Translator* 16 (1965): 74 – 80.
Muilenburg, J. "Abraham and the Nations: Blessing and World History." *Interpretation* 19 (1965): 387 – 98.
Murphy, R. E. "Wisdom Literature and Biblical Theology." *Biblical Theology Bulletin* 24 (1994): 4 – 7.
North, R. "The Theology of the Chronicler." *Journal of Biblical Literature* 82 (1963): 369 – 81.
Oehler, G. F. *Theology of the Old Testament.* Vol. 1: Translated by E. D. Smith. Vol. 2: Translated by S. Taylor. Edinburgh: T & T Clark, 1882 – 83.
Orlinsky, H. M. "The Biblical Concept of the Land: Cornerstone of the Covenant between God and Israel," in *The Land of Israel: Jewish Perspectives.* Edited by L. A. Hoffman. Notre Dame, IN: University of Notre Dame Press, 1986. 27 – 64.
Payne, D. F. "The Everlasting Covenant." *Tyndale Bulletin* 7 – 8 (1961): 10 – 16.
Payne, J. B. *The Theology of the Older Testament.* Grand Rapids: Zondervan, 1962.
Perdue, L. G. *The Collapse of History: Reconstructing Old Testament Theology.* Minneapolis: Fortress, 1994.
________. *Wisdom and Creation: The Theology of the Wisdom Literature.* Nashville: Abingdon, 1994.
Peters, G. W. *A Biblical Theology of Missions.* Chicago: Moody Press, 1972.
Pokorny, P. "The Problem of Biblical Theology." *Horizons in Biblical Theology* 15 (1993): 83 – 94.
Porter, J. R. "The Legal Aspects of the Concept of 'Corporate Personality' in the Old Testament." *Vetus Testamentum* 15 (1965): 361 – 80.
Preuss, H. D. *Old Testament Theology.* Vols. 1 – 2. New York: Harper & Row, 1995 – 96.
Rendtorff, R. "Must 'Biblical Theology' Be Christian Theology?" *Biblical Review* 4 (1988): 40 – 43.
Reumann, J., ed. *The Promise and Practice of Biblical Theology.* Minneapolis: Fortress, 1991.
Reventlow, H. C. *Problems of Old Testament Theology in the Twentieth Century.* Philadelphia: Fortress, 1985.
Richardson, A. *An Introduction to the Theology of the New Testament.* London: SCM Press, 1958.
Robertson, P. "The Outlook for Biblical Theology," in *Toward a Theology for the Future.* Edited by D. F. Wells and C. H. Pinnock. Carol Stream, IL: Creation House, 1971. 65 – 91.
Rowley, H. H. *The Faith of Israel: Aspects of Old Testament Thought.* Philadelphia: Westminster, 1956.
Rylaarsdam, J. C. *Revelation in Jewish Wisdom Literature.* Chicago: University of Chicago Press, 1946.
Sailhamer, J. H. *The Pentateuch as Narrative: A Biblical-Theological Commentary.* Grand Rapids: Zondervan, 1992.

________. *Introduction to Old Testament Theology: A Canonical Approach.* Grand Rapids: Zondervan, 1995.

Sanders, E. P. *Paul and Palestinian Judaism: A Comparison of Patterns of Religion.* London: SCM Press, 1977.

Sandys-Wunsch, J., and L. Eldredge. "J. P. Gabler and the Distinction between Biblical and Dogmatic Theology: Translation, Commentary and Discussion of His Originality." *Scottish Journal of Theology* 33 (1980): 133 – 58.

Schelkle, K. H. *Theology of the New Testament.* 4 vols. Collegeville, MN: Liturgical Press, 1971 – 78.

Schrage, W. *The Ethics of the New Testament.* Philadelphia: Fortress, 1988.

Scobie, C. H. H. *The Ways of Our God: An Approach to Biblical Theology.* Grand Rapids: Eerdmans, 2003.

Smart, J. D. *The Past, Present, and Future of Biblical Theology.* Philadelphia: Westminster, 1979.

Snaith, N. H. *The Distinctive Ideas of the Old Testament.* London: Epworth, 1944.

Spriggs, D. G. *Two Old Testament Theologies.* London: SCM Press, 1974.

Stagg, F. *New Testament Theology.* Nashville: Broadman, 1962.

Stauffer, E. *New Testament Theology.* London: SCM Press, 1955).

Stein, R. H. "Kingdom of God," in *EDBT* (1996): 451 – 54.

Stewart, J. S. "On a Neglected Emphasis in New Testament Theology." *Scottish Journal of Theology* 4 (1951): 292 – 301.

Stuhlmacher, P. "The Gospel of Reconcilation in Christ — Basic Features and Issues of a Biblical Theology of the New Testament." *Horizons in Biblical Theology* 1 (1979): 161 – 90.

________. *How to Do Biblical Theology.* Alison Park, PA: Pickwick, 1995.

Sun, H. T. C. et al. *Problems in Biblical Theology: Essays in Honor of Rolf Knierim.* Grand Rapids: Eerdmans, 1997.

Tate, M. E. "Promising Paths toward Biblical Theology." *Review and Expositor* 78 (1981): 169 – 85.

Terrien, S. L. *The Elusive Presence: Toward a New Biblical Theology.* San Francisco: Harper & Row, 1978.

Van Gemeren, W. A. *The Progress of Redemption: The Story of Salvation from Creation to the New Jerusalem.* Grand Rapids: Baker, 1988.

Verhey, A. *The Great Reversal: Ethics and the New Testament.* Grand Rapids: Eerdmans, 1984.

Verhoef, P. A. "Some Thoughts on the Present-Day Situation in Biblical Theology." *Westminster Theological Journal* 33 (1970): 1 – 19.

Vischer, W. *The Witness of the Old Testament to Christ.* London: Lutterworth, 1949.

von Rad, G. *Theology of the Old Testment.* 2 vols. New York: Harper & Row, 1962, 1965.

Vos, G. *Biblical Theology: Old and New Testaments.* Grand Rapids: Eerdmans, 1948.

Vriezen, T. C. *An Outline of Old Testament Theology.* Oxford: Blackwell, 1970.

Waltke, B. K., with Charles Yu. *An Old Testament Theology.* Grand Rapids: Zondervan, 2007.

Watson, F. *Text and Truth: Redefining Biblical Theology.* Grand Rapids: Eerdmans, 1997.

Watson, P. S. "The Nature and Function of Biblical Theology." *Expository Times* 73 (1962): 195 – 200.

Watts, J. D. W. "The People of God: A Study of the Doctrine of the Pentateuch." *Expository Times* 67 (1956): 232 – 37.

Wernberg-Moeller, P. "Is There an Old Testament Theology?" *Hibbert Journal* 59 (1960): 21 – 29.

Westermann, C. "The Way of Promise through the Old Testament," in *The Old Testament and Christian Faith.* Edited by B. W. Anderson. New York: Harper & Row, 1969. 200 – 224.

________. *The Elements of Old Testament Theology.* Atlanta: John Knox, 1982.

Wright, C. J. H. *An Eye for an Eye: The Place of Old Testament Ethics Today.* Downers Grove, IL: InterVarsity Press, 1983.

________. *Knowing God the Father through the Old Testament.* Downers Grove, IL: InterVarsity Press, 2007.

Wright, G. E. *God Who Acts: Biblical Theology as Recital.* London: SCM Press, 1952.

________. *The Old Testament and Theology.* New York: Harper & Row, 1969.

Young, E. J. *The Study of Old Testament Theology Today.* London: James Clark, 1958.

Zimmerli, W. *Old Testament Theology in Outline.* Atlanta: John Knox, 1978.

Author Index

Subject Index

K

L

Index of Hebrew Words